October 7–8, 2013
Boston, Massachusetts, USA

I0037960

Association for Computing Machinery

Advancing Computing as a Science & Profession

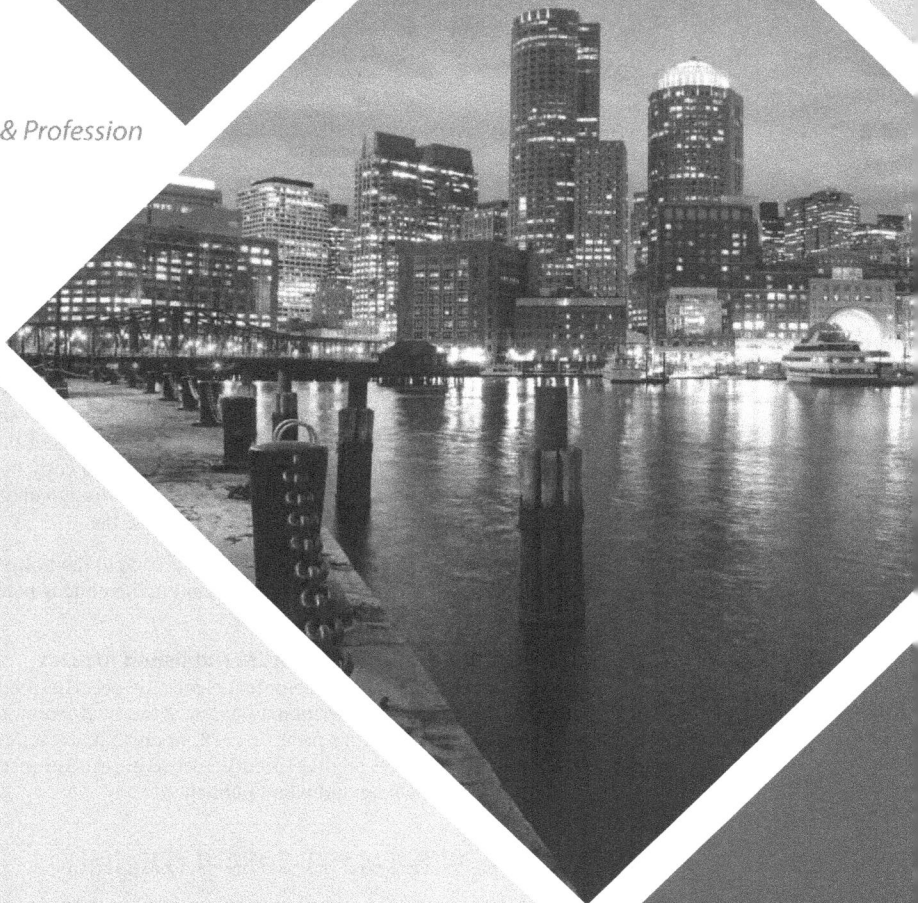

COSN'13

Proceedings of the 2013
Conference on Online Social Networks

Sponsored by:
ACM

Supported by:
NSF, Facebook, LinkedIn, Microsoft Research, Telefonica, Google, Foresight, Prof. Ram Kumar Foundation, AT&T and Akamai

Association for Computing Machinery

Advancing Computing as a Science & Profession

The Association for Computing Machinery
2 Penn Plaza, Suite 701
New York, New York 10121-0701

Notice to Past Authors of ACM-Published Articles
ACM intends to create a complete electronic archive of all articles and/or other material previously published by ACM. If you have written a work that has been previously published by ACM in any journal or conference proceedings prior to 1978, or any SIG Newsletter at any time, and you do NOT want this work to appear in the ACM Digital Library, please inform permissions@acm.org, stating the title of the work, the author(s), and where and when published.

ISBN: 978-1-4503-2084-9 (Digital)

ISBN: 978-1-4503-2673-5 (Print)

Additional copies may be ordered prepaid from:

ACM Order Department
PO Box 30777
New York, NY 10087-0777, USA

Phone: 1-800-342-6626 (USA and Canada)
+1-212-626-0500 (Global)
Fax: +1-212-944-1318
E-mail: acmhelp@acm.org
Hours of Operation: 8:30 am – 4:30 pm ET

Printed in the USA

Message from the COSN Steering Committee Chair

On behalf of the Conference on Online Social Networks Steering committee I welcome you to Boston. COSN was formed by merging six workshops covering most aspects of research in the OSN space. These workshops were held in the last five years under various auspices: SNS (Eurosys), DBSocial (SIGMOD), PSOSM (WWW), HotSocial (KDD), WOSS (VLDB), and WOSN (SIGCOMM/Usenix). COSN, as a conference, was proposed during a panel session during WOSN 2012 in Helsinki by Krishna Gummadi (MPI-SWS, Germany) and Ben Zhao (UC Santa Barbara). I agreed to organize the conference if the other workshops agreed to merge and fortunately they all agreed to do so in short order. These workshops ended in 2013 and their organizing Committees merged into COSN with the goal of bringing the disparate strands of overlapping work into a single high-quality venue. A Steering and Technical Advisory committee was formed (see the full list at http://cosn.acm.org/organization.html).

Donna Cappo, Director, Office of SIG Services in ACM (with whom I had worked earlier in the formation of Internet Measurement Conference) readily agreed to have ACM sponsor COSN and helped me throughout.

The Steering Committee selected Amr El Abbadi (UC Santa Barbara) and me to be the Program Committee chairs for COSN 2013. On behalf of the COSN Steering Committee, I thank the diverse program committee for reviewing a record number of papers in an extraordinarily short time and generating an excellent technical program. You can read all the details in our PC chairs welcome message next.

Ponnurangam Kumaraguru (IIIT Delhi) who served as COSN Publicity chair, created and managed the COSN website and related social media. Christo Wilson (Northeastern University) handled registrations ably. Alan Mislove (Northeastern University) readily agreed to convince his university to host COSN. He and his band of volunteers worked tirelessly to organize the venue you are enjoying now.

Our corporate and other supporters were critical for enabling student travel grants and for the low registration rates. At the Gold level our supporters are Facebook, LinkedIn, and Microsoft Research. At the Silver level are Foresight–the UK Government office for Science, Google, Telefonica, and the Professor Ram Kumar Memorial Foundation. AT&T and Akamai joined as supporters of the Conference reception.

At the Platinum level, the National Science Foundation provided funding for travel, hotel, and registration for US-based graduate students. I am indebted to Farnam Jahanian, Assistant Director of CISE/NSF for his prompt help in this regard and to the program manager William Bainbridge. We are grateful to NSF for their strong endorsement of this inter-disciplinary conference at its seed stage. Ben Zhao served as the student travel grant chair. The Steering Committee evaluated the applications and thanks to NSF and our corporate supporters, we were able to fund registration, shared hotel accommodation, and travel costs for 17 students from six countries.

Various staff members in ACM were quite helpful throughout the process. Maritza Nichols helped me with preparing the budget. Stephanie Sabal assisted me in conference venue-related negotiations ably. Debra Venedam took over the managing role from Donna and helped me with various issues: web site, changes to budget, corporate supporters etc. The publications chair Xiaoming Fu (University of Goettingen) with the help of Adrienne Griscti of ACM, ensured timely delivery of final versions of the papers.

I thank Jaron Lanier for readily acceding to my invitation to give the keynote at the first COSN. I also thank the staff at Steven Barclay agency for their assistance in this regard.

Above all, we want to thank the OSN technical community for submitting a large number of high quality papers. We thank you for attending and based on the results of the first COSN, we feel that it is well on its way to becoming a successful conference.

Balachander Krishnamurthy
AT&T Labs–Research

Chair, ACM COSN Steering Committee
http://www.research.att.com/ bala/papers

ACM COSN 2013 Chairs' Welcome

Welcome to the first ACM Conference on Online Social Networks - COSN! We are very excited that COSN is taking place in Boston MA, on October 7 and 8, 2013. We are proud to present its proceedings. The conference starts with a keynote by Jaron Lanier, a scientist, musician, visual artist and author of "Who owns the Future", followed by 22 technical paper presentations.

As mentioned in the Steering Committee Chair's welcome message, COSN was formed by merging six different workshops and the submissions reflected that. We received 138 submissions from over 20 countries, roughly as many submissions as the six workshops combined! We had solicited full papers (up to 12 pages) describing original research in detail and short papers (6 pages) conveying promising work and high-level vision. We received 103 long submissions and 35 short submissions. Both the high number of submissions and especially the number of long submissions clearly show that the community needs COSN and the time is ripe for COSN. The final program includes 4 short papers and 18 long papers. The acceptance rate is 16% (22 of 138 candidates) overall, 17.5% (18 of 103 candidates) for long papers and 11.5% (4 out of 35 candidates) for short papers. These rates reflect the high quality that we sought. The program reflects the broad coverage that was envisioned in merging the workshops: including papers in understanding social behavior, privacy, social graphs, trending topics, advertisements, applications, and crowdsourcing.

The PC consisted of 24 members (including the two of us). In addition, we sought and received additional reviews for some papers from over 20 external reviewers. The reviewing period was just four weeks, due to the exigencies of a first time conference with specific time constraints. Five papers were filtered out for being out of scope and a small handful was rejected based on two strongly negative reviews. Each of the remaining papers received at least three reviews with several receiving 4 or 5. In all, we had over 440 reviews within four weeks---showing the diligence of the PC and external reviewers. The reviewing process included extensive on-line discussions.

On July 29, we held a face-to-face day long program committee meeting at Columbia University. 50 papers with positive reviews and consensus after the on-line discussion were discussed extensively. The face to face PC meeting was beneficial as it brought various representatives of the OSN community together, some of whom were meeting others for the first time. The accepted papers cover a diversity of topics spanning the various research areas of the OSN community. The papers also reflect the globalization of the community, covering papers with author affiliations from 13 countries: Australia, Austria, Brazil, China, Germany, India, Italy, Japan, Korea, Spain, Switzerland, United Kingdom, and United States. Virtually all but one of the accepted papers were shepherded to ensure compliance with specific outcomes from the reviews and the discussions.

We would like to thank all the PC members and reviewers for their hard work. The load was high, the reviewing period was short, and that too in the middle of summer. The overall quality of the reviews was excellent. We also would like to thank all the authors, who submitted more papers beyond our wildest expectation. This clearly shows that the field of online social networks has reached maturity and clearly needed a top-rated venue for the presentation and discussion of state of the art results. We also thank Eddie Kohler for designing and providing HotCRP, Faisal Nawab for helping us administer HotCRP, Christopher Riederer for his help during the PC meeting, both Augustin Chaintreau and Jon Crowcroft for handling an out-of-band paper with which we were conflicted, and to Augustin Chaintreau for hosting the PC meeting at Columbia.

We hope that you find the COSN 2013 program exciting and thought-provoking and that the conference facilitates stimulating discussions with other researchers and practitioners from around the world. Enjoy the first COSN!

Amr El Abbadi   **Balachander Krishnamurthy**
UC Santa Barbara   *AT&T Labs--Research*

Table of Contents

Session 6: Ads and Apps

Session 7: Crowdsourcing

Session 8: Trending Topics and Interests

Author Index

2013 ACM Conference on Online Social Networks (COSN'13) Organization Committee

General Chair: Muthu Muthukrishnan *(Microsoft & Rutgers University, USA)*

Publicity Chair: Ponnurangam Kumaraguru *(IIIT Delhi, India)*

Student Travel Grant Chair: Ben Zhao *(UC Santa Barbara, USA)*

Local Arrangements Chair: Alan Mislove *(Northeastern University, USA)*

Registration Chair: Christo Wilson *(Northeastern University, USA)*

Proceedings Chair: Xiaoming Fu *(University of Goettingen, Germany)*

Steering Committee Chair: Balachander Krishnamurthy *(AT&T Labs-Research, USA)*

Steering Committee: Virgilio Almeida *(Federal University of Minais Gerais, Brazil)*
Xiaoming Fu *(University of Goettingen, Germany)*
Jon Crowcroft *(University of Cambridge, UK)*
Balachander Krishnamurthy *(AT&T Labs-Research, USA)*
Ben Zhao *(UC Santa Barbara, USA)*

Technical Advisory Committee: Rakesh Agrawal *(Microsoft Search Labs, USA)*
Krishna Gummadi *(MPI-SWS, Germany)*
Anne-Marie Kermarrec *(INRIA, France)*
Jon Kleinberg *(Cornell University, USA)*
Ponnurangam Kumaraguru *(IIIT Delhi, India)*

COSN'13 Technical Program Committee

Program Committee Chairs: Amr El Abbadi *(UC Santa Barbara, USA)*
Balachander Krishnamurthy *(AT&T Labs-Research, USA)*

Program Committee: Rakesh Agrawal *(Microsoft Research, USA)*
Jussara Almeida *(Federal University of Minais Gerais, Brazil)*
Lerone Banks *(Federal Trade Commission, USA)*
Steven Bellovin *(Columbia University / FTC, USA)*
Smriti Bhagat *(Technicolor Palo Alto, USA)*
Augustin Chaintreau *(Columbia University, USA)*
Meeyoung Cha *(KAIST, Korea)*
Graham Cormode *(University of Warwick, UK)*
Jon Crowcroft *(University of Cambridge, UK)*
Nilesh Dalvi *(Facebook, USA)*
Amr El Abbadi *(UC Santa Barbara, USA)*
Tina Eliassi-Rad *(Rutgers University, USA)*
Peter Gloor *(MIT, USA)*
Matthias Grossglauser *(EPFL, Lausanne, Switzerland)*
Krishna Gummadi *(MPI-SWS, Germany)*
Anne-Marie Kermarrec *(INRIA, France)*
Balachander Krishnamurthy *(AT&T Labs-Research, USA)*
Silvio Lattanzi *(Google New York, USA)*
Cecilia Mascolo *(University of Cambridge, UK)*
Muthu Muthukrishnan *(Microsoft & Rutgers University, USA)*
Daniele Quercia *(Yahoo! Research, Barcelona, Spain)*
Alessandra Sala *(Bell Labs, Dublin, Ireland)*
Jie Tang *(Tsinghua University, China)*
Ben Zhao *(UC Santa Barbara, USA)*

COSN'13 External Reviewers

Jisun An *(University of Cambridge, UK)*
Martin Arlitt *(HP Labs, USA)*
Robert Bell *(AT&T Labs-Research, USA)*
Bobby Bhattacharjee *(University of Maryland, USA)*
Petko Bogdanov *(UC Santa Barbara, USA)*
Ceren Budak *(Microsoft Research, USA)*
Emiliano De Cristofaro *(Xerox PARC, USA)*
Nick Duffield *(AT&T Labs-Research, USA)*
Cynthia Dwork *(Microsoft Research, USA)*
Brian Eriksson *(Technicolor, USA)*
Ramesh Govindan *(University of Southern California, USA)*
Saikat Guha *(Microsoft Research, USA)*
Yifan Hu *(AT&T Labs-Research, USA)*
Lee Humphreys *(Cornell University, USA)*
Jon Kleinberg *(Cornell University, USA)*
Nick Koudas *(University of Toronto, Canada)*
Arvind Krishnamurthy *(University of Washington, USA)*
Markus Kuhn *(University of Cambridge, UK)*
Kristina Lerman *(Information Sciences Institute, USA)*
Harsha V. Madhyastha *(UC Riverside, USA)*
Bruce Maggs *(Duke University, USA)*
Alan Mislove *(Northeastern University, USA)*
Arvind Narayanan *(Princeton University, USA)*
James Salter *(GCHQ, UK)*
Vyas Sekar *(SUNY Stonybrook, USA)*
Dawn Song *(UC Berkeley, USA)*
Jia Wang *(AT&T Labs-Research, USA)*
Craig Wills *(Worcester Polytechnic Institute, USA)*
Yinghui Wu *(UC Santa Barbara, USA)*
Xifeng Yan *(UC Santa Barbara, USA)*

COSN'13 Sponsor & Supporters

Sponsor:  Association for Computing Machinery

Advancing Computing as a Science & Profession

Supporters:

Platinum

Gold

Silver  Google

Government Office for Science

Conference Reception Supported By

COSN'13 Keynote Speaker

Jaron Lanier
Microsoft Research

Biography

A Renaissance Man for the 21st century, Jaron Lanier is a computer scientist, composer, artist, and author who writes on numerous topics, including high-technology business, the social impact of technology, the philosophy of consciousness and information, Internet politics, and the future of humanism. In 2010, Lanier was named one of the 100 most influential people in the world by Time Magazine. He has also been named one of top one hundred public intellectuals in the world by Prospect and Foreign Policy magazines, and one of history's 300 or so greatest inventors in the Encyclopedia Britannica. In 2009 Jaron Lanier received a Lifetime Career Award from the IEEE, the preeminent international engineering society. A pioneer in virtual reality (a term he coined), Lanier founded VPL Research, the first company to sell VR products, and led teams creating VR applications for medicine, design, and numerous other fields. He is currently a computer scientist at Microsoft Research.

In January 2010, Knopf published Lanier's book You Are Not a Gadget, A Manifesto, which became a New York Times, Los Angeles Times, and Boston Globe bestseller.

You Are Not a Gadget was chosen as one of the best books of the year by Time Magazine and The New York Times, among others.

Lanier's writing appears in Discover, The Wall Street Journal, Forbes, Harpers Magazine, Atlantic, Wired Magazine (where he was a founding contributing editor), and Scientific American. He has appeared on TV shows such as PBS NewsHour, Nightline and Charlie Rose, and has been profiled on the front pages of The Wall Street Journal and The New York Times multiple times. Jaron Lanier is also a musician and artist. He has been active in the world of new "classical" music since the late '70s, and writes chamber and orchestral works. He is a pianist and a specialist in unusual and historical musical instruments, and maintains one of the largest and most varied collections of actively played instruments in the world. Recent works include a symphony with full choral settings about William Shakespeare's contemporary and friend Amelia Lanier, commissioned for the Bach Festival Society of Winter Park. He has performed with a wide range of musicians, including Philip Glass, Yoko Ono, Ornette Coleman, George Clinton, and Steve Reich. He composes and performs frequently on film soundtracks.

COSN'13, October 7–8, 2013, Boston, Massachusetts, USA.
ACM 978-1-4503-2084-9/13/10.

We Know How You Live:
Exploring the Spectrum of Urban Lifestyles

Nicholas Jing Yuan[†], Fuzheng Zhang[*†], Defu Lian[*†], Kai Zheng[‡], Siyu Yu[§], Xing Xie[†]

[†]Microsoft Research Asia
[*]School of Computer Science and Technology, University of Science and Technology of China
[‡]School of Information Technology & Electrical Engineering , The University of Queensland
[§]Department of Sociology, University of California, Berkeley
{nicholas.yuan, v-fuz, v-delian, xing.xie} AT microsoft.com,
kevinz AT itee.uq.edu.au, syyu AT berkeley.edu

ABSTRACT

An incisive understanding of human lifestyles is not only essential to many scientific disciplines, but also has a profound business impact for targeted marketing. In this paper, we present **LifeSpec**, a *computational* framework for exploring and hierarchically categorizing urban lifestyles. Specifically, we have developed an algorithm to connect multiple social network accounts of millions of individuals and collect their *publicly available* heterogeneous behavioral data as well as social links. In addition, a nonparametric Bayesian approach is developed to model the lifestyle spectrum of a group of individuals. To demonstrate the effectiveness of LifeSpec, we conducted extensive experiments and case studies, with a large dataset we collected covering 1 million individuals from 493 cities. Our results suggest that LifeSpec offers a powerful paradigm for 1) revealing an individual's lifestyle from multiple dimensions, and 2) uncovering lifestyle commonalities and variations of a group with various demographic attributes, such as vocation, education, gender, sexual orientation, and place of residence. The proposed method provides emerging implications for personalized recommendation and targeted advertising.

Categories and Subject Descriptors

H.2.8 [**Database Management**]: Data mining; J.4 [**Social and Behavioral Science**]: Sociology

Keywords

LifeSpec, lifestyles, living patterns, human behavior

1. INTRODUCTION

Understanding human lifestyles is essential to many scientific disciplines as varied as sociology [4], biomedicine [1], and economics [37]. In marketing research, understanding individual lifestyles is particularly crucial since consumer lifestyles are strong indicators of their buying behaviors [24]. Hence, if you know more about your

consumer's lifestyles, you can reach your targets faster, and more effectively.

In the past, it was quite costly (in both time and money) for social scientists to investigate human lifestyles, since such studies depended heavily on large-scale demographic data, e.g., by surveying thousands of participants. The National Census dataset might be a good resource for studying individual lifestyles. However, the typical time cycle between two consecutive censuses is extremely long (10 years for both the U.S and China) and the data at the individual level is usually not available to the public (refer to the 72-years rule[1]). In short, both the time lag and data granularity limit the effectiveness and efficiency of traditional survey-based approaches for understanding dynamic urban lifestyles[24]. In addition, all the survey-based approaches rely on retrospective self-reports and thus are vulnerable to memory error, not to mention the well-known experimenter effects[31].

That is now changing. The emerging era of "big data" provides unprecedented (in terms of both breadth and depth) potential for us to uncovering the underlying patterns of our everyday lives. Imagine a typical day in your life: You are awakened on a Friday morning by the alarm clock, a bit earlier than usual due to an early meeting on that day (the alarm is synced with your online calendar). You rush to take a taxicab to your company (the GPS trajectories are logged by the transportation center) and arrive on time. After a boring meeting that takes up the whole morning, you decide to have a good lunch. So you search on Yelp for a high-scoring restaurant, and you check-in (the process of announcing your arrival at a place and sharing it on a social network) at the restaurant on Foursquare in order to get a discount. After work, you book yourself a ticket for a movie at night that has a high score at IMDB. It ends up being a fantastic Friday evening–not just because of the movie, but because you come across a wonderful woman/man at the theater after posting to Twitter about the movie and catching her attention when she clicked the "Who's Nearby" button.

As can be seen in the above example, many of us already live in an online world. During the past few years, mobile devices, ubiquitous sensing technologies, and various kinds of social networks have proliferated tremendously, which has turned out to be the most important catalyst for bridging our offline world with the online world. The meetings we attend, the restaurants we go to, the movies we see, the people we meet–everything we do during a day–will eventually produce behavioral data stored somewhere in the "Cloud." Intentionally or not, this data mirrors our daily lives, just as the digital *footprints* we leave in the online world. Some of these footprints reveal our movements in the physical world, such

---

[1]http://1.usa.gov/ZS5T0s

as check-ins and cell-phone traces. Moreover, a footprint can also be generated without the necessity of mobility. A diverse range of data falls into this scope, e.g., posting a tweet, sharing a link to a song, purchasing a book online, rating a movie and so forth. If we understand footprints as the linkages between *human* and *entities* (locations, music, videos, etc.), another kind of link–social link–is the connection between humans that are impatiently migrating from offline to online, even more rapidly than digital footprints.

Given the overwhelming heterogeneous behavioral data of individuals, it is tempting to think that exploring their lifestyles through such data should be easy. This is, however, still not the case. The major challenges of this work are:

- How to *connect* multiple network accounts of a user and *collect* users' *publicly available*[2] footprints (as many as possible) residing in different online networks?

- How to *computationally* model the lifestyle of an individual and a group of individuals, by integrating users' heterogeneous behavioral data?

To address the above challenges, in this paper, we propose a data-driven framework termed **LifeSpec**, to explore urban lifestyles with users' heterogeneous behavioral data and social links. Our exploration ranges from the **specification** of an individual's daily lifestyle as shown in Figure 1, to the lifestyle **spectrum** (will be explicitly defined later) within a group of individuals. This model is flexible enough to deal with groups with various sizes, e.g., a group can either be as small as hundreds of students in a university, or as large as the whole population in a megacity.

To the best of our knowledge, LifeSpec is the first attempt to investigate and model human lifestyles in a *computational* way, based on *millions* of people's *heterogeneous* behavioral data. Our main contributions are summarized as follows:

- We have developed an algorithm for connecting multiple network accounts of users, based on our key observations of users' *self-disclosure* behavior and social "hub sites." In turn, we built a data platform which successfully crawled a large dataset covering 997,500 users (identified to be unique) from 493 cities including their profiles, footprints, and social links. (Section 3)

- We have derived a nonparametric Bayesian approach to computationally model the lifestyle spectrum for a group of individuals, as well as the lifestyle of an individual. This method provides an automatic and data-driven way of generating a hierarchical lifestyle segmentation for a group of individuals. (Section 4)

- We present in-depth analytics on the collected behavioral dataset. Based on this dataset, we conducted extensive experiments and user studies to validate the effectiveness and flexibility of LifeSpec for different groups of users, considering a variety of demographic attributes, such as *vocation*, *education*, *gender*, *sexual orientation*, and *place of residence*. (Section 5)

2. RELATED WORK

Lifestyle Research in Social Science. Human lifestyles have long been studied in social science [16]. In 1967, Ansbacher [3] provided a historical and systematic review of lifestyle research in social science literatures, in which they recognized the similarities among different individuals' lifestyles and suggested the existence of lifestyle *typologies*. Furthermore, they discussed three differ-

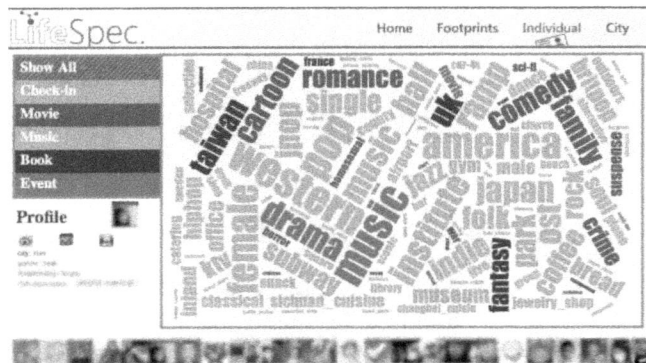

Figure 1: A screenshot of the individual view in the LifeSpec system, where the categories and frequency of footprints are indicated with different colors and sizes. A user can also switch to the city view for exploring the lifestyle spectrum (as detailed later) of a city by clicking either the user's place of residence or the menu above.

ent levels of aggregation of lifestyles, including "an *individual*," "a *group*," and a "*(generic) class or category*." While there is a broad range of lifestyle research focusing on the US, European, and India markets [26, 36, 23], we have found there is little research on systematically studying the lifestyles in contemporary China. The targeted population in this work, people who were mostly born in the 1980s and 1990s, have experienced profound changes during their lives. As the most lucrative target for the market, their lifestyles significantly differ from their previous generations. Discovering the dynamics and variations of their lifestyles will have a far-reaching impact for both marketers and governments.

Cross-domain User Linking. Linking users from different domains is crucial for targeted advertising and personalization. IP and/or Cookie-based user identification and personalization approaches have been used for years [17]. Some recent methods addressed this problem with various new solutions [25, 21, 14]. These approaches have shown a powerful ability to identify the same user from different networks. However, in most existing methods, a user's different accounts are identified and linked in a *passive* way. In other words, a user might have no intention of being linked from different networks or websites. As a result, these approaches may sometimes raise privacy concerns among users and thus become controversial. In addition, these methods are successful in a probabilistic sense, which means that an error rate (i.e., mis-linking) is inevitable. Our method, however, is based on users' *explicit* and *active* self-disclosure (detailed later) of the connections between their different accounts. Instead of *inferring* any links between their accounts–we *discover* their linked accounts.

Bridging Online and Offline. Recent studies converge to suggest that the barrier between individuals' online and offline lives is tremendously blurred. Such trend is still being accelerated by the advance in ubiquitous sensing, social networks, and big data [11, 12, 39, 2, 29]. For example, Cranshaw et al. [10] showed that human mobility patterns have strong connections with the structure of their underlying social network. Recently, Kosinski et al. [19] reported that the "Like" behavior in Facebook can be used to predict users' psychological traits with a surprisingly high accuracy. However, we have found that there is still a lack of research into human lifestyles that leverages the emerging heterogeneous behavioral data mirroring users' offline behavior from multiple dimen-

---

[2]In accordance to the United States Code of Federal Regulations defining Human Subjects Research (45 CFR 46), our collection of publicly available data would be considered exempt from Institutional Review Board (IRB) review. We anonymized the IDs of each user on each website when collecting the data, and removed all the identities before the experiments.

sions. Our work takes one more step forward towards the goal of bridging the offline world and the online world.

3. COLLECTING AND CONNECTING

This section first presents some observations that enables us to connect multiple accounts of a user from heterogeneous online networks (Section 3.1). Next, we detail the methodology for connecting users' accounts while collecting the data (Section 3.2).

3.1 Observations

Many people have multiple social network (or website) accounts, e.g., one person is likely to have both a Twitter account and a Foursquare account. There might be a number of reasons behind this, while the most obvious one is that users sign up for different social networks to fulfill different needs. It is because of the heterogeneity of online networks that we have heterogeneous behavioral data, i.e., footprints. A critical challenge for collecting users' cross-domain footprints is the identification of users' multiple social network accounts. Unlike existing approaches that leverage machine learning or rule-based methods to "infer" the connection between a single user's different accounts (which is not 100% accurate and may also be deemed to be a serious invasion of users' privacy), we identify the connection with strong "evidence" that users *actively* and *explicitly* disclose. Specifically, our method is based on the following observations:

O1. Hub site. Some websites function as a *hub* to serve for users' other social networks or websites. Here, we call a website "hub site" if it satisfies the following conditions: 1) It supports indexing users by entities or categories, e.g., places (by Foursquare), and songs (by Last.fm); 2) Users can sync their contents to other networks. For example, Foursquare can usually sync users' check-ins to Facebook and Twitter, once authenticated by users themselves. Other examples of hub sites include About.me and Klout.

O2. Self-disclosure. Many users explicitly display their other network accounts on their profile pages of one/multiple social networks. For example, many users' Facebook ID and Twitter ID are easy to identify from their Foursqaure profiles. This is also true for Jiepang (known as China's Foursquare).

3.2 Methods

Assume we have a set of known social networking sites Ψ (e.g., $\Psi = \{$Facebook, Twitter, Foursqure$\}$) and a hub site $h \in \Psi$. Based on observation O1, we can obtain a set of profile pages in h by querying h with a list of entities. Given the profile pages in h as seeds, we have developed an algorithm (Algorithm 1) to efficiently connect users' accounts on Ψ, as well as to collect their publicly available footprints and social links from different social networks. Note that in this paper, we consider a friendship relationship (either directed or undirected) identified from any network as a social link.

Accessibility and Connectivity. Given a user u's profile page p belonging to a website in Ψ (where p can be accessed by a URL), let Q_p be all the profile page URLs displayed on p, including both her own profile URLs (note p's URL is also in Q_p) and her friends' profile URLs (i.e., social links). We say q is **directly accessible** from p if $q \in Q_p$. If there is a *path* that starts from p, and reaches another profile page p' by traversing only through *directly accessible* URLs (one by one), we say p' is **accessible** from p, denoted as $p \triangleright p'$.

Furthermore, let Q be the set of all profile pages in Ψ. For each website $W \in \Psi$, by inspecting the structure of a user's profile page, we can identify whether a user discloses her accounts (profile page URLs) of other websites in Ψ based on observation O1 and O2

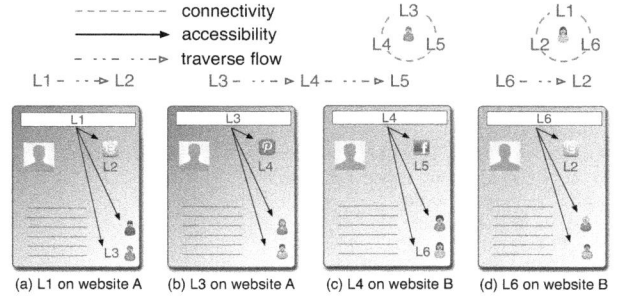

Figure 2: Accessibility relationships and connectivity relationships among users' different profile pages.

(since profile pages in W follow a certain HTML template). For any $q_1, q_2 \in Q$, we say q_1 and q_2 are **directly connected** (or with a *direct connectivity* relation) if there exist a profile page p and a user u, such that $q_1, q_2 \in Q_p^u$, where $Q_p^u \subset Q_p$ denotes u's self-disclosed profile URLs on p. Then we define the **connectivity** relation between any pair of profile pages in Q as the *transitive closure* [32] of the *direct connectivity* relation.

To explain the connectivity relation in a more natural way, we can regard each profile page in Q as a node in an undirected graph G. For any two nodes $q_1, q_2 \in Q$, there is an undirected edge between q_1 and q_2 if q_1 and q_2 are *directly connected* in some profile page p of user u. Thus, the connectivity relationship defined above is equivalent to the common sense of connectivity in an undirected graph, i.e., there exist a path connecting q_1 and q_2 in G. Since the connectivity relation is reflexive, symmetric and transitive, it is an *equivalence* relation. Hence our problem is formulated as:

*Given a set of profile pages h, find **all equivalence classes** U from all **accessible** profile pages of h.*

Actually, when all nodes (profile pages) in G are known in advance, this problem can be efficiently solved using the Union-Find algorithm [33]. In our situation, however, both the nodes and edges are unknown. To address this issue, we propose the ICONNECT algorithm (Algorithm 1) to keep track of all the equivalence classes (unique users) in real time as we discover new nodes (accessible profile pages).

Specifically, as formally presented in Algorithm 1, a queue P_U stores all unvisited profile pages, and each iteration starts by traversing from a popped profile page p (line 6), which contains a user's *directly connected* profile URLs (e.g., URL $L2$ in Fig.2a). Here, we traverse only through these *directly connected* and *directly accessible* profile pages to obtain *connected* profile pages D of this user until we encounter previously visited profile pages P_O (line 8). Since all these profile pages are *connected* with each other, we merge all the original profile pages in P_O as one user (line 9) using the Union-Find structure with almost constant time [34]. For example, $L1, L2, L6$ and $L3, L4, L5$ are merged into two equivalence classes respectively, as shown in Fig.2. Meanwhile, we collect all the footprints and social links obtained from p. In particular, if we discover new hub sites (e.g., another check-in service provider) from the footprints (typically indicated by the patterns in the URL, such as "I'm AT"), we can further add them into the hub site set (line 18), and enqueue discovered new users (line 15 and line 17). Iteratively, we crawl more profiles, footprints, and social links.

Here, to prevent potential confusion between connectivity and accessibility, we note that in Algorithm 1, accessibility relation is merely leveraged for discovering new profile pages (i.e., nodes in the undirected graph G), while we traverse from one profile page

---

Algorithm 1: IdentifyConnectedUsers (ICONNECT)

Input: seed hub site h
Output: users U, where each user $u \in U$ is a set of profile pages;
        footprints $\mathcal{F}$; social links $\mathcal{L}$, hub sites H

1 $H \leftarrow \varnothing$; $H.\mathrm{add}(h)$;
2 $\mathcal{F} \leftarrow \varnothing$; $\mathcal{L} \leftarrow \varnothing$;
3 A queue storing unvisited profile pages $P_U \leftarrow h.\mathrm{getAllUsers}()$;
4 A set of visited profile pages $P_V \leftarrow \varnothing$;
5 **while** $P_U.length > 0$ **do**
6      $p \leftarrow P_U.\mathrm{dequeue}()$;
7      $D \leftarrow \varnothing, P_O \leftarrow \varnothing$;
8      $(D, P_O) \leftarrow \mathrm{VisitProfile}(p, P_V, D, P_O, \mathcal{F}, \mathcal{L})$;
9   Merge $\{u \in U | P_O \cap u \neq \varnothing\}$ to u';
10    $P_V \leftarrow P_V \cup D$; $P_U \leftarrow P_U \setminus D$;
11   **if** $u' = \varnothing$ **then** $u' \leftarrow U.\mathrm{createUser}()$;
12   **foreach** $d \in D$ **do**
13        $u'.\mathrm{add}(d)$;
14        $H_0 \leftarrow$ hub sites obtained from $\mathcal{F}(d)$;
15        $P_U.\mathrm{enqueue}(\mathcal{L}(p).\mathrm{getProfiles}() \setminus (P_V \cup P_U))$;
16   **foreach** $h' \in H_0 \setminus H$ **do**
17           $P_U.\mathrm{enqueue}(h'.\mathrm{getAllUsers}() \setminus (P_V \cup P_U))$;
18        $H \leftarrow H_0 \cup H$;

19 **return** $U, \mathcal{F}, \mathcal{L}, H$

Procedure VisitProfile$(p, P_V, D, P_O, \mathcal{F}, \mathcal{L})$

Input: profile page p, visited pages P_V, newly discovered pages D,
       previously visited pages $P_O \subset P_V$, footprints $\mathcal{F}$, social links $\mathcal{L}$
Output: D, P_O

1 $D.\mathrm{add}(p)$;
2 $\mathcal{F}(p) \leftarrow$ footprints obtained from the account of p;
3 $\mathcal{L}(p) \leftarrow$ social links obtained from the account of p;
4 $P' \leftarrow$ other profile pages displayed on p or $\mathcal{F}(p)$, *directly connected* with p;
5 **foreach** $p' \in P'$ and $p' \notin D$ **do**
6   **if** $p' \in P_V$ **then** $P_O.\mathrm{add}(p')$;
7   **else** VisitProfile $(p', P_V, D, P_O, \mathcal{F}, \mathcal{L})$;

8 **return** (D, P_O)

---

to another only if they are *directly connected* (i.e., an edge in G), which means that we can maintain equivalence classes (connected users) in real time by traversing each profile page once. The correctness and complexity of this algorithm are given in Theorem 1.

THEOREM 1. *Algorithm 1 keeps track of all connected users in currently visited profile pages after each loop (line 18) by accessing each profile page once, and finally finds all connected users from all accessible profile pages $h_\triangleright$ of hub site h, with time complexity $O(|h_\triangleright|\alpha(|h_\triangleright|))$, where α is the inverse Ackermann function*[3] *(the proof is left to Appendix A).*

Another benefit of this algorithm is that we can stop it at any time, while still guarantee having numerous unique users (instead of one single user's different profile pages). Specifically, at any time, we can obtain a set of users $U = \{u_i\}_{i=1}^N$ with disjoint profile pages on heterogeneous networks. Let U^W denote the users who have profile pages on website W. Assuming a single user does not have two profile pages on W (which is usually true), theoretically we have in total $|U^W|$ different users. Note that choosing a different W may lead to a different number of users as well as their footprints and social links. In our method, we have chosen a W which maximizes the number of footprints. Hence, the total number of footprints is

$$\max_W \left| \bigcup_{u \in U^W} \bigcup_{p \in u} \mathcal{F}(p) \right|. \tag{1}$$

Based on this algorithm, we developed a data platform, to incrementally and continuously identify new users, connect their accounts on different networks, and collect their heterogeneous behavioral data as well as social links, which in turn supports our further exploration of their lifestyles.

4. MODELING LIFESTYLES AND LIFESTYLE SPECTRUM

This section first explicitly clarifies some related concepts in our model (Section 4.1), then tackles the challenge of integrating het-

---
[3] A quasi-constant function, which grows incredibly slowly [34].

erogeneous footprints and social links to learn the lifestyle spectrum of a group of individuals (Section 4.2).

4.1 Preliminary

A **footprint** f of an individual u is a combination of domain-specific tokens or tags, which discriminatingly describe the behavior of individual u on a certain domain at a particular time. The granularity of a footprint can vary according to different demands and the data format obtained from the data providers. For example, a mobility-related footprint can be represented with a timestamp and a geo-coordinates, or a POI category, such as "shopping mall" and "office"; a movie-related footprint can be a movie's exact name, or the category of that movie, e.g., "drama and romance".

A **living pattern** S is a combination of frequently co-occurring footprints. For example, an individual may often listen to British pop music and read sci-fi fictions. Note that different individuals may share some typical living patterns and different living patterns may also share some common footprints.

Given a group of individuals, A **lifestyle spectrum** $\mathcal{T}$ is a tree-structured hierarchy summarizing the living patterns of these individuals, where each node of $\mathcal{T}$ is a living pattern. The higher nodes in this tree stand for more commonly shared living patterns and the lower nodes are variations. Thus, a specific **lifestyle** l is a path from the root to a leaf in $\mathcal{T}$, i.e., a sequence of living patterns, ordered by the degree of commonality.

For example, Fig.3 shows the lifestyle spectrum of 100,000 Beijing citizens (sampled from the data we collected). As is shown, Node 1 is the most common living pattern (each living pattern is represented with the top 3 frequent footprints). Node 2, 3, and 4 are various living patterns pertaining to subgroups, e.g., Node 2 is a typical living pattern for an office worker and Node 3 is common for students. The path connecting $1 \rightarrow 2 \rightarrow 7$ forms a typical lifestyle for urban-dwelling office workers who love coffee, western-food and frequent bars at night. Here, the size of a node in the spectrum indicates the number of people who own such a living pattern (the larger, the more). As a result, we can easily target a subgroup of individuals with a certain lifestyle (path) in $\mathcal{T}$. Since a large group (e.g., a megacity) usually contain millions or even tens of millions of citizens, many people may share similar lifestyles, compared with a flat model or simple enumerations, the hierarchical topology of lifestyle spectrum inherently captures the similarity and difference between members in a group.

4.2 Learning the Lifestyle Spectrum

Given millions of footprints and social links of a group of individuals, we leverage topic modeling to learn their lifestyles and lifestyle spectrum, where a "topic" is a distribution of words in a document [6]. As shown in Fig. 4, this is established by building an analogue from the lifestyle spectrum to a hierarchical topic struc-

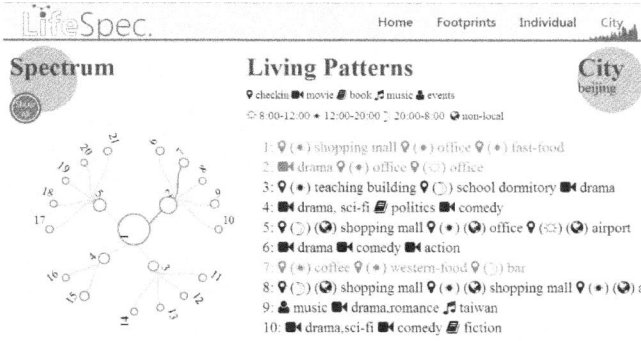

Figure 3: A screenshot of LifeSpec showing the lifestyle spectrum and living patterns (partially presented) of Beijing citizens.

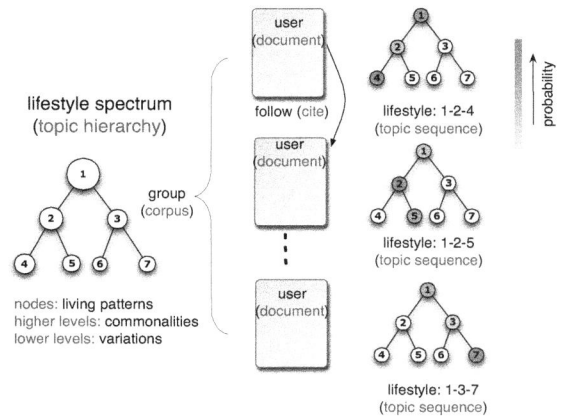

Figure 4: From lifestyle spectrum to a topic hierarchy.

ture as follows: Given a group of users as a *corpus*, we regard all the users in this group as *documents*, where the *words* in each document are an individual's footprints. Just as a topic is described using a collection of words, a living pattern is represented by a set of footprints (recall the definition of living pattern), so it can be considered as a latent *topic* in a document. Here, the lifestyle spectrum is a *hierarchical topic tree* in which each node is a topic. Each document can exhibit multiple topics, which are derived as a path (containing a set of nodes) from the topic tree. In this tree, more commonly shared topics are near the root and more specified topics are close to the leaves.

Blei et al. [7] proposed the hierarchical Latent Dirichlet Allocation (hLDA) for the above model. This model is powerful in the sense that it allows both the parameters and the structure of the model to be automatically adapted as more data is observed. For example, this model can support arbitrary branches and depth of the tree-structured spectrum. This is achieved with the aid of the "nested-Chinese restaurant process" (nCRP), which is widely used in Bayesian nonparametric statistics (refer to [15] for details of this process).

Nevertheless, hLDA still does not take the full advantage of our data, since another important signal that we have captured–the social graph–has not been considered. Actually, social psychologists have found that "perceived and real activity similarity would be equally good predictors of liking." [38] Inspired by this theory, we model a social link between two individuals as a function of their similarity with respect to their living patterns. Given the living patterns $\mathbf{x}_u = \{x_{u,1}, x_{u,2} \dots, x_{u,n}\}$ of individual u, we calculate the empirical living pattern distribution of u by $\bar{\mathbf{x}}_u = \frac{1}{n} \sum_i x_{u,i}$ (where each $x_{u,i}$ is a distribution over the vocabulary of footprints). For any pair of individuals u, u', the probability that u *follows* u' on a social network is given by

$$\exp(\zeta^\top \left(\frac{\bar{\mathbf{x}}_u \circ \bar{\mathbf{x}}'_u}{|\bar{\mathbf{x}}_u|} \right) + \upsilon), \qquad (2)$$

where $\circ$ is the Hadamard product and ζ, υ are parameters that need to be learned from the data.

Intuitively, we can deem social links between individuals as citations between documents, e.g., a paper usually cite papers that are similar or related. Several approaches have been developed to deal with the citation relationships between documents, such as the Relational Topic Model (RTM) [8, 9], however, they are for flat topic models instead of a hierarchical topic structure.

To integrate the signals from footprints and social links for learning the lifestyle spectrum, we propose a hybrid model, termed Re-

lational Hierarchical Latent Dirichlet Allocation (RH-LDA), which is a generalization of both hLDA and RTM. Specifically, the generative process of RH-LDA is as follows:
1. For each node k in the spectrum tree $\mathcal{T}$
   (a) Draw a living pattern $\beta_k \sim \text{Dirichlet}(\eta)$.
2. For each individual $d \in \{1, 2, \dots, D\}$
   (a) Draw a path $\mathbf{c}_d \sim \text{nCRP}(\gamma)$.
   (b) Draw a distribution over levels in the tree, $\theta_d|(m, \pi) \sim \text{GEM}(m, \pi)$[27].
   (c) For each footprint,
      i. Choose level $Z_{d,n}|\theta_D \sim \text{Discrete}(\theta)$.
      ii. Choose footprint $W_{d,n}|\{z_{d,n}, \mathbf{c}_d, \beta\} \sim \text{Discrete}(\beta_{c_d})$, which is parameterized by the living pattern in position $z_{d,n}$ on the path $\mathbf{c}_d$.
3. For each pair of individuals d, d',
   (a) Draw binary link with a probability given by Equation (2).
Note that Step 3 differs from the approach proposed in [9], where we extend the original RTM to directed graph by Eq. 2 (social links are usually directed). The inference of this model is implemented using collapsed Gibbs Sampling (refer to Appendix B) and the Metropolis-Hasting(MH) algorithm.

5. EXPERIMENTS

In this section, we first describe and analyze the data we collected using Algorithm 1 (Section 5.1). Later, based on this huge dataset, we conduct experiments to explore lifestyle spectrums of different groups in terms of various demographic attributes (Section 5.2), as well as a user study on the lifestyle spectrum of different cities (Section 5.3).

5.1 Data Description and Analytics

We chose Jiepang (China's Foursquare) as a hub site. We first crawled the city list and retrieved all the Points of Interest (POI) for each city. Then, for each POI, we obtained all the users who have checked-in at that POI. Using Algorithm 1 and choosing Jiepang as the W which maximizes Eq. 1, we eventually obtained a collection of 997,500 unique users from 439 cities all over China (note some users do not indicate their places of residence on their profile pages), with their 53 million footprints, as well as 3,094,965 social links. Among these users, 99.1% users have at least 2 network accounts and 33.7% users have at least 3 network accounts. We crawled users' *publicly available* profiles, footprints, and social links from the following 4 social networking sites: Jiepang,

Table 1: Summarization of collected footprints for different cities (partially presented due to page limit).

city	Shanghai	Beijing	Guangzhou	Tianjin	Hangzhou	Hongkong	Xiamen	Suzhou	Nanjing	Chengdu	Wuhan	Xian
users	417,681	162,764	53,089	15,490	34,322	12,599	10,123	19,673	21,558	23,372	20,975	15,261
check-in	25,178,189	5,898,447	1,092,138	392,943	619,219	424,650	369,231	560,274	414,202	327,634	321,646	229,678
movie	1,661,214	1,466,479	171,789	118,775	238,721	57,003	70,172	89,706	174,664	191,042	166,337	123,223
music	766,165	737,254	85,953	60,658	103,936	30,313	29,716	39,701	82,513	88,426	76,316	62,876
book	402,318	387,138	51,913	28,188	57,835	18,117	18,516	19,521	44,345	42,241	44,804	28,435
event	609,076	803,158	101,246	52,133	78,587	18,277	20,889	27,400	46,788	66,640	44,764	72,902
total	28,616,962	9,292,476	1,503,039	652,697	1,098,298	548,360	508,524	736,602	762,512	715,983	653,867	517,114

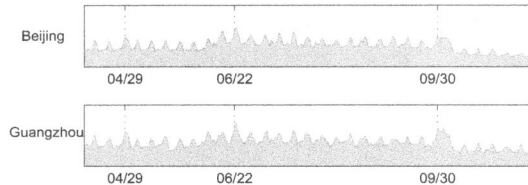

Figure 5: Daily trends of check-ins in different cities.

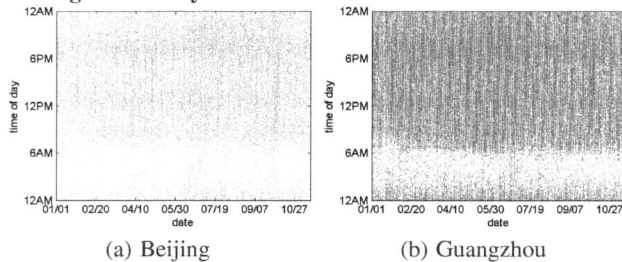

(a) Beijing   (b) Guangzhou

Figure 6: Diurnal distribution users' check-ins.

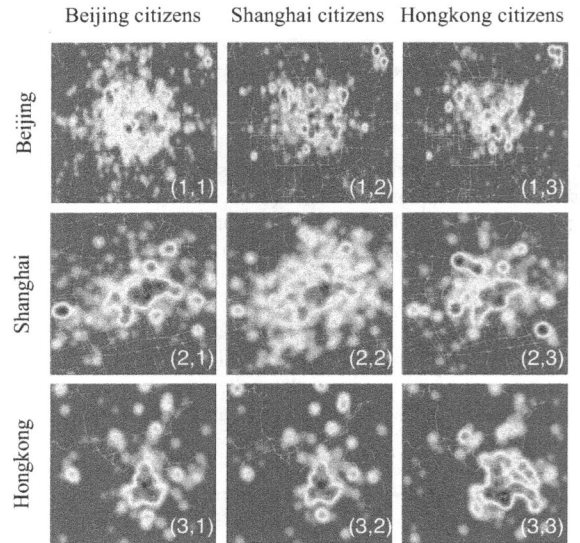

Figure 7: Check-in density distribution of 3 cities showing where people check-in in each other's cities. The diagonal subplots (local citizens) show significantly higher diversity than other subplots (travelers).

Sina Weibo (China's Twitter), Douban (an interest-based social network), Dianping (China's Yelp).

Check-ins. We collected in total 39,358,679 check-ins, where each check-in was represented with a timestamp, a latitude, a longitude, and a POI category. Since these physical footprints are extremely crucial for understanding individual lifestyles, we analyzed them in several dimensions.

For example, Fig. 5 shows the daily trends (during Apr. 9, 2012 to Nov. 15, 2012) of the total number of check-ins with respect to two major cities in north and south China respectively (Beijing and Guangzhou). As is shown, the number of check-ins periodically rises on weekends and falls on weekdays. Here, the dates that we have labeled on the x-axis are important public holidays (at least three days) in China, including Labor Day (3 days), Dragon Boat Day (3 days), and National Day (8 days). On these days, the number of check-ins is relatively higher than normal weekends, especially on National Day, which has a clearly longer peak than other holidays. This is mainly because that a lot of people travel with their families and friends during this long holiday.

We further examined the diurnal distribution of people's check-in behavior by sampling the 1000 individuals in different cities and analyzing their diurnal check-in distributions, as shown in Fig. 6. Unlike the aggregated daily trends, the diurnal distribution varies in different cities. For example, Fig. 6a and Fig. 6b reveal that people in Guangzhou check in earlier than people in Beijing in the morning (7AM), and later in the evening (12AM). This result conforms

very well to a recent survey [4] with 1 million respondents performed by Chinese Medical Doctor Association, which shows that the average bedtime of Guangzhou citizens is 23:08pm and 22:15pm for Beijing.

Fig. 7 plots the density distribution of check-ins posted by Beijing, Shanghai and Hongkong citizens when they are in each other's city, e.g., grid (1,2) in the 3×3 grids tells us where Shanghai citizens check-in at Beijing. This figure clearly indicates that the check-ins of local citizens are much more diverse than those of travelers (as expected), and people in different cities have differentiated preferences when traveling in other cities. e.g., the hot spots in grid (2,1) and grid (2,3) are quite different.

Movies/Music/Books/Events. We collected in total 82,451 movies, 477,712 songs , 406,564 books, and 407,950 social events/gatherings. All of the above entities have their taxonomies, which were also crawled and leveraged for constructing the footprints. Note these are the number of entities, not footprints. In terms of footprints, we crawled 6,241,036 movie footprints, 3,075,305 music footprints, 1,560,206 book footprints, and 2,596,252 event footprints. Table 1 summarizes the different kinds of footprints for different cities.

---

[4] http://bit.ly/14cvnem

📍 checkin 🎬 movie 📖 book 🎵 music 👥 events   ☼ 8:00-12:00 ☀ 12:00-20:00 🌙 20:00-8:00 🌐 non-local

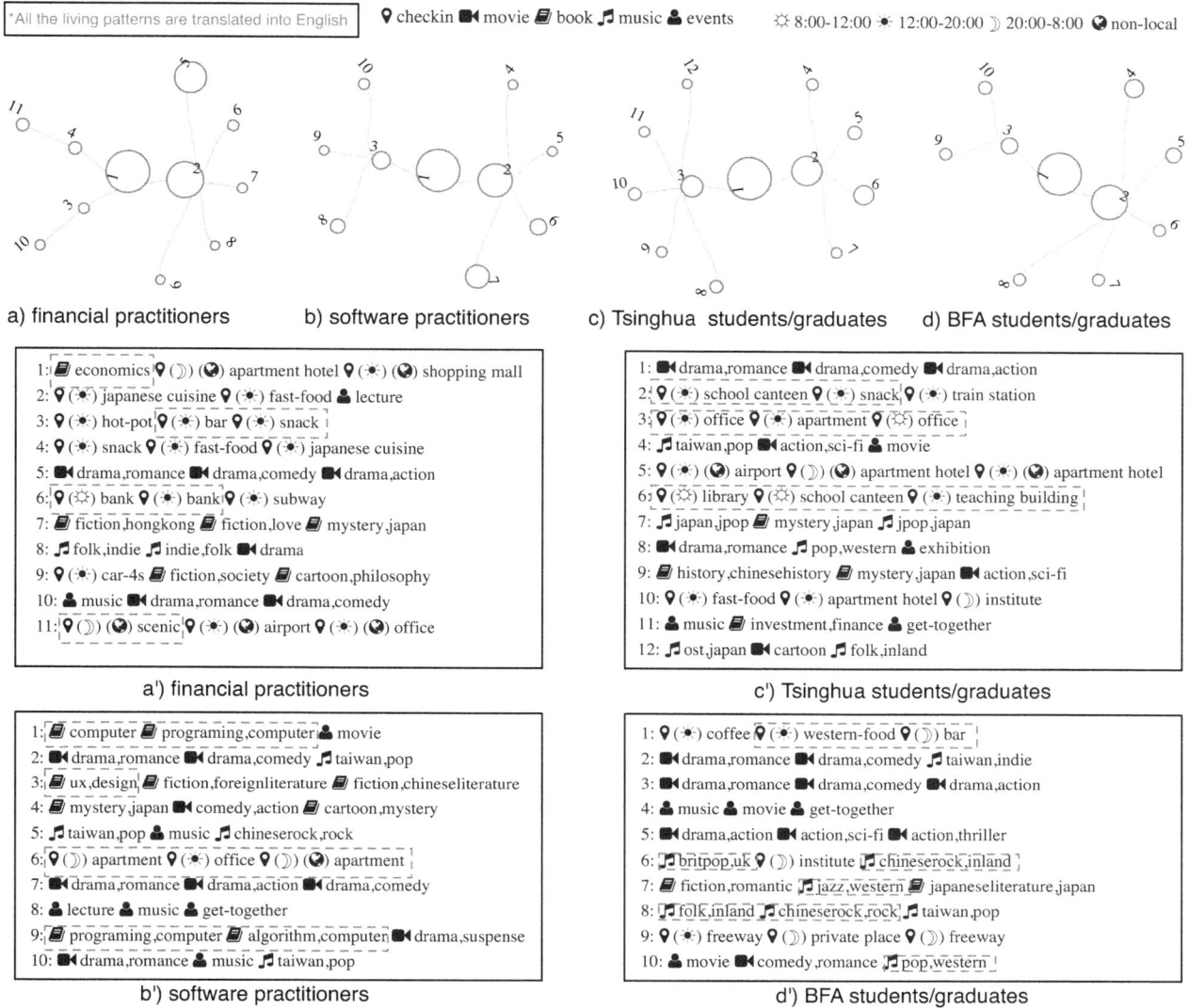

a) financial practitioners   b) software practitioners   c) Tsinghua students/graduates   d) BFA students/graduates

a') financial practitioners

1: 📖 economics 📍(🌙) (🌐) apartment hotel 📍(☀) (🌐) shopping mall
2: 📍(☀) japanese cuisine 📍(☀) fast-food 👥 lecture
3: 📍(☀) hot-pot 📍(☀) bar 📍(☀) snack
4: 📍(☀) snack 📍(☀) fast-food 📍(☀) japanese cuisine
5: 🎬 drama,romance 🎬 drama,comedy 🎬 drama,action
6: 📍(☼) bank 📍(☀) bank 📍(☀) subway
7: 📖 fiction,hongkong 📖 fiction,love 📖 mystery,japan
8: 🎵 folk,indie 🎵 indie,folk 🎬 drama
9: 📍(☀) car-4s 📖 fiction,society 📖 cartoon,philosophy
10: 👥 music 🎬 drama,romance 🎬 drama,comedy
11: 📍(🌙) (🌐) scenic 📍(☀) (🌐) airport 📍(☀) (🌐) office

c') Tsinghua students/graduates

1: 🎬 drama,romance 🎬 drama,comedy 🎬 drama,action
2: 📍(☀) school canteen 📍(☀) snack 📍(☀) train station
3: 📍(☀) office 📍(☀) apartment 📍(☼) office
4: 🎵 taiwan,pop 🎬 action,sci-fi 👥 movie
5: 📍(☀) (🌐) airport 📍(🌙) (🌐) apartment hotel 📍(☀) (🌐) apartment hotel
6: 📍(☼) library 📍(☼) school canteen 📍(☀) teaching building
7: 🎵 japan,jpop 📖 mystery,japan 🎵 jpop,japan
8: 🎬 drama,romance 🎵 pop,western 👥 exhibition
9: 📖 history,chinesehistory 📖 mystery,japan 🎬 action,sci-fi
10: 📍(☀) fast-food 📍(☀) apartment hotel 📍(🌙) institute
11: 👥 music 📖 investment,finance 👥 get-together
12: 🎵 ost,japan 🎬 cartoon 🎵 folk,inland

b') software practitioners

1: 📖 computer 📖 programing,computer 👥 movie
2: 🎬 drama,romance 🎬 drama,comedy 🎵 taiwan,pop
3: 📖 ux,design 📖 fiction,foreignliterature 📖 fiction,chineseliterature
4: 📖 mystery,japan 🎬 comedy,action 📖 cartoon,mystery
5: 🎵 taiwan,pop 👥 music 🎵 chineserock,rock
6: 📍(🌙) apartment 📍(☀) office 📍(🌙) (🌐) apartment
7: 🎬 drama,romance 🎬 drama,action 🎬 drama,comedy
8: 👥 lecture 👥 music 👥 get-together
9: 📖 programing,computer 📖 algorithm,computer 🎬 drama,suspense
10: 🎬 drama,romance 👥 music 🎵 taiwan,pop

d') BFA students/graduates

1: 📍(☀) coffee 📍(☀) western-food 📍(🌙) bar
2: 🎬 drama,romance 🎬 drama,comedy 🎵 taiwan,indie
3: 🎬 drama,romance 🎬 drama,comedy 🎬 drama,action
4: 👥 music 👥 movie 👥 get-together
5: 🎬 drama,action 🎬 action,sci-fi 🎬 action,thriller
6: 🎵 britpop,uk 📍(🌙) institute 🎵 chineserock,inland
7: 📖 fiction,romantic 🎵 jazz,western 📖 japaneseliterature,japan
8: 🎵 folk,inland 🎵 chineserock,rock 🎵 taiwan,pop
9: 📍(☀) freeway 📍(🌙) private place 📍(🌙) freeway
10: 👥 movie 🎬 comedy,romance 🎵 pop,western

Figure 8: Lifestyle spectrums of different groups in terms of vocation and education.

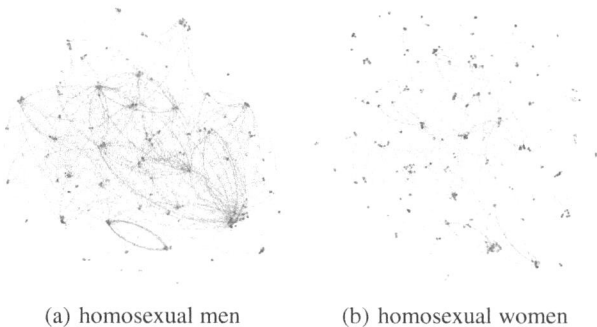

(a) homosexual men   (b) homosexual women

Figure 9: Social graphs of homosexual men and women in our dataset, where different colors indicate different places of residence.

5.2 Results on Different Demographic Groups

We extract profiles from users' multiple networks, such as gender, place of residence, sexual orientation, education, and vocation. We note that all these networks have privacy options for users to hide their profiles from others, and we only crawled *public profiles*. Based on which, we segmented users into different groups and generated the lifestyle spectrums for each group. Due to space limit, we only present part of our findings and results here. For each lifestyle spectrum, we show the top-3 levels, where each living pattern is presented by the top-3 frequent footprints.

Vocation and Education. Fig. 8a,b present the lifestyle spectrums for two vocational groups: financial practitioners and software practitioners, both containing 1,000 samples. As is shown, the most common living pattern for these financial practitioners is reading economics books and checking-in at apartment hotel (indicating that they are often on business trips). However, for software practitioners, reading programming books is their most-typical living pattern, which makes perfect sense. Node 6 (N6 for short, similarly hereinafter) in Fig. 8a targets a subgroup of individuals who are probably working for banks. Compared with software practitioners, the result suggests that these financial practitioners live a chicer life, e.g., more often they show at bars and scenic places (N3, N11 of Fig. 8a), while the software engineers are still coding or reading programming books at apartment or office (N6, N9 of Fig. 8b).

Fig. 8c and Fig. 8d are lifestyle spectrums of graduates and students from two universities: Tsinghua University (known as one of the best science and engineering university in China) and Beijing Film Academy (BFA), which graduated many famous alumni in filming industry such as Yimou Zhang and Kaige Chen. The results (generated with 300 samples for each group) show that their lifestyles widely differ from each other, e.g., N1 in Fig 8c reveal that most students/graduates in BFA go to bar and western food restaurants frequently and their music tastes are more diverse than Tsinghua students/graduates. In addition, students and graduates from Tsinghua are automatically categorized into two subgroups: Living patterns rooted at N2 reveal many characteristics of a student such as "teaching-building"; while the living pattern of N3 is commonly shared by working people.

Gender and sexual orientation. Gender and sexual orientation differences were intensely studied in sociology and social psychology[28]. Based on self-identified sexual orientation provided in users' *public* profiles, we randomly sampled 500 homosexual men and women to generate the lifestyle spectrums, as depicted in Fig. 10a,b. In 2006, China was estimated to have 5–9 million homosexual men among 452 million adult males (aged 15 to 64)[13]. To be comparable, we sampled 45,000 heterosexual men and women (for each), and generated their lifestyle spectrums. As a result, some characteristic living patterns for homosexual men/women are prominently revealed, e.g., watching homosexual movies, gym, and reading tanbi books (describing the love between boys). For homosexual women, however, the living pattern "watching homosexual movie" is not as dominant as for homosexual men. Another remarkable signal implied by the result is that a certain number of homosexual men are students (N10 in Fig. 10a). Note that social links are also leveraged in our model for learning lifestyle spectrums. Fig. 9 is a visualization of their social graphs (using OpenOrd layout [22] for edge-cutting and community clustering), where we removed 21 isolated nodes for homosexual men and 27 for homosexual women. It's clear that the gay community has a much stronger social connection than the lesbian community.

The gender difference between heterosexual men and women is also significant, e.g., men watch more sci-fi and action movies while women prefer romance movies (N1 of Fig. 10c,d). N2 and N4 of Fig. 10c may refer to two kinds of men: men who spend more time on career vs. men who spend more time with family. For women, regardless of which subgroup they belong to, they all love shopping (N1 of Fig. 10d). A majority group of females like Taiwan or western pop-style music (N2 of Fig. 10d). Many typical living patterns for Chinese women are also brought to light, such as shoe-store, hot-pot, snack, bread and KTV (N3,4,7,11,13 of Fig. 10d).

Place of Residence. We generated the lifestyle spectrum of 15 cities in China using 10,000 sampled citizens for each city, e.g., Fig. 3 shows the result of Beijing (results of other cities are not visualized here due to space limit). Meanwhile, we calculated the similarity of lifestyle spectrums between different cities based on Hausdorff distance [30], which is commonly used as a similarity measure between two sets.

Specifically, a lifestyle spectrum $\mathcal{T}$ can be represented by a set containing all the lifestyles (i.e., paths), as modeled in Section 4.1. Consider a lifestyle l as a point in a m-dimension space, where m is the number of unique footprints. For each footprint f that occurs in some living pattern $S \in l$, we assign the dimension in l that cor-

Table 2: Average recognition ratio

Method	RTM	hLDA	RH-LDA
Check-in	0.361	0.500	0.667
+Movie	0.389	0.556	0.694
++Music	0.444	0.583	0.722
+++Book	0.472	0.639	0.806
++++Events	0.472	0.667	0.833

responds to f with the proportion of people who exhibit lifestyle l. Then the distance between any two lifestyles can be calculated using the Euclidean distance. Hence, the Hausdorff distance between $\mathcal{T}_1$ and $\mathcal{T}_2$ is defined as

$$d_H(\mathcal{T}_1, \mathcal{T}_2) = \max(\max_{l \in \mathcal{T}_1} \min_{l' \in \mathcal{T}_2} d(l, l'), \max_{l' \in \mathcal{T}_2} \min_{l \in \mathcal{T}_1} d(l, l')).$$

Fig. 11 shows the similarity matrix of these cities, where green cubes indicate a smaller distance (i.e., similar) and red cubes stand for a larger distance. Many similarities found in this matrix can be explained by geographical proximity and culture homology. For example, Chengdu and Chonqing have similar lifestyles, which is widely known to the public since they are geographically close to each other and they share the root of Ba-Shu Culture[5]. Another example is Shanghai and Tianjin, the two major seaports in China, which were both colonized in the 19th century, and for both of them, there is a "mother" river flowing through their hinterlands (Haihe River[6] and Huangpu River[7]). It has been found long ago that a river plays a key-role in a city's economy, civilization and culture development [18].

5.3 User Study

In order to further validate our method in the field, we performed a user study, which focused on evaluating the lifestyle spectrum of a city. Our study is guided by the following questions: 1) Whether our model can capture the characteristics of lifestyles in a city, thus reveal the intergroup difference between different cities? 2) Whether our method can reveal diverse lifestyles of a city, thus can uncover the intragroup variations?

Participants. We recruited 36 participants (aged 21–45, 20 males and 16 females) who reside in 6 cities, including Beijing (BJ), Shanghai (SH), Guangzhou (GZ), Hangzhou (HZ), Chengdu (CD), and Xiamen (XM) (6 participants for each city), and all of them have lived in their cities for more than 8 years.

Baselines. In terms of learning the lifestyle spectrum, we compared our model (RH-LDA) with two baselines: 1) The hLDA model, which only considers words of a document (i.e., footprints). 2) The RTM model, which only leverages social links and does not support a hierarchical structure of topics. Thus the lifestyle spectrum generated by RTM is a list of topics instead of a tree-structure. In addition, RTM requires the number of topics n to be fixed beforehand. To make RTM comparable with hLDA and RH-LDA, we fixed n to be identical to the number of living patterns generated by hLDA and RH-LDA respectively, and chose the best performance between them as the result of RTM. All these models were inferred using collapsed Gibbs sampling, and the hyper parameters were learned through Metropolitan Hasting [7].

Intergroup Difference. Using each of the 3 methods, we generated lifestyle spectrums of these cities and visualized them to the participants, without telling them which city each spectrum stands

---
[5] http://bit.ly/15B2Qvm
[6] http://bit.ly/ZSHO9T
[7] http://bit.ly/10tpl5U

📍 checkin 🎬 movie 📖 book 🎵 music 👤 events   ☼ 8:00-12:00 ☀ 12:00-20:00 ☽ 20:00-8:00 🌐 non-local

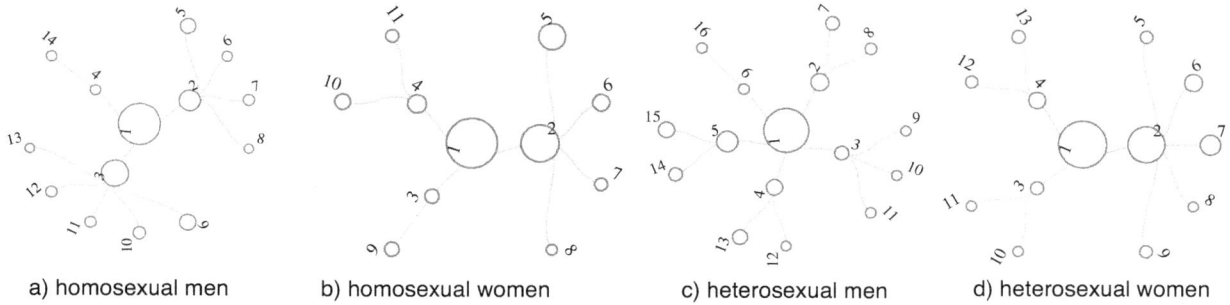

a) homosexual men   b) homosexual women   c) heterosexual men   d) heterosexual women

a') homosexual men

1: 🎬 drama,comedy 🎬 drama,romance 🎬 drama,homosexual
2: 🎬 drama 🎬 drama,romance 🎬 drama,suspense
3: 🎵 pop,western 🎵 western,pop 🎵 pop,america
4: 📍(☽) western-food 🎬 suspense 📖 fiction,tanbi
5: 🎬 drama,comedy 🎬 drama,suspense 🎬 drama,romance
6: 📍(☀)(🌐) fast-food 📍(☀)(🌐) subway 📍(☀)(🌐) supermarket
7: 🎵 japan,jpop 🎵 jpop,japan 🎬 horror
8: 👤 music 👤 get-together 🎵 britpop,uk
9: 🎵 taiwan,pop 🎬 comedy,cartoon 🎵 taiwan,chinese
10: 📍(☽) teaching building 📍(☀) teaching building 📍(☼) teaching building
11: 👤 get-together 👤 lecture 👤 exhibition
12: 📍(☀) gym 📍(☼) gym 📍(☀) library
13: 🎵 taiwan,indie 📖 fiction,youth 🎵 taiwan,pop
14: 👤 movie 👤 lecture 👤 get-together

b') homosexual women

1: 🎬 drama,romance 🎬 drama,comedy 🎬 drama
2: 👤 music 👤 get-together 👤 exhibition
3: 👤 lecture 📍(☀) office 📍(☼) office
4: 🎵 taiwan,pop 🎵 taiwan,indie 🎵 hongkong,cantonese
5: 🎬 drama,homosexual 📖 fiction,hongkong 🎬 drama,action
6: 👤 music 👤 lecture 👤 movie
7: 🎵 britpop,uk 🎵 electronica 🎬 cartoon
8: 📍(☀) apartment 📍(☽) school dormitory 📍(☽) apartment
9: 📍(☀) coffee 📍(☽) apartment 📍(☽) coffee
10: 👤 music 🎵 taiwan,indie 👤 exhibition
11: 👤 music 🎵 britpop,uk 👤 movie

c') heterosexual men

1: 🎬 drama,action 🎬 drama,comedy 🎬 sci-fi,action
2: 📍(☀) office 📍(☀) coffee 📍(☀) apartment hotel
3: 🎵 jpop,japan 🎵 japan,jpop 🎵 taiwan,pop
4: 📍(☽) apartment 📍(☀) apartment 📍(☀) subway
5: 🎬 drama,romance 🎵 taiwan,pop 🎬 drama
6: 📍(☀) scenic 📖 english 📍(☀) electronics
7: 👤 music 👤 lecture 👤 get-together
8: 📍(☽) shopping mall 📍(☀) shopping mall 📍(☽)(🌐) apartment hotel
9: 🎵 taiwan,pop 🎵 pop,western 🎵 hongkong,cantonese
10: 🎬 cartoon 🎵 ost,japan 📖 cartoon,japan
11: 📍(☽) private place 📍(☽) fast-food 📍(☀) subway
12: 📖 fiction,youth 📖 japaneseliterature,japan 📖 fiction,foreignliterature
13: 📍(☀) office 📍(☀) shopping mall 📍(☼) office
14: 📍(☽)(🌐) shopping mall 📍(☀)(🌐) shopping mall 📍(☽)(🌐) office

d') heterosexual women

1: 🎬 drama,romance 📍(☀) shopping mall 🎬 comedy,romance
2: 🎵 taiwan,pop 🎵 pop,western 🎵 taiwan,indie
3: 📍(☀) shoe store 📍(☀) shopping mall 📍(☀)(🌐) train station
4: 📍(☀)(🌐) coffee 📍(☀)(🌐) hot-pot 📍(☀)(🌐) scenic
5: 🎵 taiwan,pop 📖 romantic,fiction 📖 fiction,youth
6: 🎵 japan,jpop 🎬 drama,comedy 🎬 comedy,romance
7: 📍(☀) shopping mall 📍(☀) office 📍(☀) snack
8: 📍(☽) coffee 📍(☽) bar 📍(☀) coffee
9: 📍(☽) apartment 📍(☀) subway 📍(☽) subway
10: 👤 lecture 📖 fiction,chineseliterature 👤 exhibition
11: 📍(☽) ktv 📍(☀) ktv 📍(☀) airport
12: 👤 music 👤 lecture 👤 get-together
13: 📍(☀)(🌐) shopping mall 📍(☽)(🌐) shopping mall 📍(☀)(🌐) bread

Figure 10: Lifestyle spectrum of hetero- and homosexual men and women.

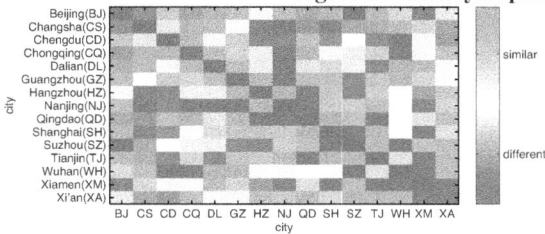

Figure 11: Similarity matrix w.r.t 15 cities.

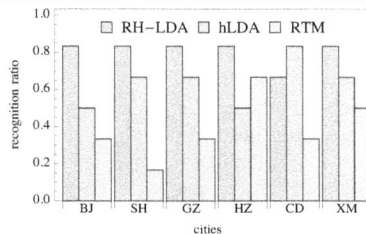

Figure 12: Recognition ratio.

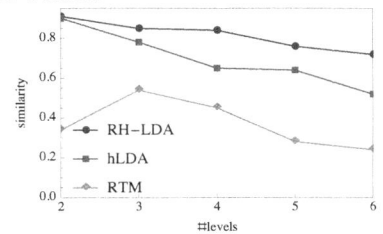

Figure 13: Jaccard Similarity.

for. Then each participant picked one among the 6 different spectrums, which she believed is most likely to be her place of residence (we had told them to consider not only their own lifestyles but the variations of lifestyles according to their knowledge of their cities). Later, we calculated the recognition ratio (RR) (the number of users who successfully identified the spectrum of their cities divided by the number of users) for each model. Fig.12 shows the recognition ratio for each city when we leveraged all kinds of footprints. We further studied how well these models can perform if we reduce the heterogeneity of footprints. Table 2 summarizes the average recognition ratio for all the considered cities, given different types of footprints including checkins, movies, songs, books, and offline events. Clearly, the performance of these models were all improved by increasing the diversity of footprints. However, for each setting, RH-LDA achieves the highest recognition ratio, which suggests that our model is more effective than competing methods in terms of the ability to summarize the lifestyles of a city and uncover the intergroup differences.

Intragroup Variation. For studying the effectiveness of our model in terms of capturing lifestyle variations within a group, we asked the participants for their online network accounts, and collected their footprints. Among them, 23 participants own multiple social network accounts. We used the trained model for each city to infer these participants' lifestyles beforehand. Then we compared the generated lifestyle (a path on the spectrum for RH-LDA and hLDA, and a set of living patterns for RTM) with their own lifestyles chosen by themselves for each model pertaining to their own cities. We then calculated their similarity by extracting the top-5 footprints for each related living pattern of these two sequences (lifestyles), and compared their average Jaccard Similarity (JS). Furthermore, we studied the effect induced by the number of levels in the spectrum (the number of topics for RTM is determined as before), as shown in Fig.13. As a result, our model outperforms the competitors significantly, however, when the number of levels increases, the similarity between the inferred lifestyle and the user's perceived lifestyle decreases for all the models. In particular, when the number of level goes from 3 to 4, the performance of the other methods declines precipitously, nevertheless, our method is relatively more stable and robust. According to users' feedback, when the number of levels becomes too large, it's not easy for them to choose the most relevant lifestyles.

6. DISCUSSIONS

• **Limitations.** While showing the potential to leverage massive behavioral data for learning lifestyles, we are aware that this method has several limitations. First, human lifestyle is complicated. It is still possible that the actual lifestyle of a person deviates from what reflected in the behavioral data. Second, the targeted population mainly consists of young people who use online social networks extensively, which may bias the lifestyle spectrum. However, this is actually induced more by the limitation of the data rather than the model. Note that conventional social studies might also suffer from sampling bias [5], with much smaller scale and coverage (e.g., dozens of college students) compared to the dataset used in this work. We believe by employing more types of footprints that mirror users' offline behaviors, e.g., credit card transactions and public transit records, this framework can cover a broader demographic and attain a more faithful understanding of their lifestyles.

• **Privacy.** We re-emphasize that in this work we only collected users' *publicly available* data (i.e., visible to everyone on the web) including profiles, social links, and footprints. Besides, the connections between users' different accounts are identified from their self-disclosed contents (refer to Section 3.1). However, we remind that some users may have no intention to (or carelessly) disclose the connections of their different accounts (e.g., by adopting the default privacy options of some websites, or by posting a tweet with location check-in automatically embedded). Thus, we suggest both the users and social networking sites re-consider their privacy policy in terms of the linkage between multiple accounts, which may potentially be exploited by attackers and thus bring privacy risk [20] to the users.

7. CONCLUSION

We have presented LifeSpec, a data-driven framework for exploring and hierarchically summarizing urban lifestyles. In this framework, we have built a data platform to connect users' heterogeneous behavioral data and their social links. Given the behavioral data as digital footprints, we have formally modeled the lifestyle spectrum of a group and generalized a probabilistic model to learn the lifestyle spectrum. We conducted a series of experiments and user studies to validate the usability and flexibility of this framework.

Please note that this framework is not designed to replace traditional methods in lifestyle research. Instead, we believe that these methods can complement each other (actually this work is also a collaboration with sociologists) to enable a better and more comprehensive understanding of human lifestyles, which is not only important for advancing the lifestyle research in social science, but also essential to *personalized* recommendation and *targeted* advertising.

References

[1] A. Agarwal, N. R. Desai, R. Ruffoli, and A. Carpi. Lifestyle and testicular dysfunction: a brief update. *Biomedicine & Pharmacotherapy*, 62(8):550–553, 2008.

[2] M. Allamanis, S. Scellato, and C. Mascolo. Evolution of a location-based online social network: analysis and models. In *Proc. ACM conference on Internet measurement conference*, pages 145–158, 2012.

[3] H. Ansbacher. Life style: a historical and systematic review. *Journal of individual psychology*, 23(2):191, 1967.

[4] M. Benson and K. O'Reilly. Migration and the search for a better way of life: a critical exploration of lifestyle migration. *The Sociological Review*, 57(4):608–625, 2009.

[5] R. A. Berk. An introduction to sample selection bias in sociological data. *American Sociological Review*, pages 386–398, 1983.

[6] D. Blei and J. Lafferty. Topic models. *Text mining: classification, clustering, and applications*, 10:71, 2009.

[7] D. M. Blei, T. L. Griffiths, and M. I. Jordan. The nested chinese restaurant process and bayesian nonparametric inference of topic hierarchies. *J. ACM*, 57(2):7:1–7:30, 2010.

[8] J. Chang and D. Blei. Relational topic models for document networks. In *Artificial Intelligence and Statistics*, pages 81–88, 2009.

[9] J. Chang and D. M. Blei. Hierarchical relational models for document networks. *The Annals of Applied Statistics*, 4(1): 124–150, 2010.

[10] J. Cranshaw, E. Toch, J. Hong, A. Kittur, and N. Sadeh. Bridging the gap between physical location and online social networks. In *Proc. Ubicomp*, pages 119–128, 2010.

[11] J. Cranshaw, R. Schwartz, J. Hong, and N. Sadeh. The livehoods project: Utilizing social media to understand the dynamics of a city. *Association for the Advancement of Artificial Intelligence*, 2012.

[12] N. Eagle and A. Pentland. Reality mining: sensing complex social systems. *Personal and Ubiquitous Computing*, 10(4): 255–268, 2006.

[13] B. Gill, Y. Huang, and X. Lu. Demography of HIV/AIDS in China. *Center for Strategic International Studies*, 2007.

[14] O. Goga, H. Lei, S. H. K. Parthasarathi, G. Friedland, R. Sommer, and R. Teixeira. Exploiting innocuous activity for correlating users across sites. In *Proc. WWW*, pages 447–458, 2013.

[15] D. Griffiths and M. Tenenbaum. Hierarchical topic models and the nested chinese restaurant process. In *Proc. NIPS*, volume 16, page 17, 2003.

[16] R. Havighurst and K. Feigenbaum. Leisure and life-style. *American Journal of Sociology*, pages 396–404, 1959.

[17] A. Juels, M. Jakobsson, and T. Jagatic. Cache cookies for browser authentication. In *IEEE Symposium on Security and Privacy*, pages 5–pp, 2006.

[18] A. Kelman. *A river and its city: The nature of landscape in New Orleans*. University of California Press, 2006.

[19] M. Kosinski, D. Stillwell, and T. Graepel. Private traits and attributes are predictable from digital records of human behavior. *PNAS*, 2013.

[20] B. Krishnamurthy. Privacy and online social networks: Can colorless green ideas sleep furiously? In *IEEE Symposium on Security and Privacy*, 2013.

[21] J. Liu, F. Zhang, X. Song, Y.-I. Song, and C.-Y. Lin. What's in a name? an unsupervised approach to link users across communities. In *Proc. WSDM*, 2013.

[22] S. Martin, W. M. Brown, R. Klavans, and K. W. Boyack. OpenOrd: an open-source toolbox for large graph layout. In *IS&T/SPIE Electronic Imaging*, pages 786806–786806, 2011.

[23] N. Mathur. Shopping malls, credit cards and global brands consumer culture and lifestyle of india's new middle class. *South Asia Research*, 30(3):211–231, 2010.

[24] R. Michman, E. Mazze, and A. Greco. *Lifestyle marketing: reaching the new American consumer*. Praeger Publishers, 2003.

[25] A. Narayanan and V. Shmatikov. De-anonymizing social networks. In *IEEE Symposium on Security and Privacy*, pages 173–187, 2009.

[26] C. Nie and L. Zepeda. Lifestyle segmentation of US food shoppers to examine organic and local food consumption. *Appetite*, 57(1):28–37, 2011.

[27] J. Pitman. Poisson–Dirichlet and GEM invariant distributions for split-and-merge transformations of an interval partition. *Combinatorics, Probability & Computing*, 11(05):501–514, 2002.

[28] S. G. Prus and E. Gee. Gender differences in the influence of economic, lifestyle, and psychosocial factors on later-life health. *Canadian Journal of Public Health*, 94(4):306–309, 2003.

[29] K. K. Rachuri, C. Efstratiou, I. Leontiadis, C. Mascolo, and P. J. Rentfrow. Metis: Exploring mobile phone sensing offloading for efficiently supporting social sensing applications. In *Proc. PerCom*. IEEE, 2013.

[30] R. T. Rockafellar and R. J-B Wets. *Variational analysis*, volume 317. Springer, 2011.

[31] R. Rosenthal. *Experimenter effects in behavioral research*. Halsted Press, 1976.

[32] G. Takeuti, W. M. Zaring, and G. Takeuti. *Introduction to axiomatic set theory*. Springer-Verlag, 1982.

[33] R. E. Tarjan. Efficiency of a good but not linear set union algorithm. *Journal of the ACM*, 22(2):215–225, 1975.

[34] R. E. Tarjan. *Data structures and network algorithms*, volume 14. SIAM, 1983.

[35] R. E. Tarjan and J. Van Leeuwen. Worst-case analysis of set union algorithms. *Journal of the ACM (JACM)*, 31(2): 245–281, 1984.

[36] P. Vyncke. Lifestyle segmentation from attitudes, interests and opinions, to values, aesthetic styles, life visions and media preferences. *European journal of communication*, 17 (4):445–463, 2002.

[37] W. Warren, R. Stevens, and C. McConkey. Using demographic and lifestyle analysis to segment individual investors. *Financial Analysts Journal*, pages 74–77, 1990.

[38] C. Werner and P. Parmelee. Similarity of activity preferences among friends: Those who play together stay together. *Social Psychology Quarterly*, pages 62–66, 1979.

[39] J. Zheng and L. M. Ni. An unsupervised framework for sensing individual and cluster behavior patterns from human mobile data. In *Proc. Ubicomp*, pages 153–162, 2012.

APPENDIX

A. PROOF OF THEOREM 1

PROOF. Since Algorithm 1 only visits each profile page once (line 2-4 of Procedure VisitProfile), and the merge operation (line 9) can be implemented using the Union-Find algorithm [33] (note that the number of connected URLs per profile page is limited by the types of networks), thus Algorithm 1 keeps the complexity of Union-Find with $O(|h_\triangleright|)$ find operations and $|h_\triangleright|$ elements, i.e., $O(|h_\triangleright|\alpha(|h_\triangleright|))$ [34, 35]. Therefore, the theorem holds when the following statements are true: 1) After termination, U contains all the profile pages in $h_\triangleright$; 2) At any time, there are no two users who have a joint profile page and 3) After each loop (line 18), for any two profile pages $p', p'' \in h_\triangleright$, where $p' \in u' \in U$ and $p'' \in u'' \in U$, if $u' \neq u''$ (i.e., p'' and p'' are merged into different classes), then p' and p'' are not connected.

The first statement is true since every visited page is added to a user in U at line 13. The second statement holds because every time, we add all the visited profile pages (line 8 of Algorithm 1) into a single user u', and no profile page is visited more than once. We assume the last statement does not hold, i.e., $u' \neq u''$ and $\exists$ an undirected path $\mathcal{W} = p_0(= p')p_1p_2 \ldots p_n(= p'')$ connecting p' and p'', where each p_ip_{i+1} are *directly connected* $\forall i = 0, 1 \ldots, n-1$ (see Section 3.2). Thus, $\forall i = 0, 1, \ldots, n-1$, $\exists$ a profile page c_i, s.t. the URLs of p_i and p_{i+1} co-occur on c_i, which leads to three cases: 1) $c_i = p_i$, thus $p_i \triangleright p_{i+1}$; 2) $c_i = p_{i+1}$, thus $p_{i+1} \triangleright p_i$; 3) $c_i \triangleright p_i$ and $c_i \triangleright p_{i+1}$. In each of the above cases, Algorithm 1 will add p_i and p_{i+1} into the same equivalence class, i.e., $u' = u''$, which yields a contradiction. Therefore, the theorem holds. $\square$

B. INFERENCE OF RH-LDA

The collapsed Gibbs sampling process is summarized as follows: Given the current state of the sampler, $\{\mathbf{c}_{1:D}^{(t)}, \mathbf{z}_{1:D}^{(t)}\}$, iteratively for each individual $d \in \{1, 2, \ldots, D\}$,

1. Randomly draw $\mathbf{c}_d^{(t+1)}$ from $p(\mathbf{c}_d|\mathbf{w}, \mathbf{c}_{-d}, \mathbf{z}, \eta, \gamma)$, which is exactly the same as given in [7].

2. For each footprint $f \in \{1, 2, \ldots, N_d\}$ of u, randomly draw $\mathbf{z}_{n,d}^{(t+1)}$ from

$$p(z_{d,f} = l | \mathbf{z}_{-(d,f)}, \mathbf{c}, \mathbf{w}, m, \pi, \eta, \zeta, \upsilon)$$

$$\propto p(z_{d,f} | \mathbf{z}_{d,-f}, m, \pi) p(w_{d,f} | \mathbf{z}, \mathbf{c}, \mathbf{w}_{-(d,f)}, \eta, \zeta, \upsilon) \quad (3)$$

$$\prod_{d' \neq d : y_{d,d'} = 1} \psi_e(y_{d,d'} = 1 | \mathbf{c}_{(d,\mathbf{z}_d)}, \mathbf{c}_{(d',\mathbf{z}'_d)}, \zeta, \upsilon) \quad (4)$$

$$\prod_{d' \neq d : y_{d,d'} = 0} \psi_e(y_{d,d'} = 0 | \mathbf{c}_{(d,\mathbf{z}_d)}, \mathbf{c}_{(d',\mathbf{z}'_d)}, \zeta, \upsilon). \quad (5)$$

Eq. (3) is the same as hLDA, given in [7].

Eq. (4)$= \displaystyle\prod_{d' \neq d : y_{d,d'} = 1} \exp\left(\frac{\eta_k N_{d'}^k}{N_d^2 N_{d'}}\right)$ and

Eq. (5)$= \displaystyle\prod_{d' \neq d : y_{d,d'} = 0} \left(1 - \exp\left(\frac{1}{N_d^2, N_{d'}} \sum_k \left(\eta_k N_d^k N_{d'}^k\right) + \upsilon\right)\right),$

where $k = \mathbf{c}_{d,l}$ is the assigned living pattern of n, N_d^k is the number of footprints assigned with living pattern k, and N_d denotes the number of footprints in u.

3. Iteratively learn the parameters ζ and υ, using the method provided in the appendix of [9].

Dynamics of Personal Social Relationships in Online Social Networks: a Study on Twitter

Valerio Arnaboldi, Marco Conti, Andrea Passarella
IIT-CNR, via G. Moruzzi, 1 - 56124 Pisa, Italy
{v.arnaboldi, m.conti, a.passarella}@iit.cnr.it

Robin Dunbar
Department of Experimental Psychology, University of Oxford
South Parks Road, Oxford OX1 3UD, United Kingdom
robin.dunbar@psy.ox.ac.uk

ABSTRACT

The growing popularity of Online Social Networks (OSN) is generating a large amount of communication records that can be easily accessed and analysed to study human social behaviour. This represents a unique opportunity to understand properties of social networks that were impossible to assess in the past. Although analyses on OSN conducted hitherto revealed some important global properties of the networks, there is still a lack of understanding of the mechanisms underpinning these properties, their relation to human behaviour, and their dynamic evolution over time. These aspects are clearly important to understand and characterise OSN and to identify the evolutionary strategy that favoured the diffusion of the use of online communications in our society.

In this paper we analyse a data set of Twitter communication records, studying the dynamic processes that govern the maintenance of online social relationships. The results reveal that people in Twitter have highly dynamic social networks, with a large percentage of weak ties and high turnover. This suggests that this behaviour can be the product of an evolutionary strategy aimed at coping with the extremely challenging conditions imposed by our society, where dynamism seems to be the key to success.

Categories and Subject Descriptors

H.3.4 [**Information Storage and Retrieval**]: Systems and Software—*information networks*; H.3.5 [**Information Storage and Retrieval**]: Online Information Services—*web-based services*

General Terms

Measurement, Human Factors

Keywords

Online social networks, Ego networks, Personal social relationships

1. INTRODUCTION

Online Social Networks (hereafter OSN) are one of the most important communication means that we use in our everyday life. They help us to maintain our social relationships with family and friends, as well as to enlarge our professional sphere and to acquire knowledge and new ideas from the network. OSN popularity is due to their ability to transform people into *active* producers of information, letting them create, access and share contents anywhere and anytime.

These unique characteristics of OSN are producing strong effects on our society, but the extent to which they are impacting on human social behaviour is still unknown. Nevertheless, there is no doubt that their role will be of primary importance in our future. For this reason, studying people's behaviour in OSN is of great value to understand how the society is evolving and how we can contribute to the process, designing future OSN able to fulfil users' needs in terms of management of social relationships through digital communications.

In this paper we analyse a Twitter data set containing communication traces of more than 2 million users to study the dynamic properties of the behaviour of OSN users and to start indicating analogies and differences between *online* and *offline* social networks, comparing our results with the findings in literature about more traditional types of social networks (e.g., face-to-face or phone calls social networks).

The novelty of our work, compared to other analysis performed on OSN, resides in the uniqueness of our data set, and in the focus on the dynamic evolution of social structures over time. In fact, we were able to obtain the last $3,200$ tweets of a large data set of users, that is in most cases enough to represent their whole communication history. This allowed us to carry out a sensitive analysis about the evolution of human social behaviour in Twitter over time (our data set covers user activities over a time span up to 7 years, and, on average, of one year). This new approach to studying the *dynamic* properties of social relationships and networks revealed many important aspects of OSN that should be considered to correctly understand their social properties. To the best of our knowledge, this is the first work that provides an extensive characterisation of the dynamic evolution of human social structures in one of the reference OSN.

The analysis of the evolution of human social behaviour in OSN has several practical implications. For example, it could be the basis of innovative applications that dynamically track the structure of the social networks of the users, helping people in the maintenance of their social relationships and suggesting possible actions to improve their social experience. Or, it could be used to classify users based on their dynamic behaviour (we show that different classes of users can be identified), and use this classification as context information for customising other OSN applications. In general, it can be used for personalising the OSN applications experience to the specific dynamic social behaviour of the users.

The results of our analysis indicate that in Twitter people behave in a significantly different way than in other kinds of social networks. One of the key results we present is that people prefer to maintain weak social relationships than strong ones, with a high turnover of contacts in their networks. This behaviour fits perfectly in our extremely dynamic society, where people must quickly adapt to cope with frequent changes in their life, from their sentimental sphere to their work. OSN like Twitter seem thus to be useful tools to have more access to new resources from the network and to manage light-weight social relationships, easy to be created, maintained and destroyed when needed. For this reason we think that this use of OSN can be seen as part of an evolutionary strategy adopted by humans to cope with the very dynamic conditions of the society we live in. Note that these results become evident only when the *dynamic* evolution over time of OSN social relationships is studied, while they remain "hidden" in static analyses (like those available in the literature) that observe the aggregate properties of social relationships over long time intervals. In addition, we also highlight the existence of different types of users, that can be broadly divided into two main categories: people who have a short, but intense, activity and people who interact with social peers for long time intervals. Different properties can be highlighted for these different classes, with the latter having smaller, but more stable, networks than the former, and much more similar to social networks found in previous analyses (such as [31]).

Finally, our results also suggest that, while there is a large number of users that abandon Twitter after a relatively short amount of time, there is a significant fraction of users that keep using it mostly at a constant rate. This suggests that the hypothesised decline in the use of OSN [26, 29] may not be present (at least in Twitter).

The paper is organised as follows: in Section 2 we introduce the related work in literature about the study of human social behaviour in social networks, from the point of view of different disciplines that analyse the subject. In Section 3 we describe the data set we collected and analysed. Then, in Section 4 we describe the methodology we used to study the data set. Hence, in Section 5 we present the main results of the analysis. Finally, in Section 6 we draw the conclusions of our work.

2. RELATED WORK

In this Section we summarise the main results about the characterisation of human behaviour in social networks found in different research fields. We classify social networks into two different categories: *offline* and *online* social networks. With the term "offline" we refer to all the social networks maintained with traditional (i.e., non-digital) communications. On the other hand, "online" is referred to social networks maintained by using digital communications (e.g., e-mail, social media applications, phone calls). This distinction helps us to identify the difference between the two worlds, and to understand how the introduction of digital communications shaped human social behaviour.

2.1 Offline social networks

The study of social networks started from the analysis of offline networks, typically extracted from questionnaires data and interviews. These kind of social networks have been primarily analysed in sociology, anthropology and evolutionary psychology.

2.1.1 Social network analysis

Social networks analysis (SNA) emerged from sociology in the 20th century. The first pioneers of SNA defined social networks as an ensemble of ties denoting the existence of a social connection between two individuals. From sociology, many important aspects of social networks have been found. Mark Granovetter discovered that our social contacts have different characteristic properties and their strength is unevenly distributed in the network. Strong ties are maintained with people close to us, while weak ties usually represent bridges between different communities and are thus important for accessing new ideas and resources [15]. Granovetter, in his seminal work, gave also an informal definition of tie strength, that is still used in many different analyses. Peter Marsden was one of the first to test the definition of tie strength given by Granovetter applying an analytic model on real data [20]. His findings revealed a strong correlation between the terms "tie strength" and "emotional closeness". Ronald Burt discovered that the social capital - that can be assimilated to the concept of quantity of resources acquired from the network - is negatively influenced by the presence of discontinuities in the distribution of social links in the network, called structural holes [5]. If a person can broker connections between otherwise disconnected segments her social capital increases.

Another important property of social networks is the average *distance*, the average shortest path length between any tho people in the network. Stanley Milgram, in his famous experiment, found that the typical distance in a social network is around 6. This property is better known as the "small world" or the "six degrees of separation" [27].

In general, sociologists focused their attention on the structural properties of the network, explaining the relation between these properties and human behaviour. For a complete description of all the known properties of social networks seen from a technical point of view we refer the reader to [10].

2.1.2 Ego networks and evolutionary psychology

A different approach to the study of social networks has been adopted by anthropologists and evolutionary psychologists. Rather then focusing on the global properties of the network they look at the local properties of personal social networks, often called *ego networks*. An ego network (depicted in Figure 1) is a simple model that describes the

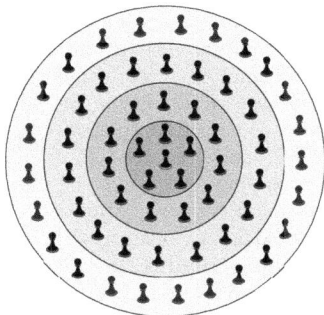

Figure 1: Ego network model

social relationships between an individual, called *ego*, and all the contacts ego has with other people, called *alters* - as defined by the standard notation in ego network analysis. The tie strength between ego and alters is modelled as the distance between them and is often estimated using the frequency of contact or the time since last contact between the people involved in the relationship [4, 16].

The most important result found on ego networks is that there is a limit on the number of alters people can actively maintain in their network, due to the cognitive constraint of human brains. This limit has been discovered by Robin Dunbar, who pioneered the study on primates, finding a positive correlation between the neocortex size - the part of the brain responsible for social activity - of different type of apes and the size of their social groups [9]. Dunbar predicted that the size of social groups in humans, given their large brain size, should be around 150 - this number is known as the *Dunbar's number*. Dunbar's hypothesis has been validated with many different experiments in offline and online social networks [4, 13, 31].

Another important result found on ego networks is that alters around ego form a layered structure with a series of inclusive concentric circles with typical characteristics and size (depicted in Figure 1). Ego can be envisioned as sitting in the centre of these circles and alters are placed around her depending on their emotional closeness. Inner circles have higher emotional closeness and frequency of contact, but lower size, since maintaining these strong relationships is extremely expensive. Moving from the inner to the outer layers, the emotional closeness decreases and the size of the layers increases, due to the lower cost of the relationships.

In anthropology and psychology literature four layers are usually identified in ego networks, as depicted in Figure 1. The first layer, called *support clique*, contains the alters to whom ego seeks advice in case of strong emotional distress or financial crisis and is usually limited to an average of 5 members. The other layers are called *sympathy* group (15 members), *affinity group* (50 members) and *active network* (150 members). The active network corresponds to the set of people that are actively maintained by ego in her network, identified by the Dunbar's number. The remarkable property of these layers is that the scaling ratio between the size of adjacent circles appears to be a constant in humans and is close to 3 [31]. The representative frequency of contact associated with these layers is *one message a week* for the support clique, *one message a month* for the sympathy group and *one message a year* for the active network. The properties of the affinity group are not accurately defined

in anthropology and have been only recently investigated in OSN [2, 3]. Other layers exist beyond the limit of the Dunbar's number, but the social relationships they contain represent only acquaintances, for which ego does not actively invest cognitive resources. For a complete ethnographic definition of the different ego network layers see [25].

Ego networks in evolutionary psychology have been studied mainly to understand the cause that induced humans to develop a large and extremely expensive brain compared to other animals. The analysis of social networks lead to the "social brain hypothesis" (SBH). SBH identifies the key factor at the basis of the evolution of human brain as the growing need for our ancestors to maintain an increasing number of social relationships with different groups to survive in the extremely challenging environmental conditions arose during the last ice age [9].

During their evolution, animals developed different mechanisms to ease the burden of maintaining their social relationships - recognised as one of the most expensive tasks in terms of cognitive resources. For example, primates use grooming to reinforce their alliance with others. Similarly, humans developed language as a convenient and light-weight instrument to maintain their relationships [8]. Language has been refined and evolved in various forms, such as *gossip* - that enables people to maintain more than one social relationship at the same time talking with friends about other friends - and *mentalisation* - the process that allows a person to understand the mental state of other people.

In this context, OSN can be seen as an example of evolution in the language domain. Using them people are able to talk directly to friends or kin, to send broadcast messages to all their contacts, to access information and news, to interact with entities other then humans (e.g., companies, institutions, associations) and to create, access and share multimedia content that can be used to express their feelings, all in one place.

Since the advent of OSN, many different studies have been done to understand the social properties of online social environments, both from a SNA perspective and from an evolutionary point of view. Despite this, we think that there is still a lack of knowledge regarding the extent to which OSN are changing human behaviour in our society and how they will contribute to the evolution of our social relationships in the future.

In this paper we contribute to fill this gap, by analysing the dynamic properties of social relationships in Twitter. This allows us to make well-grounded, though initial, hypotheses on the reasons - from an evolutionary psychology perspective - behind the results that we found. Going more in detail and validating these hypotheses is an extremely interesting subject of further investigation, that will however need custom experiments to verify individual results, and is therefore not covered in this paper.

In the following Section we summarise the most important analyses in literature about online social networks.

2.2 Online social networks

Since the advent of the digital era, humans have introduced new methods to interact within the virtual world of digital communications. The availability of digital communication traces, recorded and stored in centralised servers, paved the way for new opportunities in social network analysis. OSN data have been used to validate hypotheses that were tested on small samples collected through expensive and time consuming questionnaires, or that were simply impossible to test before the advent of OSN due to the lack of data. The typical structural properties of social networks, including the small world effect, have been found in many different OSN (see for example [17, 18]).

Besides the studies regarding the structural properties of OSN, other work has been done to characterise the local properties of social relationships in OSN. For example, in [12], the authors try to define the relationship between the tie strength - the importance of a social relationship in the network - and the different observable variables obtained through OSN communication data. The same authors applied the created model on a different medium, finding consistent results in terms of tie strength among the same social relationships in different OSN [11]. This kind of analysis has been carried out in greater detail in [4], where the authors find a connection between the definition of tie strength given by Granovetter in [15] and the composition of factors - formed of observable variables downloaded from Facebook - that explain the emotional closeness in the online relationships. The evaluation of emotional closeness collected by the authors allowed them to find a first evidence of the presence of the Dunbar's number in Facebook. Another analysis, performed on Twitter, validated the presence of an asymptotic behaviour in the communication patterns ascribable to the idea of the Dunbar's number [13]. In [2] and [3] the authors found ego network structures in Facebook and Twitter similar to those found in offline social networks, with concentric layers with compatible size and scaling factors. In [3], the authors found evidences of a difference in behaviour between separate types of users in Twitter, with those related to "humans" showing a limit ascribable to the Dunbar's number and those that appear not to be "human" who were not affected by such constraints. Recent work on phone call social networks showed that there are some important properties of OSN ascribable to human behaviour. For example, in [24], the authors found that the tie strength is not evenly distributed within ego networks, but it follows a specific shape, called "social signature", characterised by the presence of a few strong ties and many more weak ties - in line with the ego network model described in Section 2.1.2. In [21], the authors give an interesting insight into the dynamics of social relationships in phone call social networks. They identify the presence of a limited capacity each ego can devote to social activity. Moreover, social relationships are dynamically activated and deactivated over time, resulting in a constant ego network size.

Some work has been done to analyse the dynamic aspects of OSN (see for example [14,30]), but it is mainly focused on the study of the growth of the number of social relationships in the network over time. In this paper we look in detail at the the evolution of the different social structures of the ego networks of the users, that, to the best of our knowledge, has never been done before.

In [30] the authors analysed a large-scale data set obtained from a popular Chinese OSN (RenRen) studying the dynamics of the network. They found that users are most active in building their links shortly after joining the network, eventually decreasing their activity over time. They also found that the presence of communities has a significant influence on user's behaviour. In fact, users belonging to a community are more active in creating new social links, they have longer lifetime and they interact more with other peers in the same community compared to stand-alone users. In [14] the authors built a social network formed of publicly available profiles on Google+, augmenting the network with four additional attributes (i.e., school, major, employer and city) for each node. The results revealed that in some cases the network of attributes shows distributions significantly different from the plain social network. Moreover, attributes have a strong impact on social structure, with interesting differences among different attributes. In [19], a similar analysis on Google+ is presented. The study is focused (as in [14]) on the analysis of statistics about the structure of the network (e.g., clustering coefficient, degree distribution). The results are sometimes in contradiction to the findings in [14] and are focused on the relation between network properties and the geographic distribution of the users, an aspect that is orthogonal to our analysis.

Compared to our analysis, the work presented in [14,19,30] present similar results in terms of growth rate of the number of social relationships over time. Despite this, the analyses are focused on the global growth of the network and they do not consider local aspects of the ego networks of the users. Moreover, they consider only the network of social contacts (i.e., the existence of social links), without weighting the links by the interactions occurred between people. This is clearly an important aspect that must be considered to correctly analyse the social behaviour of people in online environments, even though, to the best of our knowledge there are no large-scale data sets about OSN other than Twitter with the same detailed information needed for this kind of analysis. Specifically, it is difficult to obtain the whole communication history of the users with timestamps about the single communication events needed to track the dynamics of ego networks.

Recently, a study on Twitter [23] revealed that the structure of the ego networks of the users is related, as in offline environments, to parts of one's social world (i.e., to topics, geography and emotions). The authors collected the last 200 tweets of a large sample of Twitter users (about $250,000$) and, after a detailed categorisation of the messages sent by the users into different topics, they found that users with less-constrained ego networks structures (i.e., with access to structural holes) tend to cover diverse topics. Moreover, their results highlight that the majority of the users have geographically-constrained networks and that the users are clustered according to happiness (calculated with a sentiment analysis on the communication traces). Compared to [23], we have been able to download much more data for each user (up to $3,200$ tweets), that allowed us to make a detailed analysis about the evolution of the social ego networks.

Although the work done so far on the analysis of OSN has identified some important aspects of human behaviour (see [1] for a survey on the aspects of human behaviour identified in Twitter), the dynamics of the processes governing human social behaviour in online environments are still unknown. In this paper we make a contribution to the field with a fine grained analysis of the evolution of ego networks over time in Twitter. This analysis reveals many important aspects of human behaviour in OSN.

Before introducing the analysis, we describe the data set we have collected and studied.

3. DATA SET DESCRIPTION

In this Section we describe the data set we used for the analysis. We describe the crawler we used to obtain the data from Twitter, the classifier we used to select profiles related to "humans" and the descriptive statistics of the data. Before continuing with the description of the data set, we briefly introduce Twitter and the different communication mechanisms it offers to its users.

3.1 Twitter and tweets

Twitter is an online social networking service founded in 2006 that has reached a very high popularity, with more than 500 million registered users as of 2012[1]. The main feature of Twitter is to enable its users to send short text messages called *tweets*. Tweets can be up to 140 character-long messages containing tags to reference other users, keywords to identify the topic of the message and links to web pages or multimedia content.

Users can *follow* other users to automatically receive all their tweets and visualise them in their home page. The users that a person follows are her *friends*, whereas people that follow that person are her *followers*. The act of referencing a user in a tweet is called *mention*. Mentions are direct messages sent to one or more people through the mention mechanism and are a special form of direct communication between users. Twitter enables users to directly *reply* to any tweet automatically adding a mention to the response. Replies often involve bi-directionality in the communication, since they are mostly used to reply to previously received mentions. Twitter allows the exchange of private messages as an additional mechanism for direct communications. Despite this, the content of these messages is private and cannot be accessed without the user's permission. Moreover, private messages represents only a small subset of all the messages exchanged on Twitter and therefore using only them to identify direct communications between users may result in an incomplete picture. For these reason, we do not consider them in our analysis and in the rest of the paper we refer to "direct communication" as the public direct tweets only (i.e., mention and replies). Besides direct communication, all the tweets are automatically broadcast to all the users' followers. Tweets can be *retweeted* or, in other words, forwarded by users to all their followers. Retweeting is a really efficient communication means to rapidly spread information in the network. The special tags used to assign one or more topics of a tweet are called *hashtags*, since they are characterised by the presence of the "#" character before the name of the topic, as part of the text of the tweet. Hashtags are used by Twitter to classify tweets and to cluster them into categories, browsable by the users.

3.2 Data download process

We downloaded and analysed a large sample of Twitter communication data which we used to build ego networks representing personal online social relationships of Twitter users. We collected data about Twitter user profiles and the complete history of their tweets. To obtain the data we crawled Twitter from November 2012 to March 2013, downloading a total of 2,428,647 complete user profiles. The crawler agent we used is described in more detail in [3]. The crawler uses Twitter REST API to collect data regarding

[1]According to Twitter CEO Dick Costolo in October 2012

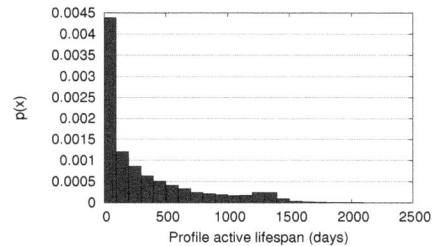

Figure 2: Distribution of active lifespan of Twitter ego networks

user profiles and all their tweets, for a maximum of 3,200 tweets per user - due to the restrictions imposed by the API. The crawler follows links between users to build a network of connected profiles[2]. Specifically, it uses the following/followers lists and the content of direct messages (i.e., replies and mentions) to identify new profiles to download. The data we obtained is an extension of the data set used in [3]. The present data set contains many more profiles, since we ran the crawler for four additional months. This allowed us to carry out a detailed analysis of the dynamics of Twitter ego networks.

3.3 Detecting humans in the crowd

Since our goal is to analyse human behaviour in Twitter, we isolated from the data set the user profiles presenting recognisable human characteristics, discarding all the other kinds of profiles that do not appear to be "humans". For example, we want to discard profiles run by companies, institutions, bots and all the other profiles that can be intuitively classified as "non-humans". Results in [3] showed that this intuitive distinction is accurate enough to separate users characterised by well-known social properties ascribable to humans (i.e., limits imposed by cognitive constraints) from users without these properties, evidently not humans. To automatically perform the separation between "humans" and "non-humans" we used a classifier, specifically a Support Vector Machine (SVM), already used in [3]. The method we used is similar to that proposed in [6], where the authors present a supervised learning approach to classify Twitter account into four different categories (i.e., organisations, journalists/bloggers, ordinary individuals and other). Our SVM uses 96 features extracted from Twitter data. These features are related both to users' profiles and their tweets (e.g., number of friends and followers, whether the profile has been verified by Twitter or not, number of tweets, retweets, replies and mentions sent by the user). We trained the SVM with 500 manually classified user accounts. The manual classification was carried out taking a random sample of profiles from Twitter and giving a binary classification based on the visual inspection of each Twitter profile page. After training the SVM we tested its accuracy on a test set of 100 accounts, which we manually classified, but that were not used during the training phase. The accuracy of the SVM is 0.813 with a 95% c.i. equal to (0.789, 0.837). Although this result could be improved using a larger training set, it is comparable with the results in [6] and is sufficient to draw significant results about human behaviour

[2]The crawl started from a very popular user, so that we could immediately have a large sample of other users at the first hop of the process.

in Twitter, while required to analyse only a very small percentage of crawled accounts.

3.4 Data set properties

After applying the SVM on the data set we obtained $1,653,155$ "human" profiles, about 68% of the total number of users in the data set. To the best of our knowledge, this is the first time the estimation of the percentage of "human" profiles is calculated on Twitter. The large number of "non-human" profiles in the data set gives us a first interesting picture of Twitter. In fact, it indicates that Twitter is an online environment where different types of users co-exist and interact. This feature makes OSN different from more traditional communication means, which often create a separation between different social environments. People using Twitter receive multiple social benefits at the same time, being able to manage more social domains in the same place.

In the first column of Table 1 we summarise the properties of the profiles in the data set, considering human users only. We report the mean values of the indicated statistics, averaged for all the profiles. The active lifespan of the profiles, the distribution of which is depicted in Figure 2, indicates the temporal length of the period in which each profile actively sent tweets. The active lifespan of a user starts with her first tweet and ends with her last tweet. Since our analysis is focused on the social activity of the users on Twitter, we think that measuring the duration of a Twitter account using its active lifespan is appropriate for this work. Of course, some of the users in Twitter could be lurkers, not actively investing their resources in the maintenance of their social relationships. Since the aim of this study is to obtain a detailed characterisation of the evolution of the social structures actively maintained in Twitter through direct communications, we are not interested in lurking-only users, for they do not actively interact with other people. Moreover, as pointed out in [22], there is not a sharp separation between lurkers and active users, since all the users alternate between lurking behaviour and active behaviour when using social-oriented virtual environments. For this reason, we think that considering direct communications is sufficient to capture the social behaviour of all the different types of users in Twitter.

To make the definition of active lifespan more clear, let us consider the following example. If a profile had been created four years before the download, but the user associated with the profile sent tweets only during the first year and then stopped using Twitter (at least for sending tweets), the resulting active lifespan of the profile is one year. The shape of the distribution in Figure 2 indicates that either most of the profiles have been created just before we downloaded the data or their activity on Twitter is very low. However, the long tail indicates that we were able to obtain profiles with a

tweet history of up to almost 7 years (i.e., the complete tweet history of some of the oldest profiles in Twitter), despite the limit of $3,200$ tweets imposed by the Twitter API. During the manual classification of the training set (described in Section 3.3), we noted that "humans" rarely generate more than $3,200$ tweets, and most of the profiles exceeding the limit were "non-humans"[3]. Indeed, only 0.02% of the "human" profiles in the data set exceed this limit. Nevertheless, the small peak in the distribution between $1,200$ and $1,400$ days could be ascribed to the presence of this limit, that prevented us from obtaining the complete active lifespan of some of the downloaded profiles. Despite this, the number of profiles affected by this problem is very low and their last $3,200$ tweets are in any case a significant sample to describe their social behaviour. For this reason, the data set we collected is well suited for our analysis.

In Table 1, we notice that the mean active lifespan of the "human" profiles in the data set (i.e., "duration" in the Table) is equal to 321.846 days. This indicates that, on average, we captured almost one year of communications for each user and this is sufficient to conduct our analysis. Replies and mentions are about 39% of the total number of tweets made by "humans" in Twitter. The exchange of these messages can be interpreted as a mechanism to actively maintain social relationships online and they should be strongly affected by our cognitive limits, since they require the users to spend cognitive resources to directly communicate with the involved people. Besides, non-direct messages take the largest part of the communication in Twitter. This kind of communication is controlled by a more *public* behaviour compared to direct messages and it should require less cognitive resources, since we expect non-direct tweets to contain a low value of emotional intensity.

The high number of replies could indicate a high number of communication threads between people. In fact, replies are usually used to reply to a previous mention and communication threads are composed by an initial mention and a series of replies to that mention. The presence of communication threads is supported by the fact that the number of replies is, on average, broadly twice the number of mentions. This is another strong indication of the maintenance of social relationships online. Retweets are largely used by Twitter users and represent the willingness of people to spread messages they are interested in within the network. Seen from an evolutionary perspective, the diffuse usage of retweets could represent a strategy used by humans to receive a global benefit from having access to more information in the network, at the cost of being active in the diffusion process.

Remarkably, non-direct tweets containing urls are less used than the other type of messages (only 4.813 tweets with urls sent on average by the users in our data set during their active lifespan). In addition, the low number of tweets with hashtags (i.e., 56.411 on average) could be ascribed to the fact that Twitter officially introduced hashtags only between 2009 and 2010.

After selecting humans from the data set, we discarded all the profiles that have not sent any tweets (i.e., with null active lifespan), reducing the number of profiles to $1,187,105$.

Table 1: Data Set Statistics

variable	mean - all	mean - active
duration (days)	321.846 [0.628]	448.201 [0.762]
replies	208.923 [0.609]	290.885 [0.801]
mentions	103.882 [0.459]	144.634 [0.625]
retweets	151.492 [0.496]	210.924 [0.661]
plain text twts	280.037 [0.773]	389.810 [1.011]
twts w urls	4.813 [0.032]	6.698 [0.045]
twts w hashtags	56.411 [0.203]	78.529 [0.273]

---

[3]Even though the SVM is not only based on this feature and is able to correctly classify cases of "non-humans" tweeting less than $3,200$ times in a period of time compatible with "human" profiles

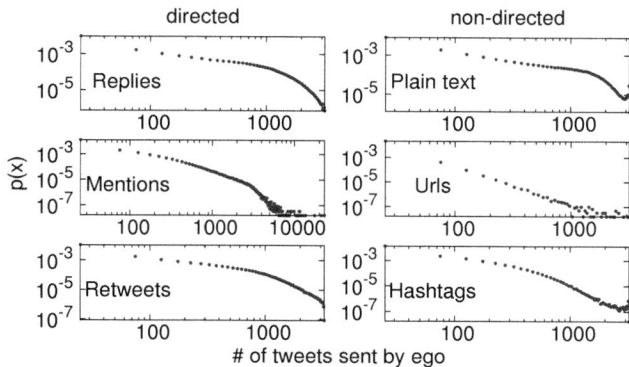

Figure 3: Distribution of the number of tweets divided by type

The statistics of these set of profiles are reported in the second column of Table 1. We can notice that all the statistics of the profiles increase when users with null active lifespan are not considered, since the removed profiles do not contribute actively to the generation of content in the network.

Figure 3 depicts the distribution of the communication variables in the data set for the profiles with positive lifespan. We separated direct and non-direct communication, with the former identifying the explicit intention of the user to mention other users in the messages. In the figure we labelled retweets as direct communication, but their nature needs further investigation. In fact, retweets are more similar to non-direct tweets, with the exception that they contain the id of the user that initially generated the message and the ids of users that retweeted it.

Mentions show a very long tail (the scale of the x axis is different than for the other graphs), with some accounts generating up to $23,104$ mentions. This high number of mentions - apparently exceeding the limit of $3,200$ tweets - is due to the fact that a single tweet can contain more than one mention at the same time, or, in other words, many people can be mentioned in the same tweet.

Before continuing with the analysis we further filtered the data set, eliminating all the profiles created less than one year before the time of their download. This reduces possible artefacts due to including recently created accounts (with respect to the end of the crawl) as well as accounts that have been active only for a short amount of time. The data set, after this selection, contains $644,014$ accounts.

3.5 From tweets to ego networks

From the set of active human users, we built a social ego network for each profile. To do so we firstly defined a measure of the strength of social links between people in Twitter. We say that a social relationship exists between two users, A and B, if A sent at least a reply or a mention to B. This definition involves a cost in terms of cognitive effort spent for the maintenance of the relationship. As an estimate of the tie strength we use the number of messages sent by A to B. In this way, tie strength grows linearly with the number of messages exchanged between two users. We think that representing tie strength in this way is, at the moment, the best possible solution, since models to study the relation between tie strength and frequency of contact are still under investigation in OSN, and the first results indicate that using linear approximations leads to sufficiently accurate results [4].

Using the standard terms in ego network analysis, we call *ego* a user associated with a profile and *alters* all the people with whom ego has a social relationship. This definition gives a "static" view of the ego networks in the data set, aggregating all the communication of the egos, as typically done in other studies [2–4,13,16]. This allowed us to make a qualitative comparison between the ego network size in our data set and that found in other studies in the literature, before moving to analysing the dynamic properties of social relationships. The total number of social relationships in the data set is $57,548,091$ with an average of 89.36 relationships per profile. This result is in accordance with the findings of other studies on OSN [2–4,13], but is considerably lower than the Dunbar's number found in offline ego networks [31]. This could be due to the fact that Twitter is only one of the many possible tools used to maintain social relationships and the time dedicated to socialising in Twitter is still limited [7].

To better understand how these ego networks evolve over time we analysed the time series of the tweets sent by ego and we studied the composition of snapshots of the ego networks considering the communication occurred in time windows of one year each. This allowed us to reveal important insights regarding human social behaviour in OSN.

4. METHODS

To perform the analysis, we studied the time series of the direct tweets (replies and mentions) and of the non-direct tweets sent by each ego. For some performance indices (i.e., new users contacted per day and total number of new users contacted) we counted the number of new alters contacted by ego each day until the network is active. Instead, for analysing the dynamics of the ego network structure, we sliced the tweets time series taking snapshots of the duration of one year each, then assessing the size and the composition of ego networks in each snapshot. We slid the one-year temporal window taking steps of one day each, looking at how ego networks change over time.

By taking temporal windows of one year we were able to capture all the active contacts maintained by each ego and their evolution over time, according to the definition of active network introduced in Section 2.1.2 that identifies as "active" friends all the alters contacted by ego at least yearly. In this way we were also able to identify relationships that the users abandoned over time. Note that we do not use the notion of "unfollowing" (i.e., the explicit request of a user to remove a person from her friends) to identify abandoned relationships, since unfollowing is an extreme action that does not capture the decline of a social link, but rather identifies sudden breach in the relationships, due to particularly negative and rare conditions.

We defined as sympathy group the set of alters contacted at least once a month (i.e., contacted at least ~ 12.17 times in one year), and as support clique the alters contacted once a week (i.e., contacted ~ 52.14 times in one year). Doing so, we were able to analyse how the different layers of the ego networks change over time. We refer the reader to Section 2.1.2 for the definitions of the different ego network layers.

To be able to analyse the average behaviour of all the ego networks we shifted the first communication of each ego network (the time when ego started to actively communicate), so that they start at the same point in time, specifically at the origin of the coordinate system of each figure reported in the following Sections.

To deeply analyse the behaviour of different users in Twitter, we divided the users in three categories on the basis of their active lifespan and we studied the differences in terms of social behaviour between these classes. To do so, we took the maximum lifespan in the data set and we divided it into three equal parts, obtaining three groups of 802 days of duration each. We decided to create exactly three categories since this choice represents a good trade-off between the accuracy of the results and their statistical significance. In fact, adding more categories would have decreased the number of users in each group, leading to low significance. After the categorisation we defined the following classes of users: (i) occasional users (lifespan $<= 802d$) ; (ii) regular users ($802d <$ lifespan $<= 1604d$) and (iii) aficionados (lifespan $> 1604d$). We expect these different categories of users to show different behaviours and different ego network properties. Our data set is composed of 63.23% of occasional users, 35.22% of regular users and 1.55% of aficionados[4].

Note that in the figures presented in Section 5, regarding the composition of ego networks in each one year snapshots (right-hand side plots in Figures 4 to 6 and 9), the value of the x axis represents the starting point of each snapshot. Thus, the maximum value of the axis is equal to the maximum lifespan of the ego networks in the considered class, minus the duration of the snapshot (one year). In the figures we report the average values as the curve in bold and the corresponding 95% confidence interval as a lighter coloured area around the curve (barely visible, most of the time).

As another contribution of this paper, we analysed the evolution of the recency of contact (i.e., time since last contact) between users, to understand how single social relationships evolve. To do so we measured the elapsed time between consecutive messages within each relationship. We averaged the results within the ego networks and then averaged for all the ego networks. While this clearly mixes the properties of different type of social relationships for a particular ego network, it provides a unique index that allows us to compare the ego networks of different classes of users, as explained in detail in Section 5.

After the analysis of the evolution of ego networks and personal social relationships over time, we measured the stability of ego networks, assessing the proportion of alters that users maintain in their networks over time. We estimated this proportion by comparing consecutive - but separated - one year snapshots and calculating their average Jaccard coefficient, then averaging the results for all the ego networks. The Jaccard coefficient is a measure of the percentage of overlap between sets defined as:

$$J(W_1, W_2) = \frac{|W_1 \cap W_2|}{|W_1 \cup W_2|} \qquad (1)$$

where W_1 and W_2 are two sets, in our case the one-year windows of the ego networks. The Jaccard coefficient can be a value between 0 and 1, with 0 indicating null overlap and 1 a complete overlap between the sets. We calculated the Jaccard coefficient for the different layers in the ego networks. This allowed us to determine the "turnover" that takes place in the ego networks. This study is fundamental

---

[4]Note anyway that we still have around 10,000 aficionados in our data set, which makes the analysis of also this class significant

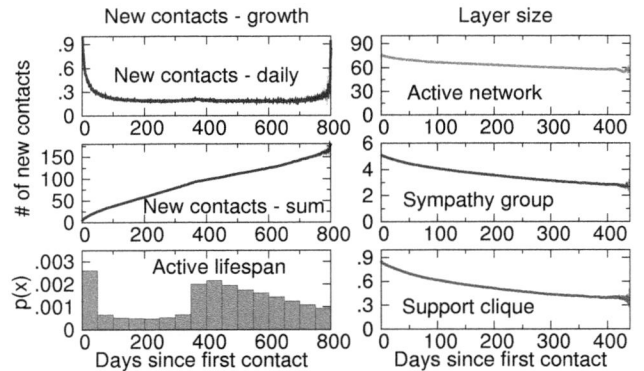

Figure 4: Ego networks properties for occasional users

for understanding whether people maintain a stable network of contacts in Twitter or they prefer to vary their social relationships over time, and allowed us to define two distinct classes of users: (i) users with structured ego networks, showing ego networks with composition and turnover similar to those found in other more traditional social networks and (ii) people without structured ego networks, showing higher turnover.

5. RESULTS

In this Section we report the results of our analysis and we interpret them from the point of view of human social behaviour. The main axes of our analysis, as identified in Section 4, are the presence of different categories of users and, on the other hand, the presence/absence of a structured ego network.

5.1 Twitter abandonment

As a first contribution of our analysis, we studied the behaviour of users that abandoned Twitter. We say that a user has abandoned Twitter if her active lifespan is followed by a period of at least six months of inactivity. In the data set, the average active lifespan of users that abandoned Twitter is 73.21 days, indicating that most of them are occasional users. In fact, over a total of 159,069 accounts that abandoned Twitter (i.e., 24.7% of our data set), 88.27% are occasional users, whilst only 11.6% are regular users and 0.13% are aficionados. From the distribution of the active lifespan of occasional users (depicted in the bottom left part of Figure 4) we can notice that there is a small number of accounts with duration between 50 and 365 days. Yet, there is a non negligible number of occasional users with a very short lifespan (i.e., $< 50d$). These accounts represent people that joined Twitter more than one year before the download, but that abandoned it after a short period of activity. This class of users can be seen as a sub-class of occasional users, who subscribed to Twitter only to "give it a try", but abandoned it very soon.

5.2 Ego networks evolution over time

5.2.1 Number of different alters contacted

The first result worth mentioning is that the number of new people that egos contact grows at a constant rate. This is true for all the categories of users and can be seen in the top left graphs in Figures 4 to 6. The graph labelled "New

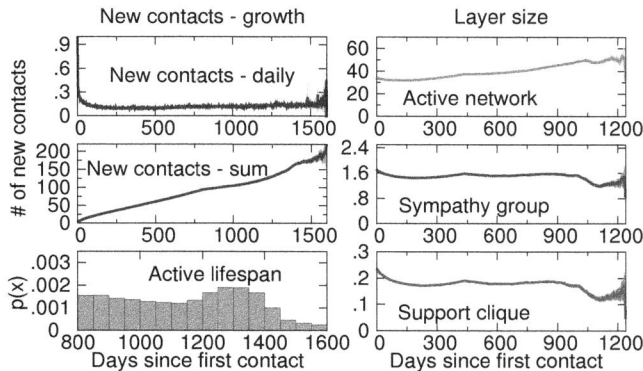

Figure 5: Ego network properties for regular users

Figure 6: Ego network properties for aficionados

contacts - daily" depicts the number of new users contacted by egos during each day of their activity (averaged over all users still active at that day), whilst "New contacts - sum" represents the cumulative number of new users contacted by ego over time (again, averaged across all active users). From these graphs it is clear that, after a first phase in which ego contacts new people at a higher rate, this number quickly converges to a constant. The value of this constant is higher for occasional users than for the other classes. The mean over time is 0.222, 0.125 and 0.112 for the three classes, respectively. This indicates that occasional users have more dynamic ego networks, with a higher number of new social links added over time compared to the other categories. We can notice that the total number of different people contacted by egos over time is, on average about 200 and it is constantly growing, with little variation between the different classes, even though the duration of the ego networks changes considerably between classes. These results are in accordance with the findings in [30], where the authors found that users in RenRen (a popular Chinese OSN) are more active in creating new social links shortly after joining the network. The users eventually approach a constant number of edges created per time unit once most offline friends have been found and linked.

The presence of a constant growth rate is an important aspect of human social behaviour, indicating high dynamism in the ego networks of the users, that are constantly contacting new people rather than maintaining a limited number of stable relationships. This behaviour is confirmed by the analysis of the set of people actively contacted within the ego networks, reported below.

To understand how the constant addition of new contacts in the ego networks impacts on the communication level with the set of existing alters, we studied the evolution of the size of the set of alters actively maintained over time, as reported in Section 5.2.2. Moreover, in Section 5.5 we report the analysis of the percentage of turnover (i.e., the degree of variation in the set of alters actively contacted) for the different layers in the ego networks.

5.2.2 Number of alters actively contacted

Even though the number of new alters contacted by egos increases over time, the number of alters that are actively maintained in the ego networks does not increase at the same rate. This fact reveals the presence of a turnover strategy within the ego networks, since the new contacts replace other relationships that are not maintained by ego. The size

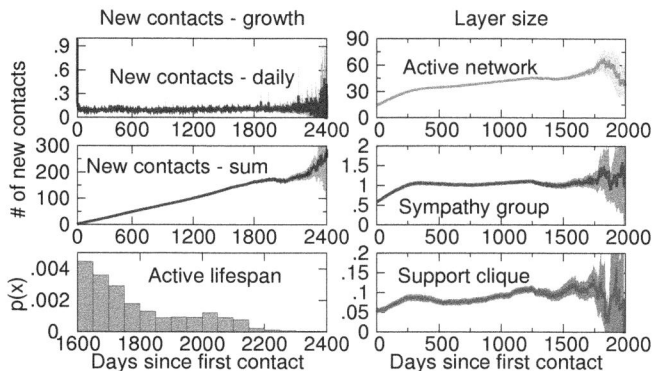

of the ego network layers are depicted in the right column of Figures 4 to 6, for the different categories of users. As far as occasional users are concerned, the size of all the layers significantly decreases over time. Specifically, the active network has a total decrease of 30.73%, the sympathy group of 45.91% and the support clique of 53.22%. Regular users show a different behaviour, with a considerable increase in the active network size (31.16% in almost 4 years), but with a decrease in the other layers (32.17% for the sympathy group and 30.42% for the support clique). It is worth noting that occasional users, compared to regular users, show a higher value of new contacts added in their ego networks daily and larger sizes in all the layers at the beginning of their lifespan, eventually approaching sizes compatible with the regular users. Aficionados show a considerable growth in size in all the ego network layers, even though the rate at which they contact new people is lower than for the other categories. These results highlight the different behaviour of the users in Twitter and indicate that occasional users have an initial boost of activity followed by a decrease or a sudden abandonment of the platform. Regular users and aficionados have a slower start, but they eventually increase the size of their active network over time. Aficionados even increase the size of their inner layers, indicating an investment in strong social relationships, maybe due to the longevity of such relationships, constantly reinforced through Twitter.

On average, the active network size lies between 30 and 80 for all the categories. This result suggests the effect of cognitive constraints of human brain in online environments, which limit the number of people that can be actively maintained over time, in line with the concept of the Dunbar's number. The small active network size, compared to offline social networks size found offline (equal to 132.5 [31]) can be related to the fact that Twitter is only a part of the complete social network of the users and the time spent on Twitter is still low compared to the time spent socialising in person, even though this discrepancy is constantly decreasing [7].

The lower growth rate shown by the sympathy group and the support clique compared to the active network (even negative for occasional users and regular users) suggests the presence of a strategy whereby people prefer dynamic ego networks formed of light-weight social relationships that give access to a larger amount of network resources [15], rather than more stable ego networks with stronger and well-consolidated relationships. Note however that for aficionados (i.e., users that spend a lot of time maintaining their social relationships in Twitter) this preference towards

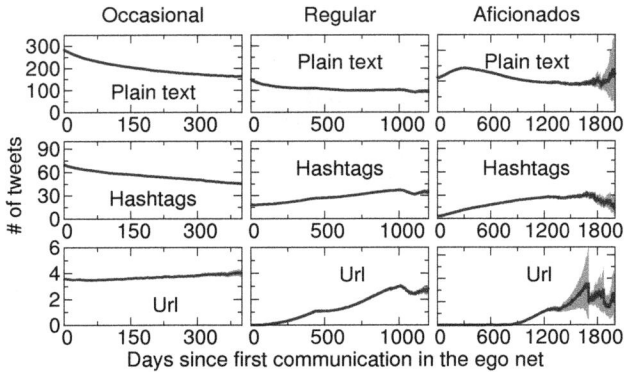

Figure 7: Non-direct communication divided by category

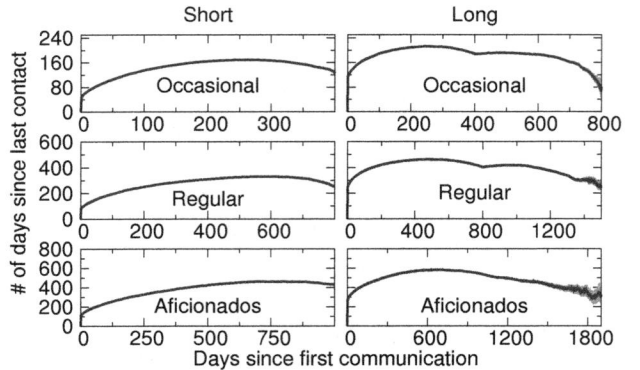

Figure 8: Days since last contact evolution over time

light-weight social relationships is way less marked, making their behaviour much more similar to the one highlighted in previous studies of social networks [31].

Finally, the rate at which egos contact new users is negatively correlated with ego networks growth rate, indicating that users spending a lot of their time adding new people to their networks do not have enough resources to maintain all these relationships over time and their layers inevitably decrease in size. This is in accordance with the idea that our social capacity is limited by cognitive constraints and going beyond our limits could even brake up our social network [25].

5.3 Non-direct communications

We studied how the number of non-direct tweets (i.e., plain text tweets, tweets with hashtags and tweets with urls) change over time for the different categories. The results are depicted in Figure 7. Occasional users significantly decrease the amount of non-direct tweets they send over time - apart from tweets with urls, although these are very limited. This category of users shows an initial boost of activity followed by a gradual decrease, as already found for direct communications. Regular users show a much more stable trend for what concerns the number of plain text tweets, with a value asymptotically converging towards ~ 100 tweets sent in each one-year window. Yet, the number of non-direct tweets is noticeably lower than for the previous category, even though it is increasing over time. This indicates that regular users are less affected by an initial boost, and they rather have a slow start. Aficionados show a similar pattern, apart from plain text tweets, which show a peak in the first two years of their active lifespan. This peak could be due to an initial enthusiasm in the platform at a global level, since this category contains some of the oldest profiles in Twitter. After this initial phase, the number of plain text tweets converges asymptotically to a value similar to the other classes.

These results tell us that whilst some users abandon Twitter after a short period of time, the activity of the egos that continue to use the platform remain stable, rejecting the hypothesis of a convergence towards the OSN decline [26, 29]. This is in contrast with the results of [28], where the authors found that, in Facebook, users are more active when they join the network, decreasing their use rate over time. Our analysis reveals that this behaviour is true only for occasional users and that there is a non negligible amount of long-term users contributing to the survival of the OSN.

5.4 Evolution of personal social relationships

To better understand how personal social relationships evolve in Twitter, we analysed how the average time since last contact changes over time for each single social link in the different categories. We divided the social relationships in each category into "short" relationships, with duration shorter than half of the maximum duration of the category, "long" relationships, with duration longer than the same threshold. Figure 8 depicts the number of days since last contact between people involved in each social relationship (on the y axis) as a function of the time since the beginning of the relationship (x axis). From the figure we can notice that all the distributions show a "bow" shaped curve. This particular shape tells us that, on the one hand, social relationships have an initial phase in which they have a shorter time since last contact (i.e., higher frequency of contact) followed by a gradual increment. On the other hand, since some social relationships disappear as time passes, the remaining social relationships have shorter time since last contact, resulting in the gradual decay in the right most part of the graphs.

It is worth noting that there is a significant variation in the values of time since last contact in the different categories of users, with occasional users having lower values compared to the other classes. Once again, this supports the idea for which occasional users have an initial boost of activity, followed by abandonment or gradual decay.

5.5 Ego network turnover

Finally, we assessed the stability over time of each layer for the different categories. To do so, we calculated the average Jaccard coefficient between separated one-year windows in each ego network. To perform this analysis we further reduced the number of ego networks in the data set, since we needed at least two years of active lifespan to calculate the Jaccard coefficient between two different non overlapping one-year windows. Thus, we selected $190, 249$ ego networks with active lifespan greater than two years. The average Jaccard coefficients for the different layers are reported in Table 2 under the label "all ego networks". The low values of Jaccard coefficient for all the layers indicate a percentage of turnover higher than 75%, with a maximum of 98.8% for the support clique of aficionados. This reveals that the average turnover in each layer is really high. Interestingly, the turnover in the inner layers is higher than the turnover in the active network. This result is in contrast with the findings on phone call records analysed in [24], where the

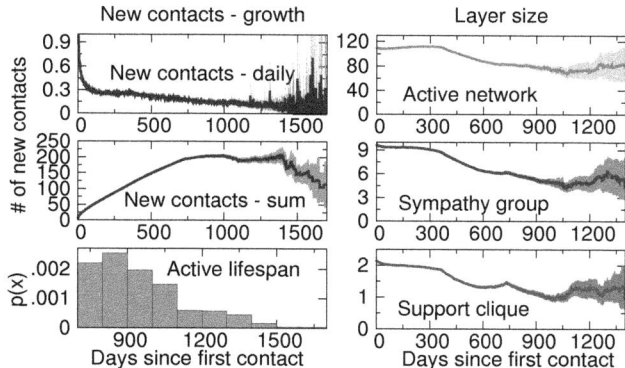

Figure 9: Ego network properties of structured ego networks

authors found that for the top 20 ranking alters in ego networks - formed of social links weighted with the number of calls between people in a fixed time period - the turnover is lower than for the rest of the ego network. It is also worth noting that occasional users show higher stability compared to the other classes. This result could be explained by the fact that the longer the lifespan, the higher is the probability that the social relationships in the ego network change due to turnover.

The low values of Jaccard coefficient in the inner layers (i.e., 0.057 for occasional users, 0.024 for regular users and 0.012 for aficionados) could be influenced by the presence of small support cliques and sympathy groups, that for many egos do not even exist. For this reason we decided to calculate the Jaccard coefficients considering only users that always maintain a structured ego network, or, in other words, that show a non empty support clique in all the sampled one-year windows. The results are reported in Table 2 under the label "structured ego network". In this case the values on the Jaccard coefficient for the different layers are higher than in the previous case and are compatible with the findings in [24]. The values of the percentage of turnover of the active networks are similar for all the different categories and are about 81% (Jaccard coefficient ~ 0.19). For what concerns the other layers, the sympathy group show a percentage of turnover between 71.3% and 63.8%, whereas the support clique 65.4% and 51.2%. These results denote a behaviour similar to other social networks, where the inner layers contain stronger relationships that should be intuitively less affected by the turnover in the network. Nevertheless, as already found in [24], also the inner layers are strongly affected by turnover. The number of ego networks that show a turnover pattern similar to those found in other social environments is 10,307, only 5.42% of the analysed egos. This is another strong indication that human behaviour in Twitter significantly differs from other social networks involving more traditional and dyadic communications. Remarkably, in structured ego networks the categories of users with longer lifespan have higher values of Jaccard coefficient, especially for the inner layers. This tells us that users that maintain structured ego network tend to reinforce their close relationships over time, instead of devoting their time to supporting weak relationships. Note that this is in accordance with the analysis of the evolution of the sizes of the layers over time for aficionados, discussed in Section 5.2.

We have further analysed the properties of these 10,307 ego networks applying the same technique used in Section 5.2.2. The results are shown in Figure 9. The active lifespan of these ego networks ranges between 730 and 1,749 days. These are the minimum and maximum active lifetimes of ego networks in our dataset that always presented a non-empty support clique. This definition allowed us to isolate users with behaviour similar to that showed in "offline" environments, where the support clique is maintained over time by the majority of people as the most important part of their networks.

Interestingly, the layers of the structured ego networks are larger than the average, resembling the layers found in [3], where the authors identify in Twitter a "super support clique", as a set containing one or two alters with very strong relationships with ego, perhaps a partner and/or a best friend. Also the sympathy group and the active network sizes are compatible with this previous study. Remarkably, all the layers decrease in size as time passes and so does the number of new alters contacted by ego. This could be explained by the presence of the initial boost of social activity of occasional users. Nevertheless, egos with longer lifespans prefer to consolidate their social relationships than adding new contacts, as indicated by the decrease in the top left graphs in Figure 9. This is in accordance with the results presented in the previous Sections.

6. CONCLUSIONS AND FUTURE WORK

In this paper we presented a detailed analysis of the dynamic processes of ego networks and personal social relationships in Twitter. The results indicate that human behaviour in Twitter significantly differs from other social networks studied in literature in different research fields. On average, compared to more traditional social networks, Twitter presents smaller ego networks with a high percentage of weak ties and a really high turnover. This fact led us to the conclusion that the general behaviour of Twitter users is to maintain a light-weight ego network formed of weak social relationships suitable to maximise the amount of resources accessible trough the network and limiting the number of strong relationships. This type of user shows an initial phase of very high activity that is inevitably followed by a gradual decay or abandonment. On the other hand, a small but noticeable set of users prefer a "slow" start with a gradual increase of activity and more stable networks. This type of user shows ego networks much more similar to those found in previous analyses of social networks, with more stable inner layers and larger active networks (with respect to the first type of users). Moreover, our results also indicate that users that do not immediately abandon Twitter tend to use it at a regular rate in terms of direct and non-direct com-

Table 2: Average Jaccard coefficient of different network layers

layer	Occasional	Regular	Aficionados
All ego networks			
active net	0.124	0.098	0.103
sympathy gr.	0.122	0.075	0.072
support cl.	0.057	0.024	0.012
Structured ego networks			
active net	0.191	0.190	0.193
sympathy gr.	0.287	0.309	0.362
support cl.	0.346	0.395	0.488

munication. This suggests that the hypothesised decline in the use of OSN might not be present, at least in Twitter.

Seen from an evolutionary perspective, the presence of a vast majority of users of the first type, and the resulting difference between the properties of their Twitter networks and conventional models of ego networks represents an interesting fact, since their behaviour seems to be adapting to the dynamism of our society, reflected in the need of new ways of acquiring information in a very dynamic way through OSN like Twitter.

Other interesting directions we are exploring at the moment include the study of the relation between ego network dynamics and the structural properties of the social network. This study could represent a further step for bridging the gap between online social network analysis and more traditional approaches derived from social sciences.

7. ACKNOWLEDGEMENTS

This work was partially funded by the European Commission under the SCAMPI (FP7-FIRE 258414), RECOGNITION (FP7 FET-AWARENESS 257756), EINS (FP7-FIRE 288021) and EIT ICT Labs MONC (Business Plan 2013) projects.

8. REFERENCES

[1] O. Aarts, P.-P. van Maanen, T. Ouboter, and J. M. Schraagen. Online Social Behavior in Twitter: A Literature Review. *ICDMW*, pages 739–746, 2012.

[2] V. Arnaboldi, M. Conti, A. Passarella, and F. Pezzoni. Analysis of Ego Network Structure in Online Social Networks. In *SocialCom*, pages 31–40, 2012.

[3] V. Arnaboldi, M. Conti, A. Passarella, and F. Pezzoni. Ego Networks in Twitter: an Experimental Analysis. In *Netscicom*, 2013.

[4] V. Arnaboldi, A. Guazzini, and A. Passarella. Egocentric Online Social Networks: Analysis of Key Features and Prediction of Tie Strength in Facebook. *Computer Communications*, 36(10-11):1130–1144, 2013.

[5] R. S. Burt. *Structural Holes versus Network Closure as Social Capital*. 2001.

[6] M. De Choudhury, N. Diakopoulos, and M. Naaman. Unfolding the event landscape on twitter: classification and exploration of user categories. In *CSCW*, pages 241–244, 2012.

[7] J. Delaney, N. Salminen, and E. Lee. Time americans spend per month on social media sites - sociallyawareblog.com, 2012.

[8] R. Dunbar. Theory of mind and the evolution of language. In *Approaches to the Evolution of Language*, chapter 6, pages 92–110. 1998.

[9] R. I. M. Dunbar. The social brain hypothesis. *Evolutionary Anthropology*, 6(5):178–190, 1998.

[10] D. Easley and J. Kleinberg. *Networks, Crowds, and Markets: Reasoning about a highly connected world.* 2010.

[11] E. Gilbert. Predicting tie strength in a new medium. In *CSCW*, pages 1047–1056, 2012.

[12] E. Gilbert and K. Karahalios. Predicting tie strength with social media. In *CHI*, pages 211–220, 2009.

[13] B. Gonçalves, N. Perra, and A. Vespignani. Modeling users' activity on twitter networks: validation of Dunbar's number. *PloS one*, 6(8):e22656, 2011.

[14] N. Z. Gong, W. Xu, L. Huang, P. Mittal, E. Stefanov, V. Sekar, and D. Song. Evolution of Social-Attribute Networks: Measurements, Modeling, and Implications using Google+. In *IMC*, pages 131–144, 2012.

[15] M. S. Granovetter. The Strength of Weak Ties. *The American Journal of Sociology*, 78(6):1360–1380, 1973.

[16] R. A. Hill and R. I. M. Dunbar. Social network size in humans. *Human Nature*, 14(1):53–72, 2003.

[17] R. Kumar, J. Novak, and A. Tomkins. Structure and evolution of online social networks. *KDD*, pages 611–617, 2006.

[18] J. Leskovec and E. Horvitz. Planetary-Scale Views on an Instant-Messaging Network. Technical report, 2007.

[19] G. Magno and G. Comarela. New kid on the block: Exploring the google+ social graph. In *Proceedings of the . . .*, pages 159–170, 2012.

[20] P. V. Marsden and K. E. Campbell. Measuring Tie Strength. *Social Forces*, 63(2):482–501, 1984.

[21] G. Miritello, R. Lara, M. Cebrian, and E. Moro. Limited communication capacity unveils strategies for human interaction. *Scientific Reports*, 3:1–7, June 2013.

[22] M. Muller, D. R. Millen, N. S. Shami, and J. Feinberg. We are all Lurkers: Toward a Lurker Research Agenda. In *CSCW*, pages 1–10, 2010.

[23] D. Quercia, L. Capra, and J. Crowcroft. The social world of twitter: Topics, geography, and emotions. *. . . AAAI Conference on Weblogs and Social . . .*, (Hansen 1999), 2012.

[24] J. Saramaki, E. Leicht, E. Lopez, S. Robetrs, F. Reed-Tsochas, and R. Dunbar. The persistence of social signatures in human communication. *arXiv preprint arXiv*, pages 1–16, 2012.

[25] A. Sutcliffe, R. Dunbar, J. Binder, and H. Arrow. Relationships and the social brain: Integrating psychological and evolutionary perspectives. *British journal of psychology*, 103(2):149–68, 2012.

[26] M. Sweney. Facebook sees first dip in UK users - guardian.co.uk, 2008.

[27] J. Travers and S. Milgram. An Experimental Study of the Small World Problem. *Sociometry*, 32(4):425, 1969.

[28] C. Wilson, A. Sala, K. P. N. Puttaswamy, and B. Y. Zhao. Beyond Social Graphs: User interactions in online social networks and their implications. *ACM Transactions on the Web*, 6(4):1–31, Nov. 2012.

[29] B. Worthen. Bill Gates quits Facebook - Wall St. Journal Online, 2008.

[30] X. Zhao, A. Sala, C. Wilson, and X. Wang. Multi-scale dynamics in a massive online social network. In *IMC*, pages 171–184, 2012.

[31] W.-X. Zhou, D. Sornette, R. a. Hill, and R. I. M. Dunbar. Discrete hierarchical organization of social group sizes. In *Biological sciences*, volume 272, pages 439–44, 2005.

Comparing and Combining Sentiment Analysis Methods

Pollyanna Gonçalves
UFMG
Belo Horizonte, Brazil
pollyannaog@dcc.ufmg.br

Matheus Araújo
UFMG
Belo Horizonte, Brazil
matheus.araujo@dcc.ufmg.br

Fabrício Benevenuto
UFMG
Belo Horizonte, Brazil
fabricio@dcc.ufmg.br

Meeyoung Cha
KAIST
Daejeon, Korea
meeyoungcha@kaist.edu

ABSTRACT

Several messages express opinions about events, products, and services, political views or even their author's emotional state and mood. Sentiment analysis has been used in several applications including analysis of the repercussions of events in social networks, analysis of opinions about products and services, and simply to better understand aspects of social communication in Online Social Networks (OSNs). There are multiple methods for measuring sentiments, including lexical-based approaches and supervised machine learning methods. Despite the wide use and popularity of some methods, it is unclear which method is better for identifying the polarity (i.e., positive or negative) of a message as the current literature does not provide a method of comparison among existing methods. Such a comparison is crucial for understanding the potential limitations, advantages, and disadvantages of popular methods in analyzing the content of OSNs messages. Our study aims at filling this gap by presenting comparisons of eight popular sentiment analysis methods in terms of coverage (i.e., the fraction of messages whose sentiment is identified) and agreement (i.e., the fraction of identified sentiments that are in tune with ground truth). We develop a new method that combines existing approaches, providing the best coverage results and competitive agreement. We also present a free Web service called iFeel, which provides an open API for accessing and comparing results across different sentiment methods for a given text.

Categories and Subject Descriptors

J.4 [**Computer Applications**]: Social and Behavioral Sciences; H.3.5 [**Online Information Services**]: Web-based services

General Terms

Human Factors, Measurement

Keywords

Sentiment analysis, social networks, public mood

1. INTRODUCTION

Online Social Networks (OSNs) have become popular communication platforms for the public to logs thoughts, opinions, and sentiments about everything from social events to daily chatter. The size of the active user bases and the volume of data created daily on OSNs are massive. Twitter, a popular micro-blogging site, has 200 million active users, who post more than 400 million tweets a day [32]. Notably, a large fraction of OSN users make their content public (e.g., 90% in case of Twitter), allowing researchers and companies to gather and analyze data at scale [12]. As a result, a big number of studies have monitored the trending topics, memes, and notable events on OSNs, including political events [29], stock marketing fluctuations [7], disease epidemics [15, 19], and natural disasters [25].

One important tool used in this context is methods for detecting sentiments expressed in OSN messages. While a wide range of human moods can be captured through sentiment analysis, a large majority of studies focus on identifying the *polarity* of a given text—that is to automatically identify if a message about a certain topic is positive or negative. Polarity analysis has numerous applications especially for real time systems that rely on analyzing public opinions or mood fluctuations (e.g., social network analytics on product launches) [17].

Broadly, there exist two types of methods for sentiment analysis: machine-learning-based and lexical-based. Machine learning methods often rely on supervised classification approaches, where sentiment detection is framed as a binary (i.e., positive or negative). This approach requires labeled data to train classifiers [22]. While one advantage of learning-based methods is their ability to adapt and create trained models for specific purposes and contexts, their drawback is the availability of labeled data and hence the low applicability of the method on new data. This is because labeling data might be costly or even prohibitive for some tasks.

On the other hand, lexical-based methods make use of a predefined list of words, where each word is associated with a specific sentiment. The lexical methods vary according to the context in which they were created. For instance, LIWC [27] was originally proposed to analyze sentiment patterns in formally written English texts, whereas

PANAS-t [16] and POMS-ex [8] were proposed as psychometric scales adapted to the Web context. Although lexical methods do not rely on labeled data, it is hard to create a unique lexical-based dictionary to be used for different contexts. For instance, slang is common in OSNs but is rarely supported in lexical methods [18].

Despite business potentials, little is known about how various sentiment methods work in the context of OSNs. In practice, sentiment methods have been widely used for developing applications without an understanding either of their applicability in the context of OSNs, or their advantages, disadvantages, and limitations in comparison with one another. In fact, many of these methods were proposed for complete sentences, not for real-time short messages, yet little eff-ort has been paid to apple-to-apple comparison of the most widely used sentiment analysis methods. The limited available research shows machine learning approaches (Naïve Bayes, Maximum Entropy, and SVM) to be more suitable for Twitter than the lexical-based LIWC method [27]. Similarly, classification methods (SVM, and Multinomial Naïve Bayes) are more suitable than SentiWordNet for Twitter [6]. However, it is hard to conclude whether a single classification method is better than all lexical methods across different scenarios nor if it can achieve the same level of coverage as some lexical methods.

In this paper, we aim to fill this research gap. We use two different sets of OSN data to compare eight widely used sentiment analysis methods: LIWC, Happiness Index, SentiWordNet, SASA, PANAS-t, Emoticons, SenticNet, and SentiStrength. As a first step comparison, we focus on determining the polarity (i.e., positive and negative affects) of a given social media text, which is an overlapping dimension across all eight sentiment methods and provides desirable information for a number of different applications. The two datasets we employ are large in scale. The first consists of about 1.8 billion Twitter messages [12], from which we present six major events, including tragedies, product releases, politics, health, and sports. The second dataset is an extensive collection of texts, whose sentiments were labeled by humans [28]. Based on these datasets, we compare the eight sentiment methods in terms of coverage (i.e., the fraction of messages whose sentiment is identified) and agreement (i.e., the fraction of identified sentiments that are in tune with results from others).

We summarize some of our main results:

1. Existing sentiment analysis methods have varying degrees of coverage, ranging between 4% and 95% when applied to real events. This means that depending on the sentiment method used, only a small fraction of data may be analyzed, leading to a bias or underrepresentation of data.

2. No single existing sentiment analysis method had high coverage and correspondingly high agreement. Emoticons achieve the highest agreement of above 85%, but have extremely low agreement of between 4% to 13%.

3. When it comes to the predicted polarity, existing methods varied widely in their agreement, ranging from 33% to 80%. This suggests that the same social media text could be interpreted very differently depending on the choice of a sentiment method.

4. Existing methods varied widely in their sentiment prediction of notable social events. For the case of an airplane crash, half of the methods predicted the relevant tweets to contain positive affect, instead of negative affect. For the case of a disease outbreak, only two out of eight methods predicted the relevant tweets to contain negative affect.

Finally, based on these observations, we developed a new sentiment analysis method that combines all eight existing approaches in order to provide the best coverage and competitive agreement. We further implement a public Web API, called iFeel (`http://www.ifeel.dcc.ufmg.br`), which provides comparative results among the different sentiment methods for a given text. We hope that our tool will help those researchers and companies interested in an open API for accessing and comparing a wide range of sentiment analysis techniques.

The rest of this paper is organized as follows. In Section 2, we describe the eight methods that are used for comparison, as we cover a wide set of related work. Section 3 outlines the comparison methodology as well as the data used for comparison, and Section 4 highlights the comparison results. In Section 5, we propose a newly combined method of sentiment analysis that has the highest coverage in handling OSN data, while having reasonable agreement. We present the iFeel system and conclude in Section 6.

2. SENTIMENT ANALYSIS METHODS

This section provides a brief description of the eight sentiment analysis methods investigated in this paper. These methods are the most popular in the literature (i.e., the most cited and widely used) and they cover diverse techniques such as the use of Natural Language Processing (NLP) in assigning polarity, the use of Amazon's Mechanical Turk (AMT) to create labeled datasets, the use of psychometric scales to identify mood-based sentiments, the use of supervised and unsupervised machine learning techniques, and so on. Validation of these methods also varies greatly, from using toy examples to a large collection of labeled data.

2.1 Emoticons

The simplest to detect the way polarity (i.e., positive and negative affect) of a message is based on the emoticons it contains. Emoticons have become popular in recent years, to the extent that some (e.g. <3) are now included in English Oxford Dictionary [3]. Emoticons are primarily face-based and represent happy or sad feelings, although a wide range of non-facial variations exist: for instance, <3 represents a heart and expresses love or affection.

To extract polarity from emoticons, we utilize a set of common emoticons from [1, 2, 4] as listed in Table 1. This table also includes the popular variations that express the primary polarities of positive, negative, and neutral. Messages with more than one emoticon were associated to the polarity of the first emoticon that appeared in the text, although we encountered only a small number of such cases in the data.

As one may expect, the rate of OSN messages containing at least one emoticon is very low compared to the total number of messages that could express emotion. A recent work has identified that this rate is less than 10% [23]. Therefore, emoticons have been often used in combination with other

Table 1: Emoticons and their variations

Emoticon	Polarity	Symbols
😀	Positive	:) :] :} :o) :o] :o} :-] :-) :-} =) =] =} =^] =^) =^} :B :-D :-B :^D :^B =B =^B =^D :') :'] :'} =') ='] ='} <3 ^.^ ^-^ ^_^ ^^ :* =* :-* ;) ;] ;} :-p :-P :-b :^p :^P :^b =P =p \o\ /o/ :P :p :b =b =^p =^P =^b \o/

😟	Negative	D: D= D-: D^: D^= :(:[
		:{ :o(:o[:^(:^[:^{
		=^(=^{ >=(>=[>={ >=(
		>:-{ >:-[>:-(>=^[>:-(
		:-[:-(=(=[={ =^[
		>:-=(>=[>=^(:'(:'[
		:'{ ='{ =') ='[=\ :\
		=/ :/ =$ o.0 0_o 0o
		:$:-{ >:-{ >=^{ :o{

😐	Neutral	:| =| :-| >.< >< >_< :o :0 =0 :@ =@ :^o :^@ -.- -.-' -_- -_-' :x =X :# =# :-x :-@ :-# :^x :^#

techniques for building a training dataset in supervised machine learning techniques [24].

2.2 LIWC

LIWC (Linguistic Inquiry and Word Count) [27] is a text analysis tool that evaluates emotional, cognitive, and structural components of a given text based on the use of a dictionary containing words and their classified categories. In addition to detecting positive and negative affects in a given text, LIWC provides other sets of sentiment categories. For example, the word "agree" belongs to the following word categories: assent, affective, positive emotion, positive feeling, and cognitive process.

The LIWC software is commercial and provides optimization options such as allowing users to include customized dictionaries instead of the standard ones. For this paper, we used the LIWC2007 version and its English dictionary, which is the most current version and contains labels for more than 4,500 words and 100 word categories. The LIWC software is available at http://www.liwc.net/. In order to measure polarity, we examined the relative rate of positive and negative affects in the feeling categories.

2.3 SentiStrength

Machine-learning-based methods are suitable for applications that need content-driven or adaptive polarity identification models. Several key classifiers for identifying polarity in OSN data have been proposed in the literature [6,21,28].

The most comprehensive work [28] compared a wide range of supervised and unsupervised classification methods, including simple logistic regression, SVM, J48 classification tree, JRip rule-based classifier, SVM regression, AdaBoost, Decision Table, Multilayer Perception, and Naïve Bayes. The core classification of this work relies on the set of words in the LIWC dictionary [27], and the authors expanded this

baseline by adding new features for the OSN context. The features added include a list of negative and positive words, a list of booster words to strengthen (e.g., "very") or weaken (e.g., "somewhat") sentiments, a list of emoticons, and the use of repeated punctuation (e.g., "Cool!!!!") to strengthen sentiments. For evaluation, the authors used labeled text messages from six different Web 2.0 sources, including MySpace, Twitter, Digg, BBC Forum, Runners World Forum, and YouTube Comments.

The authors released a tool named SentiStrengh, which implements a combination of learning techniques that produces the best results and the best training model empirically obtained [28]. Therefore, SentiStrengh implements the state-of-the-art machine learning method in the context of OSNs. We used SentiStrength version 2.0, which is available at http://sentistrength.wlv.ac.uk/Download.

2.4 SentiWordNet

SentiWordNet [14] is a tool that is widely used in opinion mining, and is based on an English lexical dictionary called WordNet [20]. This lexical dictionary groups adjectives, nouns, verbs and other grammatical classes into synonym sets called synsets. SentiWordNet associates three scores with synset from the WordNet dictionary to indicate the sentiment of the text: positive, negative, and objective (neutral). The scores, which are in the values of [0, 1] and add up to 1, are obtained using a semi-supervised machine learning method. For example, suppose that a given synset $s = [bad, wicked, terrible]$ has been extracted from a tweet. SentiWordNet then will give scores of 0.0 for positive, 0.850 for negative, and 0.150 for objective sentiments, respectively. SentiWordNet was evaluated with a labeled lexicon dictionary.

In this paper, we used SentiWordNet version 3.0, which is available at http://sentiwordnet.isti.cnr.it/. To assign polarity based on this method, we considered the average scores of all associated synsets of a given text and consider it to be positive, if the average score of the positive affect is greater than that of the negative affect. Scores from objective sentiment were not used in determining polarity.

2.5 SenticNet

SenticNet [11] is a method of opinion mining and sentiment analysis that explores artificial intelligence and semantic Web techniques. The goal of SenticNet is to infer the polarity of common sense concepts from natural language text at a semantic level, rather than at the syntactic level. The method uses Natural Language Processing (NLP) techniques to create a polarity for nearly 14,000 concepts. For instance, to interpret a message "Boring, it's Monday morning", SenticNet first tries to identify concepts, which are "boring" and "Monday morning" in this case. Then it gives polarity score to each concept, in this case, -0.383 for "boring", and +0.228 for "Monday morning". The resulting sentiment score of SenticNet for this example is -0.077, which is the average of these values.

SenticNet was tested and evaluated as a tool to measure the level of polarity in opinions of patients about the National Health Service in England [10]. The authors also tested SenticNet with data from LiveJournal blogs, where posts were labeled by the authors with over 130 moods, then categorized as either positive or negative [24, 26]. We use

SenticNet version 2.0, which is available at `http://sentic.net/`.

2.6 SASA

We employ one more machine learning-based tool called the SailAil Sentiment Analyzer (SASA) [30]. SASA is a method based on machine learning techniques such as SentiStrengh and was evaluated with 17,000 labeled tweets on the 2012 U.S. Elections. The open source tool was evaluated by the Amazon Mechanical Turk (AMT) [5], where "turkers" were invited to label tweets as positive, negative, neutral, or undefined. We include SASA in particular because it is an open source tool and further because there had been no apple-to-apple comparison of this tool against other methods in the sentiment analysis literature. We used the SASA python package version 0.1.3, which is available at `https://pypi.python.org/pypi/sasa/0.1.3`.

2.7 Happiness Index

Happiness Index [13] is a sentiment scale that uses the popular Affective Norms for English Words (ANEW) [9]. ANEW is a collection of 1,034 words commonly used associated with their affective dimensions of valence, arousal, and dominance. Happiness Index was constructed based on the ANEW terms and has scores for a given text between 1 and 9, indicating the amount of happiness existing in the text. The authors calculated the frequency that each word from the ANEW appears in the text and then computed a weighted average of the valence of the ANEW study words. The validation of the Happiness Index score is based on examples. In particular, the authors applied it to a dataset of song lyrics, song titles, and blog sentences. They found that the happiness score for song lyrics had declined from 1961 to 2007, while the score for blog posts in the same period had increased.

In order to adapt Happiness Index for detecting polarity, we considered any text that is classified with this method in the range of [1..5) to be negative and in the range of [5..9]) to be positive.

2.8 PANAS-t

The PANAS-t [16] is a psychometric scale proposed by us for detecting mood fluctuations of users on Twitter. The method consists of an adapted version of the Positive Affect Negative Affect Scale (PANAS) [31], which is a well-known method in psychology. The PANAS-t is based on a large set of words associated with eleven moods: joviality, assurance, serenity, surprise, fear, sadness, guilt, hostility, shyness, fatigue, and attentiveness. The method is designed to track any increase or decrease in sentiments over time.

To associate text to a specific sentiment, PANAS-t first utilizes a baseline or the normative values of each sentiment based on the entire data. Then the method computes the $P(s)$ score for each sentiment s for a given time period as values between $[-1.0, 1.0]$ to indicate the change. For example, if a given set of tweets contain $P(\text{"surprise"})$ as 0.250, then sentiments related to "surprise" increased by 25% compared to a typical day. Similarly, $P(s) = -0.015$ means that the sentiment s decreased by 1.5% compared to a typical day. For evaluation, we presented evidence that the method works for tweets about noteworthy events. In this paper, we consider joviality, assurance, serenity, and surprise to be positive affect and fear, sadness, guilt, hostility, shyness, and

fatigue to be negative affect. We consider attentiveness to be neutral.

Another method similar to PANAS-t is an adaptation of the Profile of Mood States (POMS) [8], a psychological rating scale that measures certain mood states consisting of 65 adjectives that qualify the following feelings: tension, depression, anger, vigor, fatigue and confusion. However, we could not include this method for comparison as it was not made publicly available upon request.

3. METHODOLOGY

Having introduced the eight sentiment analysis methods, we now describe the datasets and metrics used for comparison.

3.1 Datasets

We employ two different datasets in this paper.

3.1.1 Near-complete Twitter logs

The first dataset is a near-complete log of Twitter messages posted by all users from March 2006 to August 2009 [12]. This dataset contains 54 million users who had 1.9 billion follow links among themselves and posted 1.7 billion tweets over the course of 3.5 years. This dataset is appropriate for the purpose of this work as it contains all users who set their account publicly available (excluding those users who set their accounts private) and their tweets, which is not based on sampling and hence alleviates any sampling bias. Additionally, this dataset allows us to study the reactions to noteworthy past events and evaluate our methods on data from real scenarios.

We chose six events covered by Twitter users[1]. These events, summarized in Table 2, span topics related to tragedies, product and movie releases, politics, health and sports events. To extract tweets relevant to these events, we first identified the sets of keywords describing the topics by consulting news websites, blogs, Wikipedia, and informed individuals. Given our selected list of keywords, we identified the topics by searching for keywords in the tweet dataset. This process is very similar to the way in which mining and monitoring tools to crawl data about specific topics.

We limited the duration of each event because popular keywords are typically hijacked by spammers after a certain amount of time. Table 2 displays the keywords used and the total number of tweets for each topic. The first column contains a short name for the event, which we use to refer to them in the rest of the paper. While the table does not show the ground truth sentiment of the six events, we can utilize these events to compare the predicted sentiments across different methods.

3.1.2 Labeled Web 2.0 data

The second dataset is six sets of messages labeled as positive and negative by humans, and was made available in the SentiStrength research [28]. These datasets include a wide range of social web texts from: MySpace, Twitter, Digg, BBC forum, Runners World forum, and YouTube comments. Table 3 summarizes the number of messages in each dataset along with the fraction of positive and negative ground truth.

---

[1]Top Twitter trends at `http://tinyurl.com/yb4965e`

Table 2: Summary information of the six major topics events studied

Topic	Period	Keywords
AirFrance	06.01–06.2009	victims, passengers, a330, 447, crash, airplane, airfrance
2008US-Elect	11.02–06.2008	voting, vote, candidate, campaign, mccain, democrat*, republican*, obama, bush
2008Olympics	08.06–26.2008	olympics, medal*, china, beijing, sports, peking, sponsor
Susan Boyle	04.11–16.2009	susan boyle, I dreamed a dream, britain's got talent, les miserables
H1N1	06.09–26.2009	outbreak, virus, influenza, pandemi*, h1n1, swine, world health organization
Harry-Potter	07.13–17.2009	harry potter, half-blood prince, rowling

Table 3: Labeled datasets

Data type	# Messages	Pos / Neg
Twitter	4,242	58.58% / 41.42%
MySpace	1,041	84.17% / 15.83%
YouTube	3,407	68.44% / 31.56%
BBC forum	1,000	13.16% / 86.84%
Runners world	1,046	68.65% / 31.35%
Digg	1,077	26.85% / 73.15%

With this human-labeled data, we are able to quantify the extent to which different sentiment analysis methods can accurately predict polarity of content. We do not measure this for SentiStrength, since this method is trained on the same dataset.

3.2 Comparison Measures

In order to define the metrics used to evaluate the methods we are analyzing, we consider the following metrics:

		Actual observation	
		Positive	Negative
Predicted	Positive	a	b
expectation	Negative	c	d

Let a represent the number of messages correctly classified as positive (i.e., true positive), b the number of negative messages classified as positive (i.e., false positive), c the number of positive messages classified as negative (i.e., false negative), and d the number of messages correctly classified as negative (i.e., true negative). In order to compare and evaluate the methods, we consider the following metrics, commonly used in information retrieval: true positive rate or recall: $R = a/(a + c)$, false positive rate or precision: $P = a/(a + b)$, accuracy: $A = (a + d)/(a + b + c + d)$, and F-measure: $F = 2 \cdot (P \cdot R)/(P + R)$. We will in many cases simply use the F-measure, as it is a measure of a test's accuracy and relies on both precision and recall.

We report all the metrics listed above since they have direct interpretation in practice. The true positive rate or recall can be understood as the rate at which positive messages are predicted to be positive (R), whereas the true negative rate is the rate at which negative messages are predicted to be negative. The accuracy represents the rate at which the method predicts results correctly (A). The precision rate, also called the positive predictive rate, calculates how close the measured values are to each other (P). We also use the F-measure to compare results, since it is a standard way of summarizing precision and recall (F). Ideally, a polarity identification method reaches the maximum value of the F-measure, which is 1, meaning that its polarity classification is perfect.

Finally, we define *coverage* as the fraction of messages in a given dataset that a method is able to classify as either positive or negative. Ideally, polarity detection methods should retain high coverage to avoid bias in the results, due to the unidentified messages. For instance, suppose that a sentiment method has classified only 10% of a given set of tweets. The remaining 90% consisting of unidentified tweets may completely change the result, that is, whether the context drawn from tweets should be positive or negative. Therefore, having high coverage in data is essential in analyzing OSN data. In addition to high coverage, it is also desirable to have a high F-measure as discussed above.

4. COMPARISON RESULTS

In order to understand the advantages, disadvantages, and limitations of the various sentiment analysis methods, we present comparison results among them.

4.1 Coverage

We begin by comparing the coverage of all methods across the representative events from Twitter and also examine the intersection of the covered tweets across the methods.

For each topic described in Table 2, we computed the coverage of each of the eight sentiment analysis methods. Figure 1(a) shows the result for the AirFrance event, a tragic plane crash in 2009. As shown in the figure, SentiWordNet and SenticNet have the highest coverage with 90% and 91%, respectively, followed by SentiStrength with 69%. Emoticons and PANAS-t can interpret less than 10% of all relevant tweets. In the case of the U.S. Election event depicted in Figure 1(d), SentiWordNet, SenticNet and SASA have the highest coverage percentages with 90%, 88% and 67%, respectively.

In fact, either SentiWordNet and SenticNet had the highest coverage for every event from Table 2. In the other events SentiStrength, LIWC, and SASA had ranked in third and fourth positions.

Figure 1(e) shows the result for the outbreak of the H1N1 influenza, a worldwide epidemic declared by the World Health Organization in 2009. In this case, SentiWordNet and SenticNet have the highest coverage with 95% and 93%, respectively, followed by SentiStrength with 61%. The ranking of coverage across the methods is similar to the AirFrance event.

The analysis above shows that despite a few methods having high coverage, the percentage of tweets left unidentified is significant for most of methods, which is a serious problem for sentiment analysis. We next examine what fraction of the tweets can be identified if we combine more than one method. For each event, we combined all methods one by one, beginning from the one with the highest coverage to the one with the lowest coverage. Combining two methods, we

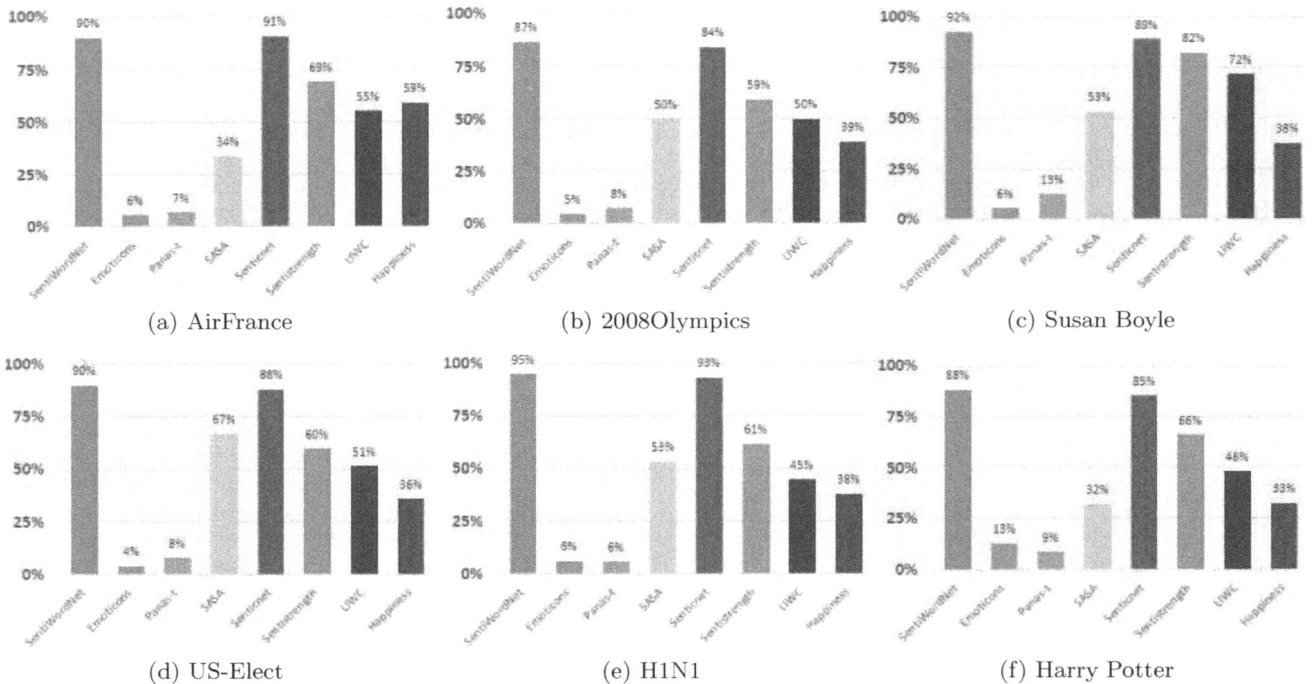

(a) AirFrance (b) 2008Olympics (c) Susan Boyle

(d) US-Elect (e) H1N1 (f) Harry Potter

Figure 1: Coverage of six events.

Table 4: Percentage of agreement between methods.

Metric	PANAS-t	Emoticons	SASA	Sentic-Net	Senti-WordNet	Happiness Index	Senti-Strength	LIWC	Average
PANAS-t	-	60.00	66.67	30.77	56.25	-	74.07	80.00	52.53
Emoticons	33.33	-	64.52	64.00	57.14	58.33	72.00	75.00	60.61
SASA	66.67	64.52	-	64.29	60.00	64.29	61.76	68.75	64.32
SenticNet	30.77	60.00	64.29	-	64.29	59.26	63.33	73.33	59.32
SentiWordNet	56.25	57.14	60.00	64.29	-	64.10	52.94	62.50	59.04
Happiness Index	-	58.33	64.29	62.50	70.27	-	65.52	71.43	56.04
SentiStrength	74.07	75.00	63.89	63.33	52.94	65.52	-	75.00	66.67
LIWC	80.00	75.00	68.97	73.33	58.82	83.33	75.00	-	73.49
Average	48.72	63.85	64.65	60.35	59.95	56.40	66.37	72.29	-

were able to increase the coverage to more than 92.75% for each of the events. We also noted that using this strategy the percentage of uncovered tweets is smaller than 7.24% for each of the events. This result is important as we will shortly demonstrate that combining methods can increase the coverage over a single method.

4.2 Agreement

Next we examine the degree to which different methods agree on the polarity of the content. For instance, when two or more methods detect sentiments in the same message it is important to check whether these sentiments are the same; this would strengthen the confidence in the polarity classification. In order to compute the agreement of each method, we calculated the intersections of the positive or negative proportion given by each method.

Table 4 presents the percentage of agreement for each method with all the others. For each method in the first column, we measure, from the messages classified for each pair of methods, for what fraction of these messages they agree. We find that some methods have a high degree of overlap as

in the case of LIWC and PANAS-t (80%), while others have very low overlap such as SenticNet and PANAS-t (30.77%). PANAS-t and Happiness Index had no intersection. The last "column" of the table shows on average to what extent each method agrees with the other seven, whereas the last "row" quantifies how other methods agree with a certain method, on average. In both situations, the method that most agrees with others and which others agree with it is LIWC, suggesting that LIWC might provide an interesting method to be used in combination with others.

In summary, the above result indicates that existing tools vary widely in terms of agreement about the predicted polarity, with scores ranging from 33% to 80%. This implies that the same social media text, when analyzed with different sentiment tools, could be interpreted very differently. In particular, for those tools that have lower than 50% agreement, the polarity will even change (e.g., from positive to negative, or vice versa).

Table 5: Average prediction performance for all labeled dataset.

Metric	PANAS-t	Emoticons	SASA	Sentic-Net	Senti-WordNet	Happiness Index	Senti-Strength	LIWC
Recall	0.614	0.856	0.648	0.562	0.601	0.571	0.767	0.153
Precision	0.741	0.867	0.667	0.934	0.786	0.945	0.780	0.846
Accuracy	0.677	0.817	0.649	0.590	0.643	0.639	0.815	0.675
F-measure	0.632	0.846	0.627	0.658	0.646	0.665	0.765	0.689

Table 6: F-measures for the eight methods.

Method	Twitter	MySpace	YouTube	BBC	Digg	Runners World
PANAS-t	0.643	0.958	0.737	0.296	0.476	0.689
Emoticons	0.929	0.952	0.948	0.359	0.939	0.947
SASA	0.750	0.710	0.754	0.346	0.502	0.744
SenticNet	0.757	0.884	0.810	0.251	0.424	0.826
SentiWordNet	0.721	0.837	0.789	0.284	0.456	0.789
SentiStrength	0.843	0.915	0.894	0.532	0.632	0.778
Happiness Index	0.774	0.925	0.821	0.246	0.393	0.832
LIWC	0.690	0.862	0.731	0.377	0.585	0.895

4.3 Prediction Performance

Next we present a comparative performance evaluation of each method in terms of correctly predicting polarity. Here we present the results for precision, recall, accuracy, and F-measure for the eight methods. To compute these metrics, we used the the ground truth provided by SentiStrength's dataset [28].

In order to compare the results of prediction performance for each method we present Table 5, which gives the average of the results obtained for each labeled dataset. For the F-measure, a score of 1 is ideal and 0 is the worst possible. The method with the best F-measure was Emoticons (0.846), which had the lowest coverage. The second best method in terms of F-measure is SentiStrength, which obtained a much higher coverage than Emoticons. It is important to note that the SentiStrength version we are using is already trained, probably with this entire dataset. Thus, running experiments with SentiStrength using this dataset would be potentially biased, as it would be training and testing with the same dataset. Instead, we compute the prediction performance metrics for SentiStrengh based on the numbers they reported in their experiments [28].

Table 6 presents the F-measures calculated for each analysis method and each of the labeled datasets we are using. Overall, we note that the eight methods yielded wide variation in their results across the different datasets. We observe better performance on datasets that contain more expressed sentiment, such as social network messages (e.g., Twitter and MySpace) and lower performance on formal datasets (e.g., BBC and Digg). For instance, on BBC posts (i.e., formal content), the highest F-measure was 0.532, from SentiStrength On the other hand, for the MySpace dataset (i.e., informal content), the highest F-measure was obtained by PANAS-t (0.958) and the average F-measure for all 8 methods was 72%. This might indicate that each method complements the others in different ways.

4.4 Polarity Analysis

Thus far, we have analyzed the coverage prediction performance of the sentiment analysis methods. Next, we provide a deeper analysis on how polarity varies across different datasets and potential pitfalls to avoid when monitoring and measuring polarity.

Figure 2 presents the polarity of each method when exposed to each labeled dataset. For each dataset and method, we computed the percentage of positive messages and the percentage of negative messages. The Y-axis shows the positive percentage minus the negative percentage. We also plot the ground truth for this analysis. The closer to the ground truth a method is, the better its polarity prediction. SentiStrength was removed from this analysis as it was trained with this dataset.

We can make several interesting observations. First, we clearly see that most methods present more positive values than the negative values, as we see few lines below the ground truth among all the datasets. Second, we note that several methods obtained only positive values, independent of the dataset analyzed. For instance, although SenticNet had a very high coverage, it identifies the wrong polarity for predominantly negative datasets.

This bias towards positive polarity showed by most of the methods might be trick for real time polarity detecting tools, as they might simply apply these methods in real time data, like Twitter streaming API, and account the rate of positive and negative message text. This would potentially show biased results due to the methods used. In order to verify this potential bias, we provide the same kind of analysis for each event we gathered from Twitter. Figure 3 shows this polarity analysis. We can see that most of the methods show very positive results, even for datasets like H1N1. While this event's data may contain jokes and positive tweets, it would be also reasonable to expect a large number of tweets expressing concerns and bad feelings. Even the event related to an airplane crash was considered positive by four methods, although the polarity difference is close to zero for most of them.

5. COMBINED METHOD

Having seen the varying degrees of coverage and agreement of the eight sentiment analysis methods, we next present a combined sentiment method and the comparison framework.

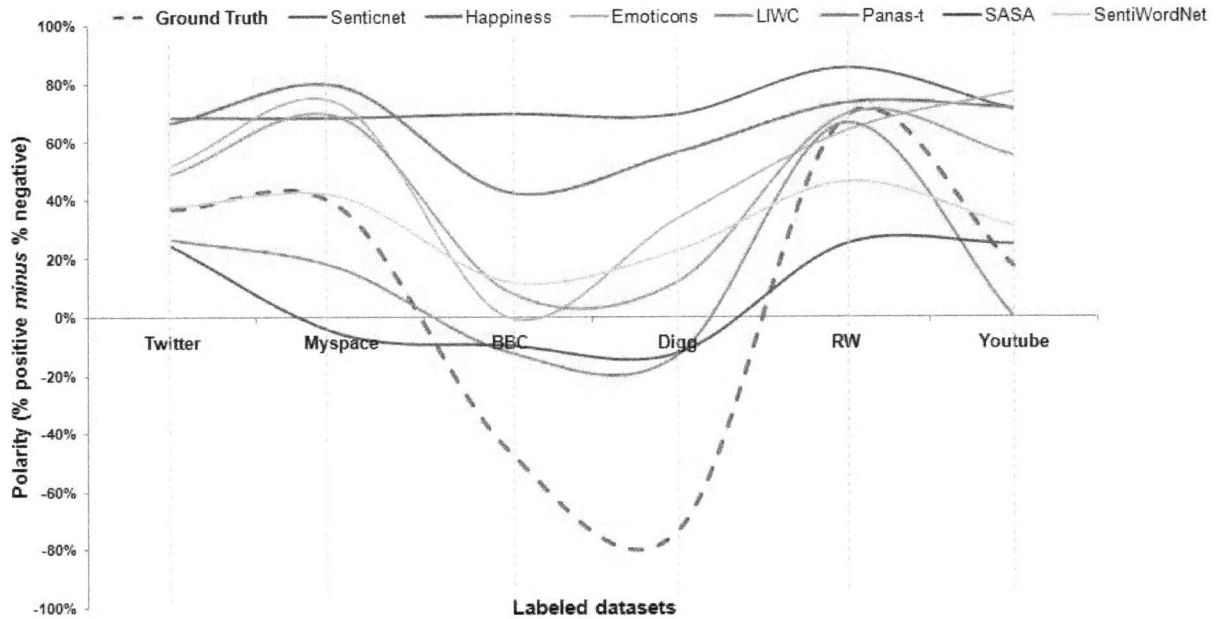

Figure 2: Polarity of the eight sentiment methods across the labeled datasets, indicating that existing methods vary widely in their agreement.

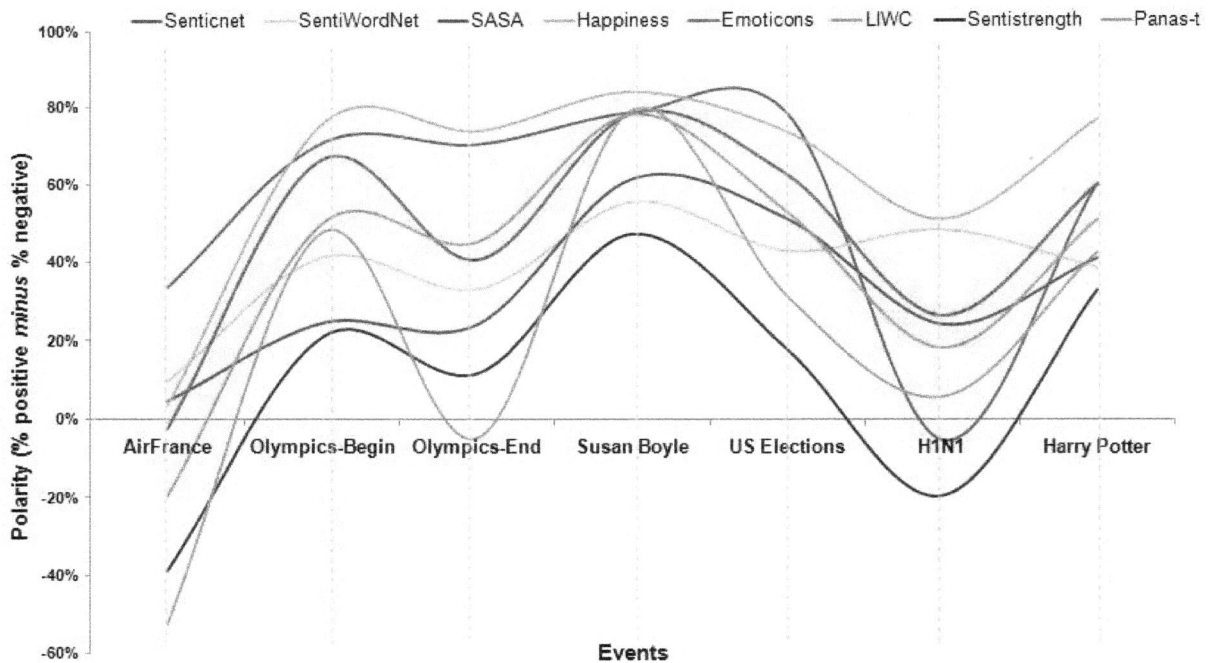

Figure 3: Polarity of the eight sentiment methods across several real notable events, indicating that existing methods vary widely in their agreement.

(a) Comparison

(b) Tradeoff

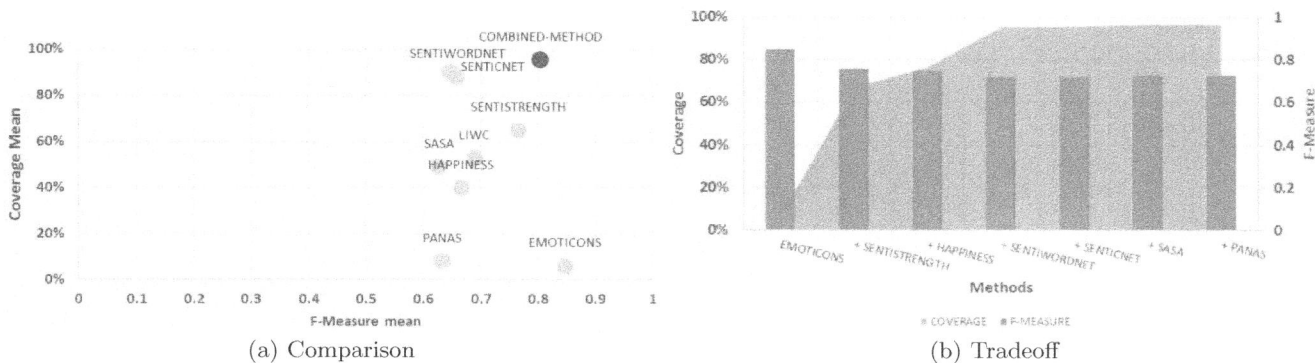

Figure 4: Trade off between the coverage vs F-measure for methods, including the proposed method

5.1 Combined-Method

We have created a combined method, which we simply call **Combined-method**. This new method relies on the following existing ones: PANAS-t, Emoticons, SentiStrength, SentiWordNet, SenticNet, SASA and Happiness Index. We omit LIWC due to copyright restrictions. The Combined-method analyzes the harmonic mean of the precision and recall for all methods and gives different weights for them (i.e., between 1 and 7). The goal is first to achieve the highest coverage, and then to achieve good agreement for a given dataset.

For evaluation, we tested the Combined-method over the SentiStrength labeled datasets [28] that consist of human-labeled Web content (through AMT) drawn from Twitter, MySpace, Runners World, BBC, Digg, and YouTube (see description in Section 3.1.2). We calculated the average F-measure and the average coverage across these Web datasets. We also computed the coverage based on the near-complete Twitter dataset, averaging results over the six notable events (see description in Section 3.1.1).

Figure 4(a) compares the coverage and the F-measure of the seven existing sentiment methods as well as the newly proposed Combined-method. The figure demonstrates the efficacy of Combined-method, in that it can detect sentiments with the highest coverage of 95%, as one might expect. Furthermore, its accuracy and precision in sentiment analysis remain relatively high, with a F-measure of 0.730. This is lower than the best performing method, Emoticons, but higher than all other the other sentiment methods.

While combining all sentiment methods would yield the best coverage, there is a diminishing return effect, in that increasing the number of methods incurs only marginal gain in coverage after some point. Figure 4(b) shows this trend, where we add methods in the order of Emoticons, SentiStrength, Happiness Index, and so on (as noted in the horizontal axis). While Emoticons gives the lowest coverage of less than 10%, the coverage increases to 70% when we add just one more method, SentiStrength (see orange shaded region in the figure). The F-measure, on the other hand, drops slightly as more sentiment methods are combined, as seen in the blue-colored bars in the figure.

As we combine more methods, the coverage increases but to a smaller extent. In fact, combining the first four methods already achieves a coverage of 95%, leaving only a small room for improvement after this point. We can also note

that, although the accuracy and precision decrease as more methods are combined, they remain in a reasonable range (an F-measure of above 0.7). This indicates that combining all of the methods is not necessarily the best strategy. The best coverage and agreement may be achieved by combining those methods best suited for a particular kind of data. For example, one might want to choose LIWC over SASA for a given data or vice versa. Reducing the amount of data needed for Combined-method to obtain good results is a desirable property for a real system deployment, given that the use of fewer methods will likely require fewer resources.

5.2 The iFeel Web System

Finally, having compared the different sentiment methods and tested the efficacy of the Combined-method, we present for the research community a Web service called iFeel. iFeel allows anyone on the Web to test the various sentiment analysis methods compared in this paper with the texts of their choice. We exclude LIWC in the set of available tools, due to copyright issues. The iFeel system was developed using Pyramid, an open source Web framework in Python based on Web Server Gateway Interface (WSGI). A beta version of the tool is available at `http://www.ifeel.dcc.ufmg.br`, and accepts short texts up to 200 characters as input.

Figure 5 shows the screen snapshot of the iFeel system for the input "I'm feeling too sad today :(". As demonstrated in this example, certain sentiment methods detect stronger degree of sentiment than others. For instance, Emoticons and PANAS-t can detect a high level of negative affect in this text, yet SenticNet and SASA do not.

In the future, we plan to extend the iFeel system to allow input files instead of input text strings, as well as supporting visualizations of different combinations of the compared results. This will not only assist researchers in reproducing the experimental results presented in this paper and other papers, but also help users to decide on the proper sentiment method for a particular dataset and application. Therefore, we hope that this system will be an important step towards applying sentiment analysis to OSN data.

6. CONCLUDING REMARKS

Recent efforts to analyze the moods embedded in Web 2.0 content have adapted various sentiment analysis methods originally developed in linguistics and psychology. Several of these methods became widely used in their knowledge fields

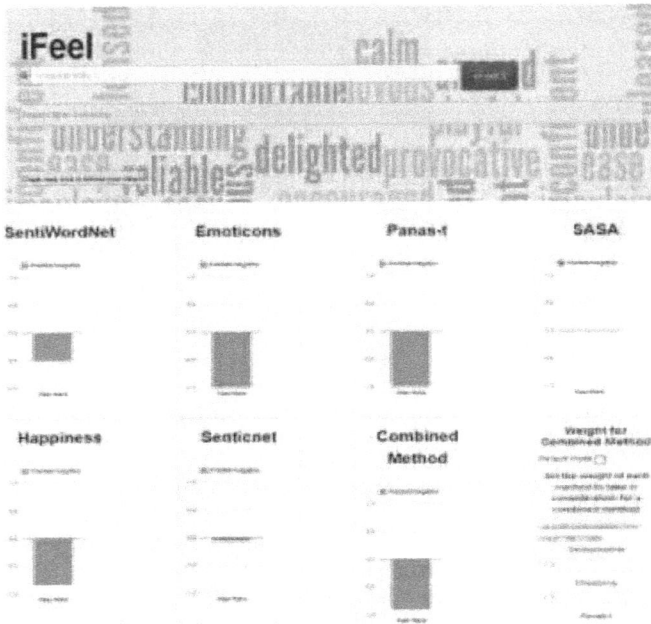

Figure 5: Screen snapshot of the iFeel web system

and have now been applied as tools to measure polarity in the context of OSNs. In this paper, we present an apple-to-apple comparison of eight representative sentiment methods: SentiWordNet, SASA, PANAS-t, Emoticons, SentiStrength, LIWC, SenticNet, and Happiness Index.

Our comparison study focused on detecting the polarity of content (i.e., positive and negative affects) and does not yet consider other types of sentiments (e.g., psychological processes such as anger or calmness). We adopted two measures of efficacy, coverage (measuring the fraction of messages whose sentiments are detected) and agreement (measuring the fraction of identified sentiments that are in tune with ground truth). We find that the eight methods have varying degrees of coverage and agreement; no single method is always best across different text sources. This led us to combine the different methods to achieve the highest coverage and satisfying agreement; we presente this tool as the Combined-method.

We also present a Web API framework, called the iFeel system, through which we would like to allow other researchers to easily compare the results of a wide set of sentiment analysis tools. The system also gives access to the Combined-method, which typically gives the highest coverage and competitive accuracy. Although preliminary, we believe this is an important step toward a wider application of sentiment analysis methods to OSN data, able to help researchers decide on the proper sentiment method for a particular dataset and application.

This work has demonstrated a framework with which various sentiment analysis methods can be compared in an apple-to-apple fashion. To be able to do this, we have covered a wide range of research on sentiment analysis and have made significant efforts to contact the authors of previous works to get access to their sentiment analysis tools. Unfortunately, in many cases, getting access to the tools was a nontrivial task; in this paper, we were only able to compare

eight of the most widely used methods. As a natural extension of this work, we would like to continue to add more existing methods for comparison, such as the Profile of Mood States (POMS) [8] and OpinionFinder [33]. Furthermore, we would like to expand the way we compare these methods by considering diverse categories of sentiments beyond positive and negative polarity.

7. ACKNOWLEDGMENTS

The authors would like to thank the anonymous reviewers for their valuable comments. This work was funded by the Brazilian National Institute of Science and Technology for the Web (MCT/CNPq/INCT grant number 573871/2008-6) and grants from CNPq, CAPES and FAPEMIG. This paper was also funded by the Basic Science Research Program through the National Research Foundation of Korea funded by the Ministry of Education, Science and Technology (Project No. 2011-0012988) and the IT R&D program of MSIP/KEIT (10045459, Development of Social Storyboard Technology for Highly Satisfactory Cultural and Tourist Contents based on Unstructured Value Data Spidering).

8. REFERENCES

[1] List of text emoticons: The ultimate resource. www.cool-smileys.com/text-emoticons.

[2] Msn messenger emoticons. http://messenger.msn.com/Resource/Emoticons.aspx.

[3] OMG! Oxford English Dictionary grows a heart: Graphic symbol for love (and that exclamation) are added as words. tinyurl.com/klv36p.

[4] Yahoo messenger emoticons. http://messenger.yahoo.com/features/emoticons.

[5] Amazon. Amazon mechanical turk. https://www.mturk.com/. Accessed June 17, 2013.

[6] A. Bermingham and A. F. Smeaton. Classifying Sentiment in Microblogs: Is Brevity an Advantage? In *ACM International Conference on Information and Knowledge Management (CIKM)*, pages 1833–1836, 2010.

[7] J. Bollen, H. Mao, and X.-J. Zeng. Twitter Mood Predicts the Stock Market. *CoRR*, abs/1010.3003, 2010.

[8] J. Bollen, A. Pepe, and H. Mao. Modeling Public Mood and Emotion: Twitter Sentiment and Socio-Economic Phenomena. *CoRR*, abs/0911.1583, 2009.

[9] M. M. Bradley and P. J. Lang. Affective norms for English words (ANEW): Stimuli, instruction manual, and affective ratings. Technical report, Center for Research in Psychophysiology, University of Florida, Gainesville, Florida, 1999.

[10] E. Cambria, A. Hussain, C. Havasi, C. Eckl, and J. Munro. Towards crowd validation of the uk national health service. In *ACM Web Science Conference (WebSci)*, 2010.

[11] E. Cambria, R. Speer, C. Havasi, and A. Hussain. Senticnet: A publicly available semantic resource for opinion mining. In *AAAI Fall Symposium Series*, 2010.

[12] M. Cha, H. Haddadi, F. Benevenuto, and K. P. Gummadi. Measuring User Influence in Twitter: The

Million Follower Fallacy. In *International AAAI Conference on Weblogs and Social Media (ICWSM)*, 2010.

[13] P. S. Dodds and C. M. Danforth. Measuring the happiness of large-scale written expression: songs, blogs, and presidents. *Journal of Happiness Studies*, 11(4):441–456, 2009.

[14] Esuli and Sebastiani. Sentwordnet: A publicly available lexical resource for opinion mining. In *International Conference on Language Resources and Evaluation (LREC)*, pages 417–422, 2006.

[15] J. Gomide, A. Veloso, W. M. Jr., V. Almeida, F. Benevenuto, F. Ferraz, and M. Teixeira. Dengue surveillance based on a computational model of spatio-temporal locality of twitter. In *ACM Web Science Conference (WebSci)*, 2011.

[16] P. Gonçalves, F. Benevenuto, and M. Cha. PANAS-t: A Pychometric Scale for Measuring Sentiments on Twitter. abs/1308.1857v1, 2013.

[17] A. Hannak, E. Anderson, L. F. Barrett, S. Lehmann, A. Mislove, and M. Riedewald. Tweetin' in the rain: Exploring societal-scale effects of weather on mood. In *Int'l AAAI Conference on Weblogs and Social Media (ICWSM)*, 2012.

[18] X. Hu, J. Tang, H. Gao, and H. Liu. Unsupervised sentiment analysis with emotional signals. In *International Conference on World Wide Web (WWW)*, 2013.

[19] A. Lamb, M. J. Paul, and M. Dredze. Separating Fact from Fear: Tracking Flu Infections on Twitter. In *Conference of the North American Chapter of the Association for Computational Linguistics: Human Language Technologies*, pages 789–795, June 2013.

[20] G. A. Miller. Wordnet: a lexical database for english. *Communications of the ACM*, 38(11):39–41, 1995.

[21] G. Paltoglou and M. Thelwall. Twitter, MySpace, Digg: Unsupervised Sentiment Analysis in Social Media. *ACM Transactions on Intelligent Systems and Technology (TIST)*, 3(4):66:1–66:19, 2012.

[22] B. Pang, L. Lee, and S. Vaithyanathan. Thumbs up?: sentiment classification using machine learning techniques. In *ACL Conference on Empirical Methods in Natural Language Processing*, pages 79–86, 2002.

[23] J. Park, V. Barash, C. Fink, and M. Cha. Emoticon style: Interpreting differences in emoticons across cultures. In *International AAAI Conference on Weblogs and Social Media (ICWSM)*, 2013.

[24] J. Read. Using emoticons to reduce dependency in machine learning techniques for sentiment classification. In *ACL Student Research Workshop*, pages 43–48, 2005.

[25] T. Sakaki, M. Okazaki, and Y. Matsuo. Earthquake shakes twitter users: real-time event detection by social sensors. In *Int'l Conference on World wide web (WWW)*, pages 851–860, 2010.

[26] S. Somasundaran, J. Wiebe, and J. Ruppenhofer. Discourse level opinion interpretation. In *Int'l Conference on Computational Linguistics (COLING)*, pages 801–808, 2008.

[27] Y. R. Tausczik and J. W. Pennebaker. The psychological meaning of words: Liwc and computerized text analysis methods. *Journal of Language and Social Psychology*, 29(1):24–54, 2010.

[28] M. Thelwall. Heart and soul: Sentiment strength detection in the social web with sentistrength. `http://sentistrength.wlv.ac.uk/documentation/SentiStrengthChapter.pdf`.

[29] A. Tumasjan, T. O. Sprenger, P. G. Sandner, and I. M. Welpe. Predicting Elections with Twitter: What 140 Characters Reveal about Political Sentiment. In *International AAAI Conference on Weblogs and Social Media (ICWSM)*, 2010.

[30] H. Wang, D. Can, A. Kazemzadeh, F. Bar, and S. Narayanan. A system for real-time twitter sentiment analysis of 2012 u.s. presidential election cycle. In *ACL System Demonstrations*, pages 115–120, 2012.

[31] D. Watson and L. Clark. Development and validation of brief measures of positive and negative affect: the panas scales. *Journal of Personality and Social Psychology*, 54(1):1063–1070, 1985.

[32] K. Wickre. Celebrating Twitter7. `http://blog.twitter.com/2013/03/celebrating-twitter7.html`. Accessed March 25, 2013.

[33] T. Wilson, P. Hoffmann, S. Somasundaran, J. Kessler, J. Wiebe, Y. Choi, C. Cardie, E. Riloff, and S. Patwardhan. Opinionfinder: a system for subjectivity analysis. In *HLT/EMNLP on Interactive Demonstrations*, pages 34–35, 2005.

Social Resilience in Online Communities: the Autopsy of Friendster

David Garcia, Pavlin Mavrodiev, and Frank Schweitzer
Chair of Systems Design, ETH Zurich
Weinbergstrasse 56/58, 8092 Zurich, Switzerland
dgarcia@ethz.ch, pmavrodiev@ethz.ch, fschweitzer@ethz.ch

ABSTRACT

We empirically analyze five online communities: Friendster, Livejournal, Facebook, Orkut, and Myspace, to study how social networks decline. We define social resilience as the ability of a community to withstand changes. We do not argue about the cause of such changes, but concentrate on their impact. Changes may cause users to leave, which may trigger further leaves of others who lost connection to their friends. This may lead to cascades of users leaving. A social network is said to be resilient if the size of such cascades can be limited. To quantify resilience, we use the k-core analysis, to identify subsets of the network in which all users have at least k friends. These connections generate benefits (b) for each user, which have to outweigh the costs (c) of being a member of the network. If this difference is not positive, users leave. After all cascades, the remaining network is the k-core of the original network determined by the cost-to-benefit (c/b) ratio. By analysing the cumulative distribution of k-cores we are able to calculate the number of users remaining in each community. This allows us to infer the impact of the c/b ratio on the resilience of these online communities. We find that the different online communities have different k-core distributions. Consequently, similar changes in the c/b ratio have a different impact on the amount of active users. Further, our resilience analysis shows that the topology of a social network alone cannot explain its success of failure. As a case study, we focus on the evolution of Friendster. We identify time periods when new users entering the network observed an insufficient c/b ratio. This measure can be seen as a precursor of the later collapse of the community. Our analysis can be applied to estimate the impact of changes in the user interface, which may temporarily increase the c/b ratio, thus posing a threat for the community to shrink, or even to collapse.

Categories and Subject Descriptors

H.1.2 [**Information Systems**]: Models and principles—*User/machine Systems*

General Terms

Human factors

Keywords

game theory; social network analysis; social resilience; rational behaviour

1. INTRODUCTION

Online Social Networks (OSN), such as `Facebook` or `Friendster`, can quickly become popular, but can also suddenly lose large amounts of users. The appearance of competing OSN, with different functionalities and designs, create unexpected shifts of users that abandon one community for another [15]. While the dynamics of growth in these online communities are an established research subject [3, 21], there are still many open questions regarding the decline of online communities, in particular related to large OSN [37]. What are the reasons behind the decision of users to stop using an OSN? What is the role of the social network in keeping user engagement, or in the spreading of user dissatisfaction? Are there network structures that lead to higher risks of massive user departures? In this article, we assess the question of the relation between the topology of the user network, and the cascades of user departures that threaten the integrity of an online community. We build on previous theoretical work on network effects [5], providing the first empirical study of this phenomenon across successful, failed, and declining OSN.

The most successful OSN attract millions of users, whose interactions create emergent phenomena that cannot be reduced back to the behavior of individual users. The OSN is a communication medium that connects a large amount of people, which would stay together only if their interaction dynamics leads to the emergent entity that we call *the community*. The OSN and its users form a socio-technical system in which the persistence of the community depends on both the social interaction between users, and the implementation and design of the OSN. In this context, the *social resilience* [1] of an online community is defined as *"The ability of the community to withstand external stresses and disturbances created by environmental changes"*. In particular, the technological component of the OSN can change the environment of the users, and create stress that threatens the cohesion of the community. As an example, changes in the user interface pose a general risk for user engagement in OSN.

The fast pace of the Internet society has already led to the total disappearance of some very large online communities. The most paradigmatic example is `Friendster`, one of the first and largest OSN, which suffered a massive exodus of users towards competing sites. This led to its closure in 2011, to reopen as an online gaming without its profile data. As a reaction, the `Internet Archive` [1] crawled as much information as possible, creating a timeless snapshot of `Friendster` right before its closure. If, on the other hand, `Friendster` was still an alive and active community, this data would have been kept private and never made accessible at such scale. Before closure, users were warned and offered to delete their data from the site, leaving all the remaining data from this community as one of the largest publicly available datasets on social behavior.

The decay of `Friendster` is commented in a comedy video of the Onion News, in which a fictitious *"Internet archaelogist"* explains `Friendster` as an ancient civilization [2]. While proposed as a satire of the speed of Internet culture, this video illustrates the opportunities that a failed OSN offers for research. The users of such a community leave traces that allow us to investigate its failure. In this sense, we can name our work as *Internet Archeology*, because we analyze non-written traces of a disappeared society, aiming at understanding the way it worked and the reasons for its demise.

In this paper, we provide a quantitative approach to the collective departure of users from OSN. We start from a theoretical perspective that, under the assumption of rational user behavior, allows us to define a new metric for the relation between network topology and massive user leaves. We apply this metric to high quality datasets from `Friendster` and `Livejournal`, comparing their social resilience with partial datasets from `Facebook`, `Orkut`, and `Myspace`. The research presented here is based on publicly available datasets, allowing the independent validation of our results, as well as the extension to further analyses [19]. We find that social resilience differs greatly across the different networks we study. Interestingly, however, more resilient networks are not necessarily more successful. This indicates that success and failure cannot be explained by topology alone. Instead, environmental factors, e.g. competition, design choices, user behaviour, etc., play a considerable role in the faith of an OSN. As an application of our analysis, we focus on the time evolution of `Friendster`, tracking the changes in its social resilience and investigating how it decayed to a complete collapse. We finish by commenting on the limitations and extensions of our approach, and outline possible future applications.

2. RELATED WORK

Recent research has focused on the question of growth and decay of activity or interest-based social groups [24]. This line of research analyzes social groups as subcommunities of a larger community, tied together due to underlying common features of their members. Such approach can be equally applied to scientific communities and online social networks [3,

38, 34], revealing patterns of diffusion and homophily that respectively spread group adoption, and increase internal connectivity. In particular, the big datasets provided by online communities allow the study of group creation and maintenance [21]. These results lead to applied techniques to predict the fate of interest-based groups, and to improve clustering analysis of social networks. Our work differs from these previous results in the scope of our analysis: Instead of looking at small to medium sized groups within larger communities, we look at the OSN as a whole. In our approach, users are not connected to each other due to certain common interest or affiliation, but through an online platform that maintains their social links and serves as communication medium.

Another research topic close to our work is the analysis of individual churn, defined as the decision of a user to stop using a service in favor of a competitor. This topic has received significant attention due to its business applications, where previous works explore how individual users disconnect from P2P networks[18], and stop using massive multiplayer online games [22]. Regarding OSN, a recent study shows the relation between social interaction and user departure in the online community `Yahoo answers` [10]. Furthermore, the same question has been addressed in a recent article [37], analyzing a mysterious online social network of which nor the name, size, nor purpose is explained. While these results are relevant for the question of user engagement, it is difficult to consider them in further research if we do not have information about the nature of the studied network. Social networks can have very different roles in online communities, requiring a differentiation between traditional social networking sites and online communities with a social network component, but where social interaction is mediated through other channels. The results of [37] reveal that 65% of the users that have no friends still remain active after three months, indicating that such social network is not precisely necessary for a user to use the site. As an example, a `Youtube` user does not need to create and maintain social contacts to interact with other users, which can be done through videos and comments independently of the social network.

Our work complements the previous results on individual user departures mentioned above, as we analyze the social resilience of the online community at the collective level. We build on these empirically validated microscopic rules of churn, to focus on cascades of departures through large OSN. We analyze the macroscopic topology of the social network and its role in the survival of the community. This kind of macroscopic effects are relevant to study the emergence of social conventions [25], an dynamics of politically aligned communities [14], in addition to the case of OSN we address here.

The particular problem of enhancing resilience by fixing nodes of a social network has been proposed and theoretically analyzed [5], aiming to prevent the *unraveling* of a social network. This implies that social resilience can be analyzed through the k-core decomposition of the social network, as explained in Section 3.1 . In addition, k-core centrality is the current state-of-the art metric to find influential nodes in general networks [23]. Regarding OSN, the k-core decomposition was applied for a global network of instant messaging [26], as well as for the Korean OSN `Cyworld` [2, 8], motivated by user centrality analysis rather than social resilience. To our knowledge, this article introduces the first empirical analysis

---

[1] http://archive.org/details/friendster-dataset-201107
[2] https://www.youtube.com/watch?v=7mFJdOsjJ0k

of social resilience, relating changes in user environment with cascades of departing users, through analysis based on the the k-core decomposition of different OSN.

3. SOCIAL RESILIENCE IN OSN

3.1 Quantifying Social Resilience

A characteristic property of any online social network is the presence of influence among friends. In particular, individual decisions regarding participating or leaving the network are, to a large extent, determined by the number of one's friends and their own engagement [3]. Therefore, users leaving a community have negative indirect effects on their friends [37]. This may trigger the latter to also leave, resulting in further cascades of departing users which may ultimately endanger the whole community. Social resilience acts to limit the spread of such cascades.

One approach to quantify social resilience is by natural removal of nodes based on some local property, for example degree [26]. By studying the network connectivity after such removals, one can identify nodes with critical importance for keeping the community connected. Importantly, by focusing on local properties we can only quantify the direct effects that a node removal has on the connectivity of the network.

In this paper, we propose an extension based on the k-core decomposition [23]. A k-core of a network is a sub-network in which all nodes have a degree $\geq k$. The k-core decomposition is a procedure of finding all k-cores, $\forall k > 0$, by repeatedly pruning nodes with degrees k. Therefore, it captures not only the direct, but also the indirect impact of users leaving the network. As an illustration consider Figure 1, which shows targeted removal of nodes with degrees < 3. On one hand,

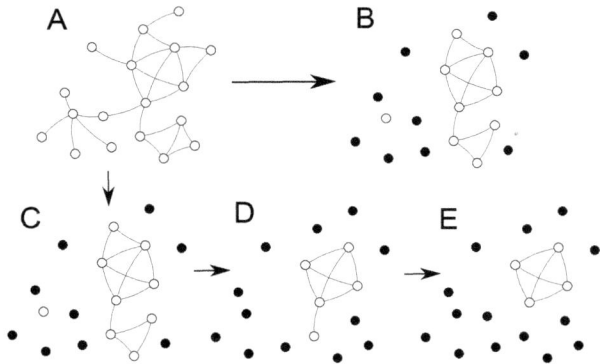

Figure 1: Effects of node removals on network connectivity as captured by degree only (A → B) and k-core decomposition (A → C → D → E)

starting from the network in A and removing all nodes with degrees < 3, produces the network in B. The black nodes in B have been removed (and thus are disconnected), and the final network consists of the 9 white nodes. The transition A → B shows only the direct effects of users with < 3 friends leaving.

On the other hand, starting again from A, and applying the k-core procedure, will repeatedly remove nodes until only

those with degrees ≥ 3 remain. The first step, A → C, removes the same black nodes as before. Continuing, C → D, removes those nodes that have been left with < 3 neighbours in C, and disconnects them as well. The final step, D → E, finishes the process by disconnecting the last white node in D that was left with < 3 friends. As a result, the final network is the fully connected network of the 4 white nodes. Hence, supposing that users leave a community when they are left with less than 3 friends, the k-core decomposition captures the full cascading effect that departing users have on the network as a whole.

We proceed by formalizing social resilience based on a *generalized* k-core decomposition. To this end, we present a theoretical model in which rational users decide simultaneously either to stay in the network or to leave it. These decisions are based on maximizing a utility function that weighs the benefits of membership against the associated costs. We show that the equilibrium network which maximizes the total payoff in the community, corresponds to a generalized k-core decomposition of the network.

3.2 Generalized k-core decomposition

Following [17], we extend the traditional k-core decomposition by recognizing that the pruning criterion need not be limited to degree only. Let us define a *property* function $\mathcal{B}_i(H)$ that given a sub-network $H \subseteq G$ associates a value, $n_i \in \mathbb{R}$, to node i. A generalized k-core of a network G is, then, defined as a sub-network $H \subseteq G$, such that $\mathcal{B}_i(H) \geq k$, $\forall i \in H$ and $k \in \mathbb{Z}$. The general form of B_i allows us to model different pruning mechanisms. For example, the traditional definition of the k-core can be recovered in the following way – for every node i take its immediate neighbourhood, $\mathcal{N}_i$, and fix $B_i(H) := |\mathcal{N}_i|$, $\forall H \subseteq G$. Other authors have also shown that considering weighted links in $\mathcal{B}_i$ can more accurately reveal nodes with higher spreading potential in weighted networks [13].

Note that by definition higher order cores are nested within lower order cores. We use this to define that a node i has *coreness* k_s if it is contained in a core of order k_s, but not in a core of order $k' > k_s$.

3.3 A rational model for OSN users

Here, we model the cost-benefit trade-off of OSN users in the following way. Assume that users in a given network, G, incur a constant integer cost, $c > 0$, for the effort they must spend to remain engaged. Accordingly, they receive a benefit or payoff from their friends in the network. Let the benefit of user i be the property function $\mathcal{B}_i(H)$ with $i \in H$. Assume non-increasing marginal benefits with respect to the size of H, i.e. $\mathcal{B}_i''(H) \leq 0$, otherwise costs are irrelevant as any cost level could be trivially overcome by increasing the size of H. This assumption is also supported by other empirical investigations of large social networks which show that the probability of a user to leave is concave with the number of friends who left [3, 37].

Users can select one of two possible actions – stay or leave. The utility of user i, is $U_i = 0$, if he chose leave or $U_i = \mathcal{B}_i(H) - c$, for stay. Finally, since users are rational, they will try to maximize their utility and so will choose stay as long as $U_i > 0$.

It is easily seen that the equilibrium network, G^*, which maximizes the total utility, $U(G) = \sum_i U_i$, is composed of users who choose stay when $c < k_s^i$, and leave otherwise. In other words, node i should remain engaged in the network as long as the cost, c, does not exceed its generalized coreness, k_s^i. In this sense, G^* corresponds to the generalized k-core of G.

To illustrate that G^* is indeed an equilibrium network, we need to show that no user has an incentive to unilaterally join it or leave it. Consider a node, $j \in G^*$ who chooses stay. This node would belong to a generalized k-core, k_s^j, and by definition, $B_j(H) - k_s^j \geq 0$. Since, j stayed in the network, it must be that $c < k_s^j$, therefore $B_j(H) - c > 0$. So, j will be forfeiting positive utility, should he decide to leave. In the same manner, consider another node $l \notin G^*$ who chooses leave, thus his coreness $k_s^l \leq c$. All his friends with the same coreness would have left the network, therefore the only benefit that l could obtain from staying would come from his connections with nodes in higher cores. The benefit, B_l, from such connections must not exceed k_s^l, otherwise l would have belonged to a higher core in the first place. Since $k_s^l \leq c$ we have $B_l < c$. This implies that l necessarily obtains negative utility from staying, so he has no incentives to do so. Moreover, G^* is optimal, as we showed that any change from the equilibrium actions of any user inevitably lowers his utility and decreases the total utility in the network. We also argue that it is reasonable to expect this equilibrium network to be reached in an actual setting, since it maximizes the utility of all users simultaneously, as well as the welfare of the network provider.

In the rest of the paper, we approximate B_i as proportional to the number of i's direct friends, N_i, i.e. $B_i = bN_i$, for some $b \in \mathbb{Z}$. Taking k_s^i to be the coreness of i, by definition it holds that $bN_i \geq k_s^i$. The maximum cost, c, that i would tolerate as a member of the community must be strictly smaller than its coreness, hence $bN_i > c$ and $N_i > c/b$. The last result implies that the minimum number of friends that a node i needs to remain engaged must be strictly larger than c/b. Therefore, $k_s^i \geq K$, i.e. the coreness of a participating user i must not fall below a critical value K with K given by:

$$K = (c/b) + 1 \qquad (1)$$

Based on the above discussion, we see that a user will remain in a network with a high c/b ratio if its coreness k_s is high. This is because, by definition, i is part of a connected network of nodes with large minimum degrees and hence large benefits. In contrast, simply having a large degree does not imply that a user will obtain large utility from staying. Note that a high-degree node may nevertheless have low coreness. This means that i would be part of a sub-network in which all nodes have low minimum degrees. As a result a lower c/b ratio would suffice to start a cascade of users departing, that can quickly leave i with no friends and thus drive it to leave too. Finally, we define social resilience of a community as the size of the K core. In other words, this is the size of the network that remains after all users with $k_s \leq c/b$ have been forced out. This definition allows us to quantify social resilience and reliably compare it across communities even for unknown c/b ratios, as shown in Section 5.

4. DATA ON ONLINE SOCIAL NETWORKS

For our empirical study of social network resilience, we use datasets from five different OSN. The choice of these datasets aims at spanning a variety of success stories across OSN, including successful and failed communities, as well as communities currently in decline. The size, data gathering methods, and references are summarized in Table 1, and outlined in the following.

Friendster
The most recent dataset we take into account is the one retrieved by the Internet Archive, with the purpose of preserving Friendster's information before its discontinuation. This dataset provides a high-quality snapshot of the large amount of user information that was publicly available on the site, including friend lists and interest-based groups. In this article, we provide the first analysis of the social network topology of Friendster as a whole.

Since some user profiles in Friendster were private, this dataset does not include their connections. However, these private users would be listed as contacts in the list of their friends who were not private. We symmetrized the Friendster dataset by adding these additional links. Due to the large size of the Friendster dataset, we symmetrized the data by using Hadoop, which we distribute under a Creative Commons license [3].

Livejournal
In Livejournal, users keep personal blogs and define different types of friendship links. The information retrieval method for the creation of this dataset combined user id sampling with neighborhood exploration [29], covering more than 95% of the whole community. We choose this Livejournal dataset for its overall quality, as it provides a view of practically the whole OSN.

Note that the design of Livejournal as an OSN deviates from the other four communities analyzed here. First, Livejournal is a blog community, in which the social network functionality plays a secondary role. Second, Livejournal social links are directed, in the sense that one user can be friend of another without being friended back. In our analysis, we only include reciprocal links, referring to previous research on its k-core decomposition [23]. By including this dataset, we aim at comparing how different interaction mechanisms and platform designs influence social resilience.

Orkut
Among declining social networking sites, we include a partial dataset on Orkut [29], which was estimated to cover 11.3% of the whole community. Far from the quality of the two previous datasets, we include Orkut in our analysis due to its platform design, as this dataset includes users that did not have a limit on their amount of friends. Furthermore, Orkut has a story of local success in Brazil[4], losing popularity against other sites at the time of writing of this article.

MySpace
One of the most famous OSN in decline is Myspace, which was the leading OSN before Facebook's success [15]. We include a relatively small dataset of 100000 users of MySpace [2], which was aimed to sample its degree distribution. This dataset was crawled through a Breadth-First Search method, providing a partial and possibly biased dataset of Myspace. We include

[3] web.sg.ethz.ch/users/dgarcia/Friendster-sim.tar.bz2
[4] http://www.digitaltrends.com/computing/facebook-taking-over-globally-with-almost-700-million-users/

Table 1: Outline of OSN and datasets

name	launch date	status in 2013	crawl date	users	links	source
Livejournal	1999	in decline	Dec 2006	5.2×10^6	2.8×10^7	[29]
Friendster	2002	discontinued	Jul 2011	1.17×10^8	2.58×10^9	Internet Archive
Myspace	2003	in decline	Oct 2006	10^5	6.8×10^6	[2]
Orkut	2004	in decline	Nov 2006	3×10^6	2.23×10^8	[29]
Facebook	2004	successful	May 2008	3×10^6	2.36×10^7	[36]

this dataset as an exercise to study the influence of sampling biases in the analysis of social resilience.

Facebook
We want to complete the spectrum of success of OSN, from the collapse of Friendster to the big success of Facebook. The last dataset we include is a special crawl which aims at an unbiased, yet partial dataset as close as possible to the whole community [36]. This dataset was retrieved based on regional networks, for which social connections among the members of that subnetwork were accessible at the time of the crawl.

The partial datasets on Orkut, MySpace, and Facebook allow us to analyze of OSN that are still "alive", in the sense that they have not been discontinued yet. As an analogy to the *autopsy* of Friendster, we provide a *biopsy* of the other OSN, taking a small sample due to their privacy and data availability issues. Our results on these datasets are valid to the extent of their publicly available data, while we can be confident that our analysis of Livejournal and Friendster are representative of their complete user bases.

5. EMPIRICS OF OSN RESILIENCE

5.1 K-core decomposition

Following the analysis of the model presented in Section 3.3, we computed the k-core decomposition for each of the OSN datasets introduced above. Among those datasets, Friendster and Livejournal cover the vast majority of their respective communities. Figure 2 shows a schematic representation of the k-core decomposition of Friendster and Livejournal. Each layer of the circles corresponds to the nodes with coreness k_s, with an area proportional to the amount of nodes with that coreness value. The color of each layer ranges from light blue for $k_s = 1$, to red for $k_s = 304$. The distribution of colors reveals a qualitative difference between both communities: Friendster has many more nodes of high coreness than Livejournal, which has a similar color range but many more nodes with low k_s. This difference indicates that, to keep together as a community, Livejournal needs to have a much lower c/b than Friendster. This scenario is rather realistic, as Livejournal is a blog community in which users create large amounts of original content.

Our theoretical argumentation, presented in Section 3.3, implies that node coreness is a more reasonable estimator for resilience than node degree. A degree of at least k_s is a necessary condition for a coreness of k_s, but a high degree does not necessarily mean a high coreness. Taking Friendster an example, Figure 3 shows the boxplot for the distribution of k_s versus node degree, indicating the spread of k_s for nodes of similar degree. The empirical data shows that a high degree does not necessarily mean a high k_s, even finding nodes with very low k_s and very high degree. Nevertheless, it is clear

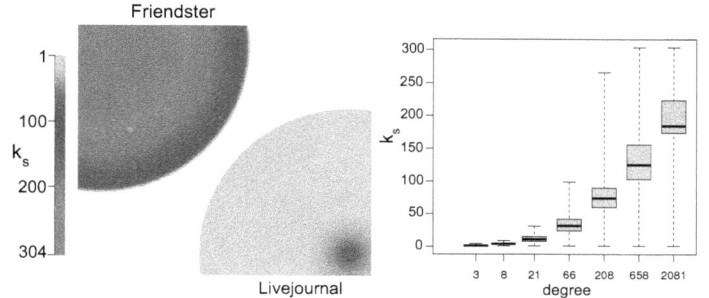

Figure 2: Left: Overview of the k-core decomposition for Friendster and Livejournal. Layers are colored according to k_s, with areas proportional to the amount of nodes with such k_s. Right: boxplot of k-shell indices by degree for Friendster. Dark lines represent the mean, and dashed bars show extreme values. Boxes are arranged in the x-axis according to the middle value of their bin.

that k_s is likely to increase with degree, but mapping degree to coreness would wrongly estimate the resilience of the community as a whole. By measuring coreness, we can detect that some nodes belong to the fringe despite their high degree, as the coreness integrates global information about the centrality of the node.

5.2 Resilience comparison

Extending the above observations, we computed the k-core decomposition of the three additional OSN, aiming at comparing their relation between their environment, measured through c/b, and the amount of users expected to be active under such conditions.

We focus our analysis on the Complementary Cumulative Density Function (CCDF) of each network, defined as $P(k_s > K)$. As shown in Section 3.3, the cost-benefit-ratio c/b corresponds to a value K that determines the nodes that leave the network, which are those k_s coreness below K (Eq. 1). Under this conditions, the CCDF of k_s measures the amount of nodes that will remain in the network under a given c/b, allowing us to compare how each OSN would withstand the same values of cost and benefit.

The right panel of Figure 3 shows the log-log CCDF of the five OSN. The first two communities to compare are Livejournal and Friendster, as the datasets on these two are the most reliable. First, the CCDF of Friendster is always above the CCDF of Livejournal. This is consistent with the structure shown in Figure 2, where it can be appreciated that Livejournal has many more nodes in the fringe than Friendster. Second, both CCDF reach comparable maximum values, re-

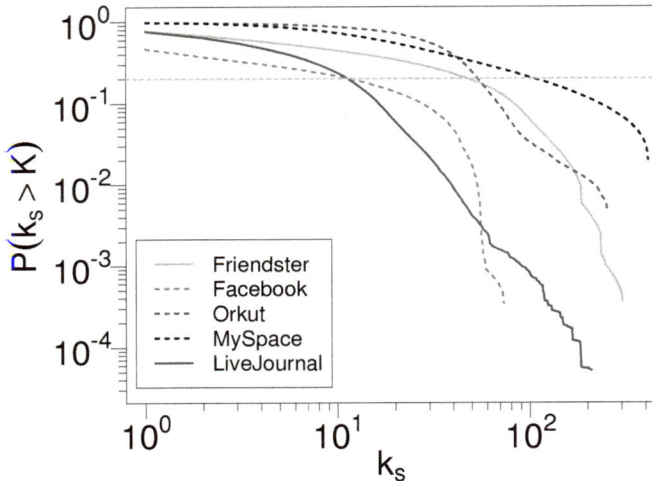

Figure 3: CCDF of k_s for all five OSN. The horizontal dashed line shows the cut at 0.2.

gardless of the fact that `Friendster` was 20 times larger than `Livejournal`. Such skewness in the coreness of `Livejournal` can be interpreted as a result of a higher competition for attention, as expected from a blog community in comparison with a pure social networking site, like `Friendster` was.

Focusing on the tails of the distributions, we can compare the patterns of resilience for environments with high K. The comparison between the resilience of these communities is heavily dependent of the value of K, as for example, `Livejournal` is less resilient than `Facebook` for values of K between 10 and 50, but more resilient below and above such interval. A similar case can be seen between `Friendster` and `Orkut`, as their CCDFS cross at 60 and 200. Thus, `Friendster` would be more resilient than `Orkut` if K lies in that interval, while `Orkut` would have a larger fraction of active nodes if $K < 60$ or $K > 200$.

It is important that these comparisons are made between the reliable datasets of `Friendster` and `Livejournal`, compared with partial datasets from the other communities. While our conclusions on the first two OSN can be seen as global findings on the community as a whole, the rest are limited to the size of the datasets available. A particularly clear example of the effect of the crawling bias is the distribution of coreness for `Myspace`, which shows an extreme resilience in comparison to all the other datasets, with the exception of `Orkut` for $K < 50$. As commented in Section 4 , the method used for `Myspace` was very biased towards nodes of high degree, leaving an unrealistic picture of the resilience of the whole community. Additionally, the low starting value of the CCDF of `Facebook` could be related to the crawling method of the dataset, restricted to regional networks. This highlights the importance of publicly available datasets for academic research: While we are able to make a major *autopsy* of `Friendster` and `Livejournal`, our analysis of the other three datasets can be considered a *biopsy*, as we can only use a small sample of them.

Regardless of any crawling bias, we found that these networks have maximum coreness numbers much higher than previous results. The maximum k_s found for the network of in-

stant messaging was limited to 68 [26], and close to 100 for the OSN Cyworld [8]. `Livejournal` has a maximum k_s of 213, `Friendster` of 304, `Orkut` of 253, and `Myspace` as a very deep core of $k_s = 414$. The exception lies in the `Facebook` dataset, where we find a maximum k_s of 74. This evidence shows that OSN can have much tighter cores than the ones found in previous research, revealing that they contain small communities with very high resilience.

As a final comparison, we focus on the values of K for the catastrophic case of the networks losing 80% of their nodes, i.e. where the CCDF has a value of 0.2. The data shows that both `Facebook` and `Livejournal` would lose 80% of their users under a value of K close to 10. For the case of the unsuccessful communities of `Orkut` and `Friendster`, it requires a much worse environment, with values of K above 60. This way, the empirical data supports the idea that, under the same environmental conditions, `Facebook` and `Livejournal` are less resilient than the three other networks, which were less successful. This means that the topology of their social network is not enough to explain their collapse, but indicates that bad decisions in design and interface changes can spread through the network and drive many users away.

6. NOT POWER-LAW DEGREE DISTRIBUTIONS

In Section 3.3, we modelled the large-scale cascades of departures as the result of rational users evaluating their net benefits of staying in the network. However, investigating if OSN have power-law degree distributions is important, as it could provide an alternative model for user exodus. In particular, networks with power-law degree distributions do not have an epidemic threshold below which a "sickness" cannot spread [32]. Instead, the sickness will survive within the network for an unbound amount of time and eventually infect most of the nodes. Such sickness could be a meme or a social norm, but could also be the decision of leaving the community.

Power-law degree distributions arise from empirically tested mechanisms of preferential attachment [26], and bursty behavior in link creation [11, 30]. Numerous previous works have reported power-law degree distributions in social networks [2, 8, 26, 29]. Nevertheless, most of these works rely on goodness of fit statistics, and do not provide a clear test of the power-law hypothesis. It states that the degree distribution follows the equation $p(d) = \frac{\alpha-1}{\deg_{min}} \left(\frac{d}{\deg_{min}} \right)^{-\alpha}$ for $d \geq \deg_{min}$. This is usually described as $p(d) \propto d^{-\alpha}$, and often argued as valid if metrics such as R^2, or F_1 are high enough. While a high goodness of fit could be sufficient for some practical applications, the power-law hypothesis can only be tested, and eventually rejected, through the result of a statistical test, assuming a reasonable confidence level.

We followed the state-of-the-art methodology to test power laws [9], which roughly involves the following steps. First, we created Maximum Likelihood (ML) estimators $\hat{\alpha}$ and $\widehat{\deg_{min}}$ for $p(d)$. Second, we tested the empirical data above $\widehat{\deg_{min}}$ against the power law hypothesis and we recorded the corresponding KS-statistics (D). Third, we repeated the KS test for 100 synthetic datasets that follow the fitted power law above $\widehat{\deg_{min}}$. The p-value is then the fraction of the synthetic D values that are larger than the empirical one. Thus, for each

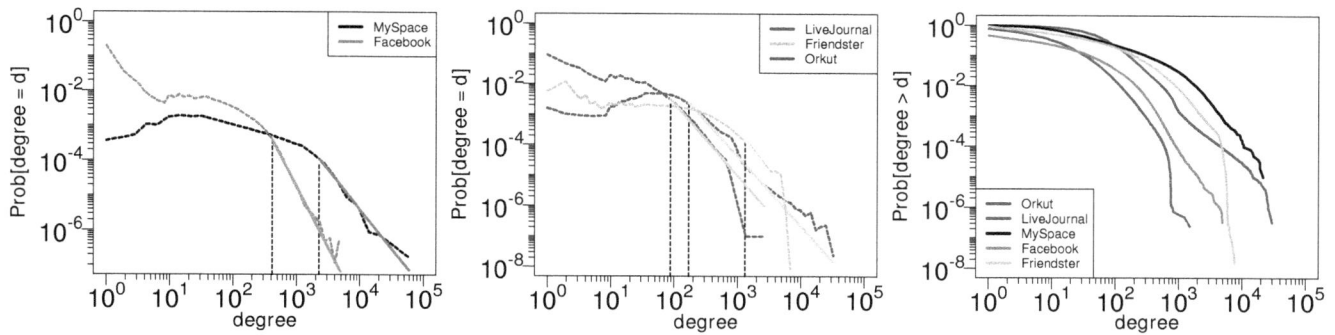

Figure 4: Complementary cumulative density function (cdf) and probability density functions (pdf) of node degree in the five considered communities. For each pdf, lighter lines show the ML power-law fits from $\widehat{\deg}_{\min}$. Vertical dotted lines indicate $\widehat{\deg}_{\min}$.

degree distribution, we have the ML estimates $\widehat{\deg}_{\min}$ and $\hat{\alpha}$, which define the best case in terms of the KS test, with an associated D value, and the p-value.

Ultimately, a power law hypothesis cannot be rejected if (i) the p-value of the KS-test is above a chosen significance level [9], and (ii) there is a sufficiently large amount of datapoints from $\deg_{\min}$ to $\deg_{\max}$ [33]. We found that the degree distributions of Facebook, Friendster, Orkut and Livejournal have p-values well below any reasonable significance threshold, showing an extremely reliable empirical support to reject the power-law hypothesis (Table 2).

Table 2: Power law fits of the degree distributions of the analyzed networks.

dataset	$\widehat{\deg}_{\min}$	$\hat{\alpha}$	n_{tail}	D	p
Friendster	1311	3.6	2.9×10^5	4.59	$< 10^{-15}$
LiveJournal	88	3.3	81141	0.02	$< 10^{-15}$
Facebook	423	4.6	4918	0.14	$< 10^{-15}$
Orkut	171	3	2.8×10^5	0.02	$< 10^{-15}$
MySpace	2350	3.6	623	0.03	0.22

For the case of Myspace, a KS test gives a p-value of 0.22, which can be considered high enough to not reject the power-law hypothesis [9]. Therefore Myspace satisfies the first criterion, but when looking at the range of values from $\deg_{\min}$ to $\deg_{\max}$ (roughly one order of magnitude), and the low amount of datapoints included, this KS-test composes a merely anecdotal evidence of the extreme tail of Myspace. If accepted, the power-law distribution would explain just 0.623% of the Myspace dataset. In addition, BFS methods have been shown to bias the macroscopic properties of the datasets they produce [31]. This leads to the conclusion that, while we cannot fully reject the power-law hypothesis, we can safely state that the dataset does not support the hypothesis otherwise. Figure 4 shows the degree distributions and their CCDF. For each OSN, we show how the typical log-log plot of the PDF is misleading, as a simple eye inspection would suggest power-law distributions, but a robust statistical analysis disproves this possibility.

7. THE TIME EVOLUTION OF FRIENDSTER

In this section, we describe a *post hoc* case study of the way how Friendster rose and collapsed, using the available timing information in the dataset.

7.1 Social growth mechanism

The Friendster dataset does not provide the date of creation of user accounts or social links, but it includes a user id that increased sequentially since the creation of the site. We analyzed the time series of Friendster in an event time scale, where each timestamp corresponds to the id of each user. We measured the time distance of an edge e, which connects users u_1 and u_2, as the difference between the ids of these users $d(e(u_1, u_2)) = |id(u_1) - id(u_2)|$. In the following, we show how early users connected to later users, making the network grow.

We divided the network in time slices of a width of 10 million user ids, with a last smaller slice of 7 million ids. Each of these 12 slices contains a set of nodes that have connections i) to nodes that joined the community before, ii) to nodes that joined the network afterwards, and iii) internally within the slice. This way, for the slice of time period t we can calculate its internal average degree $2|E_{in}(t)|/|N(t)|$, where $E_{in}(t)$ is the set of edges between nodes in the slice t, noted as $N(t)$.

As an extension, we define $E_p(t)$ and $E_f(t)$ as the sets of edges towards nodes that joined the community before t (past nodes), and nodes that joined after t (future nodes). We measured the time range of connections to the past $P(t)$ as the mean distance of the edges in $E_p(t)$, and the rage of connections to the future $F(t)$ as the mean distance of their future counterpart $E_f(t)$. By definition, the amount of past nodes for the first slice is 0, equally to the amount of future nodes for the last slice. If the process of edge creation was completely independent of these timestamps, the network would have some arbitrary sequence of node ids. In such network, $P(t)$ would steadily increase with each slice, having an expected value of $|N|/2$ for the last one, where $|N|$ is the size of the network. Similarly, $F(t)$ would decrease from $|N|/2$ at the first slice, converging at 0 in the last one.

The time evolution of the range of connections to past and future is shown in the left panel of Figure 5. Each circle represents a slice of the network, with growing t from left to right.

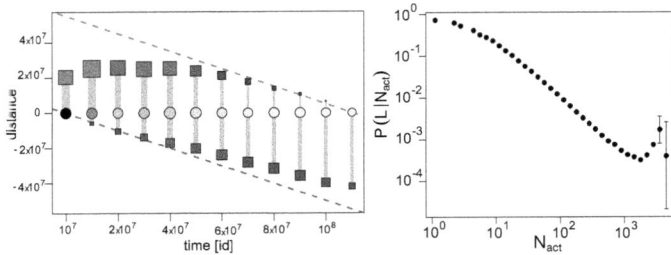

Figure 5: Left: Schema of connectivity of Friendster users across time. Each circle represents a slice of the network of width of 10 million user ids. Blue squares represent past users and red squares represent future users, with a distance from their slice according to $P(t)$ and $F(t)$ respectively. The dashed lines show the expectation of these two metrics in a random id sequence of the network. **Right:** Likelihood of a Friendster user to leave, given the amount of active friends of the user. The decreasing likelihood validates the assumption that users are more likely to leave when they do not have enough active friends.

Their horizontal alignment represents the present with respect to the slice, and each circle is connected to a blue square on the below that represents past nodes, and a red square above that represents future nodes. Circles have a size proportional to $N(t)|$, which keep approximately constant throughout time. The darkness of each circle is proportional to its internal connectivity $|E_{in}(t)|$, and the width of the connections from circles to past and future squares are proportional to $|E_p(t)|$ and $E_f(t)|$ respectively. Internal connectivities decrease through time, as early slices had significantly higher $|E_{in}(t)|$. This indicates that the initial root of users of Friendster was much more tightly connected among themselves than towards other nodes, creating a denser subcommunity of old users. A possible explanation for this pattern is that Friendster started as an OSN for dating, and its design was later shifted towards generalized networking as it became popular.

The squares of Figure 5 left are positioned according to the mean past $P(t)$ and future $F(t)$ distances of each slice. As a comparison with random network construction, dashed lines show their expected values as explained above. For early slices, the mean future distance is significantly lower than its random counterpart, revealing a connectivity pattern that limits the range of future connections. This shows a decay in the diffusion process through the offline social network, where the potential of a user to bring new users decreases through time. This suggests a possible "user expiration date" after which a user of a OSN cannot be expected to bring new users.

7.2 Microdynamics of user activity

We used the Friendster dataset to explore the empirical properties of the benefit function $\mathcal{B}_i(H)$, explained in Section 3.2. In our rational model, that function determines when a user i becomes inactive, given some quantifiable properties of its social environment H. While the dataset does not provide precise activity statistics to estimate $\mathcal{B}_i(H)$, we can estimate the conditions for users to become inactive through their sequence of ids. Following the methodology of [26], we approx-

imate the time when a user became active as its id in the sequence, and the maximum timestamp associated to its edges as the time when it became inactive. This way, we only take into account user activity as link creation in the social network, leaving out other actions such as creation of messages or sharing of pictures.

For each user, we extracted the events when a friend becomes inactive, or when a friend joins the network, calculating the amount of active friends N_{act} of the user in each of those events. This value determines the period when the user is creating new friends, until N_{act} reaches its maximum value, after which the user has decreasing amounts of active friends and ends becoming inactive itself. After this maximum value, we calculate the likelihood of a user leaving the OSN (L) given its amount of active friends $P(L|N_{act})$, in order to provide a first estimation of the social conditions for users becoming inactive in Friendster. The right panel of Figure 5 shows this likelihood, revealing that users are much more likely to leave when they have low amounts of active friends. This validates our assumption that the benefits of a user are monotonically increasing with its amount of active neighbors, as they are much less likely to leave the OSN when they have a sufficient amount of active friends.

Two additional observations can be done about the likelihood $P(L|N_{act})$. First, the shape of its dependence of N_{act} reveals high variance, despite of its fast decrease. This indicates that the likelihood of users leaving scales with connectivity, i.e. the fraction of users likely to leave the OSN does not vanish when network size and density tend to infinity. Second, there is a small trend at the tail of the likelihood, where some values seem to increase. Our statistics do not fully validate the existence of this increase, as there are very few users with so many friends, but we can observe that the monotonically decreasing behavior up to that level does not exist any more. This suggests the presence of information overload [28], in which users with very large amounts of friends might be unable to cope with all the information provided by the OSN, and thus perceiving lower benefits.

7.3 Resilience and decline of Friendster

We combined the sequence of user ids with the k-core decomposition of Friendster to study how its resilience changed over time. In particular, we explored the relation between the coreness of users and the time when they joined the community. To analyze the changes in resilience, we divided the users along the median of the distribution of coreness values, $\bar{k}_s = 6$. This way, for each period of time, there is an amount of users in the lower half of the distribution ($k_s < \bar{k}_s$). When such amount increases, the new members that joined the OSN in that period are at higher risk to leave than when they have coreness values above the median. We measure the resilience of these time-dependent parts of network as the ratio between users with $k_s < \bar{k}_s$, and the total amount of users in the slice.

We created slices of 100000 user ids, calculating a point sample estimate of $P(k_s < \bar{k}_s)$. Inset of Figure 6 shows the time evolution of this ratio, with a dark area showing 99% confidence intervals. First, we notice that the skewness of k_s does not affect our statistic, as the confidence intervals are sufficiently concentrated around the point estimates. Second, we can identify certain time periods when the new users of Friendster only connected to its fringe, having larger ratios of nodes with coreness below the median. The first moment with a peak is at the very beginning, to drop to ratios around 0.3 soon after. This shows that the set of very early users did not fully exploit the social network, and it took a bit of time for the OSN to become more resilient. The second peak is shortly after having 22 million users, which coincides with the decay of popularity of Friendster in the US. Finally, the ratio of users at risk went above 0.5 before the community had 80 million accounts, showing a lack of cohesion as its shutdown approaches, as new users do not manage to connect to the rest.

To conclude our analysis, we explored how the spread of departures captured in the k-core decomposition (see Section 3.3) can describe the collapse of Friendster as an OSN. As we do not have access to the precise amount of active users of Friendster, we proxy its value through the Google search volume of *www.friendster.com*. The inset of Figure 6 shows the relative weekly search volume from January 2009. At some point in 2009, Friendster introduced changes in its user interface, coinciding with some technical problems, and the rise of popularity of Facebook [5]. This led to the fast decrease of active users in the community, ending on its discontinuation in 2011.

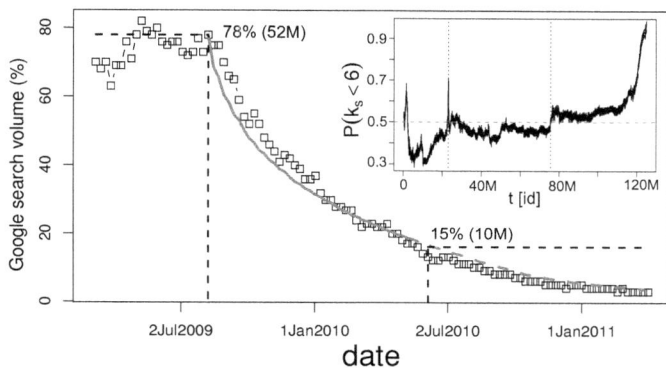

Figure 6: Weekly Google search trend volume for Friendster. The red line shows the estimation of the remaining users in a process of unraveling. Inset: time series of fraction of nodes with $k_s < 6$.

We scale the search volumes fixing 100% as the total amount of users with coreness above 0, 68 million. At the point when the collapse of Friendster started, the search volume indicates a popularity of 78% of its maximum. We take this point to start the simulation of a user departure cascade, with an initial amount of 58 million active users, i.e. users with coreness above 3. The second reference point we take is June 2010, when Friendster was reported to have 10 million active users [6], corresponding to 15% of the 68 million user reference explained above. The search volume on that date is 14%, showing the validity of the assumption that the maximum amount of active users corresponds to those with coreness above 0. Thus, these 10 million remaining users correspond to nodes with $k_s > 67$.

Given these two reference points, we can approximate the collapse of the network through its "unraveling" per k-core. Our assumption is that a critical coreness K_t, as defined in

Eq.1, starts at 3 and increases by 1 at a constant rate. Such K_t is the result of an increasing cost-to-benefit ratio, and thus all the nodes with $k_s < K_t$ would leave the community. Then, for each timestep, the amount of remaining users would correspond to the CCDF shown in Figure 3. In this simulation, K increases at a rate of 6 per month, i.e. from 3 to 67 between our two reference points.

The red line of Figure 6 shows the remaining users under this process, with dashed values after the second reference point of June 2010. We can observe that this process approximates well the decay of Friendster from the start of its decline, to its discontinuation in 2011. The R^2 value for this fit is 0.972, leaving some slight underfit through 2009. This fit show the match between two approximations: on one side the search volume as an estimation of the amount of active users, and on the other side the amount of remaining users when the c/b ratio increases constantly through time.

8. DISCUSSION

In this article, we have presented the first empirical analysis of social resilience in OSN. We approached this question using a theoretical model that relates the environment of the OSN with the cascades of user departures. We showed how a generalized version of the k-core decomposition allows the empirical measurement of resilience in OSN. Previous theoretical works [5] and empirical observations [37] suggest the existence of constant cost and monotonous benefits, which lead to a stable solution that corresponds to the k-core decomposition of the social network. Among the costs that users face when using an OSN, there are time costs to adapt to the user interface and set up privacy settings [27], including the risk of revealing private information, or sharing pictures with undesired contacts [20]. The managers and owners of OSN have thus an interest in lowering this cost, usually introducing new technologies like link recommender systems or automatized friend lists [28].

We provided an empirical study of social resilience across five influential OSN, including successful ones like Facebook and unsuccessful ones like Friendster. We have shown that the hypothesis of a power-law degree distribution cannot be accepted for any of these communities, discarding the epidemic properties of complex networks as a possible explanation for large-scale cascades of user departures. Our k-core analysis overcomes this limitation, quantifying social resilience as a collective phenomenon using the CCDF of node coreness. We found that the topologies of successful sites are less resilient than the unsuccessful ones. This indicates that the environmental conditions of an OSN play a major role for its success. Thus, we conclude that the topology of the social network alone cannot explain the stories of success and failure of the studied OSN, and it is necessary to focus future empirical analysis in additional dimensions of user activity [36]. Additionally, we found very high maximum coreness numbers for most of the OSN we studied. The existence of these superconnected cores indicates that information can be spread efficiently through these OSN [23].

As a case study, we provided a detailed analysis of the changes in Friendster through time. We detect that the range of connections towards future nodes is much lower than the expectation from a random process. We provide an estimation of the likelihood of users to leave depending on their amount of active friends, finding that users with less active friends are

[5] www.time.com/time/business/article/0,8599,1707760,00.html
[6] en.wikipedia.org/wiki/Friendster

more likely to leave. Not surprisingly, this likelihoood function reveals some heterogeneity among users in the decision when to leave, in line with previous research where personality traits, like extroversion, play a role in online activity [6]. Finally, we applied all our findings to **Friendster**'s collapse, fitting an approximated time series of active users through the spread of user departures predicted by the k-core decomposition.

Our analysis focused on the macroscopic resilience of OSN, but further research is necessary to better understand the individual conditions for users to leave an OSN. Clickstream datasets would allow to measure the time users spend in each social network, to quantify passive activity (viewing pictures, reading comments), and how they migrate across OSN [4]. This type of data would add an independent dimension of activity in the from of wall posts [35], picture shares and likes [7], allowing more precise validations of when users become inactive and under which situation.

Our formulation of a generalized k-core can be applied when user decisions are more complex than just staying or leaving the network, for example introducing heterogeneity of benefits or weights in the social links. For example, link weight can be estimated from implicit interactions [16], which can be incorporated to our k-core analysis through the formulation of [12]. Another open question is the role of directionality in the social network, and how to measure resilience when asymmetric relations are allowed. The benefits of users of these networks would be multidimensional, representing both the reputation of a user and the amount of information it receives from its neighborhood. The work presented here is theoretically limited to the study of monotonously increasing, convex objective functions of benefit versus active neighborhood. While empirical studies support this assumption [3, 37], it is possible to imagine a scenario where information overload decreases the net benefit of users with very large neighborhoods, creating nonlinearities where the generalized k-core is not a stable solution. We leave this questions open for further research, and the study of social resilience in other types of online communities.

9. ACKNOWLEDGEMENTS

The authors would like to thank the Internet Archive for their work in crawling and curating **Friendster**.

10. REFERENCES

[1] W. Adger. Social and ecological resilience: are they related? *Progress in Human Geography*, 24, 2000.

[2] Y.-Y. Ahn, S. Han, H. Kwak, S. Moon, and H. Jeong. Analysis of topological characteristics of huge online social networking services. In *WWW '07*, 2007.

[3] L. Backstrom, D. Huttenlocher, J. Kleinberg, and X. Lan. Group formation in large social networks. In *KDD '06*, 2006.

[4] F. Benevenuto, T. Rodrigues, M. Cha, and V. Almeida. Characterizing user behavior in online social networks. In *IMC '09*, 2009.

[5] K. Bhawalkar, J. Kleinberg, K. Lewi, T. Roughgarden, and A. Sharma. Preventing unraveling in social networks: the anchored k-core problem. In *ICALP'12*, 2012.

[6] C. Budak and R. Agrawal. On Participation in Group Chats on Twitter. In *WWW'13*, 2013.

[7] M. Cha, A. Mislove, and K. P. Gummadi. A measurement-driven analysis of information propagation in the flickr social network. In *WWW '09*, 2009.

[8] H. Chun, H. Kwak, Y.-H. Eom, Y.-Y. Ahn, S. Moon, and H. Jeong. Comparison of online social relations in volume vs interaction. In *IMC '08*, 2008.

[9] A. Clauset, C. R. Shalizi, and M. E. J. Newman. Power-Law Distributions in Empirical Data. *SIAM Review*, 51(4):661, 2009.

[10] G. Dror, D. Pelleg, O. Rokhlenko, and I. Szpektor. Churn prediction in new users of Yahoo! answers. In *WWW '12 Companion*, 2012.

[11] S. Gaito, M. Zignani, G. P. Rossi, A. Sala, X. Zhao, H. Zheng, and B. Y. Zhao. On the bursty evolution of online social networks. In *HotSocial '12*, pages 1–8, 2012.

[12] A. Garas, D. Garcia, M. Skowron, and F. Schweitzer. Emotional persistence in online chatting communities. *Scientific Reports*, 2:402, 2012.

[13] A. Garas, F. Schweitzer, and S. Havlin. A k-shell decomposition method for weighted networks. *New Journal of Physics*, 14:083030, 2012.

[14] D. Garcia, F. Mendez, U. Serdült, and F. Schweitzer. Political polarization and popularity in online participatory media. In *PLEAD '12*, 2012.

[15] M. Giles. A world of connections - A special report on social networking. *The Economist*, Jan 28th, 2010.

[16] M. Gupte and T. Eliassi-Rad. Measuring tie strength in implicit social networks. In *WebSci '12*, 2012.

[17] A. Harkins. Network Games with Perfect Complements. Warwick University Draft, unpublished.

[18] O. Herrera and T. Znati. Modeling Churn in P2P Networks. In *ANSS '07*, 2007.

[19] B. A. Huberman. Big data deserve a bigger audience. *Nature*, 482(7385):308, 2012.

[20] M. Johnson, S. Egelman, and S. M. Bellovin. Facebook and Privacy : It's Complicated. In *Symposium on Usable Privace and Security*, 2012.

[21] S. R. Kairam, D. J. Wang, and J. Leskovec. The life and death of online groups. In *WSDM '12*, 2012.

[22] J. Kawale, A. Pal, and J. Srivastava. Churn Prediction in MMORPGs: A Social Influence Based Approach. In *ICCSE '09*, 2009.

[23] M. Kitsak, L. K. Gallos, S. Havlin, F. Liljeros, L. Muchnik, H. E. Stanley, and H. A. Makse. Identification of influential spreaders in complex networks. *Nature Physics*, 6(11):888–893, 2010.

[24] J. Kleinberg. Analysis of large-scale social and information networks. *Philosophical transactions of the Royal Society A*, 371, 2013.

[25] F. Kooti, K. P. Gummadi, and W. A. Mason. The Emergence of Conventions in Online Social Networks. In *ICWSM '12*, 2012.

[26] J. Leskovec and E. Horvitz. Planetary-scale views on a large instant-messaging network. In *WWW '08*, 2008.

[27] Y. Liu, K. P. Gummadi, B. Krishnamurthy, and A. Mislove. Analyzing facebook privacy settings. In *IMC '11*, 2011.

[28] Y. Liu, B. Viswanath, M. Mondal, K. P. Gummadi, and A. Mislove. Simplifying friendlist management. In *WWW '12 Companion*, 2012.

[29] A. Mislove, M. Marcon, K. P. Gummadi, P. Druschel, and B. Bhattacharjee. Measurement and analysis of online social networks. In *IMC '07*, 2007.

[30] L. Muchnik, S. Pei, L. C. Parra, S. D. S. Reis, J. S. Andrade, S. Havlin, and H. A. Makse. Origins of power-law degree distribution in the heterogeneity of human activity in social networks. *Scientific reports*, 3:1783, 2013.

[31] H. Park and S. Moon. Sampling Bias in User Attribute Estimation of OSNs. In *WWW '13 companion*, 2013.

[32] R. Pastor-Satorras and A. Vespignani. Epidemic dynamics in finite size scale-free networks. *Physical Review E*, 65(3):1–4, 2002.

[33] M. P. H. Stumpf and M. A. Porter. Critical truths about power laws. *Science*, 335(6069):665–6, 2012.

[34] J. L. Toole, M. Cha, and M. C. González. Modeling the adoption of innovations in the presence of geographic and media influences. *PloS one*, 7(1):e29528, 2012.

[35] B. Viswanath, A. Mislove, M. Cha, and K. P. Gummadi. On the evolution of user interaction in Facebook. In *WOSN '09*, 2009.

[36] C. Wilson, B. Boe, A. Sala, K. P. Puttaswamy, and B. Y. Zhao. User interactions in social networks and their implications. In *EuroSys '09*, page 205, 2009.

[37] S. Wu, A. Das Sarma, A. Fabrikant, S. Lattanzi, and A. Tomkins. Arrival and departure dynamics in social networks. In *WSDM '13*, 2013.

[38] E. Zheleva, H. Sharara, and L. Getoor. Co-evolution of social and affiliation networks. In *KDD '09*, 2009.

Social Affinity Filtering

Recommendation through Fine-grained Analysis of User Interactions and Activities

Suvash Sedhain
ANU & NICTA
Canberra, Australia
ssedhain@nicta.com.au

Scott Sanner
NICTA & ANU
Canberra, Australia
ssanner@nicta.com.au

Lexing Xie
ANU & NICTA
Canberra, Australia
lexing.xie@anu.edu.au

Riley Kidd
ANU
Canberra, Australia
rileyjkidd@gmail.com

Khoi-Nguyen Tran
ANU
Canberra, Australia
kndtran@cs.anu.edu.au

Peter Christen
ANU
Canberra, Australia
peter.christen@anu.edu.au

ABSTRACT

Content recommendation in social networks poses the complex problem of learning user preferences from a rich and complex set of interactions (e.g., likes, comments and tags for posts, photos and videos) and activities (e.g., favourites, group memberships, interests). While many social collaborative filtering approaches learn from aggregate statistics over this social information, we show that only a small subset of user interactions and activities are actually useful for social recommendation, hence learning *which* of these are most informative is of critical importance. To this end, we define a novel social collaborative filtering approach termed social affinity filtering (SAF). On a preference dataset of Facebook users and their interactions with 37,000+ friends collected over a four month period, SAF learns which fine-grained interactions and activities are informative and outperforms state-of-the-art (social) collaborative filtering methods by over 6% in prediction accuracy; SAF also exhibits strong cold-start performance. In addition, we analyse various aspects of fine-grained social features and show (among many insights) that interactions on video content are more informative than other modalities (e.g., photos), the most informative activity groups tend to have small memberships, and features corresponding to "long-tailed" content (e.g., music and books) can be much more predictive than those with fewer choices (e.g., interests and sports). In summary, this work demonstrates the substantial predictive power of fine-grained social features and the novel method of SAF to leverage them for state-of-the-art social recommendation.

Categories and Subject Descriptors

H.3.3 [**Information Search and Retrieval**]: Information Filtering

Keywords

social networks; collaborative filtering; recommender systems

1. INTRODUCTION

Online social networks such as Facebook record a rich set of user preferences (likes of links, posts, photos, videos), user traits, interactions and activities (conversation streams, tagging, group memberships, interests, personal history, and demographic data). This presents myriad new dimensions to the recommendation problem by making available a rich labeled graph structure of social interactions and content from which user preferences can be learned and new recommendations can be made.

Most existing recommendation methods for social networks aggregate this rich social information into a simple measure of user-to-user interaction [9, 19, 22, 23, 32, 20, 21]. But in aggregating all of these interactions and common activities into a *single* strength of interaction, we ask whether important preference information has been discarded? Indeed, the point of departure for this work is the hypothesis that different fine-grained interactions (e.g. commenting on a wall or getting tagged in a video) and activities (e.g., being a member of a university alumni group or a fan of a TV series) *do* represent different preferential *affinities* between users, and moreover that effective *filtering* of this information (i.e., learning which of these myriad fine-grained interactions and activities are informative) will lead to improved accuracy in social recommendation.

To quantitatively validate our hypotheses and evaluate the informativeness of different fine-grained features for social recommendation, we have built a Facebook App to collect detailed user interaction and activity history available through the Facebook Graph API along with user preferences solicited by the App on a daily basis. Given this data, (1) we define a novel recommendation method called *social affinity filtering (SAF)* that learns to predict whether a user (ego) will like an item based on the surrogate item preferences of others (alters) who share fine-grained interactions or activities with the ego, and (2) we analyse the relative informativeness of these fine-grained interaction and activity features across a variety of dimensions.

In the four months that our App was active, we collected data for a set of Facebook app users and their full interactions with 37,000+ friends along with 22 distinct types of interaction and users activity for 3000+ groups, 4000+ favourites, and 10,000+ pages. In subsequent sections that outline our experimental methodology and results in detail, we make the following critical observations:

- **Overall performance:** We found that SAF significantly outperforms numerous state-of-the-art collaborative filtering and social recommender systems by over 6% in accuracy using just *page* (like) features.

- **Privacy vs. performance:** Because the reluctance of a user to install an App increases with the number of permissions requested, the above results suggest that an SAF-based social recommendation App need only request permissions for a user's *page* likes in order to achieve state-of-the-art recommendation accuracy.

- **Big data scalability:** We implement SAF as a simple linear classifier that can be globally optimised with a variety of classification methods (e.g., naive Bayes, logistic regression, SVM) and online training algorithms amenable to real-time, big data settings.

- **Cold-start capable:** Since SAF trains a single model for all users and does not require a user's preferences in order to recommend for them, we show that SAF exhibits strong *cold-start* performance for users *without* expressed item preferences as long as those users have interactions or shared activities with users who have expressed item preferences.

- **Interaction analysis:** Among *interactions*, we found that those on videos are more predictive than those on other content types (photos, post, link), and that outgoing interactions (performed by the ego on the alter's timeline) are more predictive than incoming ones (performed by alters on the ego's timeline), although the level of exposure of an ego to an alter's preferences is often more important than the directionality, modality, or action underlying the interaction with the alters.

- **Activity analysis:** The most predictive activity SAGs tend to have small memberships indicating that these informative activities represent highly specialised interests. We also found features corresponding to "long-tailed" dynamic content (such as music and books) can be more predictive than those with fewer choices that add little new content over time (e.g. interests or sports).

- **Importance of social data beyond friends:** We found that *groups*, *pages*, and *favourites* make for more informative SAGs than those defined by user-to-user interactions. This is likely because the former can be applied to SAGs *over the entire Facebook population* rather than just a user's friends (where the available preference data is considerably more sparse).

- **Social activity and item popularity vs. performance:** We analyse *how many* shared activities are needed for good performance and observe that increased activity membership correlates with increased recommendation accuracy. However, excessive item popularity among activities hurts the discriminative power of SAF to make good recommendations.

- **Fine-grained vs. aggregate social data:** Among activity features, a small subset proved to be much more informative than the rest. This suggests the value of learning *which* fine-grained features are predictive and sheds doubt on the efficacy of existing social recommendation methods that aggregate social information between two users into a single numerical value.

Subsequent sections demonstrate these findings in detail.

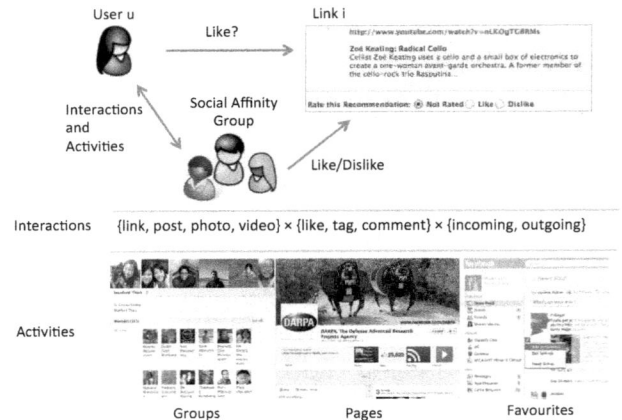

Figure 1: Overview of *social affinity filtering (SAF)*: A *social affinity group (SAG)* of user u (ego) consists of a set of alternate users $\{v\}$ (alters) who have a certain *interaction* or share an *activity* membership with u. SAF learns to classify whether user u will like item i based on the observed preferences of members of each SAG of user u toward item i.

2. SOCIAL AFFINITY FILTERING

As illustrated in Fig 1, the high-level objective of this work is to predict whether or not a user u (ego) will like an item i. Specifically, the Facebook App we have built for our experimentation collects explicit like and dislike feedback for links posted on Facebook (e.g., Youtube video, news or blog item, etc.) leading to the following preference data:

$$likes(u, i) := \begin{cases} true & u \text{ clicked } like \text{ for } i \\ false & u \text{ clicked } dislike \text{ for } i \\ unknown & u\text{'s preference for } i \text{ is unobserved} \end{cases}$$

From the observed data, *social affinity filtering (SAF)* learns to predict $likes(u, i)$ based on the surrogate link preferences $likes(v, i)$ of sets of other Facebook users v who have at least one interaction or activity in common with u. The details of SAF are outlined in the following subsections.

2.1 Interactions and Activities on Facebook

In the context of Facebook, we use the term *interactions* and *activities* to refer to the range of user-user and user-community actions, respectively.

Interactions describes communication between Facebook users and can be broken down into the following dimensions:

- **Modality:** (4 possibilities) User u can interact with another user v via *links*, *posts*, *photos* and *videos* that appear in either user's timeline.

- **Action type:** (3 possibilities) A user u can *comment* or *like* user v's item. He/she can also *tag* user v on an item, often indicating that user v is present when the content is created (for photo/video/post), or to explicitly raise user v's attention for a post — with one exception in Facebook that u cannot tag a link with users.

- **Directionality:** (2 possibilities) We look at *incoming* and *outgoing* interactions, i.e., if user u comments on, tags, or likes user v's item, then this is an *outgoing* interaction for u, and an *incoming* interaction for v. Although high correlation between *incoming* and *outgoing* interactions has been observed [26], whether interaction direction affects user preferences differently is still an open question we wish to answer in this work.

Overall there are 22 possible interaction types, namely the cross-product of modalities, actions and directions, minus the special cases of *link-tag-{incoming, outgoing}* since links cannot be tagged.

Activities are user interactions with Facebook communities like groups, pages, and favourites defined as follows:

- **Groups** on Facebook [1] are analogous to real-world community organisations. They allow users to declare membership and support people to organise activities, to post related content, and to have recurring discussions about them. Examples of groups include *Stanford Thai* (Fig 1 bottom left), or *Harvard Debate Club*.

- **Pages** on Facebook [2] are analogous to the homepages of people, organisations and events on the world-wide-web. They are publicly visible, and users can subscribe to the updates on the page, and also engage in discussions. Example pages include *DARPA* (an organisation, Fig 1 bottom middle), or *Beyonce* (a singer).

- **Favourites** are analogous to bookmarks (on physical books or on the web browser). They are a user-created list containing various items such as Facebook apps, books, music, and many other types of items (even pages) to indicate their interest. Example favourites include *Big Bang Theory* (TV series), or *FC Barcelona* (soccer club). Fig 1 bottom right shows a Facebook screenshot when a user adds a favourite. [3]

Our evaluation includes 3000+ *group*, 4000+ *page* and 10000+ *favourite* features as detailed in Sec 3.1.

2.2 Social Affinity Groups (SAGs)

With *interactions* and *activities* now defined, we proceed to define two types of *social affinity groups (SAGs)* of a user u that will be used as proxies for u's preferences:

- **Interaction Social Affinity Groups (ISAGs)**: Let the set of ISAGs be the cross-product of interaction modality, action,

---

[1]From Facebook Blog: http://www.facebook.com/blog/blog.php?post=324706977130, "Groups are the place for small group communication and for people to share their common interests and express their opinion. Groups allow people to come together around a common cause, issue or activity to organise, express objectives, discuss issues, post photos and share related content."

[2]From Facebook Blog: (http://www.facebook.com/blog/blog.php?post=324706977130 "Facebook Pages enable public figures, businesses, organisations and other entities to create an authentic and public presence on Facebook. Facebook Pages are visible to everyone on the Internet by default. Facebook users can connect with these Pages by becoming a fan and then receive their updates and interact with them."

[3]According to Facebook Blog, (https://www.facebook.com/help/232262810142682 "Facebook facilitates a wide variety of user selected favourites (Activities, Favorite Athletes, Books, Interests, Movies, Music, Sports, Favorite Teams, Television). These favourites allow a user to associate themselves with other people who share their same favourite tendencies."

and direction:

$$Interaction\text{-}Classes := \{link, post, photo, video\}$$
$$\times \{likes, tag, comment\}$$
$$\times \{incoming, outgoing\}$$

Then for $k \in Interaction\text{-}Classes$ we define

$$ISAG(u, k) := \{v | \text{user } v \text{ has had interaction } k \text{ with } u\}$$

For example,

- *ISAG(u, link-like-incoming)* is the set of all users who have liked a link posted *by* user u, and

- *ISAG(u, photo-comment-outgoing)* is the set of all users whose photos user u has commented *on*.

- **Activity Social Affinity Groups (ASAGs)**: We define ASAGs based on group membership, page likes and user favourites (of which there are over 17000 distinct activities in our data set). For any one of these activities $k \in Activity\text{-}Groups$ we define:

$$ASAG(k) := \{v | \text{user } v \text{ has taken part in activity } k\}$$

For example,

- *ASAG(page-Beyonce)* is the set of all users who have liked *Beyonce*'s Facebook *page*, and

- *ASAG(group-Harvard Debate Club)* is the set of all users who have joined the Facebook *group* for the *Harvard Debate Club*.

2.3 Social Affinity Filtering (SAF)

With SAGs now defined, we can use them to build features for a classification-based approach to social recommendation that we term *social affinity filtering (SAF)*. In SAF, our goal is to predict $likes(u, i)$ for user u and item i. As features $X_k^{u,i}$ for this classification task, we can use the observed preferences of members of each SAG k as proxies for $likes(u, i)$. Formally, we define such features as follows:

- **Interaction Social Affinity Features (ISAFs)**: We define feature $X_k^{u,i} \in \{true, false\}$ for user u, item i and interaction $k \in Interaction\text{-}Classes$ as

$$X_k^{u,i} := \begin{cases} true & \exists v \in ISAG(u, k) \wedge likes(v, i) = true \\ false & \text{otherwise} \end{cases}$$

In short, $X_k^{u,i}$ is *true* if any user sharing interaction k with u liked i. Here, v is implicitly limited to u's Facebook friends (with whom u may interact).

- **Activity Social Affinity Features (ASAFs)**: We define feature $X_k^{u,i} \in \{true, false\}$ for user u, item i and activity $k \in Activity\text{-}Groups$ as

$$X_k^{u,i} := \begin{cases} true & u \in ASAG(k) \wedge \\ & \exists v \in ASAG(k) \wedge likes(v, i) = true \\ false & \text{otherwise} \end{cases}$$

In short, $X_k^{u,i}$ is *true* if both u and some other v are a member of activity k and v has liked i. Here, v may range over all Facebook users, i.e., v need not be a friend of u to share the same public activity k.

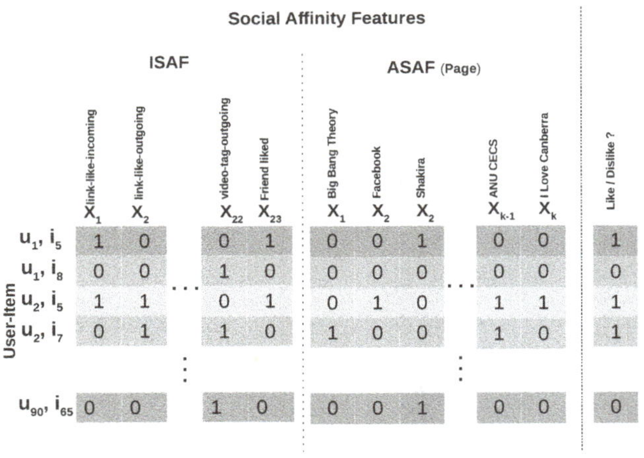

Social Affinity Features

Figure 2: SAF training data example: each row corresponds to a training data sample for a specific user-item pair (u, i) for which the prediction target $likes(u, i)$ is observed (last column). All other columns represent the value of ISAF or ASAF features evaluated relative to the (u, i) label of each row. All columns are binary-valued ($0 = false, 1 = true$).

While other non-binary definitions of ISAFs and ASAFs are certainly possible (e.g., the count or fraction of members in a SAG who like the item), simple binary features provided the best performance in our experimental evaluation.

Combining these ISAFs and ASAFs into feature vector $\mathbf{X}(u, i) = \langle \cdots, X_k^{u,i}, \cdots \rangle$ for $k \in Interaction\text{-}Classes \cup Activity\text{-}Groups$ (or any subset thereof), a SAF classifier is then simply a function

$$f : \mathbf{X}(u, i) \rightarrow likes(u, i),$$

where we restrict $likes(u, i) \in \{true, false\}$.[4] Given a dataset of historical observations $D = \{\mathbf{X}(u, i) \rightarrow likes(u, i)\}$, we can *train* f using any existing classification method; in this work we consider linear classifiers trained by an SVM, logistic regression, or naïve Bayes. For *prediction*, given user u and item i, we build the feature vector $\mathbf{X}(u, i)$ and predict $likes(u, i) = f(\mathbf{X}(u, i))$ using the trained classifier f.[5]

To understand how SAF works, it helps to visualise the training data as shown in Fig 2.

2.4 SAF vs. Other Filtering Methods

While a classification approach to recommendation might evoke comparisons to *content-based filtering* (CBF) [18], we remark that CBF is not a *social* recommendation approach and unlike CBF, SAF does not require explicit user features (e.g., age, gender, location, etc.) or item descriptors (link text, link genre, etc.); in contrast, SAF uses interaction and/or activity data for social network users to define SAGs and learns the affinities between a user (ego) and the different set of alters as defined by these SAGs. Additionally, unlike state-of-the-art *social collaborative filtering* approaches [9, 19, 20, 21, 22, 23, 32], SAF does not aggregate user-user interaction and shared activity data into a single aggregate statistic, instead it uses fine-grained distinctions in this social data to define a large

---

[4]For training purposes, we omit any unobserved cases for which the class label $likes(u, i) = unknown$. At prediction time, the binary classifier must always select a class label of *true* or *false*.

[5]Since almost all classification methods provide a score (or probability) of a classification, we can also generate the top-n item recommendations for a user u by sorting items by their score.

	App Users	Ego network of App Users
Total	119	37,872
Male	85	20,840
Female	34	17,032

Table 1: App user demographics. The *ego network* is the friend network of the App users.

App Users	Tags	Comments	Likes
Post	7,711	22,388	15,999
Link	—	7,483	6,566
Photo	28,341	10,976	8,612
Video	2,525	1,970	843
Ego network of App Users	**Tags**	**Comments**	**Likes**
Post	1,215,382	3,122,019	1,887,497
Link	—	891,986	995,214
Photo	9,620,708	3,431,321	2,469,859
Video	904,604	486,677	332,619

Table 2: Statistics on user *interactions*.

	App Users	Ego Network of App Users
Groups	3,469	373,608
Page Likes	10,771	825,452
Favourites	4,284	892,820

Table 3: Statistics on user *actions*, counted for *Groups, Pages* and *Favourites* over the App users and their ego network.

number of SAGs and learns which of these SAGs are informative for recommendation.

3. EVALUATION

3.1 Data Description

We built a Facebook App to collect explicit user like and dislike preferences back for links posted on Facebook (e.g., Youtube video, news or blog item, etc.) as well as detailed user interaction and activity history available through the Facebook Graph API. The data collection was performed with full permission from the user and in accordance with an approved Ethics Protocol #2011/142 from the Australian National University.

Our App requested to collect information on profiles (including activity memberships) and timelines (interactions) for the App users *and* their friends as required by Sec 2.2 and Sec 2.3. With such expressive permissions, many potential users were hesitant to install the App — after an intensive one month user drive at our University, we were able to attract 119 App users allowing us to collect activity and interaction data for a combined 37,872 users.[6]

We summarise basic statistics of the data in Tables 1–4. Table 1 presents user and friend demographics. Table 2 summarises the number of records for each item modality (row) and action (col-

---

[6]The issue of low App user uptake with such expressive App permissions underscores the importance of identifying the *minimal* set of permissions to obtain good recommendation performance — a question we address in our subsequent analysis.

	Friend recommendation	Non-Friend recommendation
Like	1392	1127
Dislike	895	2111

Table 4: Dataset breakdown of prediction target $like(u, i)$ by the source of the link (Friend/Non-friend) and rating (Like=$true$, Dislike=$false$).

umn) combination. Table 3 shows the group membership, page like and favourite counts for users.

Our App recommends three links to App users each day, which the users may optionally like or dislike. Recommended links are harvested from *both* friends' and non-friends' timelines. We display only three links per day in order to avoid rank-bias with preferences; each link could be independently rated. Table 4 shows App user link preference statistics.

All subsequent experimentats use offline batch data stored and analysed *after* a four month data collection period.

3.2 SAF Comparison

In this section, we compare novel SAF-based methods with a variety of (social) collaborative filtering baselines:

1. **Most Likely Class Constant Predictor (Const)**

2. **Nearest Neighbor (NN)** [6]

3. **Matrix Factorization (MF)** [27]

4. **Social Matchbox (SMB)** [23]

Here, Const serves as a lower bound on performance, NN and MF are two well-known state-of-the-art *non-social* collaborative filtering algorithms, and SMB is a state-of-the-art *social* collaborative filtering algorithm employing matrix factorization with social regularisation.

Among the novel SAF methods, we analyse four different sets of social affinity features:

1. **Interaction Social Affinity Features (ISAF)**

2. **Activity-based Social Affinity Features (ASAF)** for

   (a) **Group Memberships**

   (b) **Page Likes**

   (c) **Favourites**

Furthermore, for these four classes of features, we train one of three classifier types, leading to the following classes of SAF recommenders evaluated in our experiments:

1. **Naïve Bayes (NB-ISAF, NB-ASAF)**

2. **Support Vector Machines (SVM-ISAF, SVM-ASAF)**

3. **Logistic Regression (LR-ISAF, LR-ASAF)**

NB uses a standard Naïve Bayes implementation, SVM and LR are both implemented using *LIBLINEAR* [10].

In all experiments, we report average classification accuracy (fraction of correct classifications in held-out test data) using 10-fold cross validation and provide standard error bars corresponding to 95% confidence intervals.

Fig 3 compares the above baselines and SAF algorithms. In all of these experiments, SAF variants performed statistically significantly better than the best baseline (SMB), except for NB-ASAF

which we conjecture is due to violation of feature independence assumptions that become more pronounced as the number of features increases (n.b., NB-ISAF uses 22 features while NB-ASAF uses 1000's of features).

In terms of the best recommenders, we observe that LR-ASAF and SVM-ASAF perform comparably to each other and learn quite well despite the large size of this ASAF feature set. Overall, *LR-ASAF performs 6% better than the best baseline for page likes.* We combined all four features sets in a fifth experiment (not shown) and remark that none of NB, LR, or SVM with all features outperformed LR-ASAF with just page likes. We also note that all ISAF variants statistically significantly outperform all (social) collaborative filtering baselines. Hence, w.r.t. this Facebook dataset, we conclude that (a) *SAF with any available feature set* is sufficient to outperform existing (social) collaborative filtering baselines and that (b) if one wanted to minimise the permissions an App requests then it seems *SAF with page likes* alone is sufficient to outperform all other feature sets (alone or combined).

It is important to consider why ASAFs outperform ISAFs. We conjecture the reasons for this are quite simple: ISAFs can only see the *friends* of user u whereas ASAFs are able to look at all users, independent of u's friends. Hence, given the relative sparsity of friend-only data in Facebook compared to the greater Facebook population (at least the subset of the population the App collected) and also the relative number of ISAFs compared to ASAFs, ASAFs appear to draw on a much larger set of SAGs that in turn draw on a much larger user population. Among ASAFs, page likes are the most predictive followed by group membership and favourites. This reinforces our conjecture that data sparsity can hurt SAF since we note from Table 3 that page likes are more prevalent than groups and favourites.

Comparing SAF to the state-of-the-art in social collaborative filtering as represented by Social Matchbox (SMB) [23], we observe that SAF consistently outperforms it. We note that the key difference of SAF vs. SMB is that SAF exploits the predictiveness of fine-grained interactions and activities, whereas most social collaborative filtering approaches [9, 19, 20, 21, 22, 23, 32] instead collapse the diverse set of interactions into a single aggregate statistic for each pair of users. The performance of SAF-based recommenders suggests that the aggregation of all social information into aggregate statistics (without learning which interactions or activities are most informative) may not distinguish informative parts of the social signal from the noise.

On the computational side, we remark that SAF is implemented as a simple linear classifier that can be used in conjunction with a variety of classification methods (e.g., naïve Bayes, logistic regression, SVM) and online training algorithms amenable to real-time, big data settings. Furthermore, the linear classification methods used in SAF admit global convex optimisation w.r.t. a variety of training objectives (e.g., log loss in logistic regression, or hinge loss in SVMs) unlike (social) collaborative filtering approaches based on matrix factorization that use non-convex objectives and lack training optimality guarantees.

3.3 Cold-start Evaluation

Many collaborative filtering algorithms (e.g., NN and MF) suffer from the user *cold-start* problem, i.e., when no preference data is available for a user, these algorithms cannot perform better than the constant (most likely class) predictor since they have no way of generalising to a new unseen user. Since SAF trains a single model for all users and does *not* require a user's preferences in order to recommend for them, SAF can be used in a *cold-start* setting to recommend for users *without* expressed item preferences as long

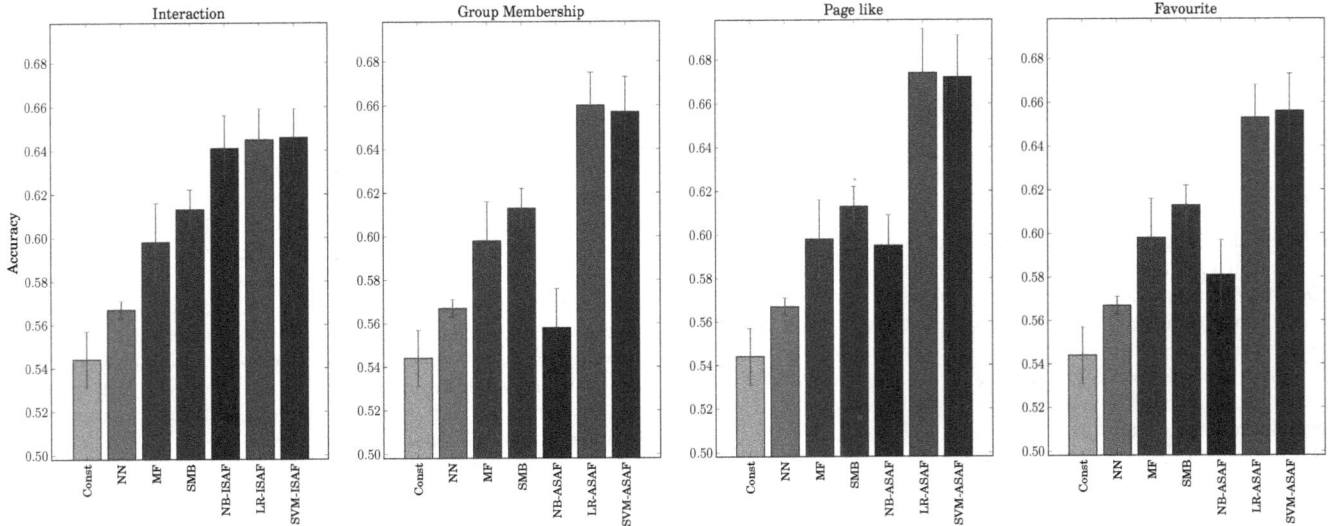

Figure 3: Comparision of a simple baseline (Const), two collaborative filtering baselines (NN and MF), a social collaborative filtering baseline (SMB) and novel SAF recommenders using different feature sets (one ISAF and three ASAF sets) and classifiers (NB,LR,SVM). The best SAF-based model (LR-ASAF) — for Page likes — significantly outperforms all baselines by at least 6%. Combining all four feature sets (not shown) does not lead to improvement over Page likes features alone.

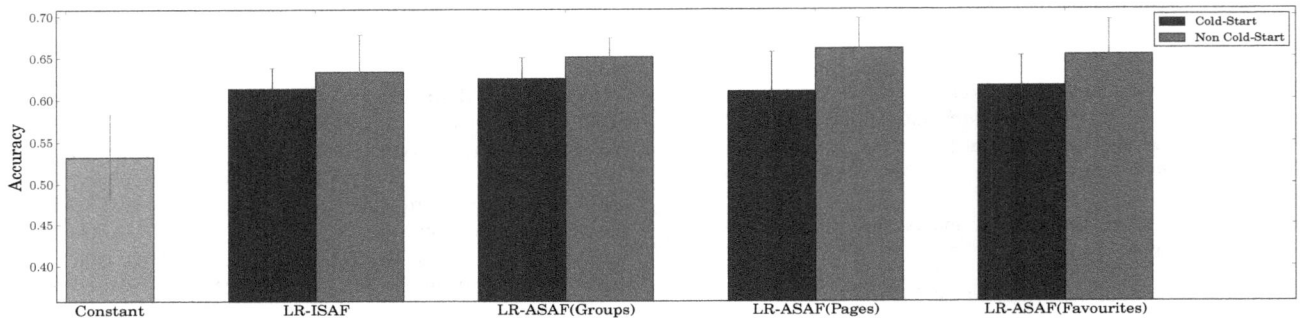

Figure 4: Cold-start evaluation of SAF: accuracy evaluated on cold-start users outperforms the most likely class (Constant) predictor baseline and is somewhat comparable to the non cold-start case when all test user data is *not* withheld from training.

as those users have interactions or shared activities with users who have expressed item preferences.

To quantitatively evaluate the cold-start performance of SAF, we run 10-fold cross validation with specially constructed folds. For *cold-start* evaluation, in each fold, we hold out a random 10% subset of the users for testing and train on the remaining 90% of users. In the test set, we further hold out 30% of the test user data. In the *non cold-start* evaluation, we test on the same data as in the *cold-start* evaluation, but we add in the 30% of held-out test user data to the *cold-start* training set thus allowing the *non cold-start* setting to train on some of the test user data. In Fig 4, we clearly see that the accuracy[7] of the SAF predictor for cold-start is significantly better than the baseline Constant predictor. Furthermore, the accuracy of the cold-start predictor is actually comparable to the non

cold-start predictor, indicating that SAF exhibits strong cold-start performance.

3.4 Interaction Analysis

In this section we analyse the informativeness of Interaction Social Affinity Features (ISAFs), namely user interactions according to their modality, type, and direction, as described in Sec 2.

A general method for measuring the amount of information that a feature $X_k^{u,i}$ provides w.r.t. predicting a user preference $likes(u,i)$ (in this case, just *true* or *false*) is to calculate its conditional entropy:

$$H(likes(u,i)|X_k^{u,i} = true)$$
$$= - \sum_{y \in (true, false)} p(likes(u,i) = y|X_k^{u,i} = true)$$
$$\cdot \ln(p(likes(u,i) = y|X_k^{u,i} = true))$$

Lower conditional entropies generally indicate more informative features. We use conditional entropy $H(likes(u,i)|X_k^{u,i} = true)$

---

[7]The slight decrease in accuracy for non cold-start case compared to Fig 3 is due to the decreased amount of test user data present in the training set for this set of experiments.

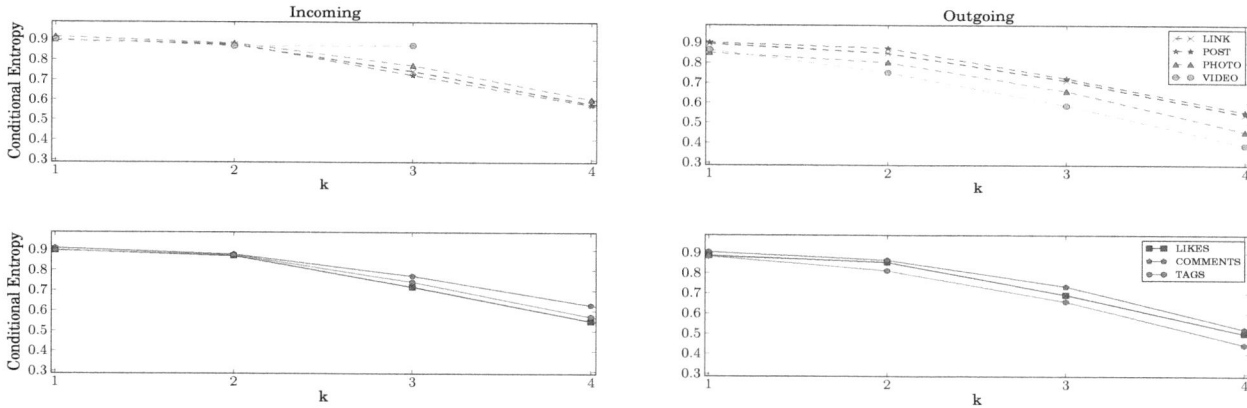

Figure 5: Conditional Entropy of modalities/activities for incoming/outgoing interactions vs. item liked by at least k friends. Increasing k generally has a stronger influence on informativeness than other features of interaction SAGs.

Table 5: Conditional entropy of various interactions (lower conditional entropies are more informative). We observe that interactions on videos are more informative than other modalities (link, post, photo), tagging is marginally more informative than commenting and liking, and outgoing interactions are slightly more informative than incoming ones. Breaking down the analysis by modality-direction and action-direction reveals finer-grained distinctions.

Modality (X)	$H(Y\|X = true)$
video	0.850
link	0.915
post	0.918
photo	0.926

Action Type (X)	$H(Y\|X = true)$
tags	0.920
comments	0.921
likes	0.924

Direction (X)	$H(Y\|X = true)$
outgoing	0.928
incoming	0.935

Modality-Direction (X)	$H(Y\|X = true)$
tags-outgoing	0.885
likes-outgoing	0.885
tags-incoming	0.900
likes-incoming	0.902
comments-outgoing	0.908
comments-incoming	0.912

Action-Direction (X)	$H(Y\|X = true)$
photo-outgoing	0.857
video-outgoing	0.863
link-outgoing	0.895
link-incoming	0.896
post-incoming	0.902
post-outgoing	0.906
video-incoming	0.915
photo-incoming	0.921

rather than mutual information $I(likes(u,i); X_k^{u,i})$, as we found that mutual information is highly correlated with (and dominated by) the frequency of the feature $X_k^{u,i} = true$ in the dataset.

First we analyse various interactions to better understand what interaction-defined SAGs have a high affinity with a user's preferences. To this end, we make a few observations from the conditional entropy analysis of Table 5:

- Interaction on *videos* indicates a stronger preferential affinity between users than other modalities (links, posts and photos). We conjecture this is because videos are time-consuming to view and hence users mainly watch the videos of those users whose preferences they share.

- Tagging has a slightly better conditional entropy than commenting and liking, potentially since tagging often results from direct social interaction (appearing in a photo or video together) indicating common interests.

- A user is more likely to share preferences with someone who she initiates the interaction with (outgoing) vs. with someone who initiates the interaction with her (incoming). E.g., we note that while outgoing photo and video interactions are *most* informative in the last table of Table 5, it appears that incoming photo and video interactions are *least* informative.

In Fig 5 we plot the conditional entropy of modality and action for incoming/outgoing interactions constrained to links liked by at least k friends in the SAG (measuring the implicit or explicit *exposure* of a user to their friends' preferences via a SAG). We note that preference affinity with any SAG increases as more people in the SAG like the item. E.g., while incoming interactions were not as predictive as outgoing interactions for the same k, we note that higher k on incoming *can be more predictive* than lower k for outgoing. Similar principles hold for modality and action vs. k — a larger k is generally more predictive than the individual variation among modality and action at a fixed k, an exception being the modality-outgoing analysis.

3.5 Activity Analysis

Now we analyse the informativeness of Activity Social Affinity Features (ASAFs) by looking at the correlation between the size and type of groups, pages and favourites.

Fig 6 provides scatter plots of conditional entropies and logistic regression weights vs. activity group size.[8] Both plots show that small activity groups *can* be highly predictive (low conditional entropy or weights that deviate extremely from zero) whereas large groups are *rarely* predictive.

In Fig 7 we plot the average conditional entropy of the top 10% of features cumulative up to the size of the activity group given on the x-axis. This graph distinctly shows that the small sizes of groups, pages and favourites have low average conditional entropy that transitions sharply to a higher average at about 50 for groups and 10^5 for pages/favourites.

We also analyse predictiveness of favourites by categories obtained from the Facebook API in Fig 8. While half of category instances in movie, books, or movies with "long-tail" (less popular, specialised) content may not be highly predictive (judging by median informativess), these categories do contain some highly predictive instances (as evidenced by the top two quartiles). On the contrary, highly generic categories (e.g. interests) and those with fewer choices (e.g. sports or fav-teams) tend to be less predictive overall. These observations of Fig 8 are also reiterated by the examples provided in Table 6 where uninformative favourites tend to have a broad appeal whereas informative favourites generally appear much more specialised. This reinforces the insight of SAF that it is important to learn which SAGs are predictive.

One might ask how the number of activities a user joins affects recommendation performance. In Fig 9, we see that on average, more user activities generally leads to higher accuracy. As an alternative analysis, Fig 2 shows performance vs. the number of *active features*, i.e., for any (user,item) recommendation in a row of Fig 2, the active features are those that are true (1). Here we see that excessive item popularity among activities hurts the discriminative power of SAF to make good recommendations.

4. RELATED WORK

This work relates to many others in inferring user preferences on social and information networks. We structure the discussion into three parts: the first is concerned with the nature and observations on user traits, interactions and diffusion mechanisms; the second is concerned with correlating these user traits and interactions to user preferences and interests; the third is concerned with methods that use these observations for predicting user interest or recommending content on social networks.

The first group of related work studies the nature of user profile, interactions, and diffusion. Profile information and demographics is correlated with user behaviour patterns. Chang *et al* [8] showed that the tendency to initiate a Facebook friendship differs quite widely across ethnic groups, while Backstorm *et al* [3] have additionally showed that female and male users have opposite tendencies for dispersing attention for within-gender and across-gender communication. Two particular measurement studies on Facebook attention [3, 31] have inspired our work. Although the average number of friends for a Facebook user is close to the human psychological limit, known as the Dunbar number [14], the findings concur that a user's attention (i.e., interactions) are divided among a much smaller subset of Facebook friends. [3] studied two types of attention: communication interaction and viewing attention (e.g. looking at profiles or photos). Users' communication attention is focused on small numbers of friends, but viewing attention is dispersed across all friends. This finding supports our approach of looking at many types of user interactions across all of a user's contact network, as a user's interest is driven by where he/she focuses attention.

The mechanisms of diffusion invite interesting mathematical and empirical investigations. The Galton-Watson epidemics model suits the basic setup of social message diffusion, and can explain real-world information cascade such as email chain-letters when adjusted with selection bias [13]. For social diffusions in a one-to-many setting, however, the epidemics model has been less accurate. Ver Steeg *et al* [29] found that online message cascades (on Digg social reader) are often smaller than prescribed by the epidemics model, seemingly due to the diminishing returns of repeated exposure. Romero *et al* [25], in an independent study, confirmed the effect of diminishing returns with Twitter hashtag cascades, and further found that cascade dynamics differ across broad topic categories such as politics, culture, or sports. Our observations on user preference on items liked by a number of Facebook friends suggest a large cumulative number of friend preferences is more predictive, although further investigation is needed to pinpoint the effect of diminishing returns on repeated exposures.

The nature of social diffusion seem to be not only democratic [2, 4], but also broadening for users [5]. While influential users are important for cascade generation [4], large active groups of users are needed to contribute for the cascade to sustain [2]. Moreover, word-of-mouth diffusion can only be harnessed reliably by targeting large numbers of potential influencers, confirmed by observations on Twitter [4] and online ads [30]. In a study facilitated by A/B testing on Facebook links, [5] found that while people are more likely to share the information they were exposed to by their strong ties rather than their weak ties, the bulk of information we consume and share comes from people with different perspectives (weak ties). SAF aims to leverage many of these insights for social recommendation by viewing affinity groups as diffusion channels. Yet, information diffusion and recommendation are distinct problems — while we observed best *recommendation* performance using ASAGs ranging across all Facebook users, the vast majority of *information diffusion* happens within one step from the source node [12].

The second group of related work tries to correlate from user interactions to preferences and tie strength. Saez-Trumper et al [26] found that incoming and outgoing activities are highly correlated on broadcast platforms such as Facebook and Twitter, and such correlation does not hold in one-to-one mode of communication such as email. Multiple studies have found that online interactions tend to correlate more with interests than with user profile. Singla *et al* [28] found that users who frequently interact (via MSN chat) tend to share (web search) interests. Anderson *et al* [1] concluded that the level of user activities correlate with the positive ratings that they give each other, i.e., it is less about what they say (content of posts) but more about who they interacted with. Such findings echo those by Brandtzag [7] that real-world interactions (e.g., appearing in the same photo evidenced by tagging) further strengthens friendship on Facebook, while virtual interactions reveal interests. Furthermore, ratings of real-world friendship strength and trust [11] seems to be better predicted from the intimacy, intensity, and duration of interactions, than from social distance and network structure. Our work is not only inspired by these observations, we also quantify the strength of correlations of user interest with a large variety of user affinities – namely, activities, and group preferences in different categories.

The third group of related work is concerned with using social network and behavior information for recommendation. Matrix factorization is one of the prevailing approaches for recommender sys-

---

[8]Here the size of a *group*, *page* and *favourite* is the number of total users in the activity group. For *pages* and *favourites* this is the total number of Facebook users, whether or not they are in the App users' ego network, while for *groups* only the number of users in the App users' ego network is visible to our App.

(a)

(b)

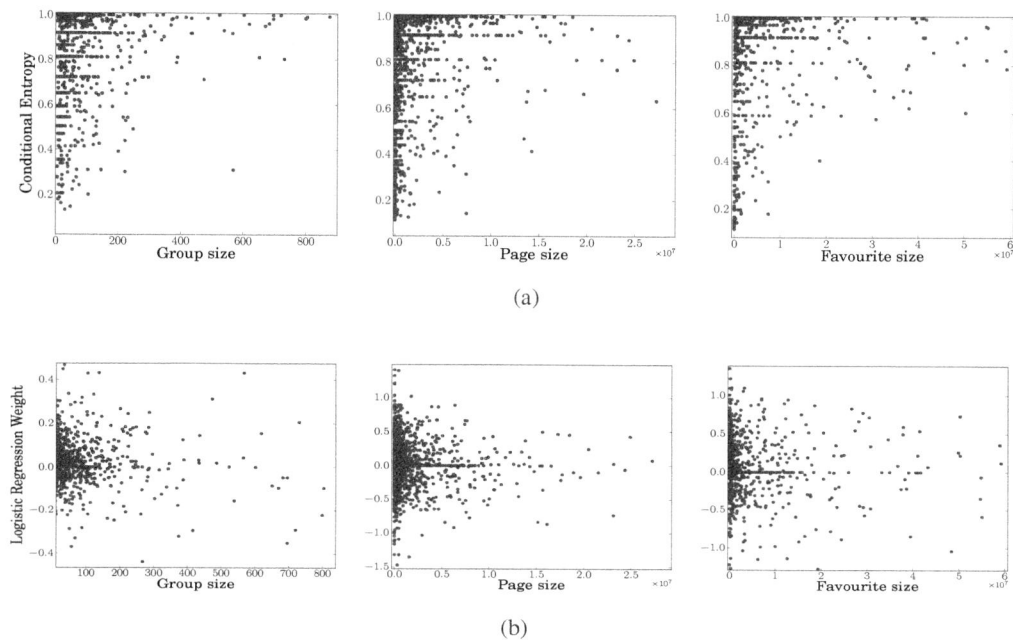

Figure 6: Conditional entropy vs. size (a); logistic regression feature weights vs size (b). In (a) we observe that the large membership ASAGs are rarely informative while the most informative SAGs tend to have low memberships. Similarly in (b) we see that the most predictive features with the largest weights (positive or negative) are concentrated toward small ASAGs.

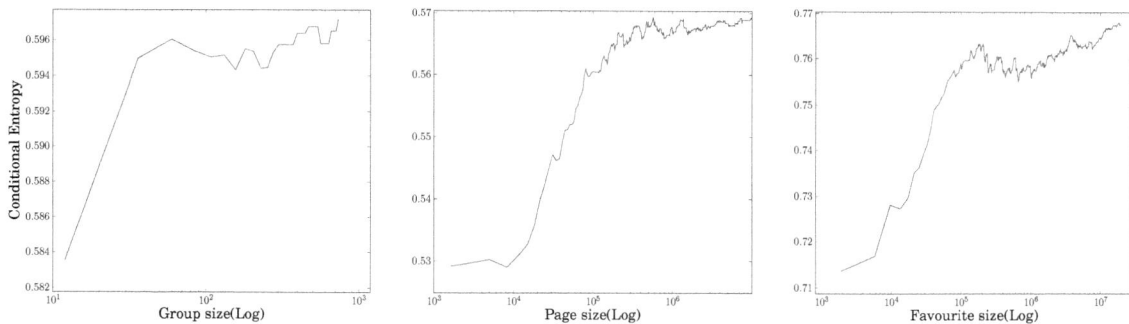

Figure 7: Average conditional entropy of top 10% groups, pages and favourite features *cumulative* over the size. Here we see that as we add in larger membership ASAGs, the average informativeness decreases substantially (entropy increases).

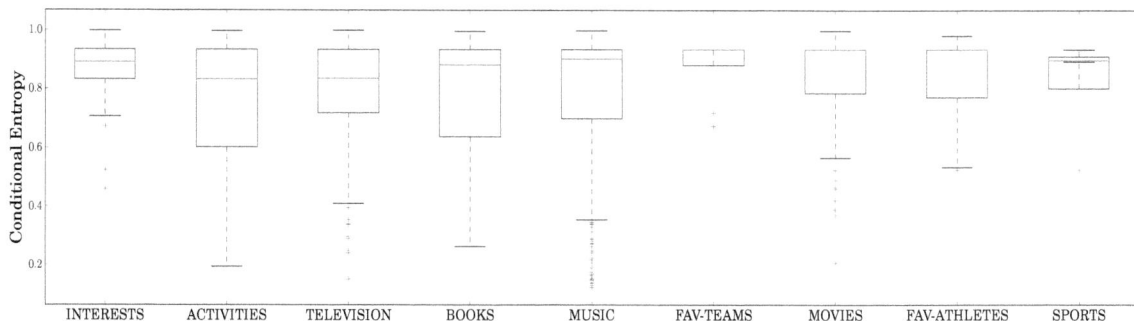

Figure 8: Conditional entropy for top 1000 favourites breakdown by categories. While at least half of ASAG categories with many options like music are not informative (judging by median values), some of the most informative ASAGs are music. This reiterates the point that it is crucial to *learn* which ASAGs are informative rather than aggregating average information.

Median Informative Favourites by Category				
Books	**Movies**	**Music**	**Television**	**Interests**
Harry Potter series	Forrest Gump	John Lennon	Futurama	Travel
A Song of Ice and Fire	Pretty Woman	U2	Star Trek	Music
Discworld	Napoleon Dynamite	AC/DC	The Trap Door	Literature
Hitchhiker's Guide To The Galaxy	Harry Potter	The Smashing Pumpkins	Drawn Together	Painting
The Hobbit	Toy Story 3	Gotye	Sherlock(Official)	Running
The Magician's Guild	The Godfather	The Rolling Stones	Hitchhiker's Guide to the Galaxy	Sports
Ranger's Apprentice	Mulan	All Axess	Buffy The Vampire Slayer	Films
Cosmos	How to Train Your Dragon	Steve Aoki	South Park	Genetics

Most Informative Favourites by Category				
Books	**Movies**	**Music**	**Television**	**Interests**
Calvin and Hobbes	Billy Madison	Avascular Necrosis	Metalocalypse	Computers
Tomorrow when the War Began	Team America: World Police	Tortured	Beast Wars	Texas HoldEm
I really like ceilings	Pan's Labyrinth	Elysian	Hey Arnold!	Programming
Angels and demons	Pirates of the Caribbean	Anno Domini	Sherlock	Economics
Magician	Aladdin	Darker Half	Hey Hey It's Saturday	Martial arts
Digital Fortress	Starship Troopers	Hellbringer	Neil Buchanan and Art Attack!	Graphic design
The Bible	Happy Gilmore	Johnny Roadkill	Breaking Bad	Cooking
Interview with the Vampire	Timon and Pumbaa	Aeon of Horus	Red vs. Blue	Klingon language

Table 6: (top) Examples of 8 items per Favourite category near the *median* conditional entropy (*median informativeness*). (bottom) Examples of top 8 items with the lowest conditional entropy (*most informative*). A general trend is that more informative favourite category ASAGs tend to be more specialised in appeal, e.g. "Avascular Necrosis" is an informative music group favourite — its members tend to share common preferences — while "John Lennon" and "U2" have a broader audience with more diverse preferences. Interestingly, "Sherlock" appears in both most and median informative table but the median informative is an official page with wide range of fans, whereas the most informative is a duplicate fan page with few fans.

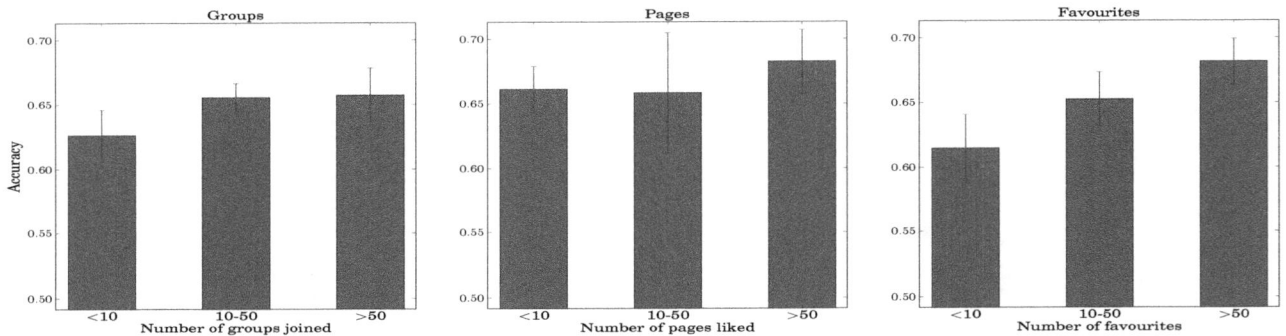

Figure 9: Accuracy of the SAF increases as users become more active in social network by joining more groups/pages/favourites. It does not appear too many activities hurts — SAF learns to discriminate when activities are predctive.

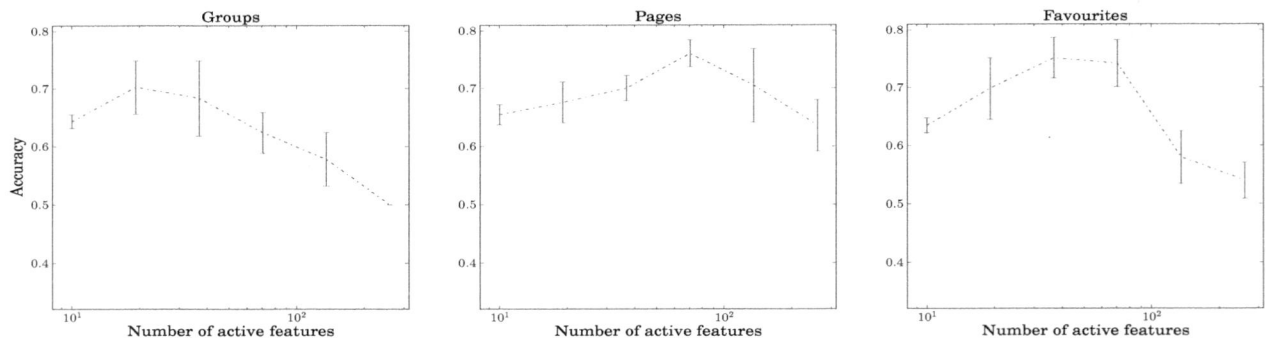

Figure 10: Accuracy increases as the number of active features increases, but then, after reaching a certain limit, it starts to decrease, i.e., excessive item popularity among activities hurts the discriminative power of SAF to make good recommendations.

tems [17, 21]. Recent advances include extending matrix factorization to user social relation in regularization [22, 19], to take into account multiple relations [24, 16], and to model social context [15]. In particular, there are different designs for using social information to regularize objective functions [32], a trust ensemble [20], a low-rank factorization of the social interactions matrix [21], or social-spectral regularization that takes into account user and item features [23]. These systems have shown very promising performance across a range of problems, but their all collapse social affinity (fine-grained interactions and group affinity) into one or a very low-dimensional representation. The point of departure of this work is to explore the predictive power of fine-grained social information.

5. FUTURE WORK

For a summary of the key contributions and insights from this work, we refer the reader back to the points outlined at the end of Sec 1. Future research directions can examine the nature of social groups via additional metrics — e.g., properties of the social network within SAGs or the activity level of SAGs. Other work might explore non-binary representations of ASAFs and ISAFs or SAF-influenced extensions of (social) collaborative filtering approaches like nearest neighbor or matrix factorization to better exploit informative fine-grained social interaction and activity features.

6. ACKNOWLEDGEMENTS

NICTA is funded by the Australian Government as represented by the Department of Broadband, Communications and the Digital Economy and the Australian Research Council through the ICT Centre of Excellence program. This work was partially funded by a Google Research Award and by the US Air Force Research Laboratory, under agreement number FA2386-12-1-4041. The U.S. Government is authorized to reproduce and distribute reprints for Governmental purposes notwithstanding any copyright notation thereon. The views and conclusions contained herein are those of the authors and should not be interpreted as necessarily representing the official policies or endorsements, either expressed or implied, of the Air Force Research Laboratory or the U.S. Government.

7. REFERENCES

[1] A. Anderson, D. Huttenlocher, J. Kleinberg, and J. Leskovec. Effects of User Similarity in Social Media. In *WSDM*, 2012.

[2] S. Asur, B. A. Huberman, G. Szabo, and C. Wang. Trends in social media: Persistence and decay. In *ICWSM*, 2011.

[3] L. Backstrom, E. Bakshy, J. Kleinberg, T. Lento, and I. Rosenn. Center of attention: How facebook users allocate attention across friends. In *ICWSM*, 2011.

[4] E. Bakshy, J. M. Hofman, W. A. Mason, and D. J. Watts. Everyone's an influencer: quantifying influence on twitter. In *WSDM*, 2011.

[5] E. Bakshy, I. Rosenn, C. Marlow, and L. Adamic. The role of social networks in information diffusion. *Facebook Report*, *http://www.scribd.com/facebook*, 2012.

[6] R. M. Bell and Y. Koren. Scalable collaborative filtering with jointly derived neighborhood interpolation weights. In *ICDM*, 2007.

[7] P. B. Brandtzaeg and O. Nov. Facebook use and social capital — a longitudinal study. In *ICWSM*, 2011.

[8] J. Chang, I. Rosenn, L. Backstrom, and C. Marlow. epluribus: Ethnicity on social networks. In *ICWSM*, 2010.

[9] P. Cui, F. Wang, S. Liu, M. Ou, and S. Yang. Who should share what? item-level social influence prediction for users and posts ranking. In *SIGIR*, 2011.

[10] R.-E. Fan, K.-W. Chang, C.-J. Hsieh, X.-R. Wang, and C.-J. Lin. Liblinear: A library for large linear classification. *JMLR*, pages 1871–1874, 2008.

[11] E. Gilbert and K. Karahalios. Predicting tie strength with social media. In *Proc. CHI*. ACM, 2009.

[12] S. Goel, D. J. Watts, and D. G. Goldstein. The structure of online diffusion networks. In *EC*, 2012.

[13] B. Golub and M. O. Jackson. Using selection bias to explain the observed structure of internet diffusions. *Proc. Nat. Academy Sci.*, 107(24), 2010.

[14] R. Hill and R. Dunbar. Social network size in humans. *Human Nature*, 14(1):53–72, 2003.

[15] M. Jiang, P. Cui, R. Liu, Q. Yang, F. Wang, W. Zhu, and S. Yang. Social contextual recommendation. In *CIKM*, 2012.

[16] M. Jiang, P. Cui, F. Wang, Q. Yang, W. Zhu, and S. Yang. Social recommendation across multiple relational domains. In *CIKM*, 2012.

[17] Y. Koren, R. Bell, and C. Volinsky. Matrix factorization techniques for recommender systems. *Computer*, 42, 2009.

[18] K. Lang. NewsWeeder: Learning to filter netnews. In *ICML*, 1995.

[19] W.-J. Li and D.-Y. Yeung. Relation regularized matrix factorization. In *IJCAI*, 2009.

[20] Ma, King, and Lyu. Learning to recommend with social trust ensemble. In *SIGIR*, 2009.

[21] H. Ma, H. Yang, M. R. Lyu, and I. King. Sorec: Social recommendation using probabilistic matrix factorization. In *CIKM*, 2008.

[22] H. Ma, D. Zhou, C. Liu, M. R. Lyu, and I. King. Recommender systems with social regularization. In *WSDM*, 2011.

[23] J. Noel, S. Sanner, K.-N. Tran, P. Christen, L. Xie, E. V. Bonilla, E. Abbasnejad, and N. Della Penna. New objective functions for social collaborative filtering. In *WWW*, 2012.

[24] S. Rendle, L. B. Marinho, A. Nanopoulos, and L. Schmidt-Thieme. Learning optimal ranking with tensor factorization for tag recommendation. In *KDD*, 2009.

[25] D. M. Romero, B. Meeder, and J. Kleinberg. Differences in the mechanics of information diffusion across topics: idioms, political hashtags, and complex contagion on twitter. In *WWW*, 2011.

[26] D. Saez-Trumper, D. Nettleton, and R. Baeza-Yates. High correlation between incoming and outgoing activity: A distinctive property of online social networks? In *ICWSM*, 2011.

[27] R. Salakhutdinov and A. Mnih. Probabilistic matrix factorization. In *NIPS*, 2008.

[28] P. Singla and M. Richardson. Yes, there is a correlation: - from social networks to personal behavior on the web. In *WWW*, 2008.

[29] G. Ver Steeg, R. Ghosh, and K. Lerman. What stops social epidemics? In *ICWSM*, 2011.

[30] D. J. Watts and P. S. Dodds. Influentials, networks, and public opinion formation. *Journal of Consumer Research*, 2007.

[31] C. Wilson, B. Boe, A. Sala, K. Puttaswamy, and B. Zhao. User interactions in social networks and their implications. In *EuroSys*, 2009.

[32] S.-H. Yang, B. Long, A. Smola, N. Sadagopan, Z. Zheng, and H. Zha. Like like alike: Joint friendship and interest propagation in social networks. In *WWW*, 2011.

On the Precision of Social and Information Networks

Reza Bosagh Zadeh
Stanford University
rezab@stanford.edu

Ashish Goel
Stanford University
ashishg@stanford.edu

Kamesh Munagala
Duke University
kamesh@cs.duke.edu

Aneesh Sharma
Twitter, Inc
aneesh@twitter.com

ABSTRACT

The diffusion of information on online social and information networks has been a popular topic of study in recent years, but attention has typically focused on speed of dissemination and recall (i.e. the fraction of users getting a piece of information). In this paper, we study the complementary notion of the *precision* of information diffusion. Our model of information dissemination is "broadcast-based", *i.e.*, one where every message (original or forwarded) from a user goes to a fixed set of recipients, often called the user's "friends" or "followers", as in Facebook and Twitter. The precision of the diffusion process is then defined as the fraction of received messages that a user finds interesting.

On first glance, it seems that broadcast-based information diffusion is a "blunt" targeting mechanism, and must necessarily suffer from low precision. Somewhat surprisingly, we present preliminary experimental and analytical evidence to the contrary: it is possible to simultaneously have high precision (i.e. is bounded below by a constant), high recall, and low diameter!

We start by presenting a set of conditions on the structure of user interests, and analytically show the necessity of each of these conditions for obtaining high precision. We also present preliminary experimental evidence from Twitter verifying that these conditions are satisfied. We then prove that the Kronecker-graph based generative model of Leskovec *et al.* satisfies these conditions given an appropriate and natural definition of user interests. Further, we show that this model also has high precision, high recall, and low diameter. We finally present preliminary experimental evidence showing Twitter has high precision, validating our conclusion. This is perhaps a first step towards a formal understanding of the immense popularity of online social networks as an information dissemination mechanism.

Categories and Subject Descriptors

H.1 [**Information Systems**]: Models and Principles

Keywords

Social networks; Precision; Recall; Modeling

1. INTRODUCTION

Modern social and information networks such as Facebook, LinkedIn and Twitter are used by hundreds of millions of users every day. There are many hypotheses as to the source of their popularity, and one popular hypothesis relates to the effectiveness of these networks as information dissemination mechanisms [10, 28]. In particular, a fundamental question about effectiveness is one of personalization: given the large number of users, one would expect them to be interested in a diverse set of content, and the network must be an effective information conduit, simultaneously, for all of them. Given that information dissemination mechanism in these networks occurs via *broadcast* (as opposed to pairwise interactions) over the network topology, it is apriori unclear whether effective information dissemination is even feasible. For instance, wouldn't users receive a large amount of un-interesting content via this mechanism? And complementarily, wouldn't users miss a large amount of content they would have potentially been interested in?

The starting point of our study is this commonly stated belief, especially in the media, that online social and information networks mostly generate information that is irrelevant for most users [24]. This claim is often based on inspecting a random tweet. However, such a claim ignores the interest-based construction of social networks: as suggested earlier, users on any social or information network have diverse interests, and tend to *follow* (i.e., receive content from) other users who share some of their interests and post content that is interesting to them. Thus, although a random tweet on Twitter is uninteresting to a random user, it could be that for any given user, the tweets in their timeline are very relevant to them.

The study of usefulness (or relevance) of content has been a primary theme in the information retrieval literature [22], but to the best of our knowledge it has not been directly studied for information diffusion on social and information networks. We adapt the widely accepted definition of relevance for networks by defining the *precision* of information in a social network: the fraction of content received by a user that is relevant to them, where relevance is captured by a match between the content and some "interest" of the user. Then we capture virality by defining two quantities: The *recall*, which is the fraction of content relevant to a user that (s)he does receive, and the *dissemination time* for content, *i.e.*, the number of hops in the graph taken for this content to spread to users who would be interested in this information.

Assuming that users have interests, and the social network is constructed according to users' interests, the following natural questions arise about the precision and recall: *What conditions (if any) on the structure of user interests are necessary for a social and information network to ensure users have high precision and recall, and dissemination time is small? Can we empirically validate these conditions as well as the conclusion on existing networks?*

We motivate this question with a preliminary empirical user study that attempts to directly measure relevance without resorting to a definition of user interests: we ask 10 active Twitter users to rate a set of 30 tweets as Relevant/Not Relevant. The users are students at Stanford University who log in at least once a week on average, follow at least 30 people, and receive at least 20 new tweets a week in their timeline. The set of 30 tweets is put together by choosing 15 tweets from the user's timeline in the past 7 days, and 15 unique randomly selected tweets out of the set of all tweet impressions (or tweet renderings) over the same 7 days[1]. The set of 30 tweets is then rendered in a random order as per usual tweet rendering guidelines [11]. The *precision* of each set of 15 tweets is then the fraction of these tweets that the user marks as being relevant. The results of the experiment for each of the 10 users is shown in Figure 1. The average precision of users for tweets drawn from their timeline is 70%. On the other hand, the precision drops to around 7% for the set of random tweets shown to the users! Even though this is too small a user study to draw a definitive conclusion about the actual value of precision on Twitter, the results lend some credence to the hypothesis that social networks such as Twitter are much more precise than one would expect if users were seeing content at random. Note that since we showed (as control) each user 15 random tweets chosen from tweet *impressions*, and got a low relevance score for this control set, it does not appear that inspection paradox[2] alone could be an adequate explanation of the high precision we see in this trial.

1.1 Necessary Conditions for Precision

In this paper, we first outline some necessary conditions for obtaining high precision. For each of these conditions, we state the hypothesis, validate it with data, and argue via modeling and analysis, why the hypothesis is necessary for obtaining high precision.

Interest-based Networks.

Our first hypothesis is a natural one: Users on social and information networks have interests, and link to other users who share some or all of these interests. This assumption is folklore in how these networks are generated –several commonly used generative models of social networks indeed use this assumption [18, 17, 7]. We define (in Section 2) an ana-

---

[1]We imposed two restrictions on the randomly selected tweets: the tweets must be in english (all the survey takers were english speakers), and the tweet must not be a reply (since a reply may not make sense outside of the full conversation, thus yielding artificially low precision).

[2]The inspection paradox is an analogue to the well-known friendship paradox [6]: high quality users have more followers and hence a random tweet impression is of higher quality than a random tweet.

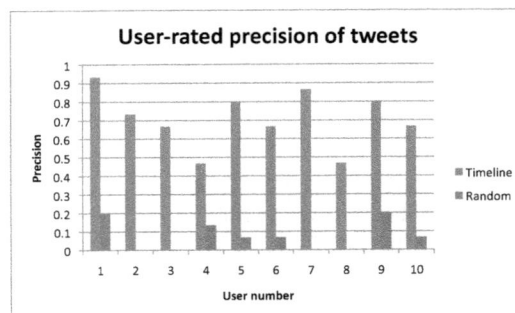

Figure 1: **Comparison of self-reported precision between tweets from a user's timeline and tweets chosen at random.**

lytic model capturing the essence of these generative models: There are a set of users V and a set of interests I. Each user $u \in V$ has a set of interests $C(u)$ that (s)he is interested in. We term these users *consumers* for interest i. Each user connects to other users based on their interests, and this yields a graph $G(V, E)$ on the users, which is the observed social network. This network could be directed (e.g., Twitter), where some users follow others and information flows along directed edges, or undirected (e.g., Facebook), where friendship is mutual, and information can flow in both directions along an edge.

In order to analyze precision in this model, we need to define which users sharing an interest $i \in I$ *produce* content related to the interest. Let $P(i)$ denote the set of users who act as producers, We show (in Section 3) that if for all interests i, $P(i) = C(i)$, which means any consumer can be a potential producer, then it is only possible to construct networks with good precision in the trivial scenario where all users have the same interests.

Production vs. Consumption.

This leads us to our second hypothesis: the production interests of a user are narrower than the consumption interests. In other words, $P(i) \subset C(i)$. We validate this assumption on Twitter (described in Section 2). We define production as either tweeting or retweeting a tweet, and consumption as clicks by the user on tweets that contain a URL. For simplicity, we refer to this as a click on a tweet. We show that the set of interests captured by clicks has larger entropy (per user) than the set capturing tweets or retweets. We note that both restricting attention only to tweets containing URLs, and requiring clicks as a measure of consumption interests are strict notions, which makes the empirical results stronger.

We also show via analysis (in Section 3) that separation of production from consumption is still insufficient to explain high precision. In particular, we show that if users choose their production and consumption interests at random from any distribution over interests (subject to mild restrictions), it is not possible to achieve even constant precision. Our result is fairly robust to the empirically observed variability in the number of user interests, and the cardinality of the interests. In Appendix A, we show the same result when users themselves have varying number of interests, as in the affiliation network models [17, 7].

Structured Interests.

The above result makes a case for interests with structure: Users do not choose interests randomly, but rather, choose them in a correlated fashion. In other words, interests have a correlation structure, and users are more likely to choose from among correlated interests than from among uncorrelated interests. We verify this assumption by measuring the correlation between interests on Twitter defined by the overlap between the sets of users having these interests. We show that the correlation is indeed much larger than what can be expected had users chosen interests at random. We then cluster the interests using these correlations, and show that these clusters have natural interpretations – sports, art, technology, etc.

It would therefore appear that users are defined by their values on various *attributes* (sports, art, etc), and interests themselves are defined either as these attributes or sets of attributes taking specific values. We finally consider a generative model of social networks that is based on users having attributes: This is the Kronecker graph model [18, 14, 21], where users connect with other users based on similarity in attribute values. We define interests using the attributes in this model, as well as producers and consumers of these interests in a natural way, so that producers are more aligned with an interest in terms of attribute similarity than consumers. We show (in Section 4) that the resulting user-user graph (or social network) has perfect precision and recall, and constant dissemination diameter for any interest.

Finally, we present (in Section 5) an empirical study to measure the precision of Twitter, defined as the fraction of the set of interests that a user receives from her friends that she is actually interested in consuming. As before, we use clicks on URLs within tweets as a proxy for consumption interest. We observe an average precision of 40%. This implies on average, users are interested in one in 2.5 topics (or interests) their neighbors tweet about. While this is already a surprisingly good number, it is worth repeating that clicks on URLs in tweets (and restricting attention to tweets with URLs) are a strict notion for capturing user interests, and it is conceivable that we are under-estimating precision in our experiments. For all our experiments, we use a classifier trained within Twitter to assign topics or interests to a tweet.

In summary, we show, both by theoretical as well as empirical analysis, that it is indeed possible for a social network to have high precision and recall for broadcast information dissemination if (a) users have interests, and connect with other users based on similarity in interests; (b) the producers of an interest are a small subset of consumers; and (c) users don't choose interests at random, but the interests have structure defined by attributes, which also define the users. We consider this to be a surprising result since a priori, a low dissemination time seems to require a well connected network which seems to trade-off with precision (this is analogous to the well studied precision-recall trade-off in Information Retrieval community).

Caveats.

We should emphasize that our results should be viewed as a first step in the understanding of the theoretical and empirical underpinnings of precision in information dissemination. For instance, our empirical measure of precision is somewhat primitive (based on broad interests) and can be refined. Though we have made use of proprietary click data in our empirical analysis of precision, we believe our user study provides an empirically better and reproducible template for measuring precision across social networks, and as future work, we plan to replicate it on a larger scale in a more principled fashion. In summary, each of our hypotheses presented above is a valid area of research in itself, deserving a more in-depth study with fine-tuned metrics, experiments, and theory. We discuss future research directions in Section 6.

1.2 Related Work

The rise of the World Wide Web and online social networks has seen an explosion of interest in the structure of these networks. In particular, researchers have made many empirical observations about network structure and posited models that could explain this structure. A comprehensive survey of these is beyond the scope of this work, but we mention some relevant works (and surveys/books, where available). There is a long line of work studying the power-law degree distributions that arise in networks [26, 3, 5]. Among other structural properties that have been studied extensively are small diameter [25, 31, 5], navigability [16, 5], densification [20] and clustering coefficients [8, 5]. It is important to note that much of the above work not only identifies the relevant structural properties, but also proposes models of phenomenon that could give rise to those properties. Among the desiderata for such models is mathematical tractability and statistical soundness in that it's assumptions and predictions match well with empirical data.

Since the focus of this paper is the interplay between network structure and information dissemination, we focus our attention to modeling approaches that seek to explain properties related to information dissemination. The empirical study of information dissemination through social networks, and the role of network structure in this process, has a long history in sociology [9, 29]. There has been an explosion of work from the computer science community in this area (sometimes known as viral marketing [19]) since the influential works of [4, 13], and we refer the interested reader to a slightly old but excellent survey of work in this area [15].

Another line of work in network modeling is relevant to us, namely one that seeks to capture the role of *user interests* in the formation of the network. The works we are aware of are the Kronecker graph model [18], the MAG model [14], the affiliation networks model [17], and a network model based on user behavior [7]. Among these, both the Kronecker graph model and the MAG model seek to be both mathematically tractable and statistically sound. On the other hand, the affiliation networks model and the model based on user behavior are theoretical.

We note that many of these models study the role of network structure in information propagation, but to the best of our knowledge none of them have studied the trade-off between precision and recall. Recall in the broadcast model has been extensively studied in the context of rumor spreading, but the goal in that line of work has typically been to maximize speed of propagation [12]. We are not aware of any work studying precision of information in social networks.

Finally, we mention that precision and recall are extremely well-studied concepts in the Information Retrieval community [22]. In particular, they are arguably the two most frequent and basic measures for information retrieval effectiveness.

2. A USER INTEREST MODEL

We start by formally describing the framework in which we analyze the precision of information diffusion. We describe a general model, folding into it the first two hypotheses presented above – that users have interests, these interests determine who they connect to, and that for any user, the set of interests for which they are the producers is a subset of the set of interests they consume (or are interested in). After presenting the model, we present an empirical rationale for the basic premise of our model.

2.1 An Interest Based Model For Precision and Recall

Interest Graph.

The set of users in the social network is denoted by set V. Every user $u \in V$ is assumed to have a fixed set of *interests*. For user u, we denote the set of interests by $C(u)$. This defines a natural *user-interest* graph $Q(V, I, F)$, where I is the set of interests, and F is the set of user-interest edges in this graph. In the discussion below, unless otherwise stated, we use $n = |V|$ and $m = |I|$.

The interests themselves are defined via the set of users that have those interests: Each interest $i \in I$ is defined by a set of *producers* $P_i \subseteq V$ and set of *consumers* $C_i \subseteq V$, such that $P_i \subseteq C_i$. The set C_i is precisely the set of neighbors of i in the graph Q, and captures all nodes interested in reading/consuming content related to interest i. The producers are a subset of these users that are sufficiently interested to produce new content or rebroadcast content associated with interest i.

We say that $Q(V, I, F)$ is *undirected* if for any interest $i \in I$, the set $P_i = C_i$, i.e., each consumer of i is a potential producer as well. If this condition is not true so that $P_i \subset C_i$, we call the graph Q as directed. We present the rationale for the separation between producers and consumers below.

User Graph.

As is customary in the literature, we represent the social network as a directed *user-user* graph $G(V, E)$. In such a network, if there is a directed edge from u to v, then we assume u *follows* v, and information broadcast by v is received by u. We call u a *follower* of v. (A user-user graph $G(V, E)$ is undirected if for any $(u, v) \in E$, u follows v and v follows u. An example of such a network is Facebook, where friendships are undirected.) This user-user graph $G(V, E)$ is constructed by the users based on the structure of the user-interest graph Q, i.e., users form links based on mutual interests in some specific manner. At the very least, for any edge $(u, v) \in E$, some interest of user u must be the same as some interest of user v. The nature of this link generation process (in addition to the structure of the interests) will be critical to how information disseminates in G.

DEFINITION 2.1. *Given a directed user-user graph $G(V, E)$, define the following quantities: Let $N(u)$ denote the set of nodes that u follows. Let $P(v) = \{i | v \in P_i\}$ and let $C(v) = \{i | v \in C_i\}$. Finally, let $S(v) = \{i | \exists (u \in N(v) \land i \in P(u))\}$, i.e. the size of the union of the production interests of the users who v follows.*

The above definition can be extended to analogous terms for undirected graphs $G(V, E)$.

Information Dissemination Metrics.

An *event* refers to a piece of information that corresponds to a single interest i, and originates at one user $v \in P_i$. This information proceeds along the edges of the social network according to the following *broadcast* process: At any time t, suppose the event has been received by a set R_t of nodes; initially, $R_0 = \{v\}$. Let $Q_t = R_t \cap P_i$ denote the nodes in R_t which are producers. These nodes broadcast the event to their followers, and the set R_{t+1} is updated by including these followers. The process terminates when the set of receivers does not increase from one step the next. Let $R_i(v)$ denote the final set of receivers if the broadcast started at node $v \in P_i$. Our model of propagation is rather simplistic, and it would be interesting to expand our results to models where resending a piece of information is based on a stochastic process or the "importance" of the information (eg. [13]).

Our goal is to study what user-interest graphs and what generative processes of user-user graphs lead to "good" information dissemination. We will make the following simplifying assumption: *The user-user graph enforces that all producers P_i of an interest i are strongly connected, so that they can both send as well as receive information related to interest i.* We capture the quality of the information dissemination via the following metrics.

DEFINITION 2.2. *Given a user-interest graph $Q(V, I, F)$ and associated user-user graph $G(V, E)$, the precision of a user v is defined as $\frac{|C(v) \cap S(v)|}{|S(v)|}$. This measures the fraction of interests that v receives that it is actually interested in. The recall of a user v is defined as $\frac{|C(v) \cap S(v)|}{|C(v)|}$. This measures the fraction of v's interests that it actually receives.*

We consolidate the above two measures into the following notion of α-PR user-interest graphs.

DEFINITION 2.3. *A user-interest graph $Q(V, I, F)$ is said to be α-PR if there exists a user-user graph $G(V, E)$ such that:*

$$\min_{v \in V} \frac{|C(v) \cap S(v)|}{|C(v) \cup S(v)|} \geq \alpha$$

Analogously, a user $v \in V$ is said to be α-PR if

$$\frac{|C(v) \cap S(v)|}{|C(v) \cup S(v)|} \geq \alpha$$

DEFINITION 2.4. *The dissemination time of the event is the number of iterations of the broadcast process before the event reaches all nodes in C_i.[3]*

The main question we ask can now be phrased formally as follows: *What kind of user-interest graphs and user-user graphs based on these interests lead to high precision and recall (captured by α-PR for constant α) and constant diameter in the above broadcast process? And is there a generative process that would allow emergence of such graphs?* An important special case of interest is the following:

---

[3]In all the models we consider, the graph is sufficiently connected that the event reaches all nodes in C_i with high probability.

DEFINITION 2.5. *A user interest-graph $\mathbb{Q}$ is PR-perfect if it is α-PR for $\alpha = 1$.*

PR-perfectness of a user-interest graph means that there is an associated user-user graph where information dissemination has 100% precision and recall, *i.e.*, all pieces of information a user receives are relevant, and furthermore, the user receives all relevant information.

2.2 Empirical Validation of Production vs Consumption Interests

A basic premise of the model described above is that users have distinct consumer and producer interests. We validate this premise empirically by using data from Twitter. As a side-effect of this analysis, we demonstrate that the production interests are in fact substantially "narrower" (i.e. have smaller entropy) than consumption interests, which plays an important role in subsequent analysis.

Experimental Setup.

We use a classifier trained within Twitter Inc. that can tag the content of a tweet with topics (which we interpret as interests for the purpose of this paper). For our classifier we used L_2 regularized Multinomial Logistic Regression trained with stochastic gradient descent over a training corpus where the number of examples for the 48 classes considered ranged from 5K to 30K. To classify tweet content we converted the text to lower case, removed embedded urls, if any, and represented each the content as a bag of character 4-grams. The set of unique feature IDs was hashed onto a 1M dimensional space but no feature selection was performed. While we have not tuned this model very extensively, it performed adequately and on par with other representations (e.g., tf-idf weighted unigrams). The training instances were collected via combination of manual labeling and manually constructed heuristic rules transferring labels from specific authors, urls, or hashtags. While we used a custom learner implementation, very similar results can be obtained with open source tools, such as Mahout, Mallet or sofia-ml [2, 23, 30].

Note that the classifier only uses features from the text of the tweet, guaranteeing that the topics tagged do not use the social network (this is going to be important later when we use the same classifier to acquire a lower bound on precision). The mean AUC (Area Under the receiver operating characteristic Curve) across the set of topics is 0.914, ranging from 0.97 down to 0.80, suggesting that the classifier is high quality. The classifier provides 48 topics, which are listed in Figure 4. The entropy for distributions over interests ranges from 0 to $\log(48) = 3.87$.

Empirical Analysis.

We now present preliminary empirical evidence that Twitter users have narrower production interests than consumption interests. As before, we generate production and consumption interests for users in the following manner: we obtain the set of production interests for a user by taking all the tweets (including retweets) produced by a user and tagging each tweet with topics with the same classifier as the one used in Section 2.2. For the consumption interests, we again resort to looking at tweets where the user explicitly expressed an interest in the tweet via clicking an URL in the tweet. Note that in order to do this, we restrict attention

only to tweets that contain an URL. To be clear, this encompasses tweets containing pictures, videos etc since their representation in tweets is via an URL. We emphasize that our definition of consumption is narrow both due to the filtered selection of tweets with URLs and also due to the fact that a click can be construed as a more definite indication of interest, as opposed to simply receiving the message. Hence, we expect (though we have not formally proved it) that the true consumption interests are wider than suggested by this study, and would further widen the separation between production and consumption interests.

We again generate a user sample of interest as before: we compute PageRank [27] on the follow graph, then from the 10 million highest PageRank users, we uniformly sample 1000 users *who have generated at least $k = 10$ tweets and clicks in a given 10 day period*. This allows us to avoid using dormant users and spammers in the analysis, and ensures we have enough tweets to analyze the production and consumption distribution. We then tag k uniform tweets that a user clicked on in their timeline in the given interval. The tags from the classifier give us a probability distribution over topics for the consumption of the user, with a corresponding entropy. Similarly, we tag k uniform random tweets that the user produced, giving a production distribution with corresponding entropy.

Distribution	Average Support	Average Entropy
Consumption Interest	7.78	1.999
Production Interest	3.96	1.242

Figure 2: The distribution of production vs consumption interests

Our results are summarized in figure 2. It is clear that in terms of both the support over interests and the entropy, the distribution of consumption interests is much broader than production interests. The average support and entropy are obtained by averaging the support/entropy of the production/consumption distribution over all users. We get similar quantitative and qualitative results when we vary the time period and k.

3. NECESSARY CONDITIONS ON THE USER-INTEREST GRAPH

Our goal in the next two sections is to understand whether it is possible to have non-trivial PR-perfect User-Interest graphs. Towards this end, we will now develop two necessary conditions that such graphs must satisfy. In the previous section, we already presented empirical evidence that users have narrower production interests than consumption interests. In this section, we first prove that if for every user, her production and consumption interests are identical, then the corresponding User-Interest graph can not be PR-perfect.

We then show that a user-interest graph that is formed by users choosing production and consumption interests uniformly at random from a distribution over interests cannot be constant-PR. This result is quite robust: In the full paper, we extend it to random graphs where the users also have non-uniform degrees. We will then empirically examine the user-interest graph of a subset of Twitter, and exhibit non-trivial structure suggesting that this graph is not drawn from a random graph model with a given degree distribution.

3.1 Production vs. Consumption

We prove that it is not possible to achieve PR-perfection with non-trivial undirected user-interest graphs (i.e. with consumption and production interests being identical).

LEMMA 3.1. *If both the user-user graph $G(V, E)$ and user-interest graph $Q(V, I, F)$ are undirected, and if $G(V, E)$ is connected, then the only PR-perfect graph is a graph where every user has identical interests.*

PROOF. If $(u, v) \in E$, then for any i such that $u \in P_i$, v receives information related to i from u. If G is PR-perfect, then $v \in C_i = P_i$. Since the graph is connected, all nodes must share the same interests. □

LEMMA 3.2. *Suppose $Q(V, I, F)$ is undirected, while $G(V, E)$ is directed. If G is PR-perfect, then for any strongly connected component $S \subseteq V$, all users in S share the same interests.*

PROOF. Suppose $v \in P_i$. Then for edge $(u, v) \in E$ so that u follows v, it must be that $v \in C_i = P_i$. Therefore, all users in a strongly connected component must have the same interests. □

The above claim can be generalized as follows: Assume $P(u) = \phi$ whenever u is a leaf of V. This corresponds to saying that if no one follows u, then u produces nothing. Then, if Q is undirected, this implies $C(u) = \phi$, but PR-perfection would imply that if $(u, v) \in E$, then $P(v) = \phi$, and so on. Therefore, PR-perfection combined with the assumption that $P(u) = \phi$ for leaves u implies either that $G(V, E)$ is strongly connected with all nodes v having the same interests, or that all nodes in G have no interests.

The above two observations justify making Q directed, *i.e.* assume $P_i \subset C_i$ for any $i \in I$ if we are looking for the existence of non-trivial PR-perfect graphs..

3.2 Independent Assortment of Interests

We continue with our question of when a user-interest graph $Q(V, I, F)$ can be α-PR for α being an absolute constant. Informed by section 3.1, we consider directed user-interest graphs, where the production interests of a user are narrower than consumption interests. We ask: *What happens if users draw their interests at random and from the same distribution as all other users?* In other words, the interests are unstructured, so that user sets of different interests have little correlation.

Our results in this section are negative: it is not possible to achieve *constant* PR with high probability in such graphs, even with a separation of production and consumption interests. We show the result when every user has the same degree in Q, while interests could have non-uniform degrees. This result is fairly robust, and extends (under mild assumptions) to the case where users have non-uniform degrees (see Appendix A). This suggests that in a constant PR-perfect user-interest graph, every user does not draw her interests from the same distribution, and can be thought of as a necessary condition.

3.2.1 Random Regular Graphs

We now show that even with the separation of producers from consumers, it is not possible to achieve PR-perfection if the user-interest graph $Q(V, I, F)$ is generated at random. We begin with the observation that different interests have different cardinalities in terms of number of users. We plot the number of producers per interest for the 48 interests on Twitter in Fig. 3. We observe that some interests are much more popular than others.

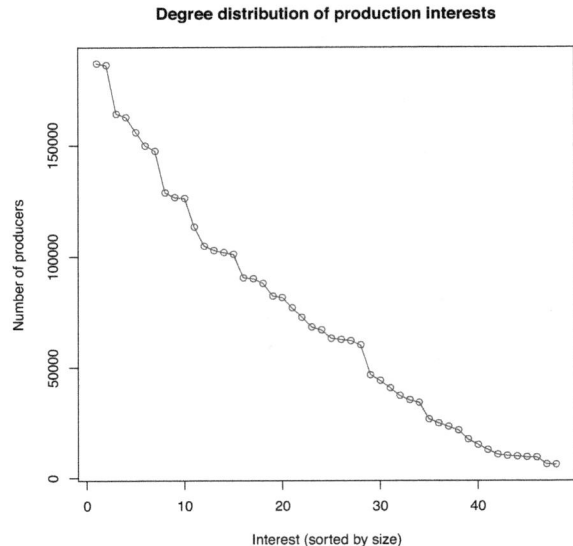

Degree distribution of production interests

Figure 3: Number of Producers per Interest

We therefore consider a random graph model where the degree distribution W of I in $Q(V, I, F)$ need not be sharply concentrated. Our negative result holds under mild assumptions that the second moment of W is order of the mean. We use the following standard method of generating such a graph. Let $n = |V|$ denote the number of users, and $m = |I|$ denote the number of interests. We generate I as follows: We generate m_d interests with degree d, where $1 \leq d \leq n^\gamma$ for constant $\gamma < 1/3$, and $\sum_d dm_d = n$. We draw m_d from an appropriately scaled version of W, so that the mean is n and second moment is $O(n)$. A canonical example is $\text{Zipf}(\beta)$ with $\beta > 3$, which follows the power law.

Let $C = |C(u)|$ and $P = |P(u)|$ denote the size of the produce and consume interests per user. Let I_d denote the interests in I with degree d. Consider a set I' where for every d, each interest $i \in I_d$ is replaced with d pseudo-interests of degree 1; note that $|I'| = \sum_d dm_d = n$. We generate the consume interests by choosing C random perfect matchings M between V and I' and taking the union of these matchings. Call this graph $M(V, I')$

After generating these matchings, consider any interest $i \in I$. Let C_i be the set of all users who were assigned to any of the d pseudo-interests corresponding to i. This defines the sets $C(u)$; note that $|C(u)| \leq C$ for all $u \in V$. Similarly, we generate the produce interests by choosing a random subset M' of size P of these matchings. Note that $|P(u)| \leq P$ for all $u \in V$. Call this graph of produce interests as $M'(V, I')$. Without loss of generality, we assume

$|C(u)| = C$ and $|P(u)| = P$ – this is achieved by assigning the remaining interests arbitrarily. This defines the graph $Q(V, I, F)$.

THEOREM 3.3. *Suppose $P = \log^\delta n$ for constant $\delta > 2$, and $C \leq n^{1/12}$. Suppose further that the second moment of the degree distribution of I is upper bounded by the mean, and that the user-user graph $G(V, E)$ has maximum degree $o(n)$. Then, the graphs $Q(V, I, F)$ as generated above are not α-PR for any constant $\alpha > 0$, with high probability.*

PROOF. Since M and M' are regular random graphs, they are expanders with probability $1 - 1/n^2$. We will argue as follows: Fix any user $u \in V$. For set $S \subseteq V$, let X_{uS} be an indicator random variable which is 1 if the following event happens: User u connects to set S **and** $|C(u) \cap (\cup_{v \in S} P(v))| \geq \alpha |C(u) \cup (\cup_{v \in S} P(v))|$. For realization r of the graph Q, let Y_{ur} be an indicator random variable which is 1 if user u can connect to some set $S \subseteq V$ such that $|C(u) \cap (\cup_{v \in S} P(v))| \geq \alpha |C(u) \cup (\cup_{v \in S} P(v))|$. Let Z_{urS} be an indicator random variable which is 1 if user u can connect to set $S \subseteq V$ such that $|C(u) \cap (\cup_{v \in S} P(v))| \geq \alpha |C(u) \cup (\cup_{v \in S} P(v))|$. Therefore, $\sum_{u,r} Y_{ur} \leq \sum_{u,r,S} Z_{urS} = \sum_{u,S} X_{uS}$. We will show that $\mathbf{E}[\sum_{u,S} X_{uS}] = o(1)$, which will imply $\mathbf{E}[\sum_{ur} Y_{ur}] = o(1)$. The latter quantity is an upper bound on the probability that a randomly chosen Q is α-PR, *i.e.*, whether there is some $G(V, E)$ so that every $u \in V$ is α-PR, which will complete the proof. Since the users are symmetric, we will simply fix a $u \in V$ and show that $\mathbf{E}[\sum_S X_S] = o(1/n)$ for this vertex.

Fix any $u \in V$. Note that $|C(u)| = C$. Consider $S = \{v_1, v_2, \ldots, v_r\}$, where $r = o(n)$. First note that since $M'(V, I')$ is an expander, with probability $1 - 1/n^2$, *every* set S of size at least $\sqrt{n}$ maps to at least $\sqrt{n}$ pseudo-interests, which must correspond to at least $\sqrt{n}/n^\gamma \geq n^{1/6}$ produce interests, since $\gamma < 1/3$. Therefore, for every such set, $|\cup_{v \in S} P(v) = \omega(|C(u)|)$, so that, restricted to sets S of this size, $\sum_{r,S} Z_{rS} = \sum_S X_S = 0$ with probability at least $1 - 1/n^2$.

Therefore, we can restrict attention to sets S of size n^μ for $\mu < 1/2$. Fix some set $S = \{v_1, v_2, \ldots, v_r\}$. Each of these r nodes has $|P(v)| = P$, so that the total number of produce interests is at most $P \times r$. For interest $i \in I$, let L_i be an indicator random variable which is 1 if $i \notin C(u)$, but there exists v_j, $j \in \{1, 2, \ldots, r\}$ such that $i \in P(v_j)$. Therefore, $L_i = 1$ is a bad event corresponding to interest i contributing to the imprecision perceived by u. Recall that I_d is the subset of I with degree d. We have

$$\Pr[L_i = 1 | i \in I_d] = \left(1 - \frac{dC}{n}\right)\left(1 - \left(1 - \frac{dP}{n}\right)^r\right)$$
$$\approx \frac{rdP}{n}\left(1 - \frac{dC}{n}\right)$$

The final approximation holds ignoring lower order terms as follows: $rdP = o(n)$ since $r, d = O(n^{1/2})$, and $P = \log^\delta n$. Therefore,

$$\mathbf{E}[\sum_i L_i] \geq \sum_d \frac{d m_d}{n} rP - \sum_d \frac{d^2 m_d}{n} \frac{PCr}{n}$$
$$= rP - o(1)$$

To see the final equality, note that $\frac{\sum_d d^2 m_d}{n} = O(1)$, since this is the ratio of the second moment to the mean is $O(1)$ by assumption. Furthermore, $r < n^{1/2}$, $P = \log^\delta n$, and

$C \leq n^{1/12}$. The variables L_i are negatively dependent, so that by an application of Chernoff bounds, for every small constant ϵ, we have:

$$\Pr\left[\sum_i L_i < rP(1 - \epsilon)\right] < e^{-rP\epsilon^2/2}$$

Therefore, the probability that there exists set $S = \{v_1, v_2, \ldots, v_r\}$ such that $\sum_i L_i < rP(1 - \epsilon)$ is at most $e^{r(\log n - P\epsilon^2/2)}$. This quantity is at most $\frac{1}{n^3}$ since $P = \Theta(\log^\delta n)$ for constant $\delta > 2$. If $\sum_i L_i < rP(1 - \epsilon)$, then u is not interested in a $(1 - \epsilon)$ fraction of the rP produce interests of set S, which implies u cannot be α-PR for constant α. This shows that $\mathbf{E}[\sum_S X_S] = o(1/n)$. Therefore, $Q(V, I, F)$ is not α-PR for any constant α with high probability. $\square$

Though the above proof assumes each user has exactly Q consume interests and P produce interests, this assumption is not critical. The proof easily generalizes to distributions over degrees of users in $Q(V, I, F)$, as long as the degrees lie in $[\log^\delta n, n^\mu]$ for suitable constants $\delta > 2$ and $\mu < 1$.

3.2.2 Extension

The above result, though very strong, assumes users have super-constant number of interests and that this distribution is uniform. Our empirical analysis suggests that many users on Twitter have very few interests. In Appendix A, we consider a simple affiliation network model in the spirit of [7, 17] where users and interests have power law degree distributions (users for interests, and interests for users), and choose to associate independently subject to the degree constraints. We show that this model is *not* constant PR when the user-user graph densifies (or has super-constant average degree), an assumption that is widely believed to hold for social networks [18, 7]. It would therefore appear that the negative result is robust as long as users choose interests independently, so that there is little correlation between the user sets for different interests. It is important to note that our model is a simplification of affiliation networks, and the full model is quite powerful. So our result does not imply that affiliation networks are not a good model of social networks.

3.3 Empirical Analysis of a User-Interest Graph

The discussion so far has shown that to achieve constant PR, it cannot be that all users draw interests independently from the same distribution. We verify this condition on Twitter as follows. For each pair of the 48 interests described earlier (and listed in figure 4), we compute the number of users who are producers for both these interests. Let n_{ij} denote this value for interests i and j. Further, let n_i denote the total number of users producing interest i, and let $n = |V|$ denote the total number of users. Then, if the graph is formed by users repeatedly sampling from a common distribution, then in expectation, approximately $e_{ij} = n_j n_j / n$ users would produce both i and j. We compute the chi-squared measure:

$$\chi_{ij} = \frac{|n_{ij} - e_{ij}|}{\sqrt{e_{ij}}}$$

We next sort the χ values in decreasing order. Let W denote the graph on the $m = 48$ interests, where there is an edge between all pairs of nodes. Let W_p denote the graph that is obtained by only adding edges (i, j) between a fraction p of the node pairs with the largest χ_{ij} values. The

label	name	label	name
1	Music and Radio	2	Technology Industry
3	Politics	4	Sports
5	Photography	6	Adult
7	Technology	8	Baseball
9	Financial Services Industry	10	Travel Industry
11	Arts and Entertainment	12	Movie/Film/TV
13	International News	14	Sports
15	Football	16	Books
17	Healthcare Industry	18	Education
19	Retail Industry	20	Application Store
21	Fiction and Literature	22	Movie/Film/TV:Adult
23	Games	24	Fashion Industry
25	Professional Services Industry	26	Alcoholic Beverages
27	Specialty	28	Non-Profit
29	Racing	30	Online Sales
31	Advertising and Marketing	32	Soccer/Futbol
33	Specialty Store	34	Food
35	Magazine	36	Artists
37	DJs	38	Hip Hop/Rap
39	Software Developers	40	Business
41	Hockey	42	Consumer/Disposable Goods Industry
43	Mixed Martial Arts	44	Beauty & Personal Care
45	Real-Estate Industry	46	Boxing
47	Religion	48	Science

Figure 4: Topic labels for topics in Figure 5

graph W_p has the same density as the Erdos Renyi graph $G(m, p)$ does in expectation. We then compute the transitivity of W_p, which is the probability that two neighbors of a node are connected. For $p = 1/12$ and $p = 1/6$, these values are 0.63 and 0.61 respectively. This shows a very high degree of clustering compared to $G(m, p)$, whose average transitivity is approximately 0.09 and 0.17 for $p = 1/12$ and $p = 1/6$ respectively. The value $1/12$ is interesting because it is just larger than $\frac{\ln 48}{48}$ ($\frac{\ln n}{n}$ is the connectivity threshold for $G(m, p)$).

We then cluster the graph $W_{\frac{1}{12}}$ (using the fastgreedy method in R with default parameters), and show the clustering in Fig. 5. Note the emergence of several natural clusters, such as sports, technology, and journalism. We find the emergence of such a natural clustering of topics to be of independent interest, which needs further study. While some clusters are unsurprising (eg. sports), some others (eg. the cluster 3, 17, 18, 28, 35, 16, 21, 47) are non-obvious.

4. ATTRIBUTE-BASED INTEREST MODEL

Our final theoretical result, somewhat surprisingly, is a positive one: we show that a natural and widely used generative model for interest-based social networks indeed achieves PR-perfection. This is the Kronecker graph model introduced in [18, 14, 21], where users are characterized by *attributes*, which are related to each other by a similarity measure. This model achieves several properties observed in social networks, such as power law degree distributions, shrinking diameter, and densification. We show a natural hierarchical definition of interests based on these attributes, which leads to PR-perfection and constant dissemination time.

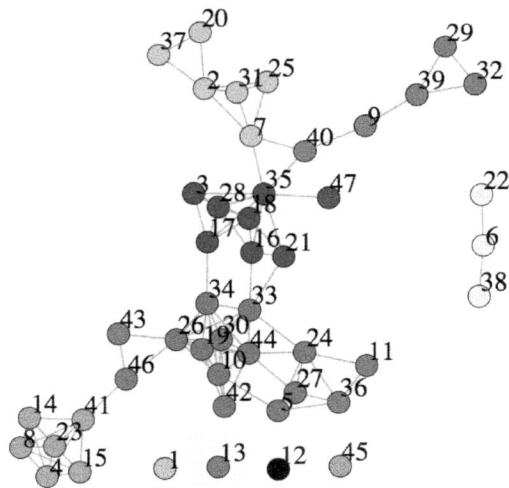

Figure 5: Communities of topics on Twitter. Yellow: Adult. Green: Sports. Pink: Consumer Retail. Dark Blue: Politics and News. Light Blue: Technology. Red: Financial.

4.1 Kronecker Graphs

In this model parametrized by a small number K, there are $|V| = n$ users, and $d = \log_K n$ attributes, each with K possible values from the set $S = \{a_1, a_2, \ldots, a_K\}$. Each node $u \in V$ maps to a d-dimensional vector of attribute values $(u_1, u_2, , u_d)$, where each $u_i \in S$. Therefore, $|V| = K^d = n$.

We define an interest as a set of pairs of attribute dimensions and their values, where a generic interest $i \in I$ has the following form:

$$i = \{\langle j_1, a_{j_1}\rangle, \langle j_2, a_{j_2}\rangle, \ldots, \langle j_r, a_{j_r}\rangle\}$$

$$\text{where } j_1, j_2, \ldots, j_r \leq K \text{ and } r \leq d$$

In other words, an interest is defined by specifying some $r \leq d$ attributes and their values. The set I is a subset of the set of all possible interests, so that $|I| \leq (K+1)^d$.

User-Interest Graph.

We now describe the mapping of users to producer and consumer interests. Treat the values in S as the K vertices of an undirected *seed graph* G_0, and denote the adjacency matrix of this graph as A. Assume $A[a_s, a_s] = 1$ for $1 \leq s \leq K$. Consider interest $i = \{\langle j_1, a_{j_1}\rangle, \langle j_2, a_{j_2}\rangle, \ldots, \langle j_r, a_{j_r}\rangle\}$. The *consumers* of this interest are defined as:

$$C_i = \{u = (u_1, u_2, \ldots, u_d) \mid A[u_j, a_j] = 1 \ \forall \langle j, a_j\rangle \in i\}$$

In other words, for each component of i of the form $\langle j, a_j\rangle$, there must be an edge between u_j and a_j in G_0. Similarly, the producers of this interest are defined as:

$$P_i = \{u = (u_1, u_2, \ldots, u_d) \mid u_j = a_j \ \forall \langle j, a_j\rangle \in i\}$$

In other words, for each component of i of the form $\langle j, a_j\rangle$, the value u_j must coincide with a_j. It is clear that $P_i \subseteq C_i$ for all i.

The above interest model has the following interpretation. Since each interest is specified by a subset of attributes along with their values, the graph G_0 and adjacency matrix A specify which interests are related, i.e. which interests specify an *interested in* relationship. Further, the interests have a natural hierarchical structure, where the *broader* interests are those specified by fewer attributes. Also note that a producer of an interest needs to align with it's attribute values on all the relevant attribute dimensions, while a consumer of an interest only needs to be *interested in* those attribute values in the relevant attribute dimensions.

We can also derive further intuition about this interpretation by examining the typical size of these interest sets are. The size of interest sets depend on the nature of the adjacency matrix A. If the degree of each node a_i in G_0 is w and $|i| = d - j$, then $|P_i| = n^{\log w / \log K}(K/w)^j$. If we set $K = O(\log n)$, $w = O(1)$, and $j = O(1)$, then $|P_i| \approx n^{1/\log\log n}$. Furthermore, $|P_i|/|C_i| = 1/w^{d-j} = o(1)$, since $d = \log_K n \approx \frac{\log n}{\log\log n}$. This means the interest sets can be reasonably small (that is, $o(n^\gamma)$ for constant γ) for suitable choice of K, w, j, but within each interest set, we have a very small number of producers relative to consumers.

User-user Graph.

The graph $G(V, E)$ is undirected, and the generation process is the same as the one described in [21, 18]. For each $u = (u_1, u_2, \ldots, u_d)$ and $v = (v_1, v_2, \ldots, v_d)$, the edge (u, v) exists iff $A[u_j, v_j] = 1$ for all $j = 1, 2, \ldots, d$. In other words,

two nodes connect iff they are interested in each other's attribute values on all attribute dimensions. It is shown in [18] that for suitably chosen adjacency matrices A, so that G_0 has constant diameter D, the graph $G(V, E)$ has multinomial degree distribution, has super-constant average degree (densifies) and the same constant diameter D as G_0. This therefore leads to a *densifying power law* graph G, and is termed the *Kronecker graph* on V using the attributes $\{1, 2, \ldots, d\}$ and seed graph G_0.

THEOREM 4.1. *Any user-interest graph $Q(V, I, F)$ and the associated user-user graph $G(V, E)$ generated by the above described process is PR-perfect with dissemination time at most $D + 1$.*

PROOF. Consider an arbitrary interest of the form $i = \{\langle j_1, a_{j_1}\rangle, \langle j_2, a_{j_2}\rangle, \ldots, \langle j_r, a_{j_r}\rangle\}$. Let $W = \{j_1, j_2, \ldots, j_r\}$, and $X = \{1, 2, \ldots, d\} \setminus W$. The set P_i has users u such that $u_j = a_j$ for $j \in W$. Consider the graph $G(P_i, E')$ induced on the set of users P_i. This graph is a Kronecker graph on the set P_i using the attributes X and seed graph G_0. This is therefore connected and has diameter at most D. This means any message originating at $u \in P_i$ reaches all of P_i in D hops. Further, it is easy to check that every neighbor of $u \in P_i$ is a $v \in C_i$, so that the precision is 100% and so is the recall. The total dissemination time is at most $D + 1$. $\square$

Theorem 4.1 shows that there is indeed a model that achieves PR-perfection while preserving the key properties of social networks such as densification, heave tailed degree distribution, and shrinking diameter. The key aspects that made PR-perfection possible in Kronecker graphs are two-fold: producers are a subset of consumers that are more aligned with that interest; and the interests have a hierarchical structure that enables users to connect to the appropriate producers. We have furthermore shown in previous sections that both these properties are necessary, including presenting empirical evidence validating their existence on Twitter.

4.2 Generalizing Kronecker Graphs

We now generalize the definition of interests in the Kronecker graph model to smoothly trade off the precision with the size of producer sets.

Consider the Kronecker graph model discussed in Section 4.1. We now show a broader definition of producers that leads to a smooth degradation in precision as the definition is broadened. Recall that K is the number of possible values an attribute can take, and that there are d attributes. Fix interest $i = \{\langle j_1, a_{j_1}\rangle, \langle j_2, a_{j_2}\rangle, \ldots, \langle j_r, a_{j_r}\rangle\}$. The *consumers* of this interest are defined as:

$$C_i = \{u = (u_1, u_2, \ldots, u_d) \mid A[u_j, a_j] = 1 \ \forall \langle j, a_j\rangle \in i\}$$

We generalize the definition of a producer as follows. Consider user $u = (u_1, u_2, \ldots, u_d)$. For interest i, let $S_i = \{j_1, j_2, \ldots, j_s\}$ be a fixed set of at most s attributes. Then u produces i only if $u \in C_i$ and $\{j | u_j \neq a_j\}| \subseteq S$. This generalizes the definition of producers used in Section 4.1, which corresponds to setting $S = \phi$.

THEOREM 4.2. *For any $s \geq 0$, the Kronecker graph model with produce interests as defined above is α-PR for $\alpha = K^{-s}$. This is constant if K and s are constant.*

PROOF. From the discussion in Section 4.1, it is clear that any user u receives all interests in $C(u)$. Therefore, $|C(u) \cap S(u)| = |C(u)|$. In order to bound $|C(u) \cup S(u)|$, consider any interest $i \in C(u)$. Corresponding to i, there are at most K^s interests in $S(u)$ that are obtained by replacing the attributes in S_i with all possible values. There are K^s such interests. These interests could be produced by a neighbor of u, and hence be received by u though these need not belong to $C(u)$. Therefore, the graph is α-PR for $\alpha \geq K^{-s}$. $\square$

A larger value of s implies producers are less aligned in attributes with the interest, *i.e.*, they are lower quality producers for that event. As is to be expected, this leads to a degradation in the precision of that interest. Therefore, this model shows a trade-off between the size of the producer set and the precision achieved, with smaller and more highly aligned producers leading to larger precision.

5. PRECISION ON TWITTER

Finally, we also present a preliminary empirical measurement of the precision observed on Twitter to build on the small user trial presented in Section 1. Since we cannot make the direct measurement as was done in the user trial (we don't have the counter-factual of random tweets for users), we define the production and consumption interests using a procedure very similar to the one in Section 2.2. Namely, the set of consumption topics is obtained using the topic distribution for tweets that contain an URL that a user *clicked on*. And the set of production topics is obtained using the topic distribution for tweets that the user tweeted (or retweeted). Also as before, we sampled 1 million users from the 10 million highest PageRank users, and within these, restrict attention to those users *who have generated at least $k = 10$ tweets and clicks in a given 10 day period*. The rationale behind this was to avoid using dormant users and spammers in the analysis, and ensure that we have enough tweets to analyze the production and consumption distribution. We then select tweets that a user clicked on in their timeline in the given interval. The tags from the classifier give us the set of consumption topics for each user u, which is the same as $C(u)$. Similarly, we tag k uniform random tweets that a user v produced, giving a production distribution $P(v)$.

We indicate the set of edges between the users as E, and define an average empirical precision of user u as:

$$\text{Precision}(u) = \frac{\sum_{(u,v) \in E} |C(u) \cap P(v)|}{\sum_{(u,v) \in E} |P(v)|}$$

The formula above is an easy to compute approximation to an unbiased estimator constructed as follows: Each user u computes the multi-set $S(u) = \uplus\{P(v)|(u,v) \in E\}$. The precision seen by u is the probability that a randomly chosen interest in $S(u)$ belongs to $C(u)$. The reason for taking a multi-set union of the produce interests as opposed to a set union is that each user follows a large number (over a hundred) producers, and therefore, it is likely every interest is represented in one of these producers. Our estimator excludes *sparse* interests that are represented in only a few producers, from being counted towards precision.

Using this measure, the average precision during the same time period was 40.5%, and the distribution of precision is presented in Fig. 6. As a baseline, since there are 48 interests and $\mathbf{E}[C(u)] \approx 8$, the average precision would be 17% had each consumer received all interests. The precision

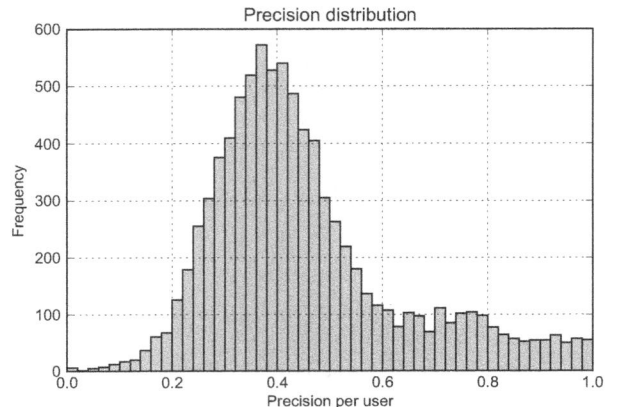

Figure 6: Distribution of Precision(u) on Twitter.

we obtain is significantly larger than the baseline, and we find this surprising given that we have only used a very narrow definition of consumption (clicks on tweets containing URLs). There are two possible explanations for this: The first is that tweets with URLs tend to be among the most interesting for users [1]; and the second is that we are measuring precision as the fraction of overlapping *interests* as opposed to the fraction of received tweets that are interesting – in this metric, we observe one in 2.5 received interests on any follow edge to be relevant on average. Nevertheless, it is clear that users read several tweets of interest without clicking on them, and as future work, we plan to determine better methods to measure precision empirically. We believe our user study provides a better and more reproducible template for performing such a study. We also re-emphasize that this measurement is not the central thesis of the paper, and is only provided as a preliminary datapoint of behavior on a real social network.

6. CONCLUSIONS AND FUTURE WORK

We have presented a definition of precision and recall for information dissemination on social networks using an interests-based framework. We also provide some necessary conditions on the structure of these interests to achieve good precision and recall, and validated these conditions on Twitter data. Somewhat surprisingly, we show that the Kronecker graph model achieves high precision and high recall while having constant dissemination time. We show preliminary empirical evidence towards the hypothesis that, despite widely held belief to the contrary, information flow on Twitter does indeed have high precision. Tying these together, the following explanation of this phenomenon emerges: users connect to other users based on similarity in interests, users produce content related to a narrower set of interests than they consume, and interests have structure so that users choose interests in a correlated fashion.

Our work is only a first step in understanding precision of information flow. Several research directions open up from this work. We have not really touched on recall or speed of dissemination, and it is *a priori* not even clear how to measure recall on Twitter. Furthermore, our measure of precision only uses a coarse set of interests, and the relation of the tweets to interests – in reality, even within an interest, tweets can have a wide range of "interestingness". This is harder to capture empirically, but is an interesting research direction. In a similar vein, we have not studied the structure of interests in Twitter in a very systematic way, since it is secondary to the main theme of this paper – this aspect will benefit from a more in-depth study.

Moving further afield, we have not considered the phenomena of *discoverability* and *coevolution*: Users need to discover other users who share their interests, and furthermore, users gradually change their links and the content they tweet based on the interests of their neighbors. These aspects need both theoretical modeling and empirical study.

7. ACKNOWLEDGMENTS

Ashish Goel acknowledges support from DARPA XDATA AND GRAPHS programs, and from the NSF award number 0904325. Kamesh Munagala is supported by an Alfred P. Sloan Research Fellowship, an award from Cisco, and by NSF grants CCF- 0745761, CCF-1008065, and IIS-0964560. Part of this work was done while the author was visiting Twitter, Inc. The authors are also grateful to Alek Kolcz for his help with the classifier used in this work.

8. REFERENCES

[1] O. Alonso, C. Carson, D. Gerster, X. Ji, and S. U. Nabar. Detecting uninteresting content in text streams. In *SIGIR Crowdsourcing for Search Evaluation Workshop*, 2010.

[2] Apache. Apache Mahout, http://mahout.apache.org.

[3] D. Chakrabarti and C. Faloutsos. Graph mining: Laws, generators, and algorithms. *ACM Computing Surveys (CSUR)*, 38(1):2, 2006.

[4] P. Domingos and M. Richardson. Mining the network value of customers. *Proc. 7th ACM SIGKDD Conference*, pages 57–66, 2001.

[5] D. Easley and J. M. Kleinberg. *Networks, crowds, and markets*, volume 8. Cambridge Univ Press, 2010.

[6] S. L .Feld. Why your friends have more friends than you do. *Amer. J. Sociology*, pages 1464–1477, 1991.

[7] I. Foudalis, K. Jain, C. H. Papadimitriou, and M. Sideri. Modeling social networks through user background and behavior. In *WAW*, pp 85–102, 2011.

[8] M. Girvan and M. E. J. Newman. Community structure in social and biological networks. *Proc. Nat. Acad. Sci.*, 99(12):7821–7826, 2002.

[9] M. S. Granovetter. The strength of weak ties. *Amer. J. Sociology*, pages 1360–1380, 1973.

[10] A. L. Hughes and L. Palen. Twitter adoption and use in mass convergence and emergency events. *Intl. J. Emergency Management*, 6(3):248–260, 2009.

[11] Twitter Inc. *Embedded Tweets*, 2013. https://dev.twitter.com/docs/embedded-tweets.

[12] R. Karp, C. Schindelhauer, S. Shenker, and B. Vocking. Randomized rumor spreading. In *Proc. 41st IEEE FOCS*, 2000.

[13] D. Kempe, J. Kleinberg, and É. Tardos. Maximizing the spread of influence through a social network. *Proc. 9th ACM SIGKDD Conf.*, 2003.

[14] M. Kim and J. Leskovec. Multiplicative attribute graph model of real-world networks. *Internet Mathematics*, 8(1-2):113–160, 2012.

[15] J. Kleinberg. Cascading Behavior in Networks: Algorithmic and Economic Issues. In N. Nisan, T. Roughgarden, E. Tardos, and V.V. Vazirani, editors, *Algorithmic Game Theory*. Cambridge University Press New York, NY, USA, 2007.

[16] J. M. Kleinberg. Navigation in a small world. *Nature*, 406(6798):845–845, 2000.

[17] S. Lattanzi and D. Sivakumar. Affiliation networks. In *Proc. 41st ACM STOC*, pages 427–434. 2009.

[18] J. Leskovec, D. Chakrabarti, J. Kleinberg, C. Faloutsos, and Z. Ghahramani. Kronecker graphs: An approach to modeling networks. *The J. Machine Learning Res.*, 11:985–1042, 2010.

[19] J. Leskovec, L. A. Adamic, and B. A. Huberman. The dynamics of viral marketing. *ACM Trans. Web*, 1(1):5, 2007.

[20] J. Leskovec, J. Kleinberg, and C. Faloutsos. Graphs over time: Densification laws, shrinking diameters and possible explanations. In *Proc. 11th ACM SIGKDD Conference*, 2005.

[21] M. Mahdian and Y. Xu. Stochastic kronecker graphs. *Random Struct. Algorithms*, 38(4):453–466, 2011.

[22] C. D. Manning, P. Raghavan, and H. Schütze. *Introduction to information retrieval*, volume 1. Cambridge University Press, Cambridge, 2008.

[23] A. K. McCallum. Mallet: A machine learning for language toolkit. 2002.

[24] P. McFedries. Technically speaking: All a-twitter. *Spectrum, IEEE*, 44(10):84–84, 2007.

[25] S. Milgram. The small world problem. *Psychology Today*, 2(1):60–67, 1967.

[26] M. Mitzenmacher. A brief history of generative models for power law and lognormal distributions. *Internet Mathematics*, 1(2):226–251, 2004.

[27] L. Page, S. Brin, R. Motwani, and T. Winograd. The pagerank citation ranking: Bringing order to the web. Technical Report 1999-66, Stanford InfoLab, November 1999.

[28] N. Park, K. F. Kee, and S. Valenzuela. Being immersed in social networking environment: Facebook groups, uses and gratifications, and social outcomes. *CyberPsychology & Behavior*, 12(6):729–733, 2009.

[29] E. M. Rogers. *Diffusion of innovations*. Free Press, 2010.

[30] D. Sculley. Combined regression and ranking. In *Proc. 16th ACM SIGKDD Conference*, pages 979–988. 2010.

[31] D. J. Watts and S. H. Strogatz. Collective dynamics of 'small-world' networks. *Nature*, 393:440–442, 1998.

APPENDIX

A. SIMPLE AFFILIATION NETWORKS

The result in Section 3.2.1 assumes all users have similar number of interests, and this number is super-constant. However, on Twitter, we observe that the number of interests per user follows a skewed distribution plotted in Fig. 7.

In order to model such behavior, we consider a fairly natural interest-based generative model of social networks termed affiliation network model [17, 7]. This model achieves many observed statistical properties of social networks (the graph $G(V, E)$), such as shrinking diameter, heave tailed de-

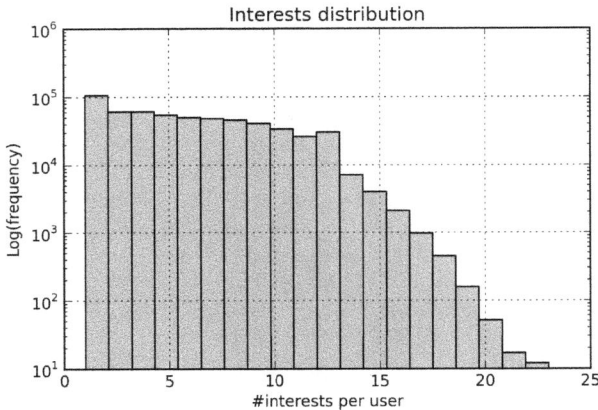

Figure 7: Histogram of number of interests per user

gree distributions, and super-constant average degree. Furthermore, it models both skewed interest degrees from Section 3.2.1, as well as the skew observed in Fig. 7.

The model we present simplifies the models presented in [17, 7], and we show this cannot be α-PR for any constant α, whenever the user-user graph $G(V, E)$ has super-constant average degree (or it densifies). Our model follows the discussion in Section 3.2.1 – the bipartite graph $Q(V, I, F)$ on users and interests is generated by the following random process. Fix two numbers $a_2 = 2 + \epsilon$, and $a_1 = 2 + 1/\epsilon$ for $0 < \epsilon < 1$. For instance, we can choose $a_2 = 2.5$ and $a_1 = 4$. There are n interest nodes I. The degrees in I are drawn from Zipf(a_2), with maximum degree n^γ for sufficiently small γ. The distribution $X =$ Zipf(a) is integer valued, with $\Pr[X = r] \propto \frac{1}{r^a}$.

User-Interest Graph.

Now imagine there is an infinite pool of user nodes, whose degrees are drawn from Zipf(a_1). Again assume the maximum degree is n^γ for sufficiently small constant γ. For a user node u of degree $d(u)$, we split it into $d(u)$ *unit user* nodes each annotated with the degree $d(u)$. Each node $q \in Q$ of degree $d(q)$ chooses $d(q)$ unit user nodes uniformly at random from this infinite pool and connects to these nodes. The unit-user nodes that are connected to are considered *marked*. At the end of the process, we generate the final set of users V and the bipartite graph Q as follows: For every degree d, we collect together all marked unit-user nodes annotated with degree d. We group these nodes into buckets of size d, and each of these buckets becomes a user $u \in U$ with degree d. Note that there could be multiple parallel edges in $Q(V, I, F)$; we retain these edges for simplicity.

By a simple application of Chernoff bounds, the number of nodes in V with degree in $[1, n^\gamma]$ for sufficiently small γ agrees with the distribution Zipf(a_2) to within a factor of 2 w.h.p., and we ignore this error in the remaining discussion.

User-User Graph.

For any interest $i \in I$, let $V(i)$ denote the set of users having an edge to this interest. We generate the user-user graph $G(V, E)$ by *folding* the graph $Q(V, I, F)$ as follows: We place an edge between $u_1, u_2 \in V(i)$ with probability

$1/r^{1-\delta}$, where $r = |V(i)|$ and $\delta > \epsilon$. The graph induced on $V(i)$ is therefore an Erdos-Renyi random graph $G(r, 1/r^{1-\delta})$.

It is shown in [17] that for the choice of parameters mentioned above, i.e., $a_1 = 2 + 1/\epsilon$, $a_2 = 2 + \epsilon$, and $0 < \epsilon < \delta \leq 1$, the resulting graph $G(V, E)$ has heavy-tailed degree distribution (since it stochastically dominates Zipf(a_1)), constant effective diameter for each interest set (since the induced graph is $G(r, 1/r^{1-\delta})$ for $\delta > 0$), and super-constant expected degree. This part requires $\delta > \epsilon$, and follows from an easy calculation that is implicit in the proof below. The canonical setting is to have $\delta = 1$, so that the graph induced on users sharing an interest is a complete graph.

We term the above model *Simple Affiliation Networks*. Since we are considering a generative process, we define the notion of expected precision:

DEFINITION A.1. *Given sets V, I, a generative process for $Q(V, I, F)$ and $G(V, E)$ is said to be α-EPR if*

$$\min_{v \in V} \frac{\mathbf{E}[|C(v) \cap S(v)|]}{\mathbf{E}[|C(v) \cup S(v)|]} \geq \alpha$$

where the expectation is over the process that generates Q, G.

We show the following theorem; our result holds for any $\delta > \epsilon$, so that the graph $G(V, E)$ densifies.

THEOREM A.2. *Assuming $|P_i| \geq 1$ for all interests i, the Simple Affiliation Network model with $\delta > \epsilon$ is not α-EPR for any constant α, regardless of the choice of P_i for each i.*

PROOF. We present the proof for the case $\delta = 1$. In the analysis below, we will focus on some user u, and condition on u having at degree (or number of interests) d. We will calculate the expected precision and recall of u conditioned on this event. Define the degree $d(\cdot)$ of a user (resp. interest) as their degrees in the bipartite graph $Q(V, I, F)$. Choose any $u \in U$, and let $|C(u)| = M \in [1, n^\gamma]$ for $\gamma < 1/10$. Now view the graph $Q(V, I, E)$ as follows: Each node $u \in V$ is $d(u)$ unit-user nodes of degree one, and each $i' \in I$ is $d(i')$ unit-nodes of degree 1. Therefore, we can view fixed $u \in V$ as M unit-nodes $u_1, u_2, \ldots, u_M$ each of which connects to an interest node at random. Fix some u_j. The interest node $i_j \in I$ connected to by u_j has degree $d(i_j)$ drawn from the distribution:

$$\Pr[\text{Degree of } i_j = d] = \frac{d \times 1/d^{a_2}}{\sum_{s=1}^{\infty} s \times 1/s^{a_2}}$$

Therefore, the degree distribution of the M users sharing interest i is Zipf($a_2 - 1$), where $a_1 = 1 + \epsilon < 2$. Consider some i_j with degree d_{i_j}, and consider some neighbor v of this interest. Then, with constant probability, the following two events happen for v: (1) Its degree is exactly 2; let the other interest shared by v be i'; and (2) the degree of i' is one, so that $v \in P(i')$. This means that for every neighbor v of i_j, with constant probability, v produces one interest. Node u receives this interest since $(u, v) \in E$ due to shared interest i_j. Therefore, the expected number of interests received by u due to interest i_j is $\Omega(d_{i_j})$. Since d_{i_j} is drawn from Zipf($a_2 - 1$), where $a_1 = 1 + \epsilon < 2$, the expected number of received interests of u is:

$$\mathbf{E}[d(u)] \left(\sum_{s=1}^{\infty} \Omega(s) \times \frac{1}{s^{a_2-1}} \right) = \omega(\mathbf{E}[d(u)])$$

Next note that $\mathbf{E}[d(u)] = \mathbf{E}[C(u)] = O(1)$ since the degree of u is distributed as Zipf(a_1). Therefore, $G(V, E)$ is not α-EPR for any constant α. $\square$

Cryptagram: Photo Privacy for Online Social Media

Matt Tierney, Ian Spiro, Christoph Bregler, Lakshminarayanan Subramanian
New York University
{tierney, spiro, bregler, lakshmi}@cs.nyu.edu

http://cryptagr.am

ABSTRACT

While Online Social Networks (OSNs) enable users to share photos easily, they also expose users to several privacy threats from both the OSNs and external entities. The current privacy controls on OSNs are far from adequate, resulting in inappropriate flows of information when users fail to understand their privacy settings or OSNs fail to implement policies correctly. OSNs may further complicate privacy expectations when they reserve the right to analyze uploaded photos using automated face identification techniques.

In this paper, we propose the design, implementation and evaluation of Cryptagram, a system designed to enhance online photo privacy. Cryptagram enables users to convert photos into encrypted images, which the users upload to OSNs. Users directly manage access control to those photos via shared keys that are independent of OSNs or other third parties. OSNs apply standard image transformations (JPEG compression) to all uploaded images so Cryptagram provides an image encoding and encryption mechanism that is tolerant to these transformations. Cryptagram guarantees that the recipient with the right credentials can completely retrieve the original image from the transformed version of the uploaded encrypted image while the OSN cannot infer the original image. Cryptagram's browser extension integrates seamlessly with preexisting OSNs, including Facebook and Google+, and currently has over 400 active users.

Categories and Subject Descriptors

K.4.1 [**Public Policy Issues**]: Privacy; K.6.5 [**Security and Protection**]: Unauthorized Access

Keywords

photo privacy; online social media

1. INTRODUCTION

Petabytes of imagery data have been posted by users to Online Social Networks (OSNs) with Facebook alone receiv-

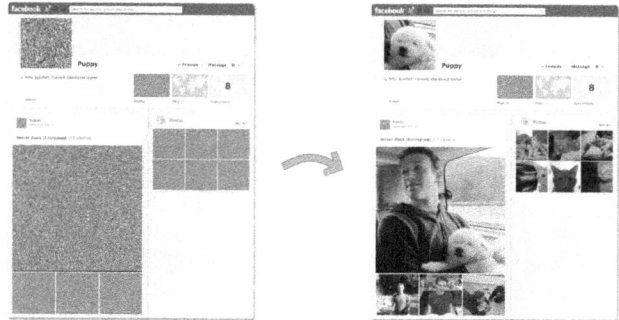

Figure 1: Example Cryptagram user experience. On the left, we show a social network with embedded Cryptagrams, uploaded by a user. A browser extension decrypts the images in place as shown on the right.

ing over 250 million photo uploads per day [24], storing 10,000 times more photos than the Library of Congress [14]. Users feel the need internally and externally (peer pressure) to share photos on OSNs given the convenience of usage and their immense popularity [21, 2, 25, 27, 34]. Users share personal and potentially sensitive photos on OSNs, thereby exposing users to a wide range of privacy threats from external entities and the OSN itself [9, 33, 31]. We consider two basic factors that trigger privacy concerns for end-users in OSNs.

User/System Errors: A user who uploads an image to an OSN may wish to share it with only a select group of people, which OSNs partially satisfy with privacy settings. Contextual integrity [23] would state that the user is attempting to implement her own notion of appropriate information flows. But a recent study confirmed that Facebook users' impression of their sharing patterns and their true privacy settings are often inconsistent [18]. Moreover, an OSN may fail to correctly enforce their privacy settings, such as the case when Facebook exposed its own CEO's private photos in a systemwide glitch [9].

Face Identification: A passive observer or a hosting OSN could extract large volumes of online photo uploads, indexing and discovering images within a corpus that belong to a specific user [33]. Mining of photo corpora can lead to the unexpected disclosure of individuals' locations or their participation in events. Facial data mining incidents have resulted in litigation against OSNs and further weakened the integrity of the relationship between the social network and the individual [31].

In this paper, we present the design, implementation and evaluation of Cryptagram, a system designed to address these photo privacy concerns in OSNs. A basic design goal of Cryptagram is to build a usable solution that can offer strong privacy guarantees for end-users that remains backwards compatible with existing OSN user interface designs. To maintain the conventional feel of an OSN, Cryptagram uses the abstraction of an image interface (RGBA pixels) to manipulate the core image formats used by OSNs. Cryptagram leverages an end-to-end encryption system to transport images, which are uploaded to OSNs. Figure 1 illustrates a specific example of how Cryptagram represents normal images as encrypted images.[1]

A challenge in the design of such an end-to-end image encryption/decryption mechanism is to be resilient to image transformations by the OSN. For instance Facebook converts all uploaded photos, regardless of original format, to JPEG, choosing quality settings without user input. The recipient of a Cryptagram image must be able to retrieve the original image from the OSN-transformed version. In this paper, we describe the notion of q, p-Recoverability (Section 3.1) which formalizes the aforementioned property that enables the assessment of embedding protocol designs. We describe a class of JPEG embedding protocols that can achieve the q, p-Recoverability property for different JPEG quality transformation levels. The top-down techniques that we discuss for designing q, p-Recoverable protocols can also be applied to lossless image compression formats.

Cryptagram addresses a problem that is fundamentally different from conventional image steganography. While steganography aims to hide data in plainsight and *avoid detection* [11], Cryptagram makes obvious that it is hiding data with the added aim of efficiently transporting bits in the image medium while being robust to image transformations. Despite the differences in problem definition, steganography does have the same mechanical use as Cryptagram for transporting bits in an image. When comparing the effective efficiency of our approach to steganography, Cryptagram packs many more bits per pixel (Section 6).

Cryptagram differs significantly from the recent work on photo privacy, P3 [29]. Unlike P3, Cryptagram operates completely in encrypted bit space and does not reveal sensitive cleartext data of photos to external entities (Section 8). Cryptagram also does not rely on third-party providers for providing photo privacy.

We present several key results in our evaluation. For JPEG Cryptagram images uploaded to Facebook, we find that JPEG compression quality for those high entropy images is in the range of 76 to 86 (for natural images, usually quality is 74). Given these recompression target ranges, we demonstrate JPEG embedding protocols that, in tandem with error-correcting codes, achieve an effective efficiency of 3.06 bits per pixel, which is 2.68× greater than the best related work. We also summarize a study of recoverability when recompressng already compressed images. We further

[1]In this example, a user has uploaded a single Cryptagram image per image in this Figure. OSNs typically recompress and resize images within their backend infrastructure, presenting the most bandwidth-friendly version (thumbnails) as they deem appropriate. In order to render the decrypted Cryptagrams for thumbnails, Cryptagram infers from URL of the thumbnail how to fetch the full-size image, which Cryptagram fetches and decompresses when a user indicates our extension should do so.

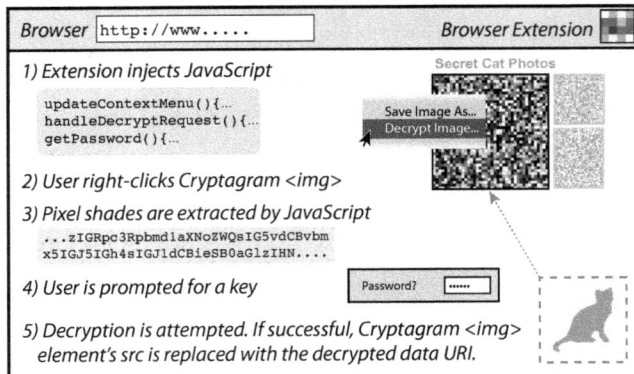

Figure 2: An overview of the Cryptagram user experience.

illustrate a design point comparison of recoverability versus filesize expansion when comparing JPEG and webp lossy compression formats.

Our end-to-end Cryptagram system has been deployed to the web. Figure 2 summarizes a user's experience with the current decoder. Our decoder browser extensions integrate seamlessly with existing OSNs including Facebook and Google+ while being compatible with their complicated DOM structures. We have nearly 400 active users of our decoder extension and over 300 users have agreed to our IRB-approved study through which they submit high-level data about their on-going image encrypting and decrypting habits with Cryptagram.

2. SYSTEM MODEL

2.1 Problem Statement

The basic problem that Cryptagram aims to address can be stated as follows: Two users U and V are members in an OSN and have a shared key k (e.g., password), independent of the OSN. U wants to use the OSN to share an image I with V but does not intend to upload I to the OSN since the OSN or other unauthorized users may also be able to view I. Instead, U needs an encryption mechanism that can transform I into an encrypted image I', which V can retrieve, decrypt and obtain I (using the shared key k). The key challenge is that when U uploads an encrypted image I', the OSN can apply image transformations and the image V downloads may significantly differ from I'. Hence, the sharing mechanism needs to be resilient to image transformations.

To better understand the transformation-resilient image encryption problem, we outline the basic image encoding and decoding steps used by Cryptagram and the property that Cryptagram aims to achieve:

• A user U encrypts a to-be-shared cleartext image, I, using a strong block cipher with a secret key, k, to produce a byte sequence, $E(I, k)$. This k may be human-readable (a password) or part of a hybrid cryptosystem in which the k is generated and shared using public key cryptography.

• An image encoding protocol, C, embeds $E(I, k)$ into the spatial domain of an image, $I_m = C(E(I, k))$ which the OSN transforms as $T(I_m)$. In this paper, we restrict T to be the identity transformation (lossless format) or a standard lossy image compression. We use JPEG for the lossy format in much of the evaluation since that is a commonly used standard across OSNs.

- An OSN user V who is an authorized recipient of the image needs to be aware of the block cipher secret key k. Using this key k and an image decoding algorithm, V should be able to successfully decode I from a transformed version $T(I_m)$. Here, we aim to achieve *recoverability* (intuitively, data integrity of the embedded message), which in the case of a lossless format is tautologically true sans other transformations. For JPEG, we aim for q, p-Recoverability property: given a minimum quality level q of the transformed image $T(I_m)$, the decoding protocol should enable V to decode the original image I with high probability, p. We denote this recoverability probability using p, where the ideal case is when $p = 1$; however, achieving $p = 1$ may not always be feasible.
- Adversary, Eve, who passively observes $T(I_m)$ should not learn anything about I.

2.2 Design Goals

The aforementioned problem statement highlights two key design goals of Cryptagram: *data confidentiality* and *probabilistic data integrity for lossy images*. For data confidentiality, Cryptagram leverages trusted algorithms that users may use to ensure that data has been encoded with a strong proofs of security. For probabilistic data integrity, since Cryptagram aims to create images for use on OSNs, we can relax the constraint of traditional information security data integrity [10] for lossy image formats such as JPEG. This relaxation enables the Cryptagram design to incorporate features that demonstrate a spectrum of data integrity when a social network transforms uploaded images.

But given these goals, should U and V use an OSN to share personal images at all? We accept as a constraint that many users desire the convenience of social networks [21]. This "convenience" constraint raises the following design goals that Cryptagram meets:

Usable: We aim to offer a system that affords users intuitive privacy on top of the images that they share on OSNs. While several offline approaches exist to preserve privacy (e.g., PGP [39]), Cryptagram makes it possible for users to create and share private photos without disrupting the OSN experience.

Widely Deployable and Applicable: To gain wide adoption, we have created a cross-browser, cross-platform, cross-image format system that enables Cryptagram to be used as both an encoder and decoder. The reduced friction to creating and accessing Cryptagram images removes the barrier to broader use of the technology.

Efficient: Compared to alternative methods, we present a system that offers significantly more data storage for a given file size or image dimensions.

2.3 Security Overview

2.3.1 Threat #1: Facial Data Mining

In this threat, the adversary is the OSN, whose aim is to execute facial data mining algorithms on uploaded images. In recent years, as social networks' corpi of images have grown dramatically, this is a serious concern for the privacy-conscious individual.

Approach. We have devised a scheme that reveals no information about the original image to the OSN. As we discuss in Section 4, the use of our embedding algorithm by nature thwarts facial data mining by embedding the cleartext (e.g., facial) data indirectly as encrypted bits in the spatial domain of the transport image.

Security Guarantees. With the use of a block cipher to transform the secret message, Cryptagram retains the strength of the underlying security properties of the chosen algorithm. With the use of public key cryptography users can retain cryptographic strength while leveraging a trusted, separate channel to bootstrap their sharing.

2.3.2 Threat #2: Misconfigured Privacy Controls

OSNs may fail to correctly deploy access control policies or users may accidentally misconfigure confusing access controls. The use of Cryptagram creates a separate channel of communication to ensure, with cryptographic strength, that only intended recipients see the cleartext photo. With the correct use of Cryptagram, an OSN could suffer a full system breach and encrypted images would remain private.

2.3.3 Limitations

Detecting and Blocking Cryptagram Images. Cryptagram does not address the problem of an OSN detecting and inhibiting the upload of all Cryptagram images. Steganography may be proposed in this scenario but problem redefinition and the tradeoff in efficiency make steganography an inappropriate application.

Unsupported Transformations. Though Cryptagram images are robust to varying degrees of JPEG compression, they does not support many other transformations. For example, cropping or rescaling a Cryptagram will generally break its encoding.

Brute-Force Cryptographic Attack. Cryptagram users who choose weak passwords in the symmetric key scheme can be attacked with dictionary or brute-force techniques. To address this limitation, we encourage users to abide by strong password creation techniques [22, 28] when using symmetric key credentials. When using public key cryptography, we encourage users to leverage the use of a public key infrastructure that is coupled with Cryptagram as we follow Key Continuity Management practices [13].

Copy and Paste. Users who gain access to cleartext images can copy and paste those images to whomever they choose. We believe this problem will persist despite any attempts, short of controlling all hardware at the disposal to humans accessing social networks.

3. IMAGE FORMATS IN OSNS

Several image formats are used across OSNs. While Facebook uses only the JPEG format to store images (and, moreover, strips uploaded images of EXIF data), Google+ and other networks allow for a variety of lossless (e.g., PNG) and lossy (e.g., webp) formats. Our goal is to design a generic photo privacy solution that can work across different image formats. While lossless compression techniques are relatively easier to handle, determining an image encryption/decryption mechanism in the face of a lossy transformation is much more challenging. Given the popularity and broad use of JPEG, we use JPEG as our primary image format to describe the design of Cryptagram. We show how Cryptagram can be easily applied for other image formats including lossy image formats like webp.

Our design primarily focuses on embedding data in the spatial dimensions of an image. We define an embedding protocol to be an algorithm that describes the creation of a sequence of bits and how those bits are embedded into the spatial domain (pixels) of an image. We design embedding algorithms that work in a top-down fashion; that is, the data to be embedded is written into the spatial domain of an image on a pixel level rather than in any protocol-specific manner. We believe that a top-down approach allows us to meet the aim for wide deployablility and applicability in terms of implementation, testing and future image formats. The top-down API means that the design of codecs can apply or be tested across multiple formats with ease. When codec design depends on DCT coefficients, for instance, there are non-intuitive programming interfaces that would be required to make that facility addressable to the PNG format and not just JPEG, webp, and other DCT-coefficient based compression algorithms.

Assuming a passive adversary, this approach is a valid solution to the security threats that we outlined in the previous section. This is an especially prudent design choice considering that lossy image transformations will most intuitively aim to preserve higher order features of an image rather than its bit-wise representation.

The generic interface to the image is thus the four possible color channels red, green, blue, and alpha as well as their corresponding bit value. For JPEG, this means up to eight bits per the first three color channels. For PNG, we have up to 16 bits per channel for all four possible channels.

3.1 Defining q,p-Recoverability for JPEG

JPEG image transformations are inherently lossy in nature. With the aim of probabilistic data integrity, we make concrete the goal of relaxing the constraints of traditional notions of information security data integrity [10] for embedding data in JPEG.

We define the q,p-*JPEG Recoverability* (or, simply q,p-*Recoverability*) property of embedding protocols as follows: given a minimum quality level q that an OSN preserves in a transformation T of an uploaded image, an authorized recipient should be able to decode the original image with high probability p, where in the ideal case $p = 1$. The concept of q,p-Recoverability can also be applied to other lossy image transformations though the corresponding attainable values of q and p are dependent on transformation T.

In the context of JPEG images, we define a Cryptagram protocol as a message-JPEG encoder G and JPEG-message decoder G'. Given an input image[2] I, the first step in Cryptagram encoding is to convert the image into an encrypted sequence of bits $m = E(I, k)$, for clear-text image I and a block cipher key k. We refer to the input to the JPEG encoder as a sequence of bits m. Given m, the protocol encodes m in the spatial domain of a JPEG image, $I_m = G(m)$. JPEG (denoted by the function T, its inverse for decompression is T') compresses I_m at quality q to produce a sequence of bits, $T(I_m, q)$.

The recipient uses a two step decoding mechanism to retrieve an encrypted set of bits m': (a) the first step involves using the decompression step T' to produce $T'(T(I_m, q))$; (b) the second step involves using the JPEG-message de-

---

[2]We mean that I is a sequence of bits that represent an image format that a browser can render. Notably, Cryptagram's embedding can be a used with any arbitrary message I for delivering a message via the spatial domain of a transport image.

$$I_m = G(m)$$

$$G'(T'(T(I_m, q))) = m' =_p m \implies$$

$$G \text{ is } q,p\text{-Recoverable}$$

Figure 3: q,p-Recoverability in a nutshell.

coder G' to retrieve an encrypted sequence of bits $m' = G'(T'(T(I_m, q)))$. Ideally, m' should match m; if they do, the recipient can use the secret key k to decrypt m' to retrieve the original input message. However given the lossy nature of the transformations, the message-JPEG encoding and JPEG-message decoding steps may not always succeed. Here, we use the term p to denote the probability that the algorithm successfully decodes the input bit sequence m. Mathematically, we denote this as: $m' =_p m$. If this constraint holds, then we define the protocol to be q,p-Recoverable. By considering a large sample set of input messages, we can statistically estimate the value of p for a given quality threshold q. The aim of Cryptagram is to identify q,p-Recoverable protocols that attain p close to one for low quality values and a high bits per pixel ratio. We summarize these ideas in Figure 3.

4. SYSTEM DESIGN

4.1 Lossy Images

To discuss how to embed data into a lossy image, we focus on the JPEG compression algorithm, though our design principles apply to other lossy formats.

How should one embed bits into the spatial domain of an image? To approach this challenge, we develop a mapping of bits to colors for specific pixels in an image. Intuitively, when choosing points (coordinates) in the color space to represent bits, we leverage the observation that the lossy codec may *shift* an initially embedded point (pixel's color) during encoding and decoding an image; however, the sphere in the color space within which that point may move does not overlap with other point-centered spheres. This is to say that when choosing what values to embed and how to coordinate pixel values, protocol designers must be sensitive to the assumption that the lossy codec will shift values within spheres in a color space. This intuition guides our JPEG design discussion below but, more importantly, is the generally applicable principle for Cryptagram protocol design.

The principal unit of embedding in Cryptagram is the Cryptagram pixel block (CPB). Multiple CPBs must fill or pack a 8×8 JPEG pixel block (JPB) for each channel of JPEG (luminance, chrominance red and chrominance blue), which is the "atomic unit" of pixels that undergoes JPEG compression [36]. We consider how to pack bits into the spatial domain of JPEG given two goals: (1) efficient bit packing (increasing the number of bits per pixel) and (2) q,p-Recoverability.

4.1.1 Embedding in the Spatial Domain

Cryptagram Pixel Blocks.

For protocol design we examine how to manipulate 64 pixels to embed bits efficiently. We embed symbols into the 64-pixel JPBs for each YC_bC_r channel with multiple Cryptagram pixel blocks (CPBs) per JPB. A CPB could be any shape that packs into a JPB, For our discussion, we consider 1×1 and 2×2 CPBs.

The composition of a CPB thus is a shape description, $w \times h$ (width, height) and a set of rules, R, for translating a symbol, x, or set of bits ($x = b_0, \ldots, b_{|x|}$) into red, green, and blue tuples (r, g, b) that we embed in each pixel of the CPB according to the appropriate $RGB \rightarrow YC_bC_r$ conversion. For simplicity, we represent the CPB embeddings for each channel as $L_{w \times h}^{R_L}$, where R_L are the rules that correspond to the channel, L, how to embed x to color values for L.

Because JPEG compression applies different downsampling and quantization matrices to luminance and chrominance channels (but applies the same compression to the two chrominance channels), we express the embedding protocol for a CPB as:

$$\left(Y_{w_Y \times h_Y}^{R_Y}, C_{w_C \times h_C}^{R_C} \right)$$

where Y corresponds to luminance and C to chrominance channels.

The rule set, R provides a large space for Cryptagram protocol designers. Intuitively, the composition of rules becomes a choice of three parameters: (1) how many bits to embed, (2) the number of discretizations to use (for which the number of bits to embed determines the lower-bound) in the color space, and (3) the choice of which discretization values from the color space to use. In short, we determine how many colors to use, what values they represent, and the resulting bitrate.

The JPEG compression algorithm compresses least the luminance channel of the three yielded by the $RGB \rightarrow Y'C_bC_r$ transformation. If we choose only to discretize values in luminance, we have an effective range of $[0, 255]$, which corresponds to "grayscale". We denote this scenario as $\left(Y_{w_Y \times h_Y}^{R_Y}, C^0 \right)$, using C^0 to denote that chrominance is not used.

On Chrominance Embedding. When considering the use of the chrominance channels in the embedding protocol, there are several complications to address in this proposal. As described in the JPEG specification, the two chrominance channels are stored with significantly less fidelity than luminance. Both chrominance channels are down-sampled (by default in `libjpeg`, 2:1) and a more aggressive quantization table is used to further reduce the number of bits that need to be stored [36]. Intuitively, the chrominance channels are less efficient for embedding data in the spatial domain.

Encoding Algorithm.

We demonstrate the embedding algorithm in Figure 4. As we discuss the embedding algorithm at a high-level, we will refer to the concrete demonstration in that figure.

The first step of the encoding algorithm transforms the input clear-text image I into a sequence of encrypted bits m using a shared key k such that $m = E(I, k)$. Here, we use a standard block cipher algorithm AES in CCM mode (128 bit keys and 64 bit tag size). The encoding algorithm from this point chooses a small collection of bits at a time and converts these bits into Cryptagram pixel blocks. Figure 4 Step A shows how our example encrypted output message m is the sequence of characters, "Security." Using the base64 representation of the character, we know that the sequence

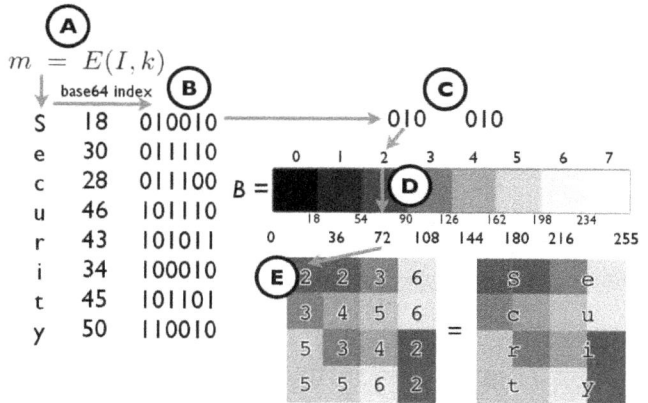

Figure 4: Encoding algorithm illustration. We demonstrate how Cryptagram maps an encrypted message's sequence of bits (Steps A-C) to color values (Step D) and how those correspond to embedded pixels (Step E).

of bits for each character is shown under Step B. We then show in Step C how the sequence of bits for the first character (S's representation as 010010) can be split into two three-bit sequences, the aforementioned "small collection of bits." Using a chunked grayscale color spectrum, we map the three-bits to an index in the array of values. The index's group representative (in this case at Step D, it's the grayscale value of 72) is what is embedded for the appropriate pixels, as shown in Step E. In this example, we continue to pluck off three bits at a time, for Steps B and C, then map those three bits values to grayscale values in Step D. Finally, we continue to embed the values left-to-right, top-to-bottom in this simple example for Step E. We have used a 2×2 CPB for this illustration, which packs perfectly into a standard 8×8 JPB. An alternative format could have used 1×1 CPBs, shading one pixel instead of four in Step E.

Figure 5 illustrates at a high-level where data is embedded in a typical Cryptagram image format.

We make the above example more concrete in the following formalism. An embedding algorithm, a, assumes that b bits will be embedded per CPB. Given b, a has a bijective mapping $B_L : \{0, 1, \ldots, 2^b\} \rightarrow L_a$ where $L_a \subseteq [0, 255]$. Given a bit sequence, s, a uses B_L to map b-length substrings of s to the corresponding L channel values that will be embedded at that particular pixel. Given the notation we have introduced, B is a more specific case of the notion of rule sets R_L we presented earlier. B_L mappings underpin the designs we present in this paper.

We can measure the efficiency of B_L based on b and the size of the channel's CPB to which the output of B_L mapped as $\frac{b}{|CPB|}$ bits per pixel, where $|CPB|$ is the number of pixels occupied by the CPB: $|CPB| = w \times h$.

From our discussion of the embedding protocol and the notion of q, p-Recoverability, we have laid the groundwork for how the designer's choice of protocol parameters ($d_{w,h}$, B, etc.) adjust the effective efficiency of the end-to-end protocol.

Example Encodings for Reasoning about q, p-Recoverability. To demonstrate the tradeoff between efficiency (number of discretizations in B per CPB size) and q, p-Recoverability that we must consider in protocol design, we present two

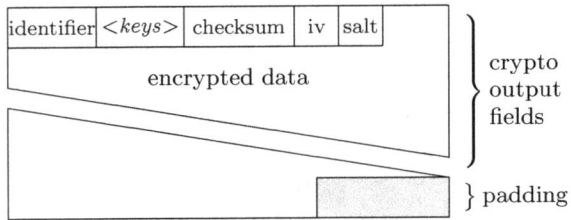

Figure 5: Layout of a Cryptagram. Each box is a sequence of shaded pixels representing the range of values for a particular protocol.

Name	Notation	Luminance-only B Mapping
Bin	$\left(Y_{1\times1}^1, C^0\right)$	$B : \{0,1\} \to \{0,255\}$
Quad	$\left(Y_{1\times1}^2, C^0\right)$	$B : \{0,1,2,3\} \to \{0,85,170,255\}$
Oct	$\left(Y_{1\times1}^3, C^0\right)$	$B : \{0,1,...,7\} \to \{0,36,73,...,255\}$
Hex	$\left(Y_{1\times1}^3, C^0\right)$	$B : \{0,1,...,15\} \to \{0,17,34,...,255\}$

Table 1: We present the B mappings for luminance-only embeddings in order to introduce the Y^n notation as well as illustrate the corresponding luminance values embedded in a Cryptagram using that mapping for the embedding protocol.

examples. The first example uses a $\left(Y_{1\times1}^B, C^0\right)$ CPB. As we translate (according to B) bits from m to successive CPBs color values, we fill the JPB from left-to-right, top-to-bottom, starting in the top-left of the 64 square pixel JPB, covering each channel independently. We can explore multiple color mappings B in order to see how q,p-Recoverability is affected by the $\left(Y_{1\times1}^B, C^0\right)$ CPB and B interaction.

We consider three mappings for B as shown in Table 1. The simplified representations for luminance will be used through this paper. The superscript is the number of bits that can be embedded given the use of equally space values in $[0, 255]$, including extremal values.

Figure 6 illustrates the q,p-Recoverability of these choices. In comparing the best of binary, quadrature, octature, and hexature bits per pixel discretizations for the $\left(Y_{1\times1}^B, C^0\right)$ CPB, we have a sense of how the mapping choices perform relative to one another. Given a social network quality value (for JPEG recompression), we want to choose an embedding that allows for p very close to 1. If we choose the target quality to be 86%, then the values that are actually at $p = 1$ are the Quad and Bin mappings. These yield two and one bits per pixel, respectively. Because we are apt to conservatively choose a quality threshold assuming an OSN may lower their thresholds slightly (e.g., the OSN finds they save enough disk space without causing user experience to suffer too much), we opt to use the Bin approach: $\left(Y_{1\times1}^1, C^0\right)$.

Figure 7 shows the results of our exploration of the chrominance CPB size and the impact of embedding in luminance and chrominance concurrently. We must use 2×2 CPBs in chrominance channels to embed one bit per channel's block (or a cumulative 0.5 bits per pixel gain). We can thus embed in chrominance as a function of the corresponding luminance values.[3] With this approach, we find that embedding more than two values per chrominance channel suffers low q,p-Recoverability. Thus while 4×4 appears to illustrate good q,p-Recoverability in the binary embedding case, we

---

[3]Notably, if the luminance values are at the extremes (0 or 255), then we do not embed a chrominance value in that pixel since no valid chrominance value exists.

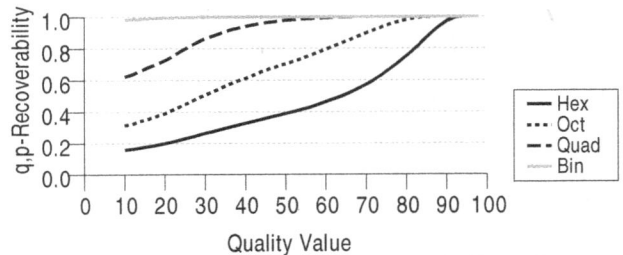

Figure 6: The relative performance of $\left(Y_{1\times1}^B, C^0\right)$ CPBs. We see that more discretizations results in weaker q,p-Recoverability as the quality to which we subject the JPEG to decreases. The tradeoff we must consider is what q,p-Recoverability we want to achieve (what minimum quality do we want a probabilistic guarantee) and how efficient we want for our embedding protocol.

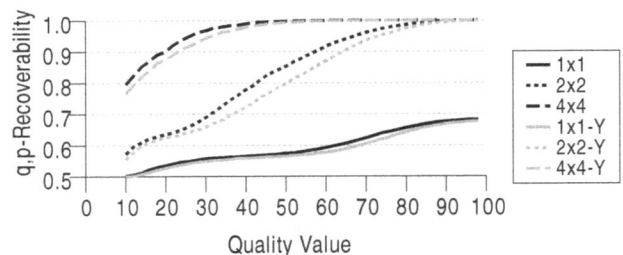

Figure 7: The feasibility of using chrominance to gain additional bits for embedding. All lines correspond to a chrominance B binary mapping. $n \times n$ corresponds to using only chrominance to embed bits using a binary mapping while keeping luminance set to 128. $n \times n$-Y embeds non-128 chrominance values along with chrominance. This plot also highlights the tension of using chrominance in tandem with luminance values. The diminished q,p-Recoverability may appear marginal when we are embedding binary data in the luminance space, but performance degrades significantly. As we explore the applicability of higher bit rates, we must carefully balance the interaction of luminance and chrominance.

think that the efficiency gain is so marginal as to be negligible. Thus we consider the of use $\left(Y_{1\times1}^3, C_{2\times2}^1\right)$ CPBs to gain an additional 0.5 bits per pixel. This gain with chrominance always requires error correction in order to attain q,p-Recoverability that is robust to OSN recompression.

On Decoding. To decode values from a Cryptagram JPEG, the decoder examines pixels in the same order as the encoder. Converting the RGB values to YC_bC_r, the decoding algorithm finds the nearest neighbor for the values in the co-domain of the B mapping for that protocol. The sequence of corresponding domain values is the decoded sequence of bits.

4.1.2 Balancing q,p-Recoverability and Efficiency with Error Correction

Since the nature of protocols that we investigate are probabilistically recoverable (the p in q,p-Recoverability), we consider the use of Error Correcting Codes (ECC) in order to improve the q,p-Recoverability of our protocols while maintaining efficiency of the embedding algorithm. Reed-Solomon codes are of interest to us for their well-understood ECC properties and space efficiency. In our case and especially in Section 6, we use $RS(255, 223)$ protocol, in which we use the $x^8 + x^7 + x^2 + x + 1$, or "0x187", field generator polynomial and 32 bytes for parity in order to recover up to 16 byte errors for a 255 byte transmission. The input to $RS(255, 223)$ is the encrypted output of the block cipher algorithm. With the application of $RS(255, 223)$ then, the q, p-Recoverable protocol directly embeds the output bit stream from $RS(255, 223)$.

From Figure 7, we note how the use of chrominance would always require ECC in order to recover from OSN recompression-induced errors for the CPB case we have highlighted: $\left(Y_{1\times1}^3, C_{2\times2}^1\right)$.

4.2 Lossless Compatibility

Our effort focuses on the JPEG format given its online prevalence, but it's worth noting that our approach is seamlessly compatible with lossless formats such as PNG [8].

In this lossless scenario, we trivially achieve recoverability. The PNG format has a maximum per pixel efficiency of 64 bits per pixel. Each of the four channels, red, green, blue, and alpha, can store 16-bit values. We take 64 bits of sequential data in m, split the 64 bits into four 16-bit segments, then write the respective 16-bit values into each of the four channels of a pixel.

4.3 Easy Key Management and Cryptography

Users have two options for managing access to their photos in Cryptagram: symmetric key cryptosystem or a hybrid (symmetric key and public key) cryptosystem.

In the case of the symmetric key cryptosystem, Cryptagram makes sharing keys easy. A single key can be used for an image, set of images, or an album, and shared amongst a group of friends. This makes key sharing easy and manageable by design, and our Cryptagram browser extension facilitates the use of a password across multiple images or an album by allowing users to store the password. Enabling a strong password to be applied across an entire album of photos means that Cryptagram makes key dissemination easy.

Employing a hybrid cryptosystem by following the principles of *key continuity management* [13] means that the Cryptagram design focuses on guiding the user to use a hybrid cryptosystem correctly. In particular, by (1) limiting the interface for the use of public keys for encryption and private keys only for decryption and (2) using strong defaults for the block cipher and public key cryptography algorithms, Cryptagram reduces the friction to secure and correct use of a hybrid cryptosystem.

For both schemes, users do not share the sensitive information through the social network. We advise users to use a separate channel (e.g., text messaging) to share sensitive credentials (e.g., an album password) so as to conform to the threat model in which Cryptagram is designed to protect users from a hosting OSN.

4.4 Usable Image Identifiers

While Cryptagram facilitates the creation of Cryptagram images, the question remains of how to identify and distinguish gray, fuzzy images for friends. We describe how we enable users to create images that are easier to identify for fellow human users.

Text Watermark: One challenge with the current format is that all output images look virtually identical. This is a problem when, for example, a user asks a friend for a Cryptagram password. Without a file name or album name,

there is no codified way to refer to images. Using a simple extension to the encoding tool, we can enable the user to specify a text or image-based watermark to render underneath the Cryptagram image. A text watermark could specify useful identifiers, such as a URL or an email address for submitting password requests.

Chrominance Watermark: In cases that we do not use the chrominance channels for data transmission, we can use these channels for identification purposes. We modify the C_b and C_r channels to add chrominance to output Cryptagrams and do so without corrupting the luminance payload.

We embed images in these chrominance channels so long as luminance remains unaffected. This watermark is not suitable for embedding most natural images since, perceptually, we rely heavily on luminance, but the technique works well with high-saturation icons or logos.

4.5 Surviving Partial Failures

The current protocol has error correction and can withstand some degree of noise from JPEG but will fail with a cropping transformation. We can extend the basic design to provide cropping robustness by dividing a Cryptagram's payload into smaller units. We encrypt each block with the same password and decryption will involve individually decrypting and concatenating all blocks. If one block fails to decode correctly due to cropping, the integrity of other blocks and their sequence within the original JPEG remain unharmed. Such an approach, however, does not apply to storing arbitrary bit streams, but for images one can replace unrecoverable blocks with zeroes in order to display as much of the original image as possible as shown in Figure 8.

5. IMPLEMENTATION AND DEPLOYMENT

In this section we describe the current state of the applications deployed under the Cryptagram name, including several components and continuously evolving inner protocols. The code is open source and online:

http://github.com/prglab/cryptagram.

5.1 Microbenchmarks

As of the submission of this paper, Cryptagram has over 400 active users (installed and currently present on the user's system) of its Chrome extension, distributed through the Chrome webstore. We request user-consent for an IRB-approved study to gather non-identifying log reports and consent has been granted from 373 unique browser installations.

We built the Chrome Extension with the Closure framework [15], requiring approximately 4000 Source Lines of Code (SLOC) [7, 38], porting the core components to a Firefox add-on with some additional code.

Our benchmarking framework consists of an ECC implementation and benchmarking code, and relies on the Reed-Solomon kernel module code ported to userspace, libjpeg-turbo codec, and a corresponding image interface ported from the Google Chromium browser [35]) (3000 SLOC).

The iOS App uses WebKit's JavaScriptCore to leverage the same cryptographic library as our JavaScript extension whereas the Android App achieves JavaScript integration through a WebKitView (2300 SLOC). These applications enable local Cryptagram encoding and decoding – we do not currently integrate with OSNs. While we do not have

(a) Quality 78　　　　　　(b) Quality 74　　　　　　(c) Quality 70
Figure 8: Partial failure resiliant protocol.

user data for the mobile versions of Cryptagram at this time to present, we have challenges in engineering and usability to consider. With respect to engineering we have found that configuring native cryptographic libraries to be compatible across languages can be a difficult sea to navigate: our wrapping JavaScript libraries results in a performance penalty but simplifies the assurance of algorthmic parity across platforms. We also encounter usability challenges with respect to accessing user's OSN photos from a third-party application. The current aim is to seamlessly integrate with a user's existing social workflow rather than require users to use our product to access their OSNs. If Cryptagram were to be a self-sufficient entity, then we could foresee aiming to encourage user's to see Cryptagram as a portal to their OSNs. Of course, then one must balance the terms of service requirements of OSNs with the information our product reveals or does not reveal to those OSNs.

5.2 Browser Extension Decoder

We implemented the first version of the software as a browser extension, a framework supported by Chrome and Firefox browsers, which allows us to augment the user experience on any website by JavaScript injection.

For our first deployment of Cryptagram we adopted an embedding protocol with a $\left(Y_{2\times2}^3, C^0\right)$ CPB. This protocol also embeds a checksum for verifying the integrity of the decoded encrypted bits. The checksum is not of the cleartext data; it is a checksum of the encrypted data and embedded adjacent to the encrypted data for data integrity purposes.

Decoding in place. Extensions can access pixel data of images on a website. The extensions perform image processing to produce new images to insert into the original image's container, as shown in figure 2. We add a contextual menu item so a user can right-click any image and attempt to decrypt it as a Cryptagram. With the correct credentials, the extension decrypts the original image, which pops into place.

5.3 Web-based Encoder

We wrote the web-based encoder in JavaScript with the Closure Framework, sharing much of the codebase with the decoder extensions. The encoder allows users to drag-and-drop cleartext images onto the encoder page. The drag-and-drop triggers an event to prompt users for a strong password (in the symmetric key case) as well as desired settings (e.g., the preferred tradeoff of a high-resolution, low-quality image or low-resolution, high-quality image). The encryption, encoding, and produced download zip requires no server interaction and thus allows for complete offline operation by end-users.

6. EVALUATION

We now explore the evaluation of the Cryptagram system. We begin with microbenchmarks as well as observations that serve as background for the subsequent evaluations. In particular, we will present the efficiency performance of protocols that we find to be the most useful for end-users and reason about the utility of the current deployment.

6.1 Efficiency Microbenchmarks

With microbenchmarks, we aim to establish a sense of the tangible weight that Cryptagram adds to the user experience of sharing photos as well as the system overhead.

On Browser Performance. We found that the input file size to the encoder and decoder correlated linearly with time to execute. The approximate ratio of time to complete the operation (milliseconds) to input filesize (KB) was 2.684 for the encoder and 1.989 for the decoder on an iMac with 2 x 2.26 Quad Core processors in the Chrome browser (one core for the browser process). While the noticeable human visual reaction time is in the range of 190 to 330 milliseconds [19], the results demonstrate that the overhead of using Cryptagram for viewing OSN photos is marginal.

On File Size. Since the high entropy of Cryptagram counteracts the compressive power of JPEG, the output file size depends entirely on the chosen embedding protocol and constraints imposed by the OSN. For Google+ and Facebook, uploading images have a cap based solely on image dimensions. The authors have found that the maximum upload dimensions in these OSNs is 2048×2048. This means that for a scheme that attains an efficiency of three bits per pixel, we can store at most 1.5 MB in the spatial domain of an uploaded JPEG image.

How does the size of the input data relate to the output Cryptagram image size? The nature of JPEG compression complicates this question. The output Cryptagram image may be saved at 100% quality, creating a large filesize footprint. While this may seem necessary given that we examine q, p-Recoverability with respect to the compression applied by an OSN, the composition of JPEG compression is neither idempotent nor cleanly-defined recursively. Instead, as we explore later in this section, we consider the observed error rates of compressing already-compressed Cryptagram images (simulating what an OSN would do).

Table 2 shows the expansion ratio from a given input size. For the case of a $\left(Y_{1\times1}^3, C^0\right)$ CPB with an output Cryptagram image with JPEG compression 70, the filesize on disk inflation is $1.4\times$.

For the sake of minimizing upload bandwidth, users may opt to export Cryptagram images with less than 100% quality and Cryptagram will still guarantee q, p-Recoverability within a certain range.

6.2 Compressing the Compressed

Apropos to the question of file size expansion, we examine the implications of a recompressed Cryptagram JPEG on q, p-Recoverability. Figure 9 shows the effects of exporting

	$(Y_{1\times1}^3, C^0)$			$(Y_{1\times1}^1, C^0)$		
Quality:	90	80	70	90	70	50
Expansion:	2.25	1.75	1.40	7.82	5.29	4.39

Table 2: We present the tabular data that illustrates the file size expansion when using various protocol choices in the Cryptagram framework.

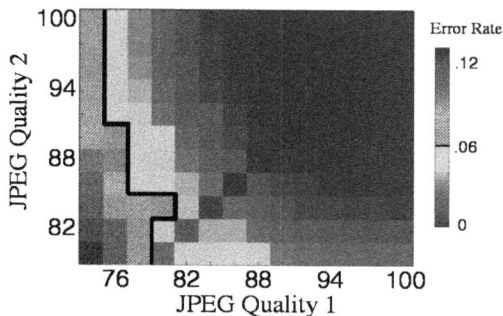

Figure 9: The effects of recompressing a compressed JPEG. The x-axis shows the quality of the original Cryptagram JPEG. The y-axis shows the recompressed quality of the JPEG. The line separating striped versus unstriped values is the q, p-Recoverability threshold we encounter with $RS(255, 223)$. Any values to the right of the 0.06 line show the successive recompressions that Cryptagram can tolerate for $(Y_{1\times1}^3, C^0)$. Error rates were determined by testing approximately 2,400 pseudorandom 8×8 images at each combination of quality levels.

a Cryptagram to a JPEG Quality 1 and then (as an OSN would do) recompressing the image at JPEG Quality 2. The error rate indicates the fraction of CPBs that were broken through successive recompression. This data indicates that we can export Cryptagram JPEGs to 82% quality and OSNs' recompression still permits recoverability, assuming that we leverage $RS(255, 223)$ ECC.

6.3 OSN Photo Quality

As much of our evaluation relates error rates to JPEG quality level, we want to know the JPEG settings employed by popular OSNs. To estimate these quality levels, we exported a variety of images as quality 95 JPEGs, uploaded those images to both Facebook and Google+, then re-downloaded the images for analysis.

On Google+, 30 such test images came back bitwise identical, meaning images were not recompressed.[4]

Facebook, on the other hand, applies JPEG compression to save disk space. After downloading images from Facebook, we looked for evidence of quality in the JPEG headers. Out of 30 natural images, 25 came back with a JPEG quantization matrix exactly equivalent to that of a quality 74 JPEG, the other five having matrices equivalent to JPEG qualities in the range of 76 to 86.

Fortunately for Cryptagram, high entropy images all appear similarly to the JPEG algorithm and are treated predictably when uploaded to Facebook. All test Cryptagrams uploaded then downloaded came back with the quantization matrix from a quality 85 or 87 JPEG, which we measured by explicitly examining the quantization tables of the down-

---

[4]Google+ does recompress images for quicker display during album browsing but it is trivial to convert any such hyperlinks to their full-resolution equivalents.

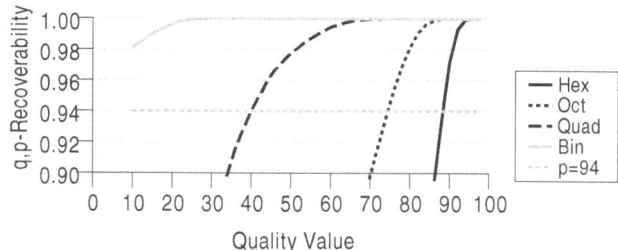

Figure 10: This indicates to us the feasibility of leveraging $RS(255, 223)$ to improve the q, p-Recoverability with various $(Y_{1\times1}^B, C^0)$ embedding protocols.

loaded JPEG file. This quality level puts us safely above the necessary threshold of our deployed embedding protocol.

6.4 Embeddings with ECC

In this section, we examine the benefit of using ECC to reconcile the tradeoffs we must consider between efficiency and q, p-Recoverability. We presented in Section 4 the performance of the $(Y_{1\times1}^B, C^0)$ CPB for various B mappings. From that experience, we conclude that a protocol without error correction is limited to using quad or bin mapping strategies.

We examine the utility of applying our ECC algorithm of choice for embedding data to measure q, p-Recoverability in lower quality regimes of JPEG compression. With the use of $RS(255, 223)$ for ECC, we note that we embed 14% extra data for the recovery so our subsequent evaluation considers the effective efficiency of a system that adds this data overhead.

Figure 10 allows us to explore the design space of applying ECC to evaluate the q, p-Recoverability for given $(Y_{1\times1}^B, C^0)$ luminance-only embedding schemes. We see that the Bin, Quad and Oct embedding schemes perform above p=94 in the regime around 85%, thus enabling us to achieve q, p-Recoverability on Facebook.

Figure 11 illustrates the benefit of using luminance and chrominance embeddings in order to achieve 3.5 bits per pixel embedding efficiency for q, p-Recoverability that satisfies OSN recompression and ECC. In the interest of saving space, we do not show the q, p-Recoverability curves, but instead summarize the details relevant to the ECC discussion in Table 3. Given that ECC with $RS(255, 223)$ recovers up to 16 bytes ($\approx 6.27\%$) of damaged bytes for every 255 bytes of data, we can establish our target recoverability probability at $\approx 94\%$; in other words, if less than 6% of bytes break then applying ECC enables us to use that particular encoding scheme. We highlight in Table 3 the q, p-Recoverable protocol that we choose for Cryptagram.

This efficiency is superior to X-pire! [1], which had a capacity of two bits per pixel with ECC. We have $1.75\times$ this capacity, significant considering the size and quality of images this enables users to upload to OSNs.

Comparison with Steganographic Efficiency.
Though the goals of steganography and Cryptagram differ, both embed data in images, so we can compare the two in terms of bits/pixel efficiency.

Related work has expounded on the efficiency of steganographic embeddings [5, 37], reducing the approach to one embedding p message bits into $2^p - 1$ pixels, yielding a rela-

		Without ECC		With ECC ($RS(255,223)$)			
lum $\lvert B \rvert$		q, 100-Rec (quality)	Efficiency (bits/pix)	q, 94-Rec (quality)	Effective Efficiency	Lum+Chrom q, 94-Rec	Efficiency (bits/pix)	Effective Efficiency
Hex		-	-	90	3.5	90	4.5	3.94
Oct		90	3	76	2.62	77	3.5	3.06
Quad		80	2	44	1.75	66	2.5	2.19
Bin		< 20	1	< 10	0.87	38	1.5	1.31

Table 3: Summary of the results that inform how to proceed with applying $RS(255,223)$ FEC for embedding values in JPEGs that are recompressible.

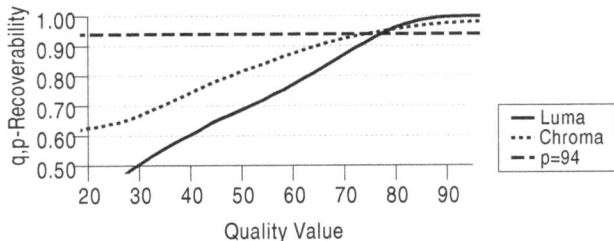

Figure 11: This indicates the feasibility of leveraging $RS(255,223)$ to improve the q,p-Recoverability of a $\left(Y_{1\times1}^3, C_{2\times2}^1\right)$ protocol.

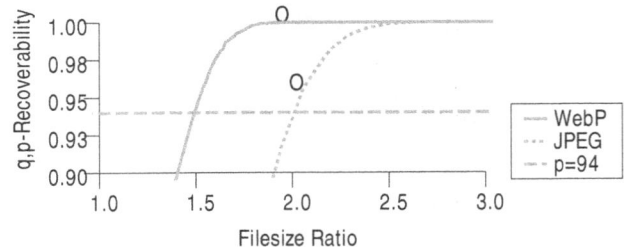

Figure 12: Showing the comparison of JPEG and lossy webp recoverability vs. filesize ratio. We draw the reader's attention to the $p = 94$ threshold as a point of comparison with the ECC studies in the rest of this paper. We acknowledge that JPEG and webp quality settings are not related and cannot be directly compared. However, this figure shows that for a similar notion of q,p-Recoverability, webp has a smaller filesize expansion than JPEG to achieve the same probability of recovery. To note the distinction in the meaning of "quality" between libjpeg and webp, we highlight the points along the curves where quality is 74 for each codec.

tive payload of $\alpha = p/(2^p - 1)$. While steganography choose slightly higher values of p a low value of p yields 0.42 bits per pixel for $p = 3$. In the highlighted row, our effective efficiency is 3.06 bits per pixel. In comparison, our approach represents a minimum 7.5× improvement.

6.5 File Format Embedding Comparison

In Figure 12, we show the q,p-Recoverability versus filesize ratio of JPEG versus webp image compression formats. By file ratio, we mean the on-disk size of the output image format for the same image canvas input. Notably, the embeddings are always three bits per pixel in the Figure. We see that for the same probability of recovery, p, webp has a much smaller filesize ratio than JPEG. As OSNs besides Google+ begin to experiment with webp deployment [32], the opportunity for lower bandwidth and storage requirements while maintaining q,p-Recoverability means that Cryptagram can be applied as improved media compression formats are adopted.

6.6 Deployment Usage Data

At the time of submission, Cryptagram has nearly 400 active installations, with 373 users agreeing to participate in our IRB-approved study. Through this study, we receive high-level data about the Cryptagram encryption and decryption habits of our users. The following data does not include the authors' own tests or images. We have had more than 3,300 Cryptagram image decryption events with more than 160 unique encrypted images generated. Of the decrypted images, we can confirm that 102 unique images have been decrypted from Facebook and 217 unique images from Google+.

7. DISCUSSION

Applicability of q,p-Recoverability to Lossy Formats. OSNs continue to use lossy image formats in order to reduce demands on storage infrastructure and reduce delivery latencies to end-users. Recently developed formats shoud be considered given these goals. We have begun to examine the webp [16] format for Cryptagram. The tool of q,p-Recoverability applies in the analysis of these formats given that the spatial domain pixel value is the key component of Cryptagram communication.

Transformations. We aim to handle a variety of transformations with the development of q,p-Recoverable protocols. In previous sections, we discussed the design and evaluated our protocols' q,p-Recoverability with respect to the JPEG transformation. We have begun prototyping our approach to cropping and noising transformations on images produced by Cryptagram as well, leveraging blocking algorithms coupled with ECC. While we do not address rotation explicitly, we do not consider such a transformation intractable as we apply techniques from QR Codes (two dimensional barcodes) by orienting corner features in future iterations.

Scaling transformations are of interest given the pervasiveness of lower resolution images (e.g., thumbnails) to partially depict images on a social networking website. We have considered the integration of pyramid representations [3, 6] in the design of future embedding protocols to meet this transformation request.

The Economics of Privacy. Our culture values greatly the power of images to document and record in ways that words simply cannot. We say *seeing is believing*. Images convey a range of human experience, and unfortunately, that includes images that can irrevocably damage a person's reputation.

OSNs offer privacy features and third parties have even developed commercial products to address photo privacy. McAfee Social Protection lets users store cleartext photos on their server while uploading blurred versions to Facebook, then facilitates access requests [30]. This superficially addresses photo privacy, but in the end, amounts to an escrow service that redirects trust from one third party to another.

Our optimistic vision for this project is that its adoption could articulate to OSNs that users desire increased ownership over personal data. We envision a scenario in which an OSN embraces the philosophy of Cryptagram and provides client-side tools to make end-to-end encryption feasible. Wide adoption of Cryptagram would require more storage for the encrypted files and may create less potential for targeted advertising.

8. RELATED WORK

P3 [29] examined the use of non-colluding services to store minimally-revealing cleartext images in one service and encrypted versions of DCT coefficients of JPEG images in another service. Their system experienced a 10-20% file size increase from the original compressed image when one follows their recommended privacy-preserving settings by setting the DCT-hiding threshold in the range $T \in [10, 20]$. The authors acknowledged their technique's vulnerability to face identification when $T \geq 35$. Cryptagram fundamentally differs from P3 in two ways. First, Cryptagram completely avoids the use of third parties. Secondly, Cryptagram works only in the encrypted bit space and does not expose any unencrypted data to the end-user. Unless users' keys are compromised, users cannot have their faces detected with any of our embedding protocols.

Steganography. Cryptagram is superficially reminiscent of various attempts to embed cryptographic data in JPEG through traditional steganographic techniques [11], but differs significantly from conventional JPEG steganography. Cryptagram makes obvious that it is hiding data to attain greater efficiency, and furthermore, does so in a way that is robust to image compression, which steganography generally is not. Attempts to achieve lossy compression tolerant steganography are early works with inefficient results [17].

One recent work attempted to embed data in JPEG DCT coefficients without the steganographic constraint of being hidden. The non-linearities of DCT quantization and rounding in standard compression and decompression required very conservative data embedding that resulted in efficiency significantly lower than what we were able to achieve [1].

Li et al. [20] address the concern of hiding data within DCT coefficients but shuffle the DCT coefficients between blocks that then are quantized during the JPEG compression algorithm. Likewise, Poller et al. demonstrate that DCT coefficient permutation and spatial domain permutation do provide some security features but do not address efficiency or prove the correctness of their security mechanism [26].

A formalization for the description of the embeddings that we use in Cryptagram have been explored by Galand and Kabatiansky [12] but the authors do not explore how to construct such protocols.

But Cheddad et al. [4] claim that spatial domain techniques are not robust against noise, only work in bitmap-formatted images, and are not robust against lossy compression and image filters. Cryptagram overcomes all of these drawbacks in spatial domain embedding and demonstrates the useful privacy and security properties that can be available for OSN photo sharing. Cryptagram achieves

q, p-Recoverability in the face of the complete recompression of the JPEG image containing sensitive information.

9. CONCLUSIONS

The advent of popular online social networking has resulted in the compromise of traditional notions of privacy, especially in visual media. In order to facilitate convenient and principled protection of photo privacy online, we have presented the design, implementation, and evaluation of Cryptagram, a system that efficiently and correctly protects users photo privacy across popular OSNs. We have introduced q, p-Recoverability and demonstrated Cryptagram's ability to embed cryptographic primitives correctly to attain q, p-Recoverability through JPEG compression in our implementation.

Acknowledgments: We would like to thank Helen Nissenbaum, Alex Rubinsteyn, David Iserovich, the members of the NYU Networking and Wide-area Systems Group, the members of the NYU Privacy Research Group, our shepherd Steven Bellovin, and the anonymous COSN reviewers for their helpful comments. This work was supported in part by the NSF (grant 0966187) and in part by the ONR (contract N000141210327). The views and conclusions contained in this document are those of the authors and should not be interpreted as necessarily representing the official policies, either expressed or implied, of any of the sponsors.

10. REFERENCES

[1] BACKES, J., BACKES, M., DÜRMUTH, M., GERLING, S., AND LORENZ, S. X-pire! - a digital expiration date for images in social networks. *CoRR abs/1112.2649* (2011).

[2] BOYD, D. M., AND ELLISON, N. B. Social network sites: Definition, history, and scholarship. *Journal of Computer-Mediated Communication 13*, 1 (2007), 210–230.

[3] BURT, P. J. Fast filter transform for image processing. *Computer graphics and image processing 16*, 1 (1981), 20–51.

[4] CHEDDAD, A., CONDELL, J., CURRAN, K., AND MC KEVITT, P. Digital image steganography: Survey and analysis of current methods. *Signal Processing 90*, 3 (2010), 727–752.

[5] CRANDALL, R. Some notes on steganography. *Posted on steganography mailing list* (1998).

[6] CROWLEY, J. L. A representation for visual information. Tech. Rep. CMU-RI-TR-82-07, Robotics Institute, Pittsburgh, PA, November 1981.

[7] DANIEL, A. CLOC: Count Lines of Code. http://cloc.sourceforge.net/.

[8] DUCE, D., AND BOUTELL, T. Portable network graphics (png) specification. *Information technology ISO/IEC 15948* (2003), 2003.

[9] DUELL, M. Mark Zuckerberg's private Facebook photos revealed: Security 'glitch' allows web expert to access billionaire's personal pictures. *The Daily Mail (MailOnline)* (December 2011). http://www.dailymail.co.uk/news/article-2070749/Facebook-security-glitch-reveals-Mark-Zuckerbergs-private-photos.html.

[10] FINKENZELLER, K. *Data Integrity*. Wiley Online Library, 2003.

[11] FRIDRICH, J. *Steganography in Digital Media: Principles, Algorithms, and Applications*. Cambridge University Press, 2009.

[12] GALAND, F., AND KABATIANSKY, G. Information hiding by coverings. In *Information Theory Workshop,*

2003. *Proceedings. 2003 IEEE* (2003), IEEE, pp. 151–154.

[13] GARFINKEL, S. L., AND MILLER, R. C. Johnny 2: a user test of key continuity management with s/mime and outlook express. In *Proceedings of the 2005 symposium on Usable privacy and security* (2005), ACM, pp. 13–24.

[14] GOOD, J. How many photos have ever been taken? http://blog.1000memories.com/94-number-of-photos-ever-taken-digital-and-analog-in-shoebox.

[15] GOOGLE. Closure Tools. https://developers.google.com/closure/.

[16] GOOGLE. webp: A new image format for the Web. https://developers.google.com/speed/webp/.

[17] HWANG, R.-J., SHIH, T., KAO, C.-H., AND CHANG, T.-M. Lossy compression tolerant steganography. In *The Human Society and the Internet Internet-Related Socio-Economic Issues*, W. Kim, T.-W. Ling, Y.-J. Lee, and S.-S. Park, Eds., vol. 2105 of *Lecture Notes in Computer Science*. Springer Berlin / Heidelberg, 2001, pp. 427–435.

[18] JOHNSON, M., EGELMAN, S., AND BELLOVIN, S. M. Facebook and privacy: it's complicated. In *SOUPS '12: Proceedings of the Eighth Symposium on Usable Privacy and Security* (2012).

[19] KOSINSKI, R. J. A literature review on reaction time. *Clemson University 10* (2008).

[20] LI, W., AND YU, N. A robust chaos-based image encryption scheme. In *Multimedia and Expo, 2009. ICME 2009. IEEE International Conference on* (2009), IEEE, pp. 1034–1037.

[21] LIN, K.-Y., AND LU, H.-P. Why people use social networking sites: An empirical study integrating network externalities and motivation theory. *Computers in Human Behavior 27*, 3 (2011), 1152–1161.

[22] MICROSOFT SAFETY SECURITY CENTER. Create strong passwords, 2013. http://www.microsoft.com/security/online-privacy/passwords-create.aspx.

[23] NISSENBAUM, H. *Privacy in context: Technology, policy, and the integrity of social life*. Stanford Law Books, 2009.

[24] PARR, B. Facebook by the Numbers. http://mashable.com/2011/10/21/facebook-infographic/.

[25] PFEIL, U., ARJAN, R., AND ZAPHIRIS, P. Age differences in online social networking–a study of user profiles and the social capital divide among teenagers and older users in myspace. *Computers in Human Behavior 25*, 3 (2009), 643–654.

[26] POLLER, A., STEINEBACH, M., AND LIU, H. Robust image obfuscation for privacy protection in web 2.0 applications. In *Society of Photo-Optical Instrumentation Engineers (SPIE) Conference Series* (2012), vol. 8303, p. 1.

[27] POWELL, J. *33 million people in the room: how to create, influence, and run a successful business with social networking*. Ft Press, 2008.

[28] PRINCETON UNIVERSITY OFFICE OF INFORMATION TECHNOLOGY IT SECURITY. Tips for creating strong, easy-to-remember passwords, 2013. http://www.princeton.edu/itsecurity/basics/passwords/.

[29] RA, M.-R., GOVINDAN, R., AND ORTEGA, A. P3: Toward Privacy-Preserving Photo Sharing. In *Proceedings of the 10th USENIX Symposium on Networked Systems Design and Implementation* (2013), USENIX Association.

[30] SECURITY, M. McAfee Social Protection. https://apps.facebook.com/socialprotection/.

[31] SENGUPTA, S., AND OâĂŹBRIEN, K. J. Facebook Can ID Faces, but Using Them Grows Tricky. *The New York Times* (2012).

[32] SHANKLAND, S. Facebook tries Google's WebP image format. http://news.cnet.com/8301-1023_3-57580664-93/facebook-tries-googles-webp-image-format-users-squawk.

[33] STONE, Z., ZICKLER, T., AND DARRELL, T. Toward large-scale face recognition using social network context. *Proceedings of the IEEE 98*, 8 (2010), 1408–1415.

[34] TAPSCOTT, D. *Grown Up Digital: How the Net Generation is Changing Your World HC*, 1 ed. Mcgraw-Hill, 2008.

[35] THE CHROMIUM AUTHORS. libjpeg | The Chromium Projects. http://src.chromium.org/viewvc/chrome/trunk/src/third_party/libjpeg/.

[36] UNION, I. T. Digital Compression and Coding of Continuous-tone Still images. CCITT Rec. T.81, 1992.

[37] WESTFELD, A., AND PFITZMANN, A. High capacity despite better steganalysis (f5–a steganographic algorithm). In *Information Hiding, 4th International Workshop* (2001), vol. 2137, Pittsburgh, PA, pp. 289–302.

[38] WHEELER, D. SLOCCount. http://www.dwheeler.com/sloccount/.

[39] ZIMMERMANN, P. R. *The official PGP user's guide*. MIT press, 1995.

APPENDIX

A. APPENDIX

A.1 JPEG Review

JPEG is a lossy codec designed to provide reasonable tradeoffs between compression and recoverability of the original image [36]. We chose JPEG because of its prevalence on the web and the availability of efficient JPEG libraries. Here we review the core elements of JPEG that affect our protocol design.

Transformations.

The first step in compressing an input bitmap image, M to JPEG is a color space transformation. In particular, JPEG transforms every pixel in M from the RGB to the YC_bC_r color space through a linear transformation that converts red, green, and blue (RGB) pixel values to luminance (Y), chrominance blue (C_b), and chrominance red (C_r) values.

$$Y' = (0.299 \cdot R'_D) + (0.587 \cdot G'_D) + (0.114 \cdot B'_D)$$
$$C_B = 128 - (0.168736 \cdot R'_D) - (0.331264 \cdot G'_D) + (0.5 \cdot B'_D)$$
$$C_R = 128 + (0.5 \cdot R'_D) - (0.418688 \cdot G'_D) - (0.081312 \cdot B'_D)$$

After the color space transformation, the JPEG algorithm transforms the three color channels of YC_bC_r independently.

Subsampling.

Following the initial color space transformation, JPEG subsamples the color channels. In the default `libjpeg` codec settings, luminance is not subsampled while chrominance blue and chrominance red data undergo 2:1 subsampling vertically and horizontally, also known as "4:2:0" subsampling. This results in one-fourth the number of pixels that represent each of the original chrominance blue and chrominance red channels.

Discrete Cosine Transform.

The output matrices of subsampling are then transformed using the Discrete Cosine Transform. Since the DCT for JPEG operates only on 8×8 pixel blocks, JPEG breaks each of the subsampled spaces into non-overlapping 8×8 pixel blocks. This paper we will refer to these units as JPEG Pixel Blocks or JPBs.

The DCT is a well-understood transformation from the spatial to frequency domain. We present the two dimensional DCT here:

$$G_{u,v} = \sum_{x=0}^{7} \sum_{y=0}^{7} \alpha(u)\alpha(v)g_{x,y} \cos\left[\frac{\pi}{8}\left(x+\frac{1}{2}\right)u\right] \cos\left[\frac{\pi}{8}\left(y+\frac{1}{2}\right)v\right],$$

where $u \in \{0, 1, \ldots, 7\}$ is the horizontal spatial frequency; $v \in \{0, 1, \ldots, 7\}$ is the vertical spatial frequency;

$$\alpha(u) = \begin{cases} \sqrt{\frac{1}{8}}, & \text{if } u = 0 \\ \sqrt{\frac{2}{8}}, & \text{otherwise} \end{cases}$$

is a normalizing scale factor to maintain orthonormality; $g_{x,y}$ is the pixel value at coordinates (x, y); and $G_{u,v}$ is the DCT coefficient at coordinates (u, v). The two dimensional DCT,

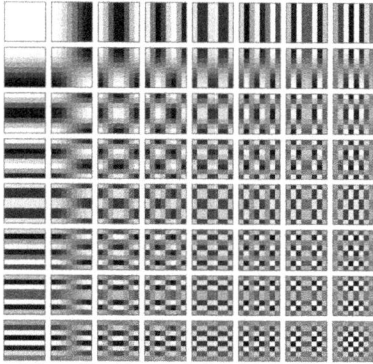

Figure 13: Visualization of the 64 DCT basis functions.

computed on each 8×8 block of pixels in an image, results in 64 coefficients per block; the visual representation of which is in Figure 13.

Quantization.

The DCT returns real values but we have to represent them on disk with limited precision. The JPEG codec stores each of the 64 coefficients not as a float but as a single 8-bit number that, combined with the quantization matrix, can approximate a real number.

Here is the standard luminance quantization table in JPEG.

$$\begin{bmatrix} 16 & 11 & 10 & 16 & 24 & 40 & 51 & 61 \\ 12 & 12 & 14 & 19 & 26 & 58 & 60 & 55 \\ 14 & 13 & 16 & 24 & 40 & 57 & 69 & 56 \\ 14 & 17 & 22 & 29 & 51 & 87 & 80 & 62 \\ 18 & 22 & 37 & 56 & 68 & 109 & 103 & 77 \\ 24 & 35 & 55 & 64 & 81 & 104 & 113 & 92 \\ 49 & 64 & 78 & 87 & 103 & 121 & 120 & 101 \\ 72 & 92 & 95 & 98 & 112 & 100 & 103 & 99 \end{bmatrix}$$

And for chrominance:

$$\begin{bmatrix} 17 & 18 & 24 & 47 & 99 & 99 & 99 & 99 \\ 18 & 21 & 26 & 66 & 99 & 99 & 99 & 99 \\ 24 & 26 & 56 & 99 & 99 & 99 & 99 & 99 \\ 47 & 66 & 99 & 99 & 99 & 99 & 99 & 99 \\ 99 & 99 & 99 & 99 & 99 & 99 & 99 & 99 \\ 99 & 99 & 99 & 99 & 99 & 99 & 99 & 99 \\ 99 & 99 & 99 & 99 & 99 & 99 & 99 & 99 \\ 99 & 99 & 99 & 99 & 99 & 99 & 99 & 99 \end{bmatrix}$$

This means, for example, that to approximate the value 99.0 for the 0th (pure DC) component, we would write the integer $\lfloor \frac{99.0}{16} \rfloor = 6$. In short, the lower the value in the quantization matrix, the greater the precision for preservation of that particular DCT coefficient. By scaling all values in the quantization table, JPEG prioritizes lower frequencies (which are more obvious to the human eye) while allowing end-users to achieve a range of qualities.

Chrominance red and chrominance blue use a separate quantization matrix which is more heavily quantized, since the human eye is less sensitive to variations in chrominance than luminance [36].

Entropy Coding.

Once JPEG computes the quantized values, JPEG losslessly writes these values to disk. This deterministic operation provides the biggest savings for bytes on disk. In particular, values are zigzag encoded, meaning that the order of values written to disk follows a zigzag pattern. Any repeated values in the zigzag ordered list JPEG writes as a compressed value; e.g., the JPEG algorithm dictates writing 20 sequential 0's as 20{0}. The benefits of this process is a reduced amount of disk space required to represent the values.

A.1.1 Decoding JPEG

Dequantization.

Given the original JPEG quantization matrix in the JPEG file, the decompression algorithm multiplies the values read from disk with the corresponding quantization matrix entries.

Inverse DCT.

JPEG applies the inverse DCT function to each set of 64 dequantized coefficients to produce the lossy output 8×8 block of pixels.

Shifting and Upsampling Chrominance.

Values in all of color spaces are then shifted up by 128 to be within the valid display ranges again. JPEG upsamples chrominance accordingly.

Conversion from YC_bC_r to RGB.

Finally, JPEG executes the last linear transformation between YC_bC_r to RGB to present a human comprehensible RGB image.

$$R = Y + 1.402 \cdot (C_R - 128)$$
$$G = Y - 0.34414 \cdot (C_B - 128) - 0.71414 \cdot (C_R - 128)$$
$$B = Y + 1.772 \cdot (C_B - 128)$$

Tweeting Under Pressure: Analyzing Trending Topics and Evolving Word Choice on Sina Weibo

Le Chen
College of Computer and
Information Science
Northeastern University
Boston, MA USA
leonchen@ccs.neu.edu

Chi Zhang
College of Computer and
Information Science
Northeastern University
Boston, MA USA
czhang79@ccs.neu.edu

Christo Wilson
College of Computer and
Information Science
Northeastern University
Boston, MA USA
cbw@ccs.neu.edu

ABSTRACT

In recent years, social media has risen to prominence in China, with sites like Sina Weibo and Renren each boasting hundreds of millions of users. Social media in China plays a profound role as a platform for breaking news and political commentary that is not available in the state-sanctioned news media. However, like all websites in China, Chinese social media is subject to censorship. Although several studies have identified censorship on Weibo and Chinese blogs, to date no studies have examined the overall impact of censorship on discourse in social media.

In this study, we examine how censorship impacts discussions on Weibo, and how users adapt to avoid censorship. We gather tweets and comments from 280K politically active Weibo users for 44 days and use NLP techniques to identify trending topics. We observe that the magnitude of censorship varies dramatically across topics, with 82% of tweets in some topics being censored. However, we find that censorship of a topic correlates with high user engagement, suggesting that censorship does not stifle discussion of sensitive topics. Furthermore, we find that users adopt variants of words (known as *morphs*) to avoid keyword-based censorship. We analyze emergent morphs to learn how they are adopted and spread by the Weibo user community.

Categories and Subject Descriptors

J.4 [**Computer Applications**]: Social and behavioral sciences; K.5.2 [**Governmental Issues**]: Censorship

Keywords

Online social networks; Sina Weibo; Trending topics

1. INTRODUCTION

In recent years, social media has risen to prominence in China. Sina Weibo (the Chinese equivalent of Twitter, abbreviated as *Weibo*) boasts 500 million users [45], and Renren (the Chinese equivalent of Facebook) boasts 172 million users [22]. Like people the world over, Chinese users flock to these platforms as places to

socialize and share content. However, social media in China also plays a more profound role as a platform for breaking news and political commentary that is not available in the state-sanctioned news media. For example, Weibo played a key role in the downfall of once-prominent politician Bo Xilai [17].

Like all websites in China, Chinese social media is subject to government-enforced content regulation policies. The primary manifestation of these regulations is censorship, which is known to impact Chinese blogs [25] and Weibo. Current work disagrees on the scope of censorship on Weibo, with estimates ranging from 0.01% [42] to 16% [7] of all "weibos" (*a.k.a.* tweets on Weibo) being censored. Users who discuss political issues [42, 49] and minority groups [7] tend to incur the brunt of censorship. In fact, it is hypothesized that Weibo employs thousands of crowdsourced workers to manually examine and censor the huge volume of tweets that are generated each day [49]. Thus, tweets may be visible for minutes, hours, or even days before they are censored, giving researchers an opportunity to download and analyze them.

Although it is no secret that tweets on Weibo are censored, how censorship is applied and the impact that it has on discourse is currently unknown. In this study, we seek to answer two key questions: *first*, what is the impact of censorship on discourse on Weibo? In other words, is censorship effective at chilling or even halting discussion on Weibo? *Second*, do Weibo users adapt in order to avoid censorship? Anecdotal evidence suggests that users may use *morphs* to avoid keyword-based censorship [7, 42], *e.g.,* 储君 (crown prince) instead of 习近平 (Xi Jinping, the current president of China). However, it is unknown whether this theory is true, and if so, what the dynamics of morph generation are. These two questions get at the heart of the conflict between information dissemination and censorship in the highly dynamic, human-driven social media space.

To answer these questions, we break our study down into three major components. *First*, we conduct a large scale crawl of Weibo for 44 days. Our crawl targeted a connected component of 280,250 users who are active on Weibo. The crawler implemented a prioritization system where users who tweet more frequently were crawled more frequently. This enabled the crawler to gather most censored tweets before they were deleted (censorship can then be identified after-the-fact). In total, our crawl gathered 36.5M tweets, 1% of which were censored. We observe that censorship is not applied uniformly, *e.g.,* 82% of tweets from one particularly contentious topic were censored, while up to 50% of tweets from some celebrity users were censored.

In addition to tweets, our crawler also gathered all of the *comments* on each tweet. Comments on Weibo function like comments on Facebook, *i.e.,* users append them to existing tweets. Unlike prior studies of censorship on Weibo, ours is the first to examine both tweets and comments. This distinction is important, because, as we show in § 4.2, there are an order of magnitude more comments than tweets on Weibo.

Second, we leverage Latent Dirichlet Allocation (LDA) [9] to extract 37 trending topics from our crawled data. Each one of these topics corresponds to a real-world event (*e.g.,* the Boston marathon bombing, Ya'an Earthquake, *etc.*), and several were heavily censored (*e.g.,* a Sichuan official who was criticized following the Ya'an earthquake, an incident between President Xi and a Beijing taxi driver, *etc.*). Across these topics, we analyze the relationship between the magnitude of censorship and the characteristics exhibited by the topic (*e.g.,* number of engaged users, tweets per user, *etc.*). Contrary to our expectations, we find that users are more active in discussing censored topics, indicating that censorship does not have a chilling effect on discussion on Weibo.

Third and finally, we examine the usage of morphs on Weibo. We find that 11 of our 37 topics include morphs, in some cases up to 5 morphs per topic. Although we observe that many uncensored topics include morphs for comedic or satirical effect (*e.g.,* 黑十字 (Black Cross) in place of 红十字 (Red Cross)), we also find that morph usage dramatically increases within censored topics. Temporal analysis reveals that morph usage increases rapidly within hours of censorship being implemented, suggesting that users adapt their word usage to circumvent censorship.

We view this study as a first step towards understanding the impact of censorship on discourse in social media, rather than simply quantifying the scope of censorship. This study lays the foundation for updating existing information dissemination models, or developing new ones, that take adversarial forces into account. Our results also point towards new techniques for identifying and predicting censorship, by using language models to observe when words usage changes (*i.e.,* morphs) in otherwise unexpected ways.

2. BACKGROUND

We begin by briefly introducing Sina Weibo, comparing its features to Twitter, and discussing government regulation of the Web in China.

2.1 Sina Weibo

Sina Weibo (referred to as Weibo) is the most popular microblogging website in China. Weibo first launched in August 2009 and by December 2012, it had ≈500 million users. Over 4.6 million users are active on a daily basis, and over 100 million weibos (*a.k.a.* a tweet on Weibo) are posted every day [44, 45]. As of April 2013, Alexa shows that Weibo is the No.6 website in China, and No.29 website globally.

Weibo provides similar functionality to Twitter. Users can *follow* other users and view their tweets in a timeline. Users post 140-Unicode-character tweets which can include URLs, pictures, videos, geotags, *retweets*, *@mentions*, and *#hashtags*. Each Weibo user has a personal profile that may include basic information (*e.g.,* hobbies, hometown, *etc.*) as well as statistics (*e.g.,* total tweets, followers, and followings). Like Twitter, Weibo users can be "verified," *i.e.,* manually vetted by Weibo staff to confirm their identity.

Weibo also offers some features that are similar to Facebook. Weibo users may *like* and/or attach *comments* to tweets. Weibo users may also prepend 140-character messages to retweets. The ability to comment gives conversations on Weibo a well-defined, multi-layered structure. Comments may contain *@mentions* and *#hashtags*, just like tweets.

Like Twitter, Weibo provides rate-limited APIs to developers. These APIs enable software to retrieve users' timelines, post and delete tweets, *etc.* However, as we discuss in § 3.1, there are significant limitations to Weibo's APIs.

2.2 Government Regulation of the Web

The Chinese government enforces several policies to regulate content on websites. As a major social hub, Sina Weibo regulates content in cooperation with these policies.

- **Real Name Policy.** In March 2012, Weibo implemented the Real Name Registration (RnR) Policy [48]. The policy states that users must use their real name when creating a Weibo account, although users may use a pseudonym as their public handle on the website.

- **Blacklists.** Weibo maintains a blacklist of words and URLs that are not permitted in tweets. For example, tweets may not contain links that leverage Google's URL shortener goo.gl.

- **Search Censorship.** Weibo does not permit users to search for tweets that contain certain words. The China Digital Times maintains an up-to-date list of words impacted by search censorship on Weibo [1].

- **Tweet Censorship.** Several studies have confirmed that Weibo censors tweets [7, 49]. Tweets may be deleted if they contain politically sensitive topics, abusive language, pornography, or rumors. It is hypothesized that Weibo employs a heterogeneous strategy for tweet censorship, ranging from keyword filtering to real-time crowdsourced monitoring [49].

Violations and Penalties. Sina Weibo enforces penalty policies against users who violate online content regulations. The *Sina Weibo Community Treaty*, launched in May 2013 [6], outlines these penalty policies. The treaty introduced a *credit* system for Weibo users where *credit* is deducted for each policy violation. Weibo accounts are permanently deleted if their *credit* reaches 0. Accounts may also be temporarily suspended at Sina Weibo's discretion. Many violations are detected and handled by Weibo's automatic security systems, *e.g.,* spam tweets, tweets that link to pornography, and tweets that include blacklisted keywords. More complex violations (such as disseminating false or misleading rumors) are handled by Weibo's *Community Board*, which is composed of well-known Weibo users that are hand-chosen by Sina.

Awareness of and Responses to Censorship. Sina Weibo users are aware that the social network censors content. Users must agree to the *Sina Weibo Community Treaty* when they register for an account, and complaints about censorship are common on Weibo, as well as on other Chinese web forums. Although the *Treaty* does not specify what topics or words are censored, there are webpages that catalogue the details of censorship on Weibo [1]. Thus, savvy web users can locate the current list of censored topics and words on Weibo.

Given this awareness of censorship, Chinese Web users have adopted a variety of obfuscation techniques to avoid censorship. In particular, users have been observed using abbreviations, anglicanizations of Chinese characters, neologisms (newly invented words), homophones (words that sound the same), and homographs (words that look similar) to avoid keyword-based censorship [25, 49]. Collectively, we refer to these words as *morphs*.

Although we cannot be certain that any given Weibo user is aware of censorship, as we show in § 6, users adopt morphs in tandem with the emergence of politically sensitive trending topics.

This morph adoption begins even before censorship is imposed, indicating that, in general, users are aware of censorship and try to avoid it preemptively.

2.3 Studies of Censorship on Weibo

Three existing studies examine censorship on Weibo. Bamman *et al.* confirmed the existence of censorship by calculating that tweets with certain words are deleted much more frequently than predicted by random chance [7]. Fu *et al.* developed statistical tools to locate censored keywords, and examined the chilling effect of RnR on Weibo [42]. However, these studies disagree on the scope of censorship on Weibo, with the former claiming that 16% of tweets are censored, and the latter claiming 0.01% of tweets are censored. These drastically different estimates may be due to different tweet sampling methodologies between the two studies. Finally, Zhu *et al.* measure the velocity of censorship, and observe that 30% of censored original tweets (*i.e.*, not retweets) are deleted within 30 minutes [49].

Censorship of Comments on Weibo. Although existing studies confirm that Weibo censors tweets, to date no studies have examined censorship of comments on Weibo. During our study, we observed that when a tweet is deleted (for any reason), the comments associated with that tweet are also deleted. We also observed Weibo deleting comments that contain malicious links and spam. However, *we have not observed any instances where Weibo has censored a comment*. We confirmed this observation by searching the Chinese Web for complaints about censorship on Weibo: although many users complain about tweet censorship, we could not find a single instance of users complaining about comment censorship. This distinction is important, because, as we show in § 4, there are an order of magnitude more comments than tweets on Weibo.

3. METHODOLOGY

The goal of this study is to examine the impact of censorship on topical discussion and word usage on Weibo. In particular, we want to address two broad questions: *first*, is censorship effective at diminishing (or even halting) discussion of particular topics? *Second*, do Weibo users adapt to try and avoid censorship (*e.g.*, by using morphs), and if so, what are the dynamics of this process?

To answer these questions, we need to collect a large corpus of tweets and comments from Weibo over a long period of time. In this section, we present our methodology for gathering this data. First, we discuss the challenges presented by collecting data from Weibo. Next, we introduce the population of users targeted by our crawler. Finally, we discuss the design of our prioritized crawler, and validate its effectiveness at gathering censored tweets.

3.1 Data Gathering: API or DIY?

There are three options for gathering data from Weibo: sampling tweets from the public timeline API, querying the tweets of individual users with the developer API, or crawling the website. We chose to crawl the Weibo site for two reasons. First, Weibo's public timeline API (which is roughly equivalent to Twitter's "spritzer" data stream) does not include retweets or comments. As we show in § 4, retweets and comments account for 97% of the content on Weibo. Thus, the public tweet API is unusable for our study.

Second, Weibo's developer APIs are inefficient for gathering tweets and comments. Each call to the API returns the most recent 100 tweets for a given user, however an additional API call is necessary to gather the comments *on each tweet*. In contrast, the Weibo site return 10 tweets per HTTP request, along with the first

10 comments on each of those tweets. As we shown in § 4, >99% of tweets accrue ≤10 comments, meaning that 10 HTTP requests is roughly equivalent to making 101 API calls.

3.2 Selecting Weibo Users

The next step in our study is identifying a subset of Weibo users to crawl. We choose to focus on a large, diverse, connected component of users rather than a random sample because studies have shown that different types of Weibo users experience dramatically different levels of censorship. For example, Fu *et al.* find that 0.01% of tweets from 350K celebrities (users with >1000 followers) are censored [42], whereas Zhu *et al.* find that 13% of tweets from 3K politically active Weibo users are censored [49].

Seed Selection. To locate a connected component of Weibo users, we first select 7 politically active Chinese celebrities as *seeds*. We then gathered all of the users who the seeds follow, most of whom are also celebrities in China. Collectively, we refer to these 3049 users as *celebrities*.

Selecting Commentors. The next step is to add normal users to the connected component. Unfortunately, it is not feasible to crawl the 33M followers of the *seeds* on a daily basis. Furthermore, it has been shown that 57% of Weibo accounts never tweet, and 90% tweet less than once per week [41]. Thus, randomly selecting from the *celebrity* followers is unlikely to uncover active users.

Instead, we select normal users from the set of users who comment on tweets from the seeds. We crawled all comments on all tweets from the 7 seeds between October 2012 and February 2013. This process located 2.8M commentors, which is still too many to crawl on a daily basis. We decided to split our resources by crawling the 177K *top commentors* and a 100K sample of *random commentors* (note that these two populations are non-overlapping). Thus, our final target population includes 280,250 users.

This split between *top* and *random* commentors allows us to crawl highly active users, as well as a less biased sample of average users. Each *top commentor* generated ≥10 comments during the measurement period, while ≈60% of the *random commentors* only commented once. We observe that *commentors* who comment more than once tend to do so at two week intervals. We compare the characteristics of our three target groups in more detail in § 4.

3.3 Crawler Design and Data Collection

Now that we have selected the target population, we must develop a strategy to crawl these users. On one hand, we want to crawl each user's tweets as often as possible, since it has been shown that censored tweets can be deleted in a matter of minutes [49]. On the other hand, the number of HTTP requests we can make to Weibo each day is rate-limited, and we want to collect data from a large number of users.

Prioritized Crawler Design. To balance these competing goals, we develop a prioritized crawler. Prior work has shown that Weibo users tweet at different rates [41]. This indicates that our crawler should visit some users more frequently than others.

To correctly allocate our resources, we need to understand the tweeting behavior of the target user population. Thus, we crawled all the tweets generated by the target users in January 2013. Figure 1 shows the inter-arrival time between tweets for *celebrities*, *top commentors*, and *random commentors*. The figure shows CDFs of minimum, average, and maximum inter-arrival times for all users. Two conclusions can be drawn from Figure 1. First, all three user populations have similar overall behavior. Second, the vast majority of users tweet between once every three hours, and once per day. A small fraction of users tweet more frequently.

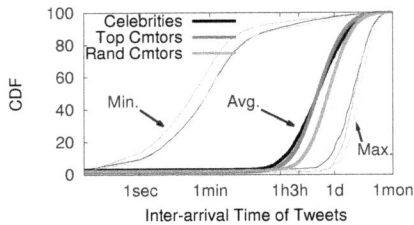

Figure 1: Inter-arrival time between tweets for our three target groups.

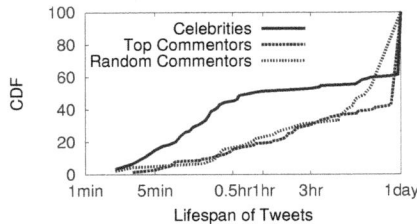

Figure 2: Lifespan of censored tweets.

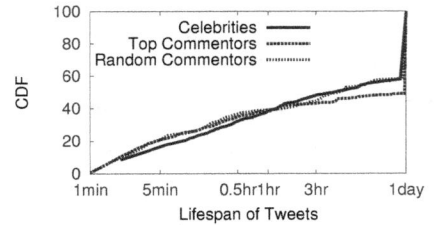

Figure 3: Lifespan of tweets deleted by their owner.

Based on the results in Figure 1, we can implement a prioritized crawler. The crawler has three buckets: one hour, three hours, and daily. A user in a given bucket is visited by the crawler at the corresponding frequency. The buckets contain 5K, 22K, and 253K users, respectively. Most users in the one and three hour buckets are *celebrities* and *top commentors*.

Data Collection. We crawled Weibo from March 30 to May 13, 2013. The crawler collected tweets from users' timelines between 8 a.m. and 2 a.m. China Standard Time. Between 2 a.m. and 8 a.m. (when users are likely to be asleep) the crawler went back and downloaded the comments attached to all tweets found the previous day. This enabled tweets to accrue comments for many hours before we collected them. We record the unique ID, content, author, and timestamp of each tweet and comment. In addition to the prioritized, targeted crawl, we also collected 700K tweets per day from Weibo public timeline API.

Identifying Censored Tweets. We conducted periodic crawls to identify censored tweets. Every two weeks, a separate crawl would revisit each targeted user's timeline and compare the contents with our historical records. Any missing tweets would be individually queried to determine if it was censored, marked as spam, or deleted by the owner. Weibo returns explicit error messages describing why tweets are deleted, enabling researchers to unambiguously identify censored tweets. Prior work also leverages this methodology to identify censored tweets [7, 42, 49].

Dealing with Spam. Weibo is now a popular target for spammers, just like Twitter [18, 8, 38, 39]. For this study, we adopted a best-effort approach to eliminating spam from our dataset. Before finalizing the set of *commentors*, we filtered out all users with obviously suspicious interaction patterns, *e.g.*, a huge amount of tweets from a recently created account, or many comments posted within seconds of each other. We manually inspected these suspicious accounts and confirmed that they were spammers.

Despite these precautions, 4459 (1.6%) of the *commentors* were suspended from Weibo during our study. It is not clear what violation(s) of the *Community Treaty* caused these suspensions. Fortunately, the number of suspended users is very small, and does not jeopardize the fidelity of our study.

3.4 Validation

Our crawling methodology makes an explicit tradeoff in favor of scope at the expense of timeliness. Specifically, our crawler gathers tweets and comments from a large number of users, at the cost of only being able to visit each user's timeline every few hours. However, prior work has shown that tweets can be censored in as little as a few minutes [49]. This raises an important question: what percentage of censored tweets is our crawler able to gather?

To answer this question and validate our methodology, we performed an experiment: we selected 500 random users from each of our three target populations and crawled their timelines once per minute for a week (April 29 to May 5, 2013). This high-fidelity crawl enables us to calculate the lifetime of deleted tweets down to the minute. During this week, we observed 25,735 tweets, 603 of which were censored, and 1,277 of which were deleted by their owners. Note that in this experiment, we only monitor tweets from the prior 24 hours for censorship/deletion.

Figure 2 plots the lifespan of censored tweets for the three target groups. For *celebrities*, ≈50% of censored tweets are deleted within one hour of their creation, while ≈40% are censored after one day. This result is similar to the findings of Zhu *et al.* [49]. However, for *commentors* <20% of censorship occurs within the first hour. It is not clear whether the different speeds of censorship occur because celebrities are more heavily monitored by the authorities, or because they generate more objectionable tweets than *commentors*.

To put the results in Figure 2 into perspective, we plot Figure 3, which shows the lifetime of tweets deleted by their owners. In this case, the lifespan of tweets is the same across all three populations: ≈40% of tweets are deleted within the first hour. This result makes intuitive sense: if a user wants to delete one of their own tweets (*e.g.*, it contains a typo or an incorrect link), they perform this action quickly.

Implications. The takeaway from this validation experiment is that our prioritized crawler will miss some censored tweets (*i.e.*, the tweets will be generated and censored before our crawler can observe them). In the worst case, the prioritized crawler may miss 50% of censored tweets from *celebrities*, since they are crawled once every hour. Similarly, in the worst case, the prioritized crawler will miss 20-40% of censored tweets from *commentors*.

Although our crawler will miss some censored tweets, this does not adversely impact our study for two reasons. *First*, our crawler captures the majority of censored tweets from the target users. This gives us a large enough sample to know, with high statistical confidence, which topics and words are being censored. This information is sufficient to support our goal of analyzing censorship's impact on topical discussion and word usage on Weibo. *Second*, as we show in § 4.2, the vast majority of content on Weibo is in comments, not tweets. Unlike previous studies of censorship on Weibo which ignore comments [7, 42, 49], our crawler is able to capture comments. We feel that this is a favorable tradeoff, *i.e.*, gathering 18M comments per day at the expense of missing some censored tweets.

4. GENERAL ANALYSIS

In this section, we analyze the overall characteristics of our Weibo dataset. *First*, we contrast the characteristics of *celebrities*, *top commentors*, and *random commentors* with a random sample of Weibo users taken from the public timeline API. This comparison enables us to quantify the differences between our target population

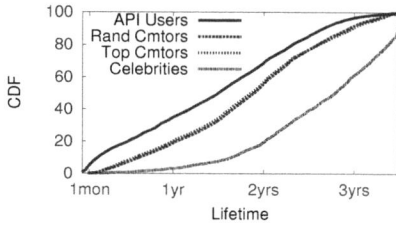

Figure 4: Lifetime of Weibo users.

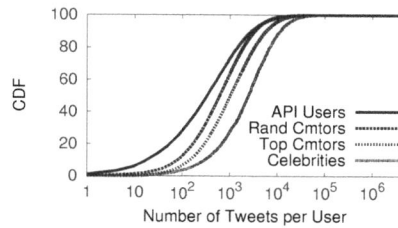

Figure 5: Total tweets per Weibo user.

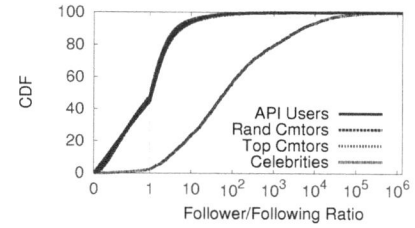

Figure 6: Follower/following ratio for Weibo users.

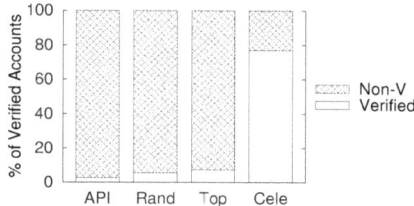

Figure 7: Percentage of verified Weibo users.

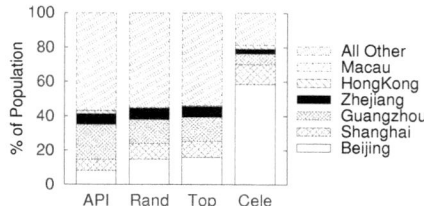

Figure 8: Location demographics for Weibo users.

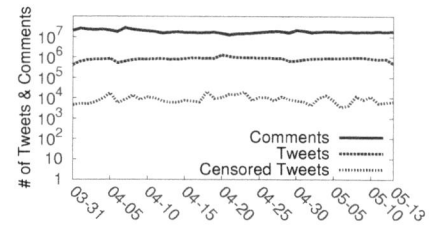

Figure 9: Tweets, comments, and censored tweets per day.

and the overall Weibo userbase. *Second*, we introduce and briefly examine the data from our daily crawls of Weibo. This sets the stage for deeper analysis of trending topics on Weibo in Section 5.

4.1 Characterizing Weibo Users

In this section, we analyze the characteristics of our three target populations by examining data from their user profiles. On Weibo, each user profile includes the date the account was created, the total number of tweets, followers, and followings for the account, whether the user is verified, and the user's self-reported geographic location. To compare the profiles of the target users with generic Weibo users, we randomly picked 1M users who appeared in the public timeline API. We refer to these users as *API users*. All profiles were crawled on February 17, 2013.

Lifetime of Accounts. First, we examine the lifetime of users in our four different groups. Since Weibo went public on August 14, 2009, the maximum user lifetime on Weibo is 1284 days. Figure 4 plots the lifetime of users in the four groups. *API users* tend to have the youngest accounts (50% are ≤1.5 years old). Given that the population of Weibo has been growing exponentially, it makes sense that many users have young accounts. In contrast, the two *commentor* groups have indistinguishable lifetime characteristics, and are older than the *API users* by several months. The *celebrities* have the oldest accounts (40% are ≥3 years old), showing that they were early adopters of Weibo.

Tweets Per User. Next, we examine how active the different user groups are by looking at the total number of tweets they generate. Figure 5 reveals that each group of users generates a different amount of tweets. The *API Users* generate the least tweets, which accords with their short lifetimes, and prior work showing that many Weibo accounts tweet infrequently [41]. *Top commentors* generate more tweets than *random commentors* despite having similar lifetimes. This corresponds to our original selection criteria, *i.e., top commentors* were chosen because they are active. *Celebrities* generate the most tweets by far because they are highly active and have the oldest accounts.

Followers vs. Followings. To gauge the impact of fame, we plot the follower/following ratio for the four user groups in

Figure 6. We filter out 17K *API users*, 348 *commentors*, and 7 *celebrities* that have 0 followings. Figure 6 demonstrates that most users on Weibo have similar ratios of followers to followings, with *celebrities* being the exceptions. 98% of *celebrities* have ratios >1, and 77% have ratios >10. In contrast, 44% of *API users* and *commentors* have ratios <1, *i.e.,* they follow many users, but have few followers.

Verified Accounts. Similar to Twitter, Weibo provides an identity verification system for famous users (not the general public). To become verified, users must submit supporting documentation to authenticate themselves, which is then manually verified by Weibo staff.

Figure 7 plots the percentage of verified users in each of our four user groups. 77% of *celebrities* are verified, which confirms our classification of these users. ≈7% of *commentors* are verified, while only 3% of *API users* are verified.

Geographic Distribution. Finally, we study the geographic distribution of the four user groups. Weibo users must list a home location on their profile, with the available options being Chinese provinces, autonomous/special administrative regions, "abroad," or "other." Note that user's locations are self-reported, and may not be accurate.

Figure 8 plots the location demographics for our four user groups. Beijing, Shanghai, Guangzhou, and Zhejiang are the top 4 locations across all groups. This is not surprising, since these coastal regions all have above average rates of Internet penetration in China [32]. 59% of *celebrities* are in Beijing, possibly because it is the capital and political center of China. In contrast, the *commentors* and *API users* have similar demographics, with the former slightly favoring Beijing, and the latter Guangzhou.

Summary. The results in this section contrast our target user groups and a random sample of active Weibo users. Overall, the *commentors* and *API users* are quite similar, *e.g.,* similar follow ratios and geographic distributions. However, the *commentors* do have older accounts than *API users*. This data suggests that the *commentors*, who are 99% of our target population, are representative of active Weibo users in general.

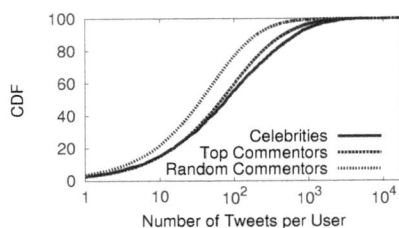

Figure 10: Tweets per user in our three target groups.

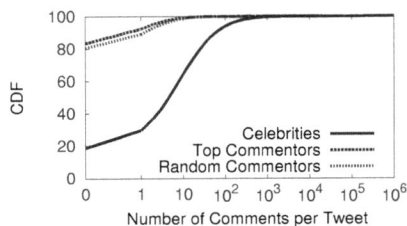

Figure 11: Comments per tweet for our three target groups.

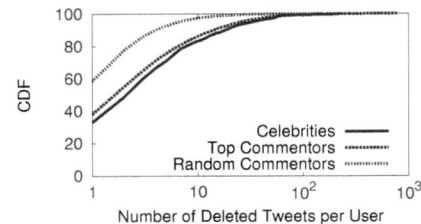

Figure 12: Censored tweets per user for our three target groups.

The *top commentor* and *random commentor* groups are extremely similar. Although we chose the *top commentors* specifically because they are very active, their overall characteristics are almost the same as the *random commentors*, who were chosen using a less biased selection process.

Unsurprisingly, the *celebrities* are very different from other Weibo users. Given that the *celebrities* only comprise 1% of our target population, these differences have little impact on the overall composition of our target population.

4.2 Daily Activity on Weibo

In this section, we provide a brief overview of the data from our daily crawls of Weibo, *i.e.,* how many tweets and comments per day, how many comments per tweet, and how many tweets are censored per day. We analyze this dataset in greater depth in § 5 and § 6.

Overall Data Collection. We conducted daily crawls of the *celebrities*, *top commentors*, and *random commentors* between March 30 and May 13, 2013. Figure 9 shows the number of tweets and comments gathered each day, along with the number of censored tweets. The number of interactions per day is roughly constant: ≈830K tweets, 18M comments, and 9K censored tweets. There are an order of magnitude more comments per day than tweets. Although it is not shown in Figure 9, there are also an order of magnitude more retweets every day than original tweets.

Figure 10 plots the number of tweets per user during our 44 days of crawled data. *Celebrities* and *top commentors* have almost identical behavior over this time period, with ≈40% of users tweeting >100 times. In contrast, the majority of *random commentors* tweet <36 times.

Figure 11 shows the number of comments attached to each tweet in our dataset. Despite the fact that *top commentors* generate more tweets than *random commentors*, both groups accrue similar amounts of comments: ≈80% of tweets receive 0 comments, and <1% receive >10 comments. In contrast, 50% of *celebrity* tweets accrue >5 comments. Clearly, *celebrity* tweets serve as hubs of discussion on Weibo.

Censorship per User. During our crawl, we observed that 1% of tweets are censored every day. However, this is a conservative estimate, given that our crawler is expected to miss some censored tweets (see § 3.4). Figure 12 plots the number of censored tweets per user in each user group. For *celebrities* and *top commentors*, ≈35% have 1 censored tweet, while ≈17% have ≥10 censored tweets. In contrast, 59% of *random commentors* only have 1 censored tweet.

5. TOPIC ANALYSIS

At this point, we have described our crawling methodology, and presented an overview of the users and timeline data gathered by

it. We now return to the first of two major questions asked in this paper: *what is the impact of censorship on discourse on Weibo?* To answer this question, we extract trending topics from our Weibo data and examine the relationship between censorship and topic-level characteristics.

We organize this section into two parts. *First*, we present our methodology for locating tweets and comments that correspond to trending topics. *Second*, we introduce the 37 trending topics we identify on Weibo (including several censored topics) and analyze the correlation between censorship and topic-level characteristics.

5.1 Locating Trending Topics

Before we can analyze topic-level characteristics, we must develop a methodology for locating trending topics amongst the 839M tweets and comments collected by our crawler. We divide this process into four phases: word segmentation, topic extraction, validation, and labeling.

Word Segmentation. The first step in our methodology is segmenting tweets and comments from Weibo into individual words. This step is necessary because the Chinese language does not include breaks between words. However, identification of individual words is a necessary precondition for using many Natural Language Processing (NLP) algorithms to extract topics from text corpora.

We segment tweets and comments using OpenCLAS [23], which is an open-source implementation of the ICTCLAS Chinese word segmentation algorithm [47]. We chose ICTCLAS because it is consistently a top contender at the SIGHAN Chinese NLP bakeoff.[1] This tournament is the de-facto benchmark for state-of-the-art Chinese NLP techniques.

The weakness of OpenCLAS is that it relies on a dictionary of 104K traditional Chinese words to perform segmentation. This dictionary does not include any of the new words or morphs present on social media. To overcome this deficiency, we augmented the OpenCLAS dictionary with 6.1M words taken from the Sogou Pinyin dictionary [4]. Sogou Pinyin is a the most popular Chinese character input software in China [5], and the dictionary of words leveraged by the software is constantly updated by users who upload new words. We manually verified that OpenCLAS with the updated dictionary was able to correctly segment 1000 randomly selected tweets from our dataset.

Topic Extraction. The second step in our methodology is to extract topics from the corpus of segmented tweets and comments. For this task, we leverage LDA [9]. Although LDA cannot usually be applied to microblog text because each tweet is too short [35, 20, 34], two factors make LDA feasible in our case. First, Chinese text is denser than English, *i.e.,* more words fit into 140-character tweets. Second, on Weibo, many tweets have associated comments.

---

[1] http://www.sighan.org/

Topic name	Topic Description	Lifespan (Days)	Tweets	Cmts	Likes	RTs	% Censored
Lushan	Derision of a Chinese official with an expensive wristwatch after the Ya'an earthquake.	6	928	8K	265	10K	81.6%
Taxi	An incident involving a taxi driver who claimed to meet President Xi.	2	2K	3K	2K	70K	36.2%
Bird Flu	Rumors about the return of SARS horrors during the emergence of H7N9 bird flu.	4	394	10K	243	5K	20.0%
Jingwen	The suicide (rumored homicide) of a young woman at Jingwen shopping mall.	5	9K	141K	4K	72K	12.2%
Obama	White House petition asking for deportation of the suspected poisoner of Ling Zhu.	3	26K	640K	23K	268K	5.8%

Table 1: Top 5 topics ranked by percentage of censored tweets.

Topic Name	Original Words	Morphs
Lushan	范继跃 (the official's name)	芦山县委书记 (Lushan secretary), 表印哥 (brother watch-print), 无表哥 (brother no-watch), 机智哥 (brother wisdom)
Taxi	郭立新 (the driver's name)	北京的哥 (Beijing taxi driver), 郭师傅 (Shifu Guo)
Bird Flu	十年前非典 (SARS, 10 years ago), 十年后禽流感 (bird flu)	*No Morphs*
Jingwen	京温 (Jingwen), 袁利亚 (the girl's name), 钟涛 (Jingwen boss' name)	京wen (partial anglicanization of Jingwen), 袁莉亚 (homograph of the girl's name), 京温老总 (Jingwen boss), 安徽女子 (girl from Anhui), 袁某 (Yuan XX)
Obama	奥巴马 (Obama), 白宫 (the Whitehouse)	美国信访办 (US petition office), 信访办主任 (director of the petition office), 奥青天 (Oba-the-sky)

Table 2: Original words and their corresponding morphs amongst the top 5 censored topics.

For the purposes of topic extraction, we combine each tweet with its comments to form a single, longer *document*.

We applied LDA to a random sample of 1.4M documents from our timeline dataset. Before processing we filtered out rare words that appear ≤ 3 times, the top 500 most common words, a stop-list of emoticons and other useless words, and URLs. These filters increase the accuracy and decrease the running time of LDA. We set the number of topics $K = 300$, $\alpha = 0.167$, and $\beta = 0.001$ (based on the parameterization from [43]), and ran LDA for 1000 iterations. The output of LDA is 300 topics, each containing 100 words ranked by how strongly they correspond to that topic.

Manual Validation. The third step in our methodology is manually vetting and validating the topics from LDA. Manual analysis of the 300 topics revealed that 36 corresponded to real-world events that took place between March 30 and May 13, 2013. We refer to these 36 as *trending topics*. The remaining topics from LDA were very general, and did not correspond to any particular real-world event. Example topics include: gender specific terms, weather related terms, emoticons, and advertising related terms.

To validate whether the trending topics from LDA cover the popular topics on Weibo during the measurement period, we compared our 36 topics to two external sources. First, we compared the LDA topics to a list of known trending topics from April and May 2013 [2, 3]. All 11 topics (10 from April, 1 from May) are included in the 36 topics. Second, we compared the words in the 36 topics to the list of censored words from China Digital Times [1]. Words from one censored topic were not included in our 36 topics; we manually added this missing topic to our collection. These tests confirm that LDA captures the vast majority of trending and censored topics on Weibo. The one manually added topic brings our complete collection to 37 trending topics.

Labeling Tweet and Comments. The final step in our methodology is to label tweets and comments with their corresponding topic. To bootstrap this process, we identified between 1 and 4 keywords in each of our 37 topics that uniquely correspond to that topic. The vast majority of these keywords are proper nouns (*e.g.*, names and places), *e.g.*, 范继跃, 郭立新, and 袁利亚. In 11 topics, we also identified between 1 and 5 unique morphs that only occur within that topic, which we also use as keywords. We revisit these morphs later in § 6. For each tweet and comment in our dataset, we label it as topic t if it contains ≥ 1 of the keywords from topic t.

5.2 Analysis of Trending Topics

In this section, we analyze the 37 trending topics in our dataset. First, we briefly introduce the trending topics and present their high-level features. Second, we use Spearman's ρ to calculate the correlation between censorship and the characteristics of trending topics on Weibo.

High-Level Overview. The 37 trending topics in our dataset cover many topical events that occurred between March 30 and May 13, 2013. This includes major world events, *e.g.*, the death of Margaret Thatcher and the Boston Marathon bombing. They also cover important events within China, *e.g.*, the dispute of over the Senkaku/Diaoyu islands, the Ya'an earthquake, H7N9 bird flu, and Chinese president Xi Jinping's "Chinese Dream" proposal. On average, each trending topics lasts 4.6 days, with the shortest lasting 2 days and the longest 14 days. The average topic includes 19K tweets and 635K comments, with min/max tweets being 394/108K, and min/max comments being 538/3.1M.

These numbers reveal that only a small fraction of the 36.5M tweets in our dataset belong to trending topics. This results is not surprising: just like on Facebook and Twitter, the vast majority of content on Weibo is random chatter.

For our study, the most interesting trending topics are ones that are censored. Table 1 lists the details of the top 5 most *censored topics* during our measurement period, ranked by the percentage of tweets in the topic that were censored. We observe that these censored topics touch on many political issues, and that the magnitude of censorship is highly variable (ranging between 82% and 6%). Of the remaining 32 trending topics, 27 exhibit <2% censorship. Table 2 lists some of the keywords in the top 5 most censored topics, as well as the corresponding morphs of those words.

Some readers may be surprised by how few topics are censored on Weibo. One reason for the lack of censorship is that the Chi-

	Avg. Comments per Tweet	Avg. Comments per User	Total Comments	Unique Commentors	Unique Tweeters
ρ	0.012	0.033	0.077	0.036	0.198
p-value	0.874	0.677	0.323	0.644	0.011

Table 3: Spearman's ρ correlation between percentage of censored tweets vs. 5 topic-level variables.

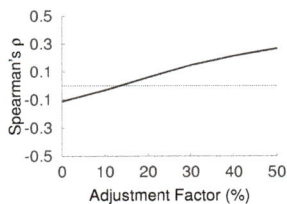

Figure 13: The Spearman's ρ between % of censored tweets vs. tweets per user.

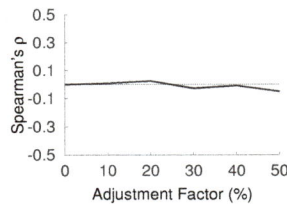

Figure 14: The Spearman's ρ between % of censored tweets vs. tweets per topic.

nese government is primarily interested in censoring content that incites public protests, not content that is critical of the government [25]. Thus, only a subset of the political discourse on Weibo is censored. Furthermore, political and news-related topics are a small percentage of the overall trending topics on social media. For example, only 17% of trending topics on Twitter are political or news-related [28]. Thus, people's limited appetite for political discussion on social media puts an upper bound on the number of topics that could potentially trigger censorship.

Impact of Censorship. We now examine the correlation between the magnitude of censorship and the characteristics exhibited by trending topics. We use Spearman's ρ for this analysis, which is a non-parametric measure of correlation between two variables. ρ is defined between -1 and 1, with $\rho > 0$ indicating positive correlation, and $\rho < 0$ indicating negative correlation. Prior work has successfully leveraged ρ to analyze correlations on social network datasets [12, 24].

Table 3 lists the correlation between the percentage of censored tweets in our 37 topics versus 5 other variables. To increase the sample size of our dataset, we divide each topic into separate days, *i.e.,* a topic with a lifetime of d days creates d separate daily samples. Thus, each test includes $n = 169$ samples. In each test, the null hypothesis is that the given variable is not impacted by censorship.

Table 3 shows that there is a weak positive correlation between the number of unique users who tweet in a topic and censorship. This suggests that Weibo users are not dissuaded from discussing sensitive topics by the threat of censorship. The other four variables presented in Table 3 do not show any correlation with censorship.

Next, we examine the correlation between censorship and the number of tweets per user. Analyzing tweets per user is challenging because our crawler misses some fraction of censored tweets (see § 3.4). To compensate, we *adjust* the number of tweets per user by assuming that some percentage of censored tweets were missed. For example, if we assume that 50% of censored tweets were missed, and user u generates 10 tweets in topic A, 2 of which are censored, then we estimate u actually generated 12 tweets in A.

Figure 13 shows the correlation between censorship and average tweets per user in our 37 topics. The x-axis denotes the *adjustment factor*, defined as the estimated percentage of censored tweets that were missed by the crawler. 0% adjustment refers to the original, unmodified average tweets per user. Interestingly, the unadjusted data shows negative correlation between censorship and

tweets per user, suggesting that censorship may be dissuading users from tweeting. However, when the missing censored tweets are taken into account, the correlation quickly becomes strongly positive. This reveals that users actually generate more tweets than normal in censored topics.

Lastly, we examine the correlation between censorship and total tweets per topic. Tweets per topic is also impacted by missing censored tweets, so we apply the same adjustment methodology used in the previous experiment. Figure 14 shows that there is no clear correlation between censorship and total tweets per topic, even when the *adjustment factor* is taken into consideration.

Discussion. Our analysis reveals surprising aspects about the impact of censorship on Weibo. Initially, we assumed that censorship caused a chilling effect that would manifest as negative correlations, *i.e.,* fewer active users, fewer tweets per user, *etc.* Instead, the data reveals the opposite effects, *i.e.,* censored topics see more active users tweeting more frequently. As shown in Table 3, censorship does not correlate with reduced overall discussion volume, nor does it impact commenting behavior (probably because comments are not censored). These results indicate that, at least for our target population on Weibo during our measurement period, censorship does not cause a chilling effect on discussions.

Our results are different from those of Fu *et al.,* who found that the Real Name Registration (RnR) policy had a chilling effect on Weibo users [42]. However, RnR was implemented on March 16, 2012, and Fu *et al.* observe that the volume of tweets returned to normal levels by June 2012. Thus, it is possible that the chilling effect of RnR has dulled over time.

6. WORD USAGE ON WEIBO

In § 5, we quantify the impact of censorship on the high-level dynamics of trending topics on Weibo. This brings us to the second major question posed in this paper: *do Weibo users adapt in order to avoid censorship?*

To answer this question, we analyze the relationship between censorship and morph usage. As mentioned in § 5, 11 of our 37 trending topics include morphs, and prior work has also observed censored topics that include morphs [7, 42]. We observe that the vast majority of morph usage in our trending topics occurs within heavily censored topics, indicating that there is a relationship between censorship and morph usage. To better understand this phenomenon, we examine the temporal usage of morphs, and the usage of morphs by different types of users (*e.g., celebrities*), in both censored and uncensored topics.

6.1 What is a Morph?

Before we analyze morphs, we must first clearly define what a morph is. A morph is an alternate form of a preexisting, original word or phrase. In conversation (online or offline), the morph can be substituted for the original.

We observe that some morphs on Weibo are existing words used as metaphors or for satirical effect. For example, some Weibo users refer to Chinese president Xi Jingping (习近平) as the "crown prince" (储君). Similarly, after several scandals involving the Red Cross (红十字) in China, Weibo users began referring to it as the Black Cross (黑十字). Alternatively, some morphs are generaliza-

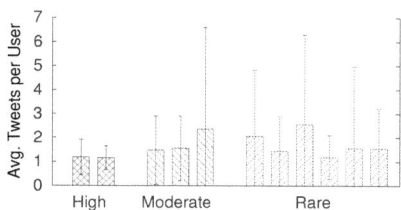

Figure 15: Average tweets per user for different topics.

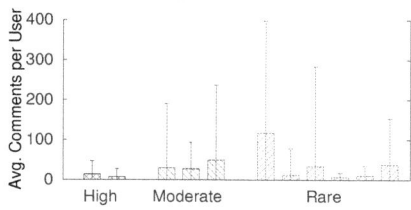

Figure 16: Average comments per user for different topics.

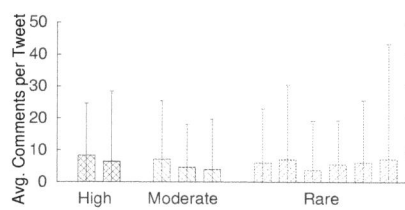

Figure 17: Average comments per tweet for different topics.

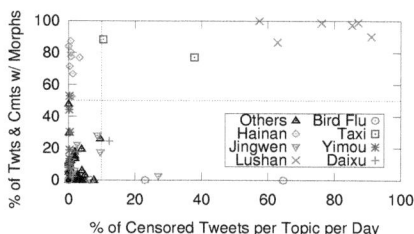

Figure 18: Morph usage versus censorship across 37 trending topics.

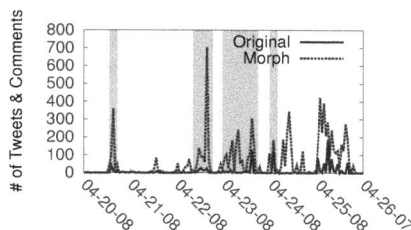

Figure 19: Original word and morph usage over time in the *Lushan* topic.

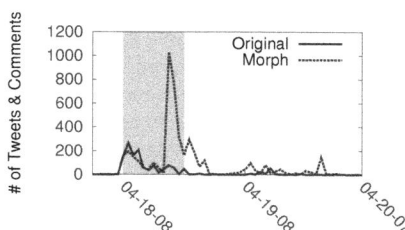

Figure 20: Original word and morph usage over time in the *Taxi* topic.

tions that only make sense in context. For example, in the *Taxi* topic in Table 2, users replaced the name of the taxi driver (郭立新) with the generic phrase "Beijing taxi driver" (北京的哥).

We also observe morphs that are entirely new words, or words used in unexpected ways. In the *Jingwen* topic in Table 2, users partially anglicize 京温 to 京*wen*. In the same topic, some users replace the girl's name (袁利亚) with a homograph (袁莉亚), *i.e.*, a word that looks similar to the original. In a topic discussing the Ling Zhu Thallium poisoning case, some users replace the girl's name (朱令) with a (in this case, offensive) homophone (猪令), *i.e.*, a word that looks different but has the same sound as the original.

Identifying Morphs. In this section, our goal is to investigate whether users adapt to censorship by inventing new morphs. Thus, we are only interested in novel morphs that were invented within our 37 trending topics. To identify novel morphs, we had two native Chinese speakers identify all morphs in the lists of 100 words associated with each of our 37 topics. We then counted the number of tweets and comments using each morph during each day of our dataset. We assume that any a morph m from topic A used >100 times prior to the start date of A was not invented during A, and is therefor not a novel morph.

In total, we identified 11 trending topics in our dataset that include novel morphs. Table 2 lists the original words and morphs in the top 5 most censored topics. Note that a single original word can correspond with multiple morphs.

General Statistics. We now briefly present some general statistics about the 11 topics that include novel morphs. We divide the 11 topics into three categories: *high*, *moderate*, and *rare* censorship. The high-censorship category includes the *Lushan* and *Taxi* topics, the moderate category includes *Jingwen*, *Obama*, and *Zhuling*, and the rare category includes the remaining six topics.

Figure 15 through 17 show that all 11 topics have similar average tweets per user, comments per user, and comments per tweet. In some cases the standard deviation is quite high, particularly for comments in Figure 16. This is due to the presence of spam accounts within the topic. Note that the values in Figures 15 and 17

are not adjusted to compensate for censored tweets missed by the crawler (see § 3.4).

6.2 Morph Usage and Censorship

The first question we address in this section is: *is there a relationship between censorship and morph usage on Weibo?* To answer this question, we plot the percentage of tweets and comments that use morphs in each of our 37 topics, versus the percentage of tweets that were censored in each topic. Figure 18 shows the results of this experiment, where each point represents one day of tweets and comments from one topic. Topics above the 50% horizontal line use more morphs than original words on that particular day.

The majority of trending topics in our dataset do not include novel morphs and are not censored, thus they cluster at the origin in Figure 18. However, several topics exhibit different behavior. The *Hainan* topic, and for one day the *Yimou* topic, appear in the top left of Figure 18, *i.e.*, morphs dominate but the topics are uncensored. In both cases, these morphs are comedic in nature. In *Hainan*, users invented a pejorative term for certain kinds of women (绿茶婊). In *Yimou*, users equivocate the one child policy with a popular Chinese children's animation (葫芦娃).

Three trending topics appear in the bottom right quadrant of Figure 18, *i.e.*, they are censored but original words dominate over morphs. The first topic corresponds to the *Jingwen* suicide/murder case. The censored point in the bottom right quadrant represents to the first day of this topic. As shown in Table 1, users did invent morphs in the *Jingwen* topic. However these morphs were not used until the latter four days of topic, when it was not censored. The same trend of first-day censorship, followed by morph introduction happens in the *Daixu* topic (about a senior colonel who posted a controversial tweet about loss of life due to bird flu). The third topic also concerns *Bird Flu*. As shown in Table 1, users did not invent any morphs within this topic.

Finally, *Lushan* and *Taxi*, the two most heavily censored topics in our dataset appear in the upper right quadrant of Figure 18. The vast majority of tweets and comments in these two topics use morphs instead of the original words.

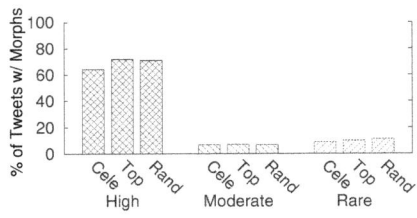

Figure 21: Morph usage in tweets by different user groups.

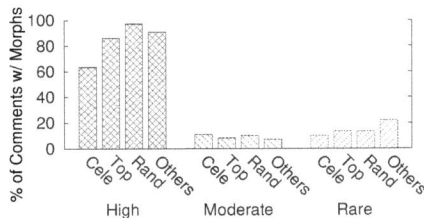

Figure 22: Morph usage in comments by different user groups.

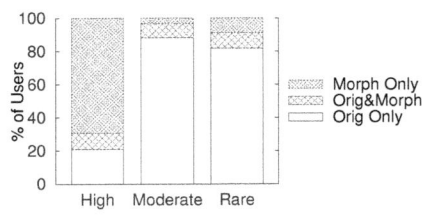

Figure 23: Use of original words and morphs by individual users.

Discussion. Figure 18 reveals that there is a direct relationship between censorship and morph usage. Morphs consistently dominate original words in *only one* of the 32 trending topics in our dataset with ≤5% censored tweets. In contrast, the two most censored topics are overwhelmingly dominated by morphs. Two of the three topics in the middle (between 5 and 20% censorship) include morphs, but usage is weighted towards original words.

One concern with Figure 18 is that our dataset is missing some censored tweets (see § 3.4). In heavily censored topics, it is possible that we may not observe many censored tweets that include original words. However, recall that there are an order of magnitude more comments than tweets on Weibo (§ 4.2), and comments are not censored. The results in Figure 18 primarily derive from word usage in comments. Thus, the results in Figure 18 are not significantly impacted by censored tweets that are missing from our dataset.

6.3 Dynamics of Morph Usage

Figure 18 indicates that users adopt morphs as a means to avoid censorship. In this section, we examine the dynamics of morph usage and adoption in greater detail.

Morph Usage Over Time. First, we examine how the use of morphs changes over time. Figures 19 and 20 plot the number of tweets and comments that use original words or morphs per hour in our top two most censored topics. Grey regions denote times when censorship was occurring. Although the *Lushan* topic is very bursty, it can be seen that the morphs exist at the start of the topic on April 20, 2013. The same observation is true for the *Taxi* topic, although the trend is clearer: initially, the original word and the morph are equally popular. However, 10 hours after tweets with the original words are censored, the popularity of the morph spikes, while the original words fall out of favor.

There are two takeaways from the results in Figures 19 and 20. First, the morphs are invented at essentially the same time the topics begin to trend, *i.e.,* users preemptively invent morphs, even before there are signs of censorship. This may indicate that Weibo users take a proactive approach to inventing morphs that can be used to avoid keyword-based censorship. Second, Figure 20 suggests that the popularity of morphs can skyrocket due to censorship of the original words. However, given that we have only observed one example of this phenomenon, we cannot rule out that some external factor is the cause of the popularity spike in Figure 20.

Morph Usage by Different Types of Users. Next, we examine how morph usage differs across different types of users. Figures 21 and 22 plot the percentage of tweets and comments that use morphs from *celebrities*, *top commentors*, and *random commentors*. As in § 6.1, the 11 topics are divided into three groups based on the censorship rate. In Figure 22, there is an additional bar for "other" users who were not crawled, but did comment on tweets we crawled.

Figures 21 and 22 reinforce our finding that morph usage is correlated with censorship. Across all user groups, morphs appear in 63-97% of tweets and comments in highly censored topics. Conversely, morph usage is very uncommon even in moderately censored topics.

The difference between Figures 21 and 22 is that morphs are more common in comments, especially among non-celebrities. We hypothesize that this occurs for two reasons. First, non-celebrities may be more willing to experiment with novel morphs whose meaning is not known to a large audience. Conversely, *celebrities* may be less willing to use novel morphs that may not be understood by their audience. Second, because tweets create a context for their attached comments, it may be easier to use novel morphs in comments. For example, if a tweet discusses Xi Jinping, it is obvious who the "crown prince" in comments refers to.

Evolution of Word Use by Individuals. Next, we seek to understand whether individual users adapt their word usage over the course of a trending topic. To analyze this, Figure 23 plots the percentage of users who use only original words, only morphs, or a combination of the two. We observe that the number of users who use both original words and morphs is only ≈9%, regardless of the magnitude of censorship of the topic. This shows that most users do not alter their word usage, *i.e.,* users choose the convention they will use when they first tweet/comment, and they do not deviate from this convention though the life of the topic.

Instead, the spikes in morph popularity observed in Figures 19 and 20 are due to *communal* adaptation. As more users join these trending topics over time, they chose to adopt either the original word or the morph convention. In the case of high-censorship topics, Weibo users joining the conversation overwhelmingly choose to adopt morphs, possibly because those tweets are less likely to be censored.

Word Correspondence. Finally, we examine the correspondence between the words used in tweets and their associated comments. We seek to answer the question: *do commentors adopt the conventions used in the associated tweet?* To answer this question, Figure 24 plots the percentage of comments that use the *same* con-

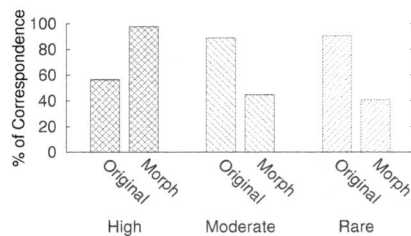

Figure 24: Correspondence between words used in tweets and their associated comments.

vention as their associated tweet, *i.e.*, comments that use the original word on tweets that also use the original word, and vice-versa.

Figure 24 reveals that the word correspondence trends are opposite for highly censored topics versus moderately and rarely censored topics. In highly censored topics, 44% of comments use morphs even when the tweet uses the original word. Conversely, in low-censorship topics, only 10% of comments use morphs when the tweet uses the original word. The trend reverses when we consider tweets that use morphs: in highly censored topics, commentors eagerly adopt the morph convention, whereas in low-censorship topics, commentors revert to using the original words.

The results in Figure 24 indicate that the conventions adopted by commentors are influenced by censorship. In high-censorship topics, commentors tend to use morphs regardless of the convention used by the tweet. Comments that use novel morphs on tweets that use original words help to establish the context of the morph for users who have not observed it before, which may help speed the adoption of the morph. In contrast, commentors are reluctant to adopt novel morphs in the absence of censorship. Without the impetus of censorship, commentors revert to using original words even when tweets include novel morphs.

7. RELATED WORK

Information Dissemination. Information dissemination on OSNs has been extensively studied in the literatures. Many studies focus on Twitter: [37] measure retweets, while [31, 40, 36, 13, 29] measure $\#hashtags$. [10, 12] investigate the impact of social influence on Facebook and Twitter. Numerous studies have applied machine learning algorithms to the prediction of trending topics and user attributes based on information dissemination patterns [33, 30, 46, 19].

Topic Models on OSNs. Several studies share the aim of extracting topics from OSN data. [34, 35] leverage Labeled LDA to extract topics from short tweets. [11] use a graph-based approach to identify emerging topics. Lastly, [20] evaluate the efficacy of several topic models (*e.g.*, TF*IDF) on Twitter data. In this work, we leverage LDA for topic extraction. Unlike Twitter, LDA is successful on Weibo because there are more words per tweet, and comments can be used to increase the length of each document.

Linguistic Evolution in Social Media. Several studies delve into how linguistic conventions change over time on social media. [14, 15, 16] study linguistic style accommodation, power differentials between users revealed through linguistics, and linguistic change over long time scales in social media. [27, 26] measure and predict the emergence of social conventions on Twitter. In our study, we also investigate the emergence of conventions (*i.e.*, morphs). However, as shown in § 6, morphs emerge over very short time scales in response to censorship, which is a different environment than that studied by prior work. [21] propose a graph-based approach for identifying the original word associated with novel morph on Weibo.

8. CONCLUSION

In this paper, we study the impact of censorship on discourse and word choice in Sina Weibo. We crawled 280K Weibo users on an hourly basis for 44 days, gathering 839M tweets and comments. Our study is the first to analyze comments on Weibo, which is crucial since there are an order of magnitude more comments than tweets. We observe that $\approx 1\%$ of all tweets are censored, although some topics are 82% censored, and some celebrity users are 50% censored.

Our analysis of trending topics reveals that there are positive correlations between censorship and user engagement. This may indicate that censorship has less of a chilling effect on discourse on Weibo than was previously suspected [42]. However, we caution that estimating the magnitude of the chilling effect, or lack thereof, is difficult given our data: although we observe many users discussing sensitive topics, it is possible that even more users would discuss these topics if there was no threat of censorship. Thus, although we observe positive correlations between censorship and user engagement, these correlations could be even higher in the complete absence of censorship.

We also observe a strong relationship between censorship and the use of morphs. Weibo users tend to introduce novel morphs into heavily censored topics within the first few hours of the topics existence, even before censorship has been implemented. This indicates that users are aware of censorship and actively adopt novel morphs as a way to avoid keyword censorship.

Taking a broader view, we see this study as a first step towards understanding the impact of censorship on discourse in social media. There are several future directions that could strengthen and extend our findings. *First*, it would be beneficial to confirm our findings over longer time scales (this study only examines two months of data) and through more diverse socio-political conditions (*e.g.*, elections, leadership changes, and natural disasters).

Second, this study analyzes the impact of censorship on the macro-scale, aggregate behavior of Weibo users. Additional work is necessary in order to understand the micro-scale dissemination of morphs through the Weibo population. Unfortunately, we cannot conduct this analysis on our Weibo dataset due to the confounding impact of comments. For example, user A can disseminate a morph to user B's followers by commenting on B's tweet, even if there are no social links between A and those followers. New information dissemination models that take these indirect information channels into account will need to be developed before we can model the dissemination of morphs on Weibo.

Lastly, we note that the point of our study is not to make value judgments for or against censorship. Our goal is simply to observe the impact these policies have on social media, as a step towards improving models and predictors of information dissemination and linguistic change.

Acknowledgments

We thank the anonymous reviewers and our shepherd, Krishna Gummadi, for their valuable time and comments. This research was supported by an Amazon Web Services in Education Grant.

9. REFERENCES

[1] Sensitive words series. China Digital Times. http://chinadigitaltimes.net/china/sensitive-words-series/.

[2] 2013年4月份网络热点事件舆情报告 (Trending Topics Report in April 2013). Mesh Media, 2013.

[3] 2013年5月份网络热点事件舆情报告 (Trending Topics Report in May 2013). Mesh Media, 2013.

[4] Sogou pinyin. Sogou, 2013. http://pinyin.sogou.com/.

[5] Sohu.com inc sohu q1 2013 earnings call transcript. Morningstar, Inc, 2013.

[6] 新浪微博社区公约 (Sina Weibo Community Treaty). Sina, 2013.

[7] BAMMAN, D., O'CONNOR, B., AND SMITH, N. A. Censorship and Deletion Practices in Chinese Social Media. *First Monday 17*, 3 (2012).

[8] BENEVENUTO, F., MAGNO, G., RODRIGUES, T., AND ALMEIDA, V. Detecting spammers on twitter. In *Proc. of CEAS* (2010).

[9] BLEI, D. M., NG, A. Y., AND JORDAN, M. I. Latent dirichlet allocation. *the Journal of machine Learning research 3* (2003).

[10] BOND, R. M., FARISS, C. J., JONES, J. J., KRAMER, A. D. I., MARLOW, C., SETTLE, J. E., AND FOWLER, J. H. A 61-million-person experiment in social influence and political mobilization. *Nature 2012* (489).

[11] CATALDI, M., DI CARO, L., AND SCHIFANELLA, C. Emerging topic detection on twitter based on temporal and social terms evaluation. In *Proc. of MDMKDD* (2010).

[12] CHA, M., HADDADI, H., BENEVENUTO, F., AND GUMMADI, K. P. Measuring user influence in twitter: The million follower fallacy. In *Proc. of ICWSM* (2010).

[13] CUNHA, E., MAGNO, G., COMARELA, G., ALMEIDA, V., GONÇALVES, M. A., AND BENEVENUTO, F. Analyzing the dynamic evolution of hashtags on twitter: a language-based approach. In *Proc. of LSM* (2011).

[14] DANESCU-NICULESCU-MIZIL, C., GAMON, M., AND DUMAIS, S. Mark my words! Linguistic style accommodation in social media.

[15] DANESCU-NICULESCU-MIZIL, C., LEE, L., PANG, B., AND KLEINBERG, J. M. Echoes of power: Language effects and power differences in social interaction.

[16] DANESCU-NICULESCU-MIZIL, C., WEST, R., JURAFSKY, D., LESKOVEC, J., AND POTTS, C. No country for old members: User lifecycle and linguistic change in online communities.

[17] GAO, H. Rumor, lies, and weibo: How social media is changing the nature of truth in china. The Atlantic, 2012.

[18] GRIER, C., THOMAS, K., PAXSON, V., AND ZHANG, M. @spam: the underground on 140 characters or less.

[19] GUO, L., TAN, E., CHEN, S., ZHANG, X., AND ZHAO, Y. E. Analyzing patterns of user content generation in online social networks.

[20] HONG, L., AND DAVISON, B. D. Empirical study of topic modeling in twitter.

[21] HUANG, H., WEN, Z., YU, D., JI, H., SUN, Y., HAN, J., AND LI, H. Resolving entity morphs in censored data. In *Proc. of ACL* (2013).

[22] INC., R. Renren announces unaudited third quarter 2012 financial results. PRNewsWire, 2012.

[23] JADESOUL. Open Chinese Lexical Analysis System. Github, 2013. https://github.com/jadesoul/openclas.

[24] JIANG, J., WILSON, C., WANG, X., HUANG, P., SHA, W., DAI, Y., AND ZHAO, B. Y. Understanding latent interactions in online social networks.

[25] KING, G., PAN, J., AND ROBERTS, M. E. How censorship in china allows government criticism but silences collective expression. *American Political Science Review* (2013).

[26] KOOTI, F., MASON, W. A., GUMMADI, P. K., AND CHA, M. Predicting emerging social conventions in online social networks. In *Proc. of CIKM* (2012).

[27] KOOTI, F., YANG, H., CHA, M., GUMMADI, P. K., AND MASON, W. A. The emergence of conventions in online social networks. In *Proc. of ICWSM* (2012).

[28] LEE, K., PALSETIA, D., NARAYANAN, R., PATWARY, M. M. A., AGRAWAL, A., AND CHOUDHARY, A. Twitter trending topic classification. In *Proc. of IEEE ICDMW* (2011).

[29] LEHMANN, J., GONÇALVES, B., RAMASCO, J. J., AND CATTUTO, C. Dynamical classes of collective attention in twitter. *CoRR* (2011).

[30] LESKOVEC, J., BACKSTROM, L., AND KLEINBERG, J. Meme-tracking and the dynamics of the news cycle.

[31] MA, Z., SUN, A., AND CONG, G. Will this #hashtag be popular tomorrow? In *Proc. of SIGIR* (2012).

[32] MARTIN, R. China internet penetration map 2012. Tech In Asia, January 2012. http://www.techinasia.com/china-internet-penetration-map/.

[33] PENNACCHIOTTI, M., AND POPESCU, A.-M. Democrats, republicans and starbucks afficionados: user classification in twitter.

[34] QUERCIA, D., ASKHAM, H., AND CROWCROFT, J. Tweetlda: Supervised topic classification and link prediction in twitter.

[35] RAMAGE, D., DUMAIS, S. T., AND LIEBLING, D. J. Characterizing microblogs with topic models. In *Proc. of ICWSM* (2010).

[36] ROMERO, D. M., MEEDER, B., AND KLEINBERG, J. Differences in the mechanics of information diffusion across topics: idioms, political hashtags, and complex contagion on twitter.

[37] STARBIRD, K., AND PALEN, L. (how) will the revolution be retweeted?: information diffusion and the 2011 egyptian uprising. In *Proc. of CSCW* (2012).

[38] STRINGHINI, G., KRUEGEL, C., AND VIGNA, G. Detecting spammers on social networks. In *Proc. of ACSAC* (2010).

[39] THOMAS, K., ET AL. Suspended accounts in retrospect: An analysis of twitter spam. In *Proc. of IMC* (2011).

[40] TSUR, O., AND RAPPOPORT, A. What's in a hashtag?: content based prediction of the spread of ideas in microblogging communities. In *Proc. of WSDM* (2012).

[41] WA FU, F., AND CHAU, M. Reality Check for the Chinese Microblog Space: A Random Sampling Approach. *PLoS ONE 8*, 3 (2013).

[42] WA FU, K., HONG CHAN, C., AND CHAU, M. Assessing censorship on microblogs in china: Discriminatory keyword analysis and the real-name registration policy. *IEEE Internet Computing 17*, 3 (2013).

[43] WALLACH, H. M. Structured topic models for language. *Unpublished doctoral dissertation, Univ. of Cambridge* (2008).

[44] WENLIN, Z. Weibo has over 300 million users, and 100 million tweets daily. Xinhua News, February 2012.

[45] WENLIN, Z. Weibo has over 500 million users, and 4.6 million active users daily. Xinhua News, February 2013.

[46] ZAMAN, T. R., HERBRICH, R., GAEL, J. V., AND STERN, D. Predicting information spreading in twitter. In *Proc. of NIPS* (2010).

[47] ZHANG, H.-P., YU, H.-K., XIONG, D.-Y., AND LIU, Q. HHMM-based Chinese lexical analyzer ICTCLAS. In *Proc. of SIGHAN workshop on Chinese language processing* (2003).

[48] ZHOU, M. 微博明日起实行实名制 用户凭有效信息才可注册 (Weibo RnR Launching Tomorrow: Users Need to Register with Valid Information). 凤凰科技讯, March 2013.

[49] ZHU, T., PHIPPS, D., PRIDGEN, A., CRANDALL, J. R., AND WALLACH, D. S. The velocity of censorship: High-fidelity detection of microblog post deletions. In *Proc. of USENIX Security* (2013).

Call Me MayBe: Understanding Nature and Risks of Sharing Mobile Numbers on Online Social Networks

Prachi Jain, Paridhi Jain and Ponnurangam Kumaraguru
Indraprastha Institute of Information Technology (IIIT-Delhi)
New Delhi, India
{prachi1107, paridhij, pk}@iiitd.ac.in

ABSTRACT

Little research explores the activity of sharing mobile numbers on OSNs, in particular via public posts. In this work, we understand the characteristics and risks of mobile numbers shared on OSNs either via profile or public posts and focus on *Indian* mobile numbers. We collected 76,347 unique mobile numbers posted by 85,905 users on Twitter and Facebook and analyzed 2,997 numbers, prefixed with +91. We observed that most users shared their own mobile numbers to spread urgent information and to market products, IT facilities and escort business. Users resorted to applications like Twitterfeed and TweetDeck to post and popularize mobile numbers on multiple OSNs. To assess risks associated with mobile numbers exposed on OSNs, we used mobile numbers to gain sensitive information (e.g. name, Voter ID) about their owners. We communicated the observed risks to the owners by calling them on their mobile number. Few users were surprised to know the online presence of their number, while few users intentionally put it online for business purposes. With these observations, we highlight that there is a need to monitor leakage of mobile numbers via profile and public posts. To the best of our knowledge, this is the first exploratory study to critically investigate the exposure of mobile numbers on OSNs.

Categories and Subject Descriptors

K.4.1 [**Public Policy Issues**]: Privacy; H.3.5 [**Online Information Services**]: Web-based services

General Terms

Measurement, Security, Design, Human Factor

Keywords

Online Social Networks, Privacy, Mobile Number, Risks

1. INTRODUCTION

Today, Online Social Networks (OSNs) have facilitated their users with variety of services. Users can easily connect to new people and re-connect to old friends, receive live feeds of their friends' activity, and share multimedia content with friends in controlled and restrictive ways. These services have attracted users to generate voluminous new content on OSNs, for instance, 46% of adult Internet users post original photos or videos online that they themselves have created. [1] User Generated Content (UGC) on online social networks is observed to have high similarities with offline interactions of users [11]. Therefore, concerns have been raised on (un)intentional mention of one's sensitive information such as age, sexual orientation, credit card details, health records, on online profile or posts [4, 8, 12].

Phone (Mobile) number is an example of identifiable information with which a real-world individual can be associated uniquely, in most cases [14]. The associated individual can become an easy target for SMS and phone-based phishing scams, [2] which may lead to annoyance, disturbance, and stalking. Such attacks can be made impactful with easy access to large number of mobile numbers shared publicly on OSNs. Mobile numbers can be shared either via profile attributes [2] or via posts (see Figure 1). Auxiliary details of mobile number owners shared along with the mobile numbers, or collected otherwise, can help attackers to launch targeted attacks against them. To examine the necessity of safeguard methods to prevent public exposure of users' mobile numbers either via profile or posts, there is a need to comprehend mobile number sharing behavior on OSNs, and the gravity of associated risks.

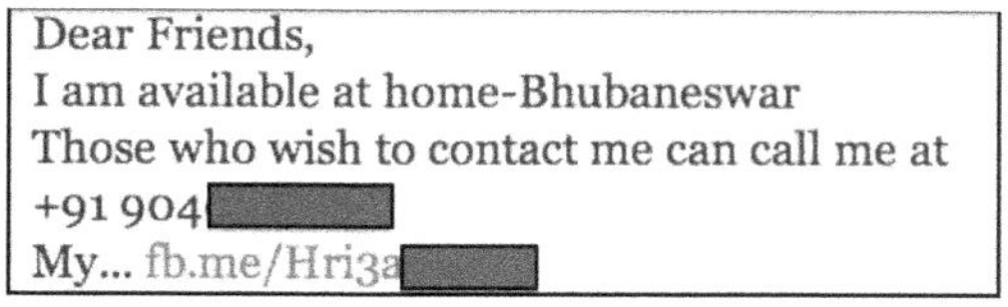

Dear Friends,
I am available at home-Bhubaneswar
Those who wish to contact me can call me at
+91 904█
My... fb.me/Hri3a█

Figure 1: Exposure of mobile number on Twitter.

India has been a popular venue for mobile and phone frauds, owing to huge telecom industry. India has the second largest mobile network in the world, with 919.17 million subscribers by Feb '13. [3] We, therefore, focus on exposure of Indian mobile numbers in this work. We explore reasons, modes and whereabouts of Indian mobile numbers shared on two most popular OSNs – Facebook and Twitter. An Indian mobile number can be used to reveal critical information about its owner such as name, age, location, which

---

[1] http://pewinternet.org/Commentary/2012/March/Pew-Internet-Social-Networking-full-detail.aspx

[2] http://www.scmagazine.com/fbi-warns-of-sms-and-phone-based-phishing-scams/article/191565/

[3] http://www.trai.gov.in/

may invite targeted identity attacks. We communicate the risks of sharing mobile numbers online to their owners by calling them on their numbers and note their reactions.

The paper is organized as follows: Section 2 presents related work on privacy leaks on OSNs. Section 3 enumerates contributions of the paper, Section 4 describes the methodology to collect mobile numbers shared on OSNs. Section 5 elaborates the analysis of leaked mobile number on OSNs. Section 6 discusses if mobile numbers can be exploited to disclose sensitive information of their owners. Section 7 presents summary of the paper, a discussion on the applicability of the results, and some limitations of our work.

2. RELATED WORK

On an OSN, a user is defined by a set of attributes e.g. name, age, education, and network. In this paper, we refer an attribute as Personally Identifiable Information (PII) if the attribute itself or in combination of other attributes can connect an online user account with a real world entity. Researchers have widely studied leakage of PII and sensitive attributes on OSNs e.g. email address [1], age [4], and phone numbers [7]. Magno *et al.* in their work on characterization of Google+, observed many Indian single males shared mobile numbers as their profile attribute. In our work, we attempt to understand the other characteristics of exposed Indian mobile numbers on OSNs. Potential risks associated with aggregation of PII and sensitive attributes from multiple social networks, have been explored in literature [2]. Krishnamurthy pointed in his work that auxiliary information collected from online sources could help in connecting an online profile uniquely to an offline entity [5]. In this work, we intend to explore the viability of the opinion. We exploit Indian mobile numbers and attempt to understand if mobile numbers can be used to gather other profile characteristics of their owners. Further, Krishnamurthy suggested that data augmentation privacy leaks could be prevented via alerting users about dispersive information sharing vulnerabilities. We follow the suggestion and attempt to communicate risks of online sharing of mobile numbers to their owners. In this work, we communicate the risks by calling a sample of users (2,492) whose mobile numbers are available on OSNs, via an Interactive Voice Response (IVR) System.

3. CONTRIBUTIONS

In the process of understanding the nature of mobile number sharing on OSNs and its associated risks, we found that – 1) Emergency, Marketing, Entertainment and Escort business were major contexts observed on Twitter while marketing IT facilities context was observed on Facebook, where mobile numbers were shared. 2) Most owners themselves shared their mobile numbers on OSNs; and users of metropolitan cities in India actively posted mobile numbers on OSNs than other locations in India. 3) Users posted mobile numbers on multiple OSNs simultaneously, evident by the use of third party applications. 4) A publically shared mobile number can be exploited to retrieve sensitive details of their owners such as number, age, voter ID, family details, and complete address from multiple data sources. We communicated the risks of online sharing of mobile numbers to their owners. We found that few users were unaware of the online presence of their number, while, few were aware and told us that they posted the number intentionally for business purposes.

4. METHODOLOGY

We deployed a three stage data collection methodology – keyword selection, data collection and data validation (see Figure 2). We collected Indian mobile numbers shared on two popular OSNs – Facebook and Twitter.

4.1 Keyword selection

A pre-requisite to collect public posts and tweets with a mobile number, was to select a set of relevant keywords [8]. To create the keyword list, we surveyed some OSN users in IIIT-Delhi to determine possible words they would use while sharing a mobile number on OSNs. We selected most commonly listed words for our initial set of 50 keywords, such as *mobile number, contact us, call me*. With the initial set of keywords, we collected 1,525 public tweets using Twitter Streaming API [4] and 1,000 public posts using Facebook Graph API. [5] We used the collected posts to identify other common keywords when mobile numbers were shared (adapting a standard technique of query expansion from Information Retrieval [13]). We tokenized the posts, removed stop words and added most frequent words to expand the seed keyword set size to 278.

4.2 Data collection

We used the final set of keywords to collect public English posts and bio [6] which shared mobile numbers, using Twitter Streaming API and Facebook Graph API. We started our data collection from Facebook on November 16, 2012 and ended on April 20, 2013, while from Twitter on October 12, 2012 and ended on April 20, 2013. We stored public bio and posts which shared mobile numbers on OSNs, along with profiles of the users who shared the number.

To tag Indian mobile numbers in users' posts and users' bio, we exploited the standard convention and structure of an Indian mobile number. It is a 10 digit number, where first digit should start with either 9 or 8 or 7. It can be prefixed with a country code (+91) or trunk code (0). [7] We used rule-based named entity recognition [9] and created a set of regular expression rules which captured Indian mobile number structure. We further observed that most users post Indian mobile numbers in different patterns. Some of the sample patterns are, numbers with no space/dash in mobile number (0999xxxxxxx), one dash after country code (+91-9xxxxx4979), three dashes (+91-9x7-1xx-02xx), and dots between digits (757.3x.52xxx). We modified our regular expressions to capture all possible ways of posting an Indian mobile number on social networks. We categorized Indian numbers prefixed with +91 as "Category +91" numbers (+91-9x7-1xx-02xx), prefixed with 0 as "Category 0" (09x71xx02xx), and prefixed with nothing "Category void" (9x7-1xx-02xx). Table 1 shows the count of mobile numbers collected from tweets or bio on Twitter and public posts or names on Facebook.

4.3 Data validation

Rule-based named entity recognition used to extract Indian mobile numbers from public posts and bio in the earlier stage, relied on a set of regular expressions and therefore misinterpreted certain other country numbers as Indian mobile numbers. Mobile number format for few countries

---

[4]https://dev.twitter.com
[5]https://developers.facebook.com/docs/reference/api
[6]referred to as "description" in Twitter API
[7]http://www.dot.gov.in/numbering_plan/nnp2003.pdf

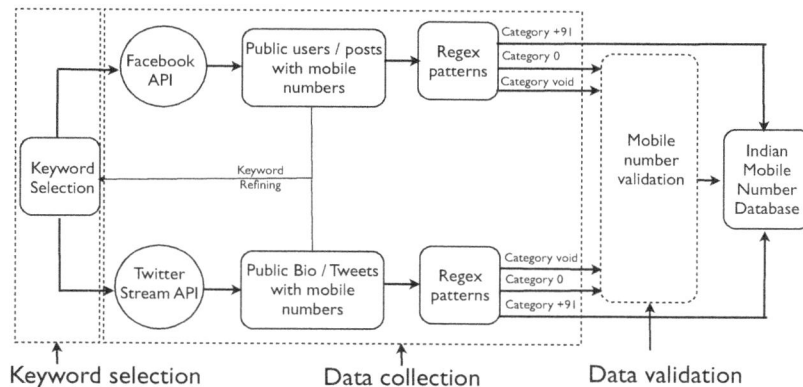

Figure 2: Data collection methodology.

Numbers	Category +91		Category 0		Category void		Total	
	Twitter	Facebook	Twitter	Facebook	Twitter	Facebook	Twitter	Facebook
Mobile numbers	885	2,191	14,909	8,873	25,566	25,294	41,360	36,358
User profiles	1,074	2,663	17,913	9,028	31,149	25,406	49,817	36,588

Table 1: Descriptive statistics of the mobile numbers collected from Twitter and Facebook.

(United Kingdom, [8] and USA [9]) is similar to that of an Indian mobile number. Mobile numbers from UK are also 10-digit numbers starting with 07, which were confused as Indian mobile numbers prefixed with 0 and starting with 7. Mobile numbers from USA also follow 10-digit format with first three digits representing area code, ranging from 2-9, therefore USA mobile numbers without country code and with area codes starting with 7, 8, 9 are similar to an Indian mobile number. To avoid any noise in our database, we ran a validation check for the Category 0 and Category void numbers. Category +91 numbers were confirmed to belong to India as they were prefixed with Indian country code. We used a service [10] which checked if a number's first four digits belonged to a valid Indian mobile number series, however the service was not updated. We observed that 19,934 mobile numbers out of 23,405 in Category 0 (85%), and 42,360 numbers out of 49,946 in Category void (85%), were confirmed to be Indian numbers by the service. After manual verification, we observed some non-Indian numbers were marked as Indian numbers by the service. We therefore, considered *only* Category +91 mobile numbers for our analysis, which were confirmed to be Indian mobile numbers. Our intent was to avoid any bias or noisy inferences by including Category 0 and Category void numbers.

5. ANALYSIS

5.1 Context analysis

To understand the context, we extracted most frequent words from the bio and posts which shared the number. We removed stop words and performed stemming to avoid repeated forms of the same root word. We manually analyzed word-clouds of the most frequent words (see Figure 3(a) and 3(b)). We observe words such as *blood, specialist, hospital, love, sexy, escort, girl, music, movie, fun, offer, reservation, ticket, hotel, seo, sale, astrologer, business* in Figure 3(a).

---

[8] http://stakeholders.ofcom.org.uk/binaries/telecoms/numbering/numbering-plan201212.pdf

[9] http://nanpa.com/enas/npaDialingPlansReport.do

[10] http://trackmobileonline.co.in

We infer that on Twitter, users post Indian mobile numbers, majorly to ask for blood donations / aid, help in emergency situations, to promote escort business, to promote entertainment, to market for travel, holiday, hotel packages, and to buy / sell products, etc. Such a behavior is understandable since Twitter is used as a news media, and marketing platform [6]. On Facebook, users post Indian mobile numbers majorly in context of Information Technology (IT) facilities and education related products, evident by the presence of words such as *price, hp, battery, dell, laptop, ibm, email, notebook, computer* (see Figure 3(b)). We infer that users post mobile numbers on social media platforms in order to benefit from social network structure and promote their business by spreading the contact information (mobile number) to large number of users.

5.2 Ownership analysis

Exposure of mobile numbers by non-owners might lead to unwanted privacy leaks and annoyance to their owners. [11] We therefore analyze if owners of the mobile numbers themselves leaked their numbers at the first place or other users posted them. For each mobile number collected from Twitter (885) and Facebook (2,191), we retrieved the first tweet (post) in our dataset sharing that mobile number on Twitter (or Facebook). The mobile number was marked as 'leaked by its owner', if the tweet (post) included a first person pronoun such as *me, my, us, mera (my in English)* along with most frequent action verbs such as *call, text, sms, ping, whatsapp, message, contact*. For instance we check for the presence of phrases like - *"call us", "text us"*. The mobile number was marked as 'leaked by a non-owner', if the tweet (post) included second person pronoun such as *you, your, yours* or third person pronoun such as *his, her, them* along with same action verbs used with first person pronouns. Researchers used only pronouns to check for ownership [8], this may give false positives like - *"You may call me at xxx"*, however we avoid it by using phrases here. We also assume that mobile

---

[11] http://thenextweb.com/media/2011/07/10/supposed-phone-number-of-news-internationals-chief-executive-leaked-on-twitter

(a) Twitter Tag-cloud

(b) Facebook Tag-cloud

Figure 3: Context in which users leaked mobile numbers on Twitter and Facebook.

numbers shared on Twitter via bio or on Facebook via name are users' own mobile numbers.

Table 2 shows the descriptive statistics of mobile numbers which were leaked by their owners and non-owners. Two hundred and ninety one mobile numbers (32.8%) were shared by their owners while only 18 mobile numbers (2.0%) were shared by non-owners on Twitter. Four hundred and eighty five mobile numbers (22%) were shared by owners, and 25 mobile numbers (1.1%) were shared by non-owners on Facebook. Example post where owner shared his mobile number is *"F1 INR 2500/- tickets are available with me..!! Limited stocks..!! Ping me or call me up on +91 989 xxx xxxx asap!"* Example post where non-owner shared the mobile number is *"@VodafoneIN My friend Debasrita took a new connection (+91-73816xxxxx), she is having issues. Please contact her at +91-9556xxxxxx"*. For remaining mobile numbers, the methodology used could not infer if the numbers were shared by the owners or non-owners. Example post is *"Need a male punjabi artist of age 35 for a ad in #chennai pls contact +91 98-41-xxxxxx"*.

Social Network	Mechanism	Mobile numbers
Twitter - Owner	Bio	155
	Tweet	136
Twitter - Non-owner	Tweet	18
Facebook - Owner	Post	468
	Name	17
Facebook - Non-owner	Message	25

Table 2: Mobile numbers shared by owners and non-owners on Twitter and Facebook.

5.3 Topographical distribution

We probe into the location of the users, who shared Indian mobile numbers on OSNs, to understand if users of few locations more actively posted mobile numbers on social networks than others. We analyzed geo-tagged posts which shared mobile numbers on both social networks. We identified only 13 geo-tagged tweets on Twitter, where 9 unique users shared 12 mobile numbers. Top states from where the numbers were posted are Delhi, Karnataka, Maharashtra and Tamil Nadu. We did not find any geo-tags in Facebook public posts which shared the number.

With few geo-tagged tweets, we investigated whether location of the users who shared mobile numbers can be estimated either via their 'location' attribute or bio description on Twitter [10]. We used Yahoo Maps [12] to trace a location present in users' location attribute or bio description, to a city, state and country. We found location of 777 users via 'location' attribute and of 747 users via their bio description. We ignored locations which did not map to real geographical locations like "Justin beiber's heart". Table 3 shows the country and state from where most Indian mobile numbers were shared, either via 'location' or 'bio' attribute. We infer that mobile numbers were largely shared by users of urban cities in India. Further, most numbers belonged to Indian metropolitan telecom circles and large cities "A" circles [13] (see Table 4). Note all 5 "A" circles appear in top 10 list.

	Location of user	Location via user bio
Country	IN,US,UK,AE,CA	US,IN,RU,BE,CA
State	IN-MH,IN-KA,IN-DL,IN-TN,IN-HR	IN-MH,US-TX,US-PA,RU-MOW,US-CA

Table 3: ISO 3166-2 code of top countries and states from where most Indian mobile numbers were shared on OSNs.

Telecom circle	Category	# of mobile numbers
Delhi	Metropolitan	582
Mumbai	Metropolitan	312
Karnataka	"A" Circle	233
Punjab	"B" Circle	226
Rajasthan	"B" Circle	171
Andhra Pradesh	"A" Circle	164
Kerala	"B" Circle	158
Maharashtra	"A" Circle	140
Gujrat	"A" Circle	135
Tamil Nadu	"A" Circle	102

Table 4: Telecom circle and count of mobile numbers associated with the circle in India.

5.4 Source analysis

We inquire the source or application by which most mobile numbers were posted on OSNs. To extract application used to post the number, we extracted 'source' attribute of the tweet, available from Twitter API, and 'application' attribute of the post, available from Facebook Graph API. On Twitter, apart from the web (234), mobile numbers were largely posted from social aggregators and other social networks such as Facebook (148), Twitterfeed (121), Google (121), LinkedIn (50), TweetDeck (22). We observe major use of social aggregators and other social networks to post mobile numbers on Twitter. Users might be sharing same mobile number not only on one OSN but on multiple OSNs simultaneously. On Facebook, most numbers were posted by Facebook mobile applications such as Facebook mobile (125), Facebook for iPhone (36 numbers), Photos (34), Facebook for Android (19), and few by social aggregators such as HootSuite (31), and Twitterfeed (3). We observe major use of social network's mobile platform to post numbers on multiple OSNs while comparatively less use of social aggregators. This could help the developers to understand other OSNs on which same mobile number was shared.

[12]http://developer.yahoo.com/maps/
[13]http://host.comsoc.org/sistersocieties/india_iete/circles.pdf

6. RISK ANALYSIS

6.1 Risks of Collation

We now turn our focus to understand how publicly shared mobile numbers can be exploited to gather critical and sensitive information about the owners. We used two online services – Truecaller [14] and OCEAN. [15] Truecaller allows to query a mobile number and returns the name of the owner as well as the network operator. OCEAN allows to query a name of a person and returns matching entries from publicly available e-government data sources, listing Voter ID, family details, age, home address, and father's name. OCEAN has data only for Delhi citizens.

We got manual annotators to extract data from Truecaller and OCEAN for Category +91 mobile numbers. For each number, they were asked to observe name of the owner, her location, and mobile number operator from Truecaller, [16] along with the name of the owner, and her location from public posts and profiles on OSNs, sharing the same number. Possible names of the mobile number owner and her possible locations were inferred for 2,997 Category +91 numbers. Name of the owners whose inferred location was Delhi, were then used to query OCEAN and matching set of Delhi citizens were recorded. Surprisingly, out of annotated 94 Delhi mobile numbers, we were able to uniquely identify 8 Delhi users with details like name, age, father's name, home location, gender, and voter ID (see Table 5). Aggregation of information extracted from OSNs with the otherwise collected information about a Delhi mobile number owner, may lead to identity theft.

Details	Shared by owner?
9873xxxxxx, X Kakrania, 24, Male, X Kakrania, "B-***, B-block, X Vihar Ph-I, Delhi", WHC17xxx63	Yes
+9199xxxx2708, X Gambhir, 23, Male, X Gambhir, "***, xxxx Bagh, Delhi", NLNxxx5696	No

Table 5: Anonymized mobile number, name, age, gender, father's name, address, Voter ID of Delhi residents who shared their mobile number on OSNs.

We also experimented with an Android application, Whatsapp, [17] to understand if we could add leaked mobile numbers and hence abuse the Address Book Matching feature of the application and get access to their status messages[3]. We added leaked mobile numbers to a phone's contact directory and ran Whatsapp application from the phone. Users leaked variety of sensitive information via their Whatsapp status updates such as travel plans, social network profile, BBM Pins. Few examples of status updates are *"100% Single"*; *"No longer in India. UK: # +44 75xx 81xxxx US#610xx xxxxx as of June 10"*; *"www.facebook.com/iakrfilms"*; *"New BBM Pin: 25C7xxxx"*. We infer that an accidental / unintentional leak of mobile number on OSNs is capable of exposing other sensitive information.

6.2 Risk Communication

With evident risks associated with leaking mobile numbers online, we attempted to communicate the observed risks to mobile number owners. Researchers suggested various channels for risk communication e.g., Short Message Service (SMS), [18] and Interactive Voice Response (IVR) system, [19] to communicate awareness information among users. Online bloggers deployed automated tools to display partially obfuscated mobile numbers onto a public web page [20] and SMS with random texts, to publicly shared mobile numbers. [21] We deployed an IVR system and communicated the risks associated with posting mobile number online by calling the owners of the numbers. We chose IVR to ensure the reach to the owners and to convince the credibility of the message to them. We now discuss the IVR deployment details, calling procedure and users' reactions to the calls.

6.2.1 IVR system design and implementation

We set up an IVR system using FreeSWITCH [22] and a Java application (see Figure 4). We called 2,492 mobile numbers from Category +91 collected from earlier mentioned methodology until 28th February '13. In India, we were not required to go through an Institutional Review Board (IRB)-type approval process before calling the users. However, we applied similar practices in this work. Prior to the actual risk communication part of the message, we informed the user that we will record the call for research purposes and log all responses and activities of callee in a database. Furthermore, participants were given options to disconnect the call and request the deletion of the audio recording, at any given point of time during the call.

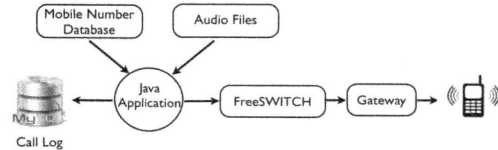

Figure 4: IVR System Design.

When a callee answered the call, for credibility purposes, we introduced ourselves as researchers from New Delhi. We then played the risk communicating message - "We found your number on X", where X was either "Facebook" or "Twitter" or "Facebook and Twitter", depending on the source from where we extracted the number of the callee. We then prompted a voice message "Posting your number online is not a good practice. Doing so will make you fall prey to various phone number frauds. Keep yourself safe and consider removing your number from the Internet." We then presented callee with the following options: "Press 1, If you did not know that your number can be leaked and now you will remove it from the Internet; Press 2, If you posted it purposefully and you will not remove it from the Internet; Press 3, if you want to hear the message again." If the user pressed either 1 or 2, we requested him to leave us a feedback and later gave him an option to end the call. We made the calls during weekdays from 11:00 IST to 16:00 IST.

6.2.2 User Reactions

Figure 5 shows how callees collectively reacted at each stage during the call. Each stage in the call is associated with a probability and the number of users who chose that

---

[14] http://truecaller.com

[15] http://precog.iiitd.edu.in/research/ocean/OCEAN.pdf

[16] As per Truecaller policy, we did not store content.

[17] http://www.whatsapp.com/

[18] http://afreak.ca/blog/being-an-avivore-and-data-mining-twitter/

[19] http://www.ddm.gov.bd/ivr.php

[20] http://www.weknowwhatyouredoing.com/

[21] http://textastrophe.com/

[22] https://wiki.freeswitch.org/wiki/IVR

stage. Sixty one percent of callees who picked the call, opted to listen to the message and six percent chose to remove their mobile numbers from OSNs. An equivalent percentage (6.2%) chose *not* to remove their numbers. Forty seven users from the 2,492 numbers that we called, left feedback on our IVR system. A few are: *"Thank you for information, I have deleted, I will not post my number online"*, *"I want to know how to remove my number and I don't know, I haven't put my number purposely but if it is there, where exactly it is there I would also like to know that. Please get in touch with me asap. Thank you"*. Some callees showed their concerns and some even requested us for help to remove their numbers from the Internet. Such user reactions urge the necessity for a safeguard solution to control the spread of personal and sensitive information on OSNs. We also received feedback saying *"I posted my number purposely for my website promotion, I usually do deal in web hosting business so that is why I want someone to contact me for hosting services"* implying intentional sharing of mobile numbers.

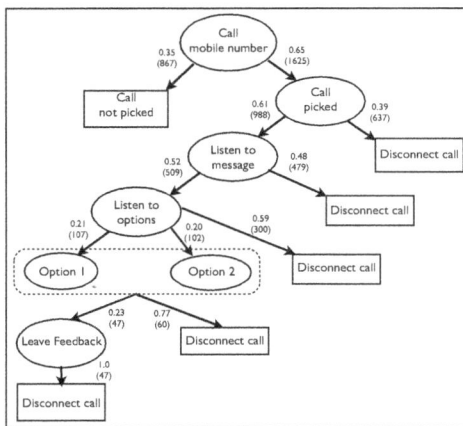

Figure 5: Callee Decision Tree.

7. DISCUSSION

In this work, we examined the exposure of Indian mobile numbers on OSNs via profile and public posts and investigated the associated privacy risks. Most mobile numbers were shared to ask for blood help, to market astrology business, IT facilities, and escort services. We observed few posts where numbers were shared in personal contexts like *"My contact no in India is +91-9958xxxxxx"*, however posts used for personal contexts had few context specific keywords, therefore, personal contexts were difficult to highlight. Users exploited social aggregators to popularize same number on multiple OSNs. Sensitive information such as Voter ID could be extracted with the use of mobile number and other information sources. To communicate the risks and vulnerabilities, we called 2,492 numbers with an IVR setup and received feedback. Few users did not know about the presence of their mobile number on OSNs while few told us that they intentionally put it to publicize their business.

Indian mobile numbers are heavily shared for non-personal contexts (e.g. marketing, emergency), even such a behavior may invite unwanted spammers / calls to marketers themselves. OSNs do not provide safeguard mechanisms to disallow sensitive and identifiable information exposure via either profile or public posts. There is a need to build technological, people and process oriented solutions to forewarn users and raise the awareness towards risks of PII leaks, so that

users can make better decisions. We speculate other information on OSNs such as Blackberry Messenger Pins (BBM), and email addresses, can also help in extracting more sensitive information about their owners. [23] We recognize the limitations of our data collection methodology and analysis. During our keyword selection phase, we used a limited set of keywords to extract posts with mobile numbers from OSNs, and refined keyword set only once. We leave the implications of iterative keyword refinement on the quality of the dataset for future work. We expect further studies to understand impact of geographical, cultural differences, and user personality traits on the practice of sharing mobile number.

8. REFERENCES

[1] Marco Balduzzi, Christian Platzer, Thorsten Holz, Engin Kirda, Davide Balzarotti, and Christopher Kruegel. Abusing social networks for automated user profiling. In *RAID '10*.

[2] Terence Chen, Mohamed Ali Kaafar, Arik Friedman, and Roksana Boreli. Is More always Merrier?: a Deep Dive into Online Social Footprints. In *WOSN '12*.

[3] Yao Cheng, Lingyun Ying, Sibei Jiao, Purui Su, and Dengguo Feng. Bind your phone number with caution: automated user profiling through address book matching on smartphone. In *ASIACCS '13*.

[4] Ratan Dey, Cong Tang, Keith W. Ross, and Nitesh Saxena. Estimating age privacy leakage in online social networks. In *INFOCOM '12*.

[5] Balachander Krishnamurthy. Privacy and Online Social Networks: Can Colorless Green Ideas Sleep Furiously? *SP '13*.

[6] Haewoon Kwak, Changhyun Lee, Hosung Park, and Sue Moon. What is Twitter, a social network or a news media? In *WWW '10*.

[7] Gabriel Magno, Giovanni Comarela, Diego Saez-Trumper, Meeyoung Cha, and Virgilio Almeida. New kid on the block: exploring the google+ social graph. In *IMC '12*.

[8] Huina Mao, Xin Shuai, and Apu Kapadia. Loose tweets: an analysis of privacy leaks on twitter. In *WPES '11*.

[9] David Nadeau and Satoshi Sekine. A survey of named entity recognition and classification. *Lingvisticae Investigationes*, 2007.

[10] T. Pontes, G. Magno, M. Vasconcelos, A. Gupta, J. Almeida, P. Kumaraguru, and V. Almeida. Beware of what you share: Inferring home location in social networks. In *ICDMW '12*.

[11] Matthew Rowe. The credibility of digital identity information on the social web: a user study. In *WICOW '10*.

[12] Yang Wang, Gregory Norcie, Saranga Komanduri, Alessandro Acquisti, Pedro Giovanni Leon, and Lorrie Faith Cranor. "I regretted the minute I pressed share": a qualitative study of regrets on Facebook. In *SOUPS '11*.

[13] Jinxi Xu and W. Bruce Croft. Query expansion using local and global document analysis. In *SIGIR '96*.

[14] Elena Zheleva and Lise Getoor. Privacy in social networks: A survey. In *Social Network Data Analytics*. 2011.

[23]We also collected BBM pins and email addresses shared on OSNs.

Hierarchical Community Decomposition Via Oblivious Routing Techniques

W. Sean Kennedy[*]
Bell Labs, Alcatel Lucent
Murray Hill, NJ
kennedy@research.bell-labs.com

Jamie Morgenstern[†]
Carnegie Mellon University
Pittsburgh, PA
jamiemmt.cs@gmail.com

Gordon Wilfong
Bell Labs, Alcatel Lucent
Murray Hill, NJ
gtw@research.bell-labs.com

Lisa Zhang[‡]
Bell Labs, Alcatel Lucent
Murray Hill, NJ
ylz@research.bell-labs.com

ABSTRACT

The detection of communities in real-world large-scale complex networks is a fundamental step in many applications, such as describing community structure and predicting the dissemination of information. Unfortunately, community detection is a computationally expensive task. Indeed, many approaches with strong theoretic guarantees are infeasible when applied to networks of large scale. Numerous approaches have been designed to scale community detection algorithms, many of which leverage local optimizations or local greedy decisions to iteratively find the communities. Solely relying on local techniques to detect communities, rather than a global objective function, can fail to detect global structure of the network.

In this work, we instead formulate a notion of a hierarchical community decomposition (HCD), which takes a more global view of hierarchical community structure. Our main contributions are as follows. We formally define a (λ, δ)-HCD where λ parametrizes the connectivity within each subcommunity at the same hierarchical level and δ parametrizes the relationship between communities across two consecutive levels. Based on a method of Räcke originally designed for oblivious routing, we provide an algorithm to construct a HCD and prove that an $(O(\log n), O(1))$-HCD can always be found for any n-node input graph. Further, our algorithm does not rely on a pre-specified number of communities or depth of decomposition. Since the algorithm is of exponential complexity, we also describe a practical efficient, yet heuristic, implementation and perform an experimental validation on synthetic and real-world networks. We experiment first with synthetic networks with well-defined "intended" decompositions, on which we verify the quality of the decompositions produced by our method. Armed with the confidence these positive results provide, we use our implementation to compute the hierarchical community structure of more complex, real-world networks.

Categories and Subject Descriptors

F.2 [**Analysis of Algorithms and Problem Complexity**]: Miscellaneous

Keywords

Community detection; hierarchical community decomposition; Räcke decompositions; approximation algorithms

1. INTRODUCTION

The recent explosion of accessible social network data, driven in part by the popularity of online social networks, has led many research, business and marketing communities to examine the resultant data sets. Mining these sets promises to create a wealth of information about how societies, objects and ideas interact. Many of these interactions are easily represented by a graph. For example, in Facebook's recently announced graph search, users are nodes and a subset of the friend relationships yields the links [17]. Of the multitude of questions surrounding the analysis of these networks, one of the most noticeable efforts focuses on *community detection*. Understanding community structure is a fundamental step in many applications, such as web search, biology, social network analysis, business structure. See for example [14, 23, 21, 24, 35, 36, 38].

The community structure of many networks is naturally hierarchical. Communities can be iteratively divided into smaller sub-communities each of which is also a good communities. Such hierarchical structures have been observed in nature, social networks, and more, see for e.g., [41, 16,

[*]Partially supported by NSERC PDF and the NIST Grant No. 60NANB10D128.

[†]Work partially done while at Bell Labs, supported in part by NSF Grant CCF-1101215 and an NSF Graduate Fellowship.

[‡]Work partially supported by the NIST Grant No. 60NANB10D128.

13, 43, 23]. Our goal is to capture the inherent hierarchical structure of such networks. Towards this end we define a *hierarchical community decomposition* (HCD) of a network. Given a network $G = (V, E)$, an HCD of G may be best described by an associated *decomposition tree* $T = (\mathcal{V}, \mathcal{E})$, where T is a rooted tree such that each node $a \in \mathcal{V}$ is labeled by a subset $V_a \subseteq V$ where these labels satisfy two properties. First, the root r is labeled by $V_r = V$, and second, for each node $a \in \mathcal{V}$ with children $c_1, c_2, ..., c_k$, the subsets $V_{c_1}, V_{c_2}, ..., V_{c_k}$ form a partition of V_a.

Informally, every node $a \in \mathcal{V}$ corresponds to a "good" community induced on V_a in G. (We discuss the question of what it means to be good below.) Furthermore, the decomposition tree also reflects the global structure of G. For example in Figure 1, community B consists of A_1, A_2, A_3 and A_4 each of which is obviously a good sub-community individually. However, $A = A_1 \cup A_2$ appears to form a natural sub-community as well. Therefore the decomposition tree shown in Figure 1.c captures the global structure more completely than the one in Figure 1.b.

This intuition leads to a basic question: *what is a good community*? Towards answering this question, many notions have been explored. From a graph theoretic viewpoint, a good community is likely to have a small diameter, i.e. the shortest path distance between any node pairs is small. Natural variations of small diameter based community detection include the k-center, k-median and k-mean clustering objectives. Alternatively, a good community is likely to be sufficiently dense; a maximal subgraph with high density reflects the nodes within the subgraph interact more with one another than with those outside the subgraph. Examples of this include high maximum and average node degrees within the community [28]. Despite simplicity these simple classes of measures do not consistently lead to good communities. As we discuss now, more sophisticated measures have proven to be more successful.

One of the most intensively studied notions of a community stems from the rich theory of graph cuts. Given a subset S of the nodes, a *cut* is the set of edges each of which has one endpoint inside S and one outside of S. Generally speaking, *conductance* (and its many variants) measures the ratio of the cut size to the number of edges inside each side of the cut. Formally, the *conductance* of $S \subseteq V$ in graph $G = (V, E)$, is

$$\varphi(S) := \frac{|\{xy \in E | x \in S, y \notin S\}|}{\min\{\sum_{v \in S} \deg(v), \sum_{v \in V - S} \deg(v)\}}.$$

A min-conductance subgraph is intuitively associated with a good community as it captures the notion of more edges within the subgraph than leaving the subgraph.

We construct hierarchical community decompositions (HCD) by adopting a scheme for oblivious routing originally designed by Harold Räcke [39]. A byproduct of Räcke's routing algorithm is a pair of connectivity conditions, each of which corresponds to our intuition of community structure. The first condition is similar to conductance and insists that any community must have ample internal connections relative to external connections. The second rule can be thought of as a conductance measure of the sub-communities ensuring that global structure is represented in the decomposition. It insists that any subset of these sub-communities must not have many inter-community connections; otherwise, this set of sub-communities should together form a larger commu-

nity. These two opposing forces guide each iteration of the algorithm, balancing between individual community quality and overall global structure.

One method to find a HCD is to determine one level of the hierarchy by applying a community detection algorithm to the original graph and then iteratively applying the algorithm to each of the sub-communities to extend the hierarchy. However, by focusing on local optimization of the choice of communities, it is easy to miss the global structure of the network. For example in Figure 1, if A_1, A_2, A_3 and A_4 are the best communities, an iterative algorithm may well find them all and put them in the same level of hierarchy, but miss the global structure that includes an extra level in which $A_1 \cup A_2$ also forms a good community A, though A is somewhat weaker than $A_1 \ldots A_4$. On the other hand, the second rule in our HCD approach based on Räcke decomposition is designed to capture such structure.

Since determining a subgraph of minimum conductance is NP-hard [44], several well-studied heuristic algorithms have been introduced. Recent work [34] makes an extensive empirical comparison of a number of these methods, and notes that they seem to present particular biases. For example spectral methods tend to find very dense subgraphs as communities which may still be well-connected to the rest of the graph, whereas some other methods may result in a small number of edges crossing the cuts between communities, but unfortunately poor internal connectivity. If a community of less desirable bias is found in one iteration, it is likely that an iterative application for community decomposition will propagate an early error. In our HCD approach, we allow multiple iterations in breaking up the potential sub-communities and recombining them until we converge to a satisfactory partition. Thus, we believe the opposing forces of partitioning and recombining provide an opportunity for patching errors that min-conductance heuristics could introduce.

1.1 Contribution and Organization

- In Section 2.1 we formally define a hierarchical community decomposition, (λ, δ)-HCD, where λ parametrizes the connectivity within every subcommunity at the same hierarchical level and δ parametrizes the relationship between communities across two consecutive levels.

- In Section 2.2 we provide an algorithm to construct a (λ, δ)-HCD and prove that an $(O(\log |V|), O(1))$-HCD can always be found for any input graph, based on Räcke's original decomposition algorithm. Since this algorithm takes exponential time (it examines an exponential number of cuts), we propose an efficient heuristic implementation via spectral cuts in Section 2.3.

- In Section 3 we detail our experimental results. We first use a small network to verify our earlier point that our algorithm is able to recover from a less-than-ideal partition provided by spectral cuts whereas performing iterative spectral cuts may not. In addition, for small enough examples that the exact algorithm is feasible, we observe that our efficient heuristic in fact returns a HCD very close to the solution given by the exact algorithm. We then proceed to "friendly" synthetic networks for which the quality of the decompositions produced by our efficient heuristics can be

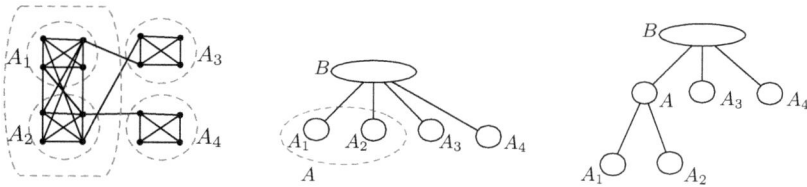

Figure 1: (a). Network B. (b) A decomposition tree that misses A in the global structure. (c) A desirable hierarchy formed by A, A_1 and A_2.

verified. We finally explore several more complex real-world networks and explore their global community structure via our heuristic. These networks consists of thousands of nodes.

1.2 Related Work

We turn to a brief overview on methods for determining communities. We do not attempt an extensive and complete review, instead referring the interested reader to [20, 10, 31, 42]. Also, Leskovek et al. [34] present a comprehensive empirical study of numerous methods for determining communities.

Communities: Hardness, Approximations & Heuristics. Many of the cut-based criteria for measuring community quality give rise to NP-hard optimization problems. See [22] or [26] for a survey (as of 1996) of approximating minimum-conductance, expansion, normalized or sparsest cuts. Flow-inspired algorithms for determining communities have been the subject of considerable study [18, 19]. Of particular interest to this work is minimum-conductance cuts. Leighton and Rao prove an $O(\log(n))$-approximation [32]; Arora et al. show an improved approximation of $O(\sqrt{\log(n)})$ [5]. Heuristics for attacking this problem use the Cheeger inequality which describes the relationship between the edge expansion of a graph and the second eigenvalue of the normalized Laplacian matrix [11]. This leads to the spectral methods to find low-conductance cuts [12].

The Nibble method by Spielman and Teng [45] finds a community of low conductance containing a starting vertex v, in time nearly linear in the size of the output community. The algorithm starts by processing a truncated distribution similar to that of a short random walk starting at v: those vertices that occur in short random walks are more likely to be a part of a low-conductance community with v. Formally, if one selects a vertex v from a community C with conductance $O(\phi^2 / \log^3(n))$, the Nibble method returns a community that is mostly contained in C with conductance at most ϕ, with a constant probability.

Local spectral methods [2] find low-conductance cuts by computing approximate PageRank vectors and conducting sweeps over those vectors. They show a mixing result for approximate PageRank vectors that implies a ϕ-conductance cut can be found provided an $\Omega(\phi^2 / \log(m))$-conductance cut exists. Extending the Nibble method, the algorithm also starts from a single vertex v and finds a low-conductance community that usually contains v. A follow-up paper [3] begins with set of well-connected seed vertices rather than a single vertex. This was inspired by the HITS algorithm [30] which begins with a seed set generated by a search engine and then does a constant-depth breadth-first-search to construct a community containing that set.

Hierarchical Community Decomposition Other than iteratively applying a community detection algorithm to find a hierarchical decomposition, a variety of more global approaches have been developed.

Consider a basic algorithm that begins with an initially empty graph on n vertices and adds edges one at a time, in the order of decreasing weight. Whenever two disconnected components are joined, they can be thought of as subcommunities in the larger community which is their union. Therefore, this basic algorithm produces decompositions that are hierarchical in nature. This approach tries to bridge the gap between scalable methods and global ones: the weights can be defined in terms of more global properties of the graph, but the algorithm itself is polynomial time. For example, the weights on these edges can be the original weights from the community graph, or a function of the number of paths between two vertices [37, 29], where longer paths are usually weighed significantly less than shorter paths. Girvan et al. [23] propose an almost dual approach by starting with the full graph and iteratively removing edges.

Balcan and Liang [6] formalize a metric to measure hierarchical community structure. They describe a bottom-up construction of stable communities: each community C must be sufficiently large, points in C must have most of their neighbors in C, and points outside C can only have a few of their neighbors in C. The authors propose an algorithm that begins with singleton sets as communities, and merges sets if there is sufficient overlap in their neighborhoods, and show the algorithm produces a hierarchy that satisfies their definition of stability.

The Louvain method [9] is a greedy modularity-based approach for constructing heirarchical community decompositions. It constructs communities in a bottom-up fashion by iteratively finding a locally maximal partition with respect to modularity, after which each partition is permanent. In contrast our method looks for the largest communities first, and at each level of the hierarchy it iterates between breaking down the potential communities and recombining them until convergence. Other work on modularity-based approaches include [27]. Work of [7, 4] also consider potentially overlapping communities.

Räcke's Decomposition. Closely related to our work is Räcke's oblivious routing algorithm and accompanying decomposition of a network [40]. This first work proves the existence of a (λ, δ) hierarchical decomposition of a network so as to allow oblivious routing with low congestion, where λ and δ are polylogarithmic. We give a formal description of this paper in Sections 2.1 and 2.2. The initial description is not polynomial-time as it considers all cuts in a graph throughout the algorithm, and computes a balanced min-cut as a subroutine. Later work [25, 8] improves this result to run in polynomial time, though these algorithms have substantially different techniques which appear to relate less directly to community detection. We therefore pursue heuristics of the original algorithm in Section 2.3.

Our philosophy of HCD also has similarity to Kannan, Vempala and Vetta [28], which generalizes the conductance-based objective to a bicriterial one. An (α, ϵ)-clustering has conductance at least α for each cluster, and has at most an ϵ-fraction of the edge weights crossing between clusters. For a graph with (α, ϵ)-clustering, [28] shows that finding a spectral cut and recurring on the two sides achieves $(f(\alpha), g(\epsilon))$-approximation guarantee for some functions f and g. One obvious difference is that [28] focuses on 1-level decomposition, not hierarchical decomposition. More importantly, the achievable values α and ϵ for a given graph are not a priori small, let alone $f(\alpha)$ and $g(\epsilon)$. In contrast, as we shall see, we guarantee a (λ, δ)-HCD with a logarithmic λ and a constant δ for *all* graphs.

2. HIERARCHICAL COMMUNITY DECOMPOSITIONS

2.1 (λ, δ)-HCD

We now give a formal definition of HCD, which stems from the first work [39] in the sequence of papers on oblivious routing by Räcke and coauthors. Let $G = (V, E)$ be an undirected weighted input graph, where w_{ij} or w_e represents the weight of an edge $e = ij \in E$. We interpret w_{ij} as the similarity between nodes i and j, the heavier the weight the more alike the two nodes. Recall an HCD of G is described by the associated *decomposition tree* $T = (\mathcal{V}, \mathcal{E})$, where T is a rooted tree such that each node $a \in \mathcal{V}$ is labeled by a subset $V_a \subseteq V$ where these labels satisfy the following:

- the root r is labelled by $V_r = V$, and

- for each node $a \in \mathcal{V}$ with children $c_1, c_2, ..., c_k$, the subsets $V_{c_1}, V_{c_2}, ..., V_{c_k}$ form a partition of V_a.

We enforce two conditions. First, if A is a good community then any subset of A must have ample connections within A relative to connections external to A; otherwise, this subset is not sufficiently connected to other nodes in A, and A is not a good community.

DEFINITION 1. *The total connections, or capacity, between two (not necessarily disjoint) subsets X and Y of V is*

$$\mathbf{cap}(X, Y) = \sum_{x \in X, y \in Y} w_{xy},$$

where $w_{xy} = 0$ whenever xy is not an edge of G.

DEFINITION 2. *Let $V' \subset V$. For $\lambda \geq 1$, a subset of $U \subset V'$ is λ-detached with respect to V' if $|U| \leq \frac{1}{2}|V'|$ and if*

$$\frac{\mathbf{cap}(U, V \setminus U)}{\mathbf{cap}(U, V' \setminus U)} \geq \lambda.$$

We say V' is λ-detachable if some subset $U \subset V'$ is λ-detached w.r.t. V'.

As argued above, for an appropriate value of λ, no good community should have a λ-detached subgraph. Hence, our first condition on the hierarchical decomposition tree T is that for each $a \in \mathcal{V}$, V_a is not λ-detachable.

The second condition takes the hierarchical view and tries to ensure that all levels of the hierarchy are present even when good smaller communities exist. Recall the example in Figure 1. Let A be a good community containing two subcommunities A_1 and A_2. Intuitively, there should exist nodes labelled by A, A_1 and A_2 in T where A is an ancestor of A_1 and A_2. Figure 1.c shows an example of a good hierarchy. In contrast, Figure 1.b demonstrates a less complete hierarchy, as it does not capture that A_1 and A_2 together form a community in addition to being separate communities themselves. We capture this notion formally in Definitions 3 and 4.

Let a be any non-leaf node of a hierarchical decomposition tree T, and let $c_1, c_2, ..., c_k$ be its children. The above intuition suggests that the only combination of the communities $V_{c_1}, V_{c_2}, ..., V_{c_k}$ that results in a good community is $V_a = \bigcup_i V_{c_i}$. To formalize this, we define the following.

DEFINITION 3. *Let $V' \subset V$. Let $\delta \geq 1$ and $P_1, P_2, ..., P_k$ be a partition of V'. An induced subgraph $R = \bigcup_{i \in I} P_i \subset V'$, where I is a subset of $\{1, 2, ..., k\}$ is δ-linked with respect to V' if $|R| \leq \frac{1}{2}|V'|$ and if*

$$\frac{\sum_{i,j \in I, i \neq j} \mathbf{cap}(P_i, P_j)}{\sum_{i \in I, j \notin I} \mathbf{cap}(P_i, P_j)} > \delta.$$

We say V' with a partition of $P_1, P_2, ..., P_k$ is δ-linkable if $R = \bigcup_{i \in I} P_i$ is δ-linked w.r.t. V' for some subset I.

Our second condition is that if $c_1, c_2, ..., c_k$ are the children of a in T then V_a with a partition of $V_{c_1}, ..., V_{c_k}$ is not δ-linkable for an appropriately chosen $\delta \geq 1$.

We are now able to describe the decomposition we are interested in finding.

DEFINITION 4. *A (λ, δ)-hierarchical decomposition of a graph $G = (V, E)$ is a decomposition tree $T = (\mathcal{V}, \mathcal{E})$ satisfying the following three properties:*

(1) For each node $a \in \mathcal{V}$, V_a is not λ-detachable.

(2) For each non-leaf node $a \in \mathcal{V}$ with children $c_1, c_2, ..., c_k$, V_a with the partition of $V_{c_1}, ..., V_{c_k}$ is not δ-linkable.

(3) For each leaf node $\ell \in \mathcal{V}$, $|V_\ell| = 1$.

Finding a decomposition satisfying only Conditions (1) and (2) is trivial. Indeed, a single node labelled by V will suffice. As we discuss in the next section, for logarithmic values of λ and constants δ there always exists a decomposition also satisfying Condition (3). These bounds on λ, δ are exponentially smaller than the range for each parameter; there exist both $(1, |E|)$ and $(|E|, 1)$ hierarchical decompositions. For example, a $(1, |E|)$-hierarchical decomposition of a graph $G = (V, E)$ is a root r labelled by $V_r = V$ and adjacent $|V|$ leaves each labeled by a unique vertex of G. On the other hand, any binary decomposition tree T defines a $(|E|, 1)$-hierarchical decomposition of a graph, since each non-leaf node a with two children c_1 and c_2 imply vacuously that V_a with partition V_{c_1} and V_{c_2} is not δ-linkable. As we discuss below, Räcke proved there always exists an $(O(\log |V|), O(\log |V|))$-hierarchical decomposition [39]. In the next section, we strengthen his result by showing that there always exists an $(O(\log |V|), O(1))$-hierarchical decomposition. Our improvement plays a key role in our practical implementation of this algorithm described in Section 2.3.

2.2 Exact Algorithms for HCD

For fixed $\lambda \geq 1$ and $\delta \geq 1$, Definition 4 suggests the outline of a algorithm to construct a (λ, δ)-hierarchical decomposition of a graph $G = (V, E)$. We iteratively build decomposition trees $T_i = (\mathcal{V}_i, \mathcal{E}_i)$, $i = 0, 1, ...$, each satisfying Conditions (1) and (2) starting with T_0 and stopping when T_i also satisfies Condition (3).

Let T_0 be a single node r labelled by V. Note that (1) holds since $V_r = V$ and so $\mathbf{cap}(U, V \setminus U) = \mathbf{cap}(U, V_a \setminus U)$ for all proper subsets U of V, and (2) holds since the unique node of T_0 is a leaf. For $i \geq 0$, assume T_i satisfies (1) and (2), but not (3). Let ℓ be a leaf node with $|V_\ell| > 1$. The key is to find a partition $P_1, ..., P_k$ of V_ℓ such that V_ℓ is not δ-linkable and that no P_i is λ-detachable; a stronger statement is captured in Lemma 6. It follows that the decomposition tree T_{i+1} found by adding children $P_1, ..., P_k$ to node ℓ in T_i, respectively labelled by $P_1, ..., P_k$, satisfies (1) and (2).

Given that we can always further partition any node satisfying (1) and (2), but not (3), there must exist some i' for which $T_{i'}$ also satisfies (3). Indeed, in each iteration we partition some leaf node a into non-empty parts each of size at most $\frac{1}{2}|V_a|$.

More rigorously, the following Theorem 5 states a (λ, δ)-hierarchical decomposition can always be found for logarithmic values of λ and constants δ. A similar and slightly weaker result is stated and proved in [39], although our proof is simpler and is phrased in terms relevant to our problem (HCD) rather than routing.

THEOREM 5. *Let $\lambda \geq 4 \log |V|$ and $\delta \geq (1 - \frac{2}{\lambda} \log |V|)^{-1}$. For any graph $G = (V, E)$ there exists an (λ, δ)-hierarchical decomposition $T = (\mathcal{V}, \mathcal{E})$.*

To prove this theorem, it is enough to prove Lemma 6 which iteratively builds the decomposition tree starting from the root, as described above.

LEMMA 6. *Assume $V' \subseteq V$ satisfies $|V'| > 1$ and is not λ-detachable. Then, there exists a partition $P_1, P_2, ..., P_k$ of V' such that*

(i) for each $i = 1...k$, $|P_i| \leq \frac{1}{2}|V'|$,

(ii) no P_i is λ-detachable, and

(iii) no subset $I \subset \{1, 2, ..., k\}$ is such that $\bigcup_{i \in I} P_i$ is δ-linkable w.r.t. V'.

In fact, Algorithms 1 and 2 find such a partition.

PROOF. Let $\mathcal{P}_0 = \{\{v\} \mid v \in V'\}$, that is, each node of V' is in its own part. Clearly, $\mathcal{P}_0$ satisfies (i) and (ii). We iteratively construct partitions $\mathcal{P}_1, \mathcal{P}_2, ..., \mathcal{P}_j, ...$ of V' each of which satisfy (i) and (ii). We stop when we find a partition $\mathcal{P}_{j'}$ also satisfying (iii). Algorithms 1 and 2 described the process in pseudocode.

We prove

LEMMA 7. *Let $\mathcal{P}_j = \{P_1, P_2, ..., P_k\}$ satisfy (i) and (ii) but not (iii) for $j \geq 0$. Then, there exists $\mathcal{P}_{j+1}$ satisfying (i) and (ii), and such that*

$$\sum_{P \in \mathcal{P}_{j+1}} \mathbf{cap}(P, V \setminus P) < \sum_{P \in \mathcal{P}_j} \mathbf{cap}(P, V \setminus P). \quad (1)$$

Algorithm 1: PARTITION

Input: $V' \subset V$ such that V' is not λ-detachable.
Output: Partition $P_1, ..., P_k$ of V' satisfying (i), (ii) and (iii).

1 **begin**
2   set $\mathcal{P} = \{\{v\} \mid v \in V'\}$
3   **while** $\exists I \subset \{1, 2, ..., |\mathcal{P}|\} \in \mathcal{P}$ **such that** $\bigcup_{i \in I} P_i$ **is** δ**-linked w.r.t.** V' **do**
4   let $\mathcal{R} = $ DETACH$(\bigcup_{i \in I} P_i)$
5   set $\mathcal{P} = (\mathcal{P} \setminus \bigcup_{i \in I}\{P_i\}) \cup \mathcal{R}$
6   **end**
7   **return** $\mathcal{P}$
8 **end**

Since the capacity of any $W \subset V$, $\mathbf{cap}(W, V \setminus W)$ is always positive, it follows that eventually, for some $\mathcal{P}_{j'}$, (iii) must also be satisfied. Hence to complete the proof of Lemma 6, we need only prove Lemma 7.

PROOF OF LEMMA 7. Since (iii) is not satisfied there exists $I \subset \{1, 2, ..., k\}$ such that $R = \mathbf{cap}_{i \in I} P_i$ is δ-linked w.r.t. V'. We show that we can partition R so that the resultant partition $R_1, ..., R_t$ satisfies (i), (ii) and

$$\sum_{j=1}^{t} \mathbf{cap}(R_t, R \setminus R_t) < \sum_{i \in I} \mathbf{cap}(P_i, R \setminus P_i). \quad (2)$$

This implies Lemma 7, since

$$\sum_{P \in \mathcal{P}_{j+1}} \mathbf{cap}(P, V \setminus P)$$
$$= \sum_{j=1}^{t} \mathbf{cap}(R_t, V \setminus R_t) + \sum_{i \notin I} \mathbf{cap}(P_i, V \setminus P_i)$$
$$= \sum_{j=1}^{t} \mathbf{cap}(R_t, V \setminus R) + \sum_{j=1}^{t} \mathbf{cap}(R_t, R \setminus R_t)$$
$$\qquad + \sum_{i \notin I} \mathbf{cap}(P_i, V \setminus P_i)$$
$$< \sum_{i \in I} \mathbf{cap}(P_i, V \setminus R) + \sum_{i \in I} \mathbf{cap}(P_i, R \setminus P_i)$$
$$\qquad + \sum_{i \notin I} \mathbf{cap}(P_i, V \setminus P_i)$$
$$= \sum_{i \in I} \mathbf{cap}(P_i, V \setminus P_i) + \sum_{i \notin I} \mathbf{cap}(P_i, V \setminus P_i)$$
$$= \sum_{P \in \mathcal{P}_j} \mathbf{cap}(P, V \setminus P),$$

where the inequality follows from Eqn. 2 and since $R_1, ..., R_t$ and $\{P_i \mid i \in I\}$ are both partitions of R. Given R we find the desired $R_1, ..., R_t$ by applying Algorithm 2. Starting with $\mathcal{R}_0 = \{R\}$, we iteratively find partitions $\mathcal{R}_1, \mathcal{R}_2, ..., \mathcal{R}_\ell, ...$.

Given $\mathcal{R}_\ell, \ell \geq 0$ we find $\mathcal{R}_{\ell+1}$ by choosing some part R^ℓ that contains a λ-detached subgraph U^ℓ with respect to R^ℓ. If no such part exists, then $\mathcal{R}_\ell$ is the desired partition. Otherwise, we set $\mathcal{R}_{\ell+1} = (\mathcal{R}_\ell \setminus \{R^\ell\}) \cup \{U^\ell, R^\ell \setminus U^\ell\}$. Since $1 \leq U^\ell \leq \frac{1}{2}|R^\ell|$, each part is nonempty and so this process eventually terminates.

Algorithm 2: DETACH

Input: $R \subset V$

Output: Partition $R_1, ..., R_t$ of R such that each R_i, $1 \le i \le t$, is not λ-detachable.

1 **begin**
2   set $\mathcal{R} = \{R\}$
3   **while** $\exists U \subset R_i \in \mathcal{R}$ **such that** U **is** λ-**detached w.r.t.** R_i **do**
4   set $\mathcal{R} = (\mathcal{R} \setminus R_i) \cup \{U, R_i \setminus U\}$
5   **end**
6   **return** $\mathcal{R}$
7 **end**

Assuming this process terminated at $\ell = \ell'$, note that we can describe this process as a set of ordered pairs $\mathcal{U} = \{(U^1, R^1), (U^2, R^2), ..., (U^{\ell'}, R^{\ell'})\}$. For each pair of parts $R_i \ne R_j$, any edge $e \in E(R_i, R_j)$ is in exactly one of the sets $E(U^\ell, R^\ell \setminus U^\ell)$ and so,

$$\sum_{j=1}^{t} \mathbf{cap}(R_t, R \setminus R_t) = 2 \sum_{(U^\ell, R^\ell) \in \mathcal{U}} \mathbf{cap}(U^\ell, R^\ell \setminus U^\ell)$$

$$\le \frac{2}{\lambda} \sum_{(U^\ell, R^\ell) \in \mathcal{U}} \mathbf{cap}(U^\ell, V \setminus U^\ell),$$

since each U^ℓ is λ-detached with respect to R^ℓ. We can split this sum as follows.

$$\frac{2}{\lambda} \sum_{(U^\ell, R^\ell) \in \mathcal{U}} \mathbf{cap}(U^\ell, V \setminus U^\ell)$$

$$= \frac{2}{\lambda} \sum_{(U^\ell, R^\ell) \in \mathcal{U}} \mathbf{cap}(U^\ell, R \setminus U^\ell)$$

$$+ \frac{2}{\lambda} \sum_{(U^\ell, R^\ell) \in \mathcal{U}} \mathbf{cap}(U^\ell, V \setminus R)$$

To finish we need a simple observation.

OBSERVATION 8. *Each vertex $v \in R$ is in at most $\log|R|$ of the U^ℓ.*

PROOF. The set of U^ℓ's containing v form a nested family of subsets each at least twice a big as the previous and all contained in R. Hence, there can be at most $\log|R|$ of them. $\square$

Observation 8 implies

$$\sum_{(U^\ell, R^\ell) \in \mathcal{U}} \mathbf{cap}(U^\ell, V \setminus R)$$

$$= \sum_{(U^\ell, R^\ell) \in \mathcal{U}} \sum_{v \in U^\ell} \mathbf{cap}(\{v\}, V \setminus R)$$

$$= \sum_{v \in R} \sum_{\substack{(U^\ell, R^\ell) \in \mathcal{U} \\ U^\ell \ni v}} \mathbf{cap}(\{v\}, V \setminus R)$$

$$\le (\log|R|) \sum_{v \in R} \mathbf{cap}(\{v\}, V \setminus R)$$

$$= (\log|R|)\mathbf{cap}(R, V \setminus R).$$

In a similar way, Observation 8 implies that every part of the final partition $R_1, ..., R_t$ is contained in at most $\log|R|$

of the U^ℓ's. Hence,

$$\sum_{(U^\ell, R^\ell) \in \mathcal{U}} \mathbf{cap}(U^\ell, R \setminus U^\ell)$$

$$\le \sum_{(U^\ell, R^\ell) \in \mathcal{U}} \sum_{R_i \subseteq U^\ell} \mathbf{cap}(R_i, R \setminus R_i)$$

$$\le \log|R| \sum_{i \in I} \mathbf{cap}(R_i, R \setminus R_i).$$

So, together we have

$$\sum_{j=1}^{t} \mathbf{cap}(R_t, R \setminus R_t)$$

$$\le \frac{2\log|R|}{\lambda} \left[\mathbf{cap}(R_i, R \setminus R_i) + \mathbf{cap}(R, V \setminus R)\right] \quad (3)$$

By assumption $R = \bigcup_{i \in I} P_i$ is δ-linked w.r.t. V' and so $\mathbf{cap}(R, V \setminus R) < \frac{1}{\delta} \sum_{i \ne j \in I} \mathbf{cap}(P_i, P_j)$. This together with our choice of λ and δ, Eqn. 3 is then equivalent to the following.

$$\sum_{j=1}^{t} \mathbf{cap}(R_t, R \setminus R_t)$$

$$< \left(1 - \frac{2\log|R|}{\lambda}\right)^{-1} \frac{1}{\delta} \sum_{i \ne j \in I} \mathbf{cap}(P_i, P_j)$$

$$< \sum_{i \ne j \in I} \mathbf{cap}(P_i, P_j).$$

This completes the proof of Lemma 7, and hence, Lemma 6. $\square$

Remark. Our proof shares many ideas with a proof of Räcke's showing that there always exists such a $(O(\log|V|), O(\log|V|))$-hierarchical decomposition tree $T = (\mathcal{V}, \mathcal{E})$ satisfying the height of T is at most $O(\log|V|)$. This additional height constraint was important in the design of his oblivious routing scheme. Note that since Condition (i) insists that each child node is at most half the size of its parent, the height of our decomposition tree is also $O(\log|V|)$.

2.3 Efficient Implementation

In this section we focus on scalable implementations of Algorithms 1 and 2. We start with Algorithm 1 where we propose replacing the exponential procedure in Line 3 with a polynomial time heuristic. Instead of checking *each* subset in Line 3, we check the subset generated by finding a spectral cut in the graph. Algorithm 3 describes the basic spectral cut method we use. Consider the reduced multigraph $G_{\mathcal{P}}$, where each part in the current partition is collapsed into a single node. A spectral cut in $G_{\mathcal{P}}$ is likely to be well-connected internally, implying the sets on one side of the cut are good candidates for δ-linkedness. If such a δ-linked subset is found we continue with Lines 4 and 5; otherwise, since Algorithm 3 is randomized, we require that it fails a fixed number of times before we assume that no δ-linkable set exists. Initially we set this failure rate to be 10, but experimentation showed that 3 was sufficient, greatly improving the runtime of our heuristic.

Similarly for Algorithm 2, a spectral cut of R_i approximates the minimum conductance cut in a graph [28]. This implies there is some measure by which the intra-connectivity of a spectral cut is low. Thus we replace checking all subsets of each R_i for λ-detachability by only checking *spectral cuts* of each R_i, where again we require that Algorithm 3 fails a fixed number of times before we assume that no λ-detachable set exists.

The proof of Lemma 7 shows that the choice of δ bounds the number of iterations of Algorithm 1 since

$$\tau(\{R_1, ..., R_t\}) := \sum_{j=1}^{t} \mathbf{cap}(R_t, R \setminus R_t)$$

decreases by at least a factor of $\frac{1}{\delta}$ in each iteration. Since $\tau(\{R_1, ..., R_t\}) \leq |E|$, by choosing $\delta \geq 2$ we can ensure there are at most $\log_2 |E|$ iterations. Additionally, our heuristic will terminate if we halt whenever $\tau(\{R_1, ..., R_t\})$ does not strictly decrease in each iteration.

Algorithm 3: SPECTRALCUT

Input: $V' \subset V$
Output: Cut (P_1, P_2) of V'.
1 begin
2 | **let** $\mathcal{L}$ = Laplacian of subgraph induced on V'
3 | **let** (u_1, u_2) = smallest 2 eigenvectors of $\mathcal{L}$
4 | **let** (C_1, C_2) be the 2-means clustering of the n columns of (u_1, u_2) (initial centers chosen randomly)
5 | **let** (P_1, P_2) be the partition of V' according to (C_1, C_2)
6 | **return** (P_1, P_2)
7 end

---

3. EXPERIMENTS

In this section, we describe some experimental results obtained by applying our method for constructing a hierarchical community decomposition (HCD). We consider the exact implementation of Algorithm 1 PARTITION and Algorithm 2 DETACH in which the all cuts are exhaustively enumerated in the while-loops, and a practical implementation in which the exhaustive enumeration is replaced by Algorithm 3 SPECTRALCUT.

There are three components to our experiments. First, we consider a very small graph for which the exact implementation of our algorithm is feasible. We observe that the decomposition produced by our practical implementation matches that produced by the exact implementation, therefore achieving the theoretical guarantees. We also observe that the first spectral cut found by the practical implementation cuts across a well-connected community. Our algorithm then corrects this mistake through the interplay of gluing together and breaking apart communities. On the other hand, a straight-forward iterative implementation of spectral cut would not be able to recover from such a mistake. Second, we present a set of synthetic graphs for which an exact implementation of our algorithm is already infeasible. However, each synthetic example has a planted hierarchical decomposition that serves as a reference point. We observe that the HCDs provided by our practical algorithms are close to the planted decompositions. Finally, we use a set of complex real-world networks for which we do not know what desired decompositions look like. We present the decompositions we find and some observations. However, our

validation on the smaller networks give us confidence in our experimental findings on the global community structure of these large networks.

We remark that the proof of Theorem 5 establishes that values of λ and δ are inversely related. This matches our intuition of the trade-offs between global and local structure. Note that in practice we do not need λ to be logarithmic. Instead we choose small values of λ and compensate with somewhat larger values of δ.

3.1 A Small Example

We begin with very small networks. Other than the exact and practical implementation of our decomposition algorithm, we also consider applying spectral cuts iteratively. By iterative spectral cuts, we mean applying SPECTRALCUT to subgraphs returned from previous applications of SPECTRALCUT.

Consider the graph illustrated in Figure 2. This graph G consists of four clique-like subgraphs C_{11}, C_{12}, C_{21} and C_{22}, each with 5 nodes, and a small number of links between these four subgraphs.

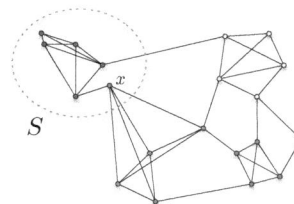

Figure 2: A 20-node graph G consists of four clique-like subgraphs. The first spectral cut yields the cut $(S, G \setminus S)$, placing vertex x not in its "best" community, the red colored vertices.

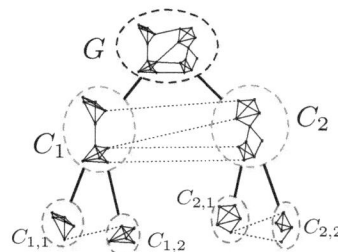

Figure 3: Applying PARTITION / DETACH to the graph G of Figure 2. Edges between communities at the same level are shown as dotted lines.

The set S of Figure 2 corresponds to the first spectral cut that incorrectly placed one red vertex x on the wrong side of the partition. Specifically, vertex x has a single neighbor inside S and three neighbors in $G - S$, thus the cut $(S - \{x\}, (G - S) \cup \{x\})$ has better conductance. If we apply spectral cut iteratively, we will never recover from this mistake of selecting S as a community.

On the other hand the practical implementation of our algorithm also initially suffers from the bad cut S, but manages to correct it due to the interplay of δ-linkedness and

λ-detachness. The former glues together nodes into one potential community and the latter breaks apart a potential community. In this example, $\{x\}$ is λ-detached with respect to S and therefore S can be corrected. Figure 3 describes our decomposition as applied to G. This highlights a key benefit of our algorithm: *the δ-linked and λ-detached conditions can correct mistakes made by spectral clustering, even when using spectral clustering as a subroutine!* Here is the progression of our algorithm.

1. $\mathcal{P} = \{\{v\} \mid v \in V\}$.

2. PARTITION discovers via SPECTRALCUT that $S = C_{1,1} \cup \{x\}$ is δ-linked. DETACH then discovers S is λ-detachable and SPECTRALCUT returns $(C_{1,1}, \{x\})$. Subsequently, P is updated to $\{C_{1,1}, \{v\} | v \in V \setminus C_{1,1}\}$.

3. PARTITION discovers via SPECTRALCUT that $C_{1,2}$ is δ-linked. $C_{1,2}$ is not λ-detachable. P is updated to $\{C_{1,1}, C_{1,2}, \{v\} | v \in V \setminus C_{1,1} \setminus C_{1,2}\}$. Similarly, PARTITION discovers via SPECTRALCUT that $C_{2,1}$ and $C_{2,2}$ are δ-linked, and P is updated to $\{C_{1,1}, C_{1,2}, C_{2,1}, C_{2,2}\}$.

4. PARTITION further discovers $\{C_{1,1}, C_{1,2}\}$ are linked which form C_1, and $\{C_{2,1}, C_{2,2}\}$ are linked which form C_2.

Finally, the exact implementation of our algorithm results in the same decomposition in this example. Hence, we know the resulting decomposition satisfies the theoretical guarantees of Theorem 5.

3.2 Larger Synthetic Examples

We now consider a set of synthetic examples, drawing inspiration from Condon and Karp's *planted partition model* [15]. These examples are sufficiently large that our exact decomposition algorithm is no longer feasible. When a graph has a clear unique hierarchical structure, we observe that the practical implementation of our algorithm returns a decomposition that matches the planted decomposition nearly perfectly. On the other hand, when a graph does not have a unique good decomposition, we observe that our algorithm may return decompositions that are different from the planted ones. However, we verify these computed decompositions are in fact sensible judging by their conductance values.

Let us first describe the construction of the synthetic examples. The *planted ℓ-partition model with probabilities $p_1 > p_2$* generates a graph G whose vertex set V can be partitioned into ℓ subsets each of size n/ℓ such that two nodes within the same partition are adjacent with probability p_1 and two nodes in different partitions are adjacent with probability p_2. For $\ell = 2$, if p_1 is substantially larger than p_2 then the minimum bisection of the graph is expected to be the planted 2-part partition [15].

To test the validity of our hierarchical decomposition algorithm, we generalize the Condon-Karp by model defining the *k-level hierarchical planted ℓ-partition model*, or (k, ℓ)-*HPPM* recursively as follows. The $(1, \ell)$-HPPM with probabilities $p_1 > p_2$ is identical to the planted ℓ-partition model with probabilities $p_1 > p_2$. A graph generated from $(2, \ell)$-HPPM with probabilities $p_1 > p_2 > p_3$ consists of ℓ graphs $G_1, G_2, ..., G_\ell$ each of which is independently generated from $(1, \ell)$-HPPM with probabilities $p_1 > p_2$, and additionally each node of G_i is adjacent to each node of G_j, $i \neq j$ with probability $p_3 < p_2$. In general, a graph G generated

from (k, ℓ)-HPPM with probabilities $p_1 > p_2 > \cdots > p_{k+1}$ consists of ℓ graphs $G_1, G_2, ..., G_\ell$ each of which is independently generated from $(k - 1, \ell)$-HPPM with probabilities $p_1 > p_2 > \cdots > p_k$ and additionally each node of G_i is adjacent to each node of G_j, $i \neq j$, with probability $p_{k+1} < p_k$.

Given a graph G generated from $(k, 2)$-HPPM with probabilities $p_1 \gg p_2 \gg ... \gg p_{k+1}$, i.e., each p_i is much smaller than its predecessor in the order, the ideal hierarchical partitioning is clear: the root should be labeled by the vertices of G where its children should be labeled by the 2 $(k - 1, 2)$-HPPM graphs used in generating G. A full decomposition is found by iterating this process.

Figure 4 gives an example of a 64-node graph $G_{1,2}$ generated using the $(1, 2)$-HPPM with $p_1 = 0.2$ and $p_2 = 0.1$. In general, spectral methods have no trouble recovering the two planted communities. It is not surprising that the practical implementation of our algorithm closely recovers the planted hierarchical decomposition. Note that the k-means procedure in Algorithm 3 SPECTRALCUT is randomized. The output therefore varies between trials. In addition the parameter choices for λ and δ also contribute to the varying output. However, none of the trials deviate far from the planted decomposition. For $\lambda = 3.0$ and $\delta = 1.0$, we see a 3-level hierarchy: the top labeled by the nodes $G_{1,2}$, its children two communities each of size $|G_{1,2}|/2 = 32$, of conductance 0.231 and 0.224, where each of these nodes have 32 singleton children. More generally, for each $k = 2, 3, ..., 8$ we gener-

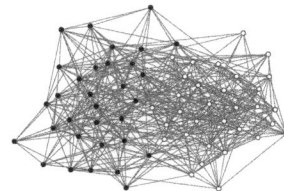

Figure 4: $G_{1,2}$: **a 64-node graph generated using the $(1, 2)$-HPPM with $p_1 = 0.2$ and $p_2 = 0.1$. The planted partition is indicated using the black and white colored nodes.**

ated $G_{k,2}$ using the $(k, 2)$-HPPM where $|G_\ell| = 32 \times 2^k$ and $p_i = \frac{0.2}{2^{i-1}}$, for $i = 1, 2, ..., k$. For each generated instance, our algorithm always recovered the planted hierarchical decomposition.

For a graph G generated from (k, ℓ)-HPPM for $\ell > 2$, even if the probabilities satisfy $p_1 \gg p_2 \gg ... \gg p_{k+1}$, good hierarchical decompositions may not be unique. For example, Figure 5 shows a 160-node graph $G_{1,5}$ generated from the $(1, 5)$-HPPM with $p_1 = 0.2$ and $p_2 = 0.05$. The first level of the hierarchical planted partition is indicated using the colored nodes, each of these five 32-node planted communities having conductance between 0.094 and 0.138. Note that each of the ten 64-node communities found by taking any two of these planted communities has conductance between 0.0712 and 0.096. Therefore, for such an example, there is no obvious unique good hierarchical structure. Specifically, it is unclear whether a flat hierarchy where each of these five planted communities hanging off the root node is superior to alternatives which include some of the larger low-

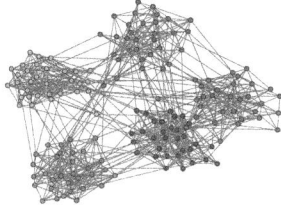

Figure 5: $G_{1,5}$: a 160-node graph generated using the $(1,5)$-HPPM with $p_1 = 0.2$ and $p_2 = 0.05$. The first level of the hierarchical planted partition is indicated using the colored nodes.

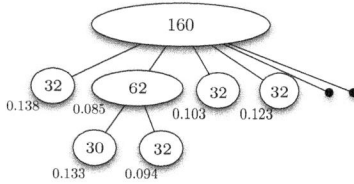

Figure 6: The hierarchical decomposition generated with $\lambda = 5$ and $\delta = 2$. Each of the non-singleton communities is labeled by its size and its conductance score. The singleton communities hanging off of the communities of size 30 and 32 are not shown.

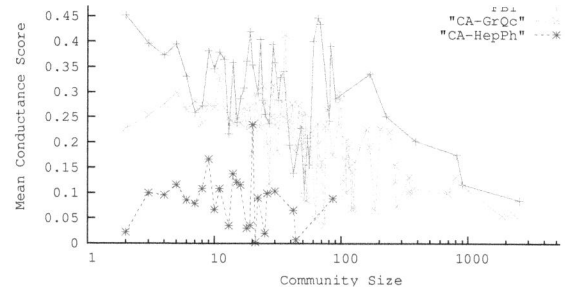

Figure 7: Mean conductance score for all non-singleton communities plotted against its size.

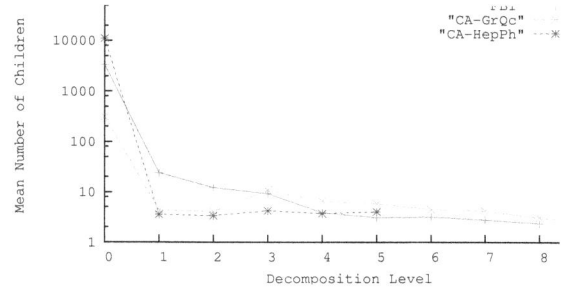

Figure 8: Number of children plotted against decomposition level.

conductance communities in the hierarchy. The trials of our algorithm reflect this by returning different decompositions. In each of these runs our algorithm does not recover the planted flat hierarchy, but instead finding a deeper decomposition which includes some of these larger low conductance communities. One such trial is depicted in Figure 6.

3.3 Real-World Experiments

We consider a set of three real-world networks each of roughly comparable size. We study one social network from Facebook, the popular online networking site. Here each node represents a unique user of the social network and two nodes are connected with a link if the two users are "friends". This network is denoted `FB1`, has 6,116 vertices, 31,374 edges and one connected component, and is an anonymized Facebook dataset derived from [46]. We study two collaboration networks from the SNAP data set [1, 33]. Each of these is built from the e-print service arXiv.org for five different scientific research communities that use this service. Nodes in these networks correspond to authors of papers, and nodes are connected by an edge whenever the corresponding authors co-authored an article. The two research communities are High Energy Physics—Phenomenology (`CA-HepPh`) and General Relativity and Quantum Cosmology (`CA-GrQc`). `CA-HepPh` has 12,008 vertices, 118,521 edges and 278 connected components, where the largest of these contains the vast majority of the vertices, specifically, 11204. `CA-GrQc` has 5,242 vertices, 14,496 edges and 355 connected components, where the largest of these is large, containing 4158 vertices.

Applying our heuristic with $\lambda = 3$ and $\delta = 1$ to `FB1` gives a rich 10-level decomposition, the average internal node in the decomposition tree having 13.4 children. In addition, the

mean conductance of the score is generally high for communities of specific sizes (see Figure 7) whilst the mean number of children decays slowly (see Figure 8). In applying our heuristic with $\lambda = 3$ and $\delta = 1$ to `CA-HepPh` and `CA-GrQc` revealed contrasting behavior. Both of the collaboration networks seemed to be characterized by stronger smaller communities that are more isolated in general. Indeed, the majority of `CA-HepPh` 12,008 vertices were placed as singletons on the first level of the decomposition. We believe this indicates the the majority of researchers in this community either published very little or collaborated with a small number of coauthors.

4. CONCLUSION

Motivated by Räcke's algorithm for oblivious routing, we define (λ, δ)-HCD together with an algorithm that computes an $(O(\log V), O(1))$-HCD for any input graph and a more efficient heuristic based on spectral methods. This heuristic performs well on friendly synthetic graphs and shows hope of scalability on larger real-world networks with thousands of nodes. We remark that this replacement with spectral methods can be thought of as a black box. In fact, any efficient method for finding good communities can be used. For future work, we have several directions to pursue. First, we intend to look into more scalable methods, such as local spectral methods, for even better scaling for larger real-world networks. Second, we also plan to systematically investigate the parameter choices of λ and δ that optimize the decomposition in practice. Our current experience shows that small values λ and δ tend to work well. Lastly, we would like to see a more extensive comparison of our approach to some existing methods such as iterative spectral methods.

Acknowledgement

The authors wish to thank Matthew Andrews for many helpful discussions.

5. REFERENCES

[1] Data archive at http://http://snap.stanford.edu/.

[2] Reid Andersen, Fan Chung, and Kevin Lang. Local graph partitioning using pagerank vectors. In *Foundations of Computer Science, 2006. FOCS'06. 47th Annual IEEE Symposium on*, pages 475–486. IEEE, 2006.

[3] Reid Andersen and Kevin J Lang. Communities from seed sets. In *Proceedings of the 15th international conference on World Wide Web*, pages 223–232. ACM, 2006.

[4] Sanjeev Arora, Rong Ge, Sushant Sachdeva, and Grant Schoenebeck. Finding overlapping communities in social networks: toward a rigorous approach. In *Proceedings of the 13th ACM Conference on Electronic Commerce*, pages 37–54. ACM, 2012.

[5] Sanjeev Arora, Satish Rao, and Umesh Vazirani. Expander flows, geometric embeddings and graph partitioning. In *Proceedings of the thirty-sixth annual ACM symposium on Theory of computing*, pages 222–231. ACM, 2004.

[6] Maria Florina Balcan and Yingyu Liang. Modeling and detecting community hierarchies. *International Workshop on Similarity Based Pattern Analysis and Recognition.*, 9(10):29–30, 2013.

[7] M.F. Balcan, C. Borgs, M. Braverman, J. Chayes, and S.H. Teng. Finding endogenously formed communities. *arXiv preprint arXiv:1201.4899*, 2012.

[8] M. Bienkowski, M. Korzeniowski, and H. Racke. A practical algorithm for constructing oblivious routing schemes. In *In Proc. of the 15th SPAA*, pages 24 – 33, 2003.

[9] V.D Blondel, J.-L. Guillaume, R. Lambiotte, and E. Lefebvre. Fast unfolding of communities in large networks. *Journal of Statistical Mechanics: Theory and Experiment*, 10, 2008.

[10] Ulrik Brandes and Thomas Erlebach. *Network analysis: methodological foundations*, volume 3418. Springer, 2005.

[11] J. Cheeger. A lower bound for the smallest eigenvalue of the Laplacian. Probl. Analysis, Sympos. in Honor of Salomon Bochner, Princeton Univ. 1969, 195-199, 1970.

[12] Fan RK Chung. Spectral graph theory. *CBMS Regional Conference Series in Math, No. 92*, 1997.

[13] Aaron Clauset, Cristopher Moore, and Mark EJ Newman. Hierarchical structure and the prediction of missing links in networks. *Nature*, 453(7191):98–101, 2008.

[14] Aaron Clauset, Mark EJ Newman, and Cristopher Moore. Finding community structure in very large networks. *Physical review E*, 70(6):066111, 2004.

[15] Anne Condon and Richard M Karp. Algorithms for graph partitioning on the planted partition model. *Random Structures and Algorithms*, 18(2):116–140, 2001.

[16] M Cosentino Lagomarsino, P Jona, B Bassetti, and H Isambert. Hierarchy and feedback in the evolution of the escherichia coli transcription network. *Proceedings of the National Academy of Sciences*, 104(13):5516–5520, 2007.

[17] Facebook. https://www.facebook.com/about/graphsearch.

[18] Gary William Flake, Steve Lawrence, and C Lee Giles. Efficient identification of web communities. In *Proceedings of the sixth ACM SIGKDD international conference on Knowledge discovery and data mining*, pages 150–160. ACM, 2000.

[19] Gary William Flake, Robert E Tarjan, and Kostas Tsioutsiouliklis. Graph clustering and minimum cut trees. *Internet Mathematics*, 1(4):385–408, 2004.

[20] Santo Fortunato. Community detection in graphs. *Physics Reports*, 486(3):75–174, 2010.

[21] Santo Fortunato and Marc Barthelemy. Resolution limit in community detection. *Proceedings of the National Academy of Sciences*, 104(1):36–41, 2007.

[22] Michael R. Garey and David S. Johnson. *Computers and Intractability: A Guide to the Theory of NP-Completeness*. W. H. Freeman & Co., New York, NY, USA, 1979.

[23] Michelle Girvan and Mark EJ Newman. Community structure in social and biological networks. *Proceedings of the National Academy of Sciences*, 99(12):7821–7826, 2002.

[24] Pablo M Gleiser and Leon Danon. Community structure in jazz. *Advances in complex systems*, 6(04):565–573, 2003.

[25] C. Harrelson, K. Hildrum, and S. Rao. A polynomial-time decomposition to minimize congestion. In *In Proc. of the 15th SPAA*, 2003.

[26] Dorit S Hochbaum. *Approximation algorithms for NP-hard problems*. PWS Publishing Co., 1996.

[27] Jianbin Huang, Heli Sun, Jiawei Han, Hongbo Deng, Yizhou Sun, and Yaguang Liu. Shrink: a structural clustering algorithm for detecting hierarchical communities in networks. In *Proceedings of the 19th ACM international conference on Information and knowledge management*, pages 219–228. ACM, 2010.

[28] R. Kannan, S. Vempala, and A. Vetta. On clusterings: Good, bad and spectral. *Journal of the ACM*, 51(3):497 – 515, May 2004.

[29] Leo Katz. A new status index derived from sociometric analysis. *Psychometrika*, 18(1):39–43, 1953.

[30] Jon M Kleinberg. Authoritative sources in a hyperlinked environment. *Journal of the ACM (JACM)*, 46(5):604–632, 1999.

[31] Andrea Lancichinetti and Santo Fortunato. Community detection algorithms: A comparative analysis. *Physical review E*, 80(5):056117, 2009.

[32] Tom Leighton and Satish Rao. Multicommodity max-flow min-cut theorems and their use in designing approximation algorithms. *J. ACM*, 46(6):787–832, November 1999.

[33] Jure Leskovec, Jon Kleinberg, and Christos Faloutsos. Graph evolution: Densification and shrinking diameters. *ACM Transactions on Knowledge Discovery from Data (TKDD)*, 1(1):2, 2007.

[34] Jure Leskovec, Kevin J Lang, and Michael Mahoney. Empirical comparison of algorithms for network community detection. In *Proceedings of the 19th international conference on World wide web*, pages 631–640. ACM, 2010.

[35] David Lusseau, Karsten Schneider, Oliver J Boisseau, Patti Haase, Elisabeth Slooten, and Steve M Dawson. The bottlenose dolphin community of doubtful sound features a large proportion of long-lasting associations. *Behavioral Ecology and Sociobiology*, 54(4):396–405, 2003.

[36] Julian McAuley and Jure Leskovec. Learning to discover social circles in ego networks. In *Advances in Neural Information Processing Systems 25*, pages 548–556, 2012.

[37] Karl Menger. Zur allgemeinen kurventheorie. *Fundamenta Mathematicae*, 10(1):96–115, 1927.

[38] Nina Mishra, Robert Schreiber, Isabelle Stanton, and Robert E Tarjan. Clustering social networks. In *Algorithms and Models for the Web-Graph*, pages 56–67. Springer, 2007.

[39] H. Racke. Minimizing congestion in general networks. In *In Proc. of the 43rd FOCS*, pages 43 – 52, 2002.

[40] Harald Racke. Minimizing congestion in general networks. In *Foundations of Computer Science, 2002. Proceedings. The 43rd Annual IEEE Symposium on*, pages 43–52. IEEE, 2002.

[41] Erzsébet Ravasz, Anna Lisa Somera, Dale A Mongru, Zoltán N Oltvai, and A-L Barabási. Hierarchical organization of modularity in metabolic networks. *Science*, 297(5586):1551–1555, 2002.

[42] Satu Elisa Schaeffer. Graph clustering. *Computer Science Review*, 1(1):27–64, 2007.

[43] Michael Schweinberger and Tom AB Snijders. Settings in social networks: A measurement model. *Sociological Methodology*, 33(1):307–341, 2003.

[44] Jiří Šíma and Satu Schaeffer. On the NP-completeness of some graph cluster measures. *SOFSEM 2006: Theory and Practice of Computer Science*, pages 530–537, 2006.

[45] Daniel A Spielman and Shang-Hua Teng. Nearly-linear time algorithms for graph partitioning, graph sparsification, and solving linear systems. In *Proceedings of the thirty-sixth annual ACM symposium on Theory of computing*, pages 81–90. ACM, 2004.

[46] Christo Wilson, Alessandra Sala, Krishna P. N. Puttaswamy, and Ben Y. Zhao. Beyond social graphs: User interactions in online social networks and their implications. *ACM Trans. Web*, pages 17:1–17:31, 2012.

On the Performance of Percolation Graph Matching

Lyudmila Yartseva   Matthias Grossglauser

School of Computer and Communication Sciences
École Polytechnique Fédérale de Lausanne (EPFL), Lausanne, Switzerland

firstname.lastname@epfl.ch

ABSTRACT

Graph matching is a generalization of the classic graph isomorphism problem. By using only their structures a graph-matching algorithm finds a map between the vertex sets of two similar graphs. This has applications in the de-anonymization of social and information networks and, more generally, in the merging of structural data from different domains.

One class of graph-matching algorithms starts with a known seed set of matched node pairs. Despite the success of these algorithms in practical applications, their performance has been observed to be very sensitive to the size of the seed set. The lack of a rigorous understanding of parameters and performance makes it difficult to design systems and predict their behavior.

In this paper, we propose and analyze a very simple percolation-based graph matching algorithm that incrementally maps every pair of nodes (i, j) with at least r neighboring mapped pairs. The simplicity of this algorithm makes possible a rigorous analysis that relies on recent advances in bootstrap percolation theory for the $G(n, p)$ random graph. We prove conditions on the model parameters in which percolation graph matching succeeds, and we establish a phase transition in the size of the seed set. We also confirm through experiments that the performance of percolation graph matching is surprisingly good, both for synthetic graphs and real social-network data.

Categories and Subject Descriptors

G.3 [**Mathematics of Computing**]: Probability and Statistics—*Probabilistic algorithms*; G.2.2 [**Discrete Mathematics**]: Graph Theory; H.1 [**Information Systems**]: Models and Principles

Keywords

Graph matching; graph sampling; bootstrap percolation; social networks; de-anonymization

1. INTRODUCTION

Social ties and interactions, interpersonal communications, and information sharing are increasingly conducted through online services and digital media. Both the risks and opportunities this brings are well known and hotly debated. The electronic traces of our patterns of communication, keyword searches, mobility, and information access, give a precise picture of many aspects of our personality and lifestyle. These sources of information are therefore heavily sought after for correlation and mining by advertisers, scientists, governments, and many other entities. In addition, when information from multiple sources and domains is combined, this usually incurs *increasing returns*: the value of a set of databases from different domains (e.g., a social network, a demographic database, and cell phone mobility traces over a given population) is significantly higher than the sum of its values in isolation. It is therefore important to understand how such information gets merged and correlated, and what unintended privacy leaks might result.

One of the most basic representations of such information is a graph, which represents pairwise relationships, potentially enriched with additional attributes. Graphs can describe our phone call patterns, Facebook friendships, relationships in a business organization, or the contact networks that drive the spread of infectious diseases. A typical individual belongs to several such networks, but might possess different identities in different networks, possibly as a deliberate measure to protect her privacy.

In this paper, we study one fundamental aspect of correlating graphs from different application domains: matching their vertex sets through structural information. If the nodes in two graphs use different labels (e.g., phone numbers and e-mail addresses) for two nodes that represent the same underlying entity (e.g., an individual), then we can ask whether the structure of the two graphs reveals the correspondence of some or all of the vertices. In other words, can we find a *matching* between (a subset of) the vertex sets of two graphs? If this is possible, then this has strong implications for privacy and for cross-domain data mining applications.

Recent work answers this question in the affirmative. Narayanan and Shmatikov [10] succeed in matching a large-scale anonymized social network to a second social network that serves as side information. Although the node identities in the first network contain no information per se, the privacy of the network is compromised through the knowledge of a correlated secondary network. In another work, a random graph model served to provide insight on the fundamental feasibility of graph matching for an adversary with unlimited computational power [11]. It turns out that under rather benign conditions, two graphs can be matched perfectly. In summary, this evolving body of work suggests that protecting graph privacy through node anonymization is inadequate.

Graph matching has other important applications in different domains. For example, using graphs to represent images, where vertices are regions and edges are adjacency relations between these regions, is widely applied in recognizing two scenes of an image and in finding similar images. In bio-informatics, modeling gene sequences as graphs and matching these graphs is applied for gene/protein networks alignment [14, 6].

The algorithm in [10] takes as input a *seed set* of pre-matched node pairs in the two graphs $G_{1,2}$ to be matched. The algorithm then iteratively expands this map, by identifying additional pairs of nodes ($i \in G_1, j \in G_2$) that can plausibly be matched. Whether (i, j) is a plausible match is computed from the position of i and j with respect to the known mapped nodes. More specifically, they consider nodes i, j in $G_{1,2}$ that are neighbors of at least two mapped nodes, and they propose various heuristics for comparing different candidate pairs. The algorithm has several parameters that need to be tuned through trial-and-error, but it has been shown to perform very well over some real datasets.

Our first key contribution in this paper is a very simple algorithm with a single tuning parameter to perform graph matching. Essentially, the algorithm matches any two nodes ($i \in G_1, j \in G_2$) that have more than r neighbors already matched to each other. Despite its deceptive simplicity, this algorithm performs very well on real data, and its operation is easy to interpret and control due to a single control nob (r). We believe that this algorithm can be viewed as the canonical placeholder for *percolation graph matching (PGM)* algorithms, which propagate a set of matched node pairs outward. The algorithms in this class differ in how candidate node pairs are compared. As such, PGM should shed light on the qualitative performance of other such algorithms.

This brings us to the second contribution of our paper. A key observation in [10] is the presence of a sharp phase transition in the performance of their algorithm as a function of the seed set size. The algorithm failed almost completely when the seed set size was below a certain threshold, but then shot up to a very high success rate (around 70% in one experiment) when the number of seeds exceeded the threshold. The authors did not speculate as to the reason for the phase transition, or try to characterize it as a function of network properties. In this paper, we formally prove the presence of a phase transition in the seed set size when the input graphs are $G(n, p; s)$. The critical value a_c for the seed set size is a function of the network parameters and of the control parameter r. This result provides a qualitative understanding of this phenomenon and provides quantitative guidelines about the feasible region in the parameter space.

This paper is organized as follows. In Section 2 we give a more in-depth overview of related research. In Section 3, we define a very simple and efficient percolation-based graph matching algorithm. We then describe a stochastic model of this matching algorithm in Section 4. The network model is the $G(n, p; s)$ model introduced in [11]: it generates two correlated Erdös-Rényi random graphs whose similarity can be controlled by a parameter s. In Section 5, we demonstrate the existence of a phase transition in the size of the seed set. When the seed set is smaller than a critical threshold a_c, the

algorithm almost certainly fails; if it is larger, the algorithm succeeds in matching almost everything. Our result relies on recent progress in the field of bootstrap percolation [5]. In Section 6, we evaluate the algorithm over both random graphs and real social network data, and we confirm the presence of the phase transition in the seed set. The algorithm also performs remarkably well over real network data. In Section 7 we conclude the paper.

2. RELATED WORK

Graph matching has many applications in several domains, including network de-anonymization, computer vision, databases, and bio-informatics. We discuss the most relevant works here.

In the privacy protection area, there have been several reported successes in matching social network data from different domains [10, 16]. Some of these are computationally expensive and therefore limited to small scales [6]; some rely on assumptions that an attacker is allowed to alter a network before publishing [2] or has access to additional side information, e.g., memberships in groups [16].

To the best of our knowledge, the methods for large-scale attacks proposed in the literature are heuristic in nature [16, 9, 10]. One of the examples of large scale attack is the work of Narayanan and Shmatikov [10]. They were the first to succeed in de-anonymizing two real, large social networks, based only on the network topology. Their approach relies on a seed set of node pairs that are pre-matched, from which they iteratively grow the map.

One key empirical observation in their work is that the size of the seed set is very important: if the seed set is too small, their algorithm tends to quickly die out. The dependence on the size of the seed set seems highly non-linear, with a sharp transition between almost complete failure and almost complete success in matching as the size of the seed set is increased. This suggests a phase transition phenomenon, which is a major focus of the study of random graphs and percolation models. In this paper, we formally prove a phase transition for a very simple instance of such a percolation graph matching algorithm, thus confirming the empirical observations in their work. Furthermore, we are able to characterize the critical value of the seed set size as a function of graph parameters, including a measure of the similarity of the two graphs to be matched.

Korula and Lattanzi [7] independently propose a graph matching algorithm similar to ours, and they provide an analysis for the $G(n, p; s)$ model as well as for preferential-attachment generator graphs. They consider a regime of dense seeds, where the mapping for a constant fraction of nodes is known a-priori. In this regime, they show that most of the network can be matched with high probability in a single propagation step. Our analysis goes further in that we prove and characterize a phase transition in the size of the seed set. We show that a sublinear seed set size can suffice for matching in some circumstances.

Graph matching also arises in other fields, such as in ontology alignment. Several automated tools were created to match sets of labels describing data [4, 15, 13]. However, the specifics of the problems assume small-scale graphs [4], and the algorithms rely heavily on the properties and attributes of the nodes, rather than on the structural features.

To shed light on the performance of seeded graph matching, we analyze a very simple percolation-based algorithm that incrementally matches pairs of nodes, based on previously matched pairs. In order to make statements about the performance of this algorithm, we need a model for the two graphs $G_{1,2}$ to be matched. For this, we rely on the random graph model introduced in [11]. This model works as follows: we first generate a random graph $G = G(n, p)$ that can be thought of as the true social network. We then derive two observable graphs $G_{1,2}$ from G, by independently including each edge of G in $G_{1,2}$ with probability s. We refer to the this model of a pair of graphs as the $G(n, p; s)$ graph-matching model, where the parameter s controls the similarity (or correlation) between $G_{1,2}$[1].

Our main theoretical contribution in this paper is to identify conditions on the model parameters (n, p, s) and on the size of the seed set a_0 (a small set of initially pre-mapped pairs of nodes) such that percolation graph matching succeeds with high probability. For this, we rely on recent advances in the analysis of bootstrap percolation in the $G(n, p)$ random graph by Janson et al. [5]. We briefly summarize their model and key results here.

Percolation theory is the study of the presence of large (or infinite) clusters in random environments, such as lattices with missing nodes or links, or random graphs. In bootstrap percolation we study systems where a node is part of a cluster only if it has at least r neighbors that belong to the cluster. This more restrictive notion of inclusion can capture, for example, the spread of influence through a social network, where an individual is convinced of an idea only if she hears this idea from several acquaintances.

In a seminal paper [5], Janson et al. succeed in analyzing this process precisely for the Erdös-Rényi ($G(n, p)$) random graph. They stated the following results for $G(n, p)$ infection spread with a threshold r. For given r, n, and p define,

$$t_c := \left(\frac{(r-1)!}{np^r} \right)^{1/(r-1)}, \quad (1)$$

$$a_c := \left(1 - \frac{1}{r} \right) t_c, \quad (2)$$

$$b_c := n \frac{(pn)^{r-1}}{(r-1)!} e^{-pn}. \quad (3)$$

They analyzed the process and estimated the size of the final active/infected set a^* depending on the size of the initially active set a_0.

THEOREM 1. *[5] Suppose that $r \geq 2$ and $n^{-1} \ll p \ll n^{-1/r}$[2].*

- *If $a_0/a_c \to \alpha < 1$, then $a^* = (\phi(\alpha) + o(1)) t_c$ w.h.p., where $\phi(\alpha)$ is the unique root in $[0, 1]$ of*

$$r\phi(\alpha) - \phi(\alpha)^r = (r - 1)\alpha. \quad (4)$$

  [For $r = 2$, $\phi(\alpha) = 1 - \sqrt{1 - \alpha}$.]
  Further, $a^*/a_0 \to \phi_1(\alpha) := \frac{r}{r-1}\phi(\alpha)/\alpha$, with $\phi_1(0) := 1$.

- *If $a_0/a_c \geq 1 + \delta$, for some $\delta > 0$, then $a^* = n - o(n)$ w.h.p.; in other words, w.h.p. the process almost percolates. More precisely, $a^* = n - O(b_c)$ w.h.p.*

We use this theorem to analyze the percolation-based matching algorithm in the $G(n, p; s)$ graph model. Although the criterion for propagation is the same in the graph matching process and in the bootstrap percolation ($\geq r$ neighbors infected), the objects of interest in our algorithm are *pairs of nodes* rather than individual nodes as in the Janson et al. model. In other words, in our algorithm, a node pair is mapped if it has at least r neighboring node pairs that are already matched. See the details of the algorithm in the next section.

One key result in the present paper is establishing an equivalence between the percolation process over node pairs for matching and bootstrap percolation, which makes the machinery of [5] available to analyze this process. One subtlety concerns mapping errors: They make the process hard to analyze; and they can propagate, thus reducing the quality of the mapping. To conclude that the algorithm is correct, we need to show two facts: (i) that the matching process percolates and touches "most" nodes, and (ii) that the algorithm matches nodes correctly.

3. PERCOLATION GRAPH MATCHING ALGORITHM

We now describe the graph-matching algorithm, whose analysis is the main contribution of this paper. We are given two graphs G_1 and G_2, both with n nodes[3]. We assume a true but hidden equivalence between nodes in the two graphs, which we can assume w.l.g. to be the identity, with $V_1 = V_2 = V$. The edge sets E_1 and E_2 are in general different, but are correlated. Informally, this means that if an edge (u, v) exists in E_1, it is likely to exist in E_2 as well, and vice versa. The matching algorithm has access only to the structure of the two graphs, i.e., it sees *unlabeled* versions of $G_{1,2}$. Its purpose is to find a map, i.e., a set of tuples $A \subset V_1 \times V_2$ such that each node in $V_{1,2}$ appears in at most one tuple[4]. The map is correct if every element of A is of the form (i, i); for a map with errors, we call $|(i, j) : i \neq j, (i, j) \in A|/|A|$ the *error rate* of the map, and we call $|A|$ the *size* of the map.

Several graph-matching algorithms proposed in the literature assume side information in the form of a known *seed set A_0* of mapped pairs. These algorithms try to iteratively expand this map by identifying additional pairs of nodes (i, j) in the "vicinity" of the set of confirmed pairs; this process continues until it runs out of pairs to add. Our goal in this paper is to define an algorithm that is simple enough to be tractable, but that also has good matching performance in real scenarios. We refer to our algorithm, and more generally to the class of algorithms that iteratively propagate a map from a seed set, as *percolation graph-matching* (PGM) algorithms, as they rely on a threshold rule reminiscent of bootstrap percolation models [1]. Simply put, a pair (i, j) is added to the set of mapped pairs if there are at least r mapped pairs that are neighbors of (i, j)[5].

We now describe our PGM algorithm more formally. The input of the algorithm is the following:

---

[1]Note that $G_{1,2} = G(n, ps)$, but their edge sets $E_{1,2}$ are correlated.

[2]In this paper, $f \ll g$ and $f \gg g$ mean $f = o(g)$ and $f = \omega(g)$, respectively.

[3]It is easy to remove the assumption of equal size; its purpose is mainly for notational simplicity.

[4]I.e., A is a matching between the subset of mapped nodes in G_1 and the subset of mapped nodes in G_2.

[5]More precisely, two pairs (i, j) and (i', j') are neighbors iff $(i, i') \in E_1$ and $(j, j') \in E_2$.

- Two graphs $G_1 = (V_1, E_1)$ and $G_2 = (V_2, E_2)$;

- A seed set A_0 of size a_0, consisting of tuples (i, i) of known pairs of matched nodes.

The algorithm we propose and analyze simply maps any two nodes with at least r neighboring pairs already mapped. An equivalent description emphasizes the incremental nature of the process: we associate with every pair of nodes ($i \in V_1, j \in V_2$) a count of marks $M_{i,j}$. At each time step t, the algorithm *uses* exactly one unused but already mapped pair (i_t, j_t). This pair adds one mark to each neighboring pair, i.e., to every pair in $N_1(i_t) \times N_2(j_t)$. As soon as any pair gets r marks, it is added to the current map; if for some node i there are several nodes j such that all (i, j) have r marks, one pair is picked at random. The process iterates until there are no more unused pairs.

The set $A(t)$ consists of the map built until time t, and the set $Z(t) \subset A(t)$ consists of mapped pairs that have been *used* until t, in the following way:

- At time $t = 0$, $A(0) = A_0$ and $Z(0) = \emptyset$,

- At time step t the algorithm randomly selects a pair $(i_t, j_t) \in A(t-1) \setminus Z(t-1)$ and adds one credit mark to all pairs $(i', j') \in V_1 \times V_2$ such that there exist $(i_t, i') \in E_1$ and $(j_t, j') \in E_2$ (cf. Fig. 1).

If a pair (i', j') has more than r marks then it is added to the map $A(t)$; furthermore, all other candidates (i'', j') and (i', j'') are permanently removed from consideration.

Let $\Delta A(t)$ be the set of pairs with r marks, which are added to the map at time t. Then

$$A(t) = A(t-1) \cup \Delta A(t)$$

and

$$Z(t) = Z(t-1) \cup \{(i_t, j_t)\}.$$

Note that $a(t) \geq z(t) = t$.

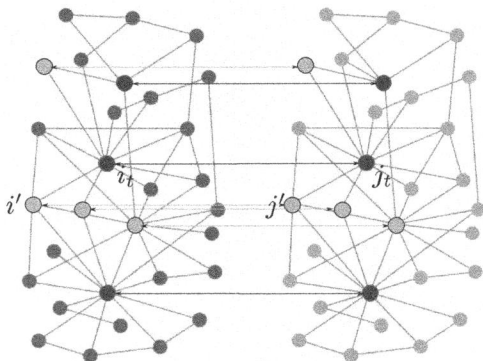

Figure 1: Red nodes are the seeds, green nodes are the set of mapped pairs after the first three iterations, for $r = 2$.

The process stops when $A(t) \setminus Z(t) = \emptyset$, which happens when all pairs from the map $A(t)$ are used. Denote this time step by $T = \min(t \geq 0 \text{ s.t. } A(t) \setminus Z(t) = \emptyset)$. The final map is $A^* = A(T) = Z(T)$ and its size is $a^* = T$.

The role of the parameter r is important: it controls the amount of evidence in favor of a pair of nodes, before these nodes are matched permanently. There is a tradeoff between two types of errors. If r is chosen too low, the probability of a false match increases. If r is chosen too high, then the algorithm may simply run out of candidate pairs to match and stop early.

3.1 Deferred Matching Variant

The algorithm as defined above leads to a tractable probabilistic model, and in particular, can be analyzed using the bootstrap percolation results from [5], as shown below. The basic algorithm greedily matches any candidate pair as soon as it reaches r credits, *even if $A(t) \setminus Z(t)$ is not empty*. This is obviously not optimal in most circumstances, as the credits yet to be generated by the remaining pairs in $A(t) \setminus Z(t)$ might improve the credit counts $M_{i,j}$ and avoid matching errors. There is an easy fix to this, which we describe here; we use this variant of the algorithm in the experiments in Section 6.

The modified algorithm works as follows. Whenever $A(t) \setminus Z(t)$ is nonempty, we are conservative and continue to attribute credits to candidate pairs, without forming any new couples. Once $A(t) \setminus Z(t)$ is empty, we form exactly one couple (i, j) that has the maximum $M_{i,j}$ of all candidates (provided this is also above the threshold r; otherwise we stop), and add it to $A(t)$; and so forth.

This variant has the advantage of being conservative about matching new couples: it first uses all the available evidence by using all unused pairs before making irreversible decisions. Also, it makes the choice of the parameter r somewhat less important. In particular, if r is chosen too low, the maximum rule ensures that only the best candidate pairs *relative to other candidates* are matched. Our simulation results show that the variant performs well, but exhibits the same phase transition in r as the basic (greedy) approach.

Formally, at each time-step t,

- The algorithm processes a mapped pair $(i_t, j_t) \in A(t-1) \setminus Z(t-1)$ and adds one credit to every neighboring pair, as in the basic algorithm;

- If $A(t) \setminus Z(t) = \emptyset$, the algorithm takes a pair whose number of credits is maximal and at least r, and adds it to $A(t)$; if there are several such pairs it picks one at random.

The algorithm stops when there are no more pairs with at least r marks.

Our experiments show that this optimization decreases the error rate in certain scenarios, but exhibits similar threshold behavior in the seed set size as the basic version. For more details see Section 6.

4. MODEL

In this section we define the model used for analysis of the PGM algorithm. In the work of Janson [5], the authors proved phase transitions of the size of the final mapping a^* in the initial seed set size a_0. In our model, we show similar phase transitions for PGM.

As we mentioned, we assume the ground-truth network graph G is $G(n, p)$, and two networks are obtained from G as follows: each edge of G is present in the observed network with probability s, independently of everything else. We refer to this probability space as the $G(n, p; s)$ graph matching model [11]. Thus an input of the problem is the following:

- Two graphs $G_1 = (V, E_1)$ and $G_2 = (V, E_2)$, obtained as a realization of the $G(n, p; s)$ graph matching model;

- A seed set $A_0 \subset V \times V$ of size $a_0 = |A_0|$.

Our goal is to explore the following question: Under what conditions on the model parameters n, p, s, a_0 and r does the algorithm propagate and match the two graphs (almost) correctly?

4.1 Properties of the Propagation Process

Let $E(i, i')$ denote the event that the edge (i, i') is present in G; and $E_1(i, i')$ and $E_2(j, j')$ are the events that edges (i, i') and (j, j') occur in G_1, G_2, respectively.

OBSERVATION 1. *Since the graph G is $G(n, p)$, the unconditional edge probability $P\{E_1(i, i')\} = P\{E_2(j, j')\} = ps$. Butsince G_1 and G_2 are sampled from the same generator,*

$$P\{E_1(i, i')|E_2(i, i')\} = s.$$

For convenience of notation, we omit the reference to the graph when it is clear from the context, and we refer to the nodes of G_1 by index i and to nodes of G_2 by index j. We write $E_1(i, i_t)$ as $E_{i,t}$ and $E_2(j, j_t)$ as $E_{j,t}$. $i = j$ means that i and j correspond to the same node of G.

Let $I_{i,j}(t)$ be an indicator of the event that a pair (i, j) received a mark at time step t, as a result of using a pair (i_t, j_t). This is equivalent to the event that there exist edges $(i, i_t) \in G_1$ and $(j, j_t) \in G_2$. Hence its probability is

$$P\{I_{i,j}(t) = 1\} = P\{E_{i,t}, E_{j,t}\}.$$

We state the following lemma about the increments at time t, conditional on no matching errors so far:

LEMMA 1. *Conditional on $i_\tau = j_\tau$ for all $\tau \leq t$*

1. $P\{I_{i,j}(t) = 1\} = \begin{cases} (ps)^2, & i \neq j \\ ps^2, & i = j \end{cases}$

2. *For a fixed t, the $\{I_{i,j}(t)\}_{i,j,i \neq j}$ are not independent.*

3. *For a fixed t, the $\{I_{i,i}(t)\}_i$ are independent.*

4. *For fixed $t_1 \neq t_2$ and i, j, the $I_{i,j}(t_1)$ and $I_{i,j}(t_2)$ are independent.*

PROOF. Conditional on $i_\tau = j_\tau$ for all $\tau \leq t$

1. If at time t, a seed is mapped correctly, the nodes i_t and j_t are sampled from the same node of G, then by Observation 1,

$$P\{I_{i,j}(t) = 1\} = P\{E_{i,t}, E_{j,t}\} = \begin{cases} (ps)^2, & i \neq j \\ ps^2, & i = j \end{cases}$$

2. For $i \neq j$ and $i_1 \neq j$:

$$P\{I_{i,j}(t) = 1|I_{i_1,j}(t) = 1\} =$$
$$= P\{E_{i,t}, E_{j,t}|E_{i_1,t}, E_{j,t}\}$$
$$= P\{E_{i,t}|E_{i_1,t}\} = P\{E_{i,t}\} = ps$$

3. For $i = j$ and $i_1 = j_1$ ($i_1 \neq i$):

$$P\{I_{i,j}(t) = 1|I_{i_1,j_1}(t) = 1\} =$$
$$= P\{E_{i,t}, E_{j,t}|E_{i_1,t}, E_{j_1,t}\}$$
$$= P\{E_{i,t}, E_{j,t}\} = (ps)^2$$

4. For $t_1 \neq t_2$:

$$P\{I_{i,j}(t_1) = 1|I_{i,j}(t_2) = 1\} =$$
$$= P\{E_{i,t_1}, E_{j,t_1}|E_{i,t_2}, E_{j,t_2}\}$$
$$= P\{I_{i,j}(t_1) = 1\} = (ps)^2$$

$\square$

Clause 2 states that markers obtained for two different pairs with a node in common are not independent. Given that a pair (i, j) gets a mark, the event that another pair (i_1, j) also gets a mark is more likely. Clause 3 is key for further analysis of the process. It states that correctly mapped pairs obtain marks independently. Thus, if a pair (i, i) got a mark at time t, it does not correlate with (j, j) getting a mark. Clause 4 asserts that each seed spreads its marks independently. In other words, at a time step t, a pair gets a mark independently of other time steps.

The count $M_{i,j}(t)$ is the number of marks of (i, j) at time t:

$$M_{i,j}(t) = \sum_{s=1}^{t} I_{i,j}(s).$$

Under the conditions of Lemma 1, each $M_{i,j}(t)$ is the sum of i.i.d. Bernoulli random variables, so it is either a $\mathsf{Bi}\left(n, (ps)^2\right)$ for $i \neq j$ or a $\mathsf{Bi}\left(n, ps^2\right)$ for $i = j$. In the following section, we develop conditions when PGM does not match wrong pairs (w.h.p.).

5. PERFORMANCE OF PGM

5.1 Main Theorems

Let $q = ps^2$ and $r \geq 2$, and note that q is the probability of an edge being sampled in both G_1 and G_2 or, equivalently, the probability of an edge to be contained in the intersection of the edge sets $E_1 \cap E_2$. Define

$$t_c = \left(\frac{(r-1)!}{nq^r}\right)^{\frac{1}{r-1}} \text{ and } a_c = \left(1 - \frac{1}{r}\right)t_c. \quad (5)$$

Here we show that t_c and a_c are the critical time horizon and the critical value of the initial size of the seed set, respectively. This means that for an initial number of seeds a_0 lower than a_c, the PGM algorithm stops earlier than t_c, with the final size at most $2a_0$; for a_0 larger than a_c, the algorithm propagates to most of the graph.

THEOREM 2 (SUBCRITICAL REGIME). *For $n^{-1} \ll ps^2 \ll sn^{-\frac{3}{2r}}$ if $a_0/a_c \to \alpha < 1$, the propagation algorithm stops with $a^* \leq t_c$ w.h.p. In particular $a^* = (\phi(\alpha) + o(1))t_c \leq \frac{r}{r-1}a_0$, where $\phi(\alpha)$ is the unique root in $[0, 1]$ of $r\phi(\alpha)) - \phi(\alpha)^r = (r-1)\alpha$.*

This means that in the subcritical regime, the final map is only slightly larger than the seed set, because the mapping process does not percolate. Now we consider at what happens above the threshold $a_0 > a_c$.

123

THEOREM 3 (SUPERCRITICAL REGIME). *For* $n^{-1} \ll ps^2 \ll sn^{-\frac{3}{2r}}$, *if* $a_0/a_c \geq 1 + \delta$ *the algorithm propagates, and the size of the final mapping is* $a^* = n - o(n)$ *w.h.p.*

In summary, there is a sharp phase transition at $a_0 = a_c$ that separates almost certain failure from almost certain success of the percolation graph matching process. We discuss the implications of this phase transition and the scaling of the main parameters in more detail in Subsection 5.4.

5.2 Proof Sketch and Bootstrap Percolation

We briefly outline the main steps of the proof and provide full details in the next subsection.

Our main goal is to prove that the couple formation process $A(t)$ defined in the previous section can be analyzed using the bootstrap percolation model introduced in [5]. In summary, [5] analyses a process where, at every time step t, objects collect a credit with probability p, independently of everything else. We want to analyze the PGM algorithm within the $G(n, p; s)$ model. However, our object of interest is not an individual node, but a pair (i, j).

At every time-step, one pair spreads credits to other node pairs. However, we do not have the critical feature that makes the analysis of [5] tractable: as shown in Lemma 1, the credit increments $I_{i,j}(t)$ are not equiprobable, and they are not independent. Therefore, the results of [5] cannot be applied directly.

Fortunately, the specific structure of the process of increments over pairs reveals a way out. The key observation is that the credits of *correct* pairs $M_{i,i}(t)$ are in fact independent of each other. Another observation of Lemma 1 is that correct pairs are more likely to get a mark. Thus, the (small) subset of pairs of the form (i, i) within all the possible pairs $V \times V$ can be analyzed using the bootstrap percolation framework.

Therefore, we first consider the event X that at any time t, a wrong pair (i, j) has collected at least r credits without either of the "competing" correct pairs (i, i) and (j, j) having collected r credits. In the case of event X, it is possible (but not guaranteed) that a matching error has occurred. In Lemma 2 below, we show that $\mathsf{P}\{X\} \to 0$ under appropriate conditions. Under these conditions, the matching algorithm does not make wrong matches (w.h.p.) and is suitable for further analysis.

It remains to be shown whether the algorithm percolates. For this, it is conservative to only consider the credits $M_{i,i}$ attributed to correct pairs, as the probability to percolate can only increase by adding additional pairs into the system. As the correct counts are independent binomials, it is then straightforward to map the problem into the bootstrap percolation framework.

5.3 Proofs of Theorems 2 and 3

In this section, we use the results from [5] to formulate our key results. We show a sharp face transitions in the final map size a depending on $a_0 < a_c$ or $a_0 > a_c$.

A key lemma bounds the probability that no error happens in the matching process. An error may occur if at some time step, a bad pair (i, j) collects r marks before its adjacent good pairs (i, i) and (j, j) have collected more than r marks. If such errors are very rare, then we can focus only on correctly mapped pairs in the analysis of $A(t)$. Let $X_{i,j}(t)$ denote the event that the algorithm made an error at time step t by

mapping a pair (i, j), $i \neq j$, where $r \leq t \leq n$. The probability of this event is

$$\mathsf{P}\{X_{i,j}(t)\} \leq$$
$$\leq \mathsf{P}\{M_{i,j}(t) = r, M_{i,i}(t) \leq r, M_{j,j}(t) \leq r\}$$

Denote by $X = \bigcup_{t, i \neq j} X_{i,j}(t)$ an event that at any time-step t an error happened.

LEMMA 2. *If* $ps \ll n^{-\frac{3}{2r}}$ *(with* $2 \leq r \leq n$*), then* $\mathsf{P}\{X\} \to 0$ *with* $n \to \infty$,

The proof of the lemma is in the appendix.

Therefore for $ps \ll n^{-\frac{3}{2r}}$, Lemma 2 guarantees that w.h.p. we need only consider the evolution of the correct counts $\{M_{i,i}\}$, to which we can apply the results of [5] directly.

PROOF THEOREM 2 AND 3. The PGM process restricted to correct pairs (i, i) is isomorphic to the bootstrap percolation process for a $G(n, q)$ random graph, with $q = ps^2$. Consider the two events $\{\{M_{i,i}\}$ percolates $\}$ and $\overline{X}$. In the supercritical case, by virtue of Theorem 1 and Lemma 2, both events occur with high probability. Therefore, PGM percolates correctly and to a set of size $n - o(n)$ w.h.p.

In the subcritical case, the process $\{M_{i,i}\}$ does not percolate. As $\mathsf{P}\{X\} \to 0$, the full PGM process over all pairs does not percolate either by virtue of Lemma 2. $\square$

5.4 Interpretation of Results

Here we look into more details on the parameters of the algorithm. In particular, we consider how the threshold a_c scales with respect to r, p and s, and we elaborate on what happens near the bounding conditions on $q = ps^2$.

The parameter r controls a tradeoff between matching errors and percolation blocking. If r is too low, then a wrong pair (i, j) might accumulate r credits before the correct pairs (i, i) and (j, j) do; if r is too high, the process might not percolate, and most nodes do not get matched. Note that r has to be at least 2 for the algorithm to work: for $r = 1$, the algorithm would match pairs of nodes with only one mapped neighbor, which would necessarily lead to ambiguity, except in degenerate cases.

The lower bound $\frac{1}{n} \ll q$ simply ensures that the intersection of the two graphs has a giant component, without which the algorithm cannot percolate. The upper bound $q \ll sn^{-\frac{3}{2r}}$ is more subtle. Of course, if q exceeds the upper bound, the algorithm still percolates, but it will make errors. This is because the ratio in the probabilities of generating correct and wrong credits is not large enough to guarantee $\overline{X}$. As expected, the threshold a_c is decreasing with increasing p and s, so denser graphs require smaller seed sets. For most scenarios of practical interest, r would be a constant. For example, if s is a constant, and the mean degree np grows sub-linearly, then there is a constant r that satisfies the upper bound $q \ll sn^{-\frac{3}{2r}}$. Specifically, if we scale $nq = n^\delta$, with $0 < \delta < 1$ a constant, then the seed set threshold then scales as $a_c \propto n^{1-\delta\frac{r}{r-1}}$. For densification slower than a power law, suppose the mean is $nq = \Theta(\log n)$ (which is the threshold for the disappearance of symmetry and of isolated vertices [3]), then a_c scales as follows: $a_c = (1 - \frac{1}{r})(r-1)!^{\frac{1}{r-1}} n(\log n)^{-r/r-1}$. With $r = 2$ this is $a_c = \frac{n}{\log^2 n}$.

6. SIMULATION RESULTS

In this section, we test the PGM algorithm over real and artificial graphs, with two goals: to validate the phase transitions predicted by theory, and to check how well the algorithm performs on real networks.

To evaluate the performance of the algorithm, we use two metrics: The first is the size of final the map a^* (the total number of mapped nodes), which says how far the algorithm propagates. The second is the error rate, i.e., the fraction of wrong pairs in the map. Recall that the error rate is $\frac{|(i,j):i\neq j,(i,j)\in A^*|}{a^*}$.

The following ground-truth network graphs are considered:

- Erdös-Rényi random graph $G(n,p)$;

- Slashdot social network;

- EPFL e-mail exchange network;

- Geometric random graph $G_{geom}(n,d)$.

We run the deferred matching version of the algorithm (see Section 3.1) with $r = 2$; however the results are qualitatively similar for the basic version. For the $G(n,p)$, Slashdot and $G_{geom}(n,d)$ random graph, we use the edge sampling model: each edge appears in the observed network with probability s. The experiment with the EPFL network is in some sense more challenging, because the two networks to be matched are in fact different observations of the social interactions within an organization at two different points in time. Figures 2 - 8 show the dependence of the performance metrics on the size of the seed set a_0. Each figure contains 3 curves for different values of the graph similarity parameter, which is either the sampling parameter s, or an estimate of s in the case of the EPFL dataset. The parameter s determines the size of the overlap of the observed networks: the intersection of the edge sets of the two graphs are of size proportional to s^2. We averaged all the results over 10 realizations.

6.1 $G(n,p;s)$ Model

To support our results, we first simulate the $G(n,p;s)$ graph matching model exactly. Specifically, in this model, the generator graph G is an Erdös-Rényi $G(n,p)$ graph with $n = 50000$ and $p = 20/n$.

We observe that when the size of the seed set is sufficiently large, the algorithm propagates to the complete mapping (see Figure 2). We also see the sharp phase transitions predicted in Theorems 2 and 3. Furthermore, the theoretically obtained threshold a_c appears very precise. According to the definition (5) of a_c, for the first curve, $s = 0.9$ the critical size of the seed set a_c is 96, for $s = 0.8$ the a_c is 152 and for $s = 0.7$ the a_c is 260. We can see that the observed transitions are close to these values. To highlight this fact, we normalize the x-axis by a_c. In Figure 3, we observe that, after re-scaling, all the curves look essentially the same.

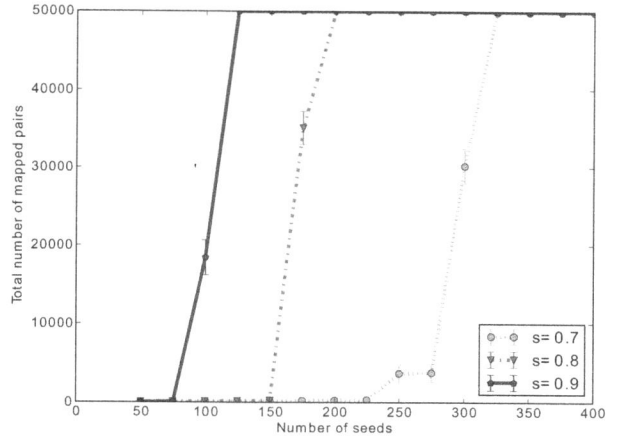

Figure 2: Total number of mapped nodes vs number of seeds for the PGM algorithm over $G(n,p)$ with $n = 50000$ and $p = 20/n$.

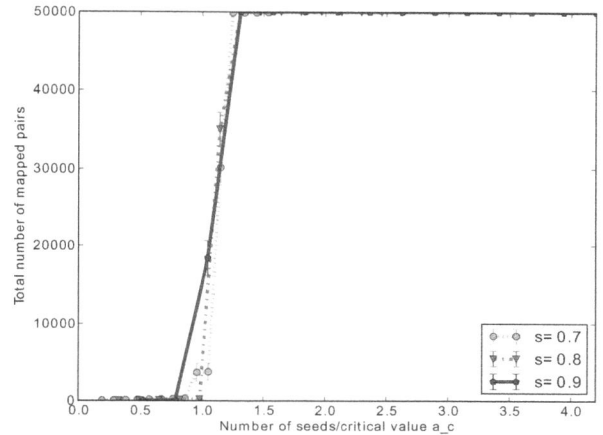

Figure 3: Total number of mapped nodes vs number of seeds for the PGM algorithm over $G(n,p)$ with $n = 50000$ and $p = 20/n$. The x-axis is rescaled according

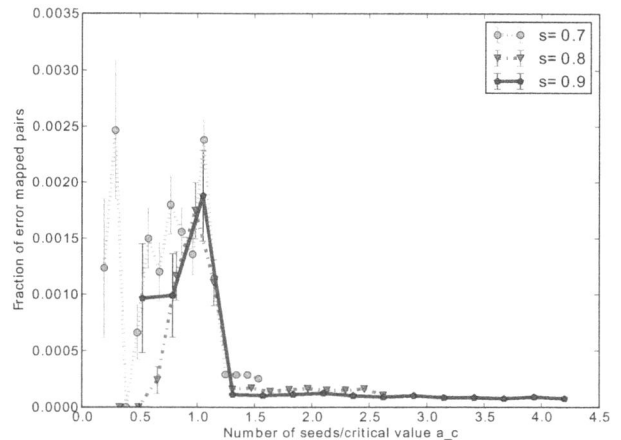

Figure 4: Error rate vs number of seeds for the PGM algorithm over $G(n,p)$ with $n = 50000$ and $p = 20/n$.

The Figure 4 provides further detail about the behavior of the PGM algorithm: if the size of the seed set a_0 is very small the PGM dies out quickly, adding only a small number of very unreliable matches to the seed set. This results in a lot of noise in the subcritical regime. For very large $a_0 \gg a_c$, the error rate goes to zero, thanks to the increasing amount of side information, as expected by Lemma 2. There appears to be a peak in the error rate just at the onset of percolation, because the algorithm matches almost the whole network, but with barely enough seeds to percolate. Errors are then more likely than for larger seed sets.

To confirm that deferred version does not change the observed phenomenons, we also ran the analogous experiments with the basic version of the PGM and observe identical threshold behavior.

6.2 Real Networks: Slashdot and E-mail Graphs

In the second set of experiments, we run PGM over large-scale social networks. First, we run the algorithm over real friend/foe links between Slashdot users [8] obtained in November 2008 (cf. Table 1).

Nodes	77360
Edges	905468
Number of components	1
Average clustering coefficient	0.0555
Diameter (longest shortest path)	10

Table 1: Slashdot dataset statistics.

To generate two observations of the network, we resort to edge sampling. In this model, when $s = 0.9$, the overlap of the two networks is less than 63000 nodes; when $s = 0.8$, the overlap is about 49000 nodes; when $s = 0.7$, it is 38000 nodes.

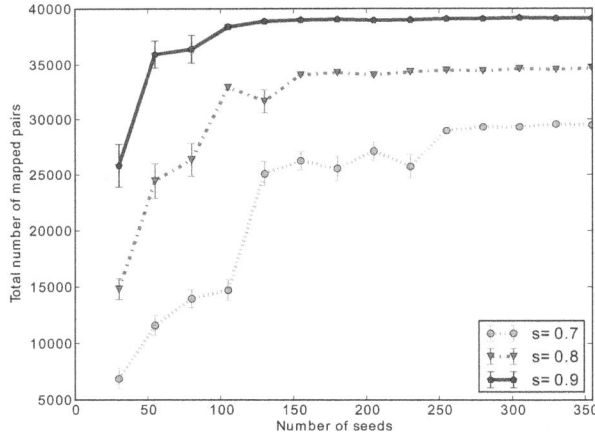

Figure 5: Total number of mapped nodes vs number of seeds for the PGM algorithm over the Slashdot network.

The results suggest phase transitions in the size of the final mapping, albeit less sharp than for $G(n; p)$ (see Figure 5). We also see that if the algorithm propagates (supercritical case), the error rate is encouragingly small (see Figure 6).

For example, for $s = 0.9$, it is enough to have 150 seeds (which is 0.2% of all nodes) for the algorithm to propagate over the majority of the graph. Figure 6 shows that the error rate drops rapidly with a_0.

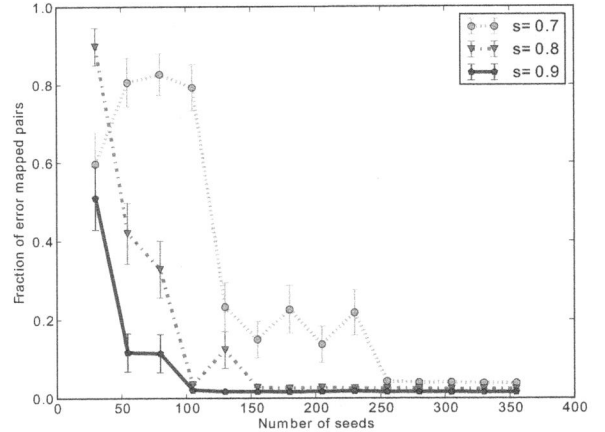

Figure 6: Error rate vs number of seeds for the PGM algorithm over the Slashdot network.

Second, we obtained snapshots of the e-mail traffic on the EPFL campus for different time periods (the week numbering starts at the beginning of year). Each node corresponds to an e-mail account, and an undirected edge means that at least one e-mail was sent between two accounts. The experiment is more realistic in the sense that we do not rely on the sampling model to generate two similar graphs $G_{1,2}$, but instead these graphs correspond to the real traffic patterns in two different time periods.

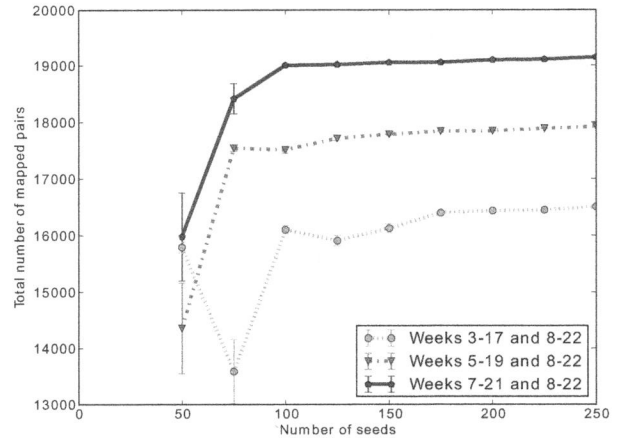

Figure 7: Total number of mapped nodes vs number of seeds for the PGM algorithm over the EPFL contact network.

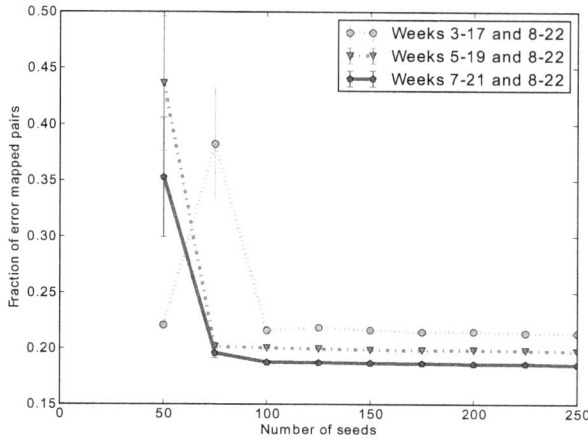

Figure 8: Error rate vs number of seeds for the PGM algorithm over the EPFL contact network.

The challenge for the algorithm is that in the considered graphs not only edge sets are different, but so are vertex sets. In other words, the PGM does not match the vertex sets of two graphs anymore, instead it identifies common subsets and matches them. If the two graphs are different enough the PGM can not separate the nodes which are not presented in both graphs and tries to match them thus increasing the error rate. Another challenge is that graphs are quite sparse, the average degree is about 7. The three curves demonstrate the behavior of the algorithm on the e-mail exchanges graphs for the following periods:

- G_1 is a graph of e-mails sent between weeks 3 and 17 and G_2 is a graph e-mails sent between weeks 8 and 12. Each graph contains approximately 60 000 nodes and 230 000 edges. The intersection graph has 50000 nodes and 160000 edges.

- For weeks 5-19 and 8-12, respectively: Each graph contains approximately 61 500 nodes and 231 000 edges. The intersection graph has 54000 nodes and 185000 edges.

- For weeks 7-21 and 8-12, respectively: Each graph contains approximately 61 500 nodes and 231 000 edges. The intersection graph has 59000 nodes and 207000 edges.

The results reveal similar phase transitions on the size of the final mapping and error rate as for those in $G(n; p)$ and Slashdot(see Figures 7 and 8).

6.3 Random Geometric Graph $G_{geom}(n, d)$

The performance of our proposed PGM algorithm is surprisingly good over both the $G(n, p; s)$ random graphs and over real social networks. We conjecture, however, that its success relies in part on the compactness of these graphs, which ensures that even with a relatively small number of seeds, every node in the network is close to some seeds, which allows to "triangulate" the nodes.

To illustrate this, we report on an experiment where the generator graph G is a random geometric graph $G_{geom}(n, d)$.

A random geometric graph is a random undirected graph which is generated by placing vertices uniformly at random on the unit square $[0, 1)^2$. Two vertices u and v are connected if and only if the distance between them is at most d [12]. The typical distance in a supercritical random geometric graph scales as $n^{1/2}$, in contrast to the logarithmic distance in $G(n, p)$ and other "small-world" networks. The average degree of a geometric graph is $\pi n d^2$. For our settings $n = 30000$ and $d = 0.01$, for an average degree of approx. 10.

Figures 9 and 10 show the experiment for $G_{geom}(n = 30000, d = 0.01)$. We observe that the algorithm does not percolate, and that it has a very high error rate within the map. While a complete understanding of the limits of percolation-based graph matching is lacking, this does suggest that PGM performs better with compact networks.

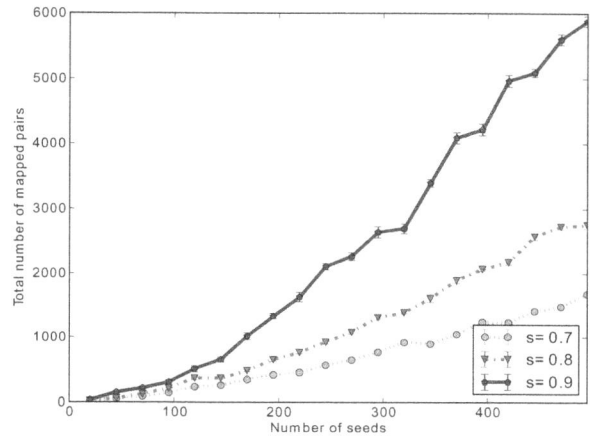

Figure 9: Total number of mapped nodes vs number of seeds for the PGM algorithm over $G(n, d)$ random geometric graph model where $n = 30000$ and $d = 0.01$.

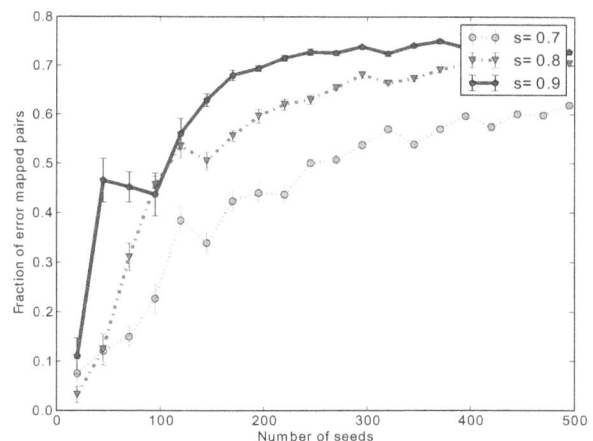

Figure 10: Error rate vs number of seeds for the PGM algorithm over $G(n, d)$ random geometric graph model where $n = 30000$ and $d = 0.01$.

7. CONCLUSION

We developed an algorithm for large-scale graph matching, and proposed a theoretical framework for its analysis. This enabled us to investigate conditions on the graph and algorithm parameters such that the algorithm percolates and performs well. One of our key contributions is a theoretical model and the identification of a phase transition in the size of the seed set, i.e., side information provided to the algorithm.

We have run experiments on several types of networks, confirming the results. We have observed two key phenomena:

- There is a sharp phase transition of the size of the final map a^*, depending on the size of the initial seed set.

- The algorithm has low complexity and performs well on real and artificial compact graphs; however, its performance was much worse on the random geometric graph, which is less compact.

The choice of r can have a significant impact on the map propagation process. A larger r means that we insist on more evidence before permanently mapping two nodes. While Lemma 2 suggests a rather benign condition on r, in more challenging scenarios (e.g., if the vertex sets V_1 and V_2 overlap only partially, or when some seeds are wrong), a larger threshold r can help compensate for such vagaries. We have also run experiments to check how robust the algorithm is with respect to these perturbations and observed that seed errors affect mostly the onset of percolation, but with a minor effect on the error rate. This agrees with the arguments in Lemma 2. An interesting related question concerns the choice of good seeds in situations where we are afforded some control.

In summary, we believe that the percolation-based graph matching algorithm proposed in this paper is both practically relevant, given its good performance and low complexity, and theoretically instructive, given the precise statements we can make about the required size of the seed set and the percolation dynamics. We hope that this work opens up new avenues for research, both into better graph-matching algorithms and richer classes of network models.

APPENDIX
Proof of Lemma 2

PROOF. First we bound the probability of mapping a wrong pair (i, j) $(i \neq j)$ at time step t, conditional on no wrong used pairs up to time $t - 1$. Note that conditioning on a correct used pair $i_\tau = j_\tau$ at time τ implies that this pair was correctly matched at some time τ' before τ, which in turn ascertains that for this pair, the correct count $M_{i_\tau, i_\tau}(\tau')$ "won" over all wrong counts $M_{i', i_\tau}(\tau')$ and $M_{i_\tau, j'}(\tau')$. Therefore, conditional on $i_\tau = j_\tau$ for $\tau < t$, correct counts are stochastically (slightly) larger, and wrong counts stochastically smaller. In the following argument, we are conservative in ignoring this bias in bounding the probability of future errors.

$$P\{X_{i,j}(t)\} \leq$$
$$\leq P\{M_{i,j}(t) = r, M_{i,i}(t) \leq r, M_{j,j}(t) \leq r\}$$
$$\leq P\{M_{i,j}(t) = r, M_{i,i}(t) \leq r\}$$

We compute this probability as follows (see Figure 11 for illustration).

1. Let L be the subset of used nodes $i_1, \ldots, i_t$ in G_1 up to time t that have an edge to i. Define $l = |L|$.

2. To have $\{M_{i,j}(t) = r\}$, there need to be r edges from used nodes $j_1, \ldots, j_t$ in G_2 to node j. This ensures that (i, j) has accumulated exactly r credits from $(i_1, j_1), \ldots, (i_t, j_t)$.

3. To have $\{M_{i,i}(t) \leq r\}$, out of the set L at most r can be connected to i in G_2.

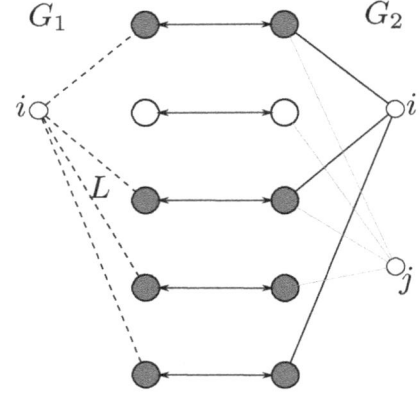

Figure 11: Edges to used nodes for pairs (i, j) and (i, i).

Thus,

$$P\{X_{i,j}(t)\} \leq$$
$$\leq \sum_{r < |L| = l < t} P\{|L| = l\} P\{M_{i,j}(t) = r, M_{i,i}(t) \leq r \mid |L| = l\}$$
$$\leq \sum_{r < l < t} P\{\mathsf{Bi}(t, ps) = l\} P\{\mathsf{Bi}(l, ps) = r\} P\{\mathsf{Bi}(l, s) \leq r\},$$

where the latter factors because the set of edges determining $M_{i,i}$ and $M_{i,j}$ are disjoint. Now we compute this probability explicitly.

$$P\{X_{i,j}(t)\} \leq$$
$$\leq \sum_l \frac{t!}{l!(t-l)!} \frac{l!}{r!(l-r)!} (ps)^l (1-ps)^{t-l} (ps)^r (1-ps)^{l-r} \cdot$$
$$\cdot P\{\mathsf{Bi}(l, s) \leq r\}$$
$$\overset{(a)}{\leq} P\{\mathsf{Bi}(t, ps) = r\} (t-r)! e^r \sum_l \frac{(ps)^l \exp(-ls/2)}{(t-l)!(l-r)!}$$
$$\overset{(b)}{\simeq} P\{\mathsf{Bi}(t, ps) = r\} (t-r)^{t-r} e^r \sum_l \frac{(ps)^l \exp(-ls/2)}{(t-l)^{t-l}(l-r)^{l-r}} \quad (6)$$

128

where (b) uses the Stirling formula for factorials, and (a) uses the following Chernoff bound for the left tail of the binomial:

$$P\{X < (1-\sigma)\mu\} \le \exp\left(\frac{-\sigma^2\mu}{2}\right).$$

Here X is $\mathsf{Bi}(l,s)$, $\mu = ls$ and $\sigma = 1 - \frac{r}{ls}$ (to make $(1-\sigma)\mu = r$). Then,

$$P\{\mathsf{Bi}(l,s) \le r\} \le \exp\left(\frac{-(1-\frac{r}{ls})^2 ls}{2}\right)$$

$$= \exp\left(-\frac{ls}{2} + r - \frac{r^2}{2ls}\right)$$

$$\le \exp\left(r - ls/2\right)$$

Now we denote by $g(l) = \frac{(ps)^l \exp(-ls/2)}{(t-l)^{t-l}(l-r)^{l-r}}$ the terms in the above sum.

We upper-bound $\sum_{r<l<t} g(l)$ in (6) by $(t-r)g(l_0)$ by virtue of Lemma 3 below:

$$g(l_0) = \frac{x^{tx+r}}{(t(1-x)+r)^{t(1-x)+r}(tx)^{tx}}$$

$$= \frac{x^r}{(t(1-x)+r)^{t(1-x)+r}(t)^{tx}}$$

$$\simeq \frac{x^r}{(t+r)^{t+r}t^{tx}}$$

Finally we upper-bound the error probability $P\{X_{i,j}(t)\}$ as follows:

$$P\{X_{i,j}(t)\} \le$$

$$\le P\{\mathsf{Bi}(t,ps) = r\}(t-r)^{t-r+1}e^r g(l_0)$$

$$\le t^r(ps)^r(t-r)^{t-r+1}e^r g(l_0)$$

$$\le (ps)^r t^{t+1} e^r g(l_0)$$

$$\simeq (psq)^r e^r \frac{t^{t+1}}{(t+r)^{t+r}t^{tq}}$$

$$\le \frac{(psq)^r}{t^{tq}}$$

$$\le (ps)^{2r}$$

Now to estimate a total probability of an error X, we take a union bound for all i,j,t. Thus we get $P(X) \le n^3(ps)^{2r}$, which provides a condition $ps \ll n^{-\frac{3}{2r}}$. $\square$

LEMMA 3. *For $x = pse^{-s/2} = o(1)$ the function $g(l)$ reaches its maximum at $l_0 = tx + r$.*

PROOF.

$$g(l) = \exp\left(l \log x - (t-l)\log(t-l) - (l-r)\log(l-r)\right)$$

We find a maximum of the function $\hat{g}(l)$, where

$$g(l) = \exp \hat{g}(l)$$

$$\hat{g}'(l) = \log x + \log(t-l) + \frac{t-l}{t-l} - \log(l-r) - \frac{l-r}{l-r}$$

$$= \log\left(\frac{(t-l)x}{l-r}\right)$$

To find an extremum, we solve $\hat{g}'(l) = 0$ or $\frac{(t-l)x}{l-r} = 1$. We get $l_0 = \frac{tx+r}{1+x} \simeq tx + r$ and it is easy to check that this is a local maximum. $\square$

Acknowledgements

The authors are grateful to Augustin Chaintreau for valuable feedback and constructive criticism.

A. REFERENCES

[1] M. Aizenman and J. L. Lebowitz. Metastability effects in bootstrap percolation. *Journal of Physics A: Mathematical and General*, 21(19), 1988.

[2] L. Backstrom, C. Dwork, and J. Kleinberg. Wherefore art thou r3579x?: anonymized social networks, hidden patterns, and structural steganography. In *Proceedings of the 16th international conference on World Wide Web*, 2007.

[3] B. Bollobás. *Random graphs*, volume 73. Cambridge University Press, 2001.

[4] P. Doshi, R. Kolli, and C. Thomas. Inexact matching of ontology graphs using expectation-maximization. *Web Semantics: Science, Services and Agents on the World Wide Web*, 7(2), 2009.

[5] S. Janson, T. Łuczak, T. Turova, and T. Vallier. Bootstrap percolation on the random graph $G_{n,p}$. *The Annals of Applied Probability*, 22(5), 2012.

[6] G. W. Klau. A new graph-based method for pairwise global network alignment. *BMC Bioinformatics*, 10(S-1), 2009.

[7] N. Korula and S. Lattanzi. An efficient reconciliation algorithm for social networks. *ArXiv e-prints*, July 2013.

[8] J. Leskovec. Stanford network analysis project. http://snap.stanford.edu/index.html.

[9] A. Mislove, B. Viswanath, K. P. Gummadi, and P. Druschel. You are who you know: inferring user profiles in online social networks. In *Proceedings of the third ACM international conference on Web search and data mining*, WSDM, pages 251–260, 2010.

[10] A. Narayanan and V. Shmatikov. De-anonymizing social networks. In *Proceedings of the 2009 30th IEEE Symposium on Security and Privacy*, 2009.

[11] P. Pedarsani and M. Grossglauser. On the privacy of anonymized networks. In *Proceedings of the 17th ACM SIGKDD International Conference on Knowledge Discovery and Data Mining*, KDD, 2011.

[12] M. Penrose. *Random Geometric Graphs*. Oxford University Press, USA, 2003.

[13] M.-E. Rosoiu, C. T. dos Santos, and J. Euzenat. Ontology matching benchmarks: generation and evaluation. In *OM*, volume 814 of *CEUR Workshop Proceedings*, 2011.

[14] Y.-K. Shih and S. Parthasarathy. Scalable global alignment for multiple biological networks. *BMC Bioinformatics*, 13(S-3), 2012.

[15] P. Shvaiko and J. Euzenat. Ontology matching: State of the art and future challenges. *IEEE Transactions on Knowledge and Data Engineering*, 25(1), 2013.

[16] G. Wondracek, T. Holz, E. Kirda, and C. Kruegel. A practical attack to de-anonymize social network users. In *IEEE Symposium on Security and Privacy*, 2010.

Scalable Similarity Estimation in Social Networks: Closeness, Node Labels, and Random Edge Lengths

Edith Cohen
Microsoft Research SVC
edith@cohenwang.com

Daniel Delling
Microsoft Research SVC
dadellin@microsoft.com

Fabian Fuchs*
KIT, Germany
fabian.fuchs@kit.edu

Andrew V. Goldberg
Microsoft Research SVC
goldberg@microsoft.com

Moises Goldszmidt
Microsoft Research SVC
moises@microsoft.com

Renato F. Werneck
Microsoft Research SVC
renatow@microsoft.com

ABSTRACT

Similarity estimation between nodes based on structural properties of graphs is a basic building block used in the analysis of massive networks for diverse purposes such as link prediction, product recommendations, advertisement, collaborative filtering, and community discovery. While local similarity measures, based on properties of immediate neighbors, are easy to compute, those relying on global properties have better recall. Unfortunately, this better quality comes with a computational price tag. Aiming for both accuracy and scalability, we make several contributions. First, we define *closeness similarity*, a natural measure that compares two nodes based on the similarity of their relations to all other nodes. Second, we show how the all-distances sketch (ADS) node labels, which are efficient to compute, can support the estimation of closeness similarity and shortest-path (SP) distances in logarithmic query time. Third, we propose the randomized edge lengths (REL) technique and define the corresponding REL distance, which captures both path length and path multiplicity and therefore improves over the SP distance as a similarity measure. The REL distance can also be the basis of closeness similarity and can be estimated using SP computation or the ADS labels. We demonstrate the effectiveness of our measures and the accuracy of our estimates through experiments on social networks with up to tens of millions of nodes.

Categories and Subject Descriptors

F.2 [**Analysis of Algorithms**]: Miscellaneous; G.2.2 [**Discrete Mathematics**]: Graph Theory; H.2.8 [**Database Management**]: Database Applications—*Data Mining*; H.3.2 [**Information Storage and Retrieval**]: Information Search and Retrieval; I.5.3 [**Pattern Recognition**]: Clustering

Keywords

Closeness Similarity; Social Networks; All-Distances Sketches; Random Edge Lengths

---

*Intern at Microsoft Research during this work.

1. INTRODUCTION

Methods that estimate the similarity of two nodes based solely on the graph structure are the heart of approaches for analyzing massive graphs and social networks [4, 21, 24, 27, 30]. These methods constitute the basic building blocks in algorithms for link prediction (friend recommendations), collaborative filtering, product placement, advertisement, and community discovery, to name a few.

The underlying *similarity measures* can be classified as *local* or *global*. Local measures are based only on the relation of immediate neighborhoods and include the number of common neighbors [28] and Adamic-Adar [4], which weighs each common neighbor inversely to the logarithm of its degree. Global measures are defined with respect to the global graph structure and include RWR (random walk with a specified restart probability) [34, 27], which extends hitting time and PageRank [10]; KATZ [24], which sums the number of distinct paths, where path contribution decreases exponentially with its length; SimRank [22], which is a recursively defined similarity measure based on neighbor similarity; resistance distance (viewing network as an electric circuit) and the related commute time (symmetric hitting time) [9]; the shortest-path (SP) distance; and the minimum cut. We refer the reader to [27] for an overview.

Local measures are fairly effective for some applications, but global measures can assign meaningful similarity scores to pairs that are more than two hops apart, and therefore have a better recall [27]. This capability comes at a price: global measures are often computationally more expensive, making them infeasible for application to networks and graphs with tens to hundreds of million of nodes, which are the norm in today's social networks, such as Twitter, Facebook, or LinkedIn.

Aiming for both accuracy and scalability, we introduce novel measures based on global properties and novel estimation techniques. Our approach consists of three components.

The first is a definition of the *closeness similarity* between nodes, which is based on the similarity of their distances to all other nodes in the network. Closeness similarity is specified with respect to three functions (*distance*, *decay*, and *weight*) and naturally extends the classic closeness centrality [31, 32] and several measures based on local and global properties.

The second component, *all-distances sketch* (ADS) labels, is a sketching technique that assigns a label to each node in the graph. ADS labels were initially developed for estimating the number of nodes reachable from (or within a certain distance of) a given node [6, 7, 12, 16, 19, 29], then extended to estimate closeness centrality [13, 15]. Although we need to compute an ADS label for each node in a graph, the above papers show that this can be done efficiently, with a logarithmic total number of traversals per edge. These computations can also be done offline, leading to extremely efficient (online) queries, consisting of simple operations on the (small) ADS labels. We show here that the ADS labels of two nodes can be used effectively to estimate both their SP distance and their closeness similarity.

As the third component in our approach, we introduce the *randomized edge lengths* (REL) technique. We define the *REL distance*, which is the expected SP distance with respect to this randomization. While both shorter path length and multiplicity strongly correlate with similarity in social networks, the SP distance does not account for multiplicity. The REL distance compensates for this semantic deficiency of SP distances while retaining the computational advantages of this benchmark similarity measure [27]. Another property of the REL distance that is not shared by the SP distance but holds for popular global measures (such as RWR, KATZ, and resistance distance) is that it can be used to identify situations in which the similarity value of two nodes highly depends on the presence of a third node (a "critical hub"). This is important because a critical hub between nodes may overstate actual similarity and also the number of pairs with respect to which a node is a critical hub can be used as a measure of betweenness centrality. Lastly, REL can be integrated with both ADSs (for efficiency) and closeness similarity (for accuracy).

We demonstrate both the effectiveness and the scalability of our approaches through a large-scale experimental study on three real social networks. The first two, DBLP and arXiv, are undirected networks representing co-authorships. The third, the so-called mention graph in Twitter, is directed and has tens of millions of nodes. We can answer arbitrary similarity queries (even global ones) on real social networks of such scale in a few *microseconds*, taking the full structure of the graph into account. Our experiments compare our approach against well-established algorithms representing both local (Adamic-Adar) and global (RWR) measures of similarity. As proxy for ground truth we use metadata associated with the networks (the text in paper titles, abstracts, and tweets), and use standard similarity measures from information retrieval to evaluate the degree of similarity between the nodes in the network. For validation, we also consider one synthetic *small world* network [26], for which we actually hold the ground truth.

In summary, the contributions of our work are:

- A definition of closeness similarity in graphs with a suitable parametrization, capable of capturing both local and global definitions.

- The application of all-distances sketch (ADS) labels to estimate distances and closeness similarities with theoretical performance guarantees.

- The application of randomized edge lengths (REL) to increase the accuracy of the similarity estimation.

- Experiments demonstrating the scalability and effectiveness of our approach on large-scale networks with comparisons to other representative approaches.

The remainder of this paper is organized as follows. We give a precise definition of ADSs and related notions in Section 2. Section 3 discusses how ADSs can be used to obtain distance estimates, and gives novel theoretical bounds for their accuracy. Section 4 introduces the notion of closeness similarity, studies two natural special cases (based on SP distances and Dijkstra ranks), and shows how they can be efficiently approximated using ADSs. Section 5

introduces the concept of randomized edge lengths (REL). The results of our experimental evaluation are provided in Section 6. We conclude with final remarks in Section 7.

2. PRELIMINARIES

We consider both directed and undirected networks. For nodes v, u, we use d_{vu} to denote the shortest-path (SP) distance from v to u. Let π_{vu} denote the *Dijkstra rank* of u with respect to v, defined as its position in the list of nodes ordered by increasing distance from v. For simplicity, we assume consistent tie-breaking to make distances distinct.

For two nodes u, v, we use the notation $\Phi_{<u}(v) = \{j | \pi_{vj} < \pi_{vu}\}$ for the set of nodes that are closer to v than u is. For $d \geq 0$ and node v, $N_d(v)$ (the d neighborhood of v) is the set of nodes of distance at most d from v, and $N_{<d}(v)$ is the set of nodes that are of distance less than d from v. We use $n_d(v) \equiv |N_d(v)|$.

For directed graphs, we distinguish between *forward* and *backward* Dijkstra ranks ($\overrightarrow{\pi}_{vi}$, $\overleftarrow{\pi}_{vi}$) and neighborhoods ($\overrightarrow{\Phi}_{<u}(v)$, $\overleftarrow{\Phi}_{<u}(v)$, $\overrightarrow{N}_d(v)$, $\overleftarrow{N}_d(v)$). The forward relations are with respect to the graph with edges oriented forward. The backward relations are with respect to the graph with edges reversed.

For a numeric function $r : X \to [0, 1]$ over a set X, the function $k_r^{th}(X)$ returns the k-th smallest value in the range of r on X. If $|X| < k$ then we define $k_r^{th}(X) = 1$.

The *all-distances sketch* (ADS) labels are defined with respect to a random rank assignment to nodes such that $\forall v, r(v) \sim U[0, 1]$, i.e, they are independently drawn from the uniform distribution on $[0, 1]$:

$$ADS(v) = \{(u, d_{vu}) \mid r(u) < k_r^{th}(\Phi_{<u}(v))\} .$$

In other words, a node u belongs to $ADS(v)$ if u is among the k nodes with lowest rank r within the ball of radius d_{vu} around v. (For simplicity, we abuse notation and often interpret $ADS(v)$ as a set of nodes, even though it is actually a set of *pairs*, each consisting of a node and a distance.) Since the inclusion probability of a node is inversely proportional to its Dijkstra rank, the expected size of $ADS(v)$ is $E[|ADS(v)|] \leq k \ln n$, where n is the number of nodes reachable from v [12, 16]. A detailed example is given in the appendix.

Moreover, a set of ADSs (one for each node) with respect to the same r can be computed efficiently, using $O(k \ln n)$ traversals per edge in expectation. The two proposed ADS computations (see overview in [13]) are based on performing pruned Dijkstra-based single-source shortest path computations [12, 16] or (for unweighted edges) dynamic programming [29, 19, 6, 7].

For a node $u \in ADS(v)$, we define

$$p_{vu} = k_r^{th}(\Phi_{<u}(v)) \tag{1}$$

to be the k-th smallest rank value amongst nodes that are closer to v than u is. By definition, $k_r^{th}(\Phi_{<u}(v)) = k_r^{th}(\{i \in ADS(v) | d_{vi} < d_{vu}\})$ (the k-th smallest amongst nodes in $ADS(v)$ that are closer to v than u is). Therefore, p_{vu} can be computed from $ADS(v)$ for all $u \in ADS(v)$. The value p_{vu} is the inclusion probability $\Pr[i \in ADS(v)]$, conditioned on fixing r on all nodes in $\Phi_{<u}(v)$ (but not fixing $r(u)$). Under this conditioning, i is included if and only if $r(i) < p_{vu}$. Since $r(i) \sim U[0, 1]$, this happens with probability p_{vu}. We use p_{vu} to obtain estimators for node centrality and pairwise relations.

Another useful function that can be computed from $ADS(v)$ with respect to a distance $x > 0$ is the threshold rank, defined as

$$\tau_v(x) = k_r^{th}(N_{<x}(v)). \tag{2}$$

The threshold rank is the maximum rank value that suffices for a node at distance x from v to be included in $\text{ADS}(v)$, fixing the ranks of all other nodes. When $u \in \text{ADS}(v)$, then $p_{vu} = \tau_v(d_{vu})$. We use τ in the analysis of our similarity estimators. The inverse function

$$\tau_v^{-1}(y) = \max\{d_{vi} \mid \text{k}_r^{\text{th}}(\Phi_{<i}(v)) > y\} \quad (3)$$

is the maximum distance for which the threshold rank is larger than y. This function gives a lower bound on the distance d_{vi} for a node $i \notin \text{ADS}(v)$. It also allows us to identify nodes that are far away from a set of nodes.

For directed graphs, we distinguish between the forward and backward ADSs: $\overrightarrow{\text{ADS}}(v)$ is computed with respect to $\overrightarrow{\Phi}_v$ and $\overleftarrow{\text{ADS}}(v)$ is computed with respect to $\overleftarrow{\Phi}_v$. Accordingly, we use the forward and backward notation with the functions p and τ ($\overrightarrow{p}_{uv}$, $\overleftarrow{p}_{uv}$, $\overrightarrow{\tau}$, $\overleftarrow{\tau}$).

As a relative error measure for the quality of our estimators we use the *coefficient of variation (CV)*, defined as the ratio of root of square error to mean.

3. DISTANCE ESTIMATION

We explore the use of ADSs as *distance labels*. Distance labels enable the computation of the SP distance d_{ij} from the labels of the nodes i and j. Node labels that have the same format as ADSs (2-hop labels [14]) have been successfully used for exact distances in road networks [3] and medium-size unweighted social graphs [5]. These exact labels, however, are much larger and much more expensive to compute than ADSs.

We show here how ADSs can be used to obtain bounds on the distance. Without loss of generality, we use the directed notation. If we are lucky and $j \in \overrightarrow{\text{ADS}}(i)$ or $i \in \overleftarrow{\text{ADS}}(j)$, we can determine the exact distance d_{ij} from $\overrightarrow{\text{ADS}}(i)$ or $\overleftarrow{\text{ADS}}(j)$. Otherwise, we can obtain upper and lower bounds, which we denote by $\overline{d}_{ij}$ and $\underline{d}_{ij}$, respectively. The upper bound is obtained by treating the ADSs as 2-hop labels [3, 5, 14], namely considering the shortest path through a node in $\overrightarrow{\text{ADS}}(i) \cap \overleftarrow{\text{ADS}}(j)$:

$$\overline{d}_{ij} \leftarrow \min\{d_{iv} + d_{vj} \mid v \in \overrightarrow{\text{ADS}}(i) \cap \overleftarrow{\text{ADS}}(j)\} \quad (4)$$

To study the quality of the upper bound given by Equation (4), we consider its *stretch*, defined as the ratio between the bound and the actual SP distance. We bound the stretch of (4) on undirected graphs as a function of the parameter k. As our first contribution, we show that the bounds on stretch, query, space, and construction time asymptotically match those of the Thorup-Zwick distance oracles [33].

THEOREM 3.1. *On undirected graphs, with constant probability,*

$$\overline{d}_{vu} \leq \left(2\left\lceil\frac{\log n}{\log k}\right\rceil - 1\right) d_{vu}.$$

PROOF. Let $d \equiv d_{vu}$. We have the relation $N_d(u) \subset N_{2d}(v) \subset N_{3d}(u) \subset N_{4d}(v) \subset \ldots$ Consider the ratio $\frac{n_{id}(v)}{n_{(i+1)d}(u)}$ for $i \geq 1$. We look at the smallest i where $\frac{n_{id}(v)}{n_{(i+1)d}(u)} > c/k$. When this holds, we are very likely to have a common node that is in $\text{ADS}(v) \cap \text{ADS}(u) \cap N_{id}(v)$. Simply, the k smallest ranked nodes in $N_{(i+1)d}(u)$ are a uniform sample, so one of them hits $N_{id}(v)$ with probability $1 - (1 - c/k)^k \approx 1 - 1/e^c$. Finally, since there are at most n nodes, we must have $i \leq \log_{k/c} n$. $\square$

This means the stretch is $\log n$ if we choose k to be constant, and $2a - 1$ if we pick $k = n^{1/a}$ (for some integer a). The bound can be

slightly tightened by looking at the maximum h such that, for some increasing $n_1 \leq n_2 \leq \ldots \leq n_h$, $k\sum_i n_i/n_{i+1} < 1$ (bounding the sum rather than the minimum ratio). This would give as stretch $\log(n)/\log\log(n)$ with fixed k.

A naive implementation of ADS intersection takes $O(k\ln n)$ time and works well in practice for small k. To improve query time when k is large (while still guaranteeing the same bound on the stretch), we further observe that the smallest ranked node in $N_{id}(v)$ is likely to be one of the k smallest in $N_{(i+1)d}(u)$. Therefore, it suffices to test for inclusion in $\text{ADS}(u)$ only the nodes in $\text{ADS}(v)$ that would have been included when $k = 1$. This would reduce query time to $O(\ln n)$. We note that asymptotic query times can be further reduced by a more careful use of the ADSs, but the details are mainly of theoretical interest and outside the scope of this work.

A clear advantage of the ADSs over the Thorup-Zwick summaries is that they are also "oracles" for other powerful measures: closeness similarity, as we show here, neighborhood sizes [12], and closeness centralities [13, 15]. In practice, the distance estimates obtained by the ADSs are much better than these worst-case bounds for arbitrary graphs. As we show in Section 6, we observe very small stretch even for directed graphs. We now provide a theoretical justification for these observations by considering structural properties of social networks.

For two nodes i, j we are likely to get a good upper bound if a good "intermediate" vertex is likely to be present at the intersection of the ADSs. More precisely, suppose nodes v_h are ordered by increasing $d_h \equiv d_{iv_h} + d_{v_h j}$, i.e., by the upper bound they yield on the distance. Note that

$$\Pr[v_h \in \text{ADS}(i) \cap \text{ADS}(j)] \geq$$
$$\min\left\{1, \frac{k}{|\overrightarrow{\Phi}_i(v_h) \cup \overleftarrow{\Phi}_j(v_h)|}\right\} \geq \frac{k}{\overrightarrow{\pi}_{iv_h} + \overleftarrow{\pi}_{jv_h}}.$$

This is because a sufficient condition for v_h to be in the intersection is that it is k-th in the random permutation induced on v_h and the nodes $\overrightarrow{\Phi}_i(v_h) \cup \overleftarrow{\Phi}_j(v_h)$. These events are negatively correlated for different nodes. Therefore, by summing over potential intermediate nodes, we are $(1 - 1/e^c)$ likely to get an upper bound at most d_s when

$$k\sum_{h=1}^{s}\frac{1}{\max\{\overrightarrow{\pi}_{iv_h}, \overleftarrow{\pi}_{jv_h}\}} \geq c.$$

A sufficient condition to obtain an upper bound d_s with probability $1 - 1/e^c$ is that there is $x < d_s$ so that the Jaccard similarity of $N_x(i)$ and $N_{d_{ij}-x}(j)$ is at least c/k.

Qualitatively, the stretch is lower when there are many potential "hub" nodes v that lie on almost shortest paths ($d_{ij} \leq (1+\epsilon)(d_{iv} + d_{vj})$). Since the presence of multiple short paths is an indicator of similarity, this suggests that the approximate distance might be better in capturing some aspects of similarity than the exact distance.

3.1 Better Bounds

Our experiments show that simply applying Equation (4) (even for fairly small values of k) is enough to obtain very accurate results for social networks. For even better upper bounds, one can use more information and trade accuracy for computation time. For example, the formula

$$\overline{d}_{ij} \leftarrow \min\{d_{ix} + d_{xz} + d_{zy} + d_{yj} \mid x \in \overrightarrow{\text{ADS}}(i), \quad (5)$$
$$y \in \overleftarrow{\text{ADS}}(j), z \in \overrightarrow{\text{ADS}}(x) \cap \overleftarrow{\text{ADS}}(y)\}$$

uses neighboring ADSs to obtain a tighter upper bound, but the associated query time is $O(k^2 \ln^2 n)$.

Moreover, we could use ADSs to obtain *lower bounds* on the distance between any two nodes as well. More precisely, the following lower bound on d_{vu} can be obtained from $r(u)$ and $ADS(v)$:

$$\Delta(u, v) = \begin{cases} d_{vu}, \text{ if } u \in ADS(v) \\ \tau_v^{-1}(r(u)), \text{ if } u \notin ADS(v). \end{cases}$$

For directed graphs we use $\overrightarrow{\Delta}$ and $\overleftarrow{\Delta}$, according to the direction of the ADS of v. A tighter bound can be obtained using both $ADS(u)$ and $ADS(v)$:

$$\underline{d}_{ij} \leftarrow \max \begin{cases} \overrightarrow{\Delta}(j, i), \\ \overleftarrow{\Delta}(i, j), \\ \forall v \in \overrightarrow{ADS}(j), \ \overrightarrow{\Delta}(v, i) - d_{jv} \\ \forall v \in \overleftarrow{ADS}(i), \ \overleftarrow{\Delta}(v, j) - d_{vi}. \end{cases} \quad (6)$$

The last two conditions state that, if there is a node v in $ADS(j)$ and distance d from v which we know has distance at least $d + x$ from i, then we get a lower bound of x on the distance between i and j.

4. CLOSENESS SIMILARITY

Using only the distance between two nodes to measure their similarity has obvious drawbacks. In this section, we introduce the concept of *closeness similarity*, which measures the similarity of two nodes based on their views of the full graph. More precisely, we consider the distance from each of these two nodes to all other nodes in the network and measure how much these two distance vectors differ. This is computationally expensive, but ADSs allow an efficient estimation of this view, as Section 4.1 will show.

Closeness similarity is specified with respect to a *distance function* δ_{ij} between nodes, a *distance decay* function $\alpha(d)$ (a monotone non-increasing function of distances), and a *weight function* $\beta(i)$ of node IDs. The basic expression for closeness similarity is

$$S_{\alpha,\beta}(v, u) = \sum_i \alpha(\max\{\delta_{vi}, \delta_{ui}\})\beta(i), \quad (7)$$

but we actually prefer the following Jaccard form, where the similarity is always in $[0, 1]$:

$$J_{\alpha,\beta}(v, u) = \frac{\sum_i \alpha(\max\{\delta_{vi}, \delta_{ui}\})\beta(i)}{\sum_i \alpha(\min\{\delta_{vi}, \delta_{ui}\})\beta(i)}. \quad (8)$$

LEMMA 4.1. *If* $\alpha(d) \geq 0$ *is monotone non-increasing and* $\beta(x) \geq 0$ *is nonnegative, then* $J_{\alpha,\beta}(u, v) \in [0, 1]$ *for all pairs* u, v, *and* $J_{\alpha,\beta}(v, v) = 1$ *for any* v.

PROOF. The first claim follows from monotonicity of α, which implies that $\alpha(\min\{\delta_{vi}, \delta_{ui}\}) \geq \alpha(\max\{\delta_{vi}, \delta_{ui}\})$. The second from $\alpha(\min\{\delta_{vi}, \delta_{vi}\}) = \alpha(\max\{\delta_{vi}, \delta_{vi}\}) = \alpha(\delta_{vi})$. $\square$

The notion of closeness similarity is quite general and extremely powerful, as this section will show. A potential drawback is that it is expensive to compute exactly, but Section 4.1 will show that we can use ADSs to approximate it accurately and efficiently for all choices of α and β and two natural choices of the distance function δ. In terms of effectiveness, our experiments will show that simply setting $\alpha(x) \equiv 1/x$, $\beta \equiv 1$, and $\delta_{vi} \equiv \pi_{vi}$ (Dijkstra ranks) is enough to obtain very good results.

In general, however, the weighting β can be anything that depends on readily-available parameters of a node, such as its degree or metadata (e.g., gender or interests obtained through text analysis). Similarity is then measured with respect to these weights.

Using $\beta \equiv 1$ weighs all nodes equally, in which case we omit β from the notation. A weight function that increases with degree can be used to emphasize contribution of highly connected nodes to the similarity. Alternatively, a decreasing β may make sense in collaborative filtering applications, where the proximity of two nodes to a third one is more meaningful when the third node is less central.

In the remainder of this section, we consider closeness similarity with respect to both *SP distance* (where $\delta_{ij} \equiv d_{ij}$), in Section 4.1.1, and *Dijkstra rank* (position in the nearest-neighbor list, with $\delta_{ij} \equiv \pi_{ij}$), in Section 4.1.2. We explain the semantic difference between these choices in Section 4.2.

The notion of closeness similarity generalizes several existing measures. In particular, when δ is the SP distance, the Adamic-Adar (AA) measure [4] can be expressed as $S_{\alpha,\beta}$ using $\alpha(x) = 0$ when $x \geq 2$ and $\alpha(x) = 1$ otherwise, and $\beta(u) = 1/\log|\Gamma(u)|$, where $|\Gamma(u)|$ is the degree of u. Using $\alpha(x) = 1/(1 + x)^c$ (for some choice of c) gives us a global variant of AA. Similarly, the intersection size of d-neighborhoods, which naturally extends the local *common neighbors* measure, can be expressed using $\beta(u) \equiv 1$ and $\alpha(x) = 1$ if $x \leq d$ and 0 otherwise.

Closeness similarity is also tightly related to the classic notion of *closeness centrality*, which measures the importance or relevance of nodes in a social network based on their distances to all other nodes. The closeness centrality $C_{\alpha,\beta}(i)$ of a node i is simply the closeness similarity $S_{\alpha,\beta}(i, i)$ between the node and itself. Use of $\alpha(x) = 1/x$ specifies Harmonic mean centrality (used in [32] with resistance distances and evaluated in [8] with SP distances) and $\alpha(x) = 2^{-x}$ specifies exponential decay with distance [20]. The number of reachable nodes from v can be expressed using $\alpha(x) = 1$. Estimators for $C_\alpha(v)$ from $ADS(v)$ were studied in [13, 15] and have coefficient of variation (CV) $\leq 1/\sqrt{2(k - 1)}$, which means that the relative error rapidly decreases with k.

In directed networks such as Twitter, we can consider closeness similarity with respect to either forward and backward edges. The forward similarity compares nodes based on how they relate to "the world," whereas backward similarity compares them based on how the world relates to them. To simplify the technical presentation, we focus on undirected graphs. Results easily extend to directed graphs by appropriately considering forward or backward paths.

4.1 Estimating Closeness Similarity

The exact computation of (7) and (8) is expensive, since it amounts to performing two single-source shortest-path searches for each pair of nodes. We will show, however, that we can obtain good estimates from $ADS(u)$ and $ADS(v)$. Since the expected time to compute the whole set of ADS labels is within a $k \ln n$ factor of a single-source shortest-path computation, this is very appealing. We also provide tight theoretical bounds on the quality of these estimates.

Our estimates $\hat{S}_{\alpha,\beta}(u, v)$ and $\hat{J}_{\alpha,\beta}(u, v)$ are obtained by separately estimating $\alpha(\max\{\delta_{vi}, \delta_{ui}\})$ and (when using the Jaccard form) $\alpha(\min\{\delta_{vi}, \delta_{ui}\})$ for each node i. We then substitute the estimate values $\hat{\alpha}(\max\{\delta_{vi}, \delta_{ui}\})$ and $\hat{\alpha}(\min\{\delta_{vi}, \delta_{ui}\})$ in the respective expressions (7) and (8). Since the estimate values are positive only for nodes $i \in ADS(u) \cup ADS(v)$, the computation is very efficient. In order to obtain a small relative error with arbitrary β, the random ranks underlying the ADS computation have to be drawn with respect to β (as done for centrality computation in [13]). This is explained in Section 4.3.

The estimates we obtain for each summand, and therefore each sum, are nonnegative. They are also unbiased for SP distances, and nearly so for Dijkstra ranks. The estimate on each summand (with respect to each node i) typically has high variance: since each ADS has expected size $k \ln n$, for most nodes i we have limited information from $\mathrm{ADS}(u)$ and $\mathrm{ADS}(v)$. We can, however, bound the error of the aggregate estimate. To do so, we consider each variant (based on SP distances and Dijkstra ranks) separately.

4.1.1 SP Distance Closeness

We use the L^* estimator of Cohen and Kaplan [17, 18], which is the unique estimator that is unbiased, nonnegative, and monotone (estimate is non-increasing with $r(i)$). The L^* estimator is also variance-optimal in a Pareto sense [17]. We explicitly derive the estimator for functions α that are monotone non-increasing with the maximum distance $\alpha(\max\{d_{vi}, d_{ui}\})$ and with the minimum distance $\alpha(\min\{d_{vi}, d_{ui}\})$. We state the estimator, as applied to $\mathrm{ADS}(u)$ and $\mathrm{ADS}(v)$, and our error bounds.

Our estimator for $\alpha(\max\{d_{vi}, d_{ui}\})$ is defined by the following lemma.

LEMMA 4.2. *The L^* estimate of $\alpha(\max\{d_{vi}, d_{ui}\})$ is*

$$\hat{\alpha}(\max\{d_{vi}, d_{ui}\}) =$$
$$\begin{cases} i \notin \mathrm{ADS}(u) \cap \mathrm{ADS}(v): & 0 \\ i \in \mathrm{ADS}(u) \cap \mathrm{ADS}(v): & \frac{\alpha(\max\{d_{vi}, d_{ui}\})}{p_{i,u,v}}, \end{cases}$$

where $p_{i,u,v} = \min\{p_{vi}, p_{ui}\}$, with p_{vi} and p_{ui} as defined in (1).

PROOF. When we have no information (no upper bound on $\max\{d_{vi}, d_{ui}\}$), the estimate is 0. The value $p_{i,u,v}$ is the conditional probability (conditioned on fixed ranks of all other nodes) of the event $i \in \mathrm{ADS}(u) \cap \mathrm{ADS}(v)$. Therefore the estimator is simply the inverse-probability estimate conditioned on fixed ranks. □

Note that we have all the information needed to compute the estimate. When $i \notin \mathrm{ADS}(u) \cap \mathrm{ADS}(v)$, the estimate is 0. When $i \in \mathrm{ADS}(u) \cap \mathrm{ADS}(v)$, we know both d_{ui} and d_{vi} and can compute p_{vi} and p_{ui}. Lastly, to estimate the sum $\sum_i \alpha(\max\{d_{vi}, d_{ui}\})\beta(i)$ it suffices to only consider nodes that belong to the intersection of the ADSs, because they are the only ones with a positive estimate.

Our estimate for $\alpha(\min\{d_{vi}, d_{ui}\})$ is defined as follows.

LEMMA 4.3. *The L^* estimate of $\alpha(\min\{d_{vi}, d_{ui}\})$ is*

$$\hat{\alpha}(\min\{d_{vi}, d_{ui}\}) = \begin{cases} i \notin \mathrm{ADS}(u) \cup \mathrm{ADS}(v): & 0 \\ i \in \mathrm{ADS}(u) \setminus \mathrm{ADS}(v): & \frac{\alpha(d_{ui})}{p_{ui}} \\ i \in \mathrm{ADS}(v) \setminus \mathrm{ADS}(u): & \frac{\alpha(d_{vi})}{p_{vi}} \\ i \in \mathrm{ADS}(u) \cap \mathrm{ADS}(v): & \\ \quad \text{if } p_{vi} \leq p_{ui}: & \\ \quad \frac{\alpha(\min\{d_{vi}, d_{ui}\}) - (p_{ui}-p_{vi})\frac{\alpha(d_{ui})}{p_{ui}}}{p_{vi}} & \\ \quad \text{if } p_{ui} < p_{vi}: & \\ \quad \frac{\alpha(\min\{d_{vi}, d_{ui}\}) - (p_{vi}-p_{ui})\frac{\alpha(d_{vi})}{p_{vi}}}{p_{ui}}. & \end{cases}$$

PROOF. We apply the general derivation of the L^* estimator, presented in [17]. In our context, we consider the outcome as a function of $r(i)$, conditioned on the ranks on all other nodes being fixed. The outcome is the occurrence of the events $i \in \mathrm{ADS}(u)$ and $i \in \mathrm{ADS}(v)$, as a function of $r(i)$. The outcome depends on the relation of $r(i)$ to the two threshold values $\tau_v(d_{vi})$ and $\tau_u(d_{ui})$ as in (2), which are solely determined by the ranks of $\Phi_{<i}(v)$ and $\Phi_{<i}(u)$. In particular, they do not depend on $r(i)$.

To obtain the L^* estimate, we need to consider the (tightest) lower bound we can obtain on $\alpha(\min\{d_{vi}, d_{ui}\})$ from the outcome. This is the infimum of the function on all possible data (distances d_{ui} and d_{vi}) that are consistent with the outcome. Note

that from the outcome for a given $r(i) = y$, we have enough information to determine the outcome, and the respective lower bound function, for all $r(i) \geq y$.

We now provide the estimator for all possible outcomes.

The first case is $i \notin \mathrm{ADS}(u) \cup \mathrm{ADS}(v)$, which happens when $r(i) > \max\{\tau_v(d_{vi}), \tau_u(d_{ui})\}$. This is consistent with i not even being reachable from v or i (or being very far). We therefore do not have an upper bound on the minimum distance (and thus do not have a lower bound on $\alpha(\min\{d_{vi}, d_{ui}\})$). We use the estimate $\hat{\alpha}(\min\{d_{vi}, d_{ui}\}) = 0$.

The second case is $i \in \mathrm{ADS}(u) \setminus \mathrm{ADS}(v)$. This can only happen if $\tau_u(d_{ui}) \geq \tau_v(d_{vi})$ and when $r(i) \in (\tau_v(d_{vi}), \tau_u(d_{ui})]$. In this case we know d_{ui}, and we have that $p_{ui} = \tau_u(d_{ui})$. Note that d_{ui} is trivially an upper bound on the minimum distance. It is also the tightest bound we can get from the information we have. We can only obtain a lower bound of $\tau_v^{-1}(r(i))$ (see Equation (3)) on d_{vi}, but we can not upper bound it. If $\tau_v^{-1}(r(i)) \geq d_{ui}$ then we know that $d_{vi} \geq d_{ui}$ and thus we know that the minimum distance is d_{ui}. Otherwise, we only know that the minimum distance is between $\tau_v^{-1}(r(i))$ and d_{ui} and the best upper bound we have is d_{ui}. Either way, whether we know the minimum distance or not, the estimate is $\hat{\alpha}(\min\{d_{vi}, d_{ui}\}) = \frac{\alpha(d_{vu})}{\tau_v(d_{ui})}$. The case $i \in \mathrm{ADS}(v) \setminus \mathrm{ADS}(u)$ is symmetric.

The remaining case is when $i \in \mathrm{ADS}(v) \cap \mathrm{ADS}(u)$. In this case we can determine d_{vi}, d_{ui}, and both thresholds $\tau_v(d_{vi}) = p_{vi}$ and $\tau_u(d_{ui}) = p_{ui}$. Assuming $\tau_v(d_{vi}) \leq \tau_u(d_{ui})$ (the other case is symmetric), the L^* estimate is the solution for x of the unbiasedness constraint: $\alpha(\min\{d_{vi}, d_{ui}\}) = (\tau_u(d_{ui}) - \tau_v(d_{vi}))\frac{\alpha(d_{ui})}{\tau_u(d_{ui})} + \tau_v(d_{vi})x$. □

Note again that we have all the information we need to compute the estimate. We know d_{vi} and p_{vi} if and only if $r(i) \leq p_{vi}$, which happens if and only if $i \in \mathrm{ADS}(v)$, and symmetrically for u.

With these estimators, the Jaccard closeness similarity can be estimated in the natural way:

$$\hat{J}_{\beta,\alpha}(v, u) = \frac{\sum_{i \in \mathrm{ADS}(u) \cap \mathrm{ADS}(v)} \hat{\alpha}(\max\{d_{vi}, d_{ui}\})\beta(i)}{\sum_{i \in \mathrm{ADS}(u) \cup \mathrm{ADS}(v)} \hat{\alpha}(\min\{d_{vi}, d_{ui}\})\beta(i)}. \quad (9)$$

The estimates for both the numerator and denominator are unbiased, since our estimates for each summand are unbiased. The estimate on the ratio is biased, but we can bound the root of the mean square error of the estimate:

THEOREM 4.1. *When $\alpha(x)$ is non-increasing and node ranks are drawn according to $\beta(i)$, the root of the expected square error of $\hat{J}_{\beta,\alpha}(v, u)$ is $O(1/\sqrt{k})$.*

PROOF. The coefficient of variation of the estimate on $\sum_i \alpha(\min\{d_{vi}, d_{ui}\})$ is bounded by $1/\sqrt{2(k-1)}$. The RMSE (square root of expected square error) on the estimate $\sum_i \alpha(\max\{d_{vi}, d_{ui}\})$ is bounded by $\sum_i \alpha(\min\{d_{vi}, d_{ui}\})/\sqrt{2(k-1)}$. □

4.1.2 Dijkstra Rank Closeness

A natural choice for the distance decay function is $\alpha = 1/x$, based on the harmonic mean. With Dijkstra ranks, we suggest the use of the variant $\alpha(x) = \min\{1, h/x\}$ for some integer $h > 1$. With $\alpha(x) = 1/x$, the weights assigned to the h closest nodes are in the range $[1/h, 1]$, which can make the measure less robust when these nodes are actually similar. By using $h > 1$, we give the h closest nodes the same α weight, increasing robustness to variations in their ordering.

We now consider the choice $h = k$. Making the appropriate substitutions in Equation (8) we have

$$J^*(u,v) = \frac{\sum_i \min\{1, \frac{k}{\max\{\pi_{vi},\pi_{ui}\}}\}}{\sum_i \min\{1, \frac{k}{\min\{\pi_{vi},\pi_{ui}\}}\}}. \quad (10)$$

It turns out that we can obtain a particularly simple estimator for J^*:

$$\hat{J}^*(u,v) = \frac{|\text{ADS}(u) \cap \text{ADS}(v)|}{|\text{ADS}(u) \cup \text{ADS}(v)|}. \quad (11)$$

This is due to the following relations:

LEMMA 4.4. *For any three nodes i, u, and v,*

$$\Pr[i \in ADS(u) \cap ADS(v)] \approx \min\left\{1, \frac{k}{\max\{\pi_{vi},\pi_{ui}\}}\right\}$$

$$\Pr[i \in ADS(u) \cup ADS(v)] \approx \min\left\{1, \frac{k}{\min\{\pi_{vi},\pi_{ui}\}}\right\}$$

PROOF. Recall that the probability that a node i appears in ADS(v) is $\min\{1, k/\pi_{vi}\}$. The probabilities that the node appears in the intersection of two or more ADSs are highly positively correlated. The joint probability is close to the minimum of the two, which is $\frac{k}{\max\{\pi_{vi},\pi_{ui}\}}$. More precisely, for $k = 1$, the joint probability is between $\frac{k}{\pi_{vi}+\pi_{ui}}$ (if the sets of preceding nodes in the permutations are disjoint) and $\frac{k}{\max\{\pi_{vi},\pi_{ui}\}}$ (if the sets of preceding nodes are maximally overlapping). Asymptotically, when k is larger, the expected size of the intersection of ADSs more closely approximates (10). □

Note that a nice property of these approximations is that we can work with a very compact representation of ADSs. Since each ADS has expected size $k \ln n$, to estimate size of union and intersection we can hash node IDs to a smaller domain of size $O(\log k + \log \log n)$. We can then store the ADS as an unordered set, obtaining a significant reduction in storage needed for the labels for very large graphs.

These approximations quickly converge with k. Using linearity of expectation, it follows that the sum with respect to $\alpha(\max\{\pi_{vi},\pi_{ui}\})$ can be approximated by the size of the intersection $|\text{ADS}(u) \cap \text{ADS}(v)|$, and the sum with respect to $\alpha(\min\{\pi_{vi},\pi_{ui}\})$ is approximated by the size of the union $|\text{ADS}(u) \cup \text{ADS}(v)|$.

We now consider estimating closeness similarity for more general forms of α. One complication is that, in contrast to the distance d_{ui}, the Dijkstra rank π_{ui} of a node i is not readily available when $i \in \text{ADS}(u)$. Fortunately, we can still obtain an estimate with good concentration:

LEMMA 4.5. *Conditioned on $i \in \text{ADS}(v)$, the estimate $\hat{\pi}_{vi} = 1 + |\widehat{\Phi_{<i}(v)}|$, where*

$$|\widehat{\Phi_{<i}(v)}| = \sum_{j \in ADS(v) \cap \Phi_{<i}(v)} \frac{1}{p_{vj}}, \quad (12)$$

is unbiased and has CV at most $1/\sqrt{2(k-1)}$.

PROOF. The Dijkstra rank $\pi_{vi} = 1 + |\Phi_{<i}(v)|$ is equal to 1 plus the number of nodes that are closer to v than i (we assume unique distances in this definition). The best estimator we are aware of for $|\Phi_{<i}(v)|$ is the RC estimator [13], which is (12). This RC estimate is equal to the exact size when $|\Phi_{<i}(v)| \leq k$ (i.e., $\pi_{vi} \leq k+1$) and an estimate that always exceeds k otherwise. The CV of the estimate is upper-bounded by $1/\sqrt{2(k-1)}$. Therefore for large k we

can get good concentration. Note that we are able to compute this estimate only when $i \in \text{ADS}(v)$ (because otherwise we can not determine the nodes in ADS(v) that are closer to v than i is). Note however that the estimate is independent of the inclusion of i in ADS(v). Therefore, we get good concentration and unbiasedness when the estimate is conditioned on $i \in \text{ADS}(v)$. □

We can then substitute the estimated Dijkstra ranks $\hat{\pi}_{vi}$ instead of distances in the SP distance closeness similarity estimators.

4.2 SP Distance versus Dijkstra Rank

We now explain the qualitative difference between closeness similarities based on distances and Dijkstra ranks, which prompted us to consider both. The measures behave differently in heterogeneous networks where nodes have different distance distributions. For intuition, we relate the problem to the classic information retrieval problem of similarity of documents. For duplicate elimination, we may want to deem documents similar based on both topic and size. When searching for query matches, we may want to factor out the size and compare only based on topic. In our social network context, the Dijkstra rank closeness captures "topic similarity": the similarity of two nodes in terms of the *relative* order of their relations to other nodes. SP distance closeness uses the absolute strength of the relations.

To make this concrete, consider measuring the similarity of two nodes u and v. Suppose that the 100 nearest neighbors of u are much closer to u than the 100 nearest neighbors of v are to v. If these sets are sufficiently similar, we may want to say that u and v are similar in that they both view the world (or, if there is direction, the world relates to them) in a similar way. In this case, we should use Dijkstra rank closeness. To identify nodes that are similar in both topic and level of involvement, we should use distance-based closeness.

In our experiments on social networks, we use TF-IDF cosine similarity as a proxy for ground truth (see Section 6.1.2). With this measure, the similarity between nodes is only based on topics (and not the number) of publications or tweets associated with them. As explained, this makes Dijkstra rank closeness (and Equation (10)) a better fit.

4.3 Using Node Weights

In order to retain the CV bound of our closeness similarity estimators of Theorem 4.1 when β is not uniform, we need to make slight modification to the ADS computation. We briefly state these modifications. The rank $r(u)$ we assign to each node u is exponentially distributed with parameter $\beta(u)$. This can be done by drawing $y \sim U[0,1]$ (independently for each node) and computing $r(u) = -\ln(y)/\beta(u)$. The intuitive explanation for this choice is that the expected rank of a node is $1/\beta(u)$. Therefore, nodes with higher $\beta(u)$, which also have a higher contribution to closeness similarity, are more likely to obtain a lower rank value $r(u)$ and therefore are more likely to be represented in the ADSs of other nodes.

The estimators we apply need to be modified accordingly, since we are using a different distribution. The only difference is the computation of the probabilities p_{ui} and p_{vi}. Instead of simply using (1), we compute the probability that an exponential random variable with parameter $\beta(u)$ is smaller than $k_r^{\text{th}}(\Phi_{<u}(v))$. We obtain

$$p_{vu} = 1 - e^{-\beta(u)k_r^{\text{th}}(\Phi_{<u}(v))}.$$

Note that, because exponential random variables are not bounded, we need to define $k_r^{\text{th}}(X) = +\infty$ when $|X| < k$. The intuition behind the analysis is that (under an appropriate scaling) a node of weight $\beta(i)$ is treated like $\beta(i)$ nodes of weight 1 under uniform scaling. Note that the mapping is not exact, as all $\beta(i)$ copies are correlated, but then the correlations between the copies work in our favor: if *any* one of the copies was represented in the decomposed problem then all of them would be represented in the weighted instance we are actually treating. For more details, we refer the reader to [12, 13, 15]. (Our problem here is more general, but the technique of handling node weights is the same)

5. RANDOMIZED EDGE LENGTHS

In this section, we introduce a similarity measure that is based on the SP distance and can be computed by SP computations, but is sensitive to path multiplicities as well as length. Our intuitive expectation from a similarity measure is that the similarity between u and v increases when there are more paths between u and v and when the paths are shorter. On the simple patterns in Figure 1, we expect similarity to increase with r (the number of paths) and decrease with ℓ (the SP distance). All common similarity measures satisfy this expectation in a *weak* sense: similarity is non-increasing with path lengths and is non-decreasing with multiplicity. Popular global measures such as KATZ, RWR, or resistance distance satisfy this expectation in a *strong* sense: similarity strictly decreases with ℓ and strictly increases with r. The SP distance and the minimum cut, however, satisfy the expectation only in a weak sense: the SP distance does not depend on r but does decrease with ℓ, whereas the minimum cut does not depend on ℓ but (for patterns B and C) increases with r. These two measures thus fail to capture some essential property of the connectivity between the nodes.

Given a network with link multiplicities w_e, we define the *REL distance* to be the *expected* shortest path distance with respect to random edge lengths that are drawn independently from an exponential distribution with parameter w_e. This is the same as assigning to each edge e a random length $-(\ln u_e)/w_e$, where $u_e \sim U[0, 1]$ are independent.

The use of the exponential distribution is natural here: if we have multiple parallel links with multiplicities $\{w_i\}$, their effect on the REL distance is the same as that of a single link with multiplicity $\sum_i w_i$, which is what we intuitively want to happen. This holds because the minimum of several exponentially distributed random variables distributes like a single exponential random variable with parameter that is the sum of the original parameters.

The REL distance can be estimated using standard SP computations: we simply draw a set of random lengths and compute SP

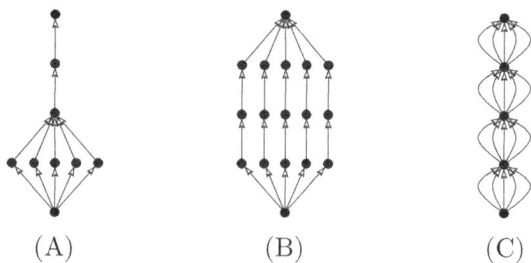

Figure 1: Connection between two nodes in simple networks. Pattern (B) consists of r disjoint paths of length ℓ. Pattern (C) has a path of length ℓ with r parallel edges between consecutive nodes. Pattern (A) has r disjoint paths of length 2 to an intermediate node and a path of length $\ell - 2$ from the intermediate node to the other end point. All paths in these examples are of integral length $\ell > 2$.

distances with respect to these lengths. We repeat this m times (for some m) for accuracy and take the average distance.

LEMMA 5.1. *The REL distance estimator is unbiased and has $CV \leq 1/\sqrt{m}$.*

PROOF. Unbiasedness is immediate. The CV does not exceed that of a single exponential random variable. □

Note that REL distance is computationally not much more expensive than SP distance, but has several advantages, which we discuss in the remainder of this section.

5.1 Edge Robustness

Intuitively, a similarity measure is more robust when it is less sensitive to removal of edges [11, 21], or additions of spurious (random) edges to the network, which connect nodes that are otherwise very dissimilar. In this sense, the REL distance is much more robust than the SP distance, and behaves more similarly to KATZ and RWR.

Consider again the patterns in Figure 1 and the relative similarity scores on these patterns by different measures. (C) is the most robust to random edge removals and (A) is the least robust. Therefore, we would like our similarity measure to have (C) $\succ$ (B) $\succ$ (A). The SP measure does not distinguish between the three cases, all having the same SP distance of ℓ, so we get (A) $\approx$ (B) $\approx$ (C). The same holds for RWR (PageRank, hitting time) regardless of the restart probability. The KATZ measure would give (C) $\succ$ (A) $\approx$ (B), since case (C) has r^ℓ paths and there are only r paths in cases (A) and (B). Thus, KATZ fails to distinguish between (A) and (B). The resistance distance is ℓ/r in both (B) and (C), thus not distinguishing between the two, but correctly giving higher resistance distance $\ell - 2 + 1/r$ in case (A). The same relation holds for the minimum cut, where the cut value is r for (B) and (C) but only 1 for (A). Thus, with both resistance distance and minimum cut, we obtain (C) $\approx$ (B) $\succ$ (A). Lastly, the REL distance gives the relation we want: (C) $\succ$ (B) $\succ$ (A). To see why, note that (C) has REL distance ℓ/r; this is much lower than (B), which has REL distance $\approx \ell - r\sqrt{\ell}$ (the standard deviation for a single length-ℓ path is $\sqrt{\ell}$ and we use an approximation for $r \ll \sqrt{\ell}$); this in turn is lower than (A), which has REL distance between $\ell - 2 + 2/r$ and ℓ.

5.2 Capturing Hub Nodes

Intuitively, when modeling or representing the relations of a node u it is important to identify when the similarity of a pair (u, w) is highly dependent on the presence of a single node v. That is, if v is removed, the similarity of (u, w) would significantly decrease. In such cases, we say that v is a *local hub* for the pair (u, w). For the relations between end points in the patterns in Figure 1, there are no local hubs in (B), all $\ell - 1$ middle nodes are local hubs in (C), and there are $\ell - 2$ local hubs in (A). We say that a similarity measure captures local hubs when we can identify that node v is a local hub for (u, w) from the similarities of (u, v), (v, w) and (u, w). We can identify local hubs with KATZ and RWR using the product relation $s_{uw} \approx s_{uv}s_{vw}$, with minimum cut using the relation $s_{uw} \approx \min\{s_{uv}, s_{vw}\}$, and with REL and resistance distance using the sum relation $s_{uw} \approx s_{uv} + s_{vw}$. SP distance, in contrast, does not capture local hubs: it is possible that $d_{uw} = d_{uv} + d_{vw}$ (as in pattern (B)) even when v is not a local hub for (u, w).

5.3 REL with ADSs

We have seen that REL has several desirable properties. As defined, however, it is very expensive to compute: it requires the computation of multiple shortest paths between two nodes, with differ-

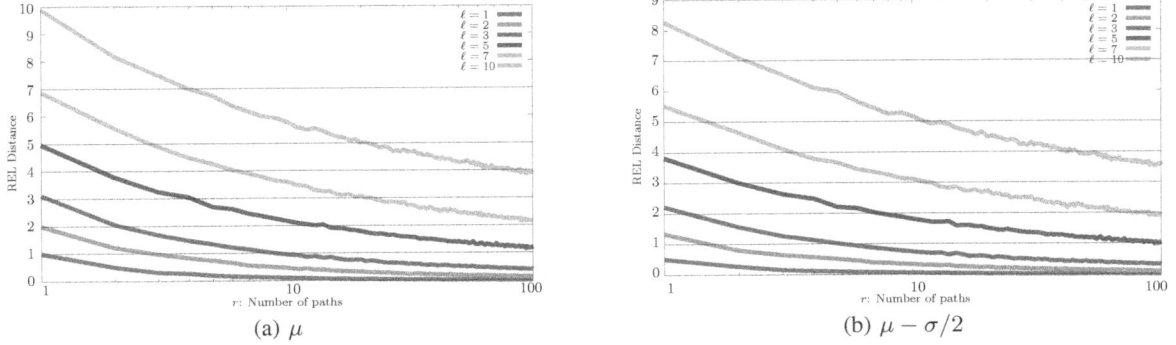

Figure 2: Variants of REL distance for two nodes connected by r **disjoint paths of length** ℓ**: (a) standard REL; (b) REL distance minus half the standard deviation.**

ent cost functions. Once again, we can use ADSs to approximate the REL computation efficiently and accurately.

We repeat the ADS computation t times, all with respect to the same random node ranking, but using different draws of edge lengths. Using the same node ranking makes the union of the ADSs more similar: a node that is included in one iteration is more likely to be included in another. That way, we can produce a single compact representation of all t sets of ADSs where each node appears with some aggregate information (average, quantile, sample SD of its distance or estimated Dijkstra rank in the different iterations). To estimate closeness similarity, we can use the t sets or work with the aggregate representation (which has a slightly different interpretation). We note that when using REL with closeness centrality estimation, we could randomize over node ranks as well. In an one-time centrality computation, the ADSs are computed but do not need to be stored [13], so there is no advantage for overlap.

A side advantage of REL when using Dijkstra ranks is that insignificant differences between nodes that can have very different Dijkstra ranks under fixed distances are ironed out. When differences are not significant, the REL distributions have significant overlap, which means that nodes would alternate relative Dijkstra rank in different repetitions.

5.4 Parametrized REL

With REL, as with other distance measures, many different patterns yield the same similarity score. We may want to be able to tune that by a parameter which controls the relative significance of different path lengths. Such a parameter is present in KATZ (the base of the exponent) and RWR (the restart probability) measures.

We propose a way to gain such control with REL. Instead of only considering the expectation of the distance, we can consider its distribution (more precisely, the variance of the REL distance random variable). Longer paths have smaller variance for the same expectation, and the sample variance and sample standard deviation σ are as easy to estimate as the sample mean μ. We propose using $\mu - c\sigma$ (for some constant $c \geq 0$) in order to increase the cost of longer paths and $\mu + c\sigma$ to achieve the opposite. Alternatively, we can also use a quantile of the distribution.

To understand this parametrization, we consider the REL distance $a(r, \ell)$ from u ro v when they are connected by r disjoint paths of length ℓ. The REL distance increases with ℓ and decreases with r (as discussed earlier, all the similarity measures we mention are non-increasing with ℓ and non-decreasing with r). Figure 2(a) shows the standard REL distance as a function of r for different values of the path length ℓ. The figure shows the relation

between paths of different lengths. For example: a single length-7 path has the same REL distance as 4 disjoint length-10 paths. A single length-1 path (single edge) has the same REL distance as 3 disjoint length-2 paths or 8 disjoint length-3 paths.

Figure 2(b) shows the relation when using a modified REL distance of $\mu - \sigma/2$, which makes longer paths have higher cost. We can see that now a single path of length 7 has the similarity of 7 length-10 paths. Similarly, it takes 6 length-2 paths or 30 length-3 paths to match a single length-1 path.

6. EXPERIMENTS

We now present experimental results that illustrate the usefulness of the concepts introduced in this paper. Our focus is on testing the most natural variant of each major concept we dealt with: distance estimation (using ADSs), closeness similarity, and randomized edge lengths. Our general approach is to compare the graph-based measures we study with independent similarity measures based on metadata associated with each node.

6.1 Setup and Methodology

Our code is written in C++ and compiled with Microsoft Visual C++ 2012. Our test machine runs Windows Server 2008 R2 and has 384 GiB of DDR3-1066 RAM and two 8-core Intel Xeon E-5-2690 2.90 GHz CPUs, each with 8×64 KB of L1, 8×256 KB of L2, and 20 MB of shared L3 cache. All executions are single-threaded and run in memory.

6.1.1 Data Sets

We consider the largest (strongly) connected component of three real-world social networks (arXiv, DBLP, and Twitter) as well as a synthetic one (small world). The first two columns of Table 1 give key statistics for these networks. (We will discuss the remaining columns in Section 6.1.4.)

Table 1: Key statistics of our data sets, together with label generation effort (time and nodes per label) and in-memory query times for label intersection ($k = 3, m = 1$**)**

graph	nodes [$\times 10^6$]	edges [$\times 10^6$]	prep. [h:m]	label size	query [μs]
arXiv	0.43	28.68	0:02	37.85	1.22
DBLP	1.06	9.16	0:02	39.09	1.64
twitter	29.64	603.87	8:05	50.82	3.51
smallworld	1.00	5.98	0:02	40.74	1.35

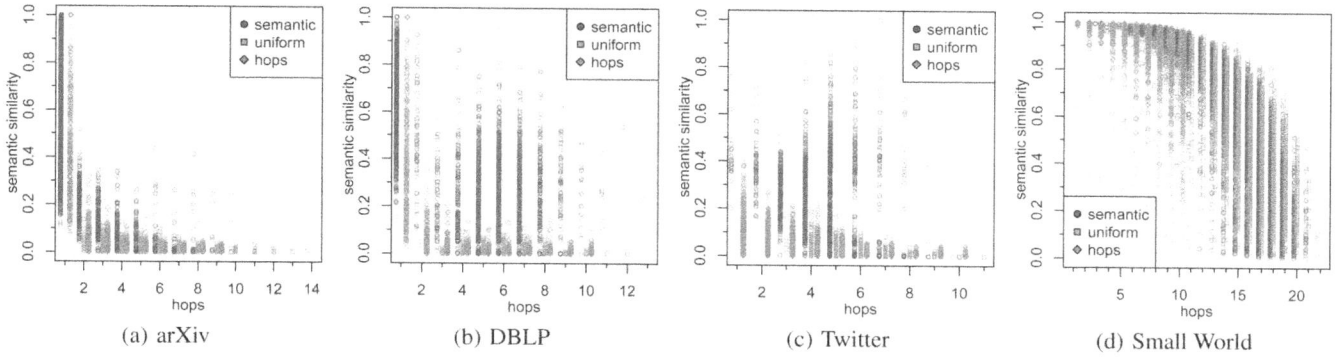

| (a) arXiv | (b) DBLP | (c) Twitter | (d) Small World |

Figure 3: Plots of all pairs sampled according to each distribution (uniform, hop-based, and semantic).

The first two networks come from DBLP and arXiv data.[1] In both cases, the raw data contains a list of articles with titles and authors; in addition, arXiv has abstracts and DBLP has venues. In the corresponding network, nodes represent authors and edges indicate co-authorship. We set the length of an edge to be the inverse of the number of common papers by the corresponding authors.

The third social network is the Twitter *mention graph*, built from tweets of December 2011. Each node represents a distinct user, and there is an edge between v and u if user v sends a tweet directed at user u (using the @ sign). This network is directed and weighted by 1/(number of mentions).

The final network we consider is a synthetic realization of a small world (SW) network [26], which is undirected and unweighted. It consists of an $N \times N$ toroidal grid with additional "long-distance" edges. For each node, we add an edge to a random node at L_1 distance d in the grid, where the probability of picking a particular value of d is proportional to d^{-2}.

6.1.2 Semantic-based Similarity

To evaluate the graph-based similarity measures we tested, we compare them against *semantic-based* similarity measures. These are based on individual properties of the entities represented by each node, with no direct information about the graph itself.

For the small world instance, we take the semantic similarity between nodes v and u to be the inverse of the L_1 distance between the corresponding points in the original metric space.

For real-world social networks, we measure semantic similarity using the metadata associated with each node. We map each node to a *document*, seen as a bag (multiset) of all terms (words) uttered by the user/author. For arXiv, this consists of the titles and abstracts of all articles written by the author; for DBLP, we use titles and venues; for Twitter, all tweets sent by the user, as long as at least two-thirds of the characters in the tweet are ASCII printable (this filters out most messages in non-Western languages, for which word-based similarity may not be an adequate ground truth). We measure the similarity between two nodes by comparing the corresponding documents. We first reweight terms using the standard TF-IDF (term frequency-inverse document frequency) method [23] (to deemphasize stop-words and other common terms), then compute the cosine similarity between the corresponding vectors.

More precisely, let $f(t, d)$ be the frequency of t, i.e., the number of times a term t appears in document d. Let the *logarithmically scaled term frequency* be $\mathrm{tf}(t, d) = \ln(f(t, d) + 1)$. The *in-*

verse document frequency is defined as $\mathrm{idf}(t, D) = \ln(|D|/|\{d \in D : t \in d\}|)$, where D is the entire corpus (set of documents). For a fixed document d and term t, $\mathrm{tfidf}(t, d, D)$ is defined as $\mathrm{tf}(t, d) \cdot \mathrm{idf}(t, D)$. Let T be the set of all terms that appear in the entire corpus. Conceptually, each document d can be seen as a $|T|$-dimensional vector $v(d)$ whose t-th entry represents $\mathrm{tfidf}(t, d, D)$. The *normalized semantic similarity* between two documents d_a and d_b is defined as the dot product of $v(d_a)$ and $v(d_b)$, divided (for normalization) by the product of the L_2 norms of $v(d_a)$ and $v(d_b)$. This is the similarity measure we use in our experiments.

6.1.3 Query Distribution

We evaluate the quality of our similarity measures on sample pairs of nodes. We pick such pairs using three distributions: *uniform*, *hop-based*, and *semantic-based*. Each has about 5000 pairs, and Figure 3 compares them. Each sampled pair (v, u) corresponds to a point; its x coordinate indicates the number of hops between v and u and its y coordinate indicates the semantic similarity. The color/shape of each point indicates the distribution it came from.

In the natural *uniform* distribution, each pair consists of two nodes picked independently and uniformly at random. Although it was often used in previous studies, this distribution is heavily biased towards pairs that are semantically quite different, since their nodes tend to be far apart in the graph.

In most real-life applications, however, we are interested in evaluating nodes that have some nontrivial degree of similarity. The *hop-based* distribution ensures that enough such pairs are evaluated, as follows. First, we pick a *center node* v uniformly at random. We then run a breadth-first search on the entire graph from v (disregarding any edge costs) and, for each $i \in \{1, 2, 3, \ldots, 10\}$, we pick a node u_i uniformly at random between all nodes that are exactly i hops away from v, creating a pair (v, u_i). We repeat this process with 500 different center nodes v.

The third distribution is *semantic-based*. Our semantic-based similarity measures are real numbers between 0 and 1. We split this range into twenty equal-width buckets $[0, 0.05), [0.05, 0.10), [0.10, 0.15), \ldots, [0.95, 1.00]$ and pick up to 250 pairs of nodes within each interval. We do so by picking pairs uniformly at random and assigning them to the appropriate bucket, keeping only the first 250 in each case. (For some inputs, the probability of hitting some of the higher buckets is extremely small; we may leave some buckets incomplete after sampling 20 million pairs unsuccessfully.)

As Figure 3 shows, most pairs in the uniform distribution are far apart and have extremely low semantic similarity. The hop-based distribution picks more pairs with higher semantic similarity, but

---

[1]Available at http://export.arxiv.org/oai2 and http://dblp.uni-trier.de/xml/.

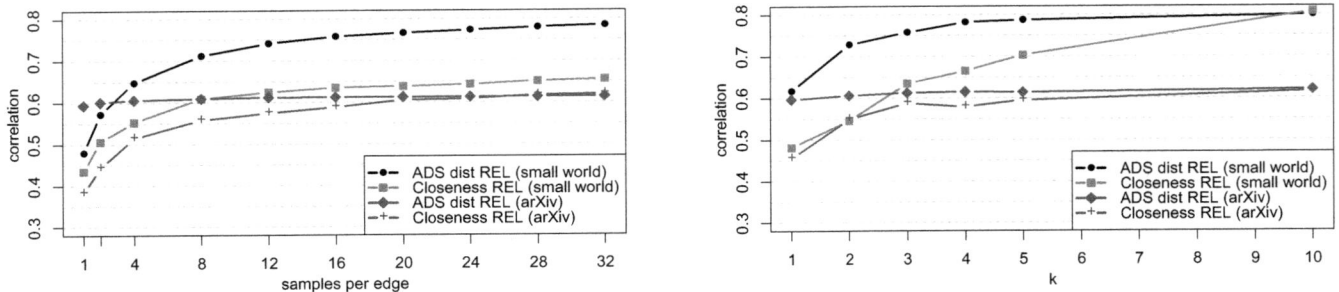

Figure 4: Parameter tests. On the left, we fix $k = 3$ and vary the number m of samples per edge. On the right, we fix $m = 16$ and vary k. For each set of parameters, we report Spearman's correlation relative to the semantic similarity.

they also tend to be very close together (in terms of hop distances). In general, the semantic-based distribution picks a more diverse set of pairs, with less correlation between hop distance and semantic similarity. We believe this distribution gives more insight into real applications.

Note that the two co-authorship networks (arXiv and DBLP) are quite different, due to different paper population and metadata. The small world network is quite distinct from other networks, with different structure, node degrees, and metadata.

6.1.4 Algorithms

To test the concepts introduced in this paper, we computed ADSs based on Dijkstra's algorithm, as described in [12, 13, 16]. Labels are represented in the obvious way, as pairs of hubs and distances, sorted by hub id to allow for a straightforward implementation of intersection in linear time [3]. Table 1 reports the time to generate labels (with $k = 3$ and $m = 1$, as defined in Sections 2 and 5) on our networks, the average number of nodes per ADS, and the average time to compute the similarity between two nodes from their ADSs. Note that preprocessing times are reasonable (a few hours for Twitter), and queries are extremely fast (a few microseconds). We want to stress that we did not tune our preprocessing code too much; our main focus is exploring the feasibility of ADS-based approaches for estimating similarity. We thus optimized our code enough to handle the Twitter data, but did not exploit further optimizations such as multi-threading or cache locality.

We implemented two ADS-based approaches to measure similarity. The first, *ADS distance*, simply computes the upper bound on the SP distance using Equation (4). Smaller distances indicate higher similarity. The second approach we consider is *closeness* similarity based on Dijkstra rank, using Equation (11).

We apply each variant to the original graph as well as to a version with randomized edge lengths (REL). For the latter, we use a single random rank function, and sample $m = 16$ lengths for each edge (see Section 6.2). The resulting preprocessing time is thus 16 times longer than those reported in Table 1.

To measure the quality of the results obtained, we compute Spearman's rank correlation coefficient [25] (or *Spearman's correlation*, for short) between each structure-based similarity measure and the appropriate semantic similarity, which we take as ground truth. Since Spearman's correlation is rank-based, it is a good fit to evaluate measures that operate on different scales. For consistency, when evaluating a similarity measure for which lower values are meant to indicate higher similarity (such as distance-based methods), we negate the similarity measure when computing Spearman's correlation. For all methods tested, therefore, positive values are better. Note that zero indicates a lack of correlation.

6.2 Parameter Setting

Both methods we study (ADS distance REL and Closeness REL) have two parameters: the threshold k for inclusion of nodes in ADS labels and the number m of samples per edge (for randomizing its length). We performed some preliminary explorations on the data to determine their values. Figure 4 shows how our similarity measures are affected (in terms of quality) when we fix one of these parameters and vary the other. As already mentioned, quality is measured in terms of Spearman's correlation to the semantic similarity (ground truth). We consider two representative graphs, small world and arXiv, and use the semantic-based distribution of pairs.

As predicted by our theoretical analysis, the trade-offs we must contend with are straightforward: increasing either parameter leads to better expected quality, at the cost extra time and space. (Recall that the preprocessing effort of the ADSs depends linearly on both k and m.) This monotonicity is very important in practice, since it eliminates the risk of overfitting to a specific input. In contrast, parameters such as the restart probability of RWR do not have this property.

Figure 4 shows that setting $k = 3$ and $m = 16$ is a reasonable trade-off between quality and efficiency. We therefore use these parameters in our experiments.

6.3 Results

Our main experimental results are reported in Tables 2, 3, and 4 (one table for each distribution of pairs described in Section 6.1.3). For each method and each graph, we give the Spearman's correlation between the similarity values they compute and the corresponding semantic similarities. The best result for each experiment (graph and distribution) is highlighted in bold.

Besides "ADS dist" and "Closeness" (and their respective versions augmented with REL), we also evaluate some competing measures. The *distance* measure is the actual graph distance between two nodes (computed explicitly with Dijkstra's algorithm). The *hops* measure is similar, but uses unit edge lengths. As a proxy for local methods, we use the *Adamic-Adar* measure [4], which adds up the number of common neighbors between v and u, weighted by the reverse logarithm of their degrees. As a proxy for global similarity measures, we consider *random walk with restarts* (RWR) [34], where the similarity between v and other nodes depends on the stationary distribution of a random walk from v, in the spirit of the rooted PageRank algorithm [10, 34]. The restart probability of this random walk must be tuned for different graphs, so we consider four different values (from 0.00 to 0.75). Our implementation of RWR is relatively slow, hence we only test it for one distribution on two networks. However, even the most efficient implementation of RWR [34] is orders of magnitude slower than ADS-based approaches.

Table 2: Uniform distribution: Spearman's correlation between each measure and semantic similarity.

measure	arXiv	DBLP	Twitter	SW
Adamic-Adar	0.097	0.034	0.107	0.000
hops	0.350	0.221	0.536	0.623
distance	**0.470**	**0.319**	0.191	0.623
ADS dist	0.462	0.318	0.196	0.519
ADS dist REL	0.419	0.314	0.242	**0.769**
Closeness	0.039	0.015	0.461	0.413
Closeness REL	0.063	0.034	**0.612**	0.666

Table 3: Hop-based distribution: Spearman's correlation between each measure and semantic similarity.

measure	arXiv	DBLP	Twitter	SW
Adamic-Adar	0.570	0.457	0.420	0.486
hops	0.645	0.468	**0.678**	0.831
distance	**0.648**	**0.507**	0.447	0.831
ADS dist	0.617	0.497	0.448	0.839
ADS dist REL	0.512	0.454	0.471	0.947
Closeness	0.379	0.249	0.518	0.877
Closeness REL	0.404	0.320	0.637	**0.949**

Table 4: Semantic distribution: Spearman's correlation between each measure and semantic similarity. (Entries marked "—" were not tested.)

measure	arXiv	DBLP	Twitter	SW
Adamic-Adar	0.626	0.746	0.548	0.000
hops	**0.752**	0.748	0.169	0.767
distance	0.590	0.634	−0.140	0.767
RWR-0.75	—	0.734	—	0.286
RWR-0.50	—	0.737	—	0.617
RWR-0.25	—	0.740	—	0.791
RWR-0.00	—	0.500	—	**0.915**
ADS dist	0.566	0.637	−0.127	0.671
ADS dist REL	0.614	0.584	−0.155	0.865
Closeness	0.641	0.742	0.613	0.609
Closeness REL	0.634	**0.752**	**0.649**	0.808

It is clear from the tables that no single measure dominates. This is to be expected, given that these are different networks that have evolved under different circumstances and with different semantics in mind. In DBLP, for example, an edge between nodes indicates an intentional collaboration that resulted in a paper. An edge in Twitter may result from a direct mention resulting from a re-tweet (which is common in some virtual chats), a casual reply, or a discussion/conversation.

There are, however, some obvious patterns we can discern. As expected, the effectiveness of local similarity measures is quite limited for arbitrary queries. Although Adamic-Adar works reasonably well for the hop-based distribution (Table 3), its performance varies wildly for other query distributions. The standard distance-based similarity tends to perform better in co-authorship and small world networks, since it can handle long-range queries appropriately. Interestingly, the hop-based measure is not far behind. In fact, on Twitter counting hops is consistently better than measuring the actual distances, indicating that the widely-used edge weighting scheme (inversely proportional to the frequency of communication) is not a good choice for this network.

The main drawback of the distance-based similarity measure is that evaluating long-range pair similarity requires costly Dijkstra computations. With ADS dist, we can approximate such distances in microseconds (see Table 1), which is orders of magnitude faster. Moreover, Tables 2 to 4 indicate that the results we obtain from both measures are comparable in quality. This is not surprising: for real-world social networks, we measured an average stretch below 10%. Adding randomized edge lengths (ADS dist REL) can lead to even better similarity estimates. This is particularly evident for small world networks, indicating that randomization is indeed effective in accounting for the underlying path multiplicity.

Remarkably, we can obtain even better results (comparable to RWR with tuned parameters) with our new ADS-based closeness similarity measure, which is just as cheap to compute. Comparing how two nodes are related to the entire network can be significantly more effective than measuring distances directly, especially when combined with randomized edge lengths. This is particularly true for Twitter. The method does have limitations, however. As Table 2 shows, closeness similarity does not work very well when nodes are far apart in the graph, as tends to be the case for pairs picked according to the uniform distribution in co-authorship networks (see Figures 3(a) and 3(b)). But in typical applications (such as community detection), when one is interested in ranking nearby (but not necessarily neighboring) nodes, ADS-based closeness similarity excels.

7. FINAL REMARKS

We have introduced global similarity measures based on all-distances sketches that are extremely efficient to compute. Our experiments on social networks with tens of millions of nodes show that these new measures are quite powerful in practice. We can compute the similarity between two arbitrary nodes in a few microseconds with accuracy that is at least as good as, and often better than, existing approaches. Another advantage is that our algorithms are simple to implement, naturally lending themselves to distributed and external memory scenarios, including within relational databases [2].

We stress that our experiments are done at full scale rather than with local subsamples of the networks. In fact, we observed that taking small samples of Twitter, for example, may significantly bias the results, leading to potentially inaccurate conclusions.

Given the diversity of social networks and their semantics, it is unrealistic to expect any single method based on structural properties of the graph to consistently dominate all others. The particular (global) approaches that we tested in our experiments are quite robust to the choice of input. That said, there are other possible instantiations of the parameters in our definitions of closeness similarity, as well as combinations with the REL techniques that we are planning to investigate and characterize further. A natural avenue for future work is to reduce the preprocessing effort (ADS computation), which is currently higher than we would like. Finally, another important direction is the extension of our techniques to computing seeded communities [1], where a group of nodes are presented and the task is to find a community spawning from this group.

8. REFERENCES

[1] I. Abraham, S. Chechik, D. Kempe, and A. Slivkins. Low-distortion inference of latent similarities from a multiplex social network. In *SODA*, pages 1853–1872, 2013.

[2] I. Abraham, D. Delling, A. Fiat, A. V. Goldberg, and R. F. Werneck. HLDB: Location-Based Services in Databases. In *GIS*, pages 339–348. ACM Press, 2012.

[3] I. Abraham, D. Delling, A. V. Goldberg, and R. F. Werneck. Hierarchical Hub Labelings for Shortest Paths. In *ESA*, volume 7501 of *LNCS*, pages 24–35. Springer, 2012.

[4] L. A. Adamic and E. Adar. How to search a social network. *Social Networks*, 27, 2005.

[5] T. Akiba, Y. Iwata, and Y. Yoshida. Fast exact shortest-path distance queries on large networks by pruned landmark labeling. In *SIGMOD*, pages 349–360, 2013.

[6] P. Boldi, M. Rosa, and S. Vigna. HyperANF: approximating the neighbourhood function of very large graphs on a budget. In *WWW*, 2011.

[7] P. Boldi, M. Rosa, and S. Vigna. Robustness of social networks: Comparative results based on distance distributions. In *SocInfo*, pages 8–21, 2011.

[8] P. Boldi and S. Vigna. Studying network structures for IR: The impact of size. http://ecir2012.upf.edu/ecir_paolo_boldi.pdf, 2012.

[9] B. Bollobás. *Modern graph theory*. Springer, 1998.

[10] S. Brin and L. Page. The anatomy of a large-scale hypertextual web search engine. In *WWW*, 1998.

[11] S. Chechik, Y. Emek, B. Patt-Shamir, and D. Peleg. Sparse reliable graph backbones. *Information and Computation*, 210:31 – 39, 2012.

[12] E. Cohen. Size-estimation framework with applications to transitive closure and reachability. *J. Comput. Syst. Sci.*, 55:441–453, 1997.

[13] E. Cohen. All-distances sketches, revisited: Scalable estimation of the distance distribution and centralities in massive graphs. Technical Report cs.DS/1306.3284, arXiv, 2013.

[14] E. Cohen, E. Halperin, H. Kaplan, and U. Zwick. Reachability and distance queries via 2-hop labels. *SIAM J. Comput.*, 32(5):1338–1355, 2003.

[15] E. Cohen and H. Kaplan. Spatially-decaying aggregation over a network: model and algorithms. *J. Comput. Syst. Sci.*, 73:265–288, 2007.

[16] E. Cohen and H. Kaplan. Summarizing data using bottom-k sketches. In *PODC*, 2007.

[17] E. Cohen and H. Kaplan. A case for customizing estimators: Coordinated samples. Technical Report cs.ST/1212.0243, arXiv, 2012.

[18] E. Cohen and H. Kaplan. What you can do with coordinated samples. In *RANDOM*, 2013.

[19] P. Crescenzi, R. Grossi, L. Lanzi, and A. Marino. A comparison of three algorithms for approximating the distance distribution in real-world graphs. In *TAPAS*, 2011.

[20] C. Dangalchev. Residual closeness in networks. *Phisica A*, 365, 2006.

[21] A. Das Sarma, S. Gollapudi, M. Najork, and R. Panigrahy. A sketch-based distance oracle for web-scale graphs. In *WSDM*, pages 401–410, 2010.

[22] G. Jeh and J. Widom. SimRank: a measure of structural-context similarity. In *KDD*. ACM, 2002.

[23] K. S. Jones. A statistical interpretation of term specificity and its application in retrieval. *Journal of Documentation*, 28(1):11–21, 1972.

[24] L. Katz. A new status index derived from sociometric analysis. *Psychometrika*, 18(1):39–43, 1953.

[25] E. S. Keeping. *Introduction to Statistical Inference*. Dover, 1962.

[26] J. M. Kleinberg. The small-world phenomenon: an algorithm perspective. In *STOC*. ACM, 2000.

[27] D. Liben-Nowell and J. Kleinberg. The link-prediction problem for social networks. *J. Am. Soc. Inf. Sci. Technol.*, 58(7):1019–1031, 2007.

[28] M. E. J. Newman. Clustering and preferential attachment in growing networks. *Phys. Rev. E 64, 025102*, 2001.

[29] C. R. Palmer, P. B. Gibbons, and C. Faloutsos. ANF: a fast and scalable tool for data mining in massive graphs. In *KDD*, 2002.

[30] R. Panigrahy, M. Najork, and Y. Xie. How user behavior is related to social affinity. In *WSDM*, pages 713–722, 2012.

[31] G. Sabidussi. The centrality index of a graph. *Psychometrika*, 31(4):581–603, 1966.

[32] K. A. Stephenson and M. Zelen. Rethinking centrality: Methods and examples. *Social Networks*, 11, 1989.

[33] M. Thorup and U. Zwick. Approximate distance oracles. In *ACM STOC*, pages 183–192, 2001.

[34] H. Tong, C. Faloutsis, and J.-H. Pan. Fast random walk with restart and its applications. In *ICDM*. IEEE, 2006.

APPENDIX

This appendix contains a detailed example of a network and corresponding ADSs. For node h in the network in Figure 5, the forward ADS for $k = 1$ is $\overrightarrow{\text{ADS}}(h) = (h, e, k, a)$. For $k = 2$ we have $\overrightarrow{\text{ADS}}(h) = (h, e, g, f, i, k, a)$. Node j has forward distance $\overrightarrow{d}_{hj} = 11$ and forward Dijkstra rank $\overrightarrow{\pi}_{hj} = 4$ with respect to h. The backwards ADS from a for $k = 1$ is $\overleftarrow{\text{ADS}}(a) = (a)$ since a is the node with lowest rank. For $k = 2$, $\overleftarrow{\text{ADS}}(a) = (a, c, d, b, e, k)$.

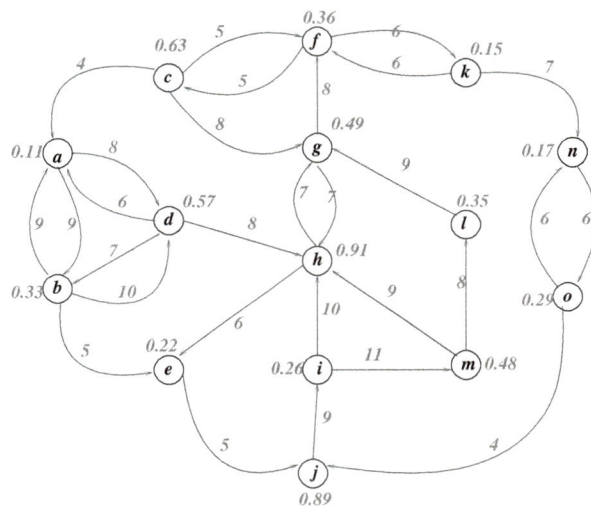

Figure 5: A directed network with lengths associated with edges and random rank values associated with its nodes. The nodes sorted by increasing distance from h, together with their distance, are $(h, 0), (e, 6), (g, 7), (j, 11), (f, 15), (c, 20), (i, 20), (k, 21), (a, 24), (n, 28), (m, 31), (b, 31), (d, 32), (o, 34), (l, 39)$. The nodes sorted by reversed increasing distance from node a are $(a, 0), (c, 4), (d, 6), (b, 9), (f, 9), (g, 12), (e, 14), (k, 15), (h, 16), (j, 19), (n, 22), (o, 23), (l, 25), (i, 28), (m, 39)$.

AppInspect: Large-scale Evaluation of Social Networking Apps

Markus Huber*†   Martin Mulazzani*

Sebastian Schrittwieser*   Edgar Weippl*

SBA Research *
Favoritenstrasse 16, 1040 Wien, Austria
{mhuber, mmulazzani, sschrittwieser, eweippl}@sba-research.org
Vienna PhD school of informatics†

ABSTRACT

Third-party apps for social networking sites have emerged as a popular feature for online social networks, and are used by millions of users every day. In exchange for additional features, users grant third parties access to their personal data. However, these third parties do not necessarily protect the data to the same extent as social network providers. To automatically analyze the unique privacy and security issues of social networking applications on a large scale, we propose a novel framework, called *AppInspect*. Our framework enumerates available social networking apps and collects metrics such as the personal information transferred to third party developers. AppInspect furthermore identifies web trackers, as well as information leaks, and provides insights into the hosting infrastructures of apps. We implemented a prototype of our novel framework to evaluate Facebook's application ecosystem. Our evaluation shows that AppInspect is able to detect malpractices of social networking apps in an automated fashion. During our study we collaborated with Facebook to mitigate shortcomings of popular apps that affected the security and privacy of millions of social networking users.

Categories and Subject Descriptors

C.2.2 [**Computer-Communication Networks**]: Network Protocols—*Applications*; D.4.6 [**Operating Systems**]: Security and Protection—*Access controls; Verification*

General Terms

Measurement, Security, Verification

Keywords

Online Social Networks; Facebook Apps; Information Leaks

1. INTRODUCTION

Third-party applications, or colloquially "apps", are used by hundreds of millions of social networking users every day. Popular apps include games, horoscopes, and quizzes. To provide additional features, app developers transfer personal information from their users to their application servers. Online social networks typically embed applications as framed websites in their own portal and thus act as proxies between users and third-party applications. The actual application code runs on third-party servers beyond the supervision of social network providers.

The modus operandi of social networking apps gives rise to unique privacy and security challenges. Applications may maliciously harvest a wealth of personal information. One of the key challenges is, therefore, to detect applications that process data in a way that may violate the security or privacy expectation of users, and to identify apps that request more permissions than actually needed for their operation. Furthermore, sensitive user data may be stored on badly maintained third-party servers, making them low-hanging fruits for attackers. Insights into applications' underlying hosting infrastructure would help to get a better understanding of these security risks. Application providers themselves rely on third parties for in-app advertising and analytics. Therefore, social networking apps may leak sensitive information to third parties, both deliberately or by accident. In the worst case, third parties may use leaked personal information to track app users across multiple websites with knowledge of their real identity. As a result, detecting information leakage is another important challenge. Previous research focused on a single challenge, namely analyzing personal information requested by social networking apps [43, 8]. As a result of the deep integration of apps into social networking platforms, users often do not understand that application developers receive and accumulate their personal information [28]. We are left with a dilemma of social networking users' misperception regarding app security and privacy, but also with little insight into third-party application ecosystems.

In this paper we outline *AppInspect*, a novel framework to systematically analyze the unique privacy and security challenges of social networking applications. Our proposed framework analyzes both information flows from social networking providers to third-party applications and information flows from social networking applications to third parties. An initial challenge in studies of online social networks lies in obtaining a meaningful sample of applications. Our *AppInspect* framework entails a number of application enumeration strategies to overcome this first obstacle. In the next step, our framework automatically fetches important attributes of enumerated applications, including their popularity and the set of requested permissions. Finally, our framework collects the network traffic of social networking apps to subsequently spot web trackers, poorly maintained application hosts, and leaking of sensitive information to third parties. The motivation of our research is to protect social networking users by automatically detecting security and privacy issues with social networking apps, as well as policy violations. The findings of our *AppInspect* framework assist both social networking providers and application developers in protecting their users. We used our *AppInspect* prototype to carry out a large-scale evaluation of Facebook's application ecosystem, which ultimately helped to detect and report a number of privacy and security shortcomings. The main contributions in this paper are the following:

- We present a novel framework for automated privacy and security analysis of social networking apps, called *AppInspect*.

- We evaluate the feasibility of our *AppInspect* framework with Facebook's application ecosystem.

- We found a number of information leaks and malpractices in popular applications and helped to fix these issues.

- We make our datasets of Facebook applications available to the research community and periodically publish updated datasets.

The rest of this paper is structured as follows: Section 2 provides a brief background on third-party applications in online social networks. Section 3 outlines the design and functionality of our proposed framework. In Section 4, we describe the evaluation of our framework on Facebook and our acquired application sample. Section 5 presents our findings on Facebook's most popular applications. We then discuss the implications of our findings in Section 6, explore related work in Section 7, and finally present our conclusions in Section 8.

2. SOCIAL NETWORKING APPS

Third-party applications are a popular feature of today's online social networks (OSNs). These "apps", as they are colloquially referred to, enrich user data to provide additional user experience and functionality. An app might, for example, query a user's birthday to create a personalized horoscope in exchange. Social networking data is hereby provided to third parties through developer application programming interfaces (APIs). At the time of writing, there are two major classes of apps. The first class consists of games, which typically incorporate aspects of social networking into their gameplay. The second class contains general

add-ons to social network platforms, ranging from simple horoscope applications to sophisticated job hunting applications. Facebook pioneered third-party applications by introducing the "Facebook Platform" in May 2007 [15]. Facebook's competitors responded with the launch of an open standard for third-party access to social networking data called "OpenSocial" in November 2007 [20]. At the time of writing, Facebook's Connect platform is the most popular and mature framework for social networking apps, which is why we use Facebook as an example of third-party platforms. Ko et al. [29] provides an overview of existing social networking APIs.

2.1 Facebook Platform

The Facebook Platform enables third parties to offer custom applications that extend Facebook's core functionality and integrate deeply into their website. Apps on Facebook are loaded inside Facebook through a "Canvas Page", which represents an *HTML iframe*. Facebook acts as a proxy for displaying the output of apps to its users through iframes, while the actual apps are hosted and executed on third-party servers. Facebook has no control over app servers but legally binds third-party developers to comply with their Platform policies [14]. Before users decide to install a specific app, they need to authorize it. Facebook uses OAuth 2.0 [22] for authentication and authorization of third-party applications. Once users authorize an application, it is granted access to *basic information* by default. Basic information includes ID, name, picture, gender, locale, and friend connections of a given user. Applications may, however, request additional permissions. At the time of writing, there are four additional permission classes available on the Facebook Platform [13], which applications may request in any combination. In total, there are 67 possible application permissions that app developers may request for their application. Permissions within the *extended permissions* class grant applications access to sensitive information such as exchanged private messages, and allows applications to post content on behalf of its users. Another important permission class is the *user and friend permissions* class. Using permissions in this class, developers may request to gather information on a user's religion, relationship status, birthday, personal email addresses, and virtually any published content. Developers may also request personal profile information from a user's friends, with the exception of private email addresses. Facebook's current default account settings allow applications to access personal information of all of a user's friends. This implies that, even if you have not installed a single application, your data may be transferred to third parties through your friends' applications. Even though users can control which information is provided to their friend's applications, users are often unaware that they share their information with apps per default. Over the course of the last five years, Facebook has also emerged as an identity provider for third-party websites. In addition to traditional canvas apps, websites leverage Facebook as an identity provider and to enhance their social experiences through JavaScript plugins. Finally, Facebook offers third-party access to mobile platforms through dedicated Android and iOS software development kits.

Before users decide to add an application, an authorization dialog with requested permissions is displayed. Hull et al. [26] claim that Facebook's privacy issues are based pri-

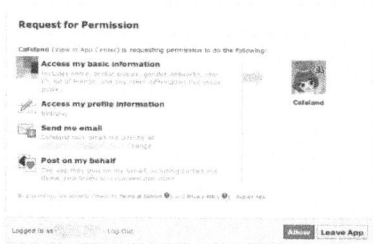

(a) Unified Auth Dialog, April 2010

(b) Enhanced Auth Dialog, January 2012

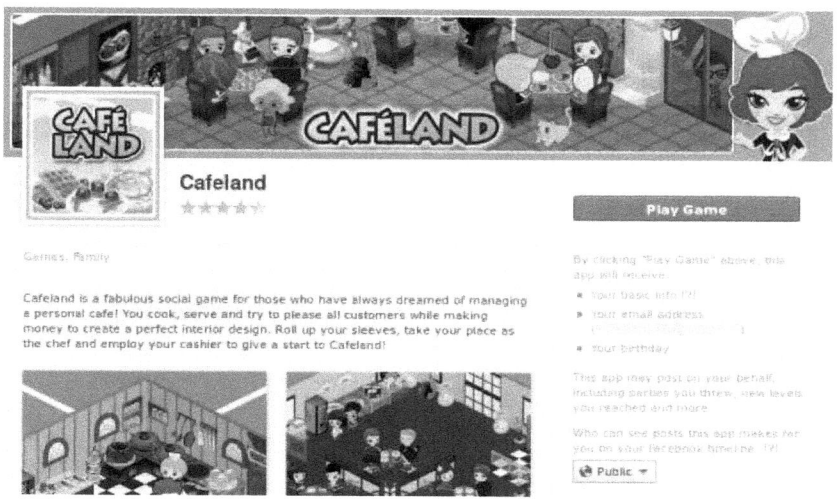

(c) App Center Auth Dialog, May 2012

Figure 1: Adjustments to Facebook's application authorization dialog over time

marily on design issues, which could be improved by making the flows of information more transparent to users. The example of Facebook's adjustments to their app authorization dialog in Figure 1, suggests that Facebook might currently invest little in making their third-party application system more transparent. In response to complaints from the privacy commissioner of Canada, Facebook introduced a unified permissions dialog in April 2010, of which Figure 1(a) provides an example. The unified dialog has been deprecated and only a small number of applications still use this dialog. In January 2012 Facebook launched a revised permissions dialog called *Enhanced Auth Dialog* (see Figure 1(b)), which replaced the unified permissions dialog. In May 2012, a third permission dialog for all applications listed in Facebook's App Center was introduced. Figure 1(c) shows an instance of this dialog. The standard authentication dialog uses pictograms and verbose descriptions for requested permissions and users may choose between *Allow* and *Leave App*. Furthermore, a directed arrow symbolizes that the requested information is transferred to a third party. Requested permissions faded from the spotlight with the enhanced authentication dialog and permissions are now presented in a bulleted list with little additional information. Facebook also changed the label of the authentication button, which reads *Play Game* instead of *Allow*. Finally, with the App Center authentication dialog, the requested permissions are hardly noticeable and a single prominent button encourages users to play the game.

2.2 Application directories and reviews

An important privacy and security challenge with social networking apps is the balance between requested data and app functionality. Horoscope apps may for example harvest a user's personal messages and photos instead of requesting only the date of birth. The Facebook Platform enables third-party developers to make their apps available to other users without requiring prior approval. Between May 2008 and December 2008, Facebook operated a verified apps program, through which it designated certain applications as "verified

apps". A verified apps badge was promised to applications that are secure and demonstrated commitment to compliance with the Facebook platform policies. An FTC report, however, found out that Facebook took no extra steps to verify the security of third-party applications and labeled the program as deceptive [19]. Until July 2011, Facebook offered a central application directory, where developers could submit their applications once they considered their software mature. Later, Facebook removed its app directory and applications are now automatically indexed once they reach 10 monthly active users (MAU) [12]. In May 2012 Facebook introduced the App Center[1], which showcases what Facebook describes as high-quality applications. At the time of writing, the App Center contains a few thousand applications. The small number of App center applications is in stark contrast to the overall number of applications. According to Facebook [38, p. 87], as of March 2012, more than nine million apps and websites were connecting to their Platform services.

3. APPINSPECT

The vast amount of available third-party social networking applications poses a challenge for large-scale security and privacy studies. In order to overcome the naïve solution of manually analyzing security and privacy issues of third-party applications, we propose a novel analysis framework, called *AppInspect*. In this section we outline the design and functionality of our framework.

Our proposed *AppInspect* framework enables automated security and privacy analysis of a target social networking app ecosystem. Figure 2 depicts the four generic processing steps to automatically analyze a given social networking provider with AppInspect. (1) First, the search module enumerates available third-party applications for a given social networking provider. (2) In a second step, the classifier module collects additional information for all enumerated apps. (3) Third, the analysis module adds the applications

---

[1]FB App Center http://www.facebook.com/appcenter

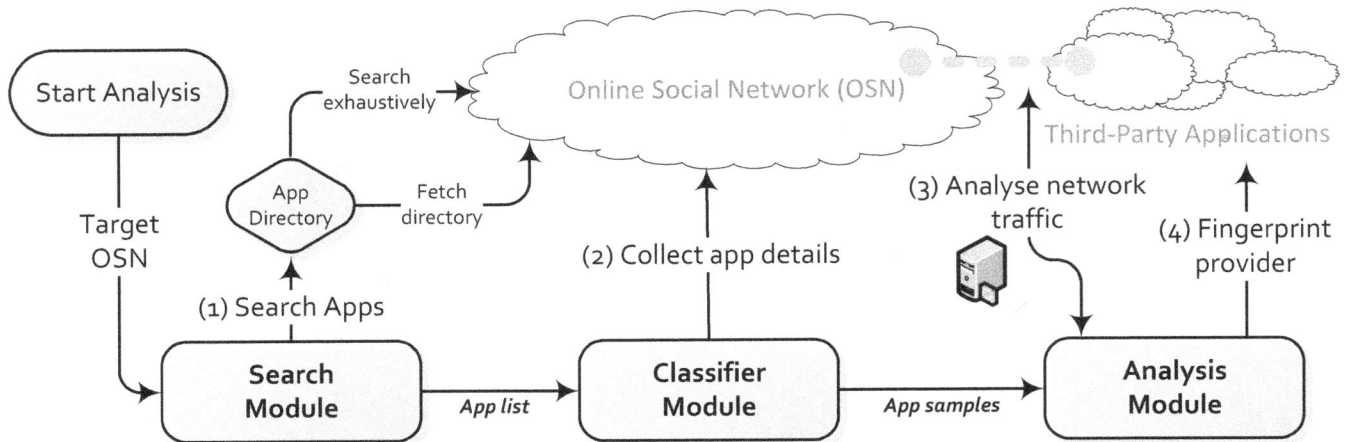

Figure 2: AppInspect, a framework for automated security and privacy analysis of social network ecosystems

to experimental accounts and collects the resulting network traffic for further analysis. (4) Finally, the analysis module fingerprints the hosting infrastructure of all applications. AppInspect uses a modular software design and its functionality is separated into three main modules. Our design enables a straightforward adaption of features for different security and privacy analyses. The three main modules and their submodules are described in the following.

3.1 Search module

The initial challenge with social networking providers consists in collecting a preferably complete list of third-party applications for further analysis in case a central app directory is missing. In the best case, the social networking provider offers a complete app directory, which contains all third-party applications. In the non-trivial case, no complete application directories exist and third-party applications have to be enumerated using exhaustive search strategies.

Exhaustive search. In case no central application directory exists, exhaustive search strategies are required. The most straightforward solution is the enumeration of unique application identifiers. This naïve approach works with social network providers with a small range of numerical application identifiers. In the case of LinkedIn, for example, all available applications are easy to enumerate by testing a small range of application identifiers. With Facebook, the exhaustive search strategy becomes a non-trivial problem because their application identifiers are not easily enumerable. Facebook assigns a unique numerical identifier to every object it stores. Objects include third-party applications but also user profiles, pictures, posts, etc. At the time of writing, Facebook's unique object identifiers are numerical values of length 14, resulting in up to 10^{14} possible combinations. This means that it is not feasible to probe the entire identifier range for third-party applications due to the resulting costs for crawling and the fact that only a subset of these IDs are for apps. However, Facebook indexes all third-party applications that have reached more than 10 monthly active users in their search feature. Hence, an exhaustive search for indexed applications opens a way to enumerate applications on Facebook. Instead of integer ranges, the exhaustive search probes the social network provider for keywords or character n-grams. For example, all trigrams for the English alphabet would result in $26^3 = 17,576$ search terms.

Castelluccia et al. [7] used this approach for a similar problem, namely the reconstruction of a users' search history. Similar to their work, our module can either use all possible character n-grams or limit the number of search terms by using Castelluccia et al.'s smart tree approach. In addition to character n-grams, lists with common words provide yet another keyword source.

Directory fetch. Some social networks offer a complete application directory. For example, Google+'s game directory[2] consists of a single webpage that contains less than 50 applications in total. In this particular case, the AppInspect framework provides a dedicated submodule to gather the list of all available third-party applications from the social network's application directory.

3.2 Classifier module

The classifier module collects additional information on applications enumerated with AppInspect's search module. Information is gathered passively from the social network provider without actually running or adding applications to profiles.

Application properties. A number of application properties are available on third-party application description pages. Important properties include the application type, popularity, and rating. This submodule implements functionality to automatically gather a set of predefined properties. The submodule opens the generic application page for every application identifier and, in addition to fetching available information, also observes the URL redirection behavior. Facebook, for example, redirects users to different targets depending on the application type. The following example redirects the user to http://yahoo.com, and the submodule therefore classifies the application as an external website.

Redirection to external website

```
GET /apps/application.php?id=194699337231859
Host: www.facebook.com
⟹ Redirects to http://yahoo.com
```

The second example of a Facebook application redirects the user to an authentication dialog that is classified as a standard application that requests additional information.

---

[2] https://plus.google.com/games/directory

146

Redirection to authentication dialog

```
GET /apps/application.php?id=102452128776
Host: www.facebook.com
⟹ Redirects to Facebook authentication dialog
```

Permissions. An important classification property of third-party applications is the set of requested permissions. This submodule collects the set of requested permissions using two different techniques: permissions are collected from rendered permission dialogs and based on parameters in permission dialog request URIs.

3.3 Analysis module

The analysis module analyses the actual application content. To this end, applications are installed on test accounts by automating a Web browser.

Web tracker identification. Social network application developers themselves rely on third-party components for analytics and advertising. In-app advertising promises revenue, while analytic products provide application developers with additional insights into their applications' users. Third-party analytics and advertising products raise major privacy concerns, because they may track users across multiple websites. The web tracker identification submodule identifies planted web trackers based on network traffic collected with the analysis module.

Information leaks. Personally identifiable information (PII) is information that can be used to uniquely identify a single individual with or without additional data sources. In case of online social networks, a user's unique identifier represents a sensitive PII. This submodule analyses whether social networking apps leak PII to third-party components, such as advertising and analytics providers. In addition to information leaks of personally identifiable information to third parties, application developers may unintentionally leak API authentication tokens through HTTP Referer. Therefore, this submodule traces leaks of tokens and unique user identifiers in the collected traffic. HTTP request (a) provides an example of leakage through an HTTP Referer header where "Super Analytics" receives a user's unique identifier as well as the app's OAuth token through the Referer header of the HTTP request. The analytics provider could then impersonate the application with the leaked access token to access the user's personal information.

(a) Information leakage via HTTP Referer

```
GET /__beacon.gif
Host: www.super-analytics.com
Referer: http://www.fbgameexample.com/flash.php
        ?oauth_token=AAA...&id=111111111&locale=
        en_US
```

HTTP request (b) provides an example of PII leakage through a URI request. In this example the third-party application transfers unique identifiers directly to a third party.

(b) Information leakage via URI request

```
GET /api/v1/ip=...&uid=111111111&data=%7B%7D
Host: api.trippleclick.net
```

Network fingerprint. The network fingerprint submodule provides network metrics of a given social networking app. The submodule first performs an analysis on the collected network traffic to determine the application's domain.

Subsequently, a number of metrics are collected on the application domain. The network fingerprint submodule furthermore performs a non-intrusive service discovery scan against the third-party systems by enumerating a list of TCP ports accepting packets and their corresponding service banners on the application host. Finally, the vulnerability search submodule determines whether a third-party host uses outdated software that might eventually compromise the security of their systems. This submodule matches discovered service types and version numbers against publicly available vulnerability databases.

4. EVALUATION AND APP SAMPLE

In this section we briefly discuss our research methodology and outline the prototype implementation of our *AppInspect* framework for Facebook. In the following we describe our enumerated third-party application sample.

4.1 Methodology

We chose to implement an instance of our *AppInspect* framework for the Facebook platform. Facebook serves as a good example due to its popularity and the plethora of available third-party applications. Facebook offers whitehat accounts[3] for security researchers, these accounts however cannot interact with third-party applications. We therefore set up a number of experimental accounts with bogus data, in order to perform automated application evaluations without processing actual personal information. Once we finished our experiments we deactivated all Facebook test accounts. In order to detect third-party products, we used traffic patterns from the Ghostery database, which contains more than 1,200 ad networks and trackers[11]. We complemented Ghostery's traffic patterns with additional trackers we identified during our traffic analysis. In order to find potential vulnerabilities of application hosts, we fingerprinted their publicly available web services in a non-intrusive way. We strictly refrained from interfering with application web services and instead based our analysis on detected service banners.

4.2 AppInspect prototype

Search Module. Facebook offers two application directories that contain a tiny subset of their third-party applications. The majority of third-party applications, however, is only retrievable with Facebook's global search feature. Therefore, we implemented three submodules to enumerate third-party applications: an exhaustive search submodule that generates application search terms and feeds them into Facebook's search, and two submodules to collect all applications from Facebook's *Timeline* and *Application Center* directories.

Classification Module. The classification module for Facebook implements the collection of application type, permissions, rating, and language. A submodule of our framework collects application properties based on application info pages. The application type is determined based on both harvested information and the application target URI. The permission submodule detects application authentication dialogs and collects the set of requested permissions. Finally, we implemented a generic language detection mod-

---

[3]https://www.facebook.com/whitehat/accounts/

ule that relies on the Google Translate API to detect and translate non-English application names.

Analysis Module. The traffic analysis submodule automates the installation of a given Facebook application on a test account and collects all traffic with a transparent HTTP(S) proxy. Moreover, our prototype implements our proposed analysis submodules. We implemented the information leaks submodule, which probes the session recordings for sensitive information. To detect information leaks we verify whether our test account's unique identifier or OAuth tokens are transmitted to detected third-party products. We inspect the collected traffic dumps for plaintext and Base64-encoded unique identifiers and authentication tokens. In order to reduce false positives of HTTP Referer leaks, the information leaks submodule verifies whether information is leaked to third parties other than application providers themselves. Furthermore, we ignore leaks to content delivery networks (CDNs) of Facebook (fbcdn.net) and application providers (e.g. zgncdn.com). Leaks to other CDNs such as Akamai or Amazon CloudFront are also less critical because they do not track their users across multiple domains using HTTP cookies. The network fingerprint submodule parses web session recordings and determines the application host based on the application's OAuth session initialization. The submodule, furthermore, uses the `tracepath` and `dig` utilities to collect network metrics. In addition to collecting network metrics, the networking fingerprint submodule also provides port scanning functionality. Finally, our prototype implements a vulnerability submodule that searches for outdated software. A number of vulnerability databases exist and we focus on databases with readily accessible exploits. The vulnerability submodule thus searches within the *Exploit Database*[36] as well as for readily available Metasploit modules[37].

4.3 Enumerated application sample

We performed an initial enumeration of applications in April 2012 with search terms based on bigrams of the English alphabet. The search module was configured to harvest information non-aggressively with a limit of 2,500 queries per day. Facebook imposes rate limits on standard accounts on a daily per-account basis. Therefore, we relied on a pool of accounts set up for the experiment, which we rotated during app analysis. Our first exhaustive search resulted in 234,597 applications. This first run helped us fine-tune our exhaustive search module. In Mid 2012, we reran the search module, this time with character trigrams based on the English alphabet and also on integers from 0 - 9. The exhaustive search module enumerated *434,687* unique applications. Our application directory submodules found 129 Timeline applications and 108 applications in Facebook's App Center. Our search module successfully verified that all Timeline and App Center applications were included in our enumerated application sample. In addition, we validated our enumerated sample against Socialbakers application statistics[4]. Our validation attempt showed that in addition to including all Socialbaker applications, our approach found a number of high-ranking applications that were missing in their sample. We observed a great disparity in the monthly active users (MAU) of the enumerated applications. Figure 3 illustrates our observation. While the great majority

---

[4] http://socialbakers.com/facebook-applications/

of applications had a MAU lower than 10,000, a small number of applications attracted a wider audience (red graph). Relative to our sample's cumulative application usage, the top 10,000 apps covered *93.16* percent (green graph) of all MAUs.

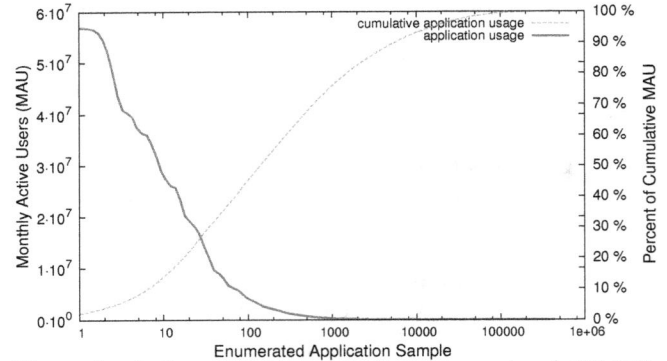

Figure 3: Active monthly users in our sample of 434,687 enumerated applications

We discarded all applications with fewer than 10,000 MAU from our subsequent analysis because of their comparably minor impact. In Autumn 2012, we performed an analysis of the 10,624 most popular apps with AppInspect's classifier module. Our selected subsample covered 94.07% of all applications relative to our samples' cumulative application usage. The results in Table 1 show the different application types observed in our sample. 44.68% or 4,747 applications belonged to the *Authentication Dialog* class. The *Authentication Dialog* class represents canvas applications that request personal information from their users. The *Canvas* class represents applications that load external content into the Facebook canvas but do not require any personal information from their users to work. *Connect* applications are external websites that leverage the Facebook API. *Connect* applications often use Facebook as an identity provider and to import Facebook content into their own portals. A number of apps responded with an error or were canceled (*Defect*). *Page Add-ons* are applications that provide add-ons to Facebook pages; these apps have access to the content of Facebook pages. The *Mobile* class, finally, represents applications that target mobile platforms such as Android or iOS.

Application Type	Applications	Total %
Authentication Dialog	4,747	44.68%
Canvas	2,365	22.26%
Connect	2,260	21.27%
Defect	865	8.14%
Page Add-ons	280	2.64%
Mobile	107	1.01%
Total	*10,624*	*100.00%*

Table 1: Classification of most popular apps (n=10,624)

The relatively high number of defective applications can be attributed to two independent observations. First, developers of less popular applications had trouble maintaining reliable applications. As a result, a number of applications responded with error codes or did not respond at all. Second, Facebook's application ecosystem is volatile and some applications are available only for a limited timespan. In the final step, the classification module leveraged the Google Translate API to detect languages used. The majority of applications were English (64.72%), followed by Spanish and German. In total, we observed 69 different languages.

5. RESULTS

This section describes the results of our extensive security and privacy analysis of third-party applications. The in-depth analysis was performed on the most popular Facebook canvas applications that requested additional information. These 4,747 apps represent a significant subsample of our enumerated applications because they impact most users.

5.1 Requested personal information

Table 2 shows the most frequently requested permissions to access personal information out of the *4,747* most popular third-party applications. The most requested permission for games was "publish posts to stream", which allows an app to post to a user's profile. In total, 51.32% of these third-party applications asked permission to publish to a user's stream. The table also shows that access to a user's personal email address was most commonly requested for generic apps and by 46.07% of all third-party applications that requested personal information. It is also interesting to observe that access to users' birth dates and photos are often requested as well.

Permission	App Category		Total %
	game	app	
Publish posts to stream	*1,617*	819	51.32%
Personal email address	1,055	*1,132*	46.07%
Publish action	435	857	27.22%
Access user's birthday	582	428	21.28%
Access user's photos	721	99	17.27%
Access data offline	517	120	13.42%
Access user likes	438	153	12.45%
Access user location	350	143	10.39%
Read stream	409	80	10.3%
Access friends' photos	319	17	7.08%

Table 2: Most common requested permissions by third-party applications (n=4,747)

We clustered applications based on their hosting domains to identify application providers. Our results showed that the 4,747 applications belonged to *1,646* distinct domains or providers. Furthermore, 73.42% or 3,485 apps belonged to a third party with more than one application. Third parties that offer multiple applications can request different personal information with different applications. Once a user installs more than one of their applications, providers can simply aggregate all collected user information. Therefore, we argue that requested permissions need to be analyzed not only based on individual apps, but also based on application providers. In this analysis, we found that the most requested permission per application provider was access to personal email addresses, which 60.24% of all providers requested. Figure 4 depicts the number of distinct permissions requested per application provider. The provider samples are hereby sorted by their monthly active users. On average, providers requested close to three permissions. As our figure illustrates, there are a number of application providers

that represent outliers because they request a vast amount of different permissions from their users.

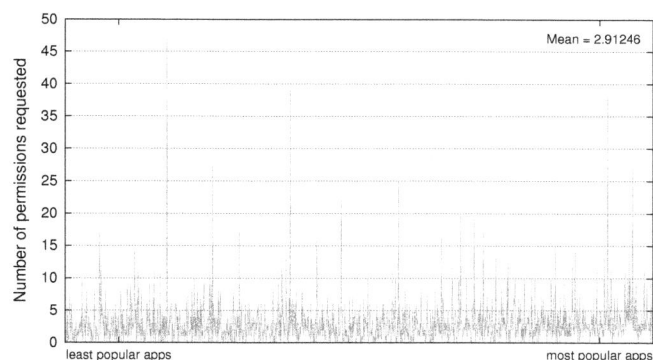

Figure 4: Number of requested permissions for 1,646 application providers

Our results show that 40 providers (2.43% of all application providers in our sample) requested more than 10 permissions. For these 40 providers, we manually verified whether the requested permissions were in required for application functionality. Our findings suggest that a number of applications genuinely required a large amount of permissions to function at all. These legitimate applications transferred large amounts of personal information to create their own specialized social networks. Examples of such applications include dating and job seeking applications. Dating applications, for example, gathered personal information to offer matchmaking features. A number of providers that requested more than 10 permissions, did, however, request more permissions than were required to function. Especially one application provider requested a excessive set of permissions. This provider offered a total of 140 applications for proverbs, quotes, and daily horoscopes in a number of different languages. The provider's most popular application was a daily horoscope in Portuguese with 2.5 million monthly users (as of November 2012). Their applications however accessed only users' basic information. The applications thus do not directly harm users by requesting 27 unnecessary permissions and it was interesting to observe the popularity of this provider's apps were not affected by the potential loss of privacy. While the provider did not misuse the requested permission to access additional personal information, leakage of access tokens would have serious implications.

5.2 Hosting environments

Our analysis of reverse DNS queries and network hops showed that developers relied upon 604 distinct Internet hosting services. Table 3 outlines the most commonly used hosting services and their geographical location. Amazon's elastic cloud service hosted 18.72% of all third-party applications in our sample. Amazon EC2 was especially popular with developers of applications that attracted a large number of active users. We also observed that the hosting services were geographically spread across 64 different countries, although our analysis showed that the majority of applications (55%) were hosted in the United States.

Our analysis module probed all 1,646 application hosts for open TCP ports and corresponding software products. All applications were accessible via HTTP but 11.5% of all applications did not offer access via HTTPS, which made

Provider	Location	Total %
Amazon EC2	US (755), IE (82), SG (52)	18.72%
SoftLayer	US (505)	10.65%
Peak Hosting	US (244)	5.14%
Rackspace	US (147), GB (11), HK (4)	3.41%
GoDaddy	SG (51), US (29), NL (6)	1.82%
Linode	US (72), GB (6), JP (2)	1.69%
OVH	FR (42), PL (7), ES (2)	1.04%
Hetzner	DE (47)	0.99%
Internap	US (35)	0.73%

Table 3: Most commonly used Internet hosting services for Facebook third-party applications

those applications inaccessible via a secure connection. Our detailed results show that 55% of web servers were powered by Apache httpd, followed by nginx (15.63%) and Microsoft IIS (9.4%). An accessible web server that handles both HTTP and HTTPS is the only requirement for a working Facebook third-party application. However, we found that third-party developers exposed a number of additional services on their application hosts. Table 4 outlines the most common publicly exposed services. It shows that 40.24% of application hosting environments allowed access via SSH and 38.91% access via FTP. The used products, together

TCP Port	Service	Hosts	% Total
22	ssh	662	40.22%
21	ftp	640	38.88%
25	smtp	572	34.75%
110	pop3	439	26.67%
143	imap	417	25.33%

Table 4: Most common additional services on application hosts

with their specific software versions, were used by the analysis module to identify hosts with potential software vulnerabilities. Our security analysis showed that HTTP and FTP services posed the highest risks. Two hosts ran an outdated nginx version that is prone to a source code disclosure vulnerability (CVE-2010-2263). Furthermore, we found two outdated versions of ProFTPD that possibly allow an attacker to execute arbitrary code on application hosts (CVE-2006-5815, CVE-2010-4221). Eight hosts were susceptible to these buffer overflow attacks via their FTP service. The most popular of the eight application hosts gathered information from an average of 1.2 million users per month. This vulnerable application provider furthermore processes sensitive personal information such as user email addresses and dates of birth.

5.3 Web trackers

Our web tracker submodule identified 139 distinct web trackers used by social apps. Table 5 outlines the most common web trackers detected in our application sample. Google dominated both with their web analytics product and their online advertising products DoubleClick and AdWords. Our analysis showed that web trackers were mostly planted by online advertising products, which are used to create additional revenue for application developers. All web bugs presented in Table 5 potentially track their users across multiple websites based on HTTP cookies.

Web bug	Type	Apps	% Total
Google Analytics	analytics	3,378	71.16%
DoubleClick	advertising	529	11.14%
Google Adsense	advertising	361	7.61%
AdMeld	advertising	276	5.81%
Cubics	advertising	153	3.22%
LifeStreet Media	advertising	94	1.98%
Google AdWords	advertising	91	1.92%
OpenX	advertising	82	1.73%
Quantcast	analytics	49	1.03%
ScoreCard Beacon	analytics	48	1.01%

Table 5: Common web trackers in third-party apps

The ranking of web trackers changes slightly when the popularity of the different applications is factored in. Based on the total number of application users exposed to web trackers, LifeStreet Media becomes the most popular advertising product. Furthermore, analytics based on BlueKai and advertising by Rubicon move to the top ten products when ranking is based on cumulative monthly active users instead of the cumulative occurrences.

5.4 Information leaks

Our findings suggest that ten advertising and analytics products directly received users' unique identifiers from social networking applications via URI requests. One advertising provider even received our test user's birthday and gender in addition to the unique identifier. The following request shows an instance of the detected application provider; however, we have replaced the actual host with a fictional name.

Information leakage via URI request

```
GET /1111111111/landingbirthday=5%2F2%2F1978&gender=
    male
Host: notdisclosed.com
```

We observed that 315 social networking applications in our sample directly transferred personally identifiable information to at least one additional third-party product via HTTP parameters. Three out of these 10 products were also previously classified as web trackers. This implies that these three third parties can track users across multiple websites with additional knowledge of their unique Facebook identifier and, thus, their real name[5]. Two advertising products that received unique user identifiers via URI requests were also approved by Facebook as valid advertising products.

Our analysis showed that 51 applications leaked unique user identifiers to third parties via the HTTP Referer header. In addition to user identifiers, 14 out of these 51 applications also leaked their API authorization tokens via HTTP Referer. Third parties could misuse leaked OAuth tokens to impersonate the leaking apps and harvest additional personal information. Referers were in both cases mainly leaked to Google Analytics and DoubleClick. It became clear that a popular game was affected by this issue, leaking on average

---

[5]The Facebook Graph API allows to query certain information without the requirement of prior authentication. Given a user's unique identifier, one can simply perform a query like: http://graph.facebook.com/4; where "4" in this example is the unique user identifier of Mark Zuckerberg.

4.7 million OAuth tokens and user identifiers per month to third-party analytics and advertising companies.

6. DISCUSSION AND LIMITATIONS

In this section we discuss the implications of our findings and possible limitations of our approach.

6.1 Detected malpractices

The evaluation of our novel AppInspect framework on the basis of Facebook shows that automated security and privacy analysis of social networking apps is feasible. Our framework detected 14 application providers that requested a disproportionate amount of personal information. These application providers offer hundreds of applications and collect sensitive personal information from millions of social networking users. Our automated analysis showed that application providers make use of 139 different web tracking and advertising products. It furthermore showed that application developers transmit personally identifiable information to third parties. 315 applications directly transferred user identifiers to third-party products via URI parameters. In addition to receiving personally identifiable information, two out of ten products set tracking cookies. Hence, a single social networking app might lead to users being tracked across multiple websites with their real name. Web tracking in combination with personal information from social networks represents a serious privacy violation that is also not transparent to social networking users. Finally, our AppInspect framework detected that a number of applications leaked personal information and authentication tokens to third-party products via HTTP Referer headers. 51 applications leaked user information and out of these, 14 applications also leaked authentication tokens. We found a popular game that suffered from this implementation bug and leaked 4.7 million authentication tokens per month on average. After we ran our automated analysis, we manually verified all detected malpractices and implementation errors. We reported our findings to Facebook in November 2012. Facebook confirmed our findings and reached out to application developers to provide implementation fixes. In May 2013, Facebook confirmed that all of our detected malpractices have been fixed by application developers.

6.2 Application hosting infrastructure

The hosting infrastructure of social networking apps is beyond the control of social networking providers and users ultimately have to trust third-party developers with protecting their personal data appropriately. Our findings show that application developers rely on a wide range of custom systems to provide social networking applications. Over one third of all application hosts maintained publicly accessible FTP and SSH services. While these services offer proper administration tools, they also increase the attack surface of application hosts. For example, both FTP and SSH are well known to be popular targets of brute-force password guessing attacks. Moreover, a number of application hosts used outdated software versions that are susceptible to remote exploits. Our findings include an application host with more than 1 million monthly active users that was susceptible to a remote buffer overflow via their FTP service. Our analysis also showed that Amazon EC2 is a popular choice for application developers. Insecure Amazon EC2 community images may pose another security risk for third-party host-

ing infrastructures. Two recent publications [6, 2] came to the conclusion that Amazon's community images contain a number of serious vulnerabilities. Our findings furthermore showed that application servers were geographically spread over 64 different countries. This geographical distribution, finally, results in non-technical challenges because a great number of different data protection laws apply.

6.3 Implications and protection strategies

Since January 2010, application developers on Facebook can request users' personal email addresses instead of proxied email addresses. It is interesting to observe that 60.24% of all providers in our third-party application sample made use of this feature and requested the personal email addresses of their application users. Both social networking providers and application developers host a pool of sensitive personal information. Large social networking providers possess the necessary resources to maintain and improve the security of their services. In contrast, our findings suggest that a considerable number of third-party developer leak personal information to third parties and fail to harden their systems. While application developers collect email addresses to contact users directly, valid email addresses are also in demand with spammers and phishers. Forbes [17] reported that 1.1 million email addresses of social networking users are sold for as little as 5 US$. According to the seller, the information was collected via a Facebook third-party application. In addition to valid email addresses, third-party developers also collect information that enables sophisticated email based attacks. For example, social phishing attacks [27] leverage the success rate of traditional phishing messages based on knowledge of a user's friend. In the case of Facebook, all applications can access friendship information by default. Context-aware spam attacks [5] might also misuse user birthdays or photos to increase the authenticity of unsolicited bulk messages. Apps might be injected into user profiles without their knowledge[24] and enable large-scale campaigns with context-aware spam [25]. Based on our findings, we propose the following protection strategies:

- Developers need to sanitize the landing page of their application and ensure that they do not pass on unique identifiers and authorization tokens via HTTP parameters.

- Developers need to provide third-party products that require a unique user identifier with random identifiers and maintain internal mappings between these random identifiers and the real Facebook user identifiers.

- Social network providers should stress that application developers should harden their hosting environments.

Finally, social network providers should follow the example of LinkedIn or iOS App Store and manually review apps before they make them available.

6.4 Dataset

We make our social networking dataset available online to the research community[6]. Furthermore, our collected dataset offers an important snapshot on application popularity, as Facebook stopped to make exact usage metrics publicly online in January 2013. *AppInspect* is designed to

---

[6]http://ai.sba-research.org

steadily provide insights into third-party application ecosystems, and we will, therefore, periodically refresh and expand our dataset.

6.5 Limitations

Our AppInspect prototype is currently limited to Facebook applications, but a number of submodules can be reused when extending our prototype to other social networking providers. In practice this would imply that both provider specific modules (enumeration, classification module) had to be adapted to the target OSNs, while we could reuse our analysis module. Another limitation is our in-depth analysis, which focused on the most popular Facebook applications. The analysis of mobile applications and websites, which leverage the Facebook API, are not included in our sample. Our findings furthermore revealed the limitations of automated security and privacy analyses of social networking apps. Our approach is unable to detect applications, which request a disproportionate amount of personal information, without additional manual reviews. Detection of information leakage to third parties is currently done by spotting unique user identifiers and authentication tokens. Hence, our framework does not automatically detect: leakage of personal data without inclusion of unique user identifiers, nor obfuscated personal information. In addition, developers of malicious apps might decide to share or sell personal information via hidden back-ends, or e.g. mail entire data collections to third parties. Finally, due to the non-intrusiveness of our performed security tests, our results indicate the vulnerability of application hosts and may contain false positives and negatives.

7. RELATED WORK

This section surveys related research regarding social networking app security and privacy.

Social application studies

To the best of our knowledge, there has been no study on security and privacy issues of social networking apps of a scope comparable to our work. Wang et al. [43] conducted the first measurement study regarding the data collection practices of third-party apps. Their study analyzed the 200 most popular applications from nine different categories of Facebook's discontinued application directory. Based on their collected dataset, their study showed the most commonly requested permissions of 1,305 Facebook applications in December 2010. The Wall Street Journal conducted an investigation into information gathered by the 100 most popular Facebook applications in May 2012 [1]. Their manual review of popular applications found that applications often seek permission to access sensitive information. Two recent studies provide additional insights into permission systems of third-party applications: Chia et al. [8] studied the effectiveness of user-consent permission systems through a data collection of Facebook apps, Chrome extensions and Android apps. They constructed a Facebook dataset with 27,029 apps by web scraping a social media analytics platform's list of Facebook applications. Chia et al. then collected the requested permissions, popularity, and ratings of apps in their dataset. The authors found that popularity and ratings are not reliable indicators of potential privacy risks associated with third-party applications. Frank et al. [18] relied on Chia et al.'s dataset and used unsupervised

learning to detect permission request patterns. Their results showed that permission patterns of low-reputation apps differed significantly from high-reputation apps.

Information leaks and web tracking

Krishnamurthy and Wills were the first to discover that online social networks leak personally identifiable information [32]. Their observation was confirmed by investigative journalism of the Wall Street Journal, which found that both advertising and tracking products received social network user identifiers [41, 40]. In May 2011, Symantec also found that third-party applications leaked OAuth tokens to third parties [42] due to a now deprecated authentication scheme of Facebook. Third-party web tracking is an extensive search area of its own. Mayer and Mitchell [35] provide an overview on current web tracking technology and policies. Krishnamurthy et al.[31] showed that 56 out of 100 popular non-OSN websites leak personal information. Mobile applications pose similar challenges for user privacy as social apps and web tracking. Evaluation of mobile apps is however facilitated by access to the runtime environment of apps. As opposed to third-party social applications, this enables taint analysis of personal information [10], as well as effective privacy protection on the client side [23]. In the following we briefly discuss social network specific protection proposals.

User protection

Related work on user protection focuses on three main research areas: security extensions to online social networks, privacy preserving third-party data access, and improved application authorization dialogs.

Generic security extensions aim to hide personal information from social network providers as well as from third parties without stopping users from sharing information. Guha et al. [21] proposed NYOB, a method to substitute personal profile information with pseudorandom content. Lucas and Borisov [33] introduced flyByNight, a tool that relies on public-key cryptography and a third-party application to exchange confidential messages via Facebook. Their concept only applies to messages; the remaining personal information is still exposed to social network providers and third-party developers. Luo et al. [34] proposed FaceCloak, where social network providers receive fake profile information and real user data is stored encrypted on a separate server. Users require passwords and a FaceCloak browser extension to restore the real information. FaceCloak's approach is similar to NYOB with the exception of requiring additional servers. Beato et al. [3] finally proposed "Scramble", a generic method to shield confidential information from social networking providers.

Felt and Evans [16] conducted a survey of the 150 most popular Facebook applications in October 2007. Based on their analysis, they proposed a privacy protection method for social networking APIs. Their method suggests providing third-party developers with no personal information at all but with a limited interface that only provides access to an anonymized social graph. Developers would use placeholders for user data, which the social network providers would replace with actual user data. Felt and Evans' design is impracticable with state-of-the-art applications because the majority of applications require personal information to work. Singh et al. [39] proposed the "xBook" framework for building privacy-preserving social networking applications. Their xBook framework is based on information flow models to control what an application provider can do with the personal information they receive. While their approach mitigates privacy and security issues of apps, it would require all third-party developers to host their applications on the xBook platform. Egele et al. [9] proposed fine-grained access control over application data requests. Their suggested solution, called "PoX", relies on a browser plugin that mediates application data access and a modified Facebook API library for application developers.

Besmer et al. [4] evaluated a user interface prototype that would help users to choose which information they want to share with third-party applications. They found that privacy-conscious users would benefit from their new user interface, while careless users would continue to expose their personal information to third-party developers. Wang et al. [43] evaluated two alternative application permission dialogs to help users understand better how third-party applications function. The authors then proposed interface design cues based on their user interface evaluation.

At the time of writing, none of the proposed generic OSN security extensions are operational nor actively used, because researchers discontinued any further development. Furthermore, none of the proposed privacy-enhancing frameworks have been adopted by social network application developers. Finally, current authentication dialogs conceal privacy-relevant information from users (see Figure 1) and are in stark contrast to suggestions from previous usability studies. In addition to missing protection strategies, previous studies either focused exclusively on requested permissions or were limited to manually verifying a small number of applications. Our AppInspect performs an automated analysis of requested permissions, information leaks, as well as application hosting infrastructures. We thus aim to establish semantic protection methods [30] for social app users by increasing the transparency of data transmission practices of third-party developers.

8. CONCLUSIONS

Social networking applications have become a popular feature of online social networks and are used by millions of users every day. In exchange for additional features, users grant social networking apps permission to transfer their personal data to third-party services.

In this paper, we proposed *AppInspect* to automatically analyze security and privacy issues of social network third-party applications. Our *AppInspect* framework first enumerates applications available for a given social network provider. Next, *AppInspect* collects application metrics from the social network provider. In a last step, *AppInspect* installs third-party applications on test accounts and analyzes their network traffic. *AppInspect* analyzes the collected network traffic for existing tracking software, information leakage to third parties, and application hosting infrastructure. We have implemented our *AppInspect* framework and used it to evaluate Facebook's application ecosystem. *AppInspect* automatically enumerated *434,687* unique Facebook applications and analyzed the most popular applications in detail. Our findings helped improve the security and privacy of social networking users. Finally, our results showed that *AppInspect* is a practicable framework for detecting common malpractices of third-party applications on a large scale.

Acknowledgements

Thanks to Balachander Krishnamurthy for shepherding this manuscript and the anonymous reviewers for their valuable feedback. This research was funded by COMET K1, FFG - Austrian Research Promotion Agency and would not have been possible without the financial support of the Vienna PhD School of informatics. The authors would also like to thank Manuel Leithner, Maciej Piec, and Sebastian Neuner for their source code contributions.

9. REFERENCES

[1] ANGWIN, J., AND SINGER-VINE, J. Selling you on facebook. *The Wallstreet Journal* (2012). last accessed 03/10/2013 http://online.wsj.com/article/SB10001424052702303302504577327744009046230.html.

[2] BALDUZZI, M., ZADDACH, J., BALZAROTTI, D., KIRDA, E., AND LOUREIRO, S. A security analysis of amazon's elastic compute cloud service. In *Proceedings of the 27th Annual ACM Symposium on Applied Computing* (2012), SAC '12, ACM.

[3] BEATO, F., KOHLWEISS, M., AND WOUTERS, K. Scramble! your social network data. In *Privacy Enhancing Technologies*, vol. 6794. Springer Berlin Heidelberg, Berlin, Heidelberg, 2011, pp. 211–225.

[4] BESMER, A., LIPFORD, H., SHEHAB, M., AND CHEEK, G. Social applications: exploring a more secure framework. In *Proceedings of the 5th Symposium on Usable Privacy and Security* (2009), ACM, p. 2.

[5] BROWN, G., HOWE, T., IHBE, M., PRAKASH, A., AND BORDERS, K. Social networks and context-aware spam. In *Proceedings of the 2008 ACM conference on Computer supported cooperative work* (2008), ACM, pp. 403–412.

[6] BUGIEL, S., NÜRNBERGER, S., PÖPPELMANN, T., SADEGHI, A.-R., AND SCHNEIDER, T. AmazonIA: when elasticity snaps back. In *Proceedings of the 18th ACM conference on Computer and communications security* (2011), CCS '11, ACM.

[7] CASTELLUCCIA, C., DE CRISTOFARO, E., AND PERITO, D. Private information disclosure from web searches. In *Privacy Enhancing Technologies* (2010), Springer, pp. 38–55.

[8] CHIA, P. H., YAMAMOTO, Y., AND ASOKAN, N. Is this app safe?: a large scale study on application permissions and risk signals. In *Proceedings of the 21st international conference on World Wide Web* (2012), WWW '12, ACM, pp. 311–320.

[9] EGELE, M., MOSER, A., KRUEGEL, C., AND KIRDA, E. Pox: Protecting users from malicious facebook applications. *Computer Communications* (2012).

[10] ENCK, W., GILBERT, P., CHUN, B.-G., COX, L. P., JUNG, J., MCDANIEL, P., AND SHETH, A. Taintdroid: An information-flow tracking system for realtime privacy monitoring on smartphones. In *OSDI* (2010), vol. 10, pp. 255–270.

[11] EVIDON. Ghostery. https://www.ghostery.com/.

[12] FACEBOOK. Getting your apps into facebook search faster. last accessed 04/27/2012 https://developers.facebook.com/blog/post/2011/07/12/getting-your-apps-into-facebook-search-faster/.

[13] FACEBOOK. Permissions reference. last accessed: 08/10/2012 `https://developers.facebook.com/docs/authentication/permissions/`.

[14] FACEBOOK. Platform policies. last accessed 04/20/2013 `https://developers.facebook.com/policy/`.

[15] FACEBOOK. Facebook platform launches, May 2007. last accessed 08/15/2012 `https://developers.facebook.com/blog/archive`.

[16] FELT, A., AND EVANS, D. Privacy protection for social networking APIs. In *W2SP '08* (2008).

[17] FORBES. Facebook investigating how bulgarian man bought 1.1 million users' email addresses for five dollars. last accessed 11/03/2012 `http://www.forbes.com/sites/andygreenberg/2012/10/25/facebook-investigating-how-bulgarian-man-bought-1-1-million-users-email-addresses-for-five-dollars/`.

[18] FRANK, M., DONG, B., FELT, A. P., AND SONG, D. Mining permission request patterns from android and facebook applications. *To appear: IEEE International Conference on Data Mining (ICDM) 2012* (2012).

[19] FTC. In the matter of facebook, inc., a corporation, Aug 2012. last accessed 06/05/2013 `http://www.ftc.gov/os/caselist/0923184/120810facebookcmpt.pdf`.

[20] GOOGLE. Google launches opensocial to spread social applications across the web, Nov 2007. last accessed 04/05/2012.

[21] GUHA, S., TANG, K., AND FRANCIS, P. Noyb: Privacy in online social networks. In *Proceedings of the first workshop on Online social networks* (2008), vol. 1, ACM, pp. 49–54.

[22] HARDT, D. The OAuth 2.0 authorization framework. last accessed 02/05/2012 `http://tools.ietf.org/html/draft-ietf-oauth-v2-31`.

[23] HORNYACK, P., HAN, S., JUNG, J., SCHECHTER, S., AND WETHERALL, D. These aren't the droids you're looking for: retrofitting android to protect data from imperious applications. In *Proceedings of the 18th ACM conference on Computer and communications security* (2011), ACM, pp. 639–652.

[24] HUBER, M., MULAZZANI, M., LEITHNER, M., SCHRITTWIESER, S., WONDRACEK, G., AND WEIPPL, E. Social snapshots: digital forensics for online social networks. In *Proceedings of the 27th Annual Computer Security Applications Conference* (2011), ACM, pp. 113–122.

[25] HUBER, M., MULAZZANI, M., WEIPPL, E., KITZLER, G., AND GOLUCH, S. Friend-in-the-middle attacks: Exploiting social networking sites for spam. *IEEE Internet Computing 15*, 3 (2011), 28–34.

[26] HULL, G., LIPFORD, H., AND LATULIPE, C. Contextual gaps: privacy issues on facebook. *Ethics and information technology 13*, 4 (2011), 289–302.

[27] JAGATIC, T., JOHNSON, N., JAKOBSSON, M., AND MENCZER, F. Social phishing. *Communications of the ACM 50*, 10 (2007), 94–100.

[28] KING, J., LAMPINEN, A., AND SMOLEN, A. Privacy: is there an app for that? In *Proceedings of the Seventh Symposium on Usable Privacy and Security* (2011), ACM, p. 12.

[29] KO, M. N., CHEEK, G., SHEHAB, M., AND SANDHU, R. Social-networks connect services. *Computer 43*, 8 (2010), 37 –43.

[30] KRISHNAMURTHY, B. Privacy and online social networks: Can colorless green ideas sleep furiously? *IEEE Security & Privacy 11*, 3 (2013), 14–20.

[31] KRISHNAMURTHY, B., NARYSHKIN, K., AND WILLS, C. Privacy leakage vs. protection measures: the growing disconnect. In *Web 2.0 Security and Privacy Workshop* (2011).

[32] KRISHNAMURTHY, B., AND WILLS, C. E. On the leakage of personally identifiable information via online social networks. In *Proceedings of the 2nd ACM workshop on Online social networks* (2009), ACM, pp. 7–12.

[33] LUCAS, M., AND BORISOV, N. Flybynight: mitigating the privacy risks of social networking. In *Proceedings of the 7th ACM workshop on Privacy in the electronic society* (2008), ACM, pp. 1–8.

[34] LUO, W., XIE, Q., AND HENGARTNER, U. Facecloak: An architecture for user privacy on social networking sites. In *Computational Science and Engineering, 2009. CSE'09. International Conference on* (2009), vol. 3, IEEE, pp. 26–33.

[35] MAYER, J., AND MITCHELL, J. Third-party web tracking: Policy and technology. In *2012 IEEE Symposium on Security and Privacy (SP)* (2012), pp. 413 –427.

[36] OFFENSIVE SECURITY. Exploits database. `http://www.exploit-db.com/`.

[37] RAPID7. Metasploit vulnerability and exploit database. `http://www.metasploit.com/modules/`.

[38] SEC. Amendment no. 4 to form s-1, facebook, inc., Apr 2012. last accessed 08/01/2012 `https://www.sec.gov/Archives/edgar/data/1326801/000119312512175673/d287954ds1a.htm`.

[39] SINGH, K., BHOLA, S., AND LEE, W. xBook: redesigning privacy control in social networking platforms. In *Proceedings of the 18th conference on USENIX security symposium* (Berkeley, CA, USA, 2009), SSYM'09, USENIX Association, p. 249âĂŞ266.

[40] STEEL, E., AND FOWLER, G. A. Facebook in privacy breach. *Wall Street Journal* (2010).

[41] STEEL, E., AND VASCELLARO, J. E. Facebook, MySpace confront privacy loophole. *Wall Street Journal* (2010).

[42] SYMANTEC. Facebook applications accidentally leaking access to third parties. last accessed 06/20/2012 `http://www.symantec.com/connect/blogs/facebook-applications-accidentally-leaking-access-third-parties-updated`.

[43] WANG, N., XU, H., AND GROSSKLAGS, J. Third-party apps on facebook: privacy and the illusion of control. In *Proceedings of the 5th ACM Symposium on Computer Human Interaction for Management of Information Technology* (2011), ACM, p. 4.

Ads by Whom? Ads about What?
Exploring User Influence and Contents in Social Advertising

Jaimie Y. Park
Division of Web Science and
Technology, KAIST, Daejeon,
Korea
jaimie@islab.kaist.ac.kr

Kyoung-Won Lee
Division of Web Science and
Technology, KAIST, Daejeon,
Korea
kyoungwon.lee@islab.kaist.ac.kr

Sang Yeon Kim
Department of Computer
Science, KAIST, Daejeon,
Korea
sangyeon@islab.kaist.ac.kr

Chin-Wan Chung
Division of Web Science and
Technology & Department of
Computer Science, KAIST,
Daejeon, Korea
chungcw@kaist.edu

ABSTRACT

Despite the growing interest in using online social networking services (OSNS) for advertising, little is understood about what contributes to the social advertising performance. In this research, we pose following questions: How many clicks do social advertisements actually receive? What are the characteristics of the advertisements that receive many clicks? What factors contribute to the clicks on advertisements? In order to answer these questions, we collect data from AdbyMe, a social media advertisement platform that connects businesses, or advertisers, with users of online social network services. Businesses can reach a large target audience through AdbyMe users who publish the advertisements on their social networks. We analyze the factors that may affect the clicks on advertisements being published on OSNS. In particular, we look into the advertised contents as well as the characteristics of users who publish the advertisements. We find that the traditional advertisement content analysis alone cannot fully explain the effectiveness of social advertisements. More importantly, we discover that in a social advertising paradigm, social influence of a publisher has a strong impact on the number of clicks on the advertisements. Our findings suggest that considering both the advertised contents and the influence of advertising publishers allows better understanding of the social advertisement phenomenon.

COSN'13, October 7–8, 2013, Boston, Massachusetts, USA.
Copyright 2013 ACM 978-1-4503-2084-9/13/10 ...$15.00.
http://dx.doi.org/10.1145/2512938.2512950.

Categories and Subject Descriptors

J.4 [**Computer Applications**]: Social and Behavioral Sciences

General Terms

Human Factors, Measurement

Keywords

Social Media Marketing; Social Network Advertising; Online Advertising; Consumer Behavior; Online Social Networks; Twitter; Content Analysis; User Influence

1. INTRODUCTION

Online social networking services (OSNS) such as Twitter and Facebook have faced a phenomenal growth in popularity. It has been reported that social networking sites have reached 82% of the world's online population, and nearly 19% of the time spent online is now spent on OSNS [9]. With the growing popularity, OSNS are used for various purposes across diverse application domains, one of which is marketing/advertising. OSNS are believed to be powerful marketing environment mainly because they consist of a tremendously large group of users worldwide who actively use the services on a daily basis, not to mention that the cost involved in connecting with these users and maintaining accounts on OSNS is fairly low. In addition, advertisements shared among social connections are expected to be persuasive because people are known to be susceptible to peer influence.

In order to leverage the marketing opportunities offered by OSNS, a new type of business platform named "social media advertising platform" has recently emerged. AdbyMe[1] is one of the many social media advertising platforms currently available on the Web. The goal of social media advertising platforms is to connect businesses, or advertisers, with

---
[1] AdbyMe. https://adby.me/

(a) Requested Advertisement

(b) Publishing the Advertisement

(c) Published Advertisement on Twitter

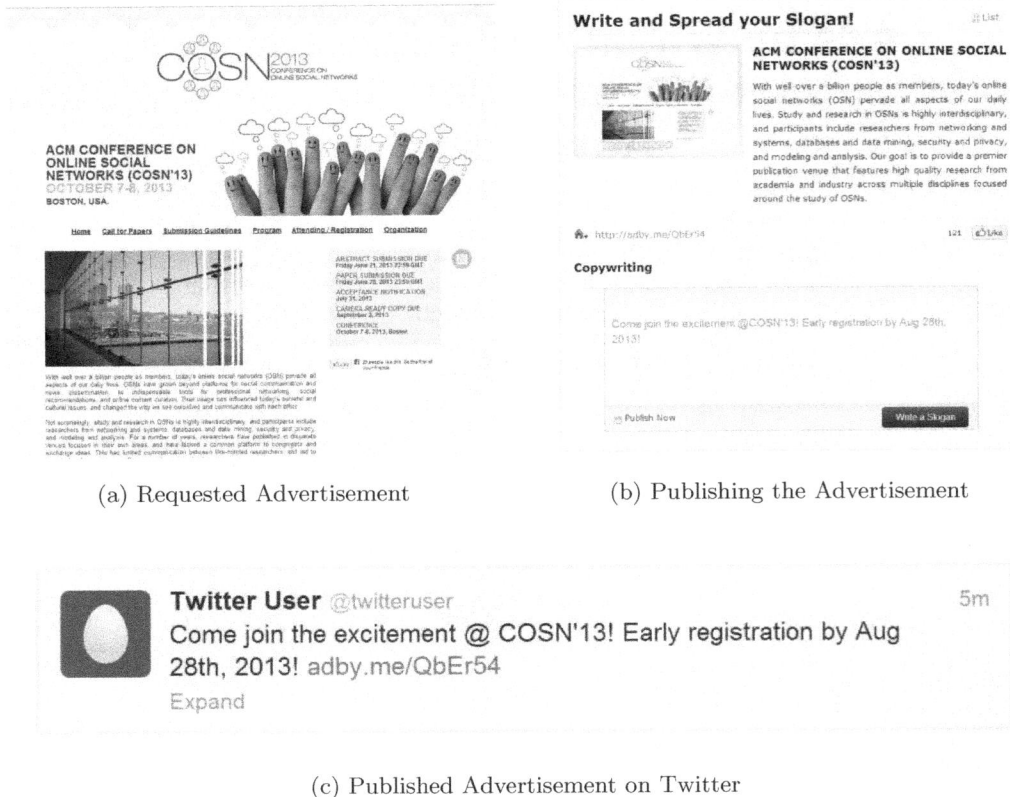

Figure 1: Social Advertising Process through AdbyMe

OSNS users who can act as social advertisement publishers. These advertisement publishers, also known as "social publishers", can be any individual who uses popular OSNS including Twitter and Facebook. In particular, OSNS users who wish to participate as publishers can register themselves on AdbyMe and specify which OSNS they will be using to publish advertisements.

Figure 1 describes the social advertising process through AdbyMe. Advertisers who wish to have their advertisements placed on OSNS make a request to AdbyMe, with a webpage specifying their products or services. Let us say COSN organizers want to advertise the upcoming conference and make a request to AdbyMe with a webpage as shown in Figure 1(a). After the request has been made, AdbyMe shows the list of advertisement requests on their system. Any user registered on AdbyMe can browse through this list and find out about the advertisements they can publish on their OSNS. Let us say a user named Twitter User decides to publish an advertisement requested by COSN and spread the information to his/her social network through Twitter. Twitter User is given an option to recreate his/her own advertisement content by typing in the slogan of his/her choice, as shown in Figure 1(b). While AdbyMe provides a default slogan, in most cases publishers choose to create a different slogan that can appeal to other Twitter users. As Figure 1(c) illustrates, a slogan is published on Twitter User's Twitter timeline, with a temporarily generated unique URL link to the advertised webpage shown in Figure 1(a). All the advertisements published through AdbyMe are associated with

this clickable URL link. Whenever a friend on Twitter User's social network clicks on the link, Twitter User gets paid a fixed amount of money as a compensation for a successful delivery of an advertisement.

By providing a systematic way for general individuals to become engaged in publishing advertisements on OSNS, social media advertising platforms are attracting a growing number of new advertisers and social publishers. In this paper, we collect and analyze social advertisement data generated by users of AdbyMe and explore factors that affect the advertisement performance measured by clicks on the advertisements. We gathered the data consisting of information on the advertised contents, advertising publishers, and resulting performance of the advertisements in terms of clicks. Click is a direct measure of "attention" of the audience, and being able to capture the attention of an audience is an important preliminary step in advertising, as described in the AIDA - Attention, Interest, Desire, and Action - marketing model [24]. Our study aims to understand the social advertising factors that trigger the attention of the target audience.

Social advertising is unique in that users are engaged in not only publishing the advertisement, but also recreating the advertisement by writing slogans as illustrated in Figure 1(b). Thus, in order to understand the factors influencing social advertising performance, we find it necessary to study both the advertised contents and advertising user. Past studies on online advertisement performance are primarily interested in content-related features that influence the success of advertisements. [14, 19, 25, 17, 21, 22, 15, 13] However, successful advertisements in this new social advertising paradigm are the results of not only effective "contents" but also influential "publishers", because even the same contents can yield different results depending on the influence of the publishers in the social context. Thereby, we look into content-related features as well as user-related features of the advertisements. Note that the terms "users" and "publishers" are used interchangeably for the rest of the paper. The contributions of this paper are as follows:

- We discover through content analysis that in social advertising paradigm, the widely-used promotional techniques do not necessarily bring improvements in advertising performance. This implies that the traditional advertisement content analysis method alone cannot fully explain the advertisement performance in social advertising.

- We verify that the users with high indegree who are presumed to be influential on OSNS do indeed show prominent performance in a social advertising setting. However, users who spawn many retweets are not necessary influential in terms of advertisement performance.

- To the best of our knowledge, our research is one of the first studies to examine the impact of both the content-related and user-related factors on social advertising performance. We perform our analysis on real-world data from a popular social media advertising platform, which realistically represents the real-life social advertising phenomenon.

2. RESEARCH PROBLEMS

In this study, we focus on studying social advertising performance through the analysis of clicks on advertisements. The research problems we address in this work are as follows:

1. What is the overall click distribution of the advertisements?
   We first want to observe how many clicks the advertisements receive through social advertising, in general. We expect the number of clicks to be unevenly distributed, with a few advertisements with high clicks, because skewness in popularity distribution is often observed in many other phenomena on the internet, such as web visits [1, 8] and video viewing activities [7]. By exploring the frequency distribution of clicks of the advertisements that are published through AdbyMe, we want to understand what portion of the population achieve high clicks, and quantify what we mean by "high" number of clicks. By exploring the frequency distribution of clicks on the advertisements that are published through AdbyMe, we also want to understand whether the advertisements on social media advertisement platforms receive similar number of clicks or not.

2. What are the characteristics of the advertisements that drive high number of clicks?
   We want to find out the features associated with the advertisements that attract users to click on the advertisements. The content-related features that we want to focus on are sweepstakes and prize giveaways, celebrity endorsement, sexual appeals, and curiosity components embedded within the advertised slogans, which were proven to be effective promotional strategies by previous studies. In addition to these content-related features, we want to examine the user-related features. In particular, we study whether the influence of a social publisher has an impact on the clicks of an advertisement. We take three different measures of user influence on Twitter: number of followers, retweet likelihood, and post count.

3. RELATED WORK

Our research is related to two bodies of research: researches on analyzing factors on advertising performance, and researches on social advertising.

3.1 Factors on Advertising Performance

Analyzing the factors that influence advertising performance has been an area of interest for many researchers and practitioners. In the past, print-based advertisements and TV commercials were major targets of interests [18, 23, 25]. Starting from the 1990s, when the commercialization of the World Wide Web was actively taking place, researches expanded their reach to online advertisements [12, 20, 11, 26].

The common research objective of these studies is to examine the different types of advertisement appeals. A large number of studies aim to analyze the verbal and visual features associated with the advertisement contents that draw the attention of users [14, 19, 25, 17, 21, 22, 15, 13]. These features include, but are not limited to, sweepstakes and prize giveaways, celebrity endorsement, sexual appeals, and curiosity components. Sweepstakes, prize giveaways, and contests are very common promotional strategies, intended to increase brand awareness by generating enthusiasm among viewers. Studies in the past show that consumer valuation of the advertised products and their response rates can be increased through the use of prizes and contests in advertisements [15, 13]. Many researchers study the effect of having well-known individuals such as pop stars or athletes using their fame to promote brands or products [14, 22, 19]. Such advertisement techniques are referred to as celebrity endorsement, and are found to be effective in arousing interests of the public. Some [25, 21] find that that more than 20% of online advertisements incorporate sexually provocative messages or images, and it increases the initial click response rate of the audience. [17] claims that advertisements that generate curiosity from the audience are shown to be more effective than the advertisements that only provides product information.

Although these promotional strategies were found to be effective by many of previous researches, it has not yet been verified if it holds true in a social advertising context. In a social advertising setting, an advertisement is delivered through a personal connection unlike in other advertising settings, and it is possible for the audience to perceive social advertising contents differently from other types of advertisements. Thus the traditional promotional strategies may result in an unexpected outcome, which makes it worthwhile for us to analyze contents in a social advertising context.

3.2 Social Advertising and Social Influence

It has only been in recent years that OSNS have introduced the new social advertising paradigm. Recent studies explore the social factors associated with the user relationships and how they impact the users' responses to advertisements in social advertising settings. [4] examine the effect of social signals on Facebook users' tendency to further spread information, and find that those who are exposed to social signals are significantly more likely to spread information. Through a large-scale observational study, [3] suggest that probability of adopting a behavior increases with the adopting peers. These studies were performed in the context of information diffusion, where the advertisement performance was measured using the likelihood of activating further information cascades. Although it may well represent the audience's perceived value of advertised content, it does not necessarily reflect how well it catches the attention of users. We use the number of clicks as a measure of advertising performance, which better represents how successful an advertisement is in grabbing the audience's attention.

[2] measures the strength of interpersonal ties between the users and its impact on consumer response to advertisements in terms of clicks, and find that effects of advertisements are greatest for strong ties. The main interests of these previous studies are in studying the egocentric network properties such as relationships among users and tie strengths. Little attention has been paid to understand how the user influence at a macro level, such as indegree, is related to the overall performance of social advertisements [6]. Do users with many friends and followers who are presumed to be influential on OSNS actually perform well in social advertising? Do users who generally spawn many cascades tend to be effective social advertisers? The purpose of this study is to answer these questions that have not yet been addresses by existing researches.

4. DATA DESCRIPTION AND COLLECTION METHODOLOGY

AdbyMe is a social media advertisement platform that serves as a bridge between advertisers and advertisement publishers. AdbyMe was founded in October 2010 in Korea, and rapidly gained popularity over the past three years. As of 2013, AdbyMe consists of 17,260 registered users who participated in publishing in total of 80,612 slogans. The vast majority of AdbyMe users are Koreans, while AdbyMe has recently expanded its business to other countries including Japan and US. Similar social media advertisement platforms around the world include, but are not limited to, Mylikes[2], Ad.ly[3], and SponsoredTweets[4].

We asked AdbyMe administrators to allow us to access their database to gather data from their service. They kindly provided an access account to their database, which allowed us to gather large amounts of data. Additionally, we collected data from Twitter using the Twitter API[5]. We focused on the registered users on AdbyMe who use Twitter as a main channel for publishing advertisements, and collected the tweets posted on their timelines.

We collected the entire set of data generated through AdbyMe in 2012. The data we collected consists of three main parts: advertisement request data, user data, and publication data. Advertisement request data contains information

[2]http://mylikes.com/
[3]http://ad.ly/
[4]http://sponsoredtweets.com/
[5]https://dev.twitter.com/

about the advertiser, title and description of the requested advertisement, and the address of the webpage displaying the full advertised content. User data contains information about the social publishers and the OSNS they mainly use for advertising. If a user mainly uses Twitter for example, his/her Twitter screenname is recorded as a part of the user information. Lastly, publication data consists of the advertisement id and the user id when he/she selects an advertisement to post on their OSNS. In addition, the publication data contains the slogan created by the user when publishing it on their OSNS as well as the unique URL assigned to the user for publishing the specified advertisement. Most importantly, publication data also contains the total number of clicks a publication received. Note that click counts are based "unique" click counts, which means that repeated clicks by a single user or duplications from a single IP are only counted as one. In total, we collected data from 3,468 users who contributed in total of 606,707 publications using 79,765 different slogans on 844 advertisement requests.

In addition, we crawled the Twitter profile and timeline of the AdbyMe users who labeled Twitter as their main advertising medium. Data from Twitter was used to measure the influence of a user on OSNS, which will be elaborated with more detail in the next section. For 98% of these users, we collected all the tweets they wrote in 2012. The remaining 2% of the population represent those who generated more than 3,200 tweets in one year. Because Twitter API only allows one to collect up to 3,200 tweets per user, we were only able to partially collect the tweets written in 2012 for these heavy-users. For the heavy users, we make estimations based on these partial data, which will be explained in further detail in the following section. Analysis was performed on anonymized and aggregated data.

5. FEATURE DESCRIPTION AND EXTRACTION METHODOLOGY

In order to understand the factors affecting the performance of social advertisements, we study the content-related features and user-related features of social advertisements. Choice of features is motivated by the findings from previous studies as well as the following questions: Are OSNS users attracted to prize giveaways displayed on advertisements? Are they sensitive to celebrity endorsement? Do curiosity and sex-appealing elements in advertised contents instigate users to click on the advertisement? Does it make a difference who publishes the advertisement? In summary, the content-related features examined in this study include *sweepstakes and prize giveaways, celebrity endorsement, sexual appeals*, and *curiosity components*.

The user-related features we are interested in are social influence measures of a user within the network which include *indegree, retweet likelihood*, and *post count*. A previous study [6] suggests that indegree represents a user's popularity and directly indicates the size of audience. Retweet indicates the ability of a user to engage others in propagating the contents. Post counts indicate the extent to which a user is actively engaged in information sharing activities on OSNS. We expect these user influence measures to have an impact on the success of an advertisement, along with the content-related features. In the following subsections, we describe in detail the methods we used to extract these features from advertised contents and publishers.

SP: Sweepstakes & Prize Giveaways   CE: Celebrity Endorsement
CC: Curiosity Components   SA: Sexual Appeal

	SP	CE	CC	SA
SP	1**			
CE	-0.043*	1**		
CC	-0.124**	0.162**	1**	
SA	-0.155**	0.051**	0.368**	1**

Table 1: Phi Correlation Coefficient among Content-Related Features (*p<0.1, **p<0.01)

5.1 Content-Related Feature Extraction and Classification

We take a semi-automatic approach to extract content-related features from the advertised contents, or slogans. We first build keyword lists pertaining to each feature for automatic extraction and classification. For example, our list of keywords related to sweepstakes and prize giveaways feature includes the following keywords: "prize", "win", "contest", "sweepstakes", and many others. The keyword lists for sweepstakes and prize giveaways, and sexual appeals were constructed collectively by the members of this research team. For the celebrity endorsement feature, we crawl the names of popular individuals in 2012 from the people search ranking list offered by Nate[6]. Nate is one of the most widely used search engines/portals in Korea, and they provide the ranked list of most searched people names on a daily basis. People on this list are mostly well-known pop stars, athletes, or politicians, and the list well represents those who are at the center of attention during the specific time period.

Based on the keywords on these lists, each advertisement is automatically assigned a binary score for each feature through keyword matching. For instance, if an advertised slogan contains messages on prizes, but does not mention any names of famous figures, it will receive a score of 1 for sweepstakes and prize giveaways feature and 0 for celebrity endorsement feature.

Keyword matching can yield false positives and false negatives due to the limitation in keyword lists as well as ambiguity of natural language. We repeatedly selected a sample of slogans and manually double-checked the results to check the false hit rate, and made sure to improve the keyword lists so that false hit rate is less than 0.05 across all features.

Extracting the curiosity components from the slogans is more complicated. We classified a slogan as the one that contains a curiosity-component if 1) the slogan does not explicitly mention the name of the advertised product, or/and 2) the slogan triggers a viewer's need to obtain further information on the advertised product. Thus, instead of building a keyword list in the aforementioned fashion, we first automatically checked whether the slogans contain the name of the advertised product through keyword matching. Then, for the slogans that do not explicitly mention the product names, we manually checked if the slogan triggers a viewer's desire to know more about the product. Manual classification was based on the majority rule, in order to maintain objectivity in our classification decision.

61% of the entire slogans contains at least one of the four content-related features, and 16% contains more than two content-related features. In order to examine the unique-

---

[6]http://www.nate.com/

F: Number of Followers   R: Retweet Likelihood
P: Tweet Post Count

	F	R	P
F	1**		
R	-0.150**	1**	
P	-0.102**	0.145**	1**

Table 2: Pearson Correlation Coefficient am ong User-Related Features (p<0.01)**

ness of these features, we perform correlation analysis among the variables. We compute Phi coefficients [10] to measure the pair-wise associations among the binary variables, where 0 indicates no relationship. We observe weak correlations among the features, as shown in table 1. Curiosity component and sexual appeal exhibit a relatively stronger correlation, mainly due to the fact that many of the sexually appealing contents also do tend to trigger curiosity. However, we find it necessary to study both factors, since not every slogan with curiosity components contain sexually appealing contents, and each factor can hold different implications. Note that the correlations are statistically significant with the indicated p-values.

5.2 User-Related Feature Extraction

The user-related features observed in this work are indegree, retweet likelihood, and post counts. On Twitter, indegree of a user is simply denoted by the number of his/her followers, which can be collected using Twitter API. To measure retweet likelihood and post counts, we have collected the Twitter timeline of AdbyMe users. We counted the number of tweets each user has written in 2012, which denotes the post counts of a user. Instead of simply counting all the tweets a user has written since the creation of his/her Twitter account, we focus on those written in 2012, because it correctly represents how active a user was engaged in using OSNS during the time he/she participated in social advertising. For the heavy users who wrote more than 3,200 tweets in a year, we estimated the post count measure based on the partial data that was collected. In particular, we determined how many tweets they generated on average in a month, or in a week depending on the total quantity, then made an estimated count of the tweets they would have generated in 2012. Retweet likelihood is measured by the portion of total tweets originally written by a user that have spawned further retweets by other users. If a user has written 10 tweets and 7 of them were retweeted by the others, the user's retweet likelihood is 0.7.

Correlation analysis is an important step in validating if it is appropriate to study the effect of each feature as an independent variable. One may, for instance, assume that the number of followers of a user and his/her post count are strongly correlated, questioning the validity of independent variables. We perform correlation analysis among the user-related features to examine the uniqueness of the features.

Table 2 shows the Pearson coefficients for every pair of user-related features. Pearson coefficient ranges from -1 to +1, where ±1 indicates perfect agreement or disagreement, and 0 indicates no relationship. The features are shown to be weakly correlated. Correlations are statistically significant with the p-value less than 0.01.

In the following section, we examine the overall distribution of advertised slogans and advertising users, in terms of the number of clicks they received. We further perform in-depth analyses of the slogans and users with respect to the extracted features.

6. CLICK DISTRIBUTION OF SOCIAL ADVERTISEMENTS

We begin our study by describing the click distribution of advertisements that were published through AdbyMe in 2012. In total we have data for 79,765 slogans and 3,468 users. We want to understand how many clicks these slogans and users received. Note that through AdbyMe platform, a user can create multiple slogans and same slogans can be used by many different users. Thus, a click distribution of slogans is different from that of users; the former is an outcome of the content-related features regarding the advertisement while the latter is an outcome of the user-related features. We now describe both distributions in detail.

6.1 Click Distribution of Slogans

Figure 2 shows the distribution of clicks on the set of slogans written in 2012. The histogram on the left show frequency, and on the right is a cumulative frequency graph. In these graphical representations, we only consider the slogans that received at least 1 click, which leaves us with 72,738 slogans. Note that the y-axis is in log scale, and as expected, we can observe the unevenly distributed clicks with a heavy-tail. The distribution shows that there are many slogans that receive only a few clicks, and a few slogans that received many clicks.

A slogan with the best advertisement performance received 13,318 clicks. We did not plot those that received more than 750 clicks on the histogram for a better visualization of the long tail effect; the rest not shown on the graph accounts for top 1% of the entire sample. Only 726 out of the 72,738 slogans received more than 750 clicks. Slogans with the top 10% performance rate receive more than 81 clicks, and top 20% receive more than 32 clicks. Approximately half of the slogans receive more than 5 clicks and half gets less than or equal to 5 clicks.

6.2 Click Distribution of Users

We take the same approach to study the click distribution of users. Once again, we only consider the users who received at least 1 click from their publications of advertisements, which are 2,443 users. As illustrated in Figure 3, users also exhibit a long-tailed distribution pattern; many users receive only a few clicks, while a few users receive many clicks. A user with the best advertisement performance received in total of 204,324 clicks. The users with the top 1% advertisement performance receive more than 27,000 clicks. The top 10% receive more than 1,250 clicks, and the top 20% receive more than 350 clicks. Approximately half of the users received more than 7 clicks.

The number of slogans that a user published on Twitter within a year varied from 1 to 297. It also follows a long-tail distribution with the median value of 10 publications. Note that we only take into consideration the users who received at least 1 click on their advertisement.

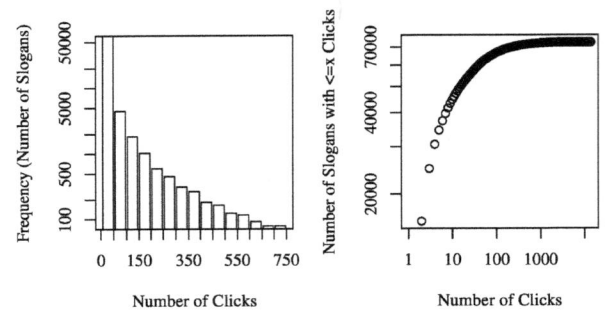

Figure 2: Overall Click Distribution of Slogans (left: frequency, right: cumulative frequency)

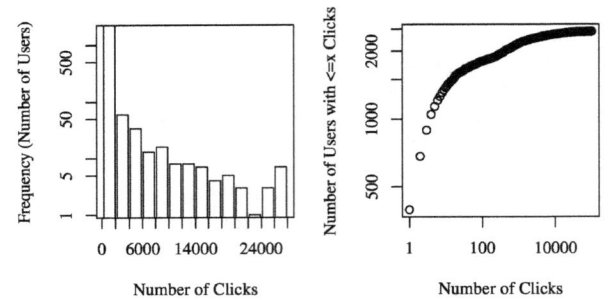

Figure 3: Overall Click Distribution of Users (left: frequency, right: cumulative frequency)

7. WHICH FACTORS IMPACT SOCIAL ADVERTISING PERFORMANCE?

We now pay attention to the content-related features and user-related features that we extracted and study how these features affect the number of clicks on advertisements.

Figure 4 shows the advertisement performance of slogans in the presence and absence of each of the four content-related features: sweepstakes and prize giveaways, celebrity endorsement, sexual appeals, and curiosity components. Because the clicks are non-normally distributed, we used Mann-Whitney U Test [16], a non-parametric statistical hypothesis test, to evaluate the differences in clicks. Note that the y-axis is in log-scale and the outliers are eliminated. The test results showed that there are statistically significant differences in the advertisement performance of slogans. Surprisingly, mentioning of sweepstakes and prize giveaways in the advertisement slogan resulted in a poorer advertising performance ($p < 0.01$), on the contrary to a common notion. Celebrity endorsement feature was found to be an effective way of improving the performance ($p < 0.05$), although the effect was not dramatic. The features that strongly affected the clicks were sexual appeal and curiosity component; the results showed that the advertising performance of slogans with and without these features differed by an order of magnitude ($p < 0.01$). Our results imply that SNS users are interested in acquiring new information, which is consistent with the previous finding that the main purpose of using microblogs is to communicate and to share information. The reason why prizes and giveaway messages resulted in poorer

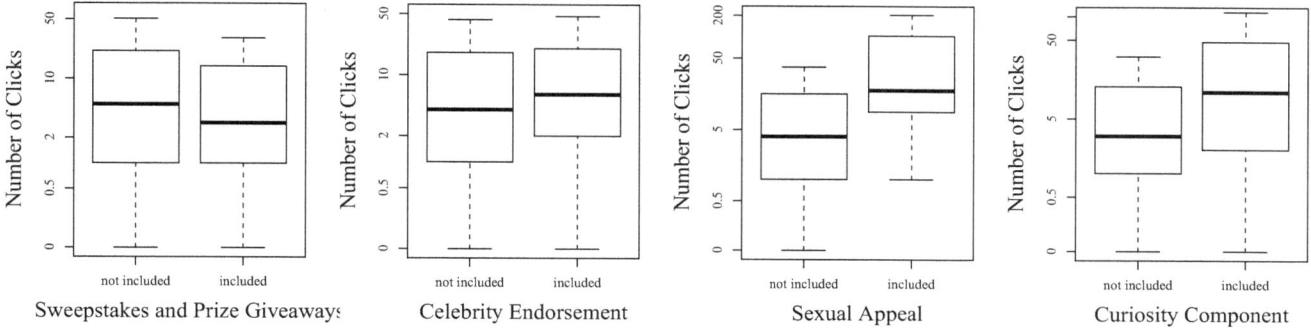

Figure 4: Click Distribution of Slogans with respect to Content-related Features

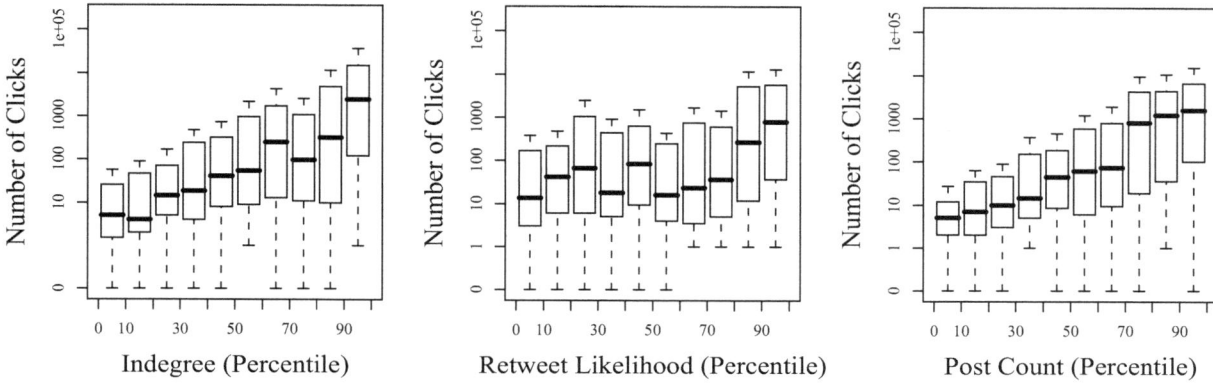

Figure 5: Click Distribution of Users with respect to User-related Features

advertisement performance may be attributed to overexposure to online phishing scams [5], while further analysis is required to understand the exact cause.

Figure 5 shows the advertisement performance of users with respect to their social influence measure on the network. We first sort the users by each measure and determine their percentile ranks, since percentile ranks are a good way of showing relative standing of an individual in a population. We then determine at which percentile range they fall into, and group the users accordingly; those at the higher percentile range indicate the ones with relatively higher indegree, retweet likelihood, and post counts.

We can immediately notice the growth in the number of clicks as the indegree and post counts go up, although slight fluctuations can be observed along the way. Overall, we see the ascending trend in clicks with respect to indegree, which indicates that users with the large target audience are likely to yield many clicks when they post advertisements. This serves as actual evidence that indegree can measure the influence of a user on a social network; we have verified that having a larger audience does indeed lead to a larger response rate in the social advertising setting. We also find that the total post counts of a user, which can represent how actively they are engaged on OSNS, is a strong indicator of their success as social publishers. We see a large gap between the number of clicks received by the top 30% of the users and the rest, in terms of post counts. At this transition, the number of clicks differed by more than an order of

magnitude. One may question whether the more number of tweets a user posts on Twitter, the more number of advertisements he/she publishes on Twitter, which can eventually affect the total number of clicks. However, the two are found to be rather weakly correlated ($r^2 = 0.19$). Furthermore, we do not find a strong correlation between the number of total advertisement publications and the total number of clicks received by a user ($r^2 = 0.21$), which indicates that it does not necessarily mean that the more advertisements a user posts, the more likely for them to received many clicks.

For retweet likelihood, we cannot find a noticeable ascending pattern up until the 80th percentile is reached. We detect a great leap in the average, or median, for those with percentile rank greater than 80, but we do not find the evidence showing that the higher the likelihood of diffusion, the higher the advertising performance. It tells us that a user's ability to prompt audience to share his/her contents is not strongly correlated with his/her ability to arouse the interests of the audience to click on the links on their contents. This also implies that the audience's interests in further sharing the content are not consistent with their interests in viewing the content.

8. CHARACTERIZING THE TOP ADVERTISEMENTS

The click distributions of advertisements showed that there are few slogans and users that receive many clicks from the

Rank	No. of Clicks	Slogan (Translated)	SP	CE	SA	CC
1	9,800	Everyone's talking about him on the messenger these days!	N	N	N	Y
2	5,804	A hot girl on the street told me to try "Clinical Pro-plex" - I asked her what it is, and this is what she showed me! lol	N	N	Y	Y
3	5,572	A secret that only Korea wasn't aware of... Gives me chills!	N	N	N	Y
4	5,286	Wow! Vega Racer2 is insane! hope iPhone5 is as good as this...	N	N	N	N
5	5,101	Shocking! A European secret that only South Korea didn't know for 30 years..	N	N	N	Y
6	4,981	never imagined this would be a true story.. brilliant!	N	N	N	Y
7	4,947	Recommended by my friends - "Sometimes Sane"... Really enjoyed this book :)	N	N	N	N
8	4,941	Sora Kang is gorgeous even when she's eating Tacos! :)	N	N	N	N
9	4,900	Vega was waiting for the right moment to compete against iPad3(New iPad)! Amazing spec!!	N	N	Y	Y
10	4,661	How can this sexy dancing queen be the wife of a Seoul city mayor?! I envy her style!	N	N	N	Y

SP: Sweepstakes & Prize Giveaways CE: Celebrity Endorsement CC: Curiosity Components SA: Sexual Appeal

Table 3: Top 10 Slogans with High Advertising Performance

Rank	No. of Clicks	Indegree	Post Count	Retweet Likelihood
1	204,324	284,484 (99.68%)	3,530 (77.67%)	4.84 (63.59%)
2	182,246	331,711 (99.79%)	8,268 (91.22%)	53.60 (97.38%)
3	102,498	243,122 (99.25%)	3,687 (78.83%)	60.19 (98.12%)
4	83,847	145,485 (97.98%)	83,328 (98.94%)	21.10 (87.53)
5	76,447	268,508 (99.47%)	2,880 (71.53%)	31.05 (92.14%)
6	68,317	215,309 (99.04%)	4,404 (83.60%)	41.65 (96.00%)
7	65,896	16,264 (82.85%)	5,566 (87.20%)	4.69 (61.97%)
8	65,652	35,970 (91.16%)	13,128 (94.39%)	62.20 (98.37%)
9	62,052	37,788 (91.91%)	9,252 (92.17%)	79.59 (99.00%)
10	41,395	18,247 (83.49%)	3,500 (77.46%)	1.82 (36.28%)

Table 4: Top 10 Users with High Advertising Performance

audience. These slogans and users can be denoted as "effective" advertisement contents and publishers. In this section, we focus on these effective advertisements at the upper right end of the distribution, and explore the characteristics associated with the effective advertisements. Slogans and users who have been ranked among the top 10 for achieving the highest advertising performance have been selected for a closer look.

Table 3 shows the list of top 10 slogans with the highest overall number of clicks. Surprisingly, none of the top 10 slogans has explicit mentions of prizes or celebrities, which contradicts a common belief that adding prize promotions and celebrities to an advertisement motivates the users to click on the advertisement. The most common content-related feature shared by the top slogans was the curiosity component feature, followed by the sexual-appeal feature. Furthermore, it is interesting to note that more than half of the top 10 slogans never actually mention the name of the product, and leaves audience with no clue of what they were advertising.

Table 4 shows the list of top 10 users who received the most clicks. Users on the list ranked high in terms of indegree; half out of the top 10 was placed within the top 1% of the indegree percentile rank, and 8 of them on the list were ranked within top 10%. The finding indicates that the publishers with high advertising performance are composed of users with a large target audience. We also find that the post counts of the top 10 publishers are relatively

Slogan Click Percentile	Slogan Count	Slogan by Top 1% Users	Slogan by Top 10% Users
0-10%	67,851	5,111 (7.53%)	22,351 (32.94%)
10-20%	2,364	694 (29.35%)	1,580 (66.83%)
20-30%	888	270 (30.40%)	569 (64.07%)
30-40%	470	162 (34.46%)	299 (63.61%)
40-50%	305	124 (40.65%)	202 (66.22%)
50-60%	233	102 (43.77%)	162 (69.52%)
60-70%	196	84 (42.85%)	127 (64.79%)
70-80%	158	73 (46.20%)	107 (67.72%)
80-90%	139	69 (49.64%)	96 (69.06%)
90-100%	133	87 (65.41%)	102 (76.69%)

Table 5: Overlap between Top Slogans & Top Users

high. Nearly half of them were within top 10% post count percentile rank, and all but one user on the top 10 list falls in the upper quartile. Retweet likelihood seems high at a first glance, for many of them falls within the top 10% percentile. However, a closer look at the list reveals that there is a high variability within the top 10 list; 2 of them have 60% percentile rank and one of them falls within the 30% percentile rank.

Observations on the top slogans and users are in accordance with the findings from the previous section, where high indegree and post counts were found to be good indicators of a successful social advertisement publisher. These observations lead to another question: are any relationships between the slogans and users? In other words, how much of top slogans are composed by top users? To measure the degree of top user involvement, we first group the slogans by the click percentile rank then count how many slogans in each group were written by the top users. Table 5 shows what portion of the slogans at each percentile range involves users with top 1% and top 10% advertising performance. The result clearly shows that the higher the percentile rank of slogan clicks, the higher the degree of top user involvement. The growing pattern is even more distinct for the top 1% users. We also find that the top users write a fairly large amount of slogans overall, which relates to the idea that effective social advertisers tend to have high post counts as shown in Figure 5. This indicates that successful advertisers are active in publishing slogans through their social networks. Our findings imply that user influence on the network plays a significant role in social advertising, suggesting that analyzing the content-related features need to be supplemented by user influence analysis.

9. DISCUSSION

The key observations of this paper are twofold: first, social advertising performance is strongly influenced by the characteristic of its publisher. We show that social advertising performance increases as the users' indegree and post counts increase, indicating that those with larger target audiences are more likely to yield successful advertising results than the others, and those who are actively engaged in social activities on OSNS generally perform better in social advertising. This reveals the truly "social" nature of social advertising; the users' social standings and activity level on the network are significant indicators of the success of the advertisement.

Second, content analysis results demonstrate that curiosity component is the main factor associated with the successful social advertisements. A majority of the top slogans did not explicitly state what it was trying to sell, and only contained slight hints or descriptions of the product. Mentions of prizes or celebrity endorsement, which are traditionally believed to be effective promotional techniques, were not shown to produce significant improvements in social advertising performance. Our findings illustrate that social advertisements can effectively capture the attention of users, even without specific references to the advertised products. Being able to capture the attention of an audience is an important preliminary step in advertising; the AIDA marketing model explains that four stages in advertising include Attention, Interest, Desire, and Action [24]. Our study on clicks on advertisements is a direct measure of "Attention" of the audience, and it tells us that social advertising can help businesses in taking the first important step in achieving their marketing goal.

We have studied the social advertising performance in terms of "attention", and another interesting issue worth exploring is on understanding the audience's "attitude" towards social advertisements. Marketing reports [5] show that too much advertisements can overwhelm the audience and reduce marketing effectiveness. This leads to the idea that users who post too many advertisements on their social network may be perceived as spammers. Interestingly, our observation from Table 5 showed that the top users were overall actively engaged in publishing top slogans. A possible explanation behind why these active users show high advertising performance may be due to the fact that they tend to post many non-advertisements as well. An in-depth analysis of the relationship between tweet post counts and advertisement post counts and how they affect the advertising performance would yield useful insights in understanding the perceived attitude towards the advertisements.

Our study is based on a single dataset from AdbyMe, in which majority of the users are Koreans who created slogans in Korean language. Thereby, one must note that, to a certain extent, there can exist cultural bias within our analyses results. For example, spam advertisements in Korea are oftentimes in the form of flashy animated banners with sweepstakes messages, which may have affected the advertisement performance. Although it is true that cultural factors cannot be ignored, we must also take into account that our study is reproducible in different cultural contexts, since existing social advertising platforms worldwide are comparable in their functions and structures. Performing cross-cultural comparisons and studying the cultural differences in perception of social advertisements would be an interesting research direction for the future.

We would also like to further examine other features not considered in this work. As a part of our study, we observed that half of the top 10 slogans were about the newly released movies. We want to study the effectiveness of social advertising across different product categories, which can lead to a better understanding of the nature of social adverting and OSNS usage. It would also be interesting to observe if there is any relationship between a user's area of interests or expertise and the contents they publish through social media advertising platform. Furthermore, our analysis on the content-related and user-related features opens up the possibility of generating models that can predict the success of an advertisement or building recommendation algorithms in the context of social advertising.

10. CONCLUSION

In this research, we study the factors that may affect the number of clicks on advertisements being published on online social networking services. We collect real-world data from a popular social media advertising platform, and perform content analysis as well as user influence analysis on the advertisement data. Surprisingly, some of the promotional techniques widely used in traditional advertising media were found to be not as effective in a social advertising setting. We also find that social advertising performance increases as the user's indegree and level of activity increase. This implies that user influence on the network plays a significant role in social advertising, suggesting that both the advertised contents and the advertising publisher need to be considered to understand the social advertising phenomenon.

11. ACKNOWLEDGEMENTS

This research was supported in part by the National Research Foundation of Korea grant funded by the Korean government (MSIP) (No. NRF-2009-0081365), and in part by WCU (World Class University) program under the National Research Foundation of Korea and funded byÂăthe Ministry of Eduation, Science and Technology of Korea (No. R31-30007).

12. REFERENCES

[1] K. Ali and M. Scarr. Robust methodologies for modeling web click distributions. In *Proceedings of the 16th international conference on World Wide Web*, WWW '07, pages 511–520, New York, NY, USA, 2007. ACM.

[2] E. Bakshy, D. Eckles, R. Yan, and I. Rosenn. Social influence in social advertising: evidence from field experiments. In *ACM Conference on Electronic Commerce*, 2012.

[3] E. Bakshy, J. M. Hofman, W. A. Mason, and D. J. Watts. Everyone's an influencer: quantifying influence on twitter. In *Proceedings of the fourth ACM international conference on Web search and data mining*, WSDM '11, pages 65–74, New York, NY, USA, 2011. ACM.

[4] E. Bakshy, I. Rosenn, C. Marlow, and L. Adamic. The role of social networks in information diffusion. In *Proceedings of the 21st international conference on World Wide Web*, WWW '12, pages 519–528, New York, NY, USA, 2012. ACM.

[5] BurstMedia. The perils of ad clutter, December 2008.

[6] M. Cha, H. Haddadi, F. Benevenuto, and P. K. Gummadi. Measuring user influence in twitter: The million follower fallacy. In *Proceedings of the Fourth International Conference on Weblogs and Social Media, ICWSM 2010, Washington, DC, USA, May 23-26, 2010*, 2010.

[7] M. Cha, H. Kwak, P. Rodriguez, Y.-Y. Ahn, and S. Moon. I tube, you tube, everybody tubes: analyzing the world's largest user generated content video system. In *Proceedings of the 7th ACM SIGCOMM conference on Internet measurement*, IMC '07, pages 1–14, New York, NY, USA, 2007. ACM.

[8] A. Clauset, C. R. Shalizi, and M. E. J. Newman. Power-law distributions in empirical data. *SIAM Reviews*, June 2007.

[9] ComScore. It's a social world. top 10 need-to-knows about social networking and where it's headed. Technical report, ComScore, 2011.

[10] H. Cramer. *Mathematical Methods of Statistics*. Princeton landmarks in mathematics and physics. Princeton University Press, 1999.

[11] D. R. Fortin and R. R. Dholakia. Interactivity and vividness effects on social presence and involvement with a web-based advertisement. *Journal of Business Research*, 58(3):387–396, 2005.

[12] C. F. Hofacker and J. Murphy. World wide web banner advertisement copy testing. *European Journal of Marketing*, 32(7-8), 1998.

[13] A. Kalra and M. Shi. Consumer Value-Maximizing Sweepstakes and Contests. *Journal of Marketing Research*, 47:287–300, 2010.

[14] M. A. Kamins, M. J. Brand, S. A. Hoeke, and J. C. Moe. Two-sided versus one-sided celebrity endorsements: The impact on advertising effectiveness and credibility. *Journal of Advertising*, 18(2):pp. 4–10, 1989.

[15] D. Kesmodel. Brand marketers return to the web, driving new growth in display ads. *The Wall Street Journal*, May 2006. May 10.

[16] H. B. Mann and W. D. R. On a test of whether one of two random variables is stochastically larger than the other. *Annals of Mathematical Statistics*, 18(1):50–60, 1947.

[17] S. Menon and D. Soman. Managing the power of curiosity for effective Web advertising strategies. *Journal of Advertising*, 31(3):1–14, 2002.

[18] A. A. Mitchell. The effect of verbal and visual components of advertisements on brand attitudes and attitude toward the advertisement. *Journal of Consumer Research*, 13(1):12, 1986.

[19] R. Ohanian. The impact of celebrity spokespersonsÊij perceived image on consumers' intention to purchase. *Journal of Advertising Research*, 31(1):46–54, 1991.

[20] J. Parsons, K. Gallagher, and K. D. Foster. Messages in the medium: An experimental investigation of web advertising effectiveness and attitudes toward web content. In *Proceedings of the 33rd Hawaii International Conference on System Sciences*.

[21] T. Reichert. Sex in advertising research: a review of content, effects, and functions of sexual information in consumer advertising. *Annual Review of Sex Research*, 13:241–273, 2002.

[22] D. Silvera and B. Austad. Factors predicting the effectiveness of celebrity endorsement advertisements. *European Journal of Marketing*, 38(11/12):1509–1526, 2004.

[23] S. N. Singh and C. A. Cole. Advertising copy testing in print media. *Current Issues and Research in Advertising*, 11(1-2):215–284, 1988.

[24] E. K. Strong Jr. Theories of selling. *Journal of applied psychology*, 9(1):75, 1925.

[25] R. Vezina and O. Paul. Provocation in advertising: A conceptualization and an empirical assessment. *International Journal of Research in Marketing*, 14(2):177 – 192, 1997.

[26] C. Y. Yoo and K. Kim. Processing of animation in online banner advertising: The roles of cognitive and emotional responses. *Journal of Interactive Marketing*, 19(4):18 – 34, 2005.

Are Trending Topics Useful for Marketing?

Visibility of Trending Topics vs Traditional Advertisement

Juan Miguel Carrascosa
Universidad Carlos III de
Madrid
jcarrasc@it.uc3m.es

Roberto González
Universidad Carlos III de
Madrid
rgonza1@it.uc3m.es

Rubén Cuevas
Universidad Carlos III de
Madrid
rcuevas@it.uc3m.es

Arturo Azcorra
Universidad Carlos III de
Madrid
Institute IMDEA Networks
azcorra@it.uc3m.es

ABSTRACT

Trending Topics seem to be a powerful tool to be used in marketing and advertisement contexts, however there is not any rigorous analysis that demonstrates this. In this paper we present a first effort in this direction. We use a dataset including more than 110K Trending Topics from 35 countries collected over a period of 3 months as basis to characterize the visibility offered by Local Trending Topics. Furthermore, by using metrics that rely on the exposure time of Trending Topics and the penetration of Twitter, we compare the visibility provided by Trending Topics and traditional advertisement channels such as newspapers' ads or radio-stations' commercials for several countries. Our study confirms that Trending Topics offer a comparable visibility to the aforementioned traditional advertisement channels in those countries where we have conducted our comparison study. Then, we conclude that Trending Topics can be useful in marketing and advertisement contexts at least in the analyzed countries.

Categories and Subject Descriptors

[**Information Systems**]: *Social Advertising*; [**Networks**]: *Online Social Networks*; [**Human-Centered Computing**]: *Social Media*.

Keywords

Trending Topics; Twitter; Marketing; Visibility

1. INTRODUCTION

Online Social Networks (OSNs) in general and Twitter in particular have changed the way in which people communicate, but also have a significant impact on the public image

of celebrities or politicians and are being used by important companies with marketing and/or advertisement purposes [25]. In particular, Twitter has its own business web page [9] and marketing on Twitter has become a business itself [20, 21]. Twitter offers a functionality, that among other uses, is of high relevance in this context named *Trending Topics* (TTs) which are officially described as: *"the hottest emerging topics (or the "most breaking" breaking news), rather than the most popular ones"* [19]. As acknowledged by experts in the field of marketing, surprise is one of the most powerful marketing tools [6]. TTs hold by definition this surprise component and marketing experts have been exploiting it. For instance, TV and radio-station shows have started to announce *hashtags*[1] so that all tweets regarding the show can be aggregated using a hashtag which eventually may become Trending Topic. If that happens it is reported as a big success. Trending Topics have been also used with marketing purposes in politics. For instance, in the last public debate for the Spanish presidency in 2011, one of the candidates became TT as a result of an orchestrated operation by his party supporters. This was used as an unequivocal proof by his party and by several media that he had won the debate [24]. In addition, some social movements such as the "occupy" movements augmented their visibility among the population after becoming TT [14]. Furthermore, the commercial interest of Trending Topics for companies is reflected by the *Promoted Trending Topics* service offered by Twitter [12]. These are a special type of TTs that can be purchased in slots of 24 hours for around $200K [22]. This service is regularly used by companies in the context of advertisement and marketing campaigns.

Finally, another symptom of the relevance of TTs is the recent movement made by Facebook to implement its own Trending Topics service that is currently available for users in United States [4].

However, to the best of the authors knowledge, this (seemingly) common idea that TTs are a useful tool in marketing contexts is not supported by any scientific or technical work. We believe that a solid scientific basis is required to allow experts in different disciplines to make informed decisions regarding the actual impact that TTs may have in market-

---

[1] A hashtag is a special type of word that starts by the symbol #. It is a common practice that people tweeting about a common topic use a common hashtag to identify it.

ing, advertisement, and related contexts. This paper constitutes a first effort in that direction in which we perform a thorough analysis of the actual *visibility* provided by TTs.

In particular, we study the visibility of World Wide Trending Topics (WW-TT), but more interestingly from the point of view of marketing[2] we analyze the visibility provided by the Local Trending Topics (Local-TT) from 35 different countries. Toward this end, we first define and implement a high resolution measurement methodology that leverages the Twitter API to collect the list of TTs with a resolution of dozens of seconds. Using this methodology we have collected 3 WW-TTs datasets between Sep 2011 and May 2013 that all together include more than 80K TTs. Using these datasets we demonstrate that the resolution provided by our methodology enables the detection of any change in the visibility of TTs. Identifying these changes is of high importance in the aforementioned marketing or advertisement contexts.

Furthermore, we use the same methodology to collect a dataset including more than 110K Local-TTs from 35 countries over a period of 3 months in 2013. We use this dataset to compare the visibility offered by TTs across these countries. In order to perform a complete comparison we define three metrics. The first one helps us to compare the *net-visibility* (i.e., the actual time of exposure) of TTs whereas the other two metrics named *potential-visibility* and *potential-online-visibility* take into account the penetration of Twitter among the population and the population with Internet access in a country, respectively. These metrics give an insight on the fraction of the population (or "online population") that the Local TTs are able to reach in a country. In addition, we use the aforementioned metrics to compare the visibility offered by TTs and traditional advertisement channels such as newspapers' ads and radio-stations' commercials for several countries with rather different demographics and cultural backgrounds. Finally, we analyze the variability offered by TTs visibility within a country and, for 3 selected countries (Ireland, New Zealand and UK) we present a more detailed analysis of the visibility: (*i*) using a novel and efficient methodology we classify the TTs of a country in different semantic categories and study which categories are more likely to become TT and which ones offer higher visibility periods; (*ii*) we study whether TTs visibility follows a diurnal pattern as Internet traffic [40] and many other online services do.

In summary, the main contributions of this paper are twofold: First, a measurement methodology that allows to monitor the visibility of TTs and its evolution over time. Second, a methodology to properly characterize the visibility of TTs within a country that permits to perform meaningful comparative analyses with other countries or with traditional advertisement channels. The utilization of these methodologies led to the following insights:
- Our results show that the median visibility of TTs is higher than that offered by radio-stations' commercials and newspapers' ads in 4 and 9 out of 10 studied countries, respectively. Hence, we conclude that (at least for the studied countries) TTs can be considered a useful tool in marketing and advertisement contexts.
- However, there is a strong variability on the visibility that TTs offer in different countries and also across Trending

[2]Marketing experts are interested on studying different regional markets.

Topics within a country. In addition, the penetration of traditional media and TTs varies substantially accross countries. Therefore, we cannot generalize the previous conclusion for all the TTs in every country.
- Our detailed examination of few countries reveals that "Hashtags" present a higher visibility than other "non-hashtaged" TTs related to "Sport Events" or "Celebrities". Furthermore, the exposure time of TTs presents a clear diurnal pattern for most of the studied countries. Specifically, TTs provide longer visibility periods during night hours when fewer users are connected.

The rest of the paper is organized as follows: Section 2 describes our measurement methodology and our datasets. Section 3 details our methodology to evaluate the visibility of TTs within a country while we devote Section 4 to put in context our analysis doing a comparison with traditional advertisement channels. Section 5 dissects the visibility of TTs within a country from a semantic perspective. Finally, we summarize the related work in Section 6 and Section 7 concludes the paper.

2. MEASUREMENT METHODOLOGY, METRICS AND DATASETS

In this section we describe our large scale measurement methodology to collect information for thousands of Trending Topics over a period of several months. Additionally, we define temporal metrics to be used in the rest of the paper. We also discuss the basic filtering techniques applied to produce meaningful datasets and finally we summarize the datasets used to conduct our analysis.

2.1 Measurement Methodology

Twitter provides different APIs to access the information available in the system [17]. In our methodology we leverage two of these APIs, namely the REST and Streaming APIs. We query the REST API to obtain the list of 10 TTs at a given instant and for a given location (e.g., a country). Since the maximum number of queries allowed by Twitter to the REST API is 150 per hour, we are able to collect the list of TTs every 24 seconds for a given location. This guarantees a fine grain time resolution in the sampling of the Trending Topics list. Furthermore, we query the Streaming API to retrieve the tweets associated to a given Trending Topic. The Streaming API offers a best effort service in which the system provides as many tweets as it can (depending on the load) including the term (i.e., Trending Topic) requested in the query. In particular, our tool uses the Streaming API to collect tweets associated to the 20 most recent TTs at any moment.

Using multiple instances of our tool we are able to collect data from World Wide (WW) Trending Topics as well as Local Trending Topics from 35 different countries in parallel.

2.2 Temporal Metrics

The visibility of a TT is basically defined by the time that it is shown to users that we refer to as *exposure time*. We use the following meaningful metrics to capture the temporal characteristics of TTs:
- *number of active periods*, this metric counts the number of times that a given topic has become TT. We refer to each one of those active periods as an *instance*.

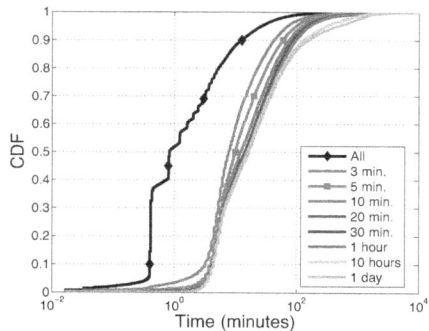

Figure 1: *Active time* **of WW-TT instances without oscillations filtering (***All***) and with oscilations filtering (filtering times from 3 min to 1 day).**

- *total active time*, this metric captures the total time a topic has been TT across one or multiple active periods, i.e., the total exposure time.
- *age*, this metric measures the total time between the first instant and the last instant a topic is a TT across one or multiple active periods.

To clarify these concepts, let us consider the following simple example: a topic that has been Trending Topic on Jan 1st 2013 between 9 AM and 9:30 AM, on Jan 1st between 6 PM and 6:20 PM and on Jan 2nd between 8:50 AM and 9 AM. Then, the *number of active periods* for this Trending Topic is 3 (or in other words this TT has 3 associated instances), the *age* is 24 hours (from 9 AM Jan 1st to 9 AM Jan 2nd) and the *total active time* is 60 min (30, 20 and 10 minutes in the first, second and third active periods, respectively).

Previous studies have considered the volume of tweets [26, 35] to analyze TTs using the Search or the Streaming API. Although, this metric does not capture the visibility of TTs as well as those presented above, it could be an interesting complementary metric for our study. Unfortunately, as demonstrated by Morstatter et al. [38], the volume of tweets obtained from the Streaming API is not a reliable metric. In particular, that study shows that due to the best effort nature of the Streaming API in those peak hours where the number of tweets associated to a topic is higher the API provides the lower number of tweets[3]. In short, using the volume of tweets as a metric may lead to wrong results and thus we do not use it for our analysis.

2.3 Data Filtering

As described before, our methodology allows to gather the list of the 10 TTs for a given location (e.g., WW or Local TTs for a country) every 24 seconds. Unexpectedly, there is a high variability in the composition of this list in a time scale of few minutes (or even seconds). We conjecture that this high variability is due to those topics that are ranked by Twitter Trending Topics selection algorithm around the 10th position that enter and leave the Top 10 list frequently. The curve labeled as *"All"* in Figure 1 shows the distribution of the *active time* for each WW-TT instance in our dataset.

---

[3]Note that this observation also applies to the search API since it provides a subset of the tweets provided by the Streaming API [23].

	Period	TT Instances	Unique TTs
WW-TT-2011	09/07/2011 - 11/30/2011	31251	13964
WW-TT-2012	12/01/2011 - 02/25/2012	80856	43985
WW-TT-2013	02/20/2013 - 05/20/2013	67221	29326
Local-TT-2013	02/20/2013 - 05/20/2013	713012	112196

Table 1: Basic statistics of Datasets.

We observe that half of the instances present an *active time* lower than 1 minute. Therefore, the Trending Topics selection algorithm works in intervals of seconds. Note that previous works considered that the list of TTs was updated in intervals of 5 minutes [35] or 20 minutes [26].

This real time selection of TTs produces a phenomenon that we refer to as *oscillations*. This occurs when a topic enters and leaves the Trending Topic list several times in a short period of time (e.g., a few minutes). However, *oscillations* are unlikely to be observed by users since neither the web interface of Twitter nor Twitter API-based applications refresh the Trending Topic information as frequently as our measurement tool. Therefore, in order to better approximate the user experience we would like to process the collected data in order to filter these short-term *oscillations*. For this purpose, we consider that a topic that presents one or more *oscillations* within a period of X minutes has been a Trending Topic during the whole X minutes period. Figure 1 shows the CDF of the *active time* of single instances of TTs after applying the described technique for X = 3, 5, 10, 20, 30, 60, 600 and 1440 minutes. The result suggests that a value of X = 5 min suffices to eliminate most of the short-term *oscillations* (i.e., those in the order of seconds or few minutes) and do not merge those long-term *oscillations* (i.e., those in the order of tens of minutes). Therefore, we filter out the *oscillations* using this value. We have repeated the experiments described along the paper with other values of X (3 and 7 minutes) obtaining similar results.

2.4 Datasets

Using the measurement methodology and data filtering technique described in this section we collected the following datasets:

WW-TT: This dataset is formed by 3 traces including all the WW-TTs in 3 different periods of approximately 3 months each.

Local-TT: This dataset was collected in parallel to our most recent WW-TT trace. It includes the Local Trending Topics for 35 countries over a period of 3 months.

The specific dates of data collection along with the number of TTs included in each trace are shown in Table 1.

2.5 Accuracy of the measurement methodology

The final goal of our measurement methodology is to accurately collect the visibility offered by TTs at any moment, expressed through the previously defined temporal metrics. Hence, the proposed methodology should be able to discover any change on the visibility of TTs.

Figure 2 presents the distribution of the number of active periods, total active time and age across TTs within our three Worldwide datasets. We observe that TTs within WW-TT-2012 and WW-TT-2013 show a similar visibility that is significantly different from that shown by TTs within WW-TT-2011. In particular, Figure 2(a) reveals that the

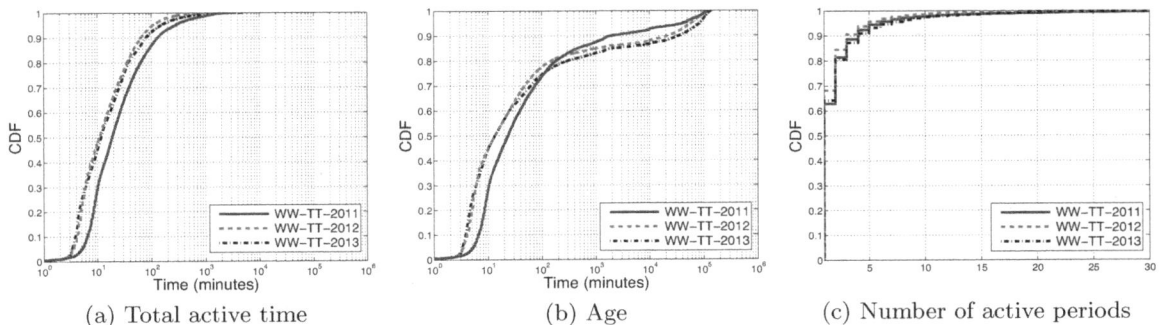

| (a) Total active time | (b) Age | (c) Number of active periods |

Figure 2: CDF of the temporal metrics of TTs within our WW-TT datasets.

median value for the total active time halves, from 20 to 10 minutes, between WW-TT-2011 and WW-TT-2012 and then remains stable in WW-TT-2013. This result suggests that the TTs selection algorithm was modified to severely reduce the visibility of TTs in December 2011, most likely during the large system upgrade process carried out by Twitter on that month [18]. However, to the best of the authors knowledge, this modification on the Trending Topics selection mechanism was not publicly announced by Twitter despite the implications that it might have.

In order to corroborate the previous observation, we have calculated the distribution of the total active time for each individual month in our Worldwide datasets but December 2011 (for being the month where the modification took place) and performed a Kolmogorov-Smirnov test [37] for each pair of distributions. The obtained results show that the distributions of Sep'11, Oct'11 and Nov'11 are similar between them and so are the distributions of Jan'12, Feb'12 and those from 2013. Specifically, the parameter K of the test varies between 0.06 and 0.15 in all cases. However, when we compare any of the first three months to any of the other months the Kolmogorov-Smirnov test concludes that the distributions are significantly different, in particular, K varies between 0.27 and 0.32.

Moreover, Figure 2(b) shows the distribution of TTs age for our three WW-TT datasets. Again, we observe that the distribution for this metric is similar for WW-TT-2012 and WW-TT-2013 and different from WW-TT-2011. This confirms the reported change in TTs visibility. In particular, the modification in the TTs selection algorithm in Dec 2011 yielded around 80% of TTs (i.e., those that have one or two close active periods) to present a lower age in our WW-TT-2012 and WW-TT-2013 than in the WW-TT-2011 dataset. However, this trend is reversed for the 20% TTs presenting a longer Age (i.e., those with several associated active periods). This suggests that the TTs selection algorithm implemented since Dec 2011, in addition to shorten the active time of TTs instances, also requires that the period of time with a relative reduced volume of tweets for a topic to become TT again to be longer. It is worth to mention that we have performed equivalent Kolmogorov-Smirnov tests for this metric as for the total active time obtaining similar results.

Finally, Figure 2(c) shows the distribution of the number of active periods (or instances) for our WW-TT datasets. The results indicate that this distribution is similar for the three datasets. Then, the modification of TTs selection al-

gorithm in Dec 2011 has not affected the ability of TTs to achieve this status multiple times, however as noted before the time between TTs instances has increased.

In summary, the results presented in this subsection confirm that the proposed measurement methodology is capable of accurately capture the visibility associated to TTs as well as identifying any change it may suffer along time.

3. METHODOLOGY TO CHARACTERIZE THE VISIBILITY OF LOCAL TTS

In this section we present a methodology to characterize the visibility of Local TTs in a country and compare it with that offered by TTs in other countries. For this purpose we define three meaningful metrics named *net-visibility*, *potential-visibility* and *potential-online-visibility*.

3.1 A first look at TTs visibility within a country

Let us use the temporal metrics defined in Section 2.2 to make a first comparison of the visibility granted by TTs across different countries.

Figure 3 shows the distribution of the *total active time* for TTs in each one of the 35 countries of our Local-TT-2013 dataset. Each distribution is represented in the form of a boxplot where the box shows the 25, 50 and 75 percentiles of the distribution and the whiskers indicate the 5 and 95 percentiles, respectively. Note that any boxplot used in the rest of the paper presents this same information unless otherwise stated.

We observe that there is an important variability in the *total active time* for the TTs within a country. We will address this issue in Section 5. Of more interest for this section is the significant difference among the distribution of *total active time* for different countries[4]. In particular, the median value of the *total active time* varies around 2 order of magnitude between 20 min in US and 1000 min in New Zealand (NZ). This observation suggests the presence of well differentiated groups of countries with respect to the visibility provided by TTs.

In order to find these groups we leverage standard clustering techniques. Specifically, we use the following 9 input variables to our clustering algorithm: 25, 50 and 75 per-

---

[4]Note that we also observe a significant variability for the *age* and the *number of active periods* across countries but we do not present the results due to space limitations.

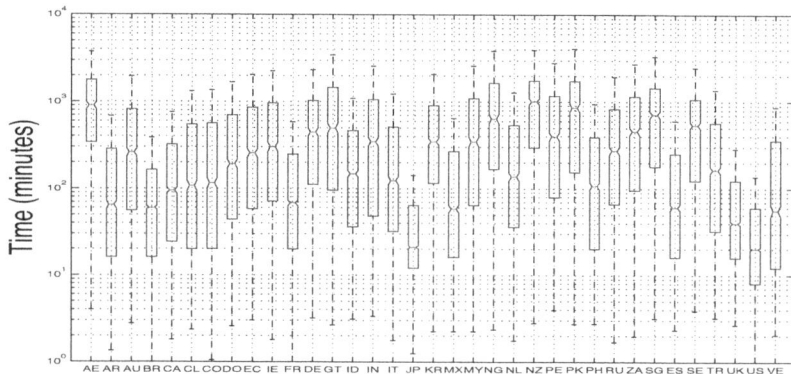

Figure 3: Distribution of Total Active Time for the TTs in each one of the 35 countries of our Local-TT-2013 dataset.

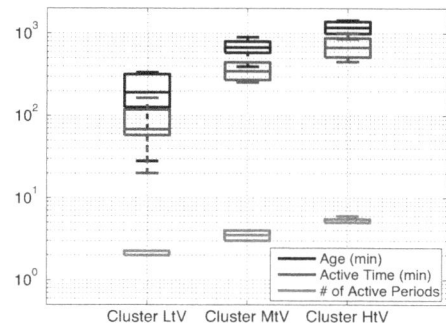

Figure 4: Summary of the distribution of temporal metrics for the HtV, MtV and LtV clusters.

centiles of the *total active time*, the *age* and the *number of active periods* for the TTs of a given country. We use the EM clustering algorithm since it provides as output the optimum number of clusters[5]. This clustering process results in 3 distinct clusters[6]. Figure 4 shows the distribution of the median value of the three temporal metrics (*total active time*, *age* and *number of active periods*) for the countries within each cluster in the form of boxplots. We can observe that the clustering algorithm produced meaningful results since the clusters are perfectly separated and thus represent three different groups that we refer to as: *High temporal Visibility* (HtV), *Medium temporal Visibility* (MtV) and *Low temporal Visibility* (LtV). In particular, the median values for the *total active time* of the HtV, MtV and LtV groups are 700, 350 and 70 min, respectively.

Note that the temporal metrics and, specifically, the *total active time* of a TT captures the *net-visibility* associated to that TT. This is the total time that the TT is visible (or exposed). In the next subsection we develop further the concept of *net-visibility*.

3.2 Net-Visibility

We define a normalized version of the *total active time* to represent the *net-visibility* associated to a TT. We refer to this metric as *net-visibility* (NV) and express it as follows:

$$NV = \frac{log(total\ active\ time)}{log(max(total\ active\ time))}\ \alpha \in [0,1] \quad (1)$$

where the *max(total active time)* is the duration of our measurement period that is the maximum active time that a TT may have in our dataset. Moreover, the list of TTs shares the bandwidth of the medium (e.g., PC or tablet screen) with other elements like the timeline or the recommendation of users to follow. Then, it is likely that some users do not pay attention to the Trending Topics while browsing through the Twitter interface. The aim of the parameter α in the previous expression is capturing this behaviour.

---

[5] The EM algorithm follows a cross-validation approach to find the optimum number of clusters [3]. Furthermore, we double-check the correlation between variables to eliminate redundant information in the clustering process.

[6] We have repeated the clustering exercise using EM and different number of seeds and for all cases we always obtain the same optimum number of clusters.

This phenomenon has been well studied in the area of online advertisement where it is refereed to as *banner blindness* [27, 33]. In a recent study, S. Heinz et al. [32] analyze the banner blindness among users who browse a web with exploratory purposes, i.e., not looking for a specific piece of information. This browsing behaviour represents well the typical browsing pattern of Twitter users. The authors quantify the banner blindness through a normalized metric of the *recognition* that captures whether a user reminds or not one (or more) banner(s) that was (were) shown during the browsing session. The value of this metric ranges between 0 (no recognition) and 1 (full recognition). The obtained results indicate that the average recognition for users performing an explorative browsing is 0.51. Given the similarity between the described scenario and ours, we will consider a value of $\alpha = 0.51$ along the paper.

Note that the *net-visibility* for a country is computed as the median of the *net-visibility* of all TTs of that country. We have computed the *net-visibility* for the 35 countries included in our Local-TT-2013 dataset. Figure 5(a) presents a ranking of countries based on their *net-visibility* (from highest to lowest). The results indicate that, as expected, countries within the HtV class present the highest *net-visibility*. Although *net-visibility* is definitely an interesting metric, it does not properly characterize the actual potential visibility offered by a TT since it does not take into account the penetration of Twitter in a country. For instance, the actual visibility granted by TTs in a country with 10K Twitter users and a *net-visibility* of 0.9 may be lower than in a country with 100M Twitter users and a *net-visibility* of 0.1. In the latter case the TTs would be visible for a shorter period of time but are (potentially) exposed to a much larger number of users.

3.3 Potential-Visibility & Potential-Online Visibility

To properly characterize the potential visibility offered by a TT we need to consider both the *net-visibility* and the penetration of Twitter in the country. Toward this end, we have defined a normalized metric that considers these two aspects. We refer to this metric as *potential-visibility* (PV) and it is expressed as follows:

$$PV = NV\frac{\#Twitter\ users}{country\ population} \in [0,1]. \quad (2)$$

169

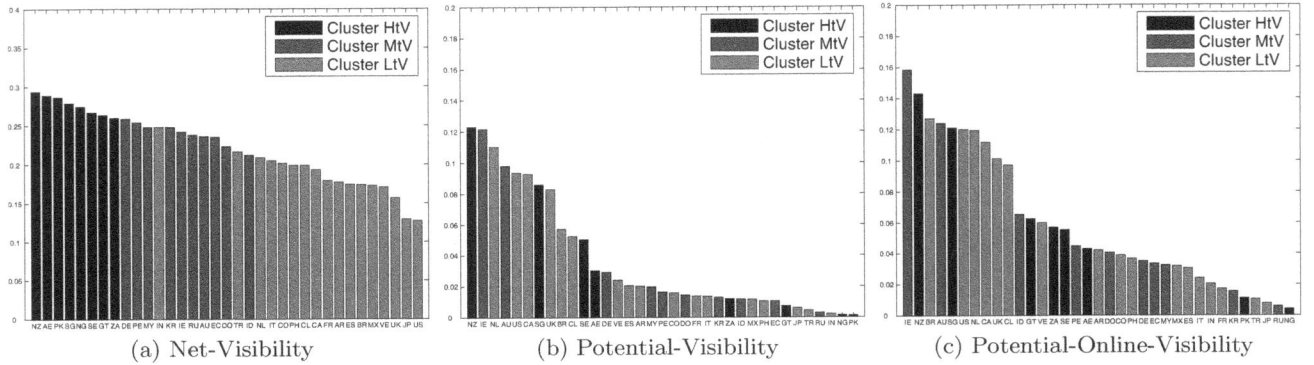

| (a) Net-Visibility | (b) Potential-Visibility | (c) Potential-Online-Visibility |

Figure 5: Trending Topics' visibility metrics for the 35 countries in our Local-TT dataset.

where, the fraction term represents the penetration of Twitter in a country. In particular, the #Twitter users is calculated as the % of registered Twitter users in a country (as obtained from our previous work [31]) multiplied by the most recent value of overall registered users reported by Twitter (554M) [15]. Furthermore, the population of each country is obtained from the Mundial Bank statistics [16]. The *potential-visibility* for a country is computed as the median of the *potential-visibility* for the TTs of that country.

We have defined a second valuable metric, the *potential-online-visibility* (PoV). This is a normalized metric that considers the penetration of Twitter among the Internet users of a country rather than among the whole country population. The number of Internet users for a country is also obtained from the Mundial Bank statistics. The expression for the PoV for a TT is the following:

$$PoV = NV \frac{\#Twitter\ users}{\#Internet\ users} \in [0, 1]. \qquad (3)$$

Differently from the *potential-visibility*, that characterizes the capacity of TTs to reach the population of a country, this metric captures the capacity of TTs to reach the Internet users of that country. Then, a person or company interested on having online presence would be more interested in this second metric[7]. Furthermore, it is worth noting that by definition the *potential-online-visibility* ≥ *potential-visibility* and the equality happens only if the Internet penetration in a country is 100% (i.e., all the citizens from a country have Internet access). Again, the *potential-online-visibility* for a country can be computed as the median of the *potential-online-visibility* for its TTs.

Figures 5(b) and 5(c) present the sorted list (from highest to lowest) of the 35 studied countries based on their *potential-visibility* and *potential-online-visibility*, respectively. These figures allow to easily identify those countries in which TTs have potential to reach a larger portion of the population (Figure 5(b)) and/or the online population (Figure 5(c)). We believe that these metrics are of high interest to

evaluate the usefulness of TTs in marketing and advertisement contexts.

As we guessed, the *potential-visibility* (and the *potential-online-visibility*) depicts a quite different picture than the *net-visibility*. For instance, Ireland (IE) that is ranked 14th based on the *net-visibility* occupies the 2nd position based on the *potential-visibility* (1st based on the *potential-online-visibility*). This occurs because despite IE has a medium *net-visibility*, it shows a high Twitter penetration and thus the potential of TTs to reach a higher portion of the population is higher than in most of other countries. We observe the opposite effect for Nigeria (NG) that has the 5th highest *net-visibility*, but due to the low penetration of Twitter in the country, it shows the 2nd lowest *potential-visibility* (the lowest *potential-online-visibility*).

Finally, it is worth to mention that we observe slight variations between the ranking of *potential-visibility* and *potential-online-visibility* metrics for most of the countries. This variability is dictated by the different penetration of Internet in different countries.

4. TRENDING TOPICS VS. TRADITIONAL ADVERTISEMENT CHANNELS

In this section we first introduce the most common metric used to measure the visibility of ads in traditional media and discuss why it is not appropriate to assess the visibility of Trending Topics. Afterwards, we leverage the methodology and metrics described in the previous section to make a comparison of the potential visibility offered by TTs and ads in traditional media.

4.1 Background on assessment of visibility in Traditional Advertisement Channels

There is a standard metric used to measure the visibility achieved by ads in traditional media (e.g., radio-stations, TV channels or newspapers). This metric is named Gross Rating Point (GRP) [29,30] and is expressed as follows:

$$GRP = frequency * reach \qquad (4)$$

Where the *reach* and the *frequency* are defined as:

- The *reach* is the ratio between the number of individuals within the target audience (e.g., men over 50) that use the specific media (e.g., a specific radio-station or TV chan-

---

[7]Note that in many cases advertisement campaigns have a specific target audience. Our metrics can be adapted to those cases. In particular, we would need to change the penetration value considering the estimated number of Twitter users belonging to the target audience and the size of the target audience in the numerator and denominator, respectively.

nel) and the total number of individuals within the target audience.

- The *frequency* is the ratio between the number of views (listenings) of an ad and the number of people who viewed (listened to) that ad. In other words, it indicates the average number of views (listenings) of an ad per user.

On the one hand, the *reach* used in the GRP is exactly the same metric as the *penetration* we use to compute our PV. On the other hand, marketing companies rely on the information provided by audiometers to compute the *frequency* for ads in TV-channels or radio-stations. These are devices installed in houses that monitor the watching (listening) activity of TV (radio-station) users. In the case of newspapers this metric is estimated based on the *Readership*. This is, the number of daily readers of a newspaper. Unfortunately, the frequency is a metric rather difficult to measure for alternative advertisement channels such as Trending Topics. Indeed, there is a controversial debate regarding the suitability of GRP for advertisement in online media [1,5].

Our PV metric considers the time of exposure of an ad, that is an objective metric (similarly to the frequency), but it can be accurately measured for both traditional advertisement channels (e.g., radio-stations' commercials or newspapers' ads) and alternative ads channels such as TTs. Hence, our PV (contrary to GRP) allows comparing the visibility of traditional and new types of advertisement channels.

4.2 Visibility of Trending Topics vs. Newspapers' ads and Radio-stations' commercials

In this subsection we apply the metrics defined in Section 3 to traditional advertisement channels such as newspapers' ads and radio-stations' commercials and compare their visibility to that offered by TTs for 10 selected countries: Canada (CA), Colombia (CO), Ireland (IE), France (FR), Germany (DE), Guatemala (GT), New Zealand (NZ), Spain (ES), United Kingdom (UK) and United States (US).

Let us focus first on newspapers' ads. We consider full-page ads for our analysis and thus α is equal to 1 because the ad uses all the bandwidth of the medium. For comparison purposes we assume that an ad appears in a newspaper every day over a period equivalent to the duration of our Local-TT-2013 dataset (90 days). Finally, R. Pieters and M. Wedel [39] report that the average time that readers dedicate to an ad in newspapers is 17.26 seconds. In particular, their results are obtained from an experimental study in which they use eye-tracking techniques on a population of slightly more than 3600 users. Using these values we can estimate the average total active time associated to newspapers' ads that would be equal to 17.26 (sec/day)* 90(days) = 25 min and 53 sec. Moreover, the information regarding newspapers' readership is typically available. In particular we have collected that information for some of the most popular newspapers in the countries under consideration[8]. The described data allows us to estimate the *net-visibility* and the *potential-visibility*[9] for popular newspapers of the studied countries.

Now, we consider the example of radio-stations' commercials. Again, α is 1 because radio stations' commercials use all the bandwidth of the medium. We consider the traditional duration of radio-stations' commercials of 60 seconds for our analysis. Note that slots of 15 or 30 seconds are typically offered by radio-stations as well [7,11]. Furthermore, radio-stations' advertisement campaigns vary between few weeks and few months depending on their goal. Then, for comparison purposes we consider the duration of our dataset (90 days) that is included in this range. Finally, the advertiser has to define a schedule for the ad. This is, the number of used slots per day and time-frames associated to those slots (morning, afternoon, evening or night). To this end, advertisement companies indicate that an ad should be listened at least 3 or 4 times by a person in order to be sure that he/she got the message [10,13]. Hence, they use this reference value to define the most suitable schedule for each specific campaign. In this paper, we consider an aggressive campaign in which the ad is played three times in every time-frame (12 times a day) so that the probability of people listening to it 4 times is high.

We can use the previous data to estimate the *total active time* associated to a radio-station's commercials as 60 (sec/commercial) *12 (commercials/day)*90 (days) = 1080 minutes. Furthermore, the audience of some of the most popular radio-stations in the considered countries is publicly available[10]. Hence, with the described data we can compute our visibility metrics for those radio-stations.

The computed *net-visibility* for radio-stations' commercials and newspapers' ads is 0.5927 and 0.2760, respectively. Comparing these results with the median *net-visibility* of TTs for the 35 countries shown in Figure 5(a) we observe that radio-stations' commercials present a significantly higher *net-visibility* that TTs in all the 35 countries. Furthermore, TTs offer a slightly higher *net-visibility* than newspapers' ads in only 3 countries: New Zealand (NZ), Arab Emirates (AE) and Pakistan (PK). Hence, we conclude that ads in traditional media enjoy longer exposure times than Trending Topics.

However, as indicated in Section 3 the *potential-visibility* is a more accurate metric since it takes into account the penetration of the specific media in the country. Figure 6 shows the *potential-visibility* associated to popular radio-stations' commercials and newspapers' ads as well as the median *potential-visibility* of TTs for the 10 considered countries. We observe that the *potential-visibility* depicts a different picture than the *net-visibility* due to the different penetration of Twitter, newspapers and radio-stations in these countries. In particular, radio-stations' commercials, Trending Topics and newspapers' ads show the highest *potential-visibility* in 5 countries (IE, FR, DE, ES and UK), 4 countries (CA, CO, NZ and US) and 1 country (GT), respectively. Moreover, in all countries, excepting Guatemala, Trending Topics show a higher *potential-visibility* than newspapers' ads. These results, indicate that despite having a lower exposure time, the higher penetration of Twitter compared to traditional media makes that Trending Topics have a higher potential visibility than radio-stations' commercials in several countries and newspapers' ads in almost every considered country.

---

[8]The references to the sources from where we obtained the data for the different newspapers' readership are available in our Technical Report [28].

[9]The *potential-online-visibility* does not make sense in this case since we are not considering online media.

[10]Again, the references to the sources from where we collect the data are available in our Technical Report [28].

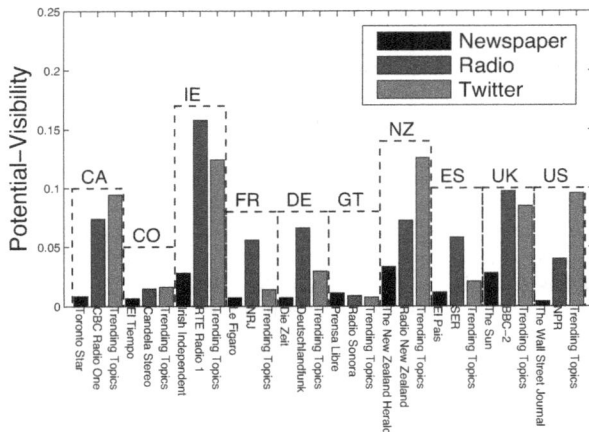

Figure 6: Potential-visibility for TTs, radio-stations' commercials and newspapers' ads for the 10 considered countries. The x-axis presents the names of the studied media for each advertisement channel and country.

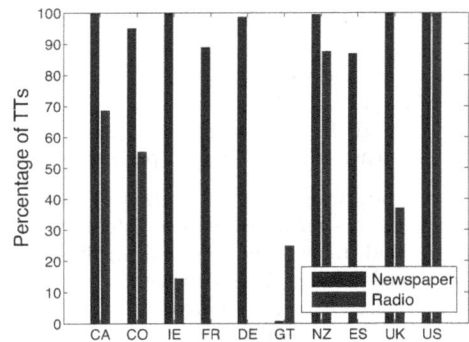

Figure 7: Percentage of TTs with higher *potential-visibility* than newspapers' ads and radio-stations' commercials for the 10 considered countries.

Therefore, we conclude that Trending Topics offer a visibility comparable to other traditional ad channels for the analyzed countries. This confirms that Trending Topics are a useful tool for marketing and advertisement purposes.

However, several considerations should be taken into account with respect to our results. First, Trending Topics should not be considered as a substitute to traditional ads channels. Instead, they should be considered a complementary tool in advertisement and marketing contexts. In particular, in traditional ad channels the advertiser buys several slots and it has the certainty that its product would be shown to the audience during those slots. However, the same advertiser may lunch a marketing campaign in Twitter but it has not the guarantee that its product will become Trending Topic. In fact, the definition of strategies to help companies to generate Trending Topics is still an unsolved matter and requires further research[11]. Second, our analysis has been conducted under certain assumptions. For instance, we have only considered popular radio-stations and newspapers in each country with a higher penetration than the average newspapers or radio-stations in those countries. Furthermore we have considered values that represent realistic advertisement campaigns in newspapers and radio-stations, but other type of campaigns are possible and may lead to different visibility results. Finally, some other subtle aspects such as how the ad support (e.g., audio vs text vs images) affects the attention of the user have not been considered.

5. ANALYSIS OF THE VARIABILITY OF TTS VISIBILITY WITHIN A COUNTRY

As Figure 3 revealed, there exists a notable difference, over an order of magnitude, in the *total active time* across Local TTs in a country. Hence, distinct TTs within a country enjoy rather different visibility. In this section we dig into this

---

[11]Note that companies have the option of purchasing Promoted Trending Topics that follow a similar business model (pay-per-slot) as traditional ad channels.

difference. In particular, we conduct the following analyses: *(i)* we present a methodology whose aim is to unveil which type of TTs are likely to provide a higher visibility and *(ii)* we study whether the visibility offered by TTs at different times of the day presents an identifiable daily pattern. Due to space limitation, we present the obtained results for three selected countries. Specifically, we have chosen one country from each one of the temporal-visibility groups defined in Section 3 to guarantee the diversity in our selection: New Zeland (NZ) from the HtV group, Ireland (IE) from the MtV group and UK from the LtV group. Note that we will refer to results for other countries when warranted.

Before going into those analyses, we would like to briefly extend our comparison between TTs and traditional advertisement channels. In the previous section we have used the median value of the different visibility metrics of TTs within a country to perform the comparison study. However, due to the high variability of TTs visibility in a country, we would like to present more statistically meaningful results. To this end, we have computed the percentage of TTs that present a higher *potential-visibility* than radio-stations' commercials and newspapers' ads for each one of the 10 countries analyzed in Section 4. Figure 7 shows the obtained results. First, at least 85% TTs present a higher *potential-visibility* than newspapers' ads in all countries but Guatemala in which due to the high penetration of the considered newspaper only the top 1% most visible Trending Topics would achieve a higher visibility than ads in that newspaper. Second, in the case of radio-stations' commercials we observe a high variability in the results. For instance, in FR, GE and ES the visibility of commercials in the considered radio-stations' is higher than for any TT whereas in US we observe the opposite effect, 99% TTs enjoy more visibility than commercials in the considered radio-station. This variability is dictated by the interplay of the penetration of different media as well as the associated *net-visibility*.

In summary, these results confirm the conclusion from Section 4: Trending Topics offer a visibility comparable to traditional ad channels and then they are useful as a tool in marketing and advertisement contexts. However, the high variability observed in the visibility of TTs across (and within) countries requires to conduct an individual analysis for each specific case to obtain accurate results.

Finally, we would like to highlight that in order to study the variability of TTs visibility within a country we use the

CLASS	CATEGORY	EXAMPLE
Hashtags	— (Self)	#FirstQuestionsAsked
Sports-Related	Athlete (DBp)	Andrew Sheridan
	Sport Events (Self)	Chelsea - Liverpool
	Other Sport Issues (DBp)	Conmebol
	College Coach (DBp)	Mike McQueary
Feelings & Emotions	Positive (Self)	Happy Birthday Britney
	Negative (Self)	RIP Perez Hilton
Places &Buildings	Architectural Structure (DBp)	US Capitol
	Administrative Region (DBp)	Northern Iowa
	Feature (DBp)	La Cartuja
	City (DBp)	Amsterdam
	Populated place (DBp)	Cannes
Celebrities	Agent (DBp)	Hugh Grant
	Office holder (DBp)	Bill Clinton
	Politician (DBp)	John McCain
	Artist (DBp)	Freddie Mercury
	Famous person (IMDb)	Christine Reyes
	Writer (DBp)	Edgar Allen Poe
Entertainment	Album (DBp)	Love After War
	Movies (IMDb)	Finding NEMO
	Book (DBp)	Geek Love
	Work (DBp)	Reservoir Dogs
	Character (IMDb)	Batman & Robin
	Video games (DBp)	Death Race
	Film (DBp)	Celda 211
	Single (DBp)	Bad Romance
	TV show (DBp)	American Idol
Companies	Organization (DBp)	RTVE, Spanair
	Privately held company (DBp)	Twitter
	Public company (DBp)	Jackson Hewitt
Others	Diseases (DBp)	HIV
	First name (DBp)	Danielle
	Wide-body aircraft (DBp)	Boeing 767
Unclassified	—	Take Facebook Down

Table 2: List of Semantic classes and categories. For each category we also indicate the source as follows: *DBp* for DBpedia, *IMDb* for IMDb and *Self* for Self-defined categories.

total-active-time in the rest of the section. Note that *net-visibility* is a normalized version of this metric and Twitter penetration, used to compute the *potential-visibility*, is the same for all TTs within a country. Then, results derived with the *total active time* and these other metrics are equivalent.

5.1 Visibility of different semantic classes of TTs

In this subsection we first define an efficient methodology to group TTs by their semantic meaning into different semantic classes. Then we apply this methodology to the Local TTs of the selected countries. Finally, we compute the distribution of the *total active time* for the TTs within each semantic class so that we can report what types of TTs offer higher visibility in each country.

5.1.1 Methodology

Our tool uses the following sources in order to assign a specific TT to a semantic category:

- *DBpedia* is a sub-project of Wikipedia that aims to create an ontology to classify different names, terms, words and expressions available in Wikipedia pages [2]. In particular, it provides a hierarchical ontology that currently covers 359 semantic categories that are described by one or more properties from a pool of 1775.

- *IMDb* is a popular database including information related to a large number of entertainment resources such as movies, TV shows, actors/actresses, etc [8]. Contrary to DBpedia, IMDb does not provide a structured classification for the stored resources.

- *Self-defined categories*: Manual inspection of TTs reveals some common semantic categories that although easily identifiable for a human being are not recognized by either DB-

pedia or IMDb. In particular, we identify two of these categories: (*i*) *Sport Events*, our manual inspection reveals that TTs are commonly used to reflect events related to different sport games, such as the score of football games. Examples of this are TTs such as 'Arsenal 1-2 Manchester United' or 'Gol de Benzema'. (*ii*) *Feelings/Emotions*, our manual inspection also suggests that TTs are used to express emotions, feelings, preferences, greetings, etc. Therefore it is common to find TTs including words such as 'Happy', 'Love' or 'Hate'. Examples of these TTs are 'Happy Birthday Andy Carroll' or 'We Love Hunger Games'. Therefore, our tool classifies those TTs that include one (or more) emotion-related word(s) and neither DBpedia nor IMDb are able to classify in the *Feelings/Emotions* class.

Moreover, we consider *Hashtags* as a separate category. As indicated in the Introduction hashtags are a special functionality of Twitter that is widely used and thus understanding whether they offer a higher/lower visibility than "non-hashtaged" topics is of high interest for commercial and advertisement purposes.

The large number of potential output categories provided by DBpedia and the lack of structure of IMBb would make infeasible to conduct a meaningful analysis of the semantic context of TTs using their provided results. To address this issue, we have performed a careful merging process in which we group semantic categories obtained from DBpedia, IMDb and our self-defined categories into a handful set of semantic *classes* that permits us to present a meaningful discussion. Note that for this process we have used as reference the 18 classes defined in [36]. Indeed, the 18 classes defined in [36] can be easily merged into the 9 classes resulting from our process (with the exception of hashtags). We have decided to define a smaller number of classes because using 18 classes results in few of them being scarcely populated.

Table 2 lists the defined semantic classes and, for each class, presents the most important categories along with its original source (i.e., DBpedia, IMDb or self-defined categories). In particular, we use the following preference order in our semantic classification process for a given TT: we first try to classify it using DBpedia in a semantic category and class. If DBpedia fails we use IMDb and in case it also fails we use our Self-defined categories. Those topics that are not classified after these three steps are added to the *Unclassified* class. Finally, our manual inspection of the TTs within the Unclassified class reveals that most of these topics correspond to complex sentences similar to some hashtags but without the initial '#'. Some examples are: 'Tomorrow is Friday', 'Bieber Fever Is Incurable', 'Ian Is Our Pride', 'M or P' and 'Lin is 6'. It can be noticed that some of them are difficult to be semantically classified even for a human being without the required context knowledge (e.g., 'M or P').

5.1.2 Performance Evaluation

We have used the described methodology to classify the TTs included in our datasets. Table 3 summarizes the percentage of TTs that have been classified as well as those that our tool is unable to classify for each analyzed country (Unclassified). The results suggest that our tool is fairly efficient since it is able to automatically classify more than 90% of the TTs in the worst considered case (UK).

However, the effectiveness of a classification tool is not measured by the percentage of resources that it is able to classify but the percentage that it is able to classify correctly.

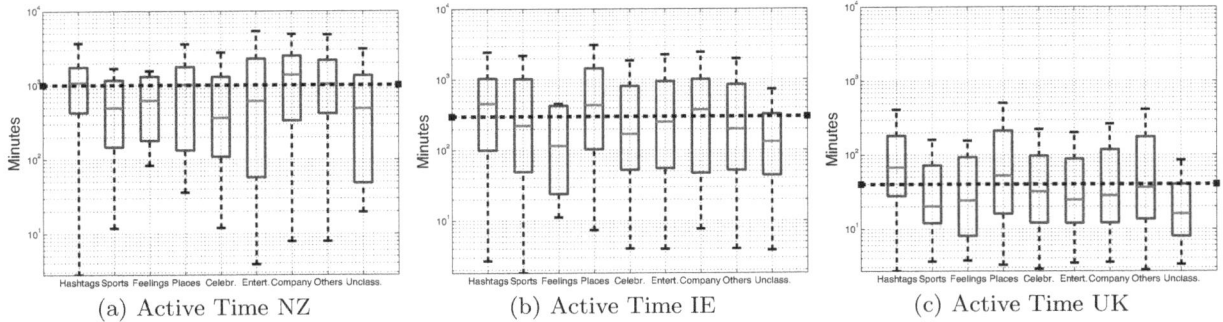

(a) Active Time NZ   (b) Active Time IE   (c) Active Time UK

Figure 8: Distribution of the *active time* across TTs within each semantic classes for NZ, IE and UK (the horizontal dashed line shows the median active time of the all the Local-TTs of the correspondent country).

In particular, we define two types of errors for our classification tool: (*i*) *false positives* are those TTs that our tool assigns to a wrong class and (*ii*) *false negatives* are those TTs that our tool was unable to classify but a human being would be able to classify in any of the defined semantic classes.

The detection of false positives and negatives needs to be done manually. Note that this is a common practice used in previous works [36, 42]. Conducting such an experiment for all the TTs from our dataset is a very tedious and time consuming task. Therefore, we have selected a random set of 1000 TTs and three different persons[12] have manually detected the false positives and negatives for this subset of TTs. Note that the differences between the classification done by these three persons over the same random set varies less than 1%. This suggests that the error introduced by human beings is negligible and thus the result of the manual classification can be considered a good approximation to the ground truth. In addition, sampling introduces an error in the proportion of Trending Topics per category used during the validation with respect to the actual proportions. This error can be computed using a hypothesis test for a proportion [41]. This is a well-known tool widely used to compute confidence intervals for the results of surveys. In particular, in our case in which we use a sample of 1K TTs, the error introduced by sampling in the proportion of Trending Topics in any class is $\leq 3.1\%$ (with 95% confidence) for any size (i.e., number of Trending Topics) of the dataset. This suggests that: first, the obtained results are reasonably accurate and, second, the used methodology scales well since manually inspecting a sample of 1000 TTs (that as we have demonstrated is doable for a human being) suffices to not incur in high errors in the considered proportions for different classes.

Our detection experiment reveals that, one the one hand, 41% of the unclassified TTs are false negatives. Since the *Unclassified* class represents less than 10% of our TTs, we conclude that overall only around 4% of the TTs corresponds to false negatives. On the other hand, false positives are also infrequent and represent only 5% of the inspected TTs. In a nutshell, these results indicate that our semantic classification tool is quite accurate and its automatic process is able to classify more than 91% of the TTs correctly.

---

[12]These three persons were not connected to our research project to guarantee the objectivity.

	NZ	IE	UK
Hashtags	53,72%	47,31%	39,13%
Sports-Related	3,46%	5,96%	10,80%
Feeling & Emotions	0,80%	0,84%	0,76%
Places & Buildings	3,86%	7,39%	4,58%
Celebrities	7,45%	9,79%	14,19%
Entertainment	8,64%	7,58%	8,85%
Companies	3,59%	3,95%	3,06%
Others	13,70%	11,67%	8,99%
Unclassified	4,79%	5,51%	9,65%

Table 3: Distribution of Local TTs from UK, IE and NZ across the defined semantic classes.

5.1.3 *Visibility of TTs across semantic classes*

Figure 8 depicts the distribution of the *total-active-time* for every semantic class of the three analyzed countries in the form of boxplot. In addition, we plot a horizontal dashed line that indicates the median *total-active-time* for all TTs in the country for reference.

First of all we observe a high variability among the visibility offered by different TTs within each class. Despite this variability, we still can derive useful observations. For instance, "Hashtags" and "Places" are the only two cateogries whose median *total active time* is above the median value of the country, for all three countries. Interestingly, this result along with results in Table 3 suggest that adding a # in front of the term to be advertised seems to increase the chances to become TT and to enjoy a longer active time. Surprisingly, categories such as "Sport" and "Celebrities" that attract a fair amount of attention from media do not appear among those offering higher visibility. This may indicate that Twitter users do not get excited about these topics for long time. Finally, we observe differences across countries that indicate that each *national market* shows preferences for different types of topics. For instance, TTs related to companies present the highest visibility in NZ whereas TTs in this category show a rather low active time in UK. Furthermore, TTs related to "Sports" present a quite low visibility in NZ and UK but not in IE.

5.2 Daily Pattern of Trending Topics Visibility

Internet traffic as well as most on-line services present a daily usage pattern bound to the daily schedule of their users [40]. In this subsection we focus on understanding whether the visibility offered by Local TTs presents an identifiable

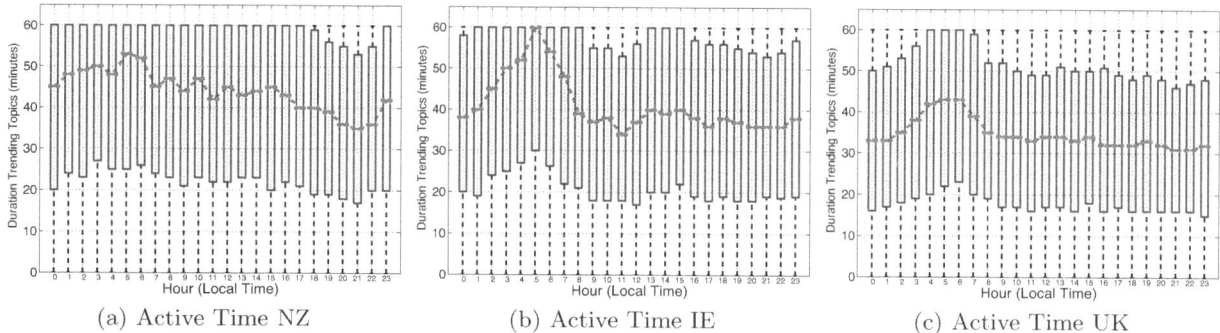

| (a) Active Time NZ | (b) Active Time IE | (c) Active Time UK |

Figure 9: Distribution of the *total active time* of TTs instances within each one of the 24-hour slots of a day.

daily pattern. For this purpose, we divide a day in its 24 one-hour slots[13] and for each slot we calculate the distribution of the *active time* for the TT instances present in that slot. Note that the maximum *active time* that a TT instance can have in a slot is 60 minutes.

Figure 9 shows the obtained results for UK, IE and NZ. The x-axis shows the 24 time slots described in the previous paragraph and the y-axis shows the distribution of the *active time* of the TTs present in each time slot in the form of boxplot. Note that the time slots represent local time for each country. We observe that there is a marked daily pattern in the distribution of the *active time* for the different hour-slots. In fact, for every country we can see the presence of few slots where TTs tend to have a higher *active time*. Specifically, these slots correspond to the night (sleeping) hours in which a lower activity of Twitter users helps TTs to remain visible longer time. However, the higher *net-visibility* enjoyed in those hours does not really lead to a higher *potential-visibility* since the number of users connected to Twitter at those hours is likely to be significantly smaller than in the morning, afternoon or evening. We have repeated this experiment for the 35 countries in our dataset. The results can be found in our TR [28]. In summary, most of the countries show the previously reported daily pattern, with few exceptions such as Japan, US and some Latin-American countries (e.g., Colombia or Venezuela), in which we observe a flatter shape. Thus, the difficulty of getting a TT in these countries is independent of the time of the day. Finally, we have separately studied the daily-pattern for week days and weekends for every country without noticing major differences.

6. RELATED WORK

Measurement and Analysis of Trending Topics: Kwak et al. [35] performed the most exhaustive characterization of Twitter so far. As part of this study the authors briefly analyze Trending Topics using coarse temporal metrics and quantitative metrics to classify Trending Topics in few externally defined (i.e., artificial) categories. Furthermore, Asur et al. [26] use quantitative metrics to analyze the formation, persistence and decay phases of Trending Topics. Both works rely on quantitative metrics that, as shown by

Morstatter et al. [38], may lead to unreliable results due to the best effort nature of Twitter APIs. Finally, Huang et al. [34] studied the differences between the tagging pattern in Twitter and other OSN systems. The authors present the phenomenon of the Twitter *micro-meme*: emergent topics for which a tag is created, used widely for a few days and then disappears. Although these papers provide initial valuable results, they focus on specific aspects of Trending Topics different to the one addressed in our paper, i.e., the characterization of the visibility offered by TTs in different countries.

Semantic classification of Trending Topics: Lee et al. [36] use a dataset formed by around 800 Trending Topics and classify them into 18 different categories using a text- and a network-based methodologies that achieve an accuracy of 65% and 70%, respectively. In our study we consider a set of Trending Topics 3 order of magnitude larger. Furthermore Zubiaga et al. [42] assign 15 different properties to Trending Topics (including some unreliable quantitative properties) to classify them into 4 classes using a similar text-based methodology as the one used in [36]. They validate their technique using a training and a test sets with 600 and 436 Trending Topics, respectively. In this case they report an accuracy of 78.4%.

7. CONCLUSION AND FUTURE WORK

Despite Trending Topics are a well-know feature regularly exploited in the context of marketing and advertisement, we still stand on preliminary ground in terms of understanding this tool. In this paper we characterize the visibility of Trending Topics across 35 countries. In particular, we present a measurement methodology along with a methodology to thoroughly analyze the visibility of Trending Topics that we believe can be of high value for experts of different disciplines in marketing and advertisement contexts. The results obtained applying these methodologies indicate that, in general, Trending Topics present a comparable visibility to other traditional advertisement channels and thus they can be considered a useful tool in marketing and advertisement contexts. However, the high variability on the visibility offered by Trending Topics across (and within) countries suggests that we should apply the described methodology to obtain accurate results for each specific case.

As future work we plan to apply our methodology to on-line advertisement in order to compare the visibility offered by TTs with that offered by other online media such as ban-

---

[13]Slot 0 includes information for the 60 minutes between 12AM and 1AM, slot 1 includes information for the 60 minutes between 1AM and 2AM and so on.

ners in popular websites. Furthermore, we will explore different strategies that companies may use to create Trending Topics in Twitter as well as their associated costs in comparison with traditional advertisement channels.

8. ACKNOWLEDGEMENTS

We would like to thank our shepherd Balachander Krishnamurthy and anonymous reviewers for their valuable feedback. The research leading to these results has been partially funded by the European Union's FP7 Program under the project eCOUSIN (318398), the Spanish Ministry of Economy and Competitiveness under the eeCONTENT project (TEC2011-29688-C02-02), and the Regional Government of Madrid under the MEDIANET project (S2009/TIC-1468).

9. REFERENCES

[1] Are gross rating points really the answer for digital? http://www.imediaconnection.com/content/32278.asp.

[2] DBpedia. http://dbpedia.org/About.

[3] EM - Weka 3. http://weka.sourceforge.net/doc/weka/clusterers/EM.htmls.

[4] Facebook friends Twitter-like Trending Topics. https://www.cnbc.com/id/100942887.

[5] Gross Rating Point Metrics Will Be Good for Online Advertising. http://www.mediapost.com/publications/article/155743/.

[6] HBR Blog Network. http://blogs.hbr.org/cs/2013/05/surprise_is_still_the_most_powerful.html.

[7] How Long is a Radio Ad. http://suite101.com/article/how-long-is-a-radio-commercial-a152539.

[8] Internet Movie Database (IMDb). http://www.imdb.com/.

[9] Marketing with Twitter. https://business.twitter.com/marketing-twitter.

[10] Optimum Scheduling for Radio Advertising. http://avenueright.com/entries/71/optimum-scheduling-for-radio-advertising-frequency-is-key.

[11] The perfect length for a radio commercial. http://danoday.com/blog/2010/11/radio-commercial-length/.

[12] Promoted Trends | Twitter for Business. https://business.twitter.com/products/promoted-trends.

[13] Radio Ad Frequency. http://www.marketingprofs.com/ea/qst_question.asp?qstid=6388.

[14] Spanish revolution. https://wiki.digitalmethods.net/Dmi/DmiSummer2011SpanishRevolution.

[15] Statistic Brain. http://www.statisticbrain.com/twitter-statistics/.

[16] The World Bank. http://www.worldbank.org/.

[17] Twitter API Documentation. https://dev.twitter.com/.

[18] Twitter Blog: Let's Fly. http://blog.twitter.com/2011/12/lets-fly.html.

[19] Twitter blog: To Trend or Not to Trend... http://blog.twitter.com/2010/12/to-trend-or-not-to-trend.html.

[20] Twitter marketing agency. http://twittermarketingagency.com/.

[21] Twitter marketing company. http://www.outsourcegeek.com/marketing-services/twitter-marketing-service/twitter-marketing-company.

[22] Twitter promoted trends tracked for one month. http://allthingsd.com/20130409/big-media-loves-promoted-trends-twitters-big-dollar-digital-billboards/.

[23] Twitter Rate Limiting. https://dev.twitter.com/docs/rate-limiting.

[24] Twitterholic Politicians. http://litteramedia.wordpress.com/2011/12/13/twitterholic-politicians/.

[25] UMD Web Site. http://www.umassd.edu/cmr/studiesandresearch/2011fortune500/.

[26] Sitaram Asur, Bernardo A Huberman, Gabor Szabo, and Chunyan Wang. Trends in social media: Persistence and decay. In *ICWSM*, 2011.

[27] Jan Panero Benway. Banner blindness: The irony of attention grabbing on the World Wide Web. In *HFES Annual Meeting*. SAGE Publications, 1998.

[28] J. Carrascosa, R. Gonzalez, R. Cuevas, and A. Azcorra. Are Trending Topics Useful for Marketing? Visibility of Trending Topics vs Traditional Advertisement. Technical report available at: http://www.it.uc3m.es/~rcuevas/techreports/TT_TR2013.pdf, Universidad Carlos III de Madrid, 2013.

[29] John A Davis. *Measuring Marketing: 110+ Key Metrics Every Marketer Needs*. Wiley. com, 2012.

[30] Paul W Farris, Neil T Bendle, Phillip E Pfeifer, and David J Reibstein. *Marketing metrics: The definitive guide to measuring marketing performance*. Pearson Education, 2010.

[31] Roberto Gonzalez, Ruben Cuevas, Angel Cuevas, and Carmen Guerrero. Understanding the locality effect in Twitter: measurement and analysis. *Personal and Ubiquitous Computing*, 2013.

[32] Silvia Heinz, Markus Hug, Carina Nugaeva, and Klaus Opwis. Online ad banners: the effects of goal orientation and content congruence on memory. In *CHI*, 2013.

[33] Guillaume Hervet, Katherine Guérard, Sébastien Tremblay, and Mohamed Saber Chtourou. Is banner blindness genuine? Eye tracking internet text advertising. *Applied Cognitive Psychology*, 2011.

[34] Jeff Huang, Katherine M Thornton, and Efthimis N Efthimiadis. Conversational tagging in twitter. In *21st ACM conference on Hypertext and hypermedia*, 2010.

[35] Haewoon Kwak, Changhyun Lee, Hosung Park, and Sue Moon. What is Twitter, a social network or a news media? In *WWW*, 2010.

[36] Kathy Lee, Diana Palsetia, Ramanathan Narayanan, Md Mostofa Ali Patwary, Ankit Agrawal, and Alok Choudhary. Twitter trending topic classification. In *ICDMW*, 2011.

[37] Hubert W Lilliefors. On the Kolmogorov-Smirnov test for normality with mean and variance unknown. *Journal of the American Statistical Association*, 1967.

[38] Fred Morstatter, Jurgen Pfeffer, Huan Liu, and Kathleen M Carley. Is the sample good enough? comparing data from twitter's streaming api with twitter's firehose. 2013.

[39] Rik Pieters and Michel Wedel. Attention capture and transfer in advertising: Brand, pictorial, and text-size effects. *Journal of Marketing*, pages 36–50, 2004.

[40] Kevin Thompson, Gregory J Miller, and Rick Wilder. Wide-area Internet traffic patterns and characteristics. *Network, IEEE*, 1997.

[41] Mario F Triola, William Martin Goodman, Gerry LaBute, Richard Law, and Lisa MacKay. *Elementary statistics*. Pearson/Addison-Wesley, 2006.

[42] Arkaitz Zubiaga, Damiano Spina, Víctor Fresno, and Raquel Martínez. Classifying trending topics: a typology of conversation triggers on twitter. In *CIKM*, 2011.

Launch Hard or Go Home!

Predicting the Success of Kickstarter Campaigns

Vincent Etter   Matthias Grossglauser   Patrick Thiran

School of Computer and Communication Sciences
École Polytechnique Fédérale de Lausanne (EPFL), Lausanne, Switzerland

firstname.lastname@epfl.ch

ABSTRACT

Crowdfunding websites such as Kickstarter are becoming increasingly popular, allowing project creators to raise hundreds of millions of dollars every year. However, only one out of two Kickstarter campaigns reaches its funding goal and is successful. It is therefore of prime importance, both for project creators and backers, to be able to know which campaigns are likely to succeed.

We propose a method for predicting the success of Kickstarter campaigns by using both direct information and social features. We introduce a first set of predictors that uses the time series of money pledges to classify campaigns as probable success or failure and a second set that uses information gathered from tweets and Kickstarter's projects/backers graph.

We show that even though the predictors that are based solely on the amount of money pledged reach a high accuracy, combining them with predictors using social features enables us to improve the performance significantly. In particular, only 4 hours after the launch of a campaign, the combined predictor reaches an accuracy of more than 76% (a relative improvement of 4%).

Categories and Subject Descriptors

H.2.8 [**Database Management**]: Database Applications—*Data Mining*

Keywords

Crowdfunding; Kickstarter; time-series classification; success prediction; social features; Twitter

1. INTRODUCTION

Kickstarter[1] is a crowdfunding website: people with a creative idea can open a campaign on the website to gather

---

[1] http://www.kickstarter.com

money to make it happen. When launching a campaign, the creator sets a funding goal and a deadline. Then, people can pledge money towards the project, and receive various rewards in return. Rewards range from the acknowledgement of a backer's participation to deep involvement in a product's design.

The fundraising model is *all or nothing*: once its deadline is reached, a campaign is considered successful if and only if it has reached its goal. In this case, backers actually pay the money they pledged and the project idea is realized. In the case where the goal is not reached, the campaign has failed and no money is exchanged.

As only 44% of campaigns reach their goal overall, it is of high interest for creators to know early on the probability of success of their campaign, to be able to react accordingly. Users whose campaigns are failing to take off might want to increase their visibility and start a social media campaign, while those whose campaigns are highly likely to succeed could already start working on them to deliver faster, or look into possible extensions of their goal.

Similarly, backers could also benefit from such a prediction. They could engage their friends and social network in backing a campaign, if its probability of success is low shortly after its launch. When the success probability is high, backers could also adjust their pledge, maybe reducing it a little in order to support another campaign, while being confident that the campaign will still succeed. Some online tools, such as *Kicktraq*[2] and *CanHeKickIt*[3], provide tracking tools and basic trend estimators, but none has yet implemented proper success predictors.

There have been several studies published on crowdfunding platforms: Mollick [4] provides insights about of the dynamics of the success and failure of Kickstater campaigns. He presents various statistics about the determinant features for success and analyzes the correlation of many campaign characteristics with its outcome. Wash [7] focuses on a different platform, called Donors Choose, where people can donate money to buy supplies for school projects. He describes how backers tend to give larger donations when it allows a campaign to reach its goal, and also studies the predictability of campaigns over time.

Greenberg et al. [3] propose a success predictor for Kickstarter campaigns based solely on their *static* attributes, i.e., attributes available at the launch of a campaign. They obtain a prediction accuracy of 68%, which we will use as baseline

---

[2] http://www.kicktraq.com
[3] http://canhekick.it

when presenting the results in Section 3. However, to the best of our knowledge, no one has studied success prediction based on *dynamic* attributes of a campaign.

Of course, predicting a time series with a finite horizon has several other applications. An obvious extension of this framework could easily be applied to online auctions, where the final amount to be reached can be predicted. Financial products, such as options, could also benefit from such predictors. We focus on building models for predicting the success of crowdfunding campaigns, using Kickstarter as an example. The techniques and results presented below however are not restricted to this platform and should apply to any similar setting.

In Section 2, we describe our dataset, its main characteristics and the preprocessing we apply. We then present our different predictors in Section 3, explaining the models and showing their individual performance. We next propose a method to combine them that significantly improves the accuracy over individual predictors. Finally, we conclude in Section 4.

2. DATASET DESCRIPTION

Our dataset consists of data scraped from the Kickstarter website between September 2012 and May 2013. It consists of 16 042 campaigns that were backed by 1 309 295 users.

2.1 Collecting the Data

New campaigns are discovered on the *Recently Launched*[4] page of Kickstarter. Once a new campaign is detected, its main characteristics, such as its category, funding goal and deadline, are collected and stored in a database. Then, a crawler regularly checks each campaign's page to record the current amount of pledged money, as well as the number of backers, until the project's funding campaign reaches its end.

In parallel, we monitor[5] Twitter for any public tweet containing the keyword *kickstarter*. For each tweet matching our search, we record all its data in the database. To determine if the tweet is related to a particular campaign, we search for a campaign URL in its text. If any is found, the tweet is identified in the database as a reference to the corresponding campaign. We thus have, for each campaign, all public tweets related to it.

Along with Twitter, Kickstarter integrates Facebook on its website, as an other way of spreading the word about campaigns. However, contrary to Twitter, most Facebook posts are not public, being usually restricted to the user's friends. As a result, a search similar to the one described above performed on Facebook usually yields very few results. For this reason, we only use Twitter in our dataset.

Finally, we regularly crawl the *Backers* page of each campaign to get the list of users who pledged money, and store them in our database. This last step being time-consuming to perform, it is done every couple of days, resulting in only a few snapshots of the list of backers and therefore a coarse resolution of the time at which each backer joined a campaign.

---

[4]http://www.kickstarter.com/discover/recently-launched

[5]We use the Twitter Streaming API to search for the keyword *kickstarter*. Because few tweets match this search query compared to the global rate of tweets, we know that we get a large uniform fraction of the relevant tweets (usually close to 100%) [6].

	Successful	Failed	Total
Campaigns	7739	8303	16042
Proportion	48.24%	51.76%	100%
Users	1 207 777	171 450	1 309 295
Pledges	2 030 032	212 195	2 242 227
Pledged $	141 942 075	16 084 581	158 026 656
Tweets	564 329	173 069	737 398

Table 1: **Global statistics of our dataset of Kickstarter campaigns. We show the values for successful and failed campaigns separately, as well as the combined total. Users are unique people who have backed at least one campaign.**

	Successful	Failed	All
Goal ($)	9595	34 693	22 585
Duration (days)	30.89	33.50	32.24
Number of backers	262	25	139
Final amount	216.60%	11.40%	110.39%
Number of tweets	73	20	46

Table 2: **Campaign statistics of our Kickstarter dataset. The average values for successful and failed campaigns are given, as well as the average over all campaigns. The final amount is relative to the campaign's goal.**

2.2 Dataset Statistics

Table 1 describes the global statistics of our dataset, for successful and failed campaigns separately, as well as the combined total. Table 2 shows average statistics for individual campaigns. As expected, failed campaigns have a much higher goal on average (close to four times higher), but it is interesting to note that they also have a longer duration[6]. Moreover, we have a nearly even split between successful and failed campaigns, with more than 48% of campaigns that reach their funding goal. The reported[7] global success rate of Kickstarter is lower, with 44% of successful campaigns overall. This difference could be explained by the fact that our dataset only contains recent campaigns, that benefit from the growing popularity of crowdsourcing websites.

2.3 Dataset Preprocessing

As explained in Section 2.1, each campaign is regularly sampled by our crawler to get its current amount of pledged money and number of backers, until it ends. On average, a campaign's *state* is sampled every 15 minutes, resulting in hundreds of samples at irregular time intervals.

To be able to compare campaigns with each other, we resample each campaign's list of states to obtain a fixed number of $N_S = 1000$ states. The time of each state is normalized with respect to the campaign's launch date and duration. We divide the current amount of money pledged of each state by the goal amount to obtain a normalized amount.

A campaign c is thus characterized by its funding goal $G(c)$, launch date $L(c)$, duration $D(c)$, final state $F(c)$ (equal to 1 if the campaign succeeded, 0 otherwise) and a series of state samples $\{\mathbf{S}_i(c)\}_{i \in \{1,2,...,N_S\}}$. Each state $\mathbf{S}_i(c)$ is itself

---

[6]Project creators can choose the duration of their campaign. The default value is 30 days, with a maximum of 60 days.

[7]http://www.kickstarter.com/help/stats

Variable	Description
$G(c)$	Funding goal
$L(c)$	Launch date
$D(c)$	Duration
$F(c)$	Final state (1 if successful, 0 otherwise)
$\{\mathbf{S}_i(c)\}$	Series of resampled states
$t_i(c)$	Sample time of the ith state
$M_i(c)$	Pledged money at time t_i
$B_i(c)$	Number of backers at time t_i

Table 3: List and description of the variables describing a campaign c. The states $\{\mathbf{S}_i(c)\}$ are resampled to obtain $N_S = 1000$ states at regular time intervals, as explained in Section 2.3.

composed of the amount of money pledged $M_i(c)$ (normalized with respect to $G(c)$) and the number of backers $B_i(c)$.

Because each campaign is resampled to have N_S evenly-spaced states, the time $t_i(c)$ of the ith state $\mathbf{S}_i(c)$ is simply defined as

$$t_i(c) = L(c) + \frac{i-1}{N_S - 1} D(c), \ i \in \{1, 2, \ldots, N_S\}.$$

Table 3 summarizes the variables describing a campaign c.

3. SUCCESS PREDICTORS

Given a campaign c and its associated variables described above, we now introduce the algorithms we chose to predict its success. Our predictors use partial information: to predict the success of c, they only consider a prefix $\{\mathbf{S}_i(c)\}_{i \in \mathcal{I}}$ of its series of states, where $\mathcal{I} = \{1, 2, \ldots, S\}$ and $1 \leq S < N_S$.

Below, we will present the results for various values of S, i.e., predictions made at different states of progress of the funding campaigns. Each result is obtained by a predictor that is trained independently. It would be possible to have predictors that are able to predict the success for several (or all) values of S, however, we chose to have separate predictors for each value of S. Global predictors would require a variable input size (as the length of the history depends on S), which is more complicated to handle.

3.1 Dataset Separation

In order to train our predictors, select their parameters and evaluate their performance, we separate the dataset into 3 parts: 70% of the campaigns are selected as the *training set*, 20% as the *validation set* and the remaining 10% as the *test set*. These sets are randomly chosen and all results presented below are averaged over 10 different assignments.

3.2 Money-Based Predictors

The first family of predictors that we define only uses the series of amounts of money pledged $\{M_i(c)\}_{i \in \mathcal{I}}$, which we call *trajectory*, to predict the outcome of a campaign c. The first predictor, described in Section 3.2.1, simply compares the trajectory of a campaign with other known campaigns and makes a decision based on the final state of the k closest ones. The second, described in Section 3.2.2, builds a probabilistic model of the evolution of trajectories and predicts the success probability of new campaigns using this model. The performances of these two predictors are shown in Section 3.2.3.

3.2.1 kNN Classifier

Our first model is a k-nearest neighbors (kNN) classifier [2]. Given a new campaign c, its partial trajectory $\{M_i(c)\}_{i \in \mathcal{I}}$ and a list of campaigns for which the ending state is known, kNN first computes the distance between c and each known campaign c'

$$d_{\mathcal{I}}(c, c') = \sqrt{\sum_{i \in \mathcal{I}} \left(M_i(c) - M_i(c')\right)^2}.$$

Then, it selects $\text{top}_{k,\mathcal{I}}(c)$, the k known campaigns that are the closest to c with respect to the distance defined above, and computes the probability of success $\phi_{\text{kNN}}(c, \mathcal{I})$ of c as the average final state of these k nearest neighbors:

$$\phi_{\text{kNN}}(c, \mathcal{I}) = \frac{1}{k} \sum_{c' \in \text{top}_{k,\mathcal{I}}(c)} F(c').$$

3.2.2 Markov Chain

Our second predictor also uses the campaign trajectories $\{M_i\}$, this time to build a time-inhomogeneous Markov Chain that characterizes their evolution over time. To do so, we first discretize the (time, money) space into a $N_S \times N_M$ grid. This means that we discretize each campaign trajectory $\{M_i(c)\}$ to map the pledged money to a set $\mathcal{M}$ of N_M equally-spaced values[8], ranging from 0 to 1. For example, if $N_M = 3$, $\mathcal{M} = \{0, 0.5, 1\}$.

We thus obtain for each campaign c a series of discretized amounts of money pledged $\{M'_i(c)\}_{1 \leq i \leq N_S}$. The Markov model defines, for each sample i, a transition probability

$$P_{m,m'}(i) = \mathbb{P}(M'_{i+1} = m' \mid M'_i = m),$$

defining a transition matrix $\mathbf{P}(i) \in [0,1]^{N_M \times N_M}$, $\forall i \in \{1, 2, \ldots, N_S - 1\}$. These transition matrices are not specific to a campaign but learned globally over all campaigns in the training set.

Success Prediction with the Markov Model.

Using the transition probabilities described above, predicting the success of a campaign c is straightforward given its discretized amount $M'_i(c)$ at time i. We compute its success probability $\phi_{\text{Markov}}(c, i)$ given its current discretized amount of pledged money $M'_i(c) = m$ as

$$
\begin{aligned}
\phi_{\text{Markov}}(c, i) &= \mathbb{P}(M'_{N_S}(c) = 1 \mid M'_i(c) = m) \\
&= \sum_{m'} \mathbb{P}(M'_{N_S}(c) = 1 \mid M'_{i+1}(c) = m') \cdot \\
&\quad \mathbb{P}(M'_{i+1}(c) = m' \mid M'_i(c) = m) \\
&= \left[\prod_{i'=i}^{N_S-1} \mathbf{P}(i') \right]_{m,1},
\end{aligned}
$$

where the last step is obtained by repeatedly applying the law of total probability.

3.2.3 Results

We select the best parameters for each predictor by doing an exhaustive search on a wide range of values and evaluating the corresponding performances on the validation set. The optimal parameters found are $k = 25$ for *kNN* and $N_M = 30$ for *Markov*.

---

[8]All values higher than 1 are mapped to 1.

(a) *kNN* predictor

(b) *Markov* predictor

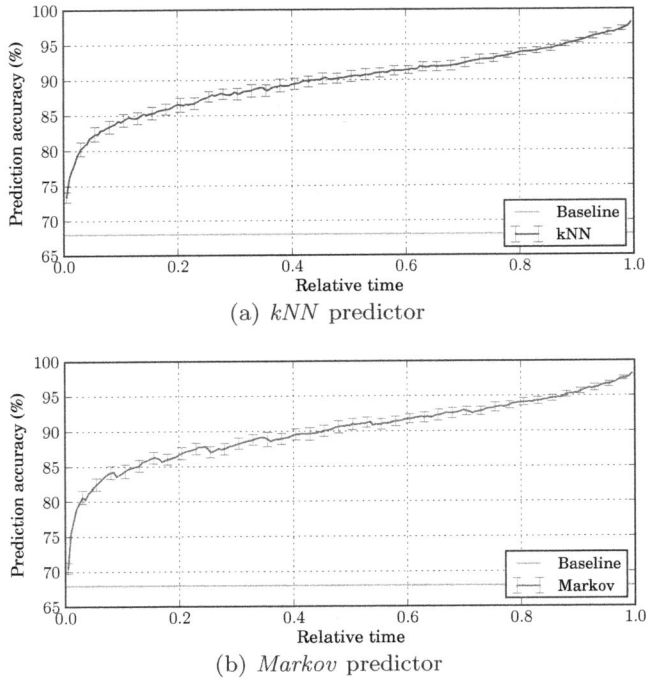

Figure 1: Prediction accuracy of the kNN and Markov predictors, along with the static baseline of Greenberg et al. [3]. For each relative time $t \in [0, 1]$, a predictor was trained using $\{M_i(c)\}_{i < \lfloor t N_S \rfloor}$ for all campaigns c in the training set. The value shown is the median accuracy over 10 runs and the error bars show the standard deviation over these runs.

Figure 1 shows the corresponding prediction accuracy over the test set for *kNN* (Figure 1a) and *Markov* (Figure 1b) predictors, along with the baseline of Greenberg et al. [3]. The baseline uses static campaign attributes, such as category, goal, and whether it has a video description or not, to predict the success of campaigns before their launch. The best accuracy obtained with this approach is 68%.

The two predictors perform similarly, and very well: after 15% of the duration of a campaign, its current amount of money pledged allows to predict its success with an accuracy higher than 85%. As time goes by, this accuracy steadily increases, to reach more than 97% in the very last moments.

However, *kNN* is very costly compared to *Markov*: it requires to keep all training samples in memory and to compute the distance to each of them when we want to classify a new sample. In contrast, *Markov* is compact, requiring to store only the matrices $\mathbf{P}(i)$, and computes the success probability of new samples very efficiently, requiring only matrix multiplications. It is thus noticeable that such a lightweight and elegant model performs as well as a more heavyweight method.

3.3 Social Predictors

Contrary to the predictors presented above, which use the amount of money pledged to predict the success of campaigns, the social predictors use side information, obtained from Twitter and Kickstarter's projects/backers graph. The first, described in Section 3.3.1, uses features extracted from the series of tweets related to a campaign, such as the number

of retweets and the number of people who tweeted. The second, described in Section 3.3.2, considers a graph linking projects and backers to extract some project features such as its number of first-time backers and the number of other projects with common backers. Both predictors then use a support vector machine (SVM) [1] to predict the campaigns' success based on the extracted features. Their results are shown in Section 3.3.3.

3.3.1 Tweets

As mentioned in Section 2, we have, for each campaign c, the list of all public tweets $\{T_i(c)\}$ that mention it. As each tweet has a timestamp, we can select the subset of tweets $\mathcal{T}_t(c) = \{T_i(c) \mid \text{timestamp}(T_i(c)) < t\}$ that were published before a time t. Using $\mathcal{T}_t(c)$, we can extract the following features:

- number of tweets, replies and retweets,
- number of users who tweeted,
- estimated number of backers[9].

We then add the campaign's goal $G(c)$ and duration $D(c)$ to these features and feed them to an SVM, resulting in a predictor $\phi_{\text{tweets}}(c, t)$.

3.3.2 Projects/Backers Graph

To extract the second set of features, we first need to build the projects/backers graph G_1. This graph contains all projects and backers in our training set as vertices, and has an edge between a project p and a backer b if and only if b backed p. The resulting graph is an undirected and unweighted[10] bipartite graph.

From G_1, we can extract the co-backers graph G_2: it is the projection of G_1 onto the project vertices. G_2 is an undirected weighted graph, where vertices are projects and the weight of an edge between two projects p_1 and p_2 is the number of backers who have pledged money to both p_1 and p_2. Figure 2 shows an example of a projects/backers graph G_1 (Figure 2a) and the corresponding co-backers graph G_2 (Figure 2b).

Using G_1 and G_2 built from our training set, we can now consider a new campaign c whose probability of success we want to estimate at some time t. To do so, we add the project p corresponding to c to G_1 and G_2, using its list of backers at time t to add the necessary edges in both graph.

Then, we extract the following features of the project p:

- number of projects with co-backers (i.e., the degree of p in G_2),
- number and proportion of these projects whose campaigns are successful,
- number of backers,
- number and proportion of first-time backers[11].

---

[9]We estimate the number of backers by counting the number of tweets that contain texts such as "I just backed project X", which is the default message proposed by Kickstarter.

[10]It would be interesting to consider a weighted version of this graph, where the weight of each edge corresponds to the amount of money pledged. Unfortunately, we do not have access to this information, and thus can only consider the unweighted version.

[11]First-time backers are users that only pledged money to the current project, and no other.

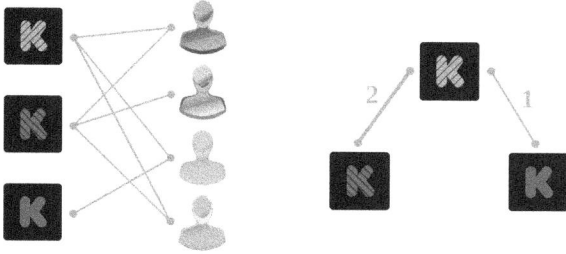

(a) Project/backers graph G_1 (b) Co-backers graph G_2

Figure 2: Example of a project/backers graph G_1 and the corresponding co-backers graph G_2. G_1 contains both projects and backers as vertices, and has an edge between a project p and a backer b if and only if b pledged money to p. G_2 is the projection of G_1 onto the project vertices, where the weight of an edge between two projects represents their number of common backers.

As with tweets, we then add the campaign's goal $G(c)$ and duration $D(c)$ to these features and feed them to an SVM, resulting in a predictor $\phi_{\text{graph}}(c, t)$.

3.3.3 Results

We train[12] the two SVMs described above using a Gaussian radial basis function (RBF) as kernel, thus having two parameters to tune:

- C: the soft margin penalty parameter,

- γ: the kernel coefficient for the RBF.

We perform an exhaustive search on a logarithmic scale for both parameters and evaluate the performance on the validation set to choose the best values. The best parameters for the *tweets* predictor are $C = 1000$ and $\gamma = 0.1$, whereas the best values for the *graph* predictor are $C = 100$ and $\gamma = 0.01$.

Figure 3 shows the corresponding prediction accuracy over the test set for the *tweets* predictor (Figure 3a) and the *graph* predictor (Figure 3b), along with the static baseline presented in Section 3.2.3. Although the performances are clearly inferior to those of the predictors that use the series of pledges, both social predictors quickly outperform the baseline performance of 68% obtained by Greenberg et al. [3]. The *graph* predictor has a fast increase in accuracy after a few time steps, then it decreases slightly towards the end. This effect could be countered by choosing the optimal values for SVM parameters independently at each time step, instead of once globally as we do now.

3.4 Combined Predictor

Predictors using the series of pledges show a good prediction accuracy, especially towards the end of the campaign. At the beginning, however, the accuracy could still be improved. Such improvement would be very useful to creators and backers, allowing them to react accordingly to correct the course of a campaign. A higher accuracy at later stages, however, would not be of high interest.

---

[12]We use a Python library [5] to train the SVMs.

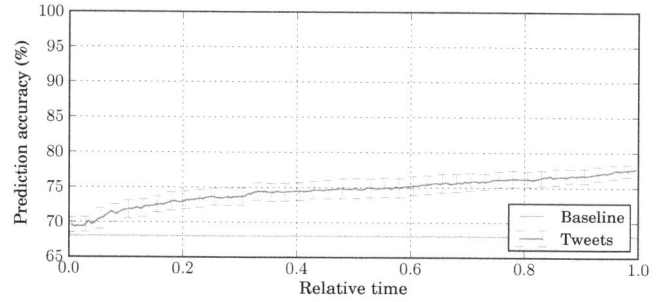

(a) *tweets* predictor

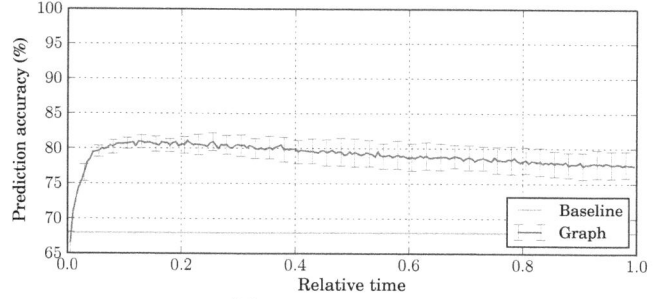

(b) *graph* predictor

Figure 3: Prediction accuracy of the *tweets* and *graph* predictors, along with the static baseline of Greenberg et al. [3]. For each relative time $t \in [0, 1]$, a predictor was trained using features extracted from tweets or the projects/backers graph at time t, for all campaigns c in the training set. The value shown is the median accuracy over 10 runs and the error bars show the standard deviation over these runs.

To improve the accuracy of the predictors presented in Sections 3.2 and 3.3, we propose to train an SVM to take the individual predictions and combine them into a final prediction. The features used by the combiner are the campaign goal $G(c)$, its duration $D(c)$, along with the probabilities of success obtained using each of the four individual predictors.

3.4.1 Results

As with the social predictors described in Section 3.3.3, we use a RBF kernel for the SVM, thus having two parameters C and γ to tune. To do so, we run an exhaustive search on a logarithmic scale for both of them. The best parameter values we obtain are $C = 100$ and $\gamma = 0.1$. Figure 4a shows the corresponding prediction accuracy of the combiner, along with the static baseline presented in Section 3.2.3. Figure 4b highlights the early-stage performance of the combined predictor. Figure 4c shows the relative improvement of the combiner with respect to the best individual predictor, at each time step.

Overall, the improvement of the combiner is the strongest at the beginning of the campaign, increasing significantly the accuracy: the first combined prediction is 4% more accurate than any individual predictor. In other words, on average 4 hours after the launch of a campaign, the combined predictor can assess the campaign's probability of success with an accuracy higher than 76%.

4. CONCLUSION

In this paper, we introduce an exclusive dataset of Kickstarter campaigns. We study the prediction of their success, based on two kinds of features: the time-series of money pledged and social attributes. We show that predictors that use the series of money pledged a reach high prediction accuracy, with more than 85% of correct predictions after only 15% of the duration of a campaign. Although the social predictors reach a lower accuracy, we propose a way of combining them with time-series predictors. The combination results in a substantial increase in prediction accuracy in the very first moments of a campaign (4%), precisely when the ability to predict success has the most value. This can provide helpful directions to both project creators and backers.

There are many future research directions we would like to pursue. First, we should study the projects/backers graph, to explore its structure and main characteristics. We are especially interested in its dynamics: can we model the "diffusion" of success across this network? Another promising direction is the Twitter graph: how does the success of a campaign depend on the spread of messages on Twitter?

For now, our predictors only output a probability of success, but act as a black box: no reason for the probable success/failure is given. While this prediction itself can already be helpful to both campaign creators and backers, as discussed in the introduction, the next step would be to give them the specific characteristics of the campaign that could be improved.

5. REFERENCES

[1] Corinna Cortes and Vladimir Vapnik. Support-vector networks. *Machine learning*, 20(3):273–297, 1995.

[2] Thomas Cover and Peter Hart. Nearest neighbor pattern classification. *IEEE Transactions on Information Theory*, 13(1):21–27, 1967.

[3] Michael D Greenberg, Bryan Pardo, Karthic Hariharan, and Elizabeth Gerber. Crowdfunding support tools: predicting success & failure. In *CHI'13 Extended Abstracts on Human Factors in Computing Systems*, pages 1815–1820. ACM, 2013.

[4] Ethan Mollick. The dynamics of crowdfunding: An exploratory study. *Journal of Business Venturing*, 2013.

[5] Fabian Pedregosa, Gaël Varoquaux, Alexandre Gramfort, Vincent Michel, Bertrand Thirion, Olivier Grisel, Mathieu Blondel, Peter Prettenhofer, Ron Weiss, Vincent Dubourg, et al. Scikit-learn: Machine learning in Python. *The Journal of Machine Learning Research*, 12:2825–2830, 2011.

[6] Twitter Developers. Frequently asked questions. Retrieved August 24, 2013 from https://dev.twitter.com/docs/faq#6861.

[7] Rick Wash. The value of completing crowdfunding projects. In *ICWSM'13: 7th International AAAI Conference on Weblogs and Social Media*, 2013.

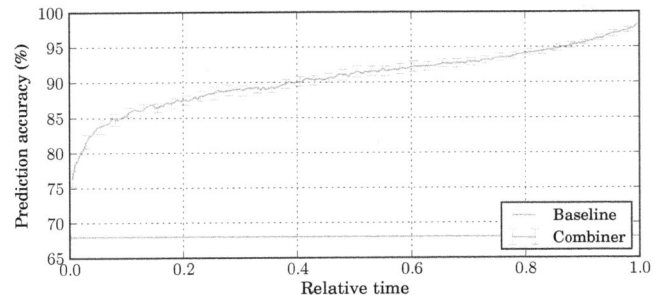

(a) Combiner performance

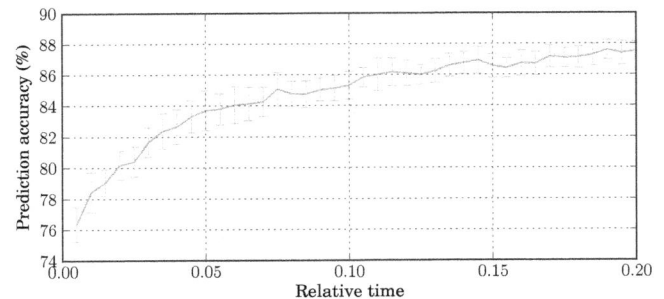

(b) Detail of early-stage combiner performance

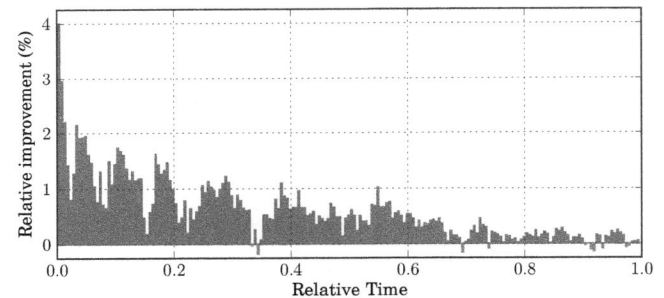

(c) Relative improvement over best predictor

Figure 4: Prediction accuracy of the combined predictor along with the static baseline of Greenberg et al. [3] (a), detail of the first 20% the campaign (b) and improvement of the combiner relative to the best individual predictor (c). For each relative time $t \in [0, 1]$, a combined predictor was trained using the the four predictions of individual predictors at time t, for all campaigns c in the training set. The value shown is the median accuracy over 10 runs and the error bars show the standard deviation over these runs.

Crowd Crawling: Towards Collaborative Data Collection for Large-scale Online Social Networks

Cong Ding[†], Yang Chen[‡], and Xiaoming Fu[†]

[†]Institute of Computer Science, University of Göttingen, 37077 Göttingen, Germany
[‡]Department of Computer Science, Duke University, Durham, NC 27708, USA
{cong, fu}@cs.uni-goettingen.de, ychen@cs.duke.edu

ABSTRACT

The emerging research for online social networks (OSNs) requires a huge amount of data. However, OSN sites typically enforce restrictions for data crawling, such as request rate limiting on a per-IP basis. It becomes challenging for an individual research group to collect sufficient data by using its own network resources. In this paper, we introduce and motivate *crowd crawling*, which allows multiple research groups to efficiently crawl data in a collaborative way. Crowd crawling is carefully designed by addressing several practical challenges including resource diversity of different partners, strict request rate limiting from OSN providers, and data fidelity. We implemented and deployed a crowd crawling prototype on PlanetLab, and demonstrated its performance through evaluations. We have made the datasets crawled in our evaluation publicly available.

Categories and Subject Descriptors

C.2.4 [**Computer-Communication Networks**]: Distributed Systems

Keywords

Online Social Network; Data Collection; Crowd Crawling

1. INTRODUCTION

Online social networks (OSNs) have witnessed an evolutionary development and deployment, which attract a lot of attention all over the world. Recently, they have become an indispensable component in people's daily life, and a hot research topic involving many professionals from a variety of fields [11]. Given the huge amount of users, most research on this field needs a high volume of data from popular OSN sites, such as Facebook [6,7], Twitter [12,16], Renren [10,13], Weibo [5,8], and Foursquare [9]. Most of the datasets used in OSN research were crawled by individual groups using their own network resources and computing clusters. However, as most of the OSN sites have very strict request rate

limiting on IP addresses and user accounts, it becomes challenging for an individual research group to crawl sufficient data covering a significant portion of an entire OSN site. A main reason is the number of IP addresses a research group owns is typically limited, especially for universities outside the United States. For example, the computer networks group at University of Göttingen owns only 14 public IPv4 addresses. It is difficult for a single group to compete against the increasing crawling requirement and unavoidable request rate limiting. For example, Weibo allows up to 1000 API requests per hour per IP address, and 150 requests per hour per user account. Moreover, different research groups might be interested in the same OSN site, while they crawl data independently nowadays. Such uncoordinated crawling may (1) waste computing and network resources as well as researchers' programming effort; (2) introduce unnecessary overhead (and extra cost) for OSN service providers; (3) lead to even stricter request rate limiting policies from OSN service providers; (4) not be able to provide universal/standard datasets as ground truth for the research community to develop and evaluate different research methods on social network analysis.

In this paper, we introduce and motivate *crowd crawling*, which leverages resources from various research groups to achieve large-scale distributed crawling. Crowd crawling allows several groups, so-called *partners*, to work in a collaborative way. In the collaboration, we require every partner to contribute crawled data beyond a pre-defined base line, if they want to benefit from the contents crawled by other partners. This collaboration framework has been used in PlanetLab in the past 10 years and proved working well [1].

We design and implement a crowd crawling prototype, and deploy it on PlanetLab to demonstrate its performance. Crowd crawling can achieve efficient data collection, while obeying OSNs' request rate limiting policies. There are three main challenges for building a crowd crawling system.

- **Resource diversity of different partners.** Different partners might allocate different amount of resources for crawling. Such diversity might include different number of crawlers, different hardware configurations of crawlers, and diverse bandwidths. These factors will lead to different data fetching efficiency. Therefore, the crawling system needs to be able to efficiently assign crawling tasks to different crawlers. Also, the system should be robust to several dynamic issues including node churning and bandwidth instability.

- **Different rate limiting policies from OSN providers.** Most OSN sites enforce request rate limiting policies. To date, mainstream OSN sites, such as Facebook, Twitter and Weibo, use IP- and account-based policies, which require careful consideration in our design. Also, for new rate limiting proposals such as link-based rate limiting [13], we introduce a compatible way to achieve efficient crawling.

- **Data fidelity.** The distributed nature of crowd crawling introduces data fidelity issue, which might be caused by malicious attacks. A straightforward motivation of such attacks is free-riding. Some partners might just want to benefit from other partners' results without contributing their own resources accordingly. Therefore, they pretend to provide enough crawled results, while in fact they just submit fake results. We propose a lightweight, flexible, and easy-to-configure solution to prevent such attacks.

The main contributions of this paper are three-fold. First, we propose and motivate crowd crawling, an integrated distributed data collection framework for online social networks. Second, we design a practical crowd crawling system, which works in an efficient and reliable way. Third, we implement a proof-of-concept prototype of crowd crawling, and deploy it on PlanetLab. We evaluate the crowd crawling prototype using a viable Weibo crawling example.

The reset of this paper is organized as follows. We introduce crowd crawling system design in Section 2. In Section 3, we provide implementation details of the proof-of-concept prototype, and discuss the evaluation result on PlanetLab. We then present related work in Section 4. Finally, Section 5 discusses several open issues for further investigations in this field, and concludes this paper.

2. SYSTEM DESIGN

In this section, we first present the high-level framework of crowd crawling (Section 2.1), by introducing three key components and describing how they collaborate. Then we discuss several practical considerations in crowd crawling.

In mainstream OSN sites like Facebook, Twitter, Weibo, Renren, and Foursquare, every user is represented by a unique identifier (UID). For instance, in Facebook, UIDs are 64bit integers. The overall crawling project is divided into small tasks, and each task consists of a set of UIDs. To crawl OSNs, we have to get UIDs first (Section 2.2). With the UIDs in hand, TAM will assign tasks to crawlers. The design of crowd crawling has to deal with the three challenges: handling resource diversity of partners' computers (Section 2.3), bypassing strict rate limiting (Section 2.4), and data fidelity (Section 2.5).

2.1 Overview

As shown in Figure 1, there are three components in the system: crawlers, task assignment module (TAM), and result collection module (RCM). Every partner is required to contribute some computers as crawlers, and provide Internet connectivity for these crawlers. For every data crawling project, we need the partners to elect a *coordinator*, which is trustworthy and responsible for assigning tasks to other partners. This coordinator is also in charge of collecting crawled results from other partners, and preparing an aggregate dataset. Both TAM and RCM are maintained by

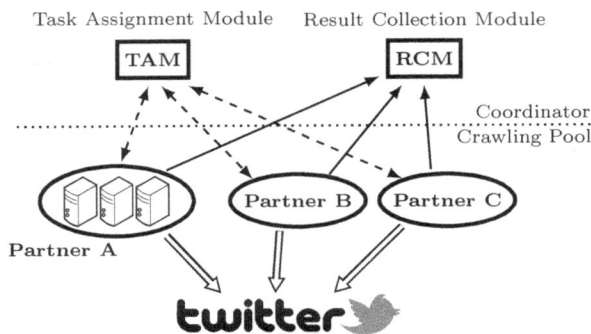

Figure 1: Crowd crawling architecture. ◄ - ► denotes task assignment, and ⟶ denotes crawled data delivery. The task assignment module (TAM) and result collection module (RCM) are controlled by the coordinator. Crawlers are owned by partners, and crawl OSNs collaboratively.

the coordinator. TAM is built based on a distributed hash table (DHT); and RCM is installed in a cluster of distributed servers to ensure scalability. TAM and RCM synchronize results periodically to ensure all the assigned tasks are finished properly and to detect prospective malicious behaviors from crawlers.

Crawlers. After getting a task from TAM, the crawler collects data of each UID in the task one by one. It sends HTTP request to the OSN site and collects data via parsing HTML documents or decoding JSON objects. Finally, the crawler sends the crawled data to RCM, and then repeats all the steps for the next task. We set every crawler's default crawling speed at a legitimate request rate (e.g., 80% of the request rate limiting), to avoid violating the request rate limiting policies.

Task assignment module. Task assignment module (TAM) acts as a controller to moderate the crawling procedure. It arranges tasks to crawlers, and obtains the latest crawling progress information from RCM. To maintain the system state, it keeps three sets of UIDs: an unassigned UID set, an assigned-but-unfinished UID set, a finished UID set. Each of these three sets is stored in a DHT. To reflect the latest system state, TAM moves UIDs between the three sets based on the status of tasks and dynamics of crawlers (Section 2.3).

Result collection module. Result collection module (RCM) is responsible for aggregating crawling results. It stores received crawling results into a local database, and updates the crawling progress to TAM. On one hand, it discovers unknown UIDs from the crawling results, i.e., social connection data of the crawled users, and reports them to TAM for further crawling (Section 2.2). On the other hand, by inspecting the fetched results, it finds out prospective malicious partners to ensure data fidelity, and reports them to TAM in real-time (Section 2.5).

2.2 Fetching UIDs

Most of the mainstream OSN sites, except Foursquare [9], assign UIDs continuously. Therefore, we need an efficient algorithm to fetch UIDs of OSN users. Conventionally, we can leverage social connections among users. It can start from a small set of known users, and fetch the UIDs of their neighbors, and neighbors' neighbors in a recursive way. There are several social graph traversal algorithms [6, 12, 17, 22], such as breadth first search (BFS), metropolis-hasting random walk (MHRW), and frontier sampling (FS). Alternatively, some OSN sites provide interfaces for keyword-based search or public global timeline. This establishes another way to fetch massive UIDs.

2.3 Handling Crawling Failure

The crawling of a task may fail due to many reasons, as the crawlers are owned by different partners and may crash unexpectedly. To keep an active view of the crawling, TAM applies a timeout policy to monitor all the crawlers. When a task has been assigned to a crawler, RCM will be notified to keep track of this task. If the crawling result of this task has not been received by RCM after the pre-defined timeout threshold, this task will be assigned to another crawler in the next task request. We use adaptive timeout here, which means the timeout threshold is adaptive to the history crawling time of this crawler. There are several adaptive timeout strategies proposed and used in Internet flow characterization [19], packet retransmission [4], etc. In our system, we extend the simple adaptive timeout algorithm used in STUN [18]. At the beginning, we set a large-enough timeout value for every crawler, which varies by the feature of target OSN sites. The coordinator can perform a crawling test to estimate the time cost for fetching each UID, to define the number of UIDs each task contains and select the initial timeout value. We adjust the timeout value based on the real crawling time of a certain crawler which decreases the failure handling cost. If the real crawling time of a task is less that $1/4$ of the current timeout for the relevant crawler, we set the timeout to be $1/2$ of the current timeout. If a timeout event happens, we double the current timeout while ensuring it is less than the initial timeout value.

2.4 Bypassing Request Rate Limiting

OSN sites enforce several request rate limiting policies to prevent aggressive crawling. Some are widely used, like IP-based rate limiting and account-based rate limiting. Some are newly proposed and emerging, like link-based rate limiting. In this section, we describe how to leverage crowd crawling to bypass them.

IP-based rate limiting. IP-based rate limiting is quite common for mainstream OSN sites such as Facebook, Twitter, and Weibo. Such limiting restricts the number of requests per hour per IP address. Crowd crawling is designed to address it in a straightforward way. As different partners own different IP blocks, they can form an aggregate pool of massive IP addresses to bypass IP-based rate limiting policies.

Account-based rate limiting. Account-based rate limiting is another common restriction. It is also used by Facebook, Twitter, and Weibo. Such limiting restricts the number of requests every hour in a per-authenticated-user basis. Account registrations are typically limited to IP addresses. For example, Weibo allows users to register up to 3 accounts per IP address per day. Benefiting from the large number of IP addresses all the partners have, it is able to create a large amount of OSN accounts.

Although we need to introduce some non-human accounts at this point, we strictly require these accounts to act properly. These accounts will never perform any harmful behaviors like spamming.

Link-based rate limiting. Different from the two typical strategies described previously, link-based rating limiting strategy is proposed in Genie [13]. The intuition behind Genie is that a legitimate user tends to visits users who are connected with or close to the user in the social graph. In contrast, Genie assumes that a crawler is not easy to create enough social links to be close to all the users whose data the crawler wants to fetch. Therefore, Genie launches rate limiting for requesting distant users' data. To bypass this prospective restriction, crowd crawling has to utilize some user accounts which are well connected in the social graph. According to our tests in Facebook and Weibo, creating social connections with legitimate users can be done quickly in an automatic way. This helps us easy to get short distances with users we are going to crawl and bypass link-based rate limiting policies. Note that we respect to users' privacy. Although the crawlers' accounts will establish some social links with legitimate users, crowd crawling would never collect the data which are configured as "visible to friends".

Facebook, the largest online social network in the world, who has the global Alexa traffic rank of 1 in August 2013, applies an undirectional friendship system. When A is B's friend, B must be in A's friend list as well. Every user can send friend requests to any other users. In January 2013, we performed two tests in Facebook: (1) sending friend requests to a random set of Facebook users; (2) sending friend requests to a tightly connected community, which means a random user with its friends, and its friends' friends. For each of the tests, we send friend requests to 1000 selected Facebook users. These requests were sent from a Facebook account manually created with a fictional profile, including an attractive picture, complete personal information, and some posted statuses. 24 hours after sending these requests, we examined how many users had accepted the friend requests. The test result shows that the acceptance rate is 4.3% for random friend requests, and 6.3% for community. The median number of friends of a Facebook user is about 100 [21]. As a result, in order to create an account having 100 friends, we can send friend requests to 2325 randomly selected users, or to 1588 users in the aforementioned tightly connected community. We can perform this automatically by leveraging Facebook's API.

Launched in August 2009, Weibo has become the largest microblogging service in China, which has the global Alexa rank of 33 in August 2013. Weibo has attracted more than 500 million registered users by 2012 [15]. Same as most microblogging services such as Twitter, the follow relationship in Weibo is directional, which means you do not have to follow your followers. Similar to what we did in Facebook, we created a fictional account with an attractive picture and appealing personal information. We also posted some tweets to this account. In January 2013, we performed three tests in Weibo: (1) following a random set of Weibo users; (2) following a selected random set of Weibo users, all of which have #followers/#followings between 0.5 and 2; (3) following a tightly connected community, which means a random user and other users who have bi-directional friendship with the random user (i.e. followed by this random user and following this user). For each of the tests, we followed 1000 Weibo users. We check the number of users following back in 24 hours. The follow-back rates are 1.9%, 3.1%, and 5.8%, respectively, for the three cases. Similar to Facebook, we can easily create a Weibo account with hundreds of followers.

2.5 Data Fidelity

As a collaborative crawling solution, we need a reliable scheme to verify the fidelity of the crawled data provided by different partners. As crawling data is a resource-intensive task, some partners might want to get benefits from other partners' results, while contributing less than what they should. For some tasks, a malicious partner might let its crawlers submit some fake results obtained by random generators, instead of performing real crawling. Therefore, we need a strategy to ensure the aggregate crawling results trustworthy. We assume that a reliable partner always tries its best to provide accurate results. Also, a malicious partner might try to escape from being detected, i.e., it might occasionally act properly.

Our solution is based on the accountability of every partner. For every completed task, the coordinator knows which partner it was assigned to. Based on this, we introduce a *redundant crawling* scheme to detect prospective malicious crawlers. This scheme is lightweight and easy to configure.

Besides TAM and RCM, we require the coordinator to have one or multiple *redundant crawler(s)*. According to the information provided by RCM, the coordinator maintains a set of recently obtained results and corresponding UIDs. According to a pre-defined percentage $p\%$ (e.g., 1%), the coordinator picks $p\%$ of these UIDs for redundant crawling, i.e., let the redundant crawler(s) perform crawling according to these randomly selected UIDs. After a round of redundant crawling, the coordinator is able to verify malicious behaviors, by comparing the results of the same UID submitted by the redundant crawlers and by a partner. For each partner i, the coordinator maintains a credit score S_i. For every round, we set an initial credit score K to each partner. During the verification procedure, once a mismatching is found, we decrease S_i by 1. Once S_i falls below zero, partner i will be regarded as malicious, and all results submitted by this partner will be treated as unreliable. Accordingly, this partner will be excluded in the final stage of result sharing.

Due to the dynamic nature of OSN sites, the desired information of a certain UID might change over time. For example, a new friend is added, or a new tweet is posted. Therefore, a mismatch might not be caused by fake crawling. On one hand, we keep the interval between two crawlings short to reduce the negative impact of the dynamic features. On the other hand, the selection of the initial credit score K provides some tolerance of mismatching.

For some partners which are found to be possibly unreliable due to historical record, the coordinator might verify a higher portion of its crawled results. However, we still ensure a minimal percentage of sampling for every partner.

3. SYSTEM IMPLEMENTATION AND PERFORMANCE EVALUATION

Our proof-of-concept prototype consists of 2,000 lines of Python code. In its TAM, we use Redis as its in-memory database benefiting from Redis's high throughput[1], and we have implemented a simple append-only database for RCM.

We deploy TAM and RCM on two servers located in Tsinghua University, China. Each of them has a 16-core 2.5GHz

---

[1]Benchmark in Linode 2048 instance shows that Redis can handle 195 thousand SET requests per second, or 250 thousand GET requests per second. More details are available in http://redis.io/topics/benchmarks.

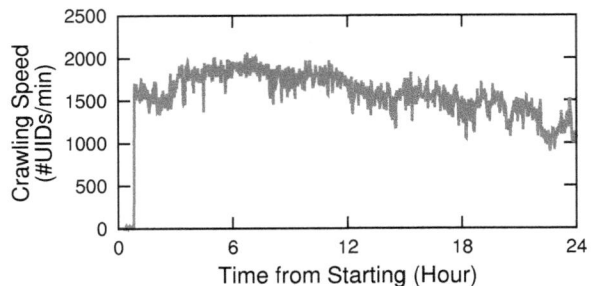

Figure 2: Overall crawling speed

processor and 64 GB memory. We use PlanetLab to emulate a number of crawling partners. By trying to connect to each PlanetLab server on August 18th, 2013 from 11am to 12pm (if not explicitly stated otherwise, the time zone is CEST), we get 472 available PlanetLab servers distributed globally, which are from 236 research institutes. There are 202 servers located in North America, 237 located in Europe, and 33 located in Asia/Oceania. These servers act as crawlers. Every crawler runs one thread for crawling and sleeps a uniformly random time between 0 and 2 seconds after finishing each HTTP request.

We utilize crowd crawling to collect data from Weibo, the largest microblogging service in China. To obtain a large number of random UIDs, we leverage Weibo's API to access the latest posted tweets in the whole site, and get the UIDs of the tweet publishers. We used 5 servers for obtaining UIDs. Each server queried this API every 2 seconds for one day (from August 17th at 2pm to 18th at 2pm). In total, we obtained 3.95 million unique UIDs. Our distributed crawling is based on these UIDs. For each user, we crawled its profile, followings, followers, and all posted tweets. We performed an aggressive crawling using crowd crawling with the 472 PlanetLab servers as its crawlers. The crawling lasted 24 hours from August 18th at 4pm to 19th at 4pm. During the 24 hours, crowd crawling collected 2.22 million users' data with the total size of 1.86 terabytes. In the following, we describe details and observations of the crawling.

Overall crawling speed. As shown in Figure 2, the crawling speed keeps relatively stable. On average, crowd crawling crawls 1.54 thousand UIDs (1.29 gigabytes data) per minute. The relatively low crawling speed in the beginning is caused by the starting time of crawlers. Interestingly, the average number of crawled UIDs per minute during the night of China is 17.1% higher than daylight, which might be caused by the longer response time of Weibo during the daytime.

Diverse crawling efficiency. From the cumulative distribution function (CDF) of number of UIDs collected by each crawler, shown in Figure 3, we can see that more than half crawlers have crawled more than 5.23 thousand users' data, while only 4.87% crawlers have crawled data of less than 100 users. We divide our crawlers into three regions, i.e., America, Europe, and Asia/Oceania. We can see the overall distribution of crawlers in America and Europe follow a similar distribution. Also, we find that Asia/Oceania contributes most of the fastest crawlers. That might be because Weibo is located in this region, which results in a high throughput.

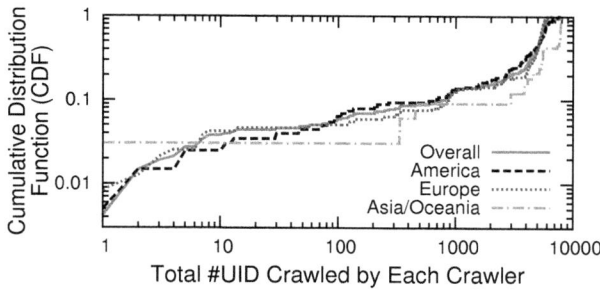

Figure 3: Crawling speed distribution

Collected data. After running crowd crawling for one day, we have obtained 2.22 million users' full content (profiles, social connections, and posted tweets). 49.2% of them are male users, while 50.8% of them are female users. The median number of a user's followings is 179, the median number of a user's followers is 140, and the median number of tweets is 333. There are 1.26% users registered in 2009, 16.8% in 2010, 27.0% in 2011, 27.4% in 2012, and 27.6% in 2013. From these users, we have obtained 1.04 billion tweets. To the best of our knowledge, the coverage of our data is significantly larger than previous work such as Fu *et al.*'s [5] (30 thousand UIDs crawled in 6 days) and Guo *et al.*'s [8] (1 million UIDs crawled in 1 month). This better coverage demonstrates the advantage of crowd crawling. The huge amount of data crawled in such a short period of time also provides a consistent snapshot of Weibo. We foresee that if we perform the crowd crawling prototype for a longer time, we will obtain the full content of tens of millions of users or even hundreds of millions. Analyzing the crawled Weibo data is left for future work.

4. RELATED WORK

Using crowdsourcing for online social network data collection is relatively new, while there is still some research on related areas.

Lots of work on distributed computing and measurement has been proposed in the past decade. They divide tasks to subtasks to achieve distributed computing and measurement, while crowd crawling utilizes this idea for distributed collaborative crawling. MapReduce [3] divides a complete computational task into subtasks, and assigns these subtasks to a number of nodes. By contributing the processor cycles, these nodes work in parallel to solve the original task. With the similar idea, crowd computing [14] provides a novel approach using mobile devices to achieve large-scale distributed computation. It combines social structure to improve performance. Dasu [20] is a distributed network measurement platform. Built as a BitTorrent extension, Dasu clients are hosted by numerous Internet end users. With Dasu, a number of network measurement activities can be conducted at the Internet's edge.

There has been some work on distributed crawling, for either web pages or OSNs. To our knowledge, all of them utilize a cluster of computers to achieve efficient crawling, without involving multiple partners. Cho *et al.* [2] present their parallel crawling system architecture. They consider several practical issues like huge amount of URLs manage-

ment and partitioning function. However, this system is designed for web page crawling, i.e., getting pages from a number of linked websites. It is significantly different from OSN crawling, which typically focuses on one particular OSN site with strict rate limiting. Gjoka *et al.* [7] demonstrate a distributed crawling system with their own server cluster. They utilize 28 servers as crawlers to collect data from Facebook. Such solution is still restricted by the IP-based rate limiting, unless the crawling organization has a large number of IP addresses.

5. CONCLUSION AND DISCUSSION

In this paper, we introduce and motivate crowd crawling, a scalable framework to enable collaborative social data collection. Crowd crawling is robust to different rate limiting manners enforced by OSN sites, and can prevent free-riders. Our evaluations on PlanetLab has demonstrated the high efficiency of OSN data collection, i.e., we can finish the crawling of 2.22 million Weibo users in 24 hours, including their profiles, social connections, and posted tweets.

As the first step of our collaborative social data collection framework, crowd crawling has been demonstrated with several advantages. At the same time, we are aware of several open issues. We would not expect the discussions in this section could reach a conclusion at this point, while we hope that our discussion would provide some insights for further investigations in this field.

First of all, different OSN sites have different terms of service (ToS). Some are stricter, while some are more flexible. However, for research purposes, different groups of people from academia continuously perform aggressive crawling in different OSN sites. As many of these crawling are duplicate, we hope our crowd crawling could at least save the load of OSN sites, while improving the crawling efficiency of research groups. In short, crowd crawling might still violate the ToS of some OSN sites, but at least it is more OSN-friendly than today's independent aggressive crawling.

Secondly, unlimited data sharing might cause ethical issues. We believe that the crawled data should be owned by the groups who contributed resources to crawling. The motivation here is similar to PlanetLab testbed. Nevertheless, if all the groups in a crawling project have reached an agreement, they have the flexibility to make the data public, or release a sampled subset. There are two noteworthy issues in making data sets public. On one hand, to preserve users' privacy, only anonymized data should be released. On the other hand, some OSN sites might prohibit public sharing of its particular contents. For instance, it is not allowed to share data crawled from Twitter [23].

Thirdly, in our current design, every partner contributes crawled data more than the pre-defined criteria can obtain the entire aggregate data set. We plan to build an incentive framework as our prospective future work, with which the partners who contribute more will be rewarded. This is desirable because all the contributions made by different partners are recorded in crowd crawling.

Finally, some researchers might want to get private data from OSN sites, while different OSN sites have different user privacy configurations. For Twitter and Weibo, if we know a user's UID, we can retrieve her entire profile, social connections, and all posted contents. Differently, for Facebook, if we know a user's but are not in her friend list, we might be only able to obtain some fields in her profile and social connections. Therefore, similar to existing individual crawlers, crowd crawling is restricted by the privacy configurations of OSN sites.

6. ACKNOWLEDGEMENTS

We are grateful to the anonymous reviewers, Ruichuan Chen and our shepherd, Anne-Marie Kermarrec, for their insightful comments.

7. REFERENCES

[1] Joining PlanetLab. http://www.planet-lab.org/joining.

[2] J. Cho and H. Garcia-Molina. Parallel crawlers. In *WWW*, 2002.

[3] J. Dean and S. Ghemawat. Mapreduce: simplified data processing on large clusters. In *OSDI*, 2008.

[4] S. W. Edge. An adaptive timeout algorithm for retransmission across a packet switching network. In *SIGCOMM*, 1984.

[5] K.-W. Fu and M. Chau. Reality check for the Chinese microblog space: a random sampling approach. *PloS ONE*, 2013.

[6] M. Gjoka, M. Kurant, C. T. Butts, and A. Markopoulou. Walking in Facebook: a case study of unbiased sampling of OSNs. In *INFOCOM*, 2010.

[7] M. Gjoka, M. Kurant, C. T. Butts, and A. Markopoulou. Practical recommendations on crawling online social networks. *JSAC*, 2011.

[8] Z. Guo, J. Huang, J. He, X. Hei, and D. Wu. Unveiling the patterns of video tweeting: a Sina Weibo-based measurement study. In *PAM*, 2013.

[9] W. He, X. Liu, and M. Ren. Location cheating: a security challenge to location-based social network services. In *ICDCS*, 2011.

[10] J. Jiang, C. Wilson, X. Wang, P. Huang, W. Sha, Y. Dai, and B. Y. Zhao. Understanding latent interactions in online social networks. In *IMC*, 2010.

[11] L. Jin, Y. Chen, T. Wang, P. Hui, and A. V. Vasilakos. Understanding user behavior in online social networks: A survey. *IEEE Communications Magazine*, 2013.

[12] H. Kwak, C. Lee, H. Park, and S. Moon. What is Twitter, a social network or a news media? In *WWW*, 2010.

[13] M. Mondal, B. Viswanath, A. Clement, P. Druschel, K. P. Gummadi, A. Mislove, and A. Post. Defending against large-scale crawls in online social networks. In *CoNEXT*, 2012.

[14] D. G. Murray, E. Yoneki, J. Crowcroft, and S. Hand. The case for crowd computing. In *MobiHeld*, 2010.

[15] J. Ong. China's Sina Weibo grew 73% in 2012, passing 500 million registered accounts. *thenextweb.com*, 2013.

[16] J. M. Pujol, V. Erramilli, G. Siganos, X. Yang, N. Laoutaris, P. Chhabra, and P. Rodriguez. The little engine(s) that could: scaling online social networks. In *SIGCOMM*, 2010.

[17] B. Ribeiro and D. Towsley. Estimating and sampling graphs with multidimensional random walks. In *IMC*, 2010.

[18] J. Rosenberg, J. Weinberger, C. Huitema, and R. Mahy. STUN–simple traversal of user datagram protocol (UDP) through network address translators (NATs). *RFC 3489*, 2003.

[19] B. Ryu, D. Cheney, and H.-W. Braun. Internet flow characterization: adaptive timeout strategy and statistical modeling. In *PAM*, 2001.

[20] M. A. Sánchez, J. S. Otto, Z. S. Bischof, D. R. Choffnes, F. E. Bustamante, B. Krishnamurthy, and W. Willinger. Dasu: pushing experiments to the Internet's edge. In *NSDI*, 2013.

[21] J. Ugander, B. Karrer, L. Backstrom, and C. Marlow. The anatomy of the Facebook social graph. *arXiv:1111.4503*, 2011.

[22] T. Wang, Y. Chen, Z. Zhang, T. Xu, L. Jin, P. Hui, B. Deng, and X. Li. Understanding graph sampling algorithms for social network analysis. In *SIMPLEX*, 2011.

[23] A. Watters. How recent changes to Twitter's terms of service might hurt academic research. *readwrite.com*, 2011.

Building Confederated Web-based Services with Priv.io

Liang Zhang
College of Computer and Information Science
Northeastern University
Boston, MA
liang@ccs.neu.edu

Alan Mislove
College of Computer and Information Science
Northeastern University
Boston, MA
amislove@ccs.neu.edu

ABSTRACT

With the increasing popularity of Web-based services, users today have access to a broad range of free sites, including social networking, microblogging, and content sharing sites. In order to offer a service for free, service providers typically monetize user content, selling results to third parties such as advertisers. As a result, users have little control over their data or privacy. A number of alternative approaches to architecting today's Web-based services have been proposed, but they suffer from limitations such as relying the creation and installation of additional client-side software, providing insufficient reliability, or imposing an excessive monetary cost on users.

In this paper, we present Priv.io, a new approach to building Web-based services that offers users greater control and privacy over their data. We leverage the fact that today, users can purchase storage, bandwidth, and messaging from cloud providers at fine granularity: In Priv.io, each user provides the resources necessary to support their use of the service using cloud providers such as Amazon Web Services. Users still access the service using a Web browser, all computation is done within users' browsers, and Priv.io provides rich and secure support for third-party applications. An implementation demonstrates that Priv.io works today with unmodified versions of common Web browsers on both desktop and mobile devices, is both practical and feasible, and is cheap enough for the vast majority users.

Categories and Subject Descriptors

C.2.4 [**Performance of Systems**]: Distributed Systems—*Distributed applications*; H.3.5 [**Information Storage and Retrieval**]: Online Information Services—*Web-based services*

Keywords

Web; privacy; online social networks; confederated services; Web browsers

1. INTRODUCTION

Users today have access to a broad range of free Web-based services (e.g., online social networks such as Facebook, microblogging services such as Twitter, content sharing sites such as Flickr). All of these services operate under a similar model: Users entrust the service provider with their personal information and content (e.g., their comments, photos, political and religious views, sexual orientation, occupations, identities of friends). In return, the service provider makes their service available for free by monetizing the user-provided information and selling the results to third parties (e.g., advertisers). Even though users are often provided with privacy controls on these sites, these controls generally only affect flow of information to other users or third-party applications; users today have no option of making their data private *from* the service provider. This model also makes it difficult for users to retrieve all of their data from the provider (e.g., if the provider closes the service [31, 32]) or remove their data entirely.

Researchers have investigated a number of approaches that provide users with greater control and privacy in such services, ranging from encrypting data uploaded to the provider [22, 38, 46] to dividing data between provider-hosted and user-hosted servers [10, 43] to implementing a fully decentralized system [11, 15, 18]. Unfortunately, none of these approaches have enjoyed widespread adoption, as they suffer from one or more of three general limitations:

- **Accessibility** Most proposals require users to install dedicated client software, such as desktop applications or browser plugins. As users typically access services from a variety of devices, these solutions require significant effort of the user (who has to install the software) and the developer (who has to build and maintain clients for various devices).

- **Reliability** Systems that rely on hosting content on end-user machines [11, 15, 18], home routers [30], or smartphones [45] maintain availability via replication. Unfortunately, such systems are known for suffering from fundamental reliability tradeoffs in dynamic environments [7].

- **Cost** Systems that require users to rent their own server from a cloud provider [43] or pay for subscription of the service [5] are likely to be too expensive for most users.

In this paper, we present Priv.io, an alternate approach to implementing Web-based services that provides users with control over their data, ensures privacy, and avoids the limitations of practicality, reliability, and cost. In Priv.io, each user provides resources necessary to support their use of the service by purchasing computing resources (storage, bandwidth, and messaging) from cloud providers such as Amazon Web Services or Windows Azure. Unfortunately, having users purchase *computation* from cloud providers is not practical in Priv.io: at the finest granularity, users still must purchase an entire virtual machine for an hour, and having an always-on server is too expensive for most users. Instead, Priv.io is built entirely in JavaScript, and all computation[1] is done within the users' Web browsers while they visit the Priv.io Web site. Priv.io works with unmodified versions of common Web browsers such as Safari, Chrome, Firefox, and Internet Explorer, as well as browsers on mobile OSes including Android and iOS.

The result is a *confederated*[2] service, where each user retains control over his or her own data. We demonstrate that services similar to Facebook, Twitter, and Flickr can be implemented in a confederated manner with very low monetary costs for most users. Thus, Priv.io provides users with an alternative to today's model of paying for Web-based services by giving up their privacy.

Priv.io provides strong guarantees of user privacy. Priv.io uses attribute-based encryption [9, 10] to encrypt all content stored on the cloud provider; this encryption is implemented in JavaScript within the user's browser. Thus, only the users' browsers ever see plaintext content. Priv.io also provides rich support for third-party applications (e.g., Farmville [53]) by providing an API that is implemented within the users' browsers. Priv.io uses browser-based sandboxing to ensure that third-party applications can only access the data that users allow and cannot leak any user information to the application provider or other third-parties.

We evaluate Priv.io using a number of techniques. *First,* we estimate the monetary cost of using Priv.io with traces from real-world content sharing sites; we demonstrate that 99% of users would pay no more than $0.95 per month if services similar to Facebook, Twitter, or Flickr were built using Priv.io. *Second,* we implement a prototype of Priv.io—available at `https://priv.io`—as well as two applications: a Facebook-like news feed application and an instant-messaging application. *Third,* we use microbenchmarks to show that downloading and uploading content is of similar speed to existing services, and that leveraging the users' browsers for computation is both efficient and practical. *Fourth,* we measure the user-perceived performance of Priv.io and demonstrate that Priv.io is practical on desktop browsers today and is likely to be sufficiently fast on mobile devices in the near future.

The remainder of this paper is organized as follows. Section 2 presents a measurement study aimed at estimating the cost of Priv.io to users of a variety of today's Web-based services. Section 3 describes the design of Priv.io and Section 4 details how Priv.io supports third-party applications in a se-

cure manner. Section 5 presents a discussion of some issues that arise when deploying Priv.io. Section 6 presents an evaluation of Priv.io, and Section 7 describes related work. Section 8 concludes.

2. OVERVIEW

Recall that our approach is to implement a Web-based service in a confederated manner, by having users provide the resources necessary to support their use of the service via cloud providers such as Amazon Web Services. While cloud providers typically offer bandwidth, storage, and messaging at relatively fine granularity, computation is still sold at a relatively coarse granularity (typically an entire virtual machine for an hour). As a result, even running the smallest of Amazon's EC2 servers (`t1.micro`) would cost a user $14.40 per month [3], not including EBS storage and I/O costs. Moreover, running an entire virtual server is overkill for most users; most of the time, this server would sit idle.

The result is that cloud services can be practically used today to provide storage, bandwidth, and messaging, but not computation. Our insight in Priv.io is to *use the user's Web browser to provide the computation needed* while they use Priv.io. Doing so provides a number of benefits: Using a user's Web browser for computation reduces costs (since users do not need to purchase computation), reduces security concerns (since content is encrypted in the browser, no third-party sees unencrypted content), and is practical (since most cloud providers allow storage and messaging services to be accessed via HTTP). However, only using browser-based computation also presents a few challenges: it results in a system where users are not always online (if a user does not have an browser window open to Priv.io, computation cannot be done on their behalf) and only provides a restricted model of computation (browser JavaScript is sandboxed, and cannot access the local disk or have unfettered access to the networking stack).

2.1 Cost study

Before we describe how we address these challenges, we briefly estimate the cost to users if services such as Facebook were implemented in a confederated manner. In other words, if each user contracted with a cloud provider to pay for their use of services such as Facebook, what would the per-user costs be? We examine this question in the context of social networking sites, microblogging sites, and content sharing sites.

Unfortunately, estimating the per-user cost is not entirely straightforward, as data availability is scarce and the costs of optimizations and overhead are hard to estimate. As a result, our goal is not to deduce the exact costs, but rather, to provide a reasonable estimate.

Social networking: Facebook To estimate the cost of storing and serving Facebook content, we use a collection of 651,539 Facebook profiles[3] from a large regional network [20]. The data includes all wall posts, status updates, photos, and videos uploaded by these users. We assume that photos are 64 KB [8], and that videos have a bitrate of 1.403 Mbps [35].

Unfortunately, our data set does not include how often content is viewed; the most detailed statistics on the viewing

---

[1]Of course, computation is also necessary on the cloud provider's side to implement the storage and messaging abstractions. For the purposes of this paper, computation refers to Priv.io and third-party application logic.

[2]We choose the adjective *confederated* rather than *federated*, as members in a confederation retain autonomy and are generally free to leave (e.g., the Articles of Confederation between the original 13 U.S. colonies).

---

[3]At the time of collection (2009), Facebook profiles were by default visible to all members of the same regional network.

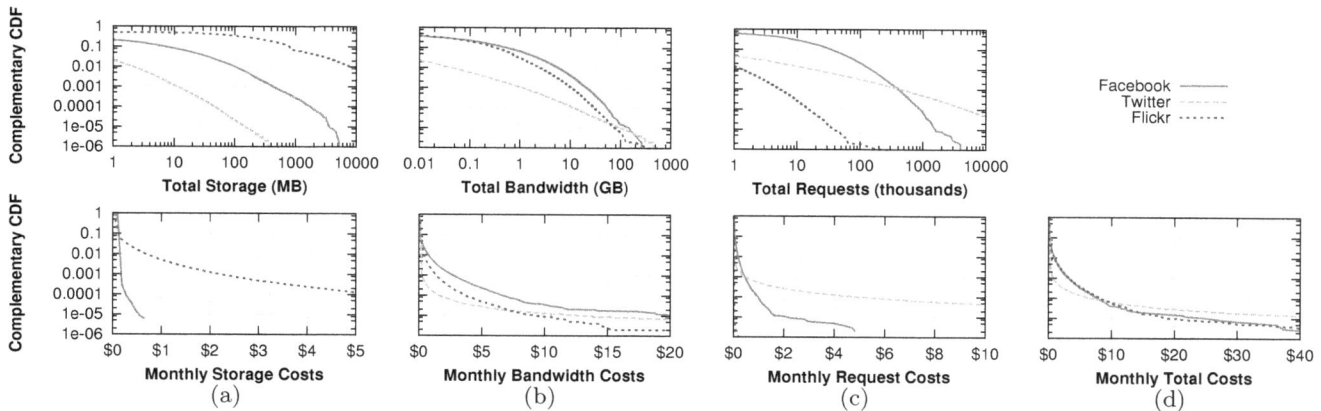

Figure 1: Complementary cumulative distributions of total monthly (a) storage, (b) bandwidth, (c) requests per user (top) and resulting costs (bottom) for Facebook, Twitter, and Flickr users (note the logarithmic scale on the y-axis). Also shown is the distribution of (d) total monthly costs. 99% of users would have to pay no more than $0.95 per month in all three scenarios.

patterns of Facebook content come from the description of Haystack [8], Facebook's photo serving system. We use the photo view distribution (Figure 7 in [8]) to parametrize our calculations.[4] We assume that videos are viewed with the same popularity distribution as photos, but at 1/20th the rate.

Microblogging: Twitter To estimate the cost of storing and serving Twitter content, we use a data set containing an almost complete set of all tweets issued up to September 2009 [12]. This data set contains 1,755,925,520 tweets issued by 54,981,152 users. We observe that the average size of a tweet (including all metadata fields) is 2551 bytes. Unfortunately, we do not have tweets view counts, but we estimate this by using the number of Twitter followers (subscribers) each issuing user has (i.e., every follower views every tweet).

Content sharing: Flickr To estimate the cost of storing and serving Flickr content, we use a data set from early 2008 consisting of 2,570,535 Flickr users sharing 260,317,120 photos [29]. This data set contains all of the users in the large, weakly connected component on Flickr. We know how many photos were uploaded by each user, but we do not know the number of times each photo was viewed. Instead, we derive the view distribution from studies by Yahoo! researchers [50]. We assume that, on average, photos require 4 MB of storage, and 2 MB of bandwidth per view (photos are typically encoded on disk in multiple sizes [8]).

Analysis We estimate the monthly per-user storage, bandwidth, and request costs for each of these three sets of users on Amazon's S3 service.[5] Figure 1 presents the comple-

mentary cumulative distributions of the total storage, bandwidth, and requests per user per month (top) and resulting costs (bottom). Figure 1(d) presents the overall cost per user per month.

We make a number of observations. *First*, the different systems show different cost characteristics: the cost of hosting Facebook content is dominated by bandwidth (due to the high average user degree, requiring distributing the same content to many friends), the cost of hosting Flickr content is dominated by storage (due to the high resolution of Flickr photos), and the cost of hosting Twitter content is dominated by requests (due to the small but frequent content). *Second*, we observe that for the vast majority of users, the total costs are quite tiny: for 99% of users, the monthly total costs are no more than $0.95 (Facebook), $0.88 (Flickr), and $0.23 (Twitter). *Third*, our calculations assume a naïve design; optimizations such as content aggregation and caching are likely to provide lower costs in practice.

3. DESIGN

We now detail the design of Priv.io, comprised of two components: *Priv.io core* and *applications*. Priv.io core provides libraries for accessing user information, manipulating the user's data, and communicating with other users; most user-facing functionality is built as applications on top of Priv.io core. When user visits https://priv.io, the Web server returns Priv.io core's JavaScript. This page allows a user to register, log in, control Priv.io settings, and install applications. It also serves as a container for hosting sandboxed applications, and provides libraries for these applications to use. Below, we describe the design of Priv.io core, followed by how applications are implemented (Section 4).

We begin by discussing the assumptions we make (Section 3.1), followed by the Priv.io building blocks (Sections 3.2 and 3.3). We then describe how these are used to implement basic Priv.io functionality (Section 3.4).

3.1 Assumptions

The Priv.io core design includes three components: the Priv.io Web server, users' Web browsers, and users' cloud providers. We briefly overview the assumptions we make

---

[4] We note that Facebook receives 120 million new photos and 100 billion photo views per day [8]. Given that photos receive 29% of their lifetime views on their first day [8] and, at the time, Facebook users had an average of 130 friends [19], we estimate that newly uploaded photos receive 1.85 views per friend of the uploader on their first day.

[5] At the time of publication, Amazon charges $0.095/GB/month for storage, $0.12/GB for outgoing bandwidth (with the first GB free each month), and $0.004 per 10,000 GET requests [4].

Provider	Storage	Messaging	REST API	Object Versioning	DNS Support	Authentication
Amazon	☑	☑	☑	☑	☑	☑
Azure	☑	☑	☑	☑	☑	☑
Google	☑	☑	☑	☑	☑	☑
HP Cloud	☑	☐	☑	☐	☐	☑
Rackspace	☑	☐	☑	☑	☑	☑
Dropbox	☑	☐	☑	☑	☐	☐

Table 1: Summary of required features in Priv.io, and their current support by major providers. Amazon, Azure, and Google support all required services today.

about each of these. We assume that some entity runs the Priv.io Web server (for now, our research group runs the server, but it could easily be run by a non-profit organization). As we will see later, the Priv.io Web server receives relatively few requests, and it is feasible to run such a server with few resources (for higher reliability, the site could be served using techniques like geo-replication or content distribution networks). We assume that users are running the latest version of a common Web browser with JavaScript and HTML5 support. We assume the security of DNS (i.e., that an attacker cannot modify Priv.io DNS entries).

We assume that the cloud provider provides certain services, listed below:

- **Storage/Messaging** We assume the provider offers both data storage and messaging (distributed queue) services.

- **REST API** We assume that operations can be performed via a REST API [42], enabling access to the API via JavaScript from the user's browser.

- **Versioning** We assume that the provider supports storing multiple versions of objects.

- **DNS support** We assume that users can access their storage containers via DNS names (e.g., bob.s3.amazonaws.com maps to Bob's storage).

- **Authentication** We assume that the provider allows permissions to be specified on stored objects.

Table 1 details which of today's providers support these features; we observe that three providers exist that can support Priv.io today. We assume that the users' cloud providers are honest-but-curious, meaning the providers faithfully implement the service that the users have contracted for (e.g., storing objects, retrieving the latest version of objects, delivering messages) but may attempt to decrypt data or messages. Finally, we assume that users' cloud providers are available, meaning the providers do not close their service without warning (users are of course free to migrate their data to new cloud providers at any time).

3.2 Attribute-based encryption

Similar to other content-sharing systems such as Persona [10], Priv.io uses attribute-based encryption (ABE) [9]. In general, ABE dramatically simplifies key management when sharing content with multiple parties. To use ABE, users first generate an ABE public key and an ABE master key (the former is made publicly available and the latter is kept private). Users can then generate ABE private keys for each of their friends, where each ABE private key is generated with one or more *attributes* such as friend, family, or yearBorn=1963.

Users can encrypt content items using expressions over attributes, and only friends whose ABE private key satisfies the given expression are able to decrypt. For example, one such expression might be

$$\text{family} \vee (\text{yearBorn} < 1980)$$

ABE is collusion-resistant [9], meaning users cannot collude to decrypt content that they could not decrypt separately. For a more detailed description of ABE, we refer the reader to the paper by Bethencourt et al. [9].

3.3 Priv.io building blocks

We now describe the building blocks used in Priv.io; a reference for the notation used is provided in Table 2. As is typical in Web-based services sites, users in Priv.io choose a username and password. Each user u has an ABE master key m_u and an ABE public key P_u. Each user also has a special ABE private key p_u^{self} with the attribute self; this allows other users to encrypt messages for u using the self attribute, similar to more traditional public key encryption.

The Priv.io Web server serves two functions. First, it distributes the Priv.io JavaScript, CSS, and images to the users when they visit https://priv.io. Second, it maintains the priv.io DNS domain, which serves as a directory for users' cloud providers.

The Priv.io JavaScript provides libraries for using the REST APIs of the cloud providers' storage and messaging services via XML HTTP Requests (XHRs). In order to use these APIs, though, the JavaScript must respect the default same-origin policy enforced by browsers (i.e., by default, the Priv.io JavaScript cannot make an XHR to alice.priv.io unless the HTML document was originally loaded from alice.priv.io). Priv.io addresses this problem in one of three ways: (a) providers such as Amazon's S3 and Windows Azure allow users to specify a Cross-Origin Resource Sharing (CORS) [17] policy, allowing such access, (b) systems like Amazon's Simple Queuing Service provide a permissive crossdomain.xml file, allowing a small embedded Flash object to make cross-domain requests, or (c) other providers like DropBox allow a stub HTML file to be placed on the target domain, which is used to load the JavaScript in a separate iframe.

Notation	Meaning
P_u	u's ABE public key
m_u	u's ABE master key
p_u^v	u's ABE private key given to friend v
p_u^{self}	u's special ABE private key with policy self
C_u^{user}	u's credentials for accessing his cloud services
C_u^{friend}	u's credentials, given to his friends, allowing limited access to his cloud services

Table 2: Notation used in the description of Priv.io.

All Priv.io encryption and decryption is implemented in JavaScript; more details are provided in Section 6.

3.4 Priv.io operations

Registration When signing up with Priv.io, a user u visits https://priv.io and provides their desired username, password, email address, cloud provider, and two sets of provider access credentials (e.g., AWS access/secret keys). The first set of credentials (C_u^{user}) are to be used by the user himself, while the second set (C_u^{friend}) are to be used by the user's friends. Of the user-provided data, *only the user's username, email address, and cloud provider* are uploaded to the Priv.io server (the email address allows the user to later change their cloud provider).

Meanwhile, the Priv.io JavaScript generates an ABE master key m_u and ABE public key P_u, as well as an ABE private key p_u^{self} with the attribute self. Then, using credentials C_u^{user}, the JavaScript creates two storage containers on the cloud provider: a publicly-readable container, and a private container that can only be read with one of the user's two credentials. Finally, the JavaScript creates the user's message queue, configured so that C_u^{friend} is only able to write to the queue.

Upon receiving the user's registration request, the Priv.io server marks the username as assigned and sets up the user's DNS entries. Each user has three DNS entries: [username].priv.io maps to the user's public container, private.[username].priv.io maps to the user's private container, and queue.[username].priv.io maps to the user's message queue.

The Priv.io JavaScript then creates two files in the publicly-readable container: public_key containing P_u, and credentials containing

$$[m_u, p_u^{\text{self}}, C_u^{\text{user}}, C_u^{\text{friend}}]$$

encrypted using the user's selected password.

Login After a user is registered, login is straightforward. The user visits https://priv.io and enters their username and password. The Priv.io JavaScript fetches [username].priv.io/credentials, and decrypts the file with the user's password. If the password was correct, the login can proceed, as the JavaScript now has all of the credentials and keys needed to operate on the user's behalf. It is worth noting that the only interaction with the Priv.io server is fetching the Priv.io root page; all others are with the user's cloud provider. A diagram is provided in Figure 2.

Friending Priv.io is built to allow users to interact with friends, and friends need not share the same storage provider. Users can discover friends either through existing friends (e.g., users can browse the list of their friends' friends), or via out-of-band means (e.g., users can exchange Priv.io usernames).

To become friends, users need to securely exchange ABE keys (p_u^v) and credentials for their cloud providers (C_u^{friend}). To do so, let us assume that Alice and Bob wish to become friends in Priv.io. Alice first fetches Bob's ABE public key from bob.priv.io/public_key. Then, Alice generates an ABE private key p_{Alice}^{Bob} for Bob, with the attributes Alice assigns to Bob (e.g., colleague). Alice then stores

$$[p_{Alice}^{Bob}, C_{Alice}^{\text{friend}}]$$

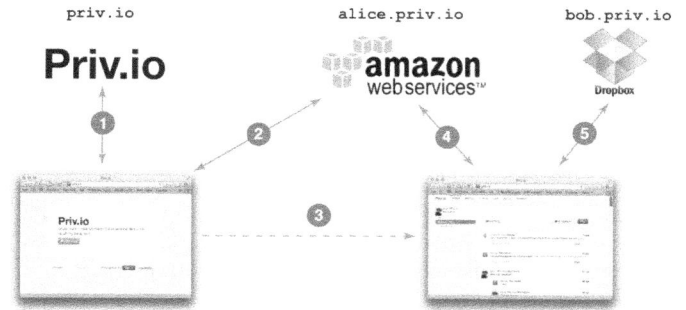

Figure 2: Diagram of login process for user Alice in Priv.io. Alice ❶ visits https://priv.io, obtaining the Priv.io JavaScript. Upon entering her username and password, her browser ❷ contacts her cloud provider S3, ❸ verifies her password , and communicates with ❹ her cloud provider as well as ❺ the cloud providers of her friends. Note that the only communication with the main Priv.io server is fetching the original JavaScript.

encrypted under Bob's ABE public key with attribute self at the location alice.priv.io/friends/bob. Bob performs similar actions for Alice.

Bob then fetches alice.priv.io/friends/bob, and decrypts it using p_{Bob}^{self}. Bob is then able to write to Alice's queue and read from Alice's private container (using $C_{Alice}^{\text{friend}}$), as well as decrypt Alice's shared objects (using p_{Alice}^{Bob}). Alice fetches bob.priv.io/friends/alice and has similar privileges. Each of the two stores a copy of the newly-acquired credentials and keys in their own private storage encrypted under the policy self, allowing each to obtain them on subsequent logins. Finally, both remove the encrypted files from their public container.

If Alice and Bob are two hops away (i.e., one of Alice's friends is also a friend of Bob), Priv.io automatically uses one of the intermediate friends to relay the request. Priv.io sends a message to the intermediate friend, who forwards it on to Bob; Bob is then automatically notified of Alice's incoming friend request. Otherwise, Alice must tell Bob using out-of-band means that she has issued the request. Since the vast majority of friendships in online social networks are established between users who are friends-of-friends [28], we expect most friend requests to be able to be relayed.

Default attributes To simplify sharing, Priv.io generates private keys for friends with two default attributes, in addition to any user-provided attributes. The first attribute is @username, which allows users to share content with only a single user (e.g., if Alice wished to share content only with Bob, she could specify the policy @bob). The second attribute is @@, which is given to all friends. This attribute allows users to share content with all of their friends.

Modifying friend permissions Users in Priv.io may want to change the permissions given to friends, either to add attributes, remove attributes, or remove the friend entirely. Adding attributes simply requires generating a new ABE private key for the friend, and giving the friend the new key. Removing a friend is the same as removing all attributes from the friend.

Removing attributes from a friend requires re-keying. To simplify this process, Priv.io assigns an integral value to each

193

ABE attribute, where the value is initialized to 0 and is incremented each time a user has that attribute removed. For example, consider user Alice with friends Bob and Charlie assigned the following attributes

> Bob   :   @@=9, @bob, work=2, soccer=1
> Charlie :   @@=9, @charlie, work=2, it_dep=3

Now, if Alice wishes to remove the work attribute from Charlie, Priv.io increments the work value to 3, and reissues an ABE private key to Bob with the attributes

> Bob   :   @@=9, @bob, work=3, soccer=1

(note that Priv.io does not need to re-issue a key to Charlie). Any new content Alice shares with the work attribute is encoded with the policy work≥3 ensuring that only friends with re-issued keys have access.[6]

Communication Priv.io uses the messaging service of users' cloud providers to enable communication with friends. After logging in, the Priv.io JavaScript connects to the user's queue and processes any messages. While online, the Priv.io JavaScript remains connected the queue and continues to process any additional messages. The only Priv.io control messages that are sent are updating ABE private keys and friendship requests; all other messages are application-level messages and are delivered to the corresponding application (discussed in the following section). Friends do not need to be online for the user to send messages to them; cloud providers typically buffer messages for multiple weeks.

Caching encryption policies ABE operations are significantly more expensive than symmetric encryption operations. To mitigate the impact of expensive ABE operations, Priv.io is configured to use ABE to only encrypt and decrypt AES keys. Actual content objects are then encrypted under AES keys. Furthermore, Priv.io caches the AES keys used for each unique encryption policy; doing so allows Priv.io to only invoke expensive ABE operations when establishing friends, modifying friends, or using a new encryption policy.

4. THIRD-PARTY APPLICATIONS

Almost all user-facing functionality in Priv.io is implemented as applications on top of the Priv.io core libraries. Similar to existing sites like Facebook, applications may be implemented by third parties, and need not be trusted. Applications are implemented using HTML and JavaScript, and are displayed to the user as part of the Priv.io Web page. Thus, the challenge in Priv.io is to provide rich support for third-party applications, while simultaneously providing strict guarantees of security and privacy for users. In particular, we wish to ensure that applications cannot leak user information back to the application provider or any other entity.

4.1 Application API

Priv.io presents an API for applications to be written against. Since Priv.io is implemented entirely within a user's browser, the API is implemented within the browser as well. Priv.io is designed to support social networking-like applications (Facebook, Twitter, and Flickr), but could also be

---

[6] Any previously-shared content will still be accessible to Charlie, as it was encoded with work≥2. If this is not desired, content can be re-encrypted with an updated policy.

Method	Description
requestPermissions(c)	Requests access for the application to methods c
getUsername()	Returns the user's username
getFriends()	Returns usernames of the user's friends
getFriends(u)	Returns usernames of friend u's friends
getAttributes()	Returns the set of attributes assigned to the user's friends
store(k, v, p)	Stores data v under key k, encrypted with policy p
retrieve(u, k)	Returns the value previously stored under key k in u's storage; may return multiple versions
send(u, m)	Sends message m to friend u's instance of this application
receive()	Receives any pending messages
delete(m)	Marks a previously received message as successfully processed

Table 3: Subset of the Priv.io application API, covering API permissions, user information, storage, and communication. All methods are protected by permissions (users must permit applications to make API calls).

used to build other applications (e.g., Web-based document editing, shared calendars, etc.). Applications in Priv.io are logically separate and cannot exchange data or messages.

Similar to the approach taken by services such as Facebook, applications must request and receive *permission from the user* to make various API calls. When requested, Priv.io presents a dialog to the user, identifying the application and the access that it desires. Priv.io records the user's response, and then uses the specified policy to allow or deny API calls by the application.

A subset of the Priv.io application API is presented in Table 3, and is discussed below:

User information Similar to the Facebook API, applications can request profile information about the current user or any of the user's friends.

Storage Applications are allowed to store and retrieve data from the user's private storage container. Each application is given a storage folder, and is only able to access its own content (applications cannot read other applications' data). When storing data, applications specify an ABE policy for encrypting the data (e.g., self for only the user, or family for all friends with the attribute family). Applications can also request to read data in friends' containers written by another instance of the same application, but can only do so if the user is able to decrypt the data.

Communication Applications are allowed to send and receive messages to and from the same application run by friends. This is implemented by sending messages to the specified friend's message queue, and reading from the user's own queue. The Priv.io code multiplexes and demultiplexes messages, and buffers any incoming messages for an application until it is run.

4.2 Managing applications

Developers register Priv.io applications with the Priv.io Web server similar to user registration; each application is given a unique name (e.g., newsfeed). The Priv.io Web server makes the application available to users from a subdomain that is hosted by the Priv.io Web server (e.g., the

Newsfeed app is available at http://newsfeed.app.priv.io/). The Priv.io Web server is responsible for serving all application HTML, JavaScript, CSS, and images.

Users install an application by providing Priv.io with the app name (e.g., newsfeed); Priv.io records all apps that a user has installed in the user's private storage, along with their permissions, and reloads the list upon each login. Users can later remove an application by asking Priv.io to delete it. Priv.io then removes the application from the user's list, and deletes any application-stored data and queued messages.

4.3 Security and privacy

Running third-party applications in Priv.io brings up two security concerns: *First*, can we restrict applications to only using the Priv.io API? In other words, can we prevent applications from accessing Priv.io JavaScript objects, or conducting attacks like cross-site scripting [33,34], frame hijacking [6], or frame busting [40]? *Second*, can we prevent applications from leaking user data obtained from the Priv.io API, either via XHRs or by loading DOM (document object model) objects?

In order to address the these concerns, Priv.io *sandboxes* all third-party application code using iframes, loading each application in a separate iframe. Applications access the Priv.io API using the postMessage [23] feature in HTML5 to send API requests to the main Priv.io frame (the application's parent frame). If the API request is allowed (based on user preferences), the response is delivered back to the application via postMessage on the application's iframe.[7] This mechanism prevents applications from directly accessing any Priv.io JavaScript objects.

However, iframes by default are allowed to load arbitrary content, meaning an application could leak user information obtained from the Priv.io API by loading DOM objects. For example, an application wishing to leak the information that user Alice is friends with Bob could request to load http://malicious-domain.com/alice-bob.png. To constrain applications from leaking data, each application's iframe is loaded with a Content Security Policy[8] (CSP). In brief, CSP allows a server to specify what client-side actions the pages it serves can take. Priv.io instructs the browser to disallow the application's iframe from making any network requests other than to [appname].app.priv.io (which is hosted by the main Priv.io server). As a result, the application is constrained to only using the Priv.io API.

4.4 Limitations

Due to the architecture of Priv.io, there are a few applications that exist on sites today that cannot be replicated. For example, any operation that requires a global view of the user data (e.g., global search) is not possible, as there is no entity in Priv.io that can view all data. Other examples include applications that allow users to interact with random users who they are not friends with (e.g., ChatRoulette).

However, many services that might appear to require global information can usually be at least partially replicated. For example, a "friend suggestion" feature could po-

---

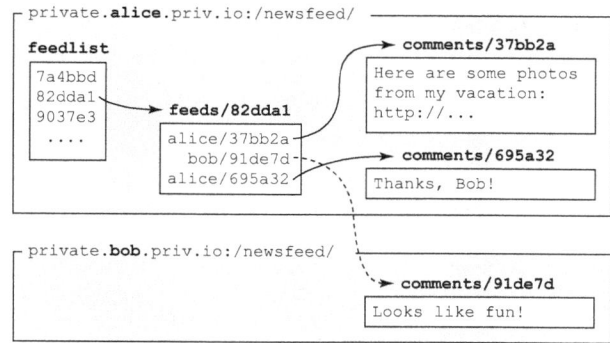

Figure 3: Diagram of how Newsfeed uses storage in Priv.io. Each user stores their own content, and the user who creates each thread stores a feed file linking together all comments.

---

tentially be implemented as an application that collects the structure of the user's local network (friends and friends-of-friends) and suggests others the user likely knows [41]. We leave a more in-depth exploration of such techniques to future work.

4.5 Demonstration applications

To demonstrate that existing Web-based services' functionality can be reproduced in Priv.io, we outline two applications that we have implemented.

Newsfeed Priv.io provides functionality similar to Facebook's News Feed via the Newsfeed application. In the application, users start a thread by posting a comment, uploading a photo, or sharing a link. Each thread is shared with a specific ABE policy, controlling which of the user's friends are able to see the thread. Friends who are able to see the thread are able to comment on the thread, and the comments are made visible to all friends for whom the thread is visible. Similar to the News Feed, the threads are sorted by creation date.

Newsfeed stores three types of objects using the storage API. Each individual comment is stored by the user who created it. The user who created the thread also stores a feed object, which simply contains references to all comments in the thread (including the user's original comment). Finally, each user has a single feedlist object that contains references to all feeds created by the user. Newsfeed uses the communication API when a user comments on a friend's feed. A message is sent to the user who owns the feed containing a reference to the comment; when the user owning the feed receives the message, Newsfeed adds the reference to the feed object, allowing other friends to then see the comment.

When users launch the Newsfeed application, it scans all of the friends' feedlists, integrating all of the visible feeds into a single news feed. A diagram showing Newsfeed's use of the storage API is presented in Figure 3.

Chat Priv.io allows users to "chat" by providing the instant messaging application Chat. The application is written entirely using the communications API. Users invite others to chat via a invitation message, and each chat message is broadcast to all other participants of the chat. As a result, Chat provides similar functionality to applications on existing sites, and could easily be extended to (optionally) archive conversations, allow file transfers, and so forth.

---

[7]Applications cannot impersonate other applications (making messages sent via postMessage appear as if they are from another origin), since the postMessage mechanism is secured by the browser [6].

[8]CSP is a new security mechanism provided in HTML5, and is supported by the latest versions of many browsers.

5. DISCUSSION

We now discuss a few deployment issues with Priv.io.

Consistency and reliability In Priv.io, users only write to their own storage location, preventing a number of consistency problems. However, users may be logged in to Priv.io from multiple locations at once, exposing Priv.io to potential consistency issues due to multiple writers. To address this problem, Priv.io leverages the object versioning (described in Section 3) supported by the cloud provider. Specifically, when Priv.io writes an updated version of an object to the user's storage location, it first checks to see if there is a newer version of the object present than the one that its pending write is based on. If such an object exists, Priv.io first downloads the updated object, and *merges* the two. Finally, Priv.io writes the new version of the object back, and deletes both of the previous versions. As a result, Priv.io itself and all applications must be able to perform merges on storage objects that may have diverged.

Priv.io allows each user to select the desired level of availability and durability for their content through the choice of their cloud provider. For example, on Amazon's S3 service, users can choose between eleven 9s of durability or four 9s of durability for content, at different price points.

Reliable message delivery Because Priv.io is implemented within a browser, the user could decide to close the window at any time, thereby killing all Priv.io JavaScript. This property makes implementing reliable message delivery for applications particularly challenging, as a message may be delivered to an application, but the Priv.io window could be closed before the application finishes processing the message. To avoid such a scenario, Priv.io requires applications to explicitly call **delete**(m) on each message m after they have finished processing it. Only at that point is the message deleted from the cloud provider's message queue.[9] Thus, Priv.io provides *at-least-once* delivery semantics for messages, and applications must be written to tolerate receiving the same message multiple times.

Security To prevent man-in-the-middle attacks on Priv.io users, all interaction with the Priv.io Web server is over HTTPS. In the future, we aim to provide support for DNSSEC to ensure the integrity of Priv.io DNS entries as well (e.g., to prevent cache poisoning attacks).

Each user's encrypted **credentials** file is stored in a publicly visible location (e.g., alice.priv.io/credentials). As a result, we are particularly concerned about brute-force password cracking attacks. To reduce the ability for an attacker to decrypt a user's **credentials** file, we first choose a random initialization vector when encrypting the credentials and salt the password, preventing attackers from using rainbow tables [36]. Second, we use the PBKDF2 password strengthener [25], which greatly raises the cost of a brute-force attack. Third, we require strong passwords for users in the form of pass phrases [37], which often possess more entropy than basic passwords.

An additional concern is whether an attacker can perform a man-in-the-middle attack during friend establishment, or intercept the exchanged friend credentials. We first note

that all friend exchange information is encrypted with the destination's ABE public key, making it unreadable by the attacker. Second, since each user is the only entity that is able to write to their public storage area, malicious users are unable to forge friend requests with credentials of their choosing.

Privacy As privacy is of paramount concern in Priv.io, we now briefly analyze what an attacker can determine about other users. We first note that the attacker can only read the user's public storage location; he cannot access the user's queue or private storage location. There are three types of objects stored in the public storage area: the **credentials** file, the **public_key** file, and the temporary friend request files discussed in Section 3.4 (recall that these files are available while a friend request is outstanding). Thus, malicious attackers are able to determine if user u is currently trying to become friends with user v. However, we note that attackers must guess the identity of v correctly (attackers cannot "list" all request files), and the window of opportunity is likely to be short.

Incremental deployment Signing up for Priv.io is more complicated than signing up for existing services like Facebook: with Priv.io, users must first sign up with a cloud provider, and then register for Priv.io using those credentials. Luckily, signing up with cloud providers is often relatively simple; for example, signing up for Amazon Web Services requires only filling out two Web forms (personal information and billing information), and much is carried over if the user already has an Amazon account. Regardless, we will continue to look for opportunities to lower the burden for signing up with Priv.io.

For social networking-like services, the network effect[10] has resulted in entrenched service providers (e.g., Facebook); being the only one of your friends to be on a new social network is unlikely to provide significant benefits. Thus, it may be difficult to initially attract significant numbers of users to Priv.io without an established user base. However, we note that Priv.io is not limited to social networking applications, as current popular Web-based applications like Google Docs could easily be implemented in Priv.io and afforded the same privacy benefits. This approach may serve as a mechanism for attracting users, who later may also use the social networking features.

Finer-granularity computation The design of Priv.io is partially driven by the high cost of purchasing computation from cloud providers. However, as new cloud providers enter the market (e.g., resellers of existing cloud providers) or the price of computation drops, purchasing computation may become feasible. If so, this would open new opportunities for Priv.io, but may also come with a different set of privacy properties. For example, if users could purchase computation at a low-enough cost, Priv.io could easily interact with existing legacy systems that cannot be supported with in-browser computation (e.g., applications such as Google Mail—requiring SMTP—could be replicated in a confederated manner). However, doing so would allow the cloud provider to potentially view raw content (as incoming emails

---

[9]Message queues like Amazon's SQS and Microsoft's Azure Queue Service support similar semantics; if a recipient dies before marking a message as processed, the message is eventually delivered again.

[10]The *network effect* describes the value of a network as the number of participants grows. In brief, it captures the notion that with each new user, the number of potential links increases, thereby increasing the value for all participants.

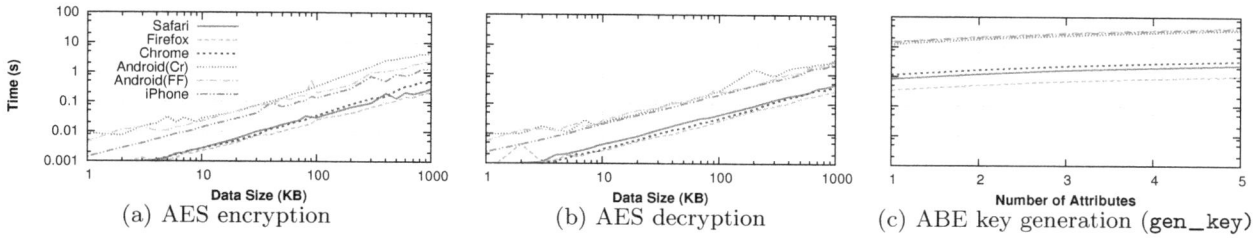

(a) AES encryption   (b) AES decryption   (c) ABE key generation (`gen_key`)

Figure 4: Priv.io encryption and decryption performance when run in different browsers. Shown is (a) AES encryption and (b) AES decryption for objects of different sizes. Also shown is (c) ABE key generation for keys with an increasing number of attributes (ABE encryptions under policies of increasing lengths shows very similar behavior).

would be observed in plaintext by the user's server). Regardless, we plan to explore ways of integrating purchased computation into Priv.io as future work.

6. EVALUATION

We now present an evaluation Priv.io, covering both microbenchmarks and measurements of Priv.io performance under different workloads.

We have implemented a prototype of Priv.io that supports almost all of the features described thus far. Priv.io currently supports using Amazon Web Services as a cloud provider, with support for SQS and S3. Support for Windows Azure and Google Cloud Platform is in progress. Priv.io supports third-party applications; both of the applications described in Section 4.5 are implemented and installed by default for each user.

Since all of Priv.io is implemented in JavaScript, it is open-source and available to the research community at `https://priv.io`. The implementation is compatible with the latest versions of common desktop Web browsers, as well as browers on Android and iOS.

The Priv.io core code represents 5,931 lines of JavaScript, excluding encryption and user interface libraries. We use the Stanford JavaScript Crypto Library for all AES operations. We used Emscripten [52] to compile the Ciphertext Policy ABE library [16] (as well as other dependencies) into JavaScript. The resulting encryption library totals 621 KB. All of these libraries are static and can easily be cached by Web browsers.

6.1 Microbenchmarks

Storage size Priv.io objects require storage on the user's cloud provider and encounter overhead, due both to encryption metadata (initialization vectors, etc.) and the base64 encoding used. The fixed overhead of using AES encryption is 145 bytes, and the fixed overhead of using ABE encryp-

tion is 345 bytes plus approximately 370 bytes per policy attribute. The base64 encoding introduces an additional 33% overhead. The ABE public keys are 1184 bytes, the encrypted `credentials` file averages 1457 bytes, and each friend request file averages 2400 bytes.

Content loading latency Loading objects in Priv.io enjoys the benefits of the user's cloud provider; we found the latency to be comparable to loading content from traditional Web sites. Using the `us-east-1` Amazon Web Services S3 storage service and loading to a client located in Boston, we found the latency of loading 64 KB objects via Priv.io to be 154 ms.

Encryption and decryption We now examine the encryption and decryption performance in Priv.io. We first focus on AES encryption. Using the latest version[11] of common browsers, we encrypt and decrypt objects of varying sizes using the AES library. We repeat each test 10 times, and report the average in Figures 4(a) and 4(b). We observe that AES encryption and decryption time correlate linearly with object size, and are fast: for 100 KB objects, both are under 43 ms for all desktops and under 327 ms for all mobile devices.

We now examine the performance of ABE. There are four ABE operations that we need to consider: `setup` (generate public and master keys), `gen_key` (generate a private key), `encrypt`, and `decrypt`. Of these, the compute time of `gen_key` and `encrypt` depend strongly on the number of attributes; the compute time of the other two is relatively constant.

We first report the performance of `setup` and `decrypt` in Table 4. We observe that the performance ranges from under 1.4 seconds on desktop browsers to about 15 seconds on mobile devices. We next examine the performance of `gen_key` and `encrypt`, shown in Figure 4(c) (the two operations show almost identical performance, so we only present the results for `gen_key` for brevity). We observe a strong linear relationship with the number of attributes used, ranging from about one second for a single attribute on desktop browsers to 45 seconds for five attributes on mobile devices. We again note that the expensive nature of ABE operations is unlikely to impact users on a regular basis, as they are only necessary when adding/modifying friends, or encrypting content

Browser	setup time (s)	decrypt time (s)
Safari	0.91	0.99
Firefox	0.63	0.36
Chrome	1.22	1.38
Android(Cr)	12.92	14.54
Android(FF)	14.63	13.08
iPhone	14.40	15.92

Table 4: Average time taken to generate an ABE master and public key (`setup`) and decrypt an ABE message (`decrypt`) in various browsers.

---

[11]Safari 6.0.4, FireFox 21.0.1 and Chrome 27.0.1453, all on OS X 10.8.3; Android Chrome 27.0.1453 and Firefox 21 on a HTC One X (AT&T); Mobile Safari 6.0 on an iPhone 5 running iOS 6.1.4. Mobile devices are connected via WiFi.

Browser	Priv.io (s)	Newsfeed (s)	Chat (s)
Safari	0.33	0.19	0.07
Firefox	0.34	0.20	0.12
Chrome	0.25	0.09	0.04
Android(Cr)	1.89	0.36	N/A
Android(FF)	2.81	0.98	0.83
iPhone	0.67	0.77	N/A

Table 5: Average time (in seconds) taken to load the basic Priv.io code after login, as well as the Newsfeed and Chat applications, in various browsers. Android Chrome and Mobile Safari do not support Flash, which is used to make cross domain request for Amazon SQS.

under a never-used-before policy (i.e., most sessions require no ABE operations).

6.2 User-perceived performance

We now examine the user-perceived performance of Priv.io. In evaluating Web services, the primary metric of interest is typically latency; we therefore focus on latency here. We are primarily concerned with three issues: *First*, what is the loading time of the basic Priv.io code when a user logs in, absent any applications? *Second*, what is the loading time of applications, both with and without subsequently loaded content? *Third*, what is the latency of sending application-level messages?

Priv.io loading time We first measure the time taken for users to log in and load the basic Priv.io code, absent any applications. To measure this, we disable all applications and measure the time taken from when a user clicks "Log in" until the Priv.io code is fully loaded. We run this experiment on all of the browsers listed above, clearing the browser cache after each experiment, and repeating the experiment 10 times. The average loading time is shown in Table 5, under the "Priv.io" column. We observe that the loading time is quite fast, between 250 and 340 ms on desktops and between 0.6 and 2.8 seconds on mobile devices.

Application loading time Next, we explore the loading time of applications. We record the time taken to load the Newsfeed and Chat applications once the Priv.io code is loaded; in each instance, the applications are empty and contain no user data (we explore the loading latency when user data is present below). The results are presented in Table 5, under the application columns. We observe that the loading time is consistent across different applications, and ranges from 90 to 200 ms on desktops to between 360 and 980 ms on mobile devices.

Next, we explore the loading time of applications when user data is present. To measure this, we use the Newsfeed application, and create users with varying amounts of Newsfeed content from varying numbers of friends. Specifically, we load up to 15 Newsfeed items (i.e., one "page" of Newsfeed items), with each friend providing three items (i.e., we create one user who loads three items from one friend, another user who loads three items each from two friends, and so on). The average loading time is presented in Figure 5. We observe that the loading time increases linearly with the number of content items loaded, and that the desktop brewers are substantially quicker in loading content, as expected. However, we observe that the loading time is reasonable in

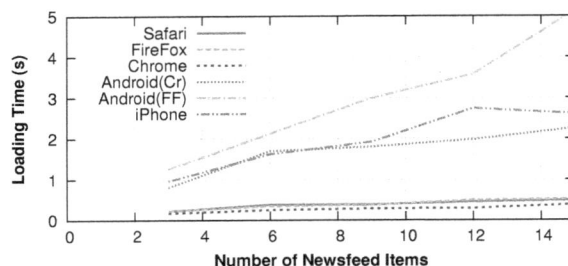

Figure 5: Average Newsfeed loading time with varying amounts of content, when content is loaded from multiple friends. We observe that the loading time increases linearly with the amount of content, as expected.

all cases: below 515 ms for desktops and below 5.1 seconds for all mobile devices.

Message latency Finally, we examine the latency of sending application-level messages. To do so, we use the Chat application, measuring the time for a user to send a message to a friend, and for the friend to reply. Both sender and receiver logged in on the same machine and browsers (note that the message itself must be delivered via the cloud provider's servers). We repeat this experiment in different browsers, and for each browser, we send 10 round trip messages and calculate the average. We find that the round trip time varies from an average of 637 ms on Chrome to 1.3 seconds on Safari[12], indicating that cloud providers' messaging can easily be used for human-timescale communication.

Overall, our results indicate that Priv.io is practical on the desktop Web browsers of today, with most user-facing loading times on the order of a second. However, mobile devices present challenges for Priv.io, as their lower computational resources result in higher latencies. Our results show that Priv.io does work on these devices, and as they become more powerful, accessing Priv.io from them will become more practical.

6.3 Small-scale deployment

We have deployed Priv.io on a small scale within our department. Unfortunately, it is difficult to measure the primary benefits of Priv.io to our users: improvements in privacy and control over data. As of this writing, 28 graduate students and professors have joined Priv.io and are using the Newsfeed and Chat applications. There were a total of 88 friendships recorded, for an average of 3.82 friends per user. Our users have accessed the service using a variety of operating systems, browsers, and desktop/mobile devices (a total of 23 different User-Agents). In total, our users have posted 221 items to Priv.io, most of which are comments in the Newsfeed application.

7. RELATED WORK

Enhancing Web browsers Over the past decade, Web browsers have become significantly more advanced. Researchers have explored using process-based models to iso-

---

[12] This latency could be further reduced if Amazon's SQS supported Cross-Origin Resource Sharing, which would eliminate the need for a Flash-based work-around.

late misbehaving Web pages [39], have examined moving beyond the same-origin policy of privilege separation [1], built systems that allow third-party code to execute while providing security and privacy guarantees [14, 24], and implemented iframe-based sandboxing [23]. We leverage many of these advances and techniques in the design of Priv.io.

Modifying existing Web services In parallel, many groups have explored ways to provide greater user privacy by re-architecting existing Web services. Developers have built subscription-based services such as app.net [5], which promise to not show ads in exchange for a yearly fee; unfortunately these simply replace one centralized provider with another. Systems have also been built that guarantee sandboxing of third-party applications [49], but these do not address hiding information from the service provider. Finally, researchers have developed approaches that enable sharing of provider-hosted content among different providers and with the user's local machine [21]; however, these do not address the issue of privacy from the centralized provider.

Others have explored retaining existing centralized providers, but hiding certain information from the provider. For example, researchers have explored encrypting uploaded content [22, 38], encrypting social relationships [47], and keeping data on user-managed devices [51]. It is unclear whether existing providers are amenable to these solutions (as they directly impact the providers' revenue stream), and deploying them independently risks users being banned by the provider.

Building new Web services Researchers have also explored new approaches that operate via the Web. For example, Persona [10] (which inspired our design, and in particular, our approach for encrypting content) stores encrypted user data on user-contracted storage services. Similar approaches include Vis-à-Vis [43] (storing data on group-based EC2 machines), Confidant [27] (storing data on friends' machines) and others [30] (storing data on users' home routers). Unfortunately, all of these solutions require client-side changes in order to work, and assume that they have a less-restricted model of computation than is available to JavaScript within the browser. In contrast, Priv.io uses many aspects of these systems' design, but does so without requiring any client-side changes and supports potentially untrusted third-party applications.

Others have explored separating Web-based services from user data. For example, W5 [26] proposed an architecture that separates Web service developers from providers that execute service code and host user data in a secure manner. While the vision of Priv.io and W5 are similar, to the best of our knowledge, W5 has not been deployed nor has any providers become available. BStore [13], provides a generic file system-like interface for Web applications, allowing users flexibility in the location of their data. Priv.io stores data on cloud providers using a number of techniques that were proposed in BStore. However, BStore is focused on providing file storage, while Priv.io also deals with challenges of sharing data with others, supporting third-party applications, and demonstrating that existing services can be replicated in a confederated manner.

Non-Web approaches Finally, researchers have presented systems that implement services in a decentralized fashion. These include PeerSoN [11], Diaspora* [18], Safebook [15],

Contrail [45], and others [2]. While similar to Priv.io in goals, all of these approaches require client software to be downloaded, and also generally face challenges in ensuring availability [7]. Others have designed protocols [48] that allow users to host their data on dedicated, secure servers of their choosing. A more detailed overview of the tradeoffs of decentralized architectures is provided in [44].

8. CONCLUSION

We presented Priv.io, a new approach to building Web-based services using a confederated architecture. In Priv.io, each user is responsible for providing the resources necessary to support their use of the service; this is accomplished by contracting with cloud providers (for storage, bandwidth, and messaging) and by using the user's Web browser (for computation). As a result, in Priv.io, users retain control of their own data, users are not required to reveal their information to any centralized entity, and users enjoy a highly reliable and available service. We demonstrated that implementing many popular services with Priv.io is both practical and affordable: Most users would pay less than $0.95 per month, and Priv.io works today on the latest versions of common Web browsers as well as (more slowly) on Android and iOS mobile devices.

Acknowledgements

We thank the anonymous reviewers and our shepherd, Ben Zhao, for their helpful comments. We also thank the Priv.io users and beta testers for their hard work and patience. This research was supported by NSF grants IIS-0964465, CNS-1054233, CNS-1319019, and an Amazon Web Services in Education Grant.

9. REFERENCES

[1] D. Akhawe, P. Sazena, and D. Song. Privilege Separation in HTML5 Applications. *USENIX ATC*, Boston, MA, 2012.

[2] J. Anderson, C. Diaz, J. Bonneau, and F. Stajano. Privacy-Enabling Social Networking Over Untrusted Networks. *WOSN*, Barcelona, Spain, 2009.

[3] Amazon EC2 Pricing. http://aws.amazon.com/ec2/pricing.

[4] Amazon S3 Pricing. http://aws.amazon.com/s3/pricing.

[5] app.net. http://join.app.net.

[6] A. Barth, C. Jackson, and J. C. Mitchell. Securing Frame Communication in Browsers. *USENIX Security*, San Jose, CA, 2008.

[7] C. Blake and R. Rodrigues. High Availability, Scalable Storage, Dynamic Peer Networks: Pick Two. *HotOS*, Lihue, HI, 2003.

[8] D. Beaver, S. Kumar, H. C. Li, J. Sobel, and P. Vajgel. Finding a needle in Haystack: Facebook's photo storage. *OSDI*, Vancouver, Canada, 2010.

[9] J. Bethencourt, A. Sahai, and B. Waters. Ciphertext-Policy Attribute-Based Encryption. *IEEE S&P*, Oakland, CA, 2007.

[10] R. Baden, A. Bender, N. Spring, B. Bhattacharjee, and D. Starin. Persona: an online social network with user-defined privacy. *SIGCOMM*, Barcelona, Spain, 2009.

[11] S. Buchegger, D. Schiöberg, L. H. Vu, and A. Datta. PeerSoN: P2P Social Networking—Early Experiences and Insights. *SNS*, Nuremberg, Germany, 2009.

[12] M. Cha, H. Haddadi, F. Benevenuto, and K. P. Gummadi. Measuring User Influence in Twitter: The Million Follower Fallacy. *ICWSM*, Washington, D.C., 2010.

[13] R. Chandra, P. Gupta, and N. Zeldovich. Separating Web Applications from User Data Storage with BStore. *WebApps*, Boston, MA, 2010.

[14] Y. Cao, Z. Li, V. Rastogi, Y. Chen, and X. Wen. Virtual Browser: a Virtualized Browser to Sandbox Third-party JavaScripts with Enhanced Security. *CCS*, Chicago, IL, 2010.

[15] L. A. Cutillo and R. Molva. Safebook: A Privacy-Preserving Online Social Network Leveraging on Real-Life Trust. *IEEE Communications*, 43(12), 2009.

[16] Ciphertext Policy Attribute-Based Encryption. http://acsc.cs.utexas.edu/cpabe.

[17] Cross-Origin Resource Sharing. http://www.w3.org/TR/cors/.

[18] Diaspora*. http://www.joindiaspora.com/.

[19] Facebook Statistics. http://on.fb.me/UtWB0.

[20] H. Gao, J. Hu, C. Wilson, Z. Li, Y. Chen, and B. Y. Zhao. Detecting and Characterizing Social Spam Campaigns. *IMC*, Melbourne, Victoria, Australia, 2010.

[21] R. Geambasu, C. Cheung, A. Moshchuk, S. D. Gribble, and a. H. M. Levy. Organizing and Sharing Distributed Personal Web-Service Data. *WWW*, Beijing, China, 2008.

[22] S. Guha, K. Tang, and P. Francis. NOYB: Privacy in Online Social Networks. *WOSN*, Seattle, WA, 2008.

[23] HTML5 Specification. http://bit.ly/3h8KZG.

[24] L. Ingram and M. Walfish. TreeHouse: JavaScript sandboxes to help Web developers help themselves. *USENIX ATC*, Boston, MA, 2012.

[25] B. Kaliski. PKCS #5: Password-Based Cryptography Specification Version 2.0. RFC 2898, IETF, 2000.

[26] M. Krohn, A. Yip, M. Brodsky, R. Morris, and M. Walfish. A World Wide Web Without Walls. *HotNets*, Atlanta, GA, 2007.

[27] D. Liu, A. Shakimov, R. Cáceres, A. Varshavsky, and L. P. Cox. Confidant: Protecting OSN Data without Locking It Up. *Middleware*, Lisbon, Portugal, 2011.

[28] A. Mislove, H. S. Koppula, K. P. Gummadi, P. Druschel, and B. Bhattacharjee. Growth of the Flickr Social Network. *WOSN*, Seattle, WA, 2008.

[29] A. Mislove, M. Marcon, K. P. Gummadi, P. Druschel, and B. Bhattacharjee. Measurement and Analysis of Online Social Networks. *IMC*, San Diego, CA, 2007.

[30] M. Marcon, B. Viswanath, M. Cha, and K. P. Gummadi. Sharing Social Networking Content from Home: A Measurement-driven Feasibility Study. *NOSSDAV*, Vancouver, Canada, 2011.

[31] R. Miller. Ma.gnolia Data is Gone for Good. http://bit.ly/tbFup.

[32] C. B. Myers. Google to finally shut down Google Buzz, along with Google Labs. *The Next Web*, 2011. http://tnw.co/pptfQp.

[33] F. Nentwich, N. Jovanovic, E. Kirda, C. Kruegel, and G. Vigna. Cross-Site Scripting Prevention with Dynamic Data Tainting and Static Analysis. *NDSS*, San Diego, CA, 2007.

[34] Y. Nadji, P. Saxena, and D. Song. Document Structure Integrity: A Robust Basis for Cross-site Scripting Defense. *NDSS*, San Diego, CA, 2009.

[35] G. Ou. Facebook slashes the quality of "HD" videos. http://bit.ly/bvx86h.

[36] P. Oechslin. Making a Faster Cryptanalytic Time-Memory Trade-Off. *CRYPTO*, Santa Barbara, CA, 2003.

[37] S. N. Porter. A password extension for improved human factors. *Comp. & Sec.*, 1(1), 1982.

[38] priv.ly. http://priv.ly.

[39] C. Reis, A. Barth, and C. Pizano. Browser security: Lessons from Google Chrome. *CACM*, 52(8), 2009.

[40] G. Rydstedt, E. Bursztein, D. Boneh, and C. Jackson. Busting frame busting: a study of clickjacking vulnerabilities at popular sites. *W2SP*, Oakland, CA, 2010.

[41] M. Roth, A. Ben-David, D. Deutscher, G. Flysher, I. Horn, A. Leichtberg, N. Leiser, Y. Matias, and R. Merom. Suggesting Friends Using the Implicit Social Graph. *KDD*, Washington, D.C., 2010.

[42] Representational State Transfer. http://en.wikipedia.org/wiki/Representational_state_transfer.

[43] A. Shakimov, H. Lim, R. Cáceres, L. P. Cox, K. Li, D. Liu, and A. Varshavsky. Vis-à-Vis: Privacy-Preserving Online Social Networking via Virtual Individual Servers. *COMSNETS*, Bangalore, India, 2011.

[44] A. Shakimov, A. Varshavsky, L. P. Cox, and R. Cáceres. Privacy, Cost, and Availability Tradeoffs in Decentralized OSNs. *WOSN*, Barcelona, Spain, 2009.

[45] P. Stuedi, I. Mohomed, M. Balakrishnan, Z. M. Mao, V. Ramasubramanian, D. Terry, and T. Wobber. Contrail: Enabling Decentralized Social Networks on Smartphones. *Middleware*, Lisbon, Portugal, 2011.

[46] A. Tootoonchian, K. K. Gollu, S. Saroiu, Y. Ganjali, and A. Wolman. Lockr: Social Access Control for Web 2.0. *WOSN*, Seattle, WA, 2008.

[47] A. Tootoonchian, S. Saroiu, Y. Ganjali, and A. Wolman. Lockr: Better Privacy for Social Networks. *CoNEXT*, Rome, Italy, 2009.

[48] tent.io. http://tent.io.

[49] B. Viswanath, E. Kıcıman, and S. Sariou. Keeping Information Safe from Social Networking Apps. *WOSN*, Helsinki, Finland, 2012.

[50] R. van Zwol. Flickr: Who is Looking? *WI*, Silicon Valley, CA, 2007.

[51] C. Wilson, T. Steinbauer, G. Wang, A. Sala, H. Zheng, and B. Y. Zhao. Privacy, Availability and Economics in the Polaris Mobile Social Network. *HotMobile*, Phoenix, AZ, 2011.

[52] A. Zakai. Emscripten: an LLVM-to-JavaScript compiler. *SPLASH*, Portland, OR, 2011.

[53] Zynga. http://zynga.com.

Fit or Unfit : Analysis and Prediction of 'Closed Questions' on Stack Overflow

Denzil Correa, Ashish Sureka
Indraprastha Institute of Information Technology
IIIT-Delhi
{denzilc, ashish} @iiitd.ac.in

ABSTRACT

Stack Overflow is widely regarded as the most popular Community driven Question Answering (CQA) website for programmers. Questions posted on Stack Overflow which are not related to programming topics, are marked as 'closed' by experienced users and community moderators. A question can be 'closed' for five reasons – *duplicate, off-topic, subjective, not a real question* and *too localized*. In this work, we present the first study of 'closed' questions on Stack Overflow. We download 4 years of publicly available data which contains 3.4 Million questions. We first analyze and characterize the complete set of 0.1 Million 'closed' questions. Next, we use a machine learning framework and build a predictive model to identify a 'closed' question at the time of question creation.

One of our key findings is that despite being marked as 'closed', *subjective* questions contain high information value and are very popular with the users. We observe an increasing trend in the percentage of closed questions over time and find that this increase is positively correlated to the number of newly registered users. In addition, we also see a decrease in community participation to mark a 'closed' question which has led to an increase in moderation job time. We also find that questions closed with the *Duplicate* and *Off Topic* labels are relatively more prone to reputation gaming. Our analysis suggests broader implications for content quality maintenance on CQA websites. For the 'closed' question prediction task, we make use of multiple genres of feature sets based on - user profile , community process, textual style and question content. We use a state-of-art machine learning classifier based on an ensemble framework and achieve an overall accuracy of 70.3%. Analysis of the feature space reveals that 'closed' questions are relatively less informative and descriptive than non-'closed' questions. To the best of our knowledge, this is the first experimental study to analyze and predict 'closed' questions on Stack Overflow.

Categories and Subject Descriptors

H.3.3 [**Information Search and Retrieval**]: Information filtering; H.3.5 [**Online Information Services**]: Web-based services; K.4.3 [**Organizational Impacts**]: Computer-supported collaborative work

Keywords

Question-answering, Question quality, Stack Overflow

1. INTRODUCTION

1.1 Research Motivation and Aim

Community driven Question Answering (CQA) websites like Stack Overflow, Quora and Yahoo! Answers are popular contemporary genre of websites on the Internet. CQA websites follow a standard Q&A format where a user asks a question on a problem she faces; while other users (who may have some prior expertise) respond with their answers on the question. Effectively, CQA websites follow a crowd sourced model in which the knowledge of experts is exploited to form a large scale knowledge base on variety of topics. Stack Exchange is a platform which provides libraries to deploy topic-based community powered Q&A websites [16]. The Stack Exchange platform is a growing network of CQA websites and currently supports 103 Q&A forums on diverse topics like code review, parenting, bicycles and audio-video production[1].

Stack Overflow is the first and most popular Stack Exchange website which caters to the benefits of professional programmers and programming enthusiasts.[2] It is a free and open Q&A website where users can ask programming related questions. Stack Overflow maintains a strong emphasis on question-answer based format of the site and strongly discourages discussion or *chit-chat*. In particular, questions on the topics which contain specific programming problems, software algorithms, coding techniques and software development tools are recommended and considered fit for its Q&A format. An intricate community based voting process is followed to reward users for good quality questions and answers. Relevant, technically challenging and good question-answers are rewarded by the community with *votes*. Similarly, answers which address the problem encountered by the original question can be voted *accepted*. This voting process allows post owners to earn a *reputation* which is a reflection of their contribution worth to the Stack Overflow community. Conversely, the same voting process can lead to penalties on the post owner's *reputation* due to low quality posts like wrong answers, spam and advertisements. *Badges* (the online equivalent of medals) are awarded to users as incentives to highlight special achievements based on community participation. This community based *reputation reward* process helps to ensure a reasonable degree of high quality content on the website and weed out low quality content.

Stack Overflow is a free, open website to all users and therefore, maintenance of content quality on such a large scale social collab-

---

[1] https://stackexchange.com
[2] http://stackoverflow.com

orative platform is a challenge [10]. Questions are an integral part of the Stack Overflow system and hence, quality control of questions play a significant role in its functioning and popularity. Stack Overflow guidelines clearly outline categories of questions which are deemed unfit for its Q&A format. Opinion-based questions and questions which have a tendency to generate discussions rather than answers are categorically considered inappropriate. Some examples of such questions include (but not limited to) homework questions, product or service recommendations, non-programming related and polls. Questions on Stack Overflow which do not fall into one of the pre-defined set of guidelines are marked 'closed' via a community-based voting system. A question can be marked as 'closed' for five reasons – *duplicate, off-topic, subjective, not a real question* and *too localized*. Section 3 contains a detailed discussion on the procedure to mark a question 'closed' and its sub-categories. Figure 1 shows an example of a 'closed' question on Stack Overflow on account of being *Too Localized*.

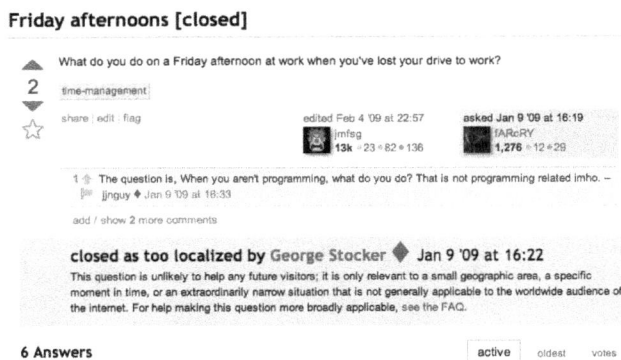

Friday afternoons [closed]

What do you do on a Friday afternoon at work when you've lost your drive to work?

2

time-management

share | edit | flag

edited Feb 4 '09 at 22:57
jmfsg
13k • 23 • 82 • 136

asked Jan 9 '09 at 16:19
fARcRY
1,276 • 12 • 29

1 The question is, When you aren't programming, what do you do? That is not programming related imho. –
jinguy ♦ Jan 9 '09 at 18:33

add / show 2 more comments

closed as too localized by George Stocker ♦ Jan 9 '09 at 16:22
This question is unlikely to help any future visitors; it is only relevant to a small geographic area, a specific moment in time, or an extraordinarily narrow situation that is not generally applicable to the worldwide audience of the internet. For help making this question more broadly applicable, see the FAQ.

6 Answers

active | oldest | votes

Figure 1: shows a screenshot of question marked 'closed' on Stack Overflow on account of being *Too Localized*.

A question is primarily marked 'closed' either due to low quality or due to irrelevance to the Stack Overflow CQA platform. The decision to 'close' a question lies completely on the shoulders of experienced users and community moderators via a systematic voting process. Due to exponential growth of Stack Overflow user base, there has been a steady increase in the workload on moderators. The process of marking a 'closed' question also requires multiple context switches [9]. Despite the existence of vibrant experienced users and self-motivated community moderators, Stack Overflow faces a continuous ongoing challenge to maintain quality of questions on their website. Therefore, it is important to analyze and study the phenomena of 'closed' questions in order to gain historical insights which can help make the future plan-of-action.

The goal of Stack Overflow is to have a knowledge base of question-answers on programming related topics. A 'closed' question is a direct feedback to the question asker that her question may be unfit or needs improvement in its current form. A system to predict a 'closed' question at post creation time can serve as an early feedback mechanism on question quality to the question asker. Such a system would also help community moderators to identify and mark 'closed' questions. Therefore, prediction of a 'closed' question at post creation time has two distinct benefits – (1) feedback to question asker and (2) community moderator assistance.

1.2 Research Contributions

We conduct the first study of 'closed' questions on Stack Overflow. We make the following research contributions –

- We present a characterization of 'closed' questions on Stack Overflow. We perform analysis on question content, answer patterns and temporal trend analysis of 'closed' question. In addition, we also make observations on community participation trends as well as analyze information quality indicators. Our analysis also throws light on content quality maintenance on CQA websites.

- We use an ensemble based machine learning framework to build a predictive model for 'closed' question prediction on Stack Overflow and report 70.3% accurate predictions. Our feature analysis reveals that 'closed' questions tend to be relatively less informative and descriptive than non-'closed' questions.

To the best of our knowledge, this is the first focussed study on analysis and prediction of 'closed' questions on Stack Overflow. The rest of the paper is organized as follows. Related work is covered in Section 2. Section 3 gives an overview of 'closed' questions, its sub-categories and procedures followed to 'close' a question. Section 4 presents our characterization study of 'closed' questions. Section 5 demonstrates a machine learning framework to predict 'closed' questions on Stack Overflow and Section 6 outlines Conclusion.

2. RELATED WORK

Stack Overflow is a popular Q&A website used by programmers all over the world to seek answers to programming related questions [21]. Besides being a question-answer website, Stack Overflow has evolved into a knowledge base for programming related tasks [11]. It has also been used for various other core and ancillary programming tasks like building crowd sourced API documentation, deficient documentation identification, identification of mobile development issues and improvement of bug tracking systems [13, 19, 20, 22]. Stack Overflow is a free and open website and has 1.29 Million registered users with 3.4 Million questions.[3] Quality control of content on such large scale community driven collaborative systems is a research challenge [10]. Questions and answers form an integral part of any CQA website and therefore, it is important to have quality checks in place for both questions and answers.

Evaluation and prediction of answer quality has attracted wide spread attention in the IR research community. Jeon *et al.* propose maximum entropy and kernel density estimation approach in conjunction with non-textual features to predict answer quality on Naver, a Korean CQA website [17]. Agichtein *et al.* model content quality in Yahoo! Answers with content and graph-based implicit user relationship features [10]. Shah *et al.* propose a classification model with features based on human assessed aspects and question-answer meta information to predict answer quality on Yahoo! Answers CQA [24]. Sakai *et al.* propose evaluation methods based on graded-relevance IR metrics to find the best answers on Yahoo! Chiebukuro (Japanese Yahoo! Answers) [23]. All the above approaches focus on answer quality on large scale CQA websites. However, it is also important to focus on question quality because prior work shows that answer quality directly depends on question quality [10]. Low quality questions have a direct impact on user experience, question retrieval, question recommendation and hence, it is important to maintain high question quality [21]. Li *et al.* analyze factors affecting question quality and propose a Mutual Reinforcement-based Label Propagation approach to predict question quality in Yahoo! Answers [18]. To the best of our knowl-

---

[3]as of August 2012

edge, this is the only work which addresses quality of questions on a large-scale CQA website. However, Stack Overflow is a programming related CQA and has appreciable differences in style, structure, organization and content from other generic CQA websites like Yahoo! Answers and Quora [21, 25].

In context of all the previous work in this area, our study differs in two main aspects – (1) we focus our attention on question quality rather than answer quality and (2) we perform our analysis on Stack Overflow which is a programming-based CQA. 'Closed' questions on Stack Overflow are considered bad for its Q&A format and hence, by definition are low quality given the context.

3. 'CLOSED' QUESTIONS ON STACK OVERFLOW

In this section, we discuss details on *who*, *how* and *why* questions are closed on Stack Overflow. We also briefly outline *what happens* once a question is 'closed' and mention the community process rules to mark a question as 'closed'. Figure 2 summarizes the details of important aspects of 'closed' questions on Stack Overflow.

What is a 'closed' a question?.

A question can be 'closed' on Stack Overflow if it is deemed unfit for its Q&A format [2]. A 'closed' question can not be answered but edits on previously posted question-answers and comments are permitted (subject to appropriate edit privileges). Question-answers can also be voted upon and are counted towards reputation points of users as well as badges.

Who can 'close' a question?.

Experienced users and community moderators can cast a vote to 'close' a question. Stack Overflow users with 3,000+ reputation points and community moderators (also called ◆ moderators) can vote for the same. In addition, users with at least 250 reputation points can vote to 'close' their own question. The *Who* block of Figure 2 corresponds to the aforementioned details.

How are questions 'closed' ?.

A question is automatically marked 'closed' if it receives 5 'close' votes. However, ◆ moderator 'close' votes are final and binding i.e. if a ◆ moderator decides to cast a 'close' vote the question is 'closed' immediately [6]. One can only vote once to 'close' a question. The *How* block of Figure 2 corresponds to this process.

Why are questions 'closed'?.

According to Stack Overflow guidelines, a question is 'closed' on Stack Overflow if it falls into one of the following five categories [2]:

1. **Exact Duplicate** – contains similar content to previously posted questions

2. **Off Topic** – unrelated to programming scope as defined by Stack Overflow

3. **Subjective (Not Constructive)** – more likely to generate debates, discussions instead of answers

4. **Not a Real Question** – ambiguous, vague questions which do not have answers

5. **Too Localized** – relevant to a very small geographic location, software or community

The *Why* block of Figure 2 corresponds to this section.

What happens to a 'closed' question?.

A 'closed' question can be 'reopened' if the question is improved from its current form. The 'reopen' voting procedure is similar to the 'close' procedure. However, if the questions are very poor in quality and beyond improvement, then they are *deleted* from Stack Overflow [2]. The *What* block of Figure 2 corresponds to this section.

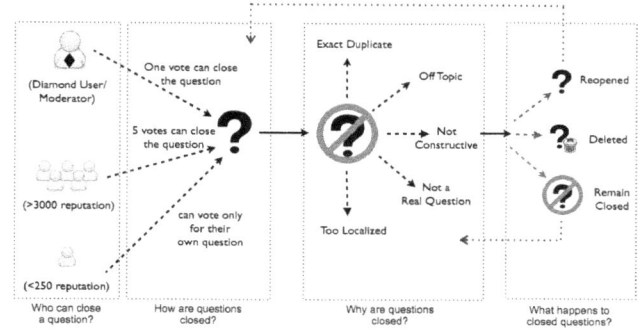

Figure 2: depicts *who*, *how* and *why* questions are marked 'closed' on Stack Overflow.

4. CHARACTERIZATION STUDY OF 'CLOSED' QUESTIONS

In the first part of our work, we perform a characterization study of 'closed' questions on Stack Overflow.

4.1 Dataset Description

Stack Overflow provides all user-generated content on its website for download under the *Creative Commons Attribute-ShareAlike* license [12]. We download Stack Overflow website data from the Stack Exchange August 2012 data dump provided by Stack Overflow which contains all data between July 31st, 2008 (the genesis of Stack Overflow) to August 31st, 2012 [7]. Table 1 outlines basic statistics for Stack Overflow August 2012 dataset used in our characterization study. The statistics show that Stack Overflow is a very popular programming CQA with 1.29M registered users, 3.4M questions and 6.8M answers.

Table 1: Stack Overflow August 2012 dataset statistics

Users	1.29M (625k askers, 443k answerers)
Questions	3.4M (62.21% with accepted answers)
Answers	6.8M (31.33% marked as accepted)
Votes	27.5M (72.35% positive, 6.81% favorites)
Ratio of Answers to Questions	2.16

In this work, we concentrate on 'closed' questions on Stack Overflow i.e. questions which are deemed unfit and therefore low quality given the context. We extract all questions from the dataset which have been marked 'closed' at least once. We find that approx. **3% (0.1 Million)** questions are marked 'closed' on Stack Overflow between August 2008 to August 2012. We use this data of **102,993** 'closed' questions to conduct our characterization study and report our findings. Table 2 contains details on 'closed' questions in Stack Overflow. [4]

---

[4] Prior to June 2011, 'Close Votes' expired 4 days after their cast and are deleted from the dataset published by Stack Overflow. This information is available only if a question is closed successfully.

Table 2: Statistics of 'Closed Questions' in Stack Overflow from August 2008 to August 2012.

	2008	2009	2010	2011	2012	Total
Closed Questions	3.8%	1.52%	1.77%	3.33%	3.82%	102, 993 (2.98%)
Closed Votes	0.03%^{3}	0.25%^{3}	0.75%^{3}	2.21%	3.9%	570,418^3 (0.2%)
Ratio of Answers to Questions	8.0	5.93	3.11	1.92	1.55	1.92

Based on the data, we can make two observations – (1) Stack Overflow maintains a very good signal-to-noise ratio as reported in previous work [21] and (2) Despite the presence of vibrant community and structured guidelines, users do post questions which are unfit for the website. A question can be closed on Stack Overflow for five reasons - *duplicate, off-topic, subjective, not a real question* and *too localized*. Figure 3 shows a pie-chart which depicts the distribution of 'closed' questions on different sub-categories or reasons. *Not a Real Question* and *Duplicate* categories are the most common reasons to close a question while *Too Localized* is the least common reason.

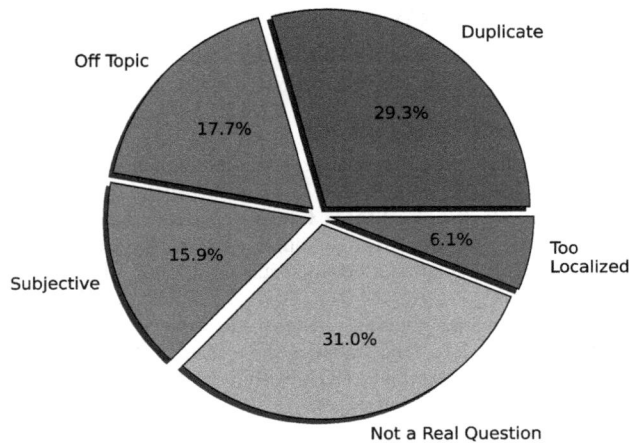

Figure 3: shows the distribution of all five sub-categories of closed questions in our dataset.

4.2 Temporal Distribution Analysis

We analyze the presence of 'closed' questions on Stack Overflow over a 48-month time window between August 2008 to August 2012. Figure 4 depicts the ratio of 'closed' questions to total questions over this time period. Overall, we find an increasing trend of the percentage of 'closed' questions in each category i.e. we find that the number of questions 'closed' over time has an upward curve. We also see that the most common categories of 'closed' questions over 48-months are *Exact Duplicate* and *Not a Real Question*. Both these categories dominate in presence over the others across time. We perform qualitative analysis of some sample questions in our dataset to understand this pattern. The high ratio of the *Exact Duplicate* category may be due to the problem

of question retrieval on Stack Overflow i.e. users are unable to efficiently locate questions which are similar to the actual problem they are faced with. The presence of such a high ratio may also be due to lethargic users who do not perform adequate searches before posting a question. Similarly, the high percentage of *Not a Real Question* category may be due to newly registered users who are yet to understand the scope, structure and guidelines of Stack Overflow. Overall, we see a sharp increase in the ratio of 'closed' questions after January 2011.

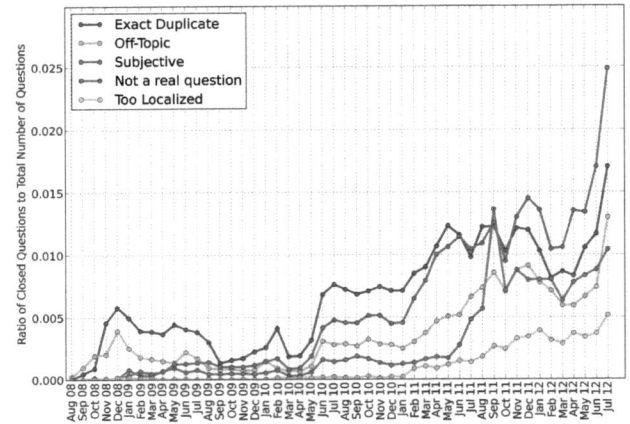

Figure 4: shows the temporal distribution plot of the ratio of 'closed questions' to total questions over a 48-month period between August 2008 to August 2012 for each sub-category.

4.3 Effect of New Registered Users

Questions are marked 'closed' on Stack Overflow if they are considered unfit for its Q&A format. Intuitively, newly registered users on the website may be indolent to existing guidelines and may ignore them in their anxiety to get a solution to a problem. Therefore, we try to understand the impact of newly registered users on the presence of 'closed' questions on Stack Overflow over time. Figure 5 shows the distribution of – (1) number of newly registered users and (2) percentage of 'closed' questions on Stack Overflow – over a 48-month period between August 2008 to August 2012. In addition, it also depicts the corresponding *Pearson Correlation Coefficient* (PCC) between the two distributions (cumulative) at each time interval. PCC calculates the linear dependence between two distributions and outputs a value between +1 (positive correlation) to -1 (negative correlation). Figure 5 shows a high correlation between the number of newly registered users and percentage of closed questions. We stress that the calculated correlation coefficient is between new registered users and the **percentage of closed questions** (and not the total number of closed questions) over time. The PCC value is +0.95 which indicates a very high correlation between the distributions with an extremely high confidence interval (p-value < 0.01). The PCC shows that newly registered users may have an immediate impact on low quality content. Here too, we find a sharp rise in PCC after January 2011.

4.4 Community Participation

Stack Overflow follows a well defined community based voting procedure to evaluate a question before closure. We analyze these voting patterns to understand *community participation* of experienced users and community moderators to weed out low quality content on the website. We recall that users with 3,000+ reputation

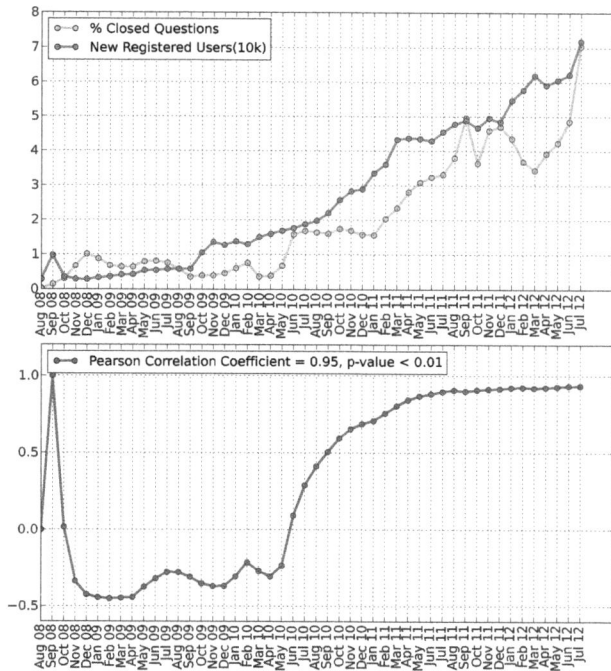

Figure 5: shows the temporal distribution plot of the percentage of 'closed questions' and newly registered users over a 48-month period from August 2008 to August 2012. In addition, the figure also shows correlation between both distributions.

points and ◆ moderators can cast a vote to close a question. A question is automatically 'closed' if it reaches 5 votes but a vote from a ◆ moderator is binding and hence, immediately closes a question. Therefore, a question can be closed with any number of 'close' votes between 1 to 5. Figure 6 shows the temporal distribution of 'close' votes on Stack Overflow between August 2008 to August 2012. Table 3 shows the distribution of number of 'close votes' on closed questions. A significant percentage($\approx$27%) of questions are closed due to a single ◆ moderator vote. More than 40% of questions require ◆ moderator intervention to close a question. We also observe a rise in the percentage of questions being closed only by ◆ moderators over time. Simultaneously, we see a decrease in percentage of questions being closed by experienced users viz. users with 3,000+ reputation points. This shows that community participation to close questions is on a decline which has led to an increase in work load for ◆ moderators on this front. A ◆ moderator on Stack Overflow has also confirmed an increase in moderation work load over the years [9]. Stack Overflow has only 16 ◆ moderators for their website out of which 13 have been elected and 3 have been appointed [8].

We now analyze the 'close vote' patterns across each category of closed questions. Figure 7 shows the 'close vote' distribution for each sub-category of closed questions on Stack Overflow between August 2008 to August 2012. We see a strong community participation on *Duplicate*, *Off Topic* and *Not a Real Question* categories. On the other hand, *Subjective* and *Too Localized* categories require a high amount of ◆ moderator intervention. We argue that the community participation behavior may be so because *Duplicate*, *Off Topic* and *Not a Real Question* questions are low hanging fruits and easy to detect. The *Subjective* category sees an equal community and ◆ moderator participation. The *Too Localized* cat-

Table 3: shows the 'Close Vote' Distribution on 'Closed' questions posted between August 2008 and August 2012. 45% questions have at least one ◆ moderator vote and 26.5% of questions are closed by a single ◆ moderator vote.

Votes	Closed Questions
1-vote	27,390 (26.59%)
2-votes	9,037 (8.77 %)
3-votes	5,436 (5.28%)
4-votes	4,030 (3.91%)
5-votes	57,117 (55.44 %)
Total	102,993

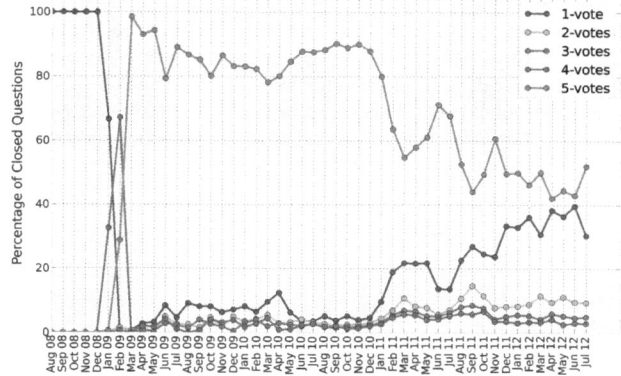

Figure 6: shows the temporal distribution of 'close votes' in closed questions over a 48-month period from August 2008 to August 2012. We observe that a high percentage of questions are closed due to a single ◆ moderator vote.

egory sees a higher ◆ moderator intervention. Since, the presence of this category is very low in our dataset, such behavior may be primarily due to low traction owing to the difficulty of identification of such questions during normal daily usage of the website.

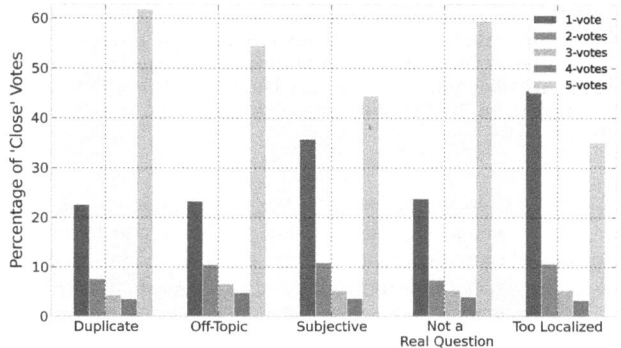

Figure 7: shows the 'close vote' distribution for each sub-category for all closed questions between August 2008 to August 2012. At least 1 out of 5 questions in each category are closed by a single ◆ moderator vote.

4.5 Content Analysis

We now characterize the content of 'closed' questions on Stack Overflow based on question tittle, question content, code snippets and topics.

Question Title, Body and Code Snippet.

Since, 'closed' questions are unfit for Stack Overflow – the presence or absence of code snippets may reveal insights about 'closed' questions. Overall, $\approx 31\%$ of 'closed' questions contain code snippets and hence, questions are 'closed' even if they contain source code. We analyze the presence of code snippets across each category to check if there are relative differences across categories. Figure 8 (left-top) shows the percentage of questions which contain code snippets for each category. We find that *Too Localized* and *Exact Duplicate* category contains a large number of questions which have code snippets in them. The *Exact Duplicate* category by definition contains duplicate information to an existing question which may explain the high number. On the other hand, *Too Localized* category by definition contains questions which are programming-related but are confined to a small community and hence, the higher percentage of questions which contain source code. We see that the *Subjective* category contains the lowest percentage of questions containing source code. This could be probably because questions in this category are open-ended and invite discussions rather than an answer to a specific problem.

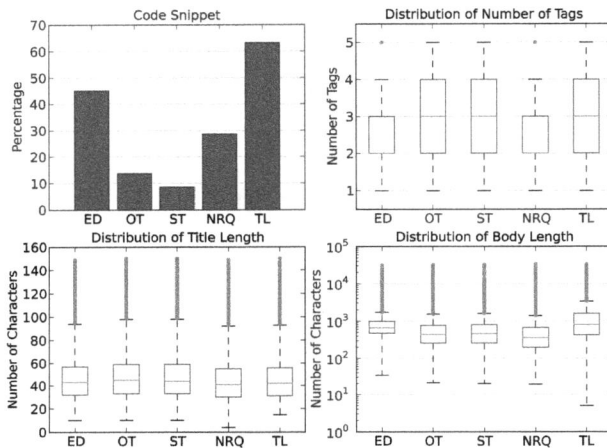

Figure 8: shows the percentage of code snippets in each subcategory and character length distributions of question title, body as well as the distribution of number of tags in form of a box-and-whisker plot.(ED = Exact Duplicate, OT = Off-Topic, ST = Subjective, NRQ = Not a Real Question, TL = Too Localized)

Figure 8 also shows the character length distribution of question title, body as well as the distribution of number of tags in form of a box-and-whisker plot. The top-right box plot shows that questions in the *Exact Duplicate* and *Not a Real Question* categories have lesser number of tags associated with it. The *Exact Duplicate* category may exhibit such a behavior due to user lethargy while questions belonging to the *Not a Real Question* category may be so as by definition the question marked with this label are non-programming related. A minimum of 1500 reputation points are required to create new tags on Stack Overflow [1]. The bottom left and bottom right box plots show the distribution of question title and question body lengths respectively. We do not observe a major difference in the length distributions either in title or body between categories. Both distributions are skewed i.e. there are may outliers (red points on the box plot) and the medians are approximately similar. However, in both of these distributions we once again see that the *Not a Real Question* has the lowest median value which indi-

cates that questions belonging to this category are a clear misfit to the Stack Overflow Q&A format even in terms of content.

Question Topics.

Each Stack Overflow question has some *tags* associated with it which is an identification of the topic of the question content. We analyze frequently occurring tags in 'closed' questions and bucket them into categories. Table 4 shows popular tags in 'closed' questions according to different categories. We see that popular tags on 'closed' questions are similar to those found overall on Stack Overflow.

Table 4: Popular Tags in Closed Questions

Type	Tags
Languages	java, c++, python, c, perl, r, ...
Web2.0	php, html5, html, css, javascript, ...
Operating Systems	iOS, unix, android, osx, windows, ...
Social	Facebook, wordpress, google, ...
Miscellaneous	books, interview-questions , homework, ...

We now analyze if 'closed' questions contain certain topics which are unique to their category viz. tags which relatively occur more frequently in 'closed' questions than otherwise. In order to do so, we normalize the occurrence of tags in 'closed' questions by calculating the **Normalized Tag Ratio (NTR)** for each tag. Let T_{CQ} be the set of all tags in 'closed' questions on Stack Overflow, and T_{NCQ} be the set of all tags in non-'closed' questions. We add the ε factor ($=2.2\times10^{-16}$) for smoothing purposes. Then,

$$\forall t_i \in T_{CQ} \quad where \quad t_i \in \{t_1 \dots t_n\}, \quad R_{CQ}^i = \frac{count(t_i)}{\sum_{i=1}^{n} count(t_i)}$$

$$\forall t_j \in T_{NCQ} \quad where \quad t_j \in \{t_1 \dots t_m\}, \quad R_{NCQ}^j = \frac{count(t_j)}{\sum_{j=1}^{m} count(t_j)}$$

$$\therefore \forall t_i \in T_{CQ} \quad NTR_{t_i} = \frac{R_{CQ}^i}{R_{NCQ}^i + \varepsilon}, \quad (T_{CQ} \cap T_{NCQ} \neq \emptyset)$$

Figure 9 shows the tags with top 30 NTR in closed questions on Stack Overflow. We can now see tags which are unique to 'closed' questions and find that these are quite different to the most popular tags. We notice that most tags are non-programming related; for example *working-conditions, career-development, fun* etc. We also notice that some of these tags are programming related but are on broad topics like *hidden-features, hints-and-tips* and *textbook*. These tags are usually attached to questions which require a discussion and may not focus on problem specific solutions.

4.6 Community Value and Information Quality

A 'closed' question is irrelevant to the Q&A format and hence, implicitly suggests that the question may be low quality in context of Stack Overflow. Here, we analyze different indicators of content quality like *Favorite Votes, Closure Time, Question Scores and Answering Patterns* and *Question Status* with respect to 'closed' questions.

Favorite Votes.

Stack Overflow provides its users a feature to *favorite* a question. A *favorite vote* is an explicit statement of approval by the user that she finds the question useful and appropriate. Table 5 shows the cumulative distribution of 'favorite votes' on overall closed questions. The data shows that $\approx 19\%$ of the overall 'closed' questions

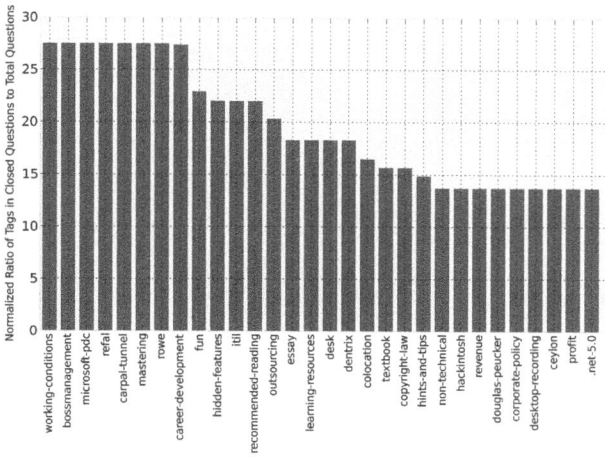

Figure 9: shows the tags of closed questions on Stack Overflow with top 30 Normalized Tag Ratios (NTR).

receive at least one *favorite vote* while $\approx 3\%$ of those receive ≥ 5 *favorite votes*.

Table 5: shows the 'Favorite Vote' Cumulative Distribution for all 'Closed' questions posted between August 2008 and August 2012. Approximately 1 out of 5 'closed' questions have at least 1 'favorite' vote and 3% have at least 5 'favorite' votes.

Votes	Closed Questions
≥ 1	19,156(18.6%)
≥ 5	3,374(3.28%)
≥ 10	1,872(1.82%)
≥ 100	206(0.2%)
≥ 500	29(0.03%)
Total	102,993

However, features such as *likes* and *favorite votes* are known to be abused by users for purposes other than their intended use. Therefore, we analyze *favorite vote* distributions on different thresholds for all sub-categories of closed questions. Figure 10 shows the distribution of *favorite votes* at different thresholds for each category of 'closed' questions. We see that the *Subjective* category attracts a very high number of *favorite votes* from users. We perform a manual qualitative analysis on these questions and notice that the *Subjective* category contains questions like Polls, Hidden Features, Books, Tricks, Interview Questions and Open ended questions. Table 6 shows examples of questions in the *Subjective* category which have ≥ 100 *favorite votes*. Note that our analysis in Section 4.5 showed that *Subjective* category had the lowest percentage of questions containing code snippets. Therefore, despite the emphasis on objectivity and source code related questions by Stack Overflow guidelines we see that some amount of programming related *Subjective* questions are encouraged and appreciated by the community members.

Closure Time.
We now analyze the time taken to 'close' questions on Stack Overflow. Figure 11 shows the closure time distribution of 'closed' question for every sub-category. The median closure times for *Exact Duplicate*, *Off Topic* and *Not a Real Question* is 6.93, 12.01 and 8.3 hours respectively. Most questions in these categories are quickly turned towards closure which may signify that their com-

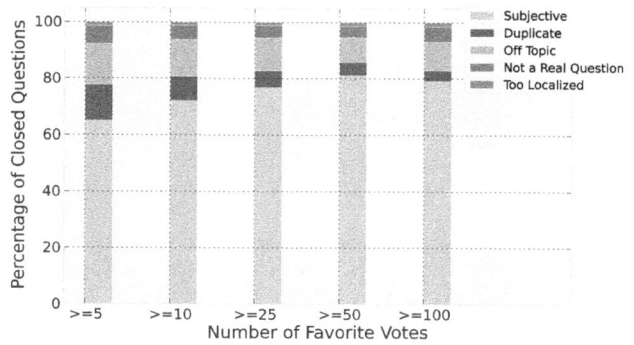

Figure 10: shows the distribution of 'favorite votes' on closed questions for each sub-category on various thresholds. *Subjective* category attracts very high number of *favorite votes* from users.

Table 6: Example questions with ≥ 100 'favorite votes' on closed questions in *subjective* category.

Favorites	Title	Answers	Views
5894	List of freely available programming books	112	569,199
2228	Hidden features of Python	100	212,589
1685	What is the best comment in source code you have ever encountered?	519	1,051,784
421	Worst security hole you've seen?	163	32,840
140	What is the most useful R trick?	34	13,197

munity value is relatively low than other categories. The *Subjective* and *Too Localized* categories have the highest median closure time ≈ 26 and 22 hours respectively. The reason for high closure time for the *Subjective* category could be because most questions (despite not being a good fit) invite discussion and opinions on broad programming related principles, guidelines, polls etc. Therefore, it takes time before these questions are answered in entirety and hence are left open for a longer time. We also notice a higher *spread* of closure times (upper quartile=586.06 days) in this category demonstrating that if a *Subjective* question is not closed within 1 day it takes a long time to close the question. The community actions indicate that these questions have not reached their maximum community value potential and hence remain open. Our prior analysis for 'close vote' distribution for *Too Localized* category in Figure 7 shows that the 66% of the questions in this category requires moderator intervention which may be one of the reasons for higher closure time. Even though *Too Localized* category has a similar median closure time (22.72 hours) to the *Subjective* category very few questions require more than 6.71 days to close. This indicates that questions in the *Too Localized* category, despite similar median closure time, reach their maximum community value potential relatively earlier than those in *Subjective* category. We also find that each category contains some outliers i.e. each category contains some questions which take a long time to be marked as 'closed'. Table 7 shows the close vote distribution pattern on questions with outlier closure times in each category.

We see that all the outlier questions have a very high percentage of ◆ moderator intervention on question closure time. This indicates that these questions are indeed outliers in terms of content too as the community prefers to keep these questions open to reach their maximum community value potential.

Question Scores and Answer Patterns.
Figure 12 shows various question scores and answer patterns on 'closed' questions in Stack Overflow. We first look into the percent-

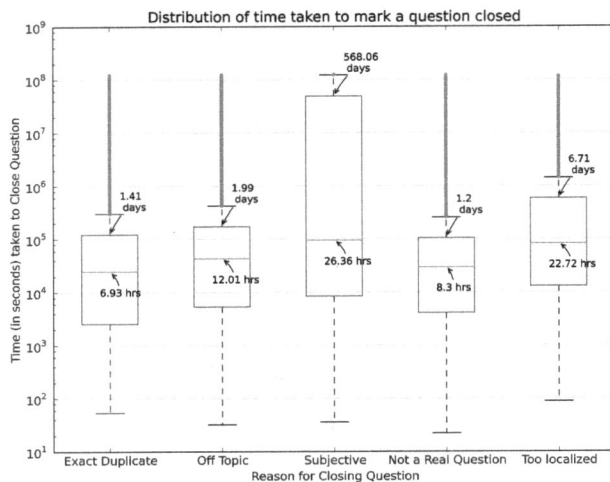

Figure 11: shows the distribution of time taken to close questions for each category in the form of a box-and-whisker plot.

Table 7: Number of Close Votes on outliers from each category

Category	1-vote	2-vote	3-vote	4-vote	5-vote
Duplicate	**55.44%**	11.68%	4.25%	2.18%	26.45%
Off-Topic	**42.06%**	16.21%	6.31%	3.47%	31.96%
Subjective	**64.64%**	16.66%	4.9%	2.26%	11.54%
Not a Real Question	**46.97%**	9.52%	6.28%	3.5%	33.74%
Too Localized	**68.22%**	11.85%	3.62%	1.86%	14.45%

age of answers (PA), percentage of accepted answers (PAA)[5] and percentage of accepted answers given an answer (PAC) on each category of 'closed' questions on Stack Overflow. We see that a large percentage of 'closed' questions receive answers from users. The *Duplicate* and *Subjective* categories also have a relatively higher PA and PAA than other categories. The higher PA and PAA on *Duplicate* questions suggest that despite the fact that the question content is an exact duplicate of others the community is eager to answer the question. Such behavior may also be exhibited by answerers to garner more reputation points in the form of answer votes and *accepted* answers. This may also explain why we see a very low PAA in the *Not a Real Question* category as users are smart enough to pick questions which have a higher probability of receiving up votes. Recall that our earlier analysis reveals that questions belonging to the *Not a Real Question* category are low in information content quality. We also analyze question score patterns on each category of 'closed' questions on Stack Overflow. We calculate percentage of questions with negative score (QN), percentage of questions with ≥ 5 score (QT) and percentage of questions with zero score (QZ). We find that *Not a Real Question* has the highest QN and once again indicates that questions in this category are very low in quality. We observe a similar pattern for *Too Localized* category and may indicate that the community in general frowns upon questions which are too confined to certain sections of the programming fraternity. We see that *Subjective* category has a very high QT and this falls in line with our earlier hypothesis that questions in this category despite being not fit to the website are immensely popular and therefore, draws large number of votes. We see similar QZ values (between 30–50%) on all categories of 'closed' questions which demonstrates that some questions do not get any approval

---

[5] A question asker can mark an answer *accepted* if the answer solves the problem faced by the question asker. Accepted answers lead to gain in reputation points to answerers.

from the community. We would like to comment that we do not observe any familiar statistical distributions like power-law on any of these question scores and answer patterns.

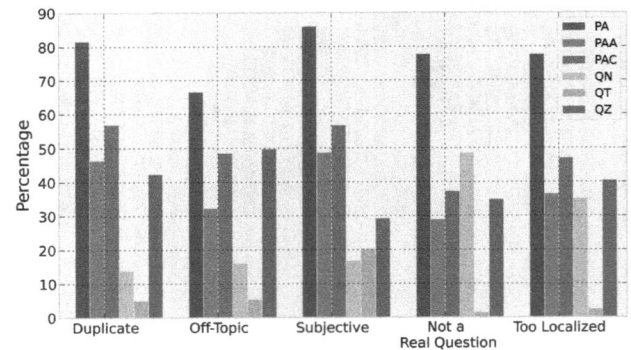

Figure 12: shows the question scores and answering patterns of users on closed questions in each category. PA = Percentage of Answers, PAA = Percentage of Accepted Answers, PAC = Percentage of Accepted Answers given that a 'closed' question has an answer, QN = Percentage of Questions with Negative Score, QT = Percentage of Questions with $\geq$ 't' Score (t=5), QZ = Percentage of Questions with Zero Score.

Question Status.

Apart from being marked as 'closed', a Stack Overflow question can also be given a *locked*, *community wiki* and *protected* label. Table 8 shows the distribution of 'closed' questions with a *locked*, *community wiki* and *protected* label. A *locked* question can not receive any new answers or any form of votes on question-answers. A question is primarily *locked* by ♦ moderator to prevent gaming or abuse of the system by users to garner reputation points [4]. We observe that *Exact Duplicate* and *Off Topic* categories are most prone to reputation gaming and therefore, marked as *locked*. A *community wiki* label is an intent to 'donate' and transfers ownership of the question from the asker to the community. The goal of Stack Overflow is to be a knowledge base of programming information and therefore *community wiki* posts play a significant role in achieving that goal [3]. We see that questions from the *Subjective* category contain a high number of *community wiki* donations. We hypothesize that this would be due to the nature of *subjective* questions as these contain discussions, opinions on programming topics which may be "never ending" (philosophical rather than factual). A *protected* label is an intent to prevent noisy answers like "Thank You", "+1" from new users who may not understand the guidelines of the forum. A *protected* label prevents newly registered users from answering these question [5]. Once again we see that a high percentage of questions from *Subjective* category are marked as *protected*. This demonstrates that *Subjective* questions are very attractive and "fun" questions to users although they may not fit into the Stack Overflow guidelines.

4.7 Characterization Summary

We now summarize key findings from our characterization study.

- We see an increasing trend in the percentage of 'closed' questions over time – in particular *Exact Duplicate* and *Not a Real Question* – with a steep rise after January 2011

- We find a positive correlation with a high confidence value between new registered users and the percentage of 'closed' questions

Table 8: shows the distribution of 'closed' Questions in the Stack Overflow with labels *locked, community wiki* and *protected*.

Category	Number of 'Closed' Questions		
	Locked	Community Wiki	Protected
Exact Duplicate	732(33.8%)	160(9.9%)	36(10.3%)
Off Topic	**1180(54.5%)**	273(16.8%)	70(20.1%)
Subjective	188(8.7%)	**978(60.3%)**	**202(58%)**
Not Real Question	50(2.3%)	192(11.8%)	28(8%)
Too Localized	114(0.6%)	10(0.6%)	12(3.4%)
Total	2,264	1,613	348

- We observe a decrease in community participation to mark a question as 'closed' over time which has probably led to increase in work load for ◆ moderators

- Popular tags on 'closed' questions are very similar to overall questions but tags unique to 'Closed' questions are vague and non-programming related

- Questions from the *Subjective* category do not follow the Q&A format but are very popular and have high community value. They also take relatively longer time to be marked as 'closed'. Questions from the *Not a Real Question* category take least amount of time to be closed and are low in community value.

- Despite a very high percentage of presence of source code, questions in *Too Localized* are not very popular in the community

- *Exact Duplicate* and *Off Topic* questions are relatively more attractive to reputation gamers

4.8 Broader Implications

Our characterization study on Stack Overflow also reveals broader implications for content quality on other CQA websites. The intricate procedures like voting, moderation etc. laid down by the Stack Overflow community helps keep low quality content to the minimum (we recall that only 3% questions are marked 'closed'). These procedures can be an important data point for other CQA websites to adopt and adapt. We observe that most low quality content on Stack Overflow is posted by newly registered users. Therefore, an early feedback mechanism to newly registered users can help with their website interaction and encourage them to post better quality content. We see that the strict adherence to guidelines by the community members leads to content being flagged for moderation despite being popular. Our analysis of 'closed' questions marked as *subjective* shows that popularity of content is not a defining factor of quality. Therefore, adherence to guidelines (and not content popularity) is a significant factor for content quality maintenance.

5. 'CLOSED' QUESTION PREDICTION

In the second part of our study, we build a predictive model to automatically detect a 'closed' question on Stack Overflow. We formulate the prediction of 'closed' questions on Stack Overflow as a binary classification task.

5.1 Features for Classification

We investigate **18** features based on *User Profile, Community Process, Question Content* and *Textual Style* for our prediction task. Table 9 shows different categories of feature sets used by our system for 'closed' question prediction. *User Profile* features are based on user's participation activity while *Community Process* features

are based on Stack Overflow community contributions in the form of votes, accepted answers etc. *Question Content* features are calculated by extracting the content from questions and *Textual Style* features characterizes the writing and posting style of the question asker. It is important to note that there may be other distinguishing features for 'closed' questions (for example - answering patterns) but the aim of the study is to predict a 'closed' question at its *creation time*. Hence, we can not make user of these features for our predictive model. The reputation of the user at question creation time is an excellent feature by intuition however, this data is not made available by Stack Overflow. Therefore, we use *Community Process* features to offset for this missing data. In addition, questions are routinely edited (title, body and tags) by experienced community users. However, there is no mechanism to get the original text of the question. All these factors make prediction of a 'closed' question difficult and challenging.

Table 9: shows the different categories of feature sets used for 'closed' question prediction

Set	Category	Number	Features
A	User Profile	3	Age of Account
			Badge Score
			Previous Posts with Negative Score
B	Community	3	Post Score
			Accepted Answer Score
			Favorite Score
C	Question Content	3	Number of URLs
			Number of Stack Overflow URLs
			Number of Popular Tags
D	Textual Style	9	Title Length
			Body Length
			Number of Tags
			Number of Punctuation Marks
			Number of Short Words
			Code Snippet Length
			Number of Special Characters
			Number of Lower Case Characters
			Number of Upper Case Characters

While most of the features are self-explanatory, below we explain some of the higher order features below (calculated at time of question creation) –

Badge Score (BS):
Let $\{b_1 \ldots b_n\}$ be the badges earned by the user, then

$$BS = \sum_{i=1}^{n} \frac{1}{\#\text{users who have } b_i}$$

Post Score (PS):
Let $\{q_1 \ldots q_n\}$ be the set of previous questions asked by the user and $\{a_1 \ldots a_m\}$ be the set of previous answers posted by the user, then

$$PS = \sum_{i=1}^{n} score(q_i) + \sum_{j=1}^{m} score(a_i)$$

Favorite Score (FS):
Let $\{fq_1 \ldots fq_n\}$ be the set of questions asked by the user which have been favourited and $\{fa_1 \ldots fa_m\}$ be the set of answers posted by the user which have been favourited, then

$$FS = \sum_{i=1}^{n} score(fq_i) + \sum_{j=1}^{m} score(fa_i)$$

Accepted Answer Score (AAS):
Let $\{aa_1 \ldots aa_n\}$ be the set of answers posted by the user which

have been accepted. We give an individual score of 15 to each accepted answer, therefore

$$AAS = \sum_{i=1}^{n} 15$$

Number of Popular Tags (#PT):
Let $T = \{t_1 \ldots t_n\}$ be the tags present in the question, and $PT = \{pt_1 \ldots pt_m\}$ our pre-derived set of popular tags on Stack Overflow[6], then

$$\#PT = \|T \cap PT\|$$

5.2 Experimental Testbed, Setup and Classification

Stack Overflow contains 102,993 'closed' questions between August 2008 to August 2012. Out of these questions, 1302 questions do not have any information about the question asker. We ignore these questions and consider the remaining **101,691** 'closed' questions as our positive class. The percentage of non-'closed' questions (negative class) is very high (97%) than 'closed' questions (3%) and therefore, leads to the formation of an imbalanced dataset. Learning with imbalanced data is a research challenge and has attracted wide spread attention of researchers in the machine learning community. Various approaches have been proposed in literature to address the nature of imbalanced datasets. One such approach is to randomly under-sample the majority class data or over-sample the minority class data to make the dataset balanced [15]. In order, to make our dataset balanced we under-sample the majority class (non-'closed' questions or -ve class) and draw **101,691** random samples. However, random sampling may result in sample bias and lead to loss of information. In order to eliminate this sample bias, we perform under-sampling by drawing several random independent subsets from the majority class (-ve class) and training multiple classifiers based on each of these -ve subsets along with the minority class (+ve class). We then evaluate our classifier across these multiple data instances and report our results. In our experiments, we draw 10 independent random subsets from **101,691** samples from the non-'closed' questions (negative majority class) and train 10 classifiers based on each of these 10 subsets along with **101,691** samples from 'closed' questions (positive minority class). Therefore, in total we have **203,382** data samples across both classes for each classification run.

Figure 13 outlines the cumulative distribution function (CDF) plots for four features – Age of Account, Code Snippet Length, Post Score and Body Length – in our experimental testbed for 'closed' and non-'closed' questions. The CDF plots strongly indicate that the features chosen for our classification task are weak discriminators. An ensemble framework gives the ability to combine the power of such weak discriminators to form a strong predictive model. Previous approaches in information and question quality prediction on CQA services have also observed good classification performance with ensemble learners like Stochastic Gradient Boosted Trees (SGBT) [10, 18]. In addition, we experimented with various classification algorithms including Support Vector Machines, Naive Bayes, Logistic Regression etc. and find that the *Stochastic Gradient Boosted Trees* gives the best performance. Stochastic Gradient Boosted Trees (SGBT) is an ensemble learning technique which combines information from *weak* predictive models (primarily built on decision trees) to form a *strong* classifier [14]. The stochastic approach randomly sub-samples the training data with-

---

[6]We obtain popular tags by calculating tag distribution of all tags in our dataset.

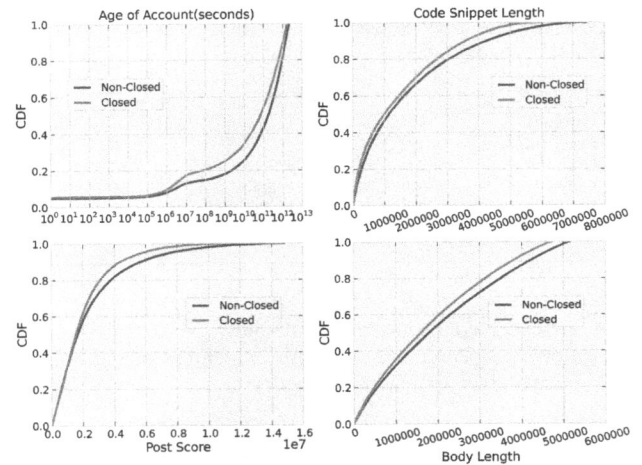

Figure 13: shows the cumulative distribution plot of four selected features used in our classification task. We see that all features are weak discriminators.

out replacement before the construction of each tree and hence, avoids over fitting on the data. Table 10 provides a summary of our testbed and experimental setup.

Table 10: Details of Experimental Setup

Dataset	203,382 questions
'Closed' (+ve class)	101,691
Non-'Closed' (-ve class)	101,691 (10-times) random sample with replacement
Classifier	Stochastic Gradient Boosted Trees
Learning Rate	0.1
Sub-sample size	0.7
Classification Runs	10 (for each +ve/-ve pair)
Feature Sets	{A}, {A, B}, {A, B, C}, {A, B, C, D}
Train-Test Split	70%-30%
Cross Validation	10-folds

We choose the most efficient parameters for learning rate (0.1) and sub-sample size (0.7) for SGBT. We use a 70-30% training-testing split and perform 10-fold cross validation on each classification run of our positive class versus random sample of negative class.

5.3 Classification Results and Evaluation

Table 11 shows the confusion matrix for our classification experiments. We are able to accurately classify 69.6% of 'closed ' questions and 70.9% of non-'closed' questions.

Table 11: Confusion Matrix – Classification Results

		Predicted	
		Closed	**Non-Closed**
True	**Closed**	**69.6%**	30.4 %
	Non-Closed	29.1%	**70.9%**

Our characterization study indicates that there is no intuitive heuristic or metric to predict a 'closed' question. Hence, in order to understand the effect of features to predict 'closed' questions, we incrementally add feature sets to our classifier and record the performance. We use three standard information retrieval metrics – F1 score, Accuracy and Area Under the ROC curve (AUC) to evaluate our classifier. Figure 14 shows the performance of our classifier on Accuracy, F1 score and AUC metrics when feature sets are incrementally added. We see that each feature set has a positive effect on the performance of the classifier across all metrics. This suggests that the all our feature sets are important for prediction.

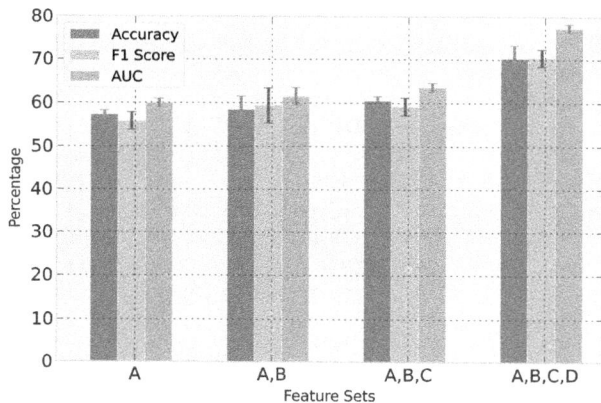

Figure 14: shows classifier performance with Accuracy, F1 and Area Under the ROC curve (AUC) metrics when feature sets are incrementally added. Note the incremental improvement in performance of our classifier on every feature set addition.

5.4 Feature Importance

One of the advantages of using SGBT is that it outputs a list of important features used for classification. Figure 15 shows the most important features for classification. Overall, we see that almost all features contribute towards our prediction model. The top five features for classification are – *Punctuation Marks*, *Special Characters*, *Code Snippet Length*, *Age of Account* and *Short Words*. We analyze the distribution of all the top five features. We observe a higher presence of *Punctuation Marks* and *Special Characters* in non-'closed' questions indicating that non-'closed' questions are more descriptive than 'closed' questions. The distribution of *Code Snippet Length* as shown in Figure 13 shows that code snippets (if present) are longer in non-'closed' questions than 'closed. This shows that code samples posted on non-'closed' questions are comparatively more detailed. The distribution of *Age of Account* in Figure 13 confirms that a newly registered user is more prone to post a 'closed' question. Overall, we see that 'closed' questions are less informative and descriptive than non-'closed' questions.

6. CONCLUSION

Stack Overflow is an extremely popular programming Community Question Answer (CQA) website for developers throughout the world. Stack Overflow uses a *karma* based incentive system to maintain the quality of content on its website. However, despite these guidelines users post questions which do not fit Stack Overflow's Q&A format. Questions which are deemed unfit for Stack Overflow are marked as 'closed' by experienced users and community moderators. We present the first study of 'closed' question on 4 years of publicly available data from Stack Overflow. We divide our study into two phases – In the first phase, we conduct a characterization of 'closed' questions posted between August 2008 to August 2012. Our characterization reveals that *subjective* 'closed'

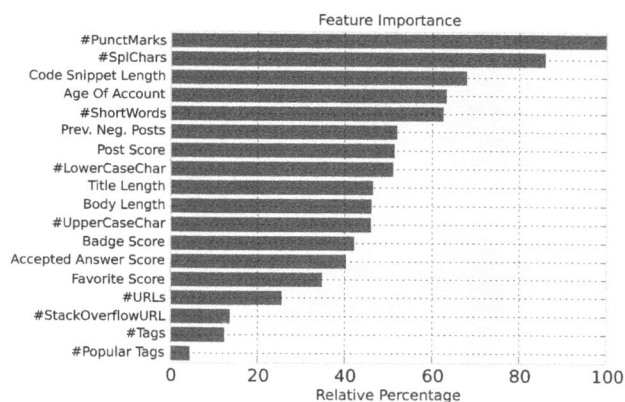

Figure 15: shows the relative feature importance of all 18 features in our predictive model.

questions are popular and high quality while *not a real question* are low in quality. We also notice decrease in community participation on question closure over time and find that *Duplicate* and *Off Topic* are more prone to reputation gaming. The analysis reveals some broader implications on content quality maintenance for CQA websites. In the second phase, we construct a predictive model for identifying a 'closed' question using an ensemble learning technique and report 70.3% accurate predictions overall. Feature analysis reveals that 'closed' questions are relatively less informative and descriptive than non-'closed' questions.

7. ACKNOWLEDGEMENTS

The authors thank Stack Overflow for providing data under the *Creative Commons Attribute-ShareAlike* license for research purposes. The authors express gratitude towards various anonymous industry sponsors for the very generous student travel grant processed via ACM. The authors would also like to thank all the anonymous reviewers for their constructive feedback on multiple drafts of the paper.

8. REFERENCES

[1] Privileges - create tags.
http://stackoverflow.com/privileges/create-tags.

[2] Why are some questions closed, and what does "closed" mean?
http://stackoverflow.com/help/closed-questions.

[3] What are "community wiki" posts?
http://meta.stackoverflow.com/questions/11740/what-are-community-wiki-posts, September 2008.

[4] What is a "locked" post? http://meta.stackoverflow.com/questions/22228/what-is-a-locked-post, September 2008.

[5] What is a "protected" question?
http://meta.stackoverflow.com/questions/52764/what-is-a-protected-question/, June 2010.

[6] Who are the diamond moderators, and what is their role?
http://meta.stackoverflow.com/a/75192/214223, January 2011.

[7] Stack exchange data dump.
http://www.clearbits.net/torrents/2076-aug-2012, August 2012.

[8] List of stack exchange moderators by sites. http://stackexchange.com/about/moderators?by=sites, June 2013.

[9] What is a day in life of a stackoverflow moderator? http://meta.stackoverflow.com/a/166630/214223, February 2013.

[10] E. Agichtein, C. Castillo, D. Donato, A. Gionis, and G. Mishne. Finding high-quality content in social media. In *Proceedings of the international conference on Web search and web data mining*, pages 183–194. ACM, 2008.

[11] A. Anderson, D. Huttenlocher, J. Kleinberg, and J. Leskovec. Discovering value from community activity on focused question answering sites: a case study of stack overflow. In *Proceedings of the 18th ACM SIGKDD international conference on Knowledge discovery and data mining*, pages 850–858. ACM, 2012.

[12] J. Atwood. Stack overflow creative commons data dump. http://blog.stackoverflow.com/2009/06/stack-overflow-creative-commons-data-dump/, June 2009.

[13] J. C. Campbell, C. Zhang, Z. Xu, A. Hindle, and J. Miller. Deficient documentation detection: a methodology to locate deficient project documentation using topic analysis. In *Proceedings of the Tenth International Workshop on Mining Software Repositories*, pages 57–60. IEEE Press, 2013.

[14] J. H. Friedman. Stochastic gradient boosting. *Computational Statistics & Data Analysis*, 38(4):367–378, 2002.

[15] H. He and E. A. Garcia. Learning from imbalanced data. *Knowledge and Data Engineering, IEEE Transactions on*, 21(9):1263–1284, 2009.

[16] J. S. Jeff Atwood. Stack exchange platform. http://stackexchange.com, September 2009.

[17] J. Jeon, W. B. Croft, J. H. Lee, and S. Park. A framework to predict the quality of answers with non-textual features. In *Proceedings of the 29th annual international ACM SIGIR conference on Research and development in information retrieval*, SIGIR '06, pages 228–235, New York, NY, USA, 2006. ACM.

[18] B. Li, T. Jin, M. R. Lyu, I. King, and B. Mak. Analyzing and predicting question quality in community question answering services. In *Proceedings of the 21st international conference companion on World Wide Web*, WWW '12 Companion, pages 775–782, New York, NY, USA, 2012. ACM.

[19] M. Linares-Vásquez, B. Dit, and D. Poshyvanyk. An exploratory analysis of mobile development issues using stack overflow. In *Proceedings of the Tenth International Workshop on Mining Software Repositories*, pages 93–96. IEEE Press, 2013.

[20] R. Lotufo, L. Passos, and K. Czarnecki. Towards improving bug tracking systems with game mechanisms. In *9th Working Conference on Mining Software Repositories (MSR'12)*, Zurich, Switzerland, 06/2012 2012. IEEE (also published as GSDLAB–TR 2011–09–29), IEEE (also published as GSDLAB–TR 2011–09–29).

[21] L. Mamykina, B. Manoim, M. Mittal, G. Hripcsak, and B. Hartmann. Design lessons from the fastest q&a site in the west. In *Proceedings of the 2011 annual conference on Human factors in computing systems*, pages 2857–2866. ACM, 2011.

[22] C. Parnin, C. Treude, L. Grammel, and M.-A. Storey. Crowd documentation: Exploring the coverage and the dynamics of api discussions on stack overflow. *Georgia Institute of Technology, Tech. Rep.*

[23] T. Sakai, D. Ishikawa, N. Kando, Y. Seki, K. Kuriyama, and C.-Y. Lin. Using graded-relevance metrics for evaluating community qa answer selection. In *Proceedings of the fourth ACM international conference on Web search and data mining*, pages 187–196. ACM, 2011.

[24] C. Shah and J. Pomerantz. Evaluating and predicting answer quality in community qa. In *Proceedings of the 33rd international ACM SIGIR conference on Research and development in information retrieval*, pages 411–418. ACM, 2010.

[25] G. Wang, K. Gill, M. Mohanlal, H. Zheng, and B. Y. Zhao. Wisdom in the social crowd: an analysis of quora.

Traveling Trends: Social Butterflies or Frequent Fliers?

Emilio Ferrara[*]

Onur Varol

Filippo Menczer

Alessandro Flammini

Center for Complex Networks and Systems Research
School of Informatics and Computing, Indiana University, Bloomington, USA

ABSTRACT

Trending topics are the online conversations that grab collective attention on social media. They are continually changing and often reflect exogenous events that happen in the real world. Trends are localized in space and time as they are driven by activity in specific geographic areas that act as sources of traffic and information flow. Taken independently, trends and geography have been discussed in recent literature on online social media; although, so far, little has been done to characterize the relation between trends and geography. Here we investigate more than eleven thousand topics that trended on Twitter in 63 main US locations during a period of 50 days in 2013. This data allows us to study the origins and pathways of trends, how they compete for popularity at the local level to emerge as winners at the country level, and what dynamics underlie their production and consumption in different geographic areas. We identify two main classes of trending topics: those that surface locally, coinciding with three different geographic clusters (East coast, Midwest and Southwest); and those that emerge globally from several metropolitan areas, coinciding with the major air traffic hubs of the country. These hubs act as trendsetters, generating topics that eventually trend at the country level, and driving the conversation across the country. This poses an intriguing conjecture, drawing a parallel between the spread of information and diseases: Do trends travel faster by airplane than over the Internet?

Categories and Subject Descriptors

[**Human-centered computing**]: Collaborative and social computing—*Social media*; [**Information systems**]: World Wide Web—*Social networks*; [**Networks**]: Network types—*Social media networks*

*Corresponding author: `ferrarae@indiana.edu`

Keywords

Social media; Twitter; trends; geography; mobility

1. INTRODUCTION

Social media and online social networks have been widely adopted as proxies to study complex social dynamics, such as the spread of information and opinions [11, 16, 25, 29, 53, 54] and the emergence of patterns of collective attention [5, 6, 26, 50]. Groundbreaking results emerged with the analysis of geographic metadata from social media, allowing for the study of human mobility patterns and social media demographics [20, 24, 31, 35, 45, 46, 8].

It has been suggested that social media may overcome the spatio-temporal limitations of traditional communication: technologically-mediated systems make it possible to ignore physical and geographic distances [12, 34]. This, however, does not imply that communication patterns on social media are not affected by physical distances and geographic borders [33, 36]. In this paper, we explicitly study the role played by geography in driving the main topics of discussion on Twitter: trending hashtags and phrases.

Trends represent interesting collective communication phenomena: they are user-generated, continually changing and mostly ungoverned (although orchestrated hijacking attempts have already been observed [9, 40, 41]). So far, trends have been studied as a proxy to detect exogenous real-world events discussed in social media, [1, 3, 17, 43], emerging topics, or news of interest for the online community [10, 27].

But trends are also strongly localized in space and time: the temporal and geographic dimensions play a crucial role to determine the success of a trend in terms of spreading and longevity. We argue that unveiling the spatio-temporal dynamics that drive trending conversations on social media is instrumental to many purposes: from designing successful advertising campaigns, to understanding virality and popularity that characterize some topics. In this paper we characterize the relation between trends and geography by tracking and analyzing trending topics on Twitter in 63 main locations of the United States and at the country level, for a period of 50 days in 2013.

Contributions and outline

Here we study the distribution, origins, and pathways of trends; the dynamics underlying trend production and consumption in different geographic areas; and the competition among trends to achieve global popularity. In the remainder of the paper we make the following contributions:

Table 1: The list of the 63 trend locations in the United States and the relative total number of trends (thousands) they generated in the period between April, 12th and the end of May 2013.

Albuquerque	6.7	Cincinnati	5.8	Greensboro	5.8	Long Beach	6.5	New Haven	5.6	Pittsburgh	5.8	San Francisco	5.7
Atlanta	5.1	Cleveland	5.4	Harrisburg	6.3	Los Angeles	5.2	New Orleans	6.2	Portland	6.4	San Jose	6.6
Austin	5.8	Colorado Springs	6.7	Honolulu	6.5	Louisville	5.9	New York	4.4	Providence	5.9	Seattle	5.9
Baltimore	5.8	Columbus	6.0	Houston	5.1	Memphis	6.5	Norfolk	6.0	Raleigh	5.3	St. Louis	5.7
Baton Rouge	6.5	Dallas-Ft. Worth	5.3	Indianapolis	5.9	Mesa	6.6	Oklahoma City	5.8	Richmond	6.2	Tallahassee	6.3
Birmingham	6.1	Denver	6.1	Jackson	6.8	Miami	5.5	Omaha	6.4	Sacramento	5.9	Tampa	5.6
Boston	5.0	Detroit	4.8	Jacksonville	6.0	Milwaukee	5.8	Orlando	5.8	Salt Lake City	6.4	Tucson	6.6
Charlotte	5.2	El Paso	6.5	Kansas City	5.7	Minneapolis	5.6	Philadelphia	5.1	San Antonio	5.8	Virginia Beach	6.8
Chicago	5.2	Fresno	6.6	Las Vegas	5.4	Nashville	6.0	Phoenix	5.9	San Diego	6.2	Washington	4.7

- In §2.2 we describe a procedure to build a directed and weighted temporal dependence network to infer the trendsetting and trend-following relationships among locations.

- In §3.1 we provide a statistical characterization of trends, describing how they are distributed in space and time.

- In §3.2 we highlight a locality effect in the trend sharing patterns: geographically close cities share similar trends. This effect of locality yields the emergence of three geographic clusters in the US, namely East coast, Midwest, and Southwest. But we also uncover a surprising fourth cluster, representing metropolitan areas spread across the country.

- The temporal dependence network is exploited to unveil the pathways that trends follow: in §3.3 we reconstruct and reveal the significant backbone of this network that carries the trends across the country.

- In §3.4 we describe two different dynamics that govern popularity of trends at the country level, one for cities in each local geographic area and one for metropolitan areas. We conclude highlighting that the major metropolitan areas shape the country trends significantly more than all other locations in the country.

- Finally, in §4 we propose an interpretation for the trendsetting role of major metropolitan areas, by noting their correspondence with air traffic hubs and conjecturing that trends travel through air passengers, just as infectious diseases.

A more extensive literature review can be found in §5.

2. EXPERIMENTAL SETUP

In this section we discuss the methodology we followed to generate a dataset of Twitter trends, and the derived temporal dependence network that allows us to unveil the dynamics of trend production and consumption.

2.1 Trends dataset

To build our dataset we monitored in real-time all trends appearing on Twitter for a period of 50 days, starting from April, 12th until the end of May 2013.

The Twitter homepage provides a trends box that contains the top 10 trending hashtags or phrases at any given moment, ranked according to their popularity. Oftentimes, a promoted trend is showed in 1st position — for our analysis we disregarded promoted trends since their popularity is artificially inflated by the advertisement.

Each Twitter user can monitor the trends at the *worldwide*, *country*, or *city* level. Twitter has identified 63 locations in the United States, displayed in Figure 4, for which it

is possible to follow local trends. The full list of locations is reported in Table 1. It is worth noting that some areas are over-represented (for example the East coast and California), while some states (namely, North and South Dakota, Montana, Wyoming, Idaho, and Alaska) are not represented at all.[1]

We deployed a Web crawler to check at regular intervals of 10 minutes the trends of each of these 63 locations and, in addition, those at the country level. We ended up collecting 11,402 different trends overall: 4,513 hashtags and 6,889 phrases. Table 1 also reports how many trends have been observed in each location.

2.2 Trend pathway backbone network

To investigate where trends usually start and how they propagate from city to city, we built a temporal dependence network of the 63 locations of the United States represented in our dataset.

This network is directed and weighted: each node corresponds to one of the 63 cities, and the weight of an arc e_{ij} from node i to node j is increased every time location i exhibits a trend before location j. The weight of arc e_{ij} therefore represents the extent to which city i precedes city j in adopting a trend: the higher the weight, the more often location i sets the trends that location j will later adopt.

Due to the fact that the adopted dataset contains a large number of trending hashtags and phrases, the network obtained using the procedure described above is fully-connected. This makes the extraction of relevant connections hard, as each location is connected with all the others and only the weight of the connections vary.

To ease the analysis we applied to this network an edge filtering technique known as multiscale backbone extraction [48]. The goal of this procedure is to retain only those connections that are statistically significant, by removing all edges whose weight does not deviate sufficiently from a null model. The significance level of an edge is determined by a threshold parameter α. Lowering α progressively removes edges and eventually causes the disruption of the network. We tuned α to obtain the backbone network with the minimum number of edges that suffices to maintain all 63 nodes connected ($\alpha = 0.3$). The resulting multiscale backbone of the network is used for the analysis of pathways of trend diffusion, and to investigate trendsetting and trend-following dynamics (see §3.3).

3. RESULTS

The results of our analysis are discussed in this section: after a statistical description of trends, discussing how they are distributed in space and time (§3.1), we explore their geographic dimension, defining what areas of the country share

---

[1]This has to do with the fact that the activity on Twitter in those states is very low.

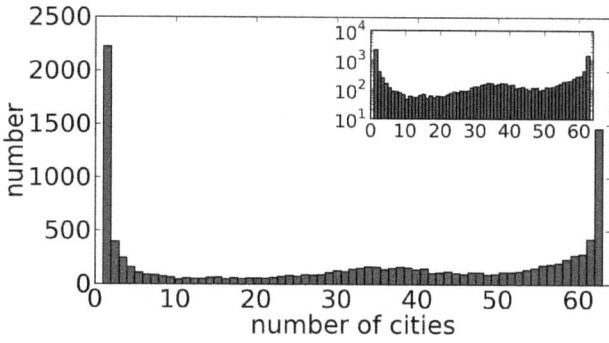

Figure 1: Histogram of the number of trends appearing in different number of places. Inset: y-axis reported in a log-scale.

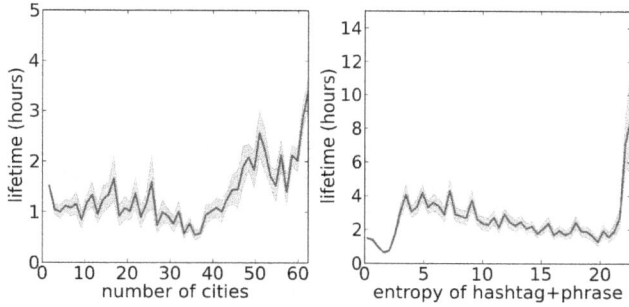

Figure 2: Lifetime of a trend. Left: as function of the number of cities in which a trend has appeared. Right: as function of its entropy. In both plots, the dark blue line is the average across trends while the standard error is depicted in light blue.

the same type of trends (§3.2); then we further investigate the temporal dimension, discussing the pathways trends follow (§3.3), and finally we characterize the trendsetting and trend-following dynamics (§3.4).

3.1 Spatio-temporal trend analysis

In our first experiment we aim to give a statistical characterization of trends: in particular, we start investigating in how many different cities trends appear. In Figure 1 we report the number of trends appearing in a given number of distinct locations. Trends follow a bimodal distribution, typically appearing either in one or few locations, or in all or most of them. We can identify three behaviors: (i) a large fraction of trends are localized and not sustained enough to spread from their originating place to others; (ii) another comparably large fraction of trends diffuse all over the cities generating a global phenomenon across the country; and (iii) the small remainder diffuse from the originating place to some other places, but fail to achieve global popularity.

The lifetime of trends is broadly distributed: short-lived topics trending for less than 20 minutes amount for more than 68% of the total, and overall trends shorter than six hours cover more than 95% of our sample. Sporadically some trends happen to live a much longer time, with only 0.3% surviving for more than a day.

We now focus on the spatio-temporal dimension of trends, aiming to determine how much time each trend spends in one or several locations. In particular, we calculate the average lifetime of a trend (the average amount of time a given hashtag or phrase is trending somewhere) as a function of the number of cities in which it appears. Figure 2 (left panel) reflects the intuition that trends reaching more places live longer.

Another way to determine the relation between the *geographic spread* of trends and their temporal patterns is to measure their lifetime as a function of *entropy*, defined as

$$\mathcal{S}^j = -\sum_i P_i^j \log P_i^j, \quad \text{with} \quad P_i^j = \frac{t_i^j}{\sum_k t_k^j}, \qquad (1)$$

where t_i^j is the time topic j has been trending in location i. The entropy is low if the trending topic is concentrated in a few places, and maximal if the topic trends for equal durations of time in all places. Figure 2 (right panel) shows that for trends with low entropy (*i.e.*, those concentrated in a single location), the expected lifetime is very short. The lifetime increases significantly (five-fold) for the maximum observed entropy. This analysis reveals a key ingredient for global trend popularity: the trending time of a topic is not only determined by its lifetime in a single location, but also by its geographic spread across many locations.

3.2 Geography of trends

Let us examine the geographic patterns of trends, namely whether geographically close cities share more similar trends than cities that are physically far apart. To determine if this locality effect exists, we first isolate, for each location i, the set of trends T_i that appeared in that location. Then, for each pair of locations i and j we compute the pairwise Jaccard similarity

$$S_{ij} = \frac{|T_i \bigcap T_j|}{|T_i \bigcup T_j|}. \qquad (2)$$

The Jaccard similarity ranges between 0 and 1: the higher the value, the more similar the trends exhibited by two different cities. These values of similarity are subsequently passed to a hierarchical clustering algorithm after being transformed in distances: $d_{ij} = 1 - S_{ij}$. This is done to determine whether it is possible to isolate clusters of locations that exhibit similar trends, and, if so, whether these locations are geographically close or spread all over the country. The result is showed in Figure 3 and discussed next.

3.2.1 Locality effects

Figure 3 is constituted by two parts: a heat-map representing the pairwise Jaccard similarity among locations, and a dendrogram generated according to an agglomerative hierarchical clustering algorithm using complete linkage. Analyzing the dendrogram we can identify three distinct clusters, whose members (reported in different colors: green, yellow and red) share a high internal similarity in the trends exhibited during the observation period. This cluster emerges applying a cut to the dendrogram for a distance value of 0.5. We can also identify a fourth cluster (in purple, emerging with a dendrogram cut corresponding to a distance value of 0.75) that exhibits a lower internal similarity and whose members show a low similarity with those of other clusters. The four clusters are reported in Table 2, and displayed in Figure 4.

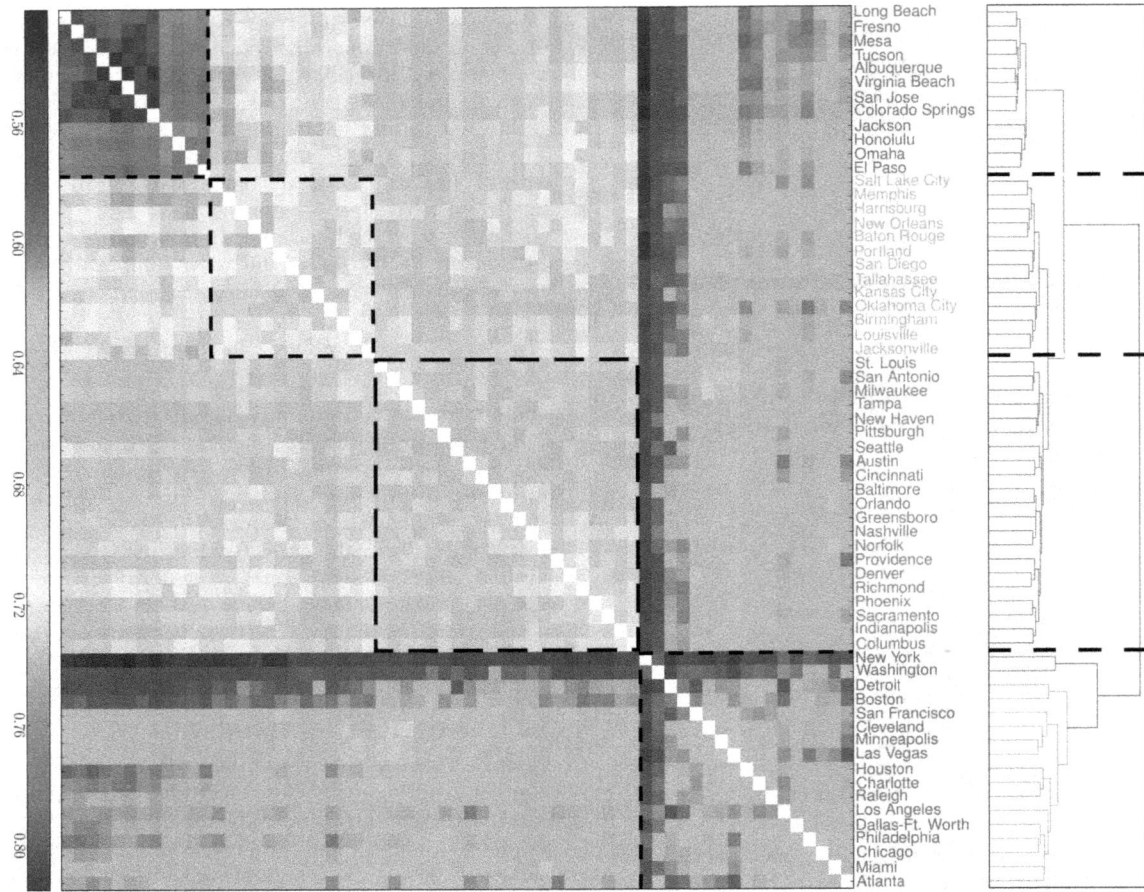

Figure 3: Shared trend similarity and hierarchical clustering of the 63 locations.

From the figure we observe that the green, yellow and red clusters are somewhat geographically localized, while the purple one is spread more or less all over the country. In detail, the green cluster, with the highest internal similarity, roughly corresponds to the Southwest of the country. The yellow cluster follows, representing the Midwest and South. The red cluster, which is less localized, matches many locations in the East coast and Midwest. The purple cluster includes several major metropolitan areas [51]; their effect on trendsetting dynamics is discussed in §3.4 and a conjecture about their role is offered in §4.

3.2.2 Significance of geographic clustering

To determine the statistical significance of the clustering obtained by using the previous method we proceeded as follows: we first computed the distribution of similarity values among all pairs of locations belonging to the same cluster (intra-cluster similarities); then, we did the same for the pairs belonging to different clusters (inter-cluster similarities). After that, we applied a kernel smoothing technique known as Kernel Density Estimation [22] to estimate the probability density functions for our similarity distributions, plotted in Figure 5 (the distribution of each cluster is represented by its color corresponding to Table 2).

We applied a t-test to determine if any given pair of distributions of intra- and inter-cluster similarity might originate

Table 2: Clusters of cities according to trend similarity.

Green	Yellow	Red	Purple
Long Beach	Memphis	St. Louis	Washington
Fresno	Salt Lake City	San Antonio	New York
Mesa	Harrisburg	Milwaukee	Detroit
Tucson	New Orleans	Tampa	Boston
Albuquerque	Baton Rouge	Pittsburgh	San Francisco
Virginia Beach	Portland	New Haven	Cleveland
San Jose	Tallahassee	Seattle	Minneapolis
Colorado Springs	San Diego	Cincinnati	Las Vegas
Jackson	Kansas City	Austin	Houston
Honolulu	Oklahoma City	Orlando	Charlotte
El Paso	Birmingham	Baltimore	Raleigh
Omaha	Louisville	Greensboro	Los Angeles
	Jacksonville	Nashville	Dallas-Ft. Worth
		Norfolk	Chicago
		Providence	Philadelphia
		Denver	Miami
		Richmond	Atlanta
		Phoenix	
		Sacramento	
		Columbus	
		Indianapolis	

from the same distribution, assessing that all distributions (and, therefore, the clusters) are significant at the 99% confidence level.

We also compared the result of the hierarchical clustering with that of two network clustering algorithms (namely, Infomap [42] and the 'Louvain method' [4]) applied to the trend pathway backbone network (described in §2.2). We obtained consistent results in all cases: the only difference

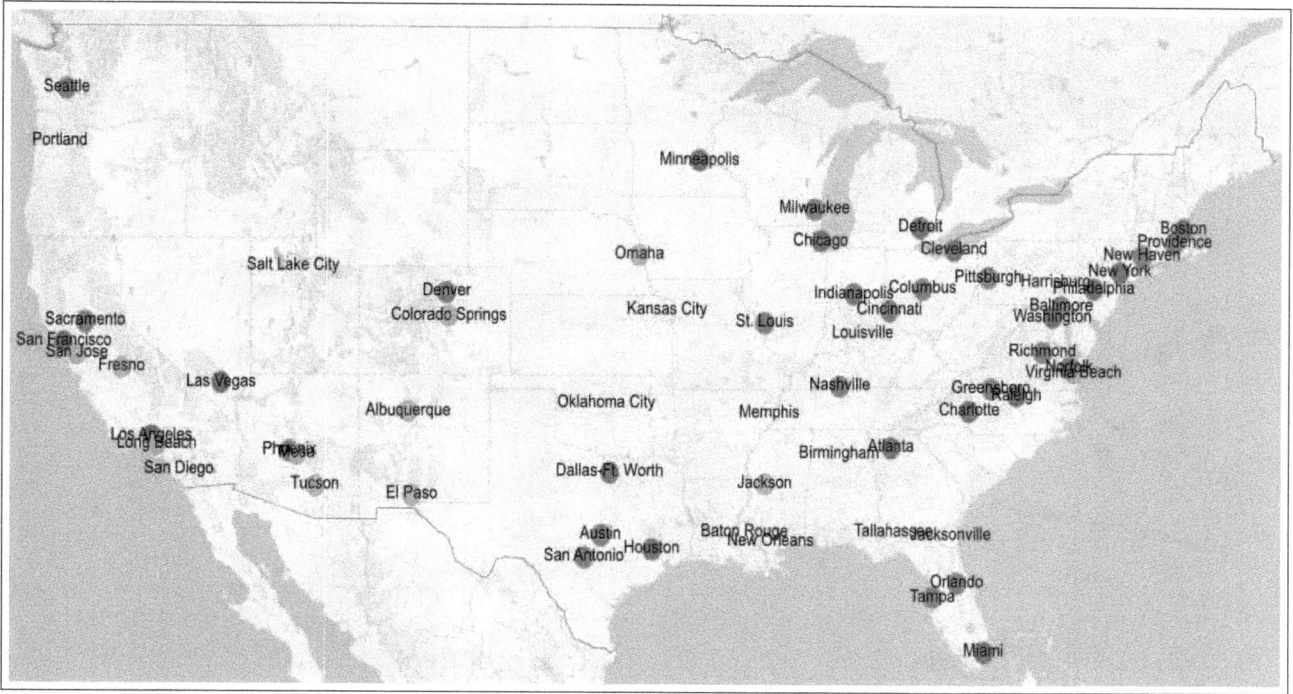

Figure 4: geographic representation of the 63 locations and respective clusters.

was that Seattle was placed in the purple cluster by both network clustering methods.

3.3 Trend pathway analysis

To establish where trends start and what pathways they follow to diffuse in the country, we analyze the multiscale trend pathway backbone network, built as described in §2.2 and represented in Figure 6 by using a divided edge bundling technique [47]. This visualization strategy has been successfully applied to other geographic networks such as the US airport traffic network (*cf.* [47]). In this node-link representation the edges are bundled taking into account directions and weights. The thicker the bundle, the higher the sum of the weights of connections wrapped in the bundle. In our case, this yields a network visualization that highlights the pathways followed by trends as they flow across

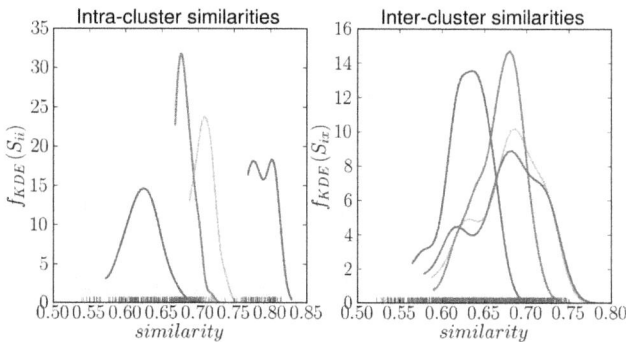

Figure 5: Kernel Density Estimation of intra- and inter-cluster similarity of the four clusters.

the country. In this figure the direction of edges represents the information flow: the tails of the bundles (in blue) show where trends start, the heads of the bundles (in red) point to where the trends arrive. From Figure 6 we can draw two observations: first, the presence of a massive backbone that carries the trend flow from the East coast to the West coast and vice-versa. Second, we observe a negligible North-South flow, except for that connecting Florida to the East coast. Moreover, the fact that the East-to-West flow is well balanced by the that in the opposite direction suggests that we are not simply observing an artifact of the time-zone effect: the West coast contributes to shaping the country trends to a similar extent that the East coast does.

In the backbone network the cities that often generate trends are those with higher fractions of outgoing edges (that is, those that spread their trends to most of the other cities); henceforth we will call them *sources*. Vice-versa, we will call *sinks* those cities with higher fraction of incoming edges. More precisely, since the network we deal with is weighted, we compute the *weighted source-sink ratio* $\omega(n)$ for each node n as

$$\omega(n) = \frac{s_{out}(n)}{s_{in}(n) + s_{out}(n)}, \quad (3)$$

where $s_{in}(n)$ (resp., $s_{out}(n)$) is the in-strength (resp., out-strength) of that node. We report in Table 3 the top 5 sources and the top 5 sinks of the backbone network. Four out of the five top sources (all but Cincinnati) also happen to be major metropolitan areas. On the other hand, all sinks belong to the Southwest and Midwest parts of the country. Los Angeles and New York (among our top sources) have also been reported in the top 5 hashtag producers worldwide in the recent work by Kamath *et al.* [23].

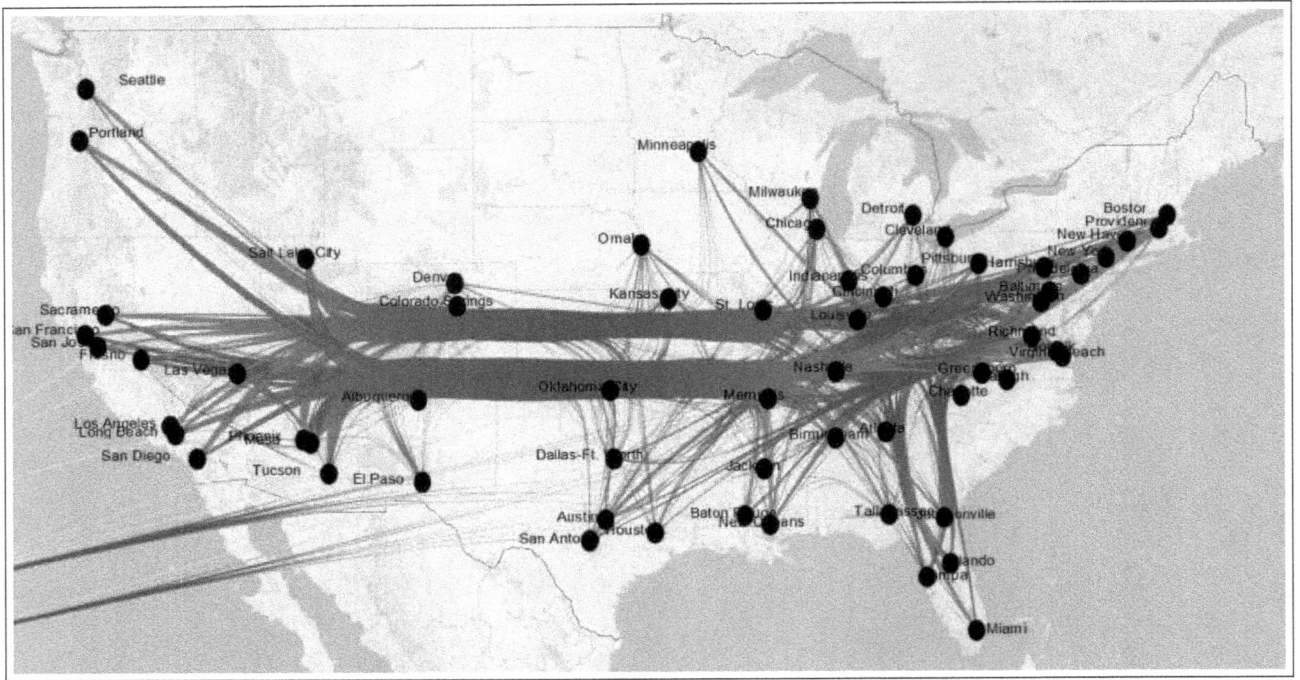

Figure 6: Trend pathways in Twitter. Trends spread in the direction from blue to red.

3.4 Trendsetters and trend-followers

The source-sink analysis presented above triggered our interest in the dynamics of trend popularity. In the following we study trendsetting and trend-following patterns, driven by the following question: *Are trending topics that become popular at the country level produced uniformly by all cities, or preferentially by some of them?*

To answer this question we selected from our dataset all those trends that at some point in time became trending at the country level. This left us with 1,724 hashtags and 2,768 phrases that achieved the highest popularity in the United States, appearing in the top 10 trending topics at the country level. We then selected the set of cities that exhibited each of these trends, and divided them in two categories: those cities in which the hashtag or phrase was trending *before* it became trending at the country level, and those cities that adopted it *after* it became trending at the country level. This allows us to determine what are the cities that contribute more to shaping the trends at the country level, and what are the cities that are more influenced by these global trends: in other words, we can identify trendsetters and trend-followers.

Figure 7 shows the result of this analysis for the hashtags. We can immediately identify two different classes of cities:

the majority of them (*i.e.*, all those in the upper-left part of the main plot) appear to influence country-level trends roughly to the same extent to which they are influenced by the global trends; a second class of cities seem to have a much stronger trendsetting role toward the country.

To assess if these two classes can be significantly distinguished, we use the Expectation Maximization algorithm to learn an optimal Gaussian Mixture Model (GMM); to determine the appropriate number of components of the mixture we perform a 5-fold cross-validation using Bayesian and Akaike information criteria as quality measures, by varying the number of components from 1 to 10. The outcome of the cross-validation determines that the optimal number of components is two, according to both criteria, matching our expectations.

The result of the GMM is showed in the inset of Figure 7: each point is assigned to one of the two components yielding two different clusters composed respectively of 11 trendsetting cities (red dots) and 52 trend-following cities (blue stars). The list of trendsetters includes (in ascending order of impact) Raleigh, Detroit, Philadelphia, Houston, New York, Dallas-Ft. Worth, Boston, Denver, Atlanta, Los Angeles, and Seattle. All of them are major metropolitan areas.

To highlight the existence of these two different dynamics we applied a regression analysis approach by fitting two different linear regressions to the points belonging to the classes of trendsetters (coefficient of determination $R^2 = 0.9455$, p-value $p = 3.9 \cdot 10^{-7}$) and trend-followers ($R^2 = 0.7063$, $p < 10^{-10}$). This points out the proportionality that exists between incoming and outgoing trend flows.

We repeated this analysis by making the model even more realistic: for example, we introduced the effect of the time lag, discounting the reward given to those cities that adopt a

Table 3: Left: top 5 sources (*i.e.*, trendsetters). Right: top 5 sinks (*i.e.*, trend-followers).

Location	Rank	$\omega(n)$	Location	Rank	$\omega(n)$
Los Angeles	1st	0.806	Oklahoma City	63rd	0.101
Cincinnati	2nd	0.736	Albuquerque	62nd	0.109
Washington	3rd	0.718	El Paso	61st	0.235
Seattle	4th	0.711	Omaha	60th	0.305
New York	5th	0.669	Kansas City	59th	0.352

1) Baton Rouge	2) Jackson	3) Chicago	4) Philadelphia	5) Denver	6) Richmond	7) Providence
8) Dallas-Ft. Worth	9) Oklahoma City	10) San Francisco	11) Birmingham	12) Los Angeles	13) Columbus	14) Indianapolis
15) Phoenix	16) Harrisburg	17) Pittsburgh	18) Sacramento	19) Nashville	20) Albuquerque	21) El Paso
22) New York	23) Baltimore	24) Honolulu	25) Atlanta	26) Memphis	27) Jacksonville	28) Tampa
29) Colorado Springs	30) Norfolk	31) Omaha	32) Charlotte	33) Miami	34) San Jose	35) Orlando
36) Kansas City	37) Detroit	38) Tucson	39) Raleigh	40) Greensboro	41) Cincinnati	42) San Diego
43) Las Vegas	44) Austin	45) Mesa	46) Virginia Beach	47) St. Louis	48) Houston	49) New Haven
50) Tallahassee	51) Fresno	52) Boston	53) Washington	54) Louisville	55) Minneapolis	56) San Antonio
57) Long Beach	58) New Orleans	59) Salt Lake City	60) Cleveland	61) Milwaukee	62) Portland	63) Seattle

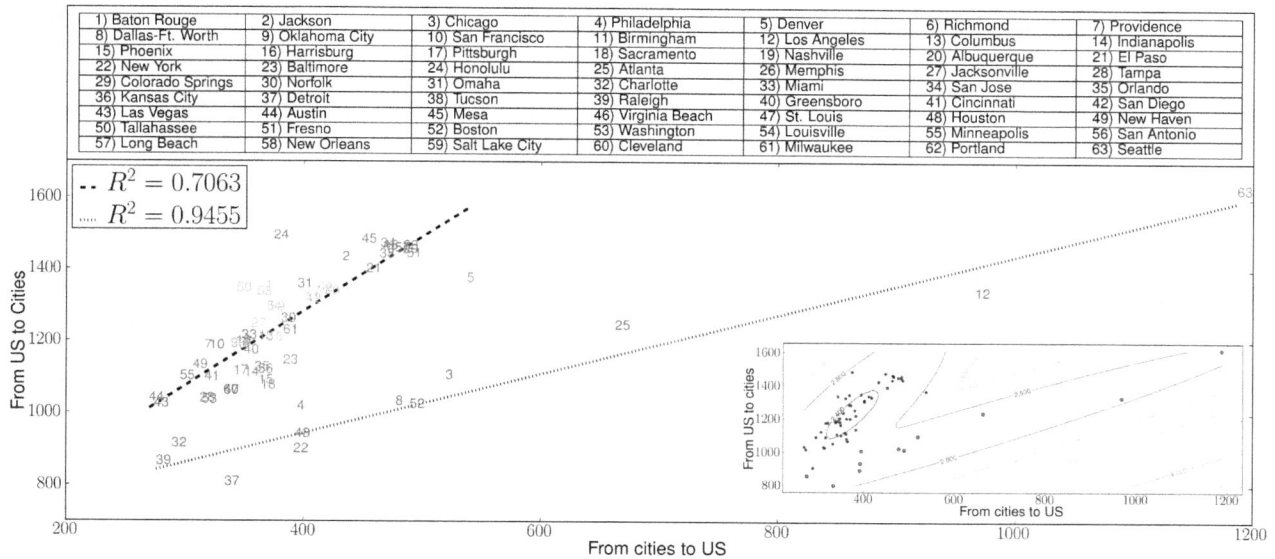

Figure 7: Trendsetting vs. trend-following cities. The x-axis shows the number of times a topic trending in a particular city later trends at the country level, while the y-axis shows the number of times of the reverse effect. The inset shows a Gaussian Mixture Model highlighting the two different trendsetting dynamics; the contours represent the standard deviations of each Gaussian distribution. In the main plot, two linear regressions are reported with the corresponding coefficient of determination R^2. City colors correspond to the cluster assignment in Table 2.

trend later with respect to the initiators; also, we rewarded only the initiators of each trend, rather than any city that exhibits a given trend before the trending point at the country level. Making the scenario more realistic did not affect the outcome: in all cases we obtained comparable results.

4. DISCUSSION

The fourth, purple cluster identified in §3.2 deserves further discussion. Differently from the others, this cluster is not geographically well defined (*cf.* Figure 4) — it contains metropolitan areas spread all over the country. Is the effect of city size sufficient to explain why these metropolitan areas are more influential than others, in the sense that they produce more national trends? It is not obvious that large populations would lead to more national trends: while a larger city produces more tweets and possibly more topic competing for popularity, the number of trends for each city at a given time is bounded to ten, irrespective of the city size. In cities with larger content production, hashtags (or phrases) must appear in more tweets to be listed as a trend, whereas a lower number of tweets is sufficient in cities with smaller content production. As a result, the effect of sheer volume is discounted by construction in the definition of Twitter trends.

Why, then, do the metropolitan areas in the purple cluster play such a trendsetting role? A possible interpretation is offered by noticing the presence in this cluster of some of the major airport hubs of the United States, such as Atlanta, Chicago, and Los Angeles. The list of top US airport hubs [52] is shown in Table 4, where we aggregated the traffic by metropolitan area. Surprisingly, 16 out of the 17 locations that constitute the cluster appear in the top 20 air traffic hubs — all of them but Cleveland. On the other hand,

Table 4: Top 20 cities ranked according to the total volume of flight traffic.

City	Cluster	Rank	Total traffic
New York (JFK, EWR, LGA)	purple	6th, 14th, 20th	54,374,758*
Atlanta (ATL)	purple	1st	45,798,809
Chicago (ORD, MDW)	purple	2nd, 25th	41,603,539*
Miami (MIA, FLL, PBI)	purple	12th, 21st, 54th	33,228,913*
Dallas-Ft. Worth (DFW, DAL)	purple	4th, 45th	31,925,398*
Washington (BWI, IAD, DCA)	purple	22nd, 23rd, 26th	31,431,854*
Los Angeles (LAX)	purple	3rd	31,326,268
Denver (DEN)	red	5th	25,799,832
Charlotte/Raleigh (CLT, RDU)	purple	8th, 37th	24,521,523*
Houston (IAH, HOU)	purple	11th, 32nd	24,082,666*
San Francisco (SFO)	purple	7th	21,284,224
Las Vegas (LAS)	purple	9th	19,941,173
Phoenix (PHX)	red	10th	19,556,189
Orlando (MCO)	red	13th	17,159,425
Seattle (SEA)	red	15th	16,121,123
Minneapolis (MSP)	purple	16th	15,943,751
Detroit (DTW)	purple	17th	15,599,877
Philadelphia (PHL)	purple	18th	14,587,631
Boston (BOS)	purple	19th	14,293,675
Salt Lake City (SLC)	yellow	24th	9,579,836

(*) Sum of the traffic volume of different airports in the same area.

some cities in the cluster that do not belong in the top 30 metropolitan areas by population (Charlotte, Raleigh, Las Vegas), do appear among the major air traffic hubs.

The presence of major air traffic hubs among the special class of cities that act as trendsetters suggests an intriguing conjecture, drawing a parallel with the spread of diseases: *Does information travel faster by airplane than over the Internet?* In other words, do conversations and trends spread following social interaction dynamics, like *social butterflies* that pass from person to person at the local level, or do they diffuse using traveling people as vectors, similarly to epidemics that take advantage of human mobility [13, 2]?

Further work is needed to explore this conjecture. One possibility would be to measure the correlation between trend overlap among pairs of cities and the corresponding air traffic.

5. RELATED WORK

Trends or aspects related to geography in socio-technical systems have been studied, directly or indirectly, in many recent studies. The present work is the first, to the best of our knowledge, that investigates the dynamics tightly binding trends and geography in online social media.

Geographic locations and physical distances have been found to be correlated to friendship behaviors in online social networks [28], to determine patterns in human mobility networks [7, 20], and to affect collaboration schemes in science networks [37].

Recent studies took advantage of platforms such as Yelp and Foursquare, which provide customized services to their users based on their physical location (e.g., recommendations of events or places), to study geographic user activity patterns [35, 44, 45, 46].

Others have used platforms such as Twitter and Facebook, that enrich user profiles with geographic information and accompany user generated content with location-based data, to map users demographics [24, 31].

Onnela et al. [36] noted that, although the probability of observing a tie between two individuals in a social network (in that case, a mobile phone call network) decreases as a power law with physical distance, the geographic spread of social groups quickly increases with the size of the group; even groups of modest dimensions ($\approx$ 30 members) span across hundreds of kilometers, suggesting that, in technologically-mediated social systems, there exist distinctive social dynamics that govern the communication among individuals.

The findings presented in this paper nicely dovetail with Onnela's work, in that we observe the existence of a class of cities, geographically spread across the country, that acts as trendsetters for all other locations. On the other hand, we highlight that also a locality effect exists: geographically concentrated areas share similar contents and trends.

The local versus global ("glocal") nature of communication has been observed before in other types of online conversation [21]. In our analysis of the Occupy Wall Street movement on Twitter [14, 15], we noted that geographically localized discussions aim at mobilizing resources (e.g., marshaling financial, material and human capital) while global discourse sets the goals of the movement and develops the narrative frames that reinforce collective purpose.

The influence of the locality effect has been also recently pointed out for innovation adoption on Twitter: Toole et al. [49] noted that homophily and physical closeness facilitate the adoption of new technological artifacts, suggesting that the effect of geographic location is critical to describe social dynamics in networked systems.

Geographic factors have also been recently found crucial in the adoption of languages and dialects [33], and in the expression of sentiment [32, 38, 39] in online social media. Mocanu et al. [33] showed how social media data can be used to characterize language geography at different levels of granularity, to highlight patterns such as linguistic homogeneity and linguistic mixture in multilingual regions.

Similarly, the study by Mitchell et al. [32] suggests that the adoption of online social media content can be instrumental to describe emotional, demographic and geographic characteristics of users of these socio-technical systems; in particular, they investigated Twitter users active in the US in terms of happiness and individual satisfaction.

Another recent research line related to our work is that of the detection of emerging trends, topics, memes, and events in online social networks and social media [1, 3, 10, 17, 19, 27, 30, 43]. Naaman et al. [34] characterized trends according to different dimensions, such as content, interaction, time-based and social features. These features were later used to classify trends, allowing for the identification of exogenous vs. endogenous trends and memes vs. retweet trends. In their analysis, the authors did not consider the geographic dimension, that is instead central in this work suggesting that it provides crucial information to characterize trends on online social media.

Finally, social media data can be used to make educated guesses on the outcome of real-word events, such as elections or competitions [18]. Ciulla et al. [12] combined trends and geographic information of Twitter data to demonstrate that online social media can be exploited to predict social events in the real-world. They collected trending hashtag and phrases related to contestants of the popular TV show *American Idol*, mapping the fan base of each candidate to different geographic regions inside and outside the US, to identify spatial patterns in attention allocation and preferences expressed on the online platform. These signals were then combined and used to predict voting behaviors of fans, achieving good accuracy.

6. CONCLUSIONS

In this work we investigated the spatial and geographic dynamics that govern trending topics in Twitter. We monitored trends from 63 different locations in the United States and, in addition, the trends at the country level, for a period of 50 days.

We sought to understand how trends are distributed in space and time and how they spread from place to place. We investigated shared trends among cities, finding that there exists a locality effect whose presence allows for the identification of three broad geographic areas where trends diffuse locally more than globally. We also identified a fourth cluster of metropolitan areas that counterbalances this locality effect. These cities, spread all over the country, act as sources of trends for other locations. They contribute much more than the others to shaping the global trends at the country level. We finally observed that these metropolitan areas coincide with the major air traffic hubs of the country, suggesting an intriguing conjecture based on a parallel between the spread of information and diseases: Do trends travel faster by airplane than over the Internet?

Our findings have broad potential applications, that include tailoring online content based on users geographic information, or designing better algorithms for geographic-aware trend prediction.

As for the future, our analysis opens new research questions that will need further attention. An example is the role of traffic hubs in trend diffusion. More in general, additional work is needed to understand how to identify locations that can be influential for the spread of a given topic and how to effectively convey the information flow to determine the success of a given commercial campaign.

Acknowledgments

This work is supported by NSF (grant CCF-1101743), DARPA (grant W911NF-12-1-0037), and the McDonnell Foundation. The funders had no role in study design, data collection and analysis, decision to publish, or preparation of the manuscript.

7. REFERENCES

[1] C. Aggarwal and K. Subbian. Event detection in social streams. In *Proceedings of SIAM International Conference on Data Mining*, 2012.

[2] D. Balcan, V. Colizza, B. Gonçalves, H. Hu, J. J. Ramasco, and A. Vespignani. Multiscale mobility networks and the spatial spreading of infectious diseases. *Proceedings of the National Academy of Sciences of the United States of America*, 106(51):21484–21489, 2009.

[3] H. Becker, M. Naaman, and L. Gravano. Beyond trending topics: Real-world event identification on Twitter. In *Proceedings of the 5th International AAAI Conference on Weblogs and Social Media*, 2011.

[4] V. D. Blondel, J.-L. Guillaume, R. Lambiotte, and E. Lefebvre. Fast unfolding of communities in large networks. *Journal of Statistical Mechanics: Theory and Experiment*, 2008(10):P10008, 2008.

[5] J. Bollen, H. Mao, and X. Zeng. Twitter mood predicts the stock market. *Journal of Computational Science*, 2(1):1–8, 2011.

[6] J. Bollen, A. Pepe, and H. Mao. Modeling public mood and emotion: Twitter sentiment and socio-economic phenomena. In *Proceedings of the 5th International AAAI Conference on Weblogs and Social Media*, pages 450–453, 2011.

[7] D. Brockmann, L. Hufnagel, and T. Geisel. The scaling laws of human travel. *Nature*, 439(7075):462–465, 2006.

[8] A. Brodersen, S. Scellato, and M. Wattenhofer. Youtube around the world: geographic popularity of videos. In *Proceedings of the 21st international conference on World Wide Web*, pages 241–250. ACM, 2012.

[9] C. Budak, D. Agrawal, and A. El Abbadi. Structural trend analysis for online social networks. *Proceedings of the VLDB Endowment*, 4(10):646–656, 2011.

[10] M. Cataldi, L. Di Caro, and C. Schifanella. Emerging topic detection on Twitter based on temporal and social terms evaluation. In *Proceedings of the 10th International Workshop on Multimedia Data Mining*, page 4. ACM, 2010.

[11] M. Cha, H. Haddadi, F. Benevenuto, and K. P. Gummadi. Measuring user influence in Twitter: The million follower fallacy. In *Proceedings of the 4th International AAAI Conference on Weblogs and Social Media*, 2010.

[12] F. Ciulla, D. Mocanu, A. Baronchelli, B. Gonçalves, N. Perra, and A. Vespignani. Beating the news using social media: the case study of American Idol. *EPJ Data Science*, 1(1):1–11, 2012.

[13] V. Colizza, A. Barrat, M. Barthélemy, and A. Vespignani. The role of the airline transportation network in the prediction and predictability of global epidemics. *Proceedings of the National Academy of Sciences of the United States of America*, 103(7):2015–2020, 2006.

[14] M. D. Conover, C. Davis, E. Ferrara, K. McKelvey, F. Menczer, and A. Flammini. The geospatial characteristics of a social movement communication network. *PloS ONE*, 8(3):e55957, 2013.

[15] M. D. Conover, E. Ferrara, F. Menczer, and A. Flammini. The digital evolution of Occupy Wall Street. *PloS ONE*, 8(5):e64679, 2013.

[16] M. D. Conover, J. Ratkiewicz, M. Francisco, B. Gonçalves, A. Flammini, and F. Menczer. Political polarization on Twitter. In *Proceedings of the 5th International AAAI Conference on Weblogs and Social Media*, 2011.

[17] A. Crooks, A. Croitoru, A. Stefanidis, and J. Radzikowski. #Earthquake: Twitter as a distributed sensor system. *Transactions in GIS*, 17:124–147, 2013.

[18] J. DiGrazia, K. McKelvey, J. Bollen, and F. Rojas. More tweets, more votes: Social media as a quantitative indicator of political behavior. *Available at SSRN: http://dx.doi.org/10.2139/ssrn.2235423*, 2013. Presented at 108th annual meeting of the American Sociological Association.

[19] E. Ferrara, M. JafariAsbagh, O. Varol, V. Qazvinian, F. Menczer, and A. Flammini. Clustering memes in social media. In *Proceedings of the 2013 IEEE/ACM International Conference on Advances in Social Networks Analysis and Mining*, 2013.

[20] M. C. Gonzalez, C. A. Hidalgo, and A.-L. Barabasi. Understanding individual human mobility patterns. *Nature*, 453(7196):779–782, 2008.

[21] K. Hampton and B. Wellman. Neighboring in netville: How the internet supports community and social capital in a wired suburb. *City & Community*, 2(4):277–311, 2003.

[22] T. Hastie, R. Tibshirani, and J. J. H. Friedman. *The elements of statistical learning*. Springer New York, 2001.

[23] K. Y. Kamath, J. Caverlee, K. Lee, and Z. Cheng. Spatio-temporal dynamics of online memes: A study of geo-tagged tweets. In *Proceedings of the 22nd International Conference on World Wide Web*, pages 667–677, 2013.

[24] J. Kulshrestha, F. Kooti, A. Nikravesh, and K. P. Gummadi. Geographic dissection of the Twitter network. In *Proceedings of the 6th International AAAI Conference on Weblogs and Social Media*, 2012.

[25] H. Kwak, C. Lee, H. Park, and S. Moon. What is Twitter, a social network or a news media? In *Proceedings of the 19th International Conference on World Wide Web*, pages 591–600. ACM, 2010.

[26] J. Lehmann, B. Gonçalves, J. Ramasco, and C. Cattuto. Dynamical classes of collective attention in Twitter. In *Proceedings of the 21st International Conference on World Wide Web*, pages 251–260, 2012.

[27] J. Leskovec, L. Backstrom, and J. Kleinberg. Meme-tracking and the dynamics of the news cycle. In

Proceedings of the 15th ACM SIGKDD International Conference on Knowledge Discovery and Data Mining, pages 497–506. ACM, 2009.

[28] D. Liben-Nowell, J. Novak, R. Kumar, P. Raghavan, and A. Tomkins. Geographic routing in social networks. *Proceedings of the National Academy of Sciences of the United States of America*, 102(33):11623–11628, 2005.

[29] A. Marcus, M. Bernstein, O. Badar, D. Karger, S. Madden, and R. Miller. Twitinfo: aggregating and visualizing microblogs for event exploration. In *Proceedings of the 2011 Annual Conference on Human Factors in Computing Systems*, pages 227–236. ACM, 2011.

[30] M. Mathioudakis and N. Koudas. Twittermonitor: trend detection over the Twitter stream. In *Proceedings of the 2010 International Conference on Management of Data*, pages 1155–1158. ACM, 2010.

[31] A. Mislove, S. Lehmann, Y.-Y. Ahn, J.-P. Onnela, and J. N. Rosenquist. Understanding the demographics of Twitter users. In *Proceedings of the 5th International AAAI Conference on Weblogs and Social Media*, 2011.

[32] L. Mitchell, K. D. Harris, M. R. Frank, P. S. Dodds, and C. M. Danforth. The geography of happiness: Connecting Twitter sentiment and expression, demographics, and objective characteristics of place. *PloS ONE*, 8(5):e64417, 2013.

[33] D. Mocanu, A. Baronchelli, N. Perra, B. Gonçalves, Q. Zhang, and A. Vespignani. The Twitter of Babel: Mapping world languages through microblogging platforms. *PloS ONE*, 8(4):e61981, Jan. 2013.

[34] M. Naaman, H. Becker, and L. Gravano. Hip and trendy: Characterizing emerging trends on Twitter. *Journal of the American Society for Information Science and Technology*, 62(5):902–918, 2011.

[35] A. Noulas, S. Scellato, C. Mascolo, and M. Pontil. An empirical study of geographic user activity patterns in foursquare. *Proceedings of the 5th International AAAI Conference on Weblogs and Social Media)*, 2011.

[36] J.-P. Onnela, S. Arbesman, M. C. González, A.-L. Barabási, and N. A. Christakis. Geographic constraints on social network groups. *PLoS ONE*, 6(4):e16939, 2011.

[37] R. K. Pan, K. Kaski, and S. Fortunato. World citation and collaboration networks: uncovering the role of geography in science. *Scientific Reports*, 2, 2012.

[38] D. Quercia. Don't worry, be happy: The geography of happiness on facebook. In *Proceedings of ACM Web Science 2013*, 2013.

[39] D. Quercia, L. Capra, and J. Crowcroft. The social world of Twitter: Topics, geography, and emotions. In *Proceedings of the 6th International AAAI Conference on Weblogs and Social Media*, 2012.

[40] J. Ratkiewicz, M. Conover, M. Meiss, B. Gonçalves, A. Flammini, and F. Menczer. Detecting and tracking political abuse in social media. In *Proceedings of the 5th International AAAI Conference on Weblogs and Social Media*, 2011.

[41] J. Ratkiewicz, M. Conover, M. Meiss, B. Gonçalves, S. Patil, A. Flammini, and F. Menczer. Truthy:

mapping the spread of astroturf in microblog streams. In *Proceedings of the 20th International Conference Companion on World Wide Web*, pages 249–252. ACM, 2011.

[42] M. Rosvall and C. T. Bergstrom. Maps of random walks on complex networks reveal community structure. *Proceedings of the National Academy of Sciences of the United States of America*, 105(4):1118–1123, 2008.

[43] H. Sayyadi, M. Hurst, and A. Maykov. Event detection and tracking in social streams. In *Proceedings of the 3rd International AAAI Conference on Weblogs and Social Media*, 2009.

[44] S. Scellato, C. Mascolo, M. Musolesi, and J. Crowcroft. Track globally, deliver locally: improving content delivery networks by tracking geographic social cascades. In *Proceedings of the 20th International Conference on World Wide Web*, pages 457–466. ACM, 2011.

[45] S. Scellato, C. Mascolo, M. Musolesi, and V. Latora. Distance matters: geo-social metrics for online social networks. *Proceedings of the 3rd Workshop on Online Social Networks*, 10, 2010.

[46] S. Scellato, A. Noulas, R. Lambiotte, and C. Mascolo. Socio-spatial properties of online location-based social networks. *Proceedings of the 5th International AAAI Conference on Weblogs and Social Media)*, pages 329–336, 2011.

[47] D. Selassie, B. Heller, and J. Heer. Divided edge bundling for directional network data. *IEEE Trans. Visualization & Comp. Graphics*, 17:2354–2363, 2011.

[48] M. Á. Serrano, M. Boguñá, and A. Vespignani. Extracting the multiscale backbone of complex weighted networks. *Proceedings of the National Academy of Sciences of the United States of America*, 106(16):6483–6488, 2009.

[49] J. L. Toole, M. Cha, and M. C. González. Modeling the adoption of innovations in the presence of geographic and media influences. *PloS ONE*, 7(1):e29528, 2012.

[50] L. Weng, A. Flammini, A. Vespignani, and F. Menczer. Competition among memes in a world with limited attention. *Scientific Reports*, 2, 2012.

[51] Wikipedia. Cities and metropolitan areas of the United States. `http://en.wikipedia.org/wiki/Cities_and_metropolitan_areas_of_the_United_States`, 2012.

[52] Wikipedia. List of the busiest airports in the United States. `http://en.wikipedia.org/wiki/List_of_the_busiest_airports_in_the_United_States`, 2012.

[53] S. Wu, J. Hofman, W. Mason, and D. Watts. Who says what to whom on Twitter. In *Proceedings of the 20th International Conference on World Wide Web*, pages 705–714. ACM, 2011.

[54] L. Xie, A. Natsev, J. R. Kender, M. Hill, and J. R. Smith. Visual memes in social media: tracking real-world news in Youtube videos. In *Proceedings of the 19th ACM International Conference on Multimedia*, pages 53–62. ACM, 2011.

Landmark-Based User Location Inference in Social Media

Yuto Yamaguchi[*]
University of Tsukuba, Japan
yuto_ymgc@
kde.cs.tsukuba.ac.jp

Toshiyuki Amagasa
University of Tsukuba, Japan
amagasa@
cs.tsukuba.ac.jp

Hiroyuki Kitagawa
University of Tsukuba, Japan
kitagawa@
cs.tsukuba.ac.jp

ABSTRACT

Location profiles of user accounts in social media can be utilized for various applications, such as disaster warnings and location-aware recommendations. In this paper, we propose a scheme to infer users' home locations in social media. A large portion of existing studies assume that connected users (i.e., friends) in social graphs are located in close proximity. Although this assumption holds for some fraction of connected pairs, sometimes connected pairs live far from each other. To address this issue, we introduce a novel concept of *landmarks*, which are defined as users with a lot of friends who live in a small region. Landmarks have desirable features to infer users' home locations such as providing strong clues and allowing the locations of numerous users to be inferred using a small number of landmarks. Based on this concept, we propose a landmark mixture model (LMM) to infer users' location. The experimental results using a large-scale Twitter dataset show that our method improves the accuracy of the state-of-the-art method by about 27%.

Categories and Subject Descriptors

H.2.8 [**Database Management**]: Database Applications—*Data Mining*; H.3.5 [**Information Storage and Retrieval**]: On-line Information Services—*Web-based services*

Keywords

location inference, user profiling, twitter, social graphs, landmarks

1. INTRODUCTION

As the use in mobile devices grows, the amount of location-related information from social media users increases. For example, Facebook users share which places they like, Twitter users transmit what happens where they are, and Foursquare users share where they visit. In such situations, users' home location profiles, which are the focus of this paper, become more important due to their usefulness in various applications (e.g., disaster warnings, location-aware recommendations, and advertisements).

However, most of users do not explicitly provide their location profiles. According to Cheng et al. [5], 76% of Twitter users do not make public their home locations at the city level. Similarly, Backstorm et al. [2] also reported that 94% of Facebook users do not provide their residential locations. These limitations reduce the usefulness of such location-aware services. Herein we deal with the problem of inferring users' home locations in social media.

In recent yeas, users' home location inference is a well-studied problem [5] [2] [14] [15]. Most major location inference methods employ user-generated contents (e.g., tweets) and/or social graphs. User-generated contents provide *local words* like the name of popular venues. These data can be utilized as clues for location inference [5]. For example, that a user who posts "rockets" may live near Houston.

Social graphs provide different clues. Major graph-based inference approaches [2] [14] [15] assume that connected users on social graphs are located near each other. Connected users in Facebook are friends where every edge is mutual, or in Twitter are either friends or followers where each edge has a direction. Although this assumption holds for some fraction of connected pairs, a significant percentage are geographically distant from each other.

Figure 1 shows the distribution of distances between home locations of mutually connected users in Twitter. 60% or more of connected pairs are at least 100km apart from each other. Hence, this *closeness assumption* between connected users may not provide us with strong clues for location inference.

Herein to improve the accuracy of the graph-based inference method, we introduce a novel concept of *landmarks*. Landmarks are users who have the following two characteristics: 1) a lot of friends and 2) the home locations of these friends are near each other. For example, if user u has a lot of friends whose locations are mostly in Boston, we regard user u as a landmark in Boston. After identifying this landmark, if another user v follows this landmark u, we infer that the user v lives in Boston. In this case, the city of Boston is this landmark's *dominance location*.

Landmarks have two desired features for location inference:

1. **Strong clues**: Due to the friends' geographical proximity, solid inferences can be made utilizing landmarks.

---

[*]Research Fellow of the Japan Society for the Promotion of Science, DC1

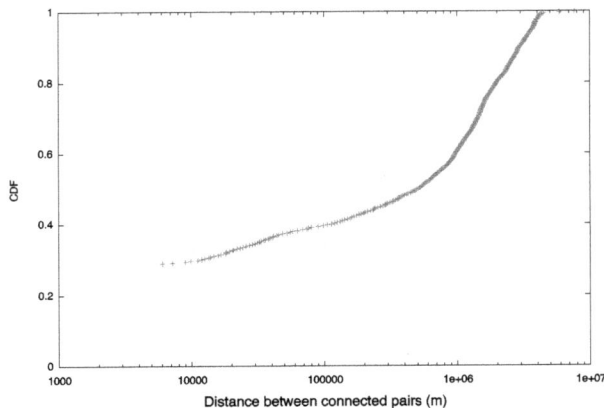

Figure 1: Distance distribution between home locations of mutually connected users in Twitter. 60% or more of connected users are at least 100km apart.

2. **Wide coverage**: Due to the large *centrality* of landmarks in a social graph, only a few landmarks are necessary to infer the most part of users in the graph.

Landmarks provide strong clues. Suppose that 80% of a Boston landmark's friends live in Boston, and these friends provide a clue with an 80% confidence level that a new friend of the landmark also lives in Boston even if the new friend's location is unavailable. Herein this is called the *concentration assumption*. Based on this concept, we propose a *landmark mixture model* (LMM) to infer users' home locations. LMM models both dominance locations of landmarks and the home locations of users as continuous probability distributions over a geographical space. Specifically, the distributions of home locations are modeled as mixtures of the distributions of dominance locations of landmarks.

Because LMM employs the concentration assumption instead of the closeness assumption, it has advantages for location inference. First, LMM allows the trade-off between precision and recall to be exploited. In this context, precision refers to the ratio of correctly inferred users, while the recall is the ratio of inferred users versus all users. Because home locations are modeled as probability distributions, decisions can be made based on the distribution shape. If the home location distribution of a user has a clear peak at certain location, the user's location can be confidently determined. On the other hand, if the distribution lacks a clear peak, the user location can be excluded to avoid an incorrect inference. This is achieved by imposing the *confidence constraint*.

Second, LMM allows the trade-off between computational cost and recall to be exploited. Because finding the mode point in the mixture model is inherently costly, location inference based on LMM may also be costly. However, LMM reduces the cost based on the observation that user locations can be inferred by using only a small number of landmarks due to their wide coverage. In other words, by imposing a *centrality constraint*, we can make reasonable inferences using a mixture model with a small number of mixed components.

The contributions of this paper can be summarized as follows:

- We introduce a novel concept of *landmarks*, which have desirable features for location inference.

- Instead of the widely adopted closeness assumption, we introduce the *concentration assumption*.

- We propose the *landmark mixture model* (*LMM*) to infer users' home locations. This model can adjust the trade-offs between precision and recall and between computational cost and recall.

Experimental results using a large Twitter dataset show that LMM successfully achieves 75.4% precision, while preserving 85.0% recall, which improves the precision of the state-of-the-art method by about 27%. The results also demonstrate that LMM flexibly adjusts the abovementioned trade-offs; raising the precision to about 90% while preserving 60% of the recall; and the cost is reduced to 10% while preserving 85% of recall.

The rest of this paper is organized as follows. Section 2 overviews related works with an emphasis on location-based social network analysis, user location inference, and applications of location-related information. Section 3 states the problem addressed in this paper and defines the terminology. The concept of landmarks are introduced in Section 4, and then our LMM is proposed in Section 5. Section 6 describes the experiments conducted to verify the effectiveness of our method compared to the other existing methods including the state-of-the-art one. Finally, Section 7 concludes the paper.

2. RELATED WORK

2.1 Location-based Social Network Analysis

Location-based social networks are attracting a lot of attention due to their large-scale location-related data and potential applications. Volkovich et al. [21] studied the relationship between the structural properties of social graphs and spatial distance. They reported that 1) users connected by strong ties are more likely to be in close proximity of each other, and 2) users in a densely connected subgraph are more likely to be located near each other.

Quercia et al. [16] investigated the geographical proximity of users in *ego-networks*, which are subgraphs composed of a user and his/her immediate neighbors. They analyzed several types of ego-networks, and found that strongly connected ego-networks (i.e., users in the ego-network are connected by strong ties or communicate with each other frequently) show a high geographical proximity.

Gao et al. [7] studied the influence of social and historical ties over users' check-ins. They proposed a method to predict users' next check-ins using a state-of-the-art language model.

Cho et al. [6] analyzed user movements in location-based social networks and proposed a method to infer a users' trajectories where trajectories are modeled as a multi-state probabilistic generative model. They reported that both geographical constraints and social influence affect users.

The observations in these works are utilized in the user location inference tasks and other location-aware applications.

2.2 User Location Inference

Most major location inference methods on social media employ user-generated contents (e.g., tweets) and/or user-relationships on social graphs. These methods can be classified into three categories: content-based, graph-based, and integrated approaches.

Content-based approaches. Content-based approaches take advantage of user-generated contents. Cheng et al. [5] inferred residential locations of Twitter users based on the *local terms* contained in tweet texts. Local terms are mainly posted by users in a specific geographical region. They are extracted using handmade training data. For example, their paper stated that the term "rockets" is a local term because it is frequently posted near Houston, Texas. Consequently, their method infers that users who post texts containing "rockets" are located near Houston.

Chang et al. [4] developed the location distributions of terms based on a *GMM* (*Gaussian Mixture Model*) to infer user locations. Unlike Cheng et al.'s method, Chang et al.'s method extracts local terms without handmade training data (i.e., unsupervised learning). Chang et al.'s experiments showed that their method, which is based on GMM, achieves a better accuracy than [5].

Kinsella et al. [10] developed a language model for each city using geotagged tweets, and proposed a location inference method. Because their language model utilizes geotagged tweets, it is more robust against user movements than methods that employ only user location profiles.

Chandra et al. [3] also dealt with the location inference task by focusing on users' *conversations*. They reported that all tweets in a conversation are on the same topic, and developed a language model where all terms in the same conversation belong to the conversation initiator. They experimentally confirmed that their inference method, which is based on their language model, shows better accuracies than models that do not consider conversations.

Unlike these methods, which utilize user-generated content, our method employs landmarks in social graphs.

Graph-based approaches. Graph-based approaches utilize user-relationships on social graphs. Backstrom et al. [2] proposed a method to infer locations of Facebook users based on the closeness assumption that connected users (i.e., friends) are likely to be located near each other. Their method calculates the likelihood of obtaining a given social graph. Locations with the largest likelihood are assigned to users as their residential locations. They achieved a better accuracy than the IP-based approach.

Clodoveu et al. [8] also proposed a graph-based method to infer location by simply considering that user u's location is where the dominant fraction of u's friends live. Users with a small number of friends may not be inferred accurately due to an insufficient number of clues. Similarly, users with many friends (e.g., celebrities, commercial accounts) may also be inferred inaccurately because their locations often lack locality.

Sadilek et al. [17] dealt with a slightly different problem for user trajectory inference. They considered that user trajectory inference and the link prediction on social graphs are mutually complementary. Their method infers user trajectories using a social graph and performs link predictions using trajectory data based on the fact that friends tend to move together.

These methods are all based on the closeness assumption. In contrast, our method is based on another observation in which users with a lot of friends in a small region (i.e., landmarks) exist. Our observation provides stronger clues than the closeness assumption.

Integrated approaches. Integrated approaches, which are the state-of-the-art methods to the best of our knowledge, use both user-generated contents and user relationships on social graphs. Li et al. [15] proposed a unified discriminative influence model (*UDI*) to infer users' home locations. UDI models user-generated contents and user-relationships as a heterogeneous graph, and assumes each node (i.e., user or venue) has its own influence scope. Nodes with larger influence scope (e.g., Lady Gaga) are more likely to be followed by distant users. Consequently, these types of nodes do not provide good clues for location inference. They have also proposed two inference methods based on UDI model, which maximize the likelihood of obtaining a heterogeneous graph.

Li et al. [14] also proposed another model, *multiple location profiling model* (*MLP*). They argue that some users have more than one locations, for example, their home location, their work location, and their former home location. Hence, MLP deals with a problem of inferring users' multiple locations. This model, which is based on the probabilistic generative model, determines its parameters are inferred using the Gibbs sampling method.

2.3 Applications of location-related information

Several studies are based on location-related information. Specifically, local event detection and location-aware searches and recommendation are receiving more attention.

Local event detection. Sakaki et al. [18] proposed a method to detect events such as earthquakes and typhoons using users' location profiles and geotagged tweets. Their method estimates event trajectories (e.g., typhoons) using the particle filter.

Lee et al. [12] proposed a local event detection method using Twitter where tweets are clustered based on Incremental DBSCAN in real time. Then the location of each cluster is inferred using users' timezones.

Walther et al. [22] developed a geospatial event detection system. They discussed what types of features are useful for event detection, and concluded that events can be detected if we examine the number of users who posts tweets in the same location and their themes. Their method uses such effective features and employs some ML methods such as decision trees to detect geospatial events.

Location-aware search and recommendation. Levandoski et al. [13] developed a location-aware recommender system (*LARDS*) after observing that users tend to prefer geographically close items (e.g., restaurants). LARDS creates a spatial grid, and provides different recommendations for each grid cell. To recommend items to moving users, LARDS developed the pyramid structure which efficiently maintain the structure of the grid.

Shaw et al. [19] proposed a spatiotemporal search scheme to support Foursquare users to *check-in* venues. To overcome the poor accuracy of GPS and the high density of urban area locations, their method exploits users' own check-in histories, friends' check-in histories and the popularity of places.

3. PROBLEM STATEMENT

This section defines the terminology and describes the problem addressed in this paper. Social graph $G = (V, E)$ is a directed graph, where each edge $e = (v_i, v_j) \in E$ is directed. Similar to Twitter's vocabulary, we adopt the terms of *follower* and *friend*. When a user *follows* another user, then the former is called a follower of the latter user, while the latter user is called a friend of the former. The vertex set is composed of two types of user set $V = U^L \cup U^N$ where U^L is a set of *labeled users* whose home locations are known in the form of latitude and longitude pairs[1], and U^N is a set of *unlabeled users* whose home locations are unavailable. Home locations are denoted as $l = (lat, longi)$

In this notation, the problem of user location inference is stated as:

PROBLEM 1 (USER LOCATION INFERENCE). *Given a social graph $G = (V, E)$, infer the home location of each unlabeled user $u \in U^N$ so that the inferred location $\hat{l_u}$ is close to the actual location l_u.*

Instead of the widely adopted closeness assumption, we employ the concentration assumption to tackle this problem. Section 4 introduces the concept of landmarks, while Section 5 describes our landmark mixture model (LMM) to solve the user location inference problem.

4. LANDMARKS

To introduce landmarks, two measurements of landmarks, *centrality* and *dispersion*, need to be defined. Centrality, which is well-known in graph theory, is a measurement to determine the relative importance of a vertex within a graph. The dispersion of user u means how far u's neighbors (i.e., friends or followers) are located from each other. Note that dispersion does not depend on user u's own home location.

Based on centrality and dispersion, we define landmarks below.

DEFINITION 1 (LANDMARKS). *A landmark is a user account u with a large centrality c_u and a small dispersion d_u.* □

In this paper, we employ the degree centrality as centrality value c_u, and 2-dimensional spatial variance with respect to latitude and longitude as dispersion value d_u. Detailed definition is described in Section 5.2.

In the context of the social media where a social graph is directed like Twitter, there are two types of landmarks, *in-landmarks* and *out-landmarks*. To deal with these two types of landmarks, we also introduce the terms of *in-centrality* c_u^{in}, *out-centrality* c_u^{out}, *in-dispersion* d_u^{in}, and *out-dispersion* d_u^{out}. In-centrality and in-dispersion are measured using a user's followers (i.e., vertices with edge directed toward the user). Inversely, out-centrality and out-dispersion are measured using a user's friends.

Preliminary experiment. To demonstrate the presence of landmarks, we investigate the centrality and the dispersion of users in our Twitter dataset, which is described in

<hr/>

[1]Practically, latitude and longitude pairs can be obtained by geocoding their location profiles.

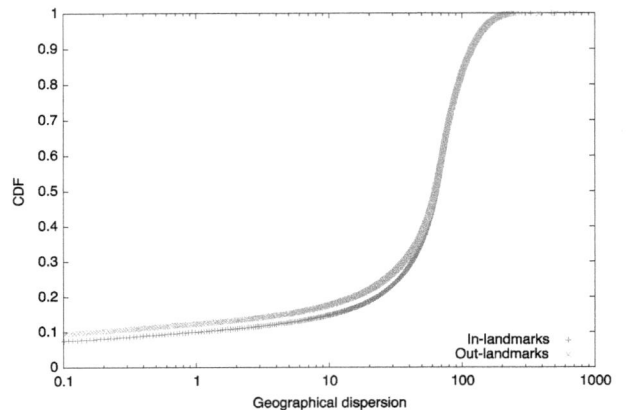

Figure 2: CDF of users over their dispersions for the top 5% users with high centralities. This figure indicates that there are $y\%$ of users have dispersions lower than x. Although most users have a large dispersion, there exist users with relatively small dispersion, which are regarded as landmarks.

Section 6.1. We employ the degree centrality for the centrality measure, and the variance of neighbors' locations for the dispersion measure (see Section 5.2).

If there exist landmarks in target dataset, we can say that the concentration assumption holds. In other words, there are some user groups whose locations are near each other and these users follow the same user (i.e., landmark). In this case, we can infer home locations of these users if their home locations are unknown, by propagate home locations of location-known users in the same group.

Figure 2 plots the CDF of users over their dispersions. This figure indicates that there are $y\%$ of users have dispersions lower than x. Note that the plotted users are limited to top 5% of users whose centralities are high in the dataset.

If we define users with dispersions less than 10 as landmarks, then 14% of plotted users in 2 can be regarded as in-landmarks and 17% as out-landmarks. Although the number of landmarks is rather small, landmarks do exist.

Figure 3 maps the above landmarks (i.e., users in the top 5% centrality, and less than 10 dispersion value). Red dots represent the home locations of all users in our dataset, while blue dots represent dominance locations of landmarks. First of all, most users, including landmarks, are located in the eastern part (e.g., east of the Mississippi River) of the United States, which is consistent with most of other works. Second, the distributions of both all users and landmarks are similar. Metropolises with a lot of users also have a lot of landmarks. Although most landmarks lie east of the Mississippi River, some cities west of the Mississippi river (e.g., Denver, Phoenix, and Salt Lake City) have a relatively large number of landmarks. Thus, landmarks can cover large segments of the user population; that is, most users can find landmarks near their home locations.

Examples. Table 1 shows some exsample landmarks in the dataset. The top two user accounts are regarded as in-landmarks, the middle two user accounts are out-landmarks, and the bottom two user accounts are both in-landmarks

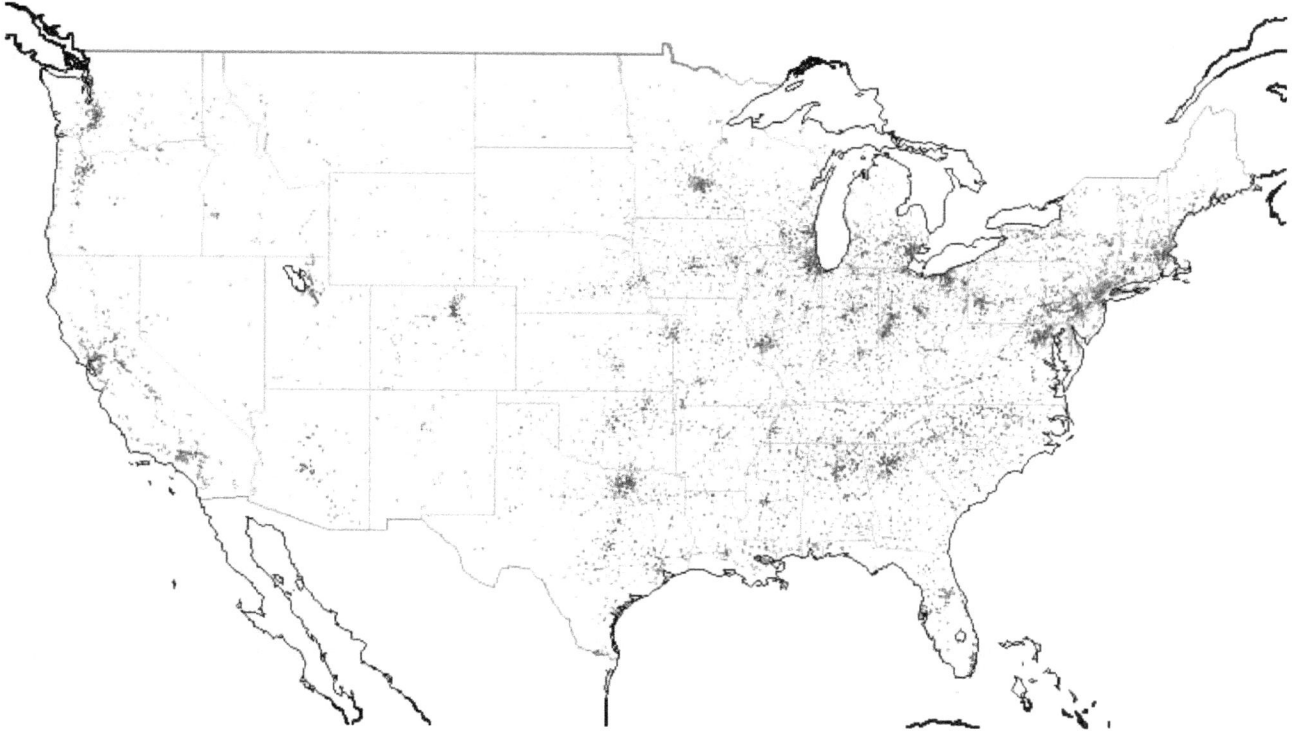

Figure 3: Distributions of both all users and landmarks. Red and blue dots represent home locations of all users in our dataset and dominance locations of landmarks, respectively. Both populations have similar distributions. Landmarks can cover a large segment of the user population; that is, most users can find a landmark near their home location.

and out-landmarks. These in- and/or out-landmarks tend to be local news accounts or commercial accounts, which are *bots* rather than *human accounts*. Specifically, most in-landmarks are local news accounts, which post about their local area. Although there are fewer out-landmarks, they tend to be commercial accounts. However, it should be noted that some user accounts can be regarded as both in-landmarks and out-landmarks. This type of landmark has a lot of followers and friends in a small region, indicating that it follows its followers back.

Our observations suggest that in-landmarks are authoritative user accounts that post useful tweets about their dominance location. Thus, in-landmarks can provide useful information about local locations. This observation provides another motivating factor to utilize in-landmarks to extract useful local information, but is beyond the scope of this paper and will be examined in the future.

On the other hand, out-landmarks are commercial accounts, including spammers, who want more followers in a small region. Although these landmarks do not post useful tweets, we can utilize them to address the home location inference problem.

5. LANDMARK MIXTURE MODEL

This section proposes the *landmark mixture model* (*LMM*) to address the user location inference problem. LMM models both the dominance locations of landmarks and the home locations of users as continuous probability distributions. Sec-

tion 5.1 formulates the model, while Section 5.2 proposes a location inference method based on this model. Finally, Section 5.3 introduces the constraints to adjust the trade-offs.

5.1 Model Formulation

According to the definition, landmarks have small dispersions, leading to clear dominance locations. Hence, LMM estimates all users' dispersions and dominance locations, and then regards users with small dispersions as landmarks.

Dominance distribution. Similar to several other studies that model the probability distribution over a geographical space [20] [23] [15], we model the dominance location as a Gaussian distribution. We call this distribution the *dominance distribution*. The underlying idea is that the Gaussian distribution has two parameters, mean and variance, which represent the dominance location and the dispersion, respectively. The value of the probability density for each location point indicates how the likelihood of a user's dominance location. A dominance distribution with a large variance (i.e., large dispersion) does not have a clear peak, indicating that the user lacks a dominance location. Consequently, the user is not a landmark.

Based on the above idea, we assign a Gaussian distribution $N(\boldsymbol{\mu_u}, \boldsymbol{\Sigma_u})$ for each user u. The mean parameter $\boldsymbol{\mu_u}$ denotes the dominance location of user u, while the covariance matrix parameter $\boldsymbol{\Sigma_u}$ denotes the dispersion of u. Herein we assume that the shape of the dominance distribution is

User Name	Profile	Center Point	Centrality (in : out)	Dispersion (in : out)
denvernews	Denver-specific news from The Denver Post. ...	39.73, -105.0 (Denver,CO)	20,526 : 7,418	0.0013 : 20.36
BostonFire	Official Twitter Boston Fire. Spring starts outdoor grilling. ...	42.32, -71.09 (Boston,MA)	34,111 : 49	0.6523 : 56.60
HomeTheaterMI	Genesis Electronics is a family-owned business ...	42.39, -83.13 (Detroit,MI)	2,331 : 1,841	16.66 : 0.0067
alabamanews1	All Alabama News!	33.52, -86.81 (Birmingham,AL)	836 : 1,523	10.51 : 0.3815
komonews	The latest breaking news, traffic, and weather from Seattle ...	47.63, -122.3 (Seattle,WA)	29,989 : 2,102	0.0107 : 0.0029
OWHnews	Updates from Omaha.com and the Omaha World-Herald ...	41.26, -96.01 (Omaha, NE)	17,400 : 9,662	0.0306 : 0.0306

symmetric, that is,

$$\Sigma_u = \begin{pmatrix} d_u & 0 \\ 0 & d_u \end{pmatrix}, \tag{1}$$

where the diagonal components are the dispersions. It should be noted that users have two types of dispersions. We assign two Gaussian distributions for each user: in-dominance distribution $N(\mu_u^{in}, \Sigma_u^{in})$ and out-dominance distribution $N(\mu_u^{out}, \Sigma_u^{out})$.

LMM. Using the dominance distributions, landmark mixture model models the home locations of users as continuous probability distributions. Following a landmark provides a strong clue for inferring a user's location because most of the landmark's neighbors are in close proximity. On the other hand, following an ordinal user (i.e., a non-landmark) does not provide a good clue because the locations of neighbors of an ordinal user are geographically dispersed.

Based on this idea, LMM is modeled as a *Gaussian mixture model (GMM)* where the dominance distributions are mixed. Specifically, a distribution of user u's home location is modeled as a GMM where each Gaussian component is the dominance distribution of u's neighbors. We call this the *location distribution*. The location distribution is denoted as:

$$P_u(x) = \sum_{v \in N_u^{out}} \pi_v^{in} N(x|\mu_v^{in}, \Sigma_v^{in}) \tag{2}$$
$$+ \sum_{w \in N_u^{in}} \pi_w^{out} N(x|\mu_w^{out}, \Sigma_w^{out}),$$

where N_u^{in} is the set of followers of u, N_u^{out} is the set of friends of u, and π_v is the mixture weight. Mixture weights are defined as:

$$\pi_v^{in} \propto \log c_v^{in}, \tag{3}$$

$$\sum_{v \in N_u^{out}} \pi_v^{in} + \sum_{w \in N_u^{in}} \pi_w^{out} = 1, \tag{4}$$

where c_v^{in} is in-degree centrality of user v. The reason that we employ the logarithm of degree centrality is degree of users in social graphs follows the *power law*. In social graphs, some users have huge degree values, which requires to moderate these values.

The probability density at a location represents the likelihood of a user's home location. Hence, if a user's location distribution has a clear peak at a specific locale, we can confidently state that identify the user's home location.

LMM does not explicitly differentiate landmarks from ordinal users in its location inference process. Instead, it imposes weights (i.e., mixture weights and variances) on all users to implicitly differentiate them. A Gaussian component with a small variance and large mixture weight, which

corresponds to a dominance distribution of a landmark, strongly affects the shape of the overall location distribution.

Consequently, our model mostly uses landmarks to determine a user's home location.

5.2 Inference Method

Given a social graph G, we initially estimate the parameters of the dominance distributions for all users. Based on the maximum likelihood criteria, the parameters are estimated using the location points of users' neighbors as

$$\hat{\mu_u^{in}} = \frac{1}{|N_u^{in}|} \sum_{v \in N_u^{in}} l_v, \tag{5}$$

$$\hat{d_u^{in}} = \frac{1}{2|N_u^{in}|} \sum_{v \in N_u^{in}} (l_v - \hat{\mu_u^{in}})^2. \tag{6}$$

The parameters for the out-dominance distributions are estimated in a similar manner.

However, noises strongly influence the mean. We found that some of the neighbors are located far from the other neighbors. To suppress the noise effect, we employ the median because the median is more robust against noises than the mean.

After the parameters of the dominance distributions are set, we can construct the users' location distributions. In this paper, we use the degree centrality for the centrality measurement because landmarks with a large number of immediate neighbors can be utilized to infer more users' locations. The estimated location distributions can be simply written as

$$P_u(x) = \sum_{v \in N_u^{out}} \pi_v^{in} N(x|\hat{\mu_v^{in}}, \hat{\Sigma_v^{in}}) \tag{7}$$
$$+ \sum_{w \in N_u^{in}} \pi_w^{out} N(x|\hat{\mu_w^{out}}, \hat{\Sigma_w^{out}}).$$

It should be noted that statistical inference methods (e.g., the EM algorithm [7]) are unnecessary because LMM simply mixes the dominance distributions. This substantially reduces the parameter estimation cost.

Based on this model, the user location is inferred as the location with the largest probability density (i.e., mode point)

$$\hat{l_u} = \arg \max_x P_u(x). \tag{8}$$

The computational complexity of finding the mode point of GMM is $O(k^2)$, where k is the number of Gaussian components of GMM. This can be explained as follows. The candidates for the mode point of GMM are limited to the center of each component because only the derivative at the center is 0. For each candidate point, we sum up the probability densities of all components at the point to determine the candidate with the largest probability density. This process has a relatively high computational cost. However, we can reduce this by imposing centrality constraint described in the next section.

5.3 Constraints to Adjust the Trade-offs

LMM can adjust the trade-offs between precision and recall, and between computational cost and recall by imposing the *confidence constraint* and *centrality constraint*, respectively.

Confidence constraint. The process to find the mode point also gives the probability density p at that point, which indicates how likely the corresponding user's home location is at that point. If p is small, the confidence of the inference is low. To avoid making an unconfident inference, we impose the *confidence constraint*.

DEFINITION 2 (CONFIDENCE CONSTRAINT). *If the probability density p_u of user u's location distribution at the mode point is less than the predefined threshold p_0, the location of user u is not inferred.* □

As the value of p_0 increases, the precision increases, but the recall decreases. On the other hand, as p_0 decreases, the opposite is true. This trade-off is examined in Section 6.3.

Centrality constraint. Because LMM does not explicitly discriminate between landmarks and ordinal users, it uses the dominance distributions of all users to infer the location. This causes a relatively expensive computational cost. Because landmarks provide the strong clues and have the wide coverage, we can infer the locations for a large segment of users using a small number of landmarks. To reduce the computational costs, we impose the *centrality constraint*.

DEFINITION 3 (CENTRALITY CONSTRAINT). *If user u's centrality c_u is lower than the predefined threshold c_0, the dominance distribution of user u is not used for the inference.* □

Because users with a low centrality are not regarded as landmarks, they do not provide good clues for location inference. The centrality constraint reduces the computational cost by eliminating the dominance distributions of these ordinal users in the location inference step.

Even if we exclude a significant fraction of users whose centralities are low, most users are connected to at least one landmark. This can be explained by the fact that the degree distribution of the Twitter social graph follows the *power law*[2] [11]. Based on *percolation theory*, in scale-free networks, the most vertices are connected even if a lot of vertices are removed as long as the degrees of removed vertices are small [1].

If the threshold c_0 is large, then it is expected that both the computational cost and recall decrease. On the other hand, if c_0 is small, then a decrease in computational costs is small and the recall remains high. This trade-off is verified in Section 6.4.

6. EXPERIMENTS

This section describes the experiments to:

1. Compare the precision and the recall of our proposed method to other existing methods.

2. Compare the precision and the recall between variations of our proposed method.

3. Evaluate the trade-offs of precision, recall, and computational cost of our method by varying the threshold values of the two constraints described in Section 5.3.

Section 6.1 explains the experimental conditions, while Sections 6.2-6.4 describe the results.

6.1 Experimental Setups

Dataset. We used the dataset from Li et al. [15]. This dataset is composed of 3,122,842 Twitter users in the United States with 284,884,514 edges. Similar to previous studies, we geocoded users' location profiles into latitude and longitude pairs using the 2010 census U.S. gazetteer[3]. Specifically, we converted location profile texts in the form of *cityName,stateName* or *cityName,stateAbbreviation* into latitude and longitude pairs. As a result, we obtained 464,794 (14.9%) labeled users. Note that misreports of location in location profiles can degrade the location inference. However, Jurgens et al. [9] experimentally show that there are not so many misreports of location. So we believe users' location profiles show their true home locations.

To evaluate the precision, we randomly divided the labeled users into a test set and a training set, where 10% were assigned to the test set and the rest were assigned to the training set.

Implementation. We implemented our proposed method and other existing methods as described in Section 6.2. Our code is available at `http://github.com/yamaguchi yuto/tomato`.

Evaluation metrics. We evaluated our method and existing methods using five metrics.

- *Precision*: The ratio of correctly inferred users versus all inferred users. If the error distance between the inferred and actual location is less than 160 km (100 miles), the inference is assumed to be accurate. This metric has been used in [4] [5] [15].

- *Recall*: The ratio of inferred users versus all labeled users in the test set.

- *F-measure*: The harmonic mean of the precision and recall, which is denoted as $F = (2 \cdot P \cdot R)/(P + R)$, where P and R are the values of precision and recall, respectively.

- *Mean E.D.*: The mean error distance between the inferred location and the actual location.

- *Median E.D.*: The median error distance between the inferred location and the actual location.

In addition, we employ *accumulative precision* at various distances, which shows that $y\%$ of users' error distances are within $x$km.

In our inference method, the dominant part in terms of computational complexity is determining the mode point of LMM, which is $O(k^2)$ where k is the number of mixed components. Hence, to evaluate the computational cost of our

---

[2]In fact, [11] reported that there are some Twitter users who have higher in-degrees than expected.

[3]`http://www.census.gov/geo/maps-data/data/gazetteer2010.html`

method, we use the average number of neighbors (i.e., the average number of mixed components in LMM) in Section 6.4.

Constraints. The threshold p_0 of the confidence constraint is varied in Section 6.3 to examine its effect on the trade-off between precision and recall. The threshold c_0 of the centrality constraint is used in Section 6.4 to examine its effect on the trade-off between recall and computational cost. If the threshold values are not clearly specified, c_0 is not used and p_0 is set to 0.003, which achieves the best F-measure.

6.2 The Performance Comparisons

This section shows the results of two experiments: one that compares our method to existing methods and the other compares variations in our method.

Comparison with existing methods. Our method is compared to a state-of-the-art method and a naive method. These two existing methods are based on the closeness assumption.

The state-of-the-art method proposed by Li et al.[15] is called UDI, which is described in Section 2. For UDI, we employ the *global prediction method*[4] as its inference method. Although their model can integrate user-generated contents and a social graph, we do not use user-generated contents because the objective of this experiment is to compare the performance of these graph-based methods.

The naive method infers user u's locations by simply calculating the medoid of locations of user u's neighbors. Note that this method uses both followers and friends as neighbors, which achieves better precision and recall than the case using only followers or friends.

Table 2 summarizes the results. Our method achieves the best precision and F-measure. Our method has an improved precision of 27% compared to the state-of-the-art method and preserves 85% of the recall. UDI shows approximately the same results as the original paper.

In addition, the mean E.D. and median E.D. of our method are substantially improved compared to the other two methods. Figure 4 shows the accumulative precision at various distances. Our method reduces the error distances. Specifically, about half of the users are located within a 1km error distance using our method.

These results indicate that our concentration assumption provides better clues than the closeness assumption. If we can find landmarks in social media, they provide the home locations of other users accurately.

The recall of our method drops to a lower value because if the probability density at the mode point is lower than p_0, our method can decide not to infer the user location. The effect of this constraint is verified in Section 6.3.

Comparison of variations of the proposed method. To examine which part of the method leads to the good results, five variations of our method are compared.

- *LMM*: Our method described as Section 5.

---

[4]The authors of [15] proposed two types of inference methods: global prediction method and local prediction method. The former achieved a higher accuracy than the latter.

Table 2: Summary of the comparison of our method to existing methods.

	LMM	UDI	Naive
Precision	**0.754**	0.594	0.445
Recall	0.850	**0.926**	0.900
F-measure	**0.799**	0.724	0.596
Mean E.D.	**297,739**	542,483	616,196
Median E.D.	**3,804**	37,363	249,982

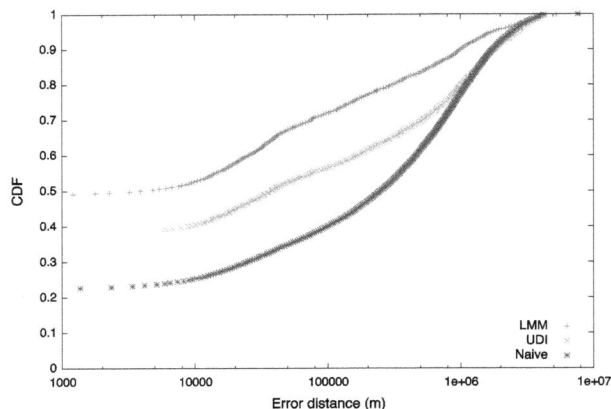

Figure 4: **Accumulative precision of our method and existing methods at various error distances. Our method successfully locates about half of the users within a 1km error distance, and outperforms the other two methods, including the state-of-the-art method.**

- *LMM w/o m*: Our method without mixture weights. This method uses the same value for all mixture weights.

- *LMM w/o mv*: Our method without mixture weights and variances. This method uses the same value for all mixture weights, and regards variances of all the Gaussian distributions as 1.

- *Medoid*: A method that simply calculates the medoid of neighbors' dominance locations. This method does not use the dominance distribution.

- *Centoid*: A method that simply calculates the centroid of neighbors' dominance locations. This method does not use the dominance distribution.

Table 3 summarizes the results. Contrary to our expectations, LMM and LMM w/o m give approximately the same results. These two methods form almost the same curve 5, indicating that the mixture weights do not improve the precision. There are three reasons that the mixture weights do not work well. 1) Even if users have relatively small centralities, they provide some clues as long as they have small dispersions. 2) Most of the users have small centralities, which results in discarding a substantial part of the clues by imposing small weights. 3) Users with large centralities are weighted heavily regardless of their dispersions. Hence, we have to carefully develop the mixture weight, and this is our future work.

Table 3: Summary of the comparison of variations of our method.

	LMM	LMM w/o m	LMM w/o mv	Medoid	Centroid
Precision	0.754	**0.757**	0.543	0.357	0.274
Recall	0.850	0.846	**0.996**	**0.996**	**0.996**
F-measure	0.799	**0.800**	0.703	0.526	0.429
Mean E.D.	297,739	**292,917**	587,857	698,769	705,689
Median E.D.	3,804	**2,694**	75,885	413,459	455,695

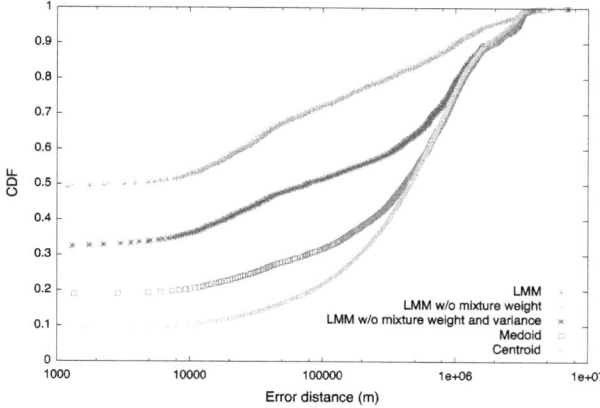

Figure 5: Accumulative precision for variations of our method at various error distances. Although considering the geographical dispersion improves the precision, considering the mixture weight does not. Medoid and Centroid do not work well because they simply use the dominant location as the points rather than as the distributions.

The other three variations do not show good results (3 and 5), indicating that employing dispersion leads to good results. Moreover, comparing LMM w/o mv and Medoid indicates that the considering the dominance location as the probability distribution rather than just a location point positively influences the results. Although not all users provide clues, users with a small dispersion provide significant clues for location inference.

6.3 Effect of the Confidence Constraint

LMM can adjust the trade-off between precision and recall by imposing the confidence constraint. This section shows the effect of the confidence constraint. Figure 6 shows the result by varying the value of threshold p_0. The x-axis denotes the value of p_0, and each line denotes the precision, recall, and F-measure. As the value of p_0 increases, the precision increases but the recall decreases. The F-measure achieves the best score around $p_0 = 0.003$. Note that even if we do not impose the confidence constraint ($p_0 = 0$), our method outperforms other methods for all these metrics.

If the probability density at the mode point is low, the overall probability distribution does not have a clear peak. In this case, we should not infer the home location of that user because there are insufficient clues to determine the location. Our method can select this option because it is based on the probability distribution.

If we require a high precision (e.g., in the case of sending disaster warnings), we can achieve that by imposing the large p_0 value. On the other hand, if we want a high recall

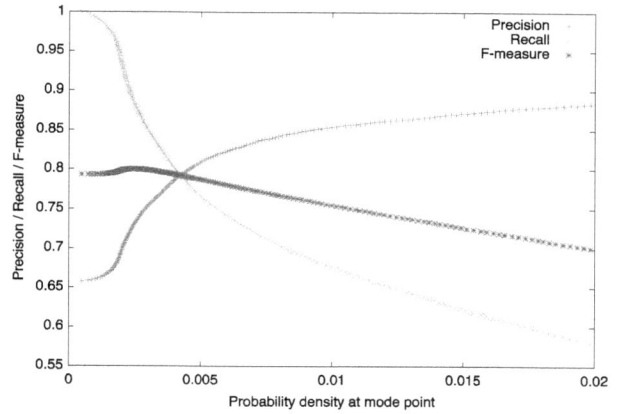

Figure 6: Effect of the confidence constraint. x-axis denotes the value of the threshold p_0. As the value of p_0 increases, the precision increases but the recall decreases. The F-measure achieves the best score around $p_0 = 0.003$, and the precision is about 0.88 at $p_0 = 0.02$.

(e.g., local advertisements), we can get that by imposing no constraint, or small p_0 value. The ability of this trade-off adjustment may expand the applications of users' home location profiles.

6.4 Effect of the Centrality Constraint

LMM can also adjust the trade-off between the computational cost and recall by imposing the centrality constraint. Varying the value of threshold c_0 demonstrates the effects of the cost, recall, and precision. The confidence constraint is not imposed in this section.

Figure 7 shows the results where the x-axis denotes the value of c_0. The left y-axis denotes the values of precision, recall, and cost, while the right y-axis denotes the average number of neighbors (or components). The ratio of the utilized landmarks means the ratio of users satisfying the centrality constraint (i.e., users with their centralities $c_u > c_0$) versus all users. The average number of neighbors means the average number of each user's neighbors, in other words, the average number of mixed components for each user's location distribution, which dominates the computational complexity of our method.

As the value of c_0 increases, the ratio of utilized landmarks decreases rapidly but the recall remains high. Hence, we conclude that our method can infer locations of almost all users with only about 5% of landmarks ($c_0 = 100$). This means only 5% of landmarks' Gaussian distributions (i.e., mean and variance parameters) and following relationships need to be stored to infer user locations.

In terms of computational cost, we can reduce the average number of neighbors to approximately 30%, preserving 85% of the recall ($c_0 = 200$). This means that because the computational complexity of our method is $O(k^2)$, where k is the number of neighbors, the cost is reduced to about 10%.

From $c_0 = 0$ to 400, the precision remains about the same value or even decreases, but from $c_0 = 500$ to 1000, it increases. Two factors may lead to such a behavior. If our method utilizes landmarks with high centrality, good results

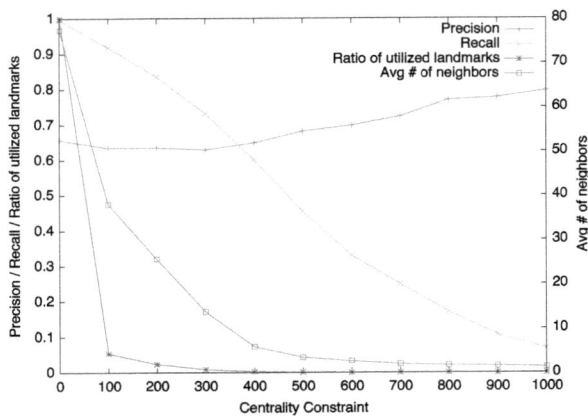

Figure 7: Effect of the centrality constraint. x-axis denotes the value of the threshold c_0. As c_0 increases, the ratio of utilized landmarks rapidly decreases, preserving the high recall value. The decrease in the average number of neighbors denotes the reduction of the computational cost of our method. The precision remains high or even increases when we utilize a small number of landmarks.

are achieved because their small dispersion values are statistically significant. On the other hand, because only a small number of landmarks have a high centrality, other users do not satisfy the centrality constraint and are not used for location inference. Ignoring these ordinal users, which is most of the users, may degrade the performance.

7. CONCLUSION

Hewein we introduce a novel concept of landmarks and propose a landmark mixture model (LMM) to address the user location inference problem. Landmarks have desirable features for location inference: strong clues and a wide coverage. LMM can adjust the trade-offs between precision and recall and between computational cost and recall. This capability may expand applications employing users' home locations. The experimental results show that our inference method outperforms other existing methods, including the state-of-the-art method. The results also demonstrate that imposing the two constraints allows our method to realize a high precision, reduce the computational cost, and preserve a high recall.

Our future work includes 1) refining our method to iteratively propagate landmark's clues to increase the inferenve coverage, 2) improving our method by integrating it with methods employing user-generated content, and 3) examining the other applications of landmarks such as recommending landmarks' tweets to travelers and searching local information utilizing landmarks.

Acknowledgements

This work was supported in part by JSPS KAKENHI, Grant-in-Aid for JSPS Fellows #242322.

8. REFERENCES

[1] R. Albert, H. Jeong, and A.-L. Barabási. Error and attack tolerance of complex networks. *Nature*, 406(6794):378–382, 2000.

[2] L. Backstrom, E. Sun, and C. Marlow. Find me if you can: improving geographical prediction with social and spatial proximity. In *WWW*, pages 61–70, 2010.

[3] S. Chandra, L. Khan, and F. B. Muhaya. Estimating twitter user location using social interactions-a content based approach. In *SocialCom/PASSAT*, pages 838–843, 2011.

[4] H.-W. Chang, D. Lee, M. Eltaher, and J. Lee. @phillies tweeting from philly? predicting twitter user locations with spatial word usage. In *ASONAM*, pages 111–118, 2012.

[5] Z. Cheng, J. Caverlee, and K. Lee. You are where you tweet: a content-based approach to geo-locating twitter users. In *CIKM*, pages 759–768, 2010.

[6] E. Cho, S. A. Myers, and J. Leskovec. Friendship and mobility: user movement in location-based social networks. In *KDD*, pages 1082–1090, 2011.

[7] H. Gao, J. Tang, and H. Liu. Exploring social-historical ties on location-based social networks. In *ICWSM*, 2012.

[8] C. A. D. Jr., G. L. Pappa, D. R. R. de Oliveira, and F. de Lima Arcanjo. Inferring the location of twitter messages based on user relationships. *T. GIS*, 15(6):735–751, 2011.

[9] D. Jurgens. That 's what friends are for: Inferring location in online social media platforms based on social relationships. In *Seventh International AAAI Conference on Weblogs and Social Media*, 2013.

[10] S. Kinsella, V. Murdock, and N. O'Hare. "i'm eating a sandwich in glasgow": modeling locations with tweets. In *SMUC*, pages 61–68, 2011.

[11] H. Kwak, C. Lee, H. Park, and S. B. Moon. What is twitter, a social network or a news media? In *WWW*, pages 591–600, 2010.

[12] C.-H. Lee, H.-C. Yang, T.-F. Chien, and W.-S. Wen. A novel approach for event detection by mining spatio-temporal information on microblogs. In *ASONAM*, pages 254–259, 2011.

[13] J. J. Levandoski, M. Sarwat, A. Eldawy, and M. F. Mokbel. Lars: A location-aware recommender system. In *ICDE*, pages 450–461, 2012.

[14] R. Li, S. Wang, and K. C.-C. Chang. Multiple location profiling for users and relationships from social network and content. *PVLDB*, 5(11):1603–1614, 2012.

[15] R. Li, S. Wang, H. Deng, R. Wang, and K. C.-C. Chang. Towards social user profiling: unified and discriminative influence model for inferring home locations. In *KDD*, pages 1023–1031, 2012.

[16] D. Quercia, L. Capra, and J. Crowcroft. The social world of twitter: Topics, geography, and emotions. In *ICWSM*, 2012.

[17] A. Sadilek, H. A. Kautz, and J. P. Bigham. Finding your friends and following them to where you are. In *WSDM*, pages 723–732, 2012.

[18] T. Sakaki, M. Okazaki, and Y. Matsuo. Earthquake shakes twitter users: real-time event detection by social sensors. In *WWW*, pages 851–860, 2010.

[19] B. Shaw, J. Shea, S. Sinha, and A. Hogue. Learning to rank for spatiotemporal search. In *WSDM*, pages 717–726, 2013.

[20] S. Sizov. Geofolk: latent spatial semantics in web 2.0 social media. In *WSDM*, pages 281–290, 2010.

[21] Y. Volkovich, S. Scellato, D. Laniado, C. Mascolo, and A. Kaltenbrunner. The length of bridge ties: Structural and geographic properties of online social interactions. In *ICWSM*, 2012.

[22] M. Walther and M. Kaisser. Geo-spatial event detection in the twitter stream. In *ECIR*, pages 356–367, 2013.

[23] Z. Yin, L. Cao, J. Han, C. Zhai, and T. S. Huang. Geographical topic discovery and comparison. In *WWW*, pages 247–256, 2011.

Inferring User Interests from Tweet Times

Dinesh Ramasamy, Sriram Venkateswaran and Upamanyu Madhow
Electrical and Computer Engineering Department
University of California Santa Barbara
{dineshr, sriram, madhow}@ece.ucsb.edu

ABSTRACT

We propose and demonstrate the feasibility of a probabilistic framework for mining user interests from their tweet times alone, by exploiting the known timing of external events associated with these interests. This approach allows for making inferences on the interests of a large number of users for which text-based mining may become cumbersome, and also sidesteps the difficult problem of semantic/contextual analysis required for such text-based inferences. The statistic that we propose for gauging the user's interest level is the probability that he/she tweets more frequently at certain times when this topic is in the "public eye" than at other times. We report on promising experimental results using Twitter data on detecting whether or not a user is a fan of a given baseball team, leveraging the known timing of games played by the team. Since people often interact with others who share similar interests, we extend our probabilistic framework to use the interest level estimates for other users with whom a person interacts (by referring to them in his/her tweets). We demonstrate that it is possible to significantly improve the detection probability (for a given false alarm rate) by such information pooling on the social graph.

Categories and Subject Descriptors

G.3 [**Probability and Statistics**]: Time series analysis—*Poisson Processes*; H.2.8 [**Database Applications**]: Data mining

Keywords

Twitter; metadata; online social networks; Bayesian inference

1. INTRODUCTION

The culture of Twitter, with its brief tweets, encourages users to express their *current* thoughts. In this paper, we explore whether the *timing* of a user's tweets tells us something about her/his interests, by comparing it against the

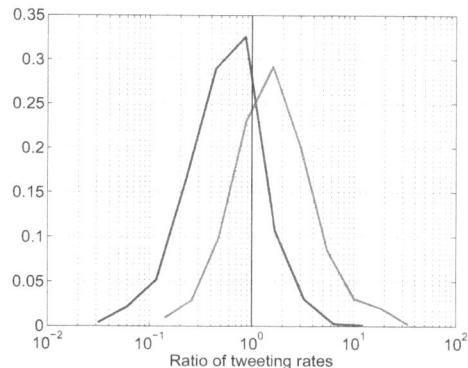

Figure 1: **Histograms of the ratio of #tweets/hour during games to #tweets/hour at other times for fans (red) and randomly picked users (blue)**

known timing of external events associated with a particular interest. As an example, consider two groups of users: (i) Fans of the San Francisco Giants baseball team (the SF-Giants), with "ground truth" based on analysis of the text of their tweets, and (ii) randomly picked users, presumed to be non-fans. In Figure 1, we plot histograms of the ratio of #tweets/hour during times when the SFGiants played a game to the #tweets/hour at other times for these two sets of users. This data was collected over a one month window. We see that a higher proportion of fans tweet more often during game times (the red curve due to fans is more to the right of the ratio = 1 line). It is clear, therefore, that there is information to be mined from the tweet times of a user. In this paper, we propose a statistical framework for doing so, and report on promising preliminary results on inferring baseball "fandom" for a given team.

Our model, motivated by the empirical findings such as those in Figure 1, is simple: a fan is likely to tweet at a higher rate in a window around game times than at other times. This leads to a statistical measure for a user's fandom which is the Bayesian posterior probability, based on measured tweet times, of the user's tweet rate during games being higher than at other times. Under our model, this probability only depends only on the *numbers* of tweets (rather than on their exact timing) during games and during other times. This makes the statistic attractive for inference in large-scale systems, both in terms of measurement and computation.

The proposed approach extends naturally to incorporate information from a given user's "neighbors," defined on the Twitter graph as follows. Most twitter accounts are public and users often label their tweets using hashtags. These hashtags bring tweets to the attention of other users who are interested in the *content* of the tweet, even when they do not necessarily follow the user who authored the tweet. In this manner, Twitter encourages conversation among individuals who share a common interest. We define the neighbors of a Twitter user as those who are mentioned in his/her tweets (this information is available in the tweet metadata, and does not require parsing of the tweet). We show that pooling measurements from neighbors enhances the reliability of detecting fandom.

Most prior work on mining user interests from Twitter employs text analysis on their tweets (we mention some selected references shortly). This is significantly more expensive than our approach in terms of computation, and hence more difficult to scale to large numbers of users. We view our minimalistic approach as complementary to such text-based approaches; for example, user interests predicted by our approach could be verified by more detailed text-based analysis. It is worth noting, however, text-based analysis is by no means an infallible gold standard. The brief (limited to 140 characters) and ephemeral nature of tweets forces upon them a context-dependent language, making text analysis difficult. For example, people can talk about baseball in their tweets by mentioning the stand, usher, pitcher, bat, ball, etc. All of these words have broad and in some cases multiple meanings. It is therefore difficult to interpret such words without context, and it is difficult to build context from the few words in a tweet. Thus, even if there were no computational bottlenecks, there may be considerable value to hybrid techniques that use dynamics, as we do, along with text-based analysis, to enhance the reliability of mining user interests.

Prior work

Prior work on mining Twitter feeds has mostly been fed by text analysis. TwitterStand [7] maintains a news stand by parsing through different tweet feeds. The timing of tweets has been used here to help in the clustering of tweets into different news groups. The authors in [6] build a system that can locate events such as an earthquake in space and time from tweets (using tweet location and times). However, unlike the solution proposed herein, both[7, 6] rely mainly on text analysis, with tweet times being used only in the later stages. PET[3] tracks the evolution of events, and users' interest in them, as a function of time. Unlike our approach, PET uses text analysis, and does not use the specific tweet time or its relation to external events (PET analyzes tweets collected daily to infer the evolution of topics from day to day). A method of training a classifier to do sentiment analysis of individual tweets is proposed in [5]. Here smileys are used in a bootstrapping mechanism to build a corpus of words along with an associated sentiment (positive or negative) for each word. The preceding references do not explicitly aim to mine for the interests of *a user*, which is the focus of our work. A system that employs Wikipedia as an external corpus to do word associations is proposed in [4] for mining *broad* interests on a *per user* basis. In [1], the authors observe that in identifying political affiliation of a 1000 hand-labeled users, the structure of the re-tweet graph

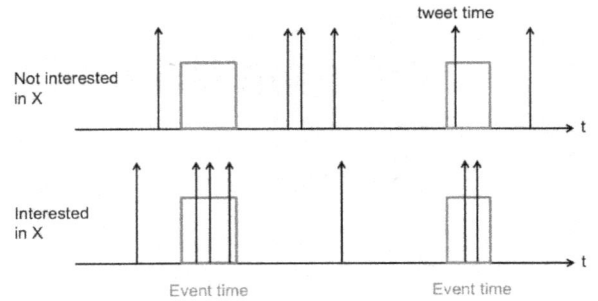

Figure 2: Tweet times of the user marked by arrows. Event times are marked in red. All other times are non-event times. Top: Tweeting behavior of a person not interested in X. Bottom: A person interested in X

is more useful than the text in the tweets themselves. They arrive at this conclusion by implementing a text based classifier and comparing it with the results obtained merely by identifying the community structure in the re-tweet graph.

2. TWEET TIMES MODEL

In this section we present a probabilistic model for tweet times of a user over an observation time window (this need not consist of contiguous intervals) . Our basic premise is the following: a user who is interested in topic X (say the SFGiants baseball team) tweets more often at times when X is in the "public eye" (SFGiants play a baseball game) than at other times. Thus, we partition the observation window into two complementary sets:

1. **Event times** are times within the observation window when X is in the "public eye" (which, according to our hypothesis, stimulates users interested in X to engage in conversations on Twitter).

2. **Non-event times:** All other times over the observation window.

This partitioning, along with the behaviors we expect for users who are interested (or not) in the topic X, is shown in figure 2.

The tweet times of a user are modeled as a homogeneous Poisson process of rate λ_1 tweets per unit time during event times and an *independent* homogeneous Poisson process of rate λ_0 tweets per unit time during non-event times. As depicted in figure 2, we expect that $\lambda_1 > \lambda_0$ for users interested in topic X.

A homogeneous Poisson process is parameterized by a single parameter, its rate λ. Such a parsimonious model for the tweet times of a user has two advantages: robustness (heterogeneity among twitter users may make more detailed usage profiles, such as allowing for tweet rates dependent on the time of day, counterproductive) and simplicity (e.g., the decision statistics we obtain require aggregate tweet counts rather than individual tweet times). For a Poisson process of constant rate λ tweets/unit time, the number of tweets N made in a time interval of length T (need not be contiguous) is a Poisson random variable with mean $\lambda \times T$. i.e., the probability that the user puts out n tweets in T time units is given by

$$\Pr\left[N=n\,|\,\lambda\right] = \frac{e^{-\lambda T}\,(\lambda T)^n}{n!},\ n = 0,1,2,\ldots,\infty.$$

Further, under the Poisson model, the number of tweets put out by the user in non-overlapping time intervals are independent random variables.

3. INFERRING INTEREST LEVELS FROM TWEET TIMES

We propose a statistic that measures our confidence in the assertion that the user tweets more *frequently* during event times than other times. i.e., his/her tweet rate during event times is larger than the rate at other times. This statistic is our metric for the user's interest level in the topic X. We use knowledge of the event and non-event times to estimate the probability distributions of the corresponding tweet rates λ_1 and λ_0 from the tweet times of the user, and then compute the statistic from these posterior distributions.

Under our Poisson model, the posterior distribution of λ_1 given the tweet times depends only on the total number of tweets put out by the user during event times, which we denote by N_1. The tweet times themselves do not matter. Similarly, to make probabilistic inferences on λ_0, all we need is the total number of tweets during non-event times, denoted by N_0. In the language of estimation theory, N_1 and N_0 are *minimal sufficient statistics* for estimation of λ_1 and λ_0, respectively. Let the total time span of the event times and non-event times be T_1 and T_0 respectively.

Continuing with our minimalism in modeling, we assume a *non-informative* prior on the rates λ_1 and λ_0, assuming that the prior density $p(\lambda_1,\lambda_0) \propto 1/\sqrt{\lambda_1\lambda_0}$ for all $\lambda_1 > 0, \lambda_0 > 0$ (the corresponding marginal priors are $p(\lambda_i) \propto 1/\sqrt{\lambda_i}$ for $\lambda_i > 0$, $i = 0,1$). Of course, this prior cannot exist over an infinite support, since densities must integrate to one, but this is a standard trick in Bayesian estimation when the ground truth on priors is difficult to determine. This joint prior is the Jeffreys non-informative prior on the rate parameters (λ_1,λ_0) [2]. In our case, accurately estimating priors for each topic X would require the ground truth on the interests of a large number of users, which goes counter to our objective of mining for these interests. Furthermore, we would need to constantly revise our ground truth data set for a heterogeneous population of Twitter users with dynamically evolving interests, which is clearly infeasible.

Since we assume that the two Poisson processes corresponding to the event times and non-event times are independent, the corresponding counts N_1 and N_0 are conditionally independent given λ_1,λ_0. Putting this together with our assumption of non-informative prior on λ_1,λ_0, we obtain, using Bayes' rule, that the posterior distributions of λ_1,λ_0 also factor and are given by $p(\lambda_i|N_i) \propto \Pr\left[N_i|\lambda_i\right]p(\lambda_i) \propto \lambda_i^{N_i-0.5}e^{-T_i\lambda_i}$, $\lambda_i > 0$. Normalizing the posteriors so they integrate to one (which we can do even though we employed improper priors), we obtain

$$p\left(\lambda_i = x|N_i\right) = \begin{cases} \frac{T_i(T_ix)^{N_i-0.5}e^{-T_ix}}{\gamma(N_i+0.5)} & \text{if } x \geq 0 \\ 0 & \text{otherwise} \end{cases}, \quad (1)$$

where $\gamma(z) = \int_0^\infty t^{z-1}e^{-t}dt$ is the gamma function. The statistic which we propose to quantify the user's interest level in the topic X is $Z = \Pr\left[\lambda_1 > \lambda_0|N_1,N_0\right]$. We declare a user to be interested in X when Z exceeds a certain threshold. Thus, we conclude that the user is interested in X, when we are "confident enough" that his/her tweet rate during event times is larger than that during non-event times. Given the observations N_1, N_0, T_1, T_0, the statistic Z can be computed using the posteriors (1) as follows:

$$Z = \Pr\left[\lambda_1 > \lambda_0|N_1,N_0\right] \quad (2)$$
$$= \iint_{x>y} p\left(\lambda_1 = x|N_1\right)p\left(\lambda_0 = y|N_0\right)\ dx\,dy.$$

4. EXPLOITING USER INTERACTIONS

We use social networks to engage in conversation with others who share our interests. If a user has interacts with others who are interested in the topic X, we expect that the probability that he/she is also interested in X is higher than for a randomly picked user. We present a method that relies on this simple intuition to improve our estimates of the interest level of a "tagged" user using interest level estimates of other users mentioned in his/her tweets. During the observation time window, this tagged user may mention other users using their twitter handle (for example, the official SFGiants twitter handle @SFGiants, or another individual @johnadams2001) in his/her tweets. We call such users the "neighbors" of the tagged user. Since we will be combining the Z statistics of multiple users, we need to pay attention to scaling. In particular, we expect that we would weight the tagged user's Z statistic higher than that of his/her neighbors. We now describe a framework for motivating such scaling.

Notation: Let the index 0 denote the tagged user and the indices $i = 1,\ldots,M$ denote the neighbors. From the number of tweets during event times $N_1(i)$ and non-event times $N_0(i)$ of the i-th user ($\mathbf{N}(i)$ denotes the pair $(N_1(i), N_0(i))$), we arrive the statistic (2) which we denote by Z_i. Let $\lambda_1(i), \lambda_0(i)$ denote the tweet rates of the i-th user in the event and non-event times and Y_i denote the event that the i-th user tweets more frequently during event times than other times. i.e., $Y_i = 1$ if $\lambda_1(i) > \lambda_0(i)$ and $Y_i = 0$ otherwise (note that $Z_i = \Pr[Y_i = 1|\mathbf{N}(i)]$). Let C_i represent the true interest of i in the topic X (C_i takes the value 1 if this user is interested in X and 0 otherwise).

A user who is not interested in X may still happen to tweet more often during event times. Likewise, a user interested in X may happen to tweet less frequently during event times than at other times. Therefore, we first relate Y_i to C_i in a probabilistic manner to derive a function of the Z_i statistic for each user i (i.e., the tagged user and his/her neighbors) such that, when combined across users to make an inference regarding the tagged user, no one user has too big an influence. We then discuss a model for the dependence between the tagged users and his/her neighbors which motivates combining these individual statistics.

For the first step, let $p_t = \Pr[Y_k = 1|C_k = 1]$ denote the probability that a user interested in topic X is *timely* (i.e., tweets more frequently during event times than at other times), and let $p_f = \Pr[Y_k = 1|C_k = 0]$ denote the probability of *false alarm* (i.e., a user not interested in X happens to tweet more frequently during event times). We now compute the likelihood ratio of user k's interest in topic X based on its own measurements, defined as

$$\phi_k = \frac{\Pr[\mathbf{N}(k)|C_k = 1]}{\Pr[\mathbf{N}(k)|C_k = 0]},$$

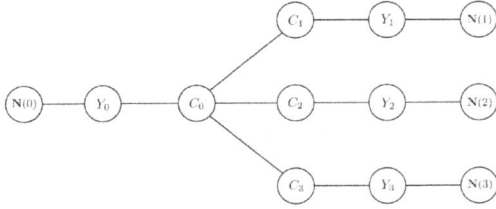

Figure 3: Markov structure of the user interests C_i, the tweet rate differentials $Y_i = \lambda_1(i) > \lambda_0(i)$ and the number of tweets $\mathbf{N}(i) = (N_1(i), N_0(i))$. The index 0 refers to the tagged user while $1, 2, 3$ denote the neighbors of this user

in terms of the statistic $Z_k = P[Y_k = 1|\mathbf{N}(k)]$, which we already know how to compute from Section 3.

Under our uninformative prior, it is easy to show that $\Pr[Y_k = 1] = \Pr[\lambda_1 > \lambda_0] = \frac{1}{2}$, Conditioning on Y_k and using the conditional independence of $\mathbf{N}(k)$ and C_k given Y_k (the Markov structure in figure 3):

$$
\begin{aligned}
\Pr[\mathbf{N}(k)|C_k] &= \Pr[Y_k = 1|C_k]\Pr[\mathbf{N}(k)|Y_k = 1] \\
&\quad + \Pr[Y_k = 0|C_k]\Pr[\mathbf{N}(k)|Y_k = 0] \\
&= 2\Pr[\mathbf{N}(k)]\Big(\Pr[Y_k = 1|C_k]Z_k \\
&\quad + \Pr[Y_k = 0|C_k](1 - Z_k)\Big),
\end{aligned}
$$

where we have used $Z_k = \Pr[Y_k = 1|\mathbf{N}(k)]$. Using the above, we obtain that

$$
\phi_k = \frac{p_t Z_k + (1 - p_t)(1 - Z_k)}{p_f Z_k + (1 - p_f)(1 - Z_k)} = \frac{1 + p_t\left(\frac{Z_k}{1 - Z_k} - 1\right)}{1 + p_f\left(\frac{Z_k}{1 - Z_k} - 1\right)}.
$$

This effectively corresponds to soft thresholding the raw likelihood ratio $\Pr[\lambda_1 > \lambda_0]/\Pr[\lambda_1 \le \lambda_0] = Z_k/(1 - Z_k)$ between an upper limit of $1/p_f$ and a lower limit of $1 - p_t$. Both ϕ_k and the raw likelihood ratio are monotone increasing in Z_k. Thus, for a single user (as considered in the previous section), threshold rules based on any of these statistics are equivalent. However, when combining across multiple users, the soft thresholding in ϕ_k is important for robustness, since it ensures that no one user has too large an influence on the outcome.

Let us now consider the second step: relating the interests of the tagged user and his/her neighbors. We expect that it is more likely that the neighbors are interested in X when the tagged user is interested in X than when the tagged user is not: Denoting $\Pr[C_k = 1|C_0 = 1]$ by α and $\Pr[C_k = 1|C_0 = 0]$ by β, we expect that $\alpha \gg \beta$. It is actually the difference in α and β that affects how we combine these statistics, rather than their raw values. For example, even if α is small (e.g., 0.1, so that there is only a 10% probability of the neighbor of a fan also being a fan), if $\beta = 10^{-4}$, then we still get very useful information from the neighbors' measurements.

We make a simplifying assumption on the structure of interactions among neighbors: The true interests of the neighbors, $\{C_i, i > 0\}$, are independent when conditioned on the interest status of the tagged user C_0: $\Pr[C_1, \ldots, C_M|C_0] = \prod \Pr[C_i|C_0]$. This is illustrated via the Markov structure depicted in figure 3 (in the figure $M = 3$). This assumption is violated when a neighbor of the tagged user refers to another neighbor of the tagged user in his/her tweets (therefore

introducing additional dependencies between the two neighbors). However, as we will see in the results section, this simple structure by itself gives us considerable gains over just using the interest level estimates Z_0 of the tagged user alone.

Our statistic that incorporates information from the neighbors is the following log likelihood ratio:

$$
S = \frac{\Pr[\mathbf{N}(0), \mathbf{N}(1), \ldots, \mathbf{N}(M)|C_0 = 1]}{\Pr[\mathbf{N}(0), \mathbf{N}(1), \ldots, \mathbf{N}(M)|C_0 = 0]}.
$$

From the Markov structure in figure 3, we observe that the true interests of the neighbors C_i given that of the tagged user C_0 are independent. This observation leads to the following simplification:

$$
S = \log\frac{\Pr[\mathbf{N}(0)|C_0 = 1]}{\Pr[\mathbf{N}(0)|C_0 = 0]} + \sum_{k=1}^{M}\log\frac{\Pr[\mathbf{N}(k)|C_0 = 1]}{\Pr[\mathbf{N}(k)|C_0 = 0]}.
$$

From Bayes' rule, for the neighbors,

$$
\begin{aligned}
\Pr[\mathbf{N}(k)|C_0] &= \Pr[\mathbf{N}(k), C_k = 1|C_0] \\
&\quad + \Pr[\mathbf{N}(k), C_k = 0|C_0] \\
&= \Pr[\mathbf{N}(k)|C_k = 1]\Pr[C_k = 1|C_0] \\
&\quad + \Pr[\mathbf{N}(k)|C_k = 0]\Pr[C_k = 0|C_0].
\end{aligned}
$$

Using the above, we obtain that:

$$
\frac{\Pr[\mathbf{N}(k)|C_0 = 1]}{\Pr[\mathbf{N}(k)|C_0 = 0]} = \frac{\alpha\phi_k + (1 - \alpha)}{\beta\phi_k + (1 - \beta)}.
$$

Therefore, the statistic S depends only on the likelihood ratios ϕ_k of the tagged user and his/her neighbors, as follows:

$$
S = \log\phi_0 + \sum_{k=1}^{M}\log\frac{1 + \alpha(\phi_k - 1)}{1 + \beta(\phi_k - 1)}.
$$

While we can tune the parameters α and β to get good performance with this statistic, in practice, we have found the following modified rule, using a single parameter to scale down the sum of the neighbors' log likelihood ratios, to work well:

$$
\tilde{S} = \log\phi_0 + \kappa\sum_{k=1}^{M}\log\phi_k. \tag{3}
$$

In our numerical results, therefore, we report on the performance of this modified statistic, with $\kappa = 1/6$ (found to work well empirically).

5. NUMERICAL RESULTS

In this section, we test our statistical framework by trying to identify whether a user is a fan of the San Francisco Giants (SFGiants) baseball team from the user's tweet times (we also briefly report on analogous results for the NY Yankees). The times when SFGiants played Major League Baseball (MLB) games are used as a natural candidate for event times. We also include a 15 minute window on either side of each game in our definition of event times to account for the buzz before and after each game when fans are expected to tweet heavily.

Dataset description: The data set is a 10% random sampling of all *public* tweets over a month (May-June) in the summer of 2011. In this one month window, SFGiants played 29 games. Each tweet, apart from its brief text, is tagged with an user ID, the time when this tweet was made and the user IDs of twitter handles mentioned in the tweet (if any).

Ground truth: In order to characterize the effectiveness of the statistic that we propose, we need to know the fandom of users on whose tweet times we apply the statistic. For this purpose, we searched the text of all tweets (in our dataset) that were made in the first and last 10 minutes of all SFGiants games for keywords associated with this baseball team. The keywords that we used were: `sfgiants`, `#sfgiants`, `rowand`, `#rowand`, `lincecum` and `#lincecum`. We identified 640 users in this manner. We assume that these users who used the keywords associated with the SFGiants baseball team are indeed their fans. We also picked a random set of 1000 users who appear in our dataset (they tweeted at least once in this one month window). None of these randomly picked users used the preceding keywords in their tweets and we assume that they are not fans of SF-Giants.

For all of the above users (fans and non-fans) we keep a list of the times at which they put out tweets in this one month window. We use these times to evaluate the statistic (2) for these users. We also keep a list of user IDs for each of these users and this list gives our per user neighbor list. The entries in this list are the users who are mentioned in the tweets of the tagged user over the one month time window (his/her neighbors). In order to compute the statistic (3) which uses estimates of the interest levels of the neighbors, we also compile a list of the tweet times of the neighbors of every user.

Interests from user times: We evaluate the statistic Z in (2) from the tweet times of the 640 fans and 1000 non-fans. When computing Z, we account for an average of ten hours of sleep daily. We do this by scaling the total one month time window $T_1 + T_0$ by $14/24$ and computing the total sleep compensated non-event times via $T_0' = (14/24) \times (T_1 + T_0) - T_1$. We assume that the user is awake during event times (thus leaving T_1 as it is). Let $\hat{\lambda}_i = N_i/T_i$ denote the empirical estimate of λ_i. We threshold the Z statistic at different values and plot the number of correctly detected fans versus the false alarms (number of randomly picked users misclassified as fans) in figure 4 (blue curve, top). Contrast this with naive ratio of empirical tweet rate estimates $\hat{\lambda}_1/\hat{\lambda}_0 = (N_1 T_0)/(N_0 T_1)$ that is plotted in black. When we are interested in small false alarm rates, $\hat{\lambda}_1/\hat{\lambda}_0$ metric is not useful: for a false alarm rate of 10/1000 we detect a mere 51/640 fans when we use $\hat{\lambda}_1/\hat{\lambda}_0$, whereas, we are able to detect 137/640 fans using the statistic Z. However, when we are willing to tolerate more false alarms ($> 40/1000$), we see that the performance of Z is comparable to that of empirical tweet rate ratios $\hat{\lambda}_1/\hat{\lambda}_0$.

Incorporating neighbor tweet times: From the tweet times of the neighbors of the 640 fans and the 1000 randomly picked users, we compute their interest level statistic Z (again accounting for a per day average of ten hours of sleep). We then use the interest level estimates of the tagged user and his/her neighbors to compute the statistic $\tilde{S}$ in (3). To compute ϕ_k from the individual interest levels Z_k, we choose $p_t = 0.9$ and $p_f = 10^{-20}$. We threshold the statistic $\tilde{S}$ at different values and plot as before the number of correctly detected fans versus the false alarms in figure 4 (red curve, top). From the figure, we see that for any fixed false alarm rate, we are able to detect more fans via the consolidated statistic $\tilde{S}$ than the interest level Z_0 of the tagged user alone. For example, for a false alarm rate of 10 in a

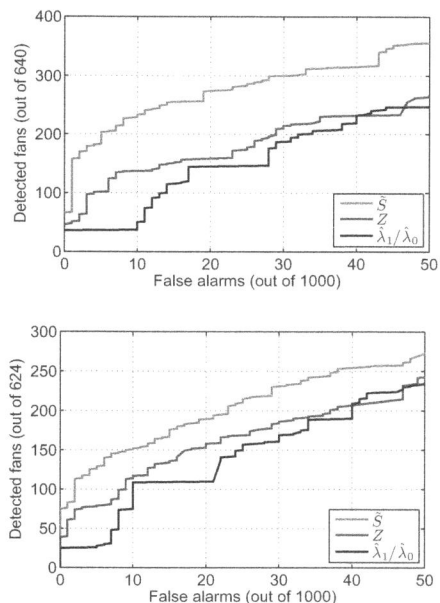

Figure 4: Number of correctly detected fans plotted versus the number of randomly picked users misclassified as fans for the statistics $Z, \tilde{S}$ and $\hat{\lambda}_1/\hat{\lambda}_0$. Top: SFGiants and Bottom: Yankees

1000, we are able to improve the detection accuracy for SF-Giants from 138/640 using Z_0 alone, to 233/640 using the consolidated statistic $\tilde{S}$ with $\kappa = 1/6$.

We run an identical analysis for 623 fans of the New York Yankees baseball team (identified in a manner similar to the SFGiants fans). These results are plotted in figure 4 (bottom). We see the same trend with the Yankees, with $\tilde{S}$ outperforming Z.

When interpreting the results summarized in figure 4, we must bear in mind the importance of operating at low false alarm rates. The proportion of "fans," or users interested in any particular topic, is expected to be small. For example, suppose 10% of the overall user population are fans. Then, for a moderately large false alarm rates of 10%, the number of misclassified non-fans is 9% of the user pool. This can overwhelm the pool of correctly classified fans, which is at most 10% for our example. This is the well known *multiple comparisons* problem, for which the natural regime of interest is low false alarm rates. From figure 4, we see that we are able to detect a significant fraction of fans for false alarm rates as small as 1%.

6. ASSUMPTIONS AND LIMITATIONS

While the numerical results on baseball fandom demonstrate the promise of the proposed approach, it is important to clearly outline its assumptions and limitations. Detecting interest in topic X from tweet times alone relies on two key assumptions: (i) Users interested in the topic X are *timely* in their tweeting habits: they respond to either the external stimulus which defines the event times (such as the baseball game played by their favorite team) or the increased chatter about X among their peers during event times, by *tweeting during event times.* (ii) Event times for topic X should not overlap significantly with event times for another interest, say Y, over the observation time interval. Otherwise, we would not be able to attribute the increased tweet rate during event times of X to interest in X *alone* but to interest in *either* X or Y. Such ambiguities get exacerbated if there are many interest groups which share the event windows.

We now give examples for which the preceding assumptions are not easily met:

Movie release times: One possible approach for identifying fans of a particular kind of movie (e.g., Sci-Fi) is to employ event windows around movie releases. However, it may take a few days for even an avid fan to find the time to watch a newly released movie. Thus, interests such as these may not elicit a timely response from fans. This may not necessarily make it difficult to employ the proposed statistic to identify fans of Sci-Fi flicks. It may just mean that we need to use a large window (e.g., a few days) around each movie release when defining event times. However, a large event window may require a large observation window, in order to collect statistics over enough event and non-event windows. This is because many unrelated events may transpire over a window of few days, hence we may require many event windows (movie releases) in order to "average out" the effects due to unmodeled interests which "interfere" with the task of inferring interest in Sci-Fi movies.

Television showtimes: Unlike movie buffs, it is reasonable to expect a timely response from fans of a TV show (say X). However, for TV shows it is possible that the air times for another TV show (say Y) overlap significantly with those of X over the observation time interval. This makes it difficult to know whether a user who tweets more often during X's air-times is indeed interested in X or whether his increased activity is due to interest in the show Y. We may be able to resolve this ambiguity if we identify sufficient additional events in the observation time window when the fans of one of the two TV shows tweet aggressively, but not the other: One example of which could be announcements regarding plans for the next season for the show X. Thus, an important topic for future work is to understand how different the times of events corresponding to two interest groups must be in order to disambiguate them.

On the other hand, for our baseball example in the previous section, both assumptions (i) and (ii) are met: it is reasonable to assume that users who are fans of a baseball team talk about the game and/or engage in conversation with other fans mostly during games (and are therefore timely) as they are expected to watch/follow the games when they are live-on-air. The timing of baseball games does not follow any specific pattern such as the daily/weekly patterns exhibited by TV shows. Therefore, *all* of the times when a particular baseball team plays its games are very unlikely to be the event times for another interest.

7. CONCLUSIONS & FUTURE WORK

We have demonstrated that significant information about a user's interest can be mined from his/her tweet times alone, by correlating these with the timing of appropriately chosen events in the external world. The Bayesian framework that we develop for extracting this information is shown to be effective in detecting baseball fandom from the tweet times of users over a one month period. Measurements from "neighbors" (in the sense of Twitter mentions) provides additional performance gains, with improvements of about 50% in detection accuracy for a false alarm rate of 1%.

We view the results in this paper as a small first step towards a broader investigation of the information that can be gleaned from spatial and temporal dynamics on social networks, and how this information can be best fused with traditional content-based analysis, while accounting for computational and privacy constraints. A Bayesian approach such as the one used here provides a natural framework for such information fusion. For the problem considered here, there are three research directions of immediate interest. As we have discussed, in order to detect interests from tweet times, users have to be timely in their tweets. Thus, an important direction for future research is to identify which interest groups exhibit such timeliness, and how to disambiguate between interest groups that share recurrent event windows. Another important direction is a deeper investigation of the problem of information pooling on the social interaction graph. In our present work, we have assumed that the interests of the neighbors of a tagged user are independent, given the interests of the tagged user. However, in practice, we expect heavy overlap among the friends of every user, so that further performance gains may be available by revisiting the independence assumption. Finally, we have assumed here that event times are known beforehand for the topic of interest. One direction for future work is to mine for these event *times* themselves from a bag of aggregate (network-wide) feeds such as Twitter's trending topics list or Google Trends. Since such an event/non-event times demarcation algorithm is topic-specific and not user-specific, it can employ sophisticated methods including text analysis on these aggregate feeds. Ideas along the lines of those in [3] can potentially be used to identify event times and this needs further study.

8. REFERENCES

[1] M. Conover, B. Goncalves, J. Ratkiewicz, A. Flammini, and F. Menczer. Predicting the Political Alignment of Twitter Users. In *2011 IEEE third international conference on social computing (SOCIALCOM) and Privacy, Security, Risk and Trust (PASSAT)*, 2011.

[2] H. Jeffreys. *Theory of probability.* Oxford University Press, 1998.

[3] C. X. Lin, B. Zhao, Q. Mei, and J. Han. PET: a statistical model for popular events tracking in social communities. In *Proceedings of the 16th ACM SIGKDD international conference on Knowledge discovery and data mining*, KDD '10, 2010.

[4] M. Michelson and S. A. Macskassy. Discovering users' topics of interest on twitter: a first look. In *Proceedings of the fourth workshop on Analytics for noisy unstructured text data*, AND '10, 2010.

[5] A. Pak and P. Paroubek. Twitter as a Corpus for Sentiment Analysis and Opinion Mining. In *Proceedings of the Seventh International Conference on Language Resources and Evaluation (LREC'10)*, may 2010.

[6] T. Sakaki, M. Okazaki, and Y. Matsuo. Earthquake shakes Twitter users: real-time event detection by social sensors. In *Proceedings of the 19th international conference on World wide web*, WWW '10, 2010.

[7] J. Sankaranarayanan, H. Samet, B. E. Teitler, M. D. Lieberman, and J. Sperling. TwitterStand: news in tweets. In *Proceedings of the 17th ACM SIGSPATIAL International Conference on Advances in Geographic Information Systems*, GIS '09, 2009.

Author Index